Japanese/Korean Linguistics

Volume 2

Japanese/Korean Linguistics

Volume 2

Edited by Patricia M. Clancy

Published for the
STANFORD LINGUISTICS ASSOCIATION
by the
Center for the Study of Language and Information
Stanford University

CSLI was founded early in 1983 by researchers from Stanford University, SRI International, and Xerox PARC to further research and development of integrated theories of language, information, and computation. CSLI headquarters and the publication offices are located at the Stanford site.

CSLI/SRI International
333 Ravenswood Ave.
Menlo Park, CA 94025

CSLI/Stanford
Ventura Hall
Stanford, CA 94305

CSLI/Xerox PARC
3333 Coyote Hill Rd.
Palo Alto, CA 94304

Printed in the United States

01 00 99 98 97 96 95 94 93 5 4 3 2 1

Library of Congress Cataloging-in-Publication Data
(Revised for volume 2)

Japanese/Korean linguistics.
Vol. 1 consists of "papers presented at the Southern California Japanese/Korean Linguistics Conference, held August 4-6, 1989 at the University of California, Los Angeles"; v. 2, of papers presented at the 1991 Conference held at the University of California, Santa Barbara. Cf. Pref., each vol.
Vol. 2 edited by Patricia M. Clancy.
Includes bibliographical references and index.
1. Japanese language--Congresses. 2. Korean language--Congresses. 3. Japanese language--Grammar, Comparative--Korean--Congresses. 4. Korean language--Grammar, Comparative--Japanese--Congresses. 5. Linguistics--Congresses. I. Hoji, Hajime. II. Clancy, Patricia Marie. III. Stanford Linguistics Association. IV. Center for the Study of Language and Information (U.S.) V. Southern California Japanese/ Korean Linguistics Conference (1989 : University of California, Los Angeles) VI. Southern California Japanese/Korean Linguistics Conference (1991 : University of California, Santa Barbara)

PL503.J36 1990 495.6 90-2550

ISBN 0-937073-56-3 (v. 1)
ISBN 0-937073-57-1 (v. 1 : pbk.)

ISBN 1-881526-14-3 (v. 2)
ISBN 1-881526-13-5 (v. 2 : pbk.)

Printed on acid-free, recycled paper

Contents

Foreword

This volume contains most of the papers presented at the Southern California Japanese/Korean Linguistics Conference, held at the University of California at Santa Barbara, September 6-8, 1991.

This conference is intended to provide a forum for presenting research in all areas of Japanese and Korean linguistics, thereby facilitating efforts to deepen our understanding of these two typologically very similar languages. Although only a few of the papers present comparative analyses, it is clear that the phenomena discussed in one language frequently have their counterparts in the other. We hope that the papers in this volume will help to advance future research in the emerging field of Japanese/Korean Linguistics and that the papers in subsequent conferences will bear the fruit of our collective endeavor.

The 1991 conference was organized by Patricia Clancy (UCSB), Hajime Hoji (USC), Noriko Akatsuka (UCLA), and Hyo-Sang Lee (Indiana University/UC Santa Barbara), with the invaluable assistance of Ryoko Suzuki, Tsuyoshi Ono, and Patricia Mayes, as well as Margaret Field, Toshihide Nakayama, Nancy Niedzielski, Hongyin Tao, and Suzanne Wash. Many thanks are also due to our large team of reviewers, for their help in selecting the papers for the conference.

The support provided by the Dept. of Linguistics at UCSB for the conference is gratefully acknowledged.

Part I

Discourse and Pragmatics

On the Clause-Linking to Construction in Japanese

SEIKO YAMAGUCHI FUJII
University of California at Berkeley

1.0. Introduction

Conditional clauses shade into temporal clauses because of the semantic overlap intrinsic to conditionals and temporals. In an attempt to clarify the semantic and pragmatic motivations for the overlap, this paper will present a case study of one specific construction — the Japanese S1-TO S2 construction, as illustrated in (1). TO is a clause-connective particle, which appears at the end of the subordinate clause, immediately preceding the main clause. As I will show in this paper, it is useful to treat the TO connective and the linked clauses as a whole as a grammatical construction, which I will call the TO construction hereafter.

1) S1 (subordinate clause) – **TO** (clause–connective particle) S2(main clause)

This construction has an interesting polysemy structure: it is typically used in generic conditionals, illustrated in (2a), and also in future–predictive conditionals, as in (2b); but another important use is to express **past specific** events, where both the antecedent and the consequent are known to have been true by the speaker, as illustrated in (2c).[1]

* At various stages of this study, I have benefited greatly from discussions with participants of the 1987 Berkeley Japanese Linguistics Seminar, the 1991 Cognitive Linguistics Workshop, and the 1991 Japanese/Korean Linguistics Conference. In particular, I wish to thank Patricia Clancy, Charles J. Fillmore, Yoko Hasegawa, Yoshiko Matsumoto, Yuko Mogami, Tsuyoshi Ono, Eve Sweetser, Sandra A. Thompson, Shigeo Tonoike, Nigel Ward, and David Zubin, for their valuable suggestions. Because of the limitation of space, I am not able to incorporate all of their suggestions in the current paper.

[1] Fujii (1990, 1991) discusses some other uses of the TO linkage which are not included in this paper.

2) the S1–TO S2 construction:
a polysemous clause-linking grammatical construction

2a) Generic conditionals
Haru–no ame–wa ittan huri–hazimeru ***TO*** *tomaranai.*
spring-GEN rain-TOPIC once rain-start IF/WHEN stop-NEG
(**If /Whenever/Once** it starts raining in spring, it won't stop for a while.)

2b) Future–predictive conditionals
Asita no paatii ni iku ***TO*** *Taroo-kun ni aeru kamosirenai.*
tomorrow GEN party DAT go IF Taroo DAT see-POTENTIAL MODAL
(**If** we go to the party tomorrow, we may be able to see Taro.)

2c) Temporals for past specific events
Kinoo uti e kaeru ***TO*** *otooto ga naite-ita.*
yesterday home to, return WHEN, brother NOM, cry-ASP-PAST
Lit.: (**When** I went home yesterday, my brother was crying.)
=> **When** I went home yesterday, [*I found*] my brother crying.

This paper will explore the third use — the temporal use of the TO construction (as exemplified in 2c), and show that it has a very specific semantic and pragmatic specialization: that of establishing the setting for a subsequent event, in particular a 'discovery' in the Japanese narratives.

My major purposes in this paper are: (i) to identify the key semantic constraints on the TO construction used in temporal expressions with past specific events (see Section 2); (ii) to describe a conceptual scheme which underlies the semantics of the TO construction, and show how this conceptual scheme motivates and accounts for the semantic constraints (Section 3); and (iii) to closely examine its uses in narratives elicited by using a picture book, paying an additional attention to its discourse functions (Section 4). To clarify these points, some comparisons will be made between the TO construction and other ordinary temporal expressions such as the ones using TOKI (NI/WA) 'when' in Japanese and WHEN in English.

2.0 Key semantic properties associated with the TO construction

We start by looking at the key semantic properties associated with the TO construction. The TO construction is used to express some temporal relations, in which the event or state expressed by the first clause (= S1) precedes the one in the second clause (= S2). But it has additional pragmatic and semantic constraints, thereby functioning as an idiomatic grammatical construction, in the sense of Fillmore, Kay, & O'Connor (1988). Our first purpose is to clarify these pragmatic and semantic constraints.

2.1.1. Uncontrollability of S2 and Switch Reference

The most basic and uncontroversial notion is that S2 usually represents a state or event that neither the speaker nor the subject of S1 can control, as illustrated in sentences (2c) and (3) through (6). As a natural result of this characteristic, S2 tends to have a subject (agent) different from that of S1, as in sentences (2c) and (3). This tendency, called 'switch-reference' from S1 to S2, is quite strong, as shown, for example, in Myhill & Hibiya (1989). However, of course, switch-reference is not required in order for S2 to be uncontrollable by the subject of S1: S2 can have the same subject if states or events expressed in S2 are unintentional or involuntary, as in sentences (4) through (6) (e.g.: (4)'I began to feel like going home'; (5) 'I was forced to read-'; (6)'I ran into somebody').

2c) *Uti e kaeru to, otooto ga naite-imasita.*
home to return TO little brother SUB cry-ASP-PAST (was crying)
(When I went home, my brother was crying;
I went home and found my brother crying.)

3) *Hamabe ni kaeru to, mura no yoosu ga*
seashore DAT return TO village GEN atmosphere NOM
sukkari kawatte-imasita.
completely change-ASP-PAST
(When I returned to the seashore, (I found that) the atmosphere there had completely changed.)

4) *Otoosan ya okaasan o omoidasu to, uti e kaeri-taku-nari-masi-ta.*
father and mother ACC recall TO home to return-want-become-PAST
(Remembering my father and mother, I began to feel like going home.)

5) *Kyoo kurasu ni iku to, sakubun o yomasareta.*
today class-DAT go TO composition-ACC read-PASSIVE-PAST
(When I went to class today, I was asked/forced to read my composition.)

6) *Kinoo teregurahu o aruite-iru to Sato-sensei ni aimasita.*
yesterday Telegraph St. ACC walk-ASP TO Sato-Prof. DAT meet-PAST
(While/When I was walking along Telegraph, I met/ran into Prof. Sato.)

2.1.2. Lexical semantics and the semantics of the TO construction

Sentences (6) and (6b) demonstrate the importance of lexical semantics in the interclausal semantics of this construction. In sentence (6), a verb, *au* (in *aimasita*), which means 'to meet', is used to express an unintentional event — 'ran into somebody' — rather than an intentional event — 'met somebody (by planning it)', although the verb by itself could have either meaning. In other words, the semantic specification of the TO construction discussed in Section 2.1.1. above automatically has us choose the unintentional meaning so that the semantics of the verb and that of the construction can be unified[2], since the sentence would not make sense otherwise.

6) *Kinoo teregurahu o aruite-iru to Sato-sensei ni aimasita.*
yesterday Telegraph ACC walk-ASP TO Sato-Prof. DAT meet-PAST
(While/When I was walking along Telegraph, I ran into Prof. Sato.)

6b) # *Kinoo teregurahu o aruite-iru to Sato-sensei o mimasita.* [3]
ACC see-PAST
(Intended Meaning: While/When I was walking along Telegraph, I saw Prof. Sato.)

In sentence (6b), another verb, *miru* (in *mimasita*), is used instead, but its meaning is inappropriate for this sentence. A Japanese verb, *miru*, is typically and mistakenly associated with an English verb, 'see', in bilingual dictionaries. But, while the English verb 'see' usually expresses passive perception (unintentional), the Japanese transitive verb *-o miru* ('-ACC look at - ') only expresses active perception (intentional), like the English expression 'look at', which clashes with the semantics of the TO construction.

2.2.1. The aspectual schemes associated with the TO construction

So far, we have discussed the basic semantic property: uncontrollability of S2 and its syntactic correlates: switch-reference. Second, we will pay attention to aspectual constraints in terms of both the grammatical aspect of the verb phrase and aspectual properties intrinsic to the meanings of verbs.

Sentences (7a) through (7f) demonstrate how importantly aspectual properties of verb phrases interact with the TO construction. In sentence (7a), the first clause, *uti o deru* 'left my house', is punctual, while the second clause, *hutte–i–masita* 'was raining', contains a progressive aspectual marker, and is thus durative. This punctual-durative combination is an acceptable scheme; this is Scheme A in Figure 1.

7a) *uti o deru TO ame ga hutte–i–masita*
home ACC left TO(WHEN) rain NOM fall–PROG–polite–PAST
(When I left my house, it was raining.)
[Punctual + Durative] : Scheme A

Sentence (7b) is also acceptable: here both the first and second clauses are successive punctual events. This is Scheme B of Figure I.

---

2 My analysis here is inspired by the unification-based Construction Grammar approach (cf. Fillmore 1985, 1988; Fillmore, Kay, & O'Connor, 1988).

3 Here and elsewhere, the notation # denotes that the sentence is anomalous. All the anomalous sentences included in this paper are taken from Japanese learners' compositions.

7b) *uti o* *deru* *TO* *ame ga* *huri–hazime–masita*
home ACC get out of TO rain NOM fall–start–polite–PAST
(When I left my house, it started raining.)
[Punctual + Punctual] : Scheme B

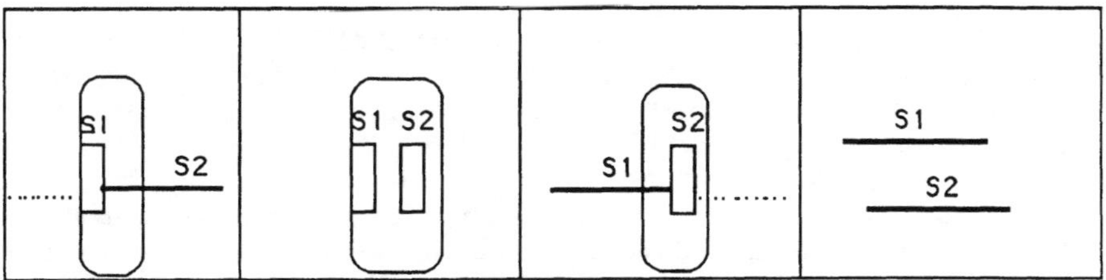

Scheme A S1: punctual S2: durative	Scheme B S1: punctual S2: punctual	Scheme C S1: durative S2: punctual	Scheme D S1: durative S2: durative
TO TOKI NI WHEN *WHILE	TO TOKI NI WHEN *WHILE	TO TOKI NI WHEN WHILE	* TO TOKI NI WHEN WHILE

FIGURE 1

Sentence (7c) is also acceptable; here the first clause represents durative event, 'be walking along the Telegraph Avenue', and the second clause punctual, 'start to rain'. This is shown in Scheme C.

7c) *Kinoo teregurahu o aruite-iru **to**, ame ga huri-hazime-masita.*
yesterday telegraph ACC walk-PROG TO rain NOM fall-start-PAST
(While/When I was walking along Telegraph Ave, it started raining.)
[Durative + Punctual] : Scheme C

Let us now compare sentence (7c) above with unacceptable sentences (7d) and (7e) below, all of which have the same antecedent, but different aspect for the verb phrases in the second clause. They all exhibit switch references; yet, only (7c) is natural and acceptable. Sentence (7d), which exhibits durative states in both the first can second clauses, is not an acceptable sentence (and does not make sense). This unacceptable scheme is shown in Scheme D in Figure 1.

7d) # *Kinoo teregurahu o aruite-iru **to**, ame ga hutte-i-masita.*
yesterday telegraph ACC walk-PROG TO rain NOM fall-PROG-PAST
Intended meaning:
While I was walking along Telegraph Avenue, it was raining.
 # [Durative + Durative] : Scheme D

7e) ?? *Kinoo tereguraḥu o aruite-iru **to**, ame ga huri-masita.*
walk-PROG fall-PAST
Intended meaning:
While/While I was walking along Telegraph Avenue, it rained.
 # [Durative + Durative]

Why is it that sentence (7c) is acceptable while sentence (7d) is not? Sentence (7c) translates as 'when I was walking along the Telegraph avenue, it started raining.' Notice here, some change of state (expressed in the second clause) happened during the durative event, and is discovered or observed by the subject of the first clause. By contrast, sentence (7d), by which non–native speakers of Japanese normally mean that 'while/when I was walking along the Telegraph Avenue, it was raining,' involves neither an observable discovery, nor a change of state. Similarly, sentence (7e) is at most marginally grammatical since the aspect of the second clause *huri-masita* ('it rained') does not express a change of state explicitly.

What is excluded from the uses of the TO construction is Scheme D, where the time span of the state expressed in S1 overlaps with that of the state expressed in S2, and where no perceptual or cognitive change occurs on the part of the subject of the S1 or the speaker during the overlapping time span. In English, although the connective WHILE is normally used to express such overlapped time spans, the connective WHEN can also be used (as in 'When I was walking along Telegraph avenue, it was raining'). On the other hand, the Japanese temporal expression using TO cannot be used to express this case. Instead, those durative clauses must be linked by an ordinary temporal construction, S1-TOKI NI S2, as shown in (7f).

7f) *Kinoo teregurahu o aruite-iru **toki**, ame ga hutte-i–masita.*
walk-PROG WHEN rain NOM fall-ASP-PAST
(**While/when** I was walking along Telegraph Avenue, it was raining.)
[Durative + Durative]

2.2.2. Lexical semantics and the aspectual constraints on the TO construction

As we saw in Section 2.1.2, lexical aspects of verbs alone may be sometimes unspecified. For example, the Japanese verb *iku* 'go' could potentially refer to not only the arrival time, but also the departure time and/or the transportation time (on his/her way there). But, as shown in sentence (7g), which means that 'When I arrived at S.F., it was raining,' when the verb *iku* 'go' appears in the antecedent of the TO construction with the durative second clause, it only refers to the arrival time. In other words, even when the lexical aspect of the verbs are unspecified, its occurrence in the TO construction determines the appropriate interpretation of the verb meaning; this is more evidence that the two clauses linked by the connective-particle TO as a whole bear certain constructional meanings.

7g) *Kinoo S.F. ni iku to, ame ga hutte-i-masita.*
yesterday S.F. DAT go TO rain NOM fall-PROG-PAST
(When I went to/arrived in S.F., it was raining there.)

3. 0. A further problem and the conceptual scheme underlying the use of the TO Construction

In Section 2, we observed the aspectual constraints (Subsections 2.2.1 - 2.2.2), in addition to constraints regarding the uncontrollability of S2 (2.1.1 - 2.1.2). Even when the lexical semantics of the verb alone is unspecified in either respect, its occurrence in the TO construction determines the appropriate interpretation of the verb meaning so that the semantics of the verb and that of the construction can be unified (2.1.2 and 2.2.2). The major issue addressed in Section 3 is: What is the underlying principle governing these semantic features?

3.1. The conceptual scheme underlying the use of the TO Construction

The underlying principle that I propose, based on the preliminary analysis discussed in Section 2 and the story data analysis to be reported in Section 4, is the following canonical conceptual scheme: In the temporal TO construction, the first clause establishes a new setting (or sets up a new scene), while the second clause provides descriptions of the state of affairs made perceivable within the new setting or scene established by the first clause. Typically, the first clause establishes a new setting for a discovery described in the second clause. This can be captured in one of two ways: First, a real change (either a new event or change of state) can occur in the setting; this is the case for Scheme B or C. Second, discovery can occur simply when the subject encounters an existing state; in this case, the activity or event described in the first clause needs to enable some cognitive change in the subject of the first clause or the narrator; this is the case for Scheme A. (For Schemes A, B and C, see Figure 1.)

This conceptual scheme is necessary to explain such cases as (8) and (9), which could be puzzling otherwise. Earlier observations lead us to believe that the durative–durative scheme, which we called Scheme D, is excluded from the uses of the TO construction. Yet, sentences (8) and (9) are very natural, in spite of the fact that both the first and second clauses are grammatically durative.[4]

8)
Syuppatu no toozitu itumo no tokoro ni pasupooto ga arimasen.
(On the day of departure, I could not find my passport in the place I usually keep it.)

Uti-zyuu o hissini natte sagasite-iru to yatto arimasita.
home-around-ACC very hard look for–PROG TO finally exist-PAST
Lit. (I was looking for it very hard all around the house, and then it was there finally.)
=>(I looked for it very hard all around the house, and finally found it.)

---

4 The first clause contains a progressive marker, *-iru*. The second clause is stative in (8) (i.e., *aru*, in *arimasita*, is a stative verb, meaning 'to exist'), and is progressive in (9).

9) *Kinoo teregurahu o aruite-iru to,*
yesterday telegraph ACC walk-PROG TO

henna hito ga miti de nete-i-masita.
strange person NOM, on the street sleep-PROG-PAST

(When I was walking along Telegraph Avenue, there was a strange man sleeping on the street.)

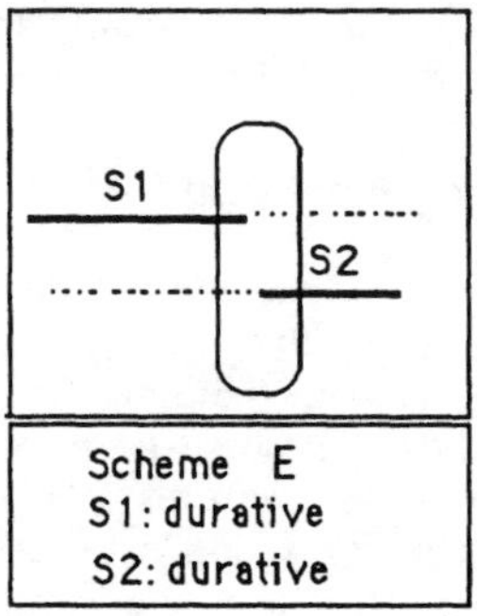

FIGURE 2

Notice that, in sentence (8) although the passport had already been there (in reality), it was only recognized and discovered at one moment--which is expressed in this construction. Similarly, in sentence (9), although the person had been sleeping on the street, it was not brought to the subject's attention until the moment profiled by this construction. Scheme E shown in Figure 2 attempts to capture this; in Scheme E, Scheme D is mapped onto Scheme B. Thus, these are quite different from the unacceptable sentence (7D), which we saw earlier, where — based on our normal world knowledge — it is difficult to imagine a situation where the subject is walking in the rain, but does not realize it until a particular point in time.

Therefore, the contrast between sentence (7D) on one hand and sentences (8) and (9) on the other reveals that the aspectual constraints on the TO construction cannot be determined simply by the grammatical aspectual marking of each clause. It also shows the contribution of the world knowledge to the processing of the sentences. More importantly, the way in which the world knowledge contributes to the processing of the TO construction is rather specific: the TO construction ensures that the first clause establishes the setting for the event described in the second clause, and that the event described in the second clause is not brought to the speaker's or subject's cognition until the time set up by the first clause and profiled by the TO construction.

Furthermore, I argue that the aforementioned semantic constraints are motivated by, or at least accounted for by the canonical conceptual scheme, which is in turn based on the event structure of a discovery. The first constraint that the second clause is uncontrollable by the subject of the first clause (or by the narrator) has to do with the fact that things we control cannot be discovered. Regarding the aspectual scheme, the durative–durative scheme is less likely to create a setting for a new discovery. In other words, the construction does not accommodate the two simultaneous durative events or states in which no cognitive change occurs in the narrator or the subject of the first clause.

Referring once again to sentence (7a), the English translation 'when I left my house it was raining' does not quite capture the meaning of the Japanese sentence *uti o deru TO ame ga hutte-imasita.* The English sentence can be interpreted in two ways: in one way, the subject was already aware that it was raining before he went out of the house. In the second interpretation, the subject discovered that it was raining only when he went out. The Japanese sentence using the TO construction exclusively expresses the second discovery meaning, presenting the events in temporal sequence with respect to the narrator's perspective. In other words, when the TO construction is used for past specific events, its use is quite limited to certain functions and meanings; this specialization distinguishes the temporal use of the TO construction from the other ordinary temporal expressions such as the English expression using WHEN and the Japanese expression using TOKI (NI) 'when'. Although WHEN and TOKI can also be used in a way similar to the TO construction, their uses are much more general, since they can accommodate various kinds of temporal relations and functions. For example, a question such as 'Why are you carrying an umbrella?' can be answered by the English sentence 'It was raining, when I left home.' But the Japanese sentence, *uti o deru TO ame ga hutte ita kara* 'because it was raining when I left home' cannot be the answer to such a question.[5] The appropriate Japanese answer would be *uti o deru TOKI WA ame ga hutte ita kara*, using TOKI instead of TO, because in answering such a question, the events do not have to be presented sequentially in a certain narrator's perspective.

3.2. Comparisons with previous studies

3.2.1. The notion of discovery

There have been previous attempts to discuss the TO clause linkage in relation to the notion of discovery. To my knowledge, Toyoda (1979) is the most extensive discussion of the ways in which the TO clause linkage expresses what is discovered.[6] Her analysis of the discovery meaning is, however, limited to examples that fall under what we call Scheme A, and in fact explicitly excludes Schemes B and C. Therefore, it does not deal with the relations among the different schemes of discovery.

Kuno's (1973) analysis is based on the idea that 'the sentence must be amenable to the paraphrase "after/while S1 happened, what do you think

[5] This was pointed out by Charles J. Fillmore.
[6] Teramura (1980) concurs with this point.

happened? I observed/discovered that S2 happened."' While this paraphrase adequately captures the important property of the TO linkage, it does not clarify the specific mechanisms of the TO construction that yield such an interpretation.[7]

In this paper, I show that, by focusing on the underlying conceptual scheme, which is in turn based on the event structure of discovery, it is possible to give a unified account of the semantic constraints and their syntactic correlates.

3.2.2. Switch-reference and perspective-shift

In an extensive study of a similar temporal use of the TARA linkage, Iwasaki (1988) also discusses the characteristics of switch-reference. He explains switch-reference in terms of the speaker's perspective-shift between the first and second clauses. I, on the other hand, explain switch-reference in terms of the canonical conceptual scheme associated with the TO construction, in particular by noting the uncontrollability of S2 where the content of a discovery is described (for details, see Subsections 2.1.1. and 3.1.). As proposed above and will further demonstrated below, it seems that what is really involved is the setting of a new perspective/cognitive space in the first clause, with the second clause being stated within that perspective/cognitive space. Because the content of a discovery is normally new, the second clause itself presents a new piece of information. Yet, this factor should be understood within the larger context that the new information (described in the second clause) is perceived within the setting expressed in the first clause.

4.0. A study of story data

Section 4 discusses some findings from a pilot study of story data, which form the basis of the aforementioned proposal (see Section 3.1). Story data were elicited by a picture story-book, entitled 'Frog, Where are You?' (Mayer, 1969). This picture story-book was used for a series of cross-linguistic studies of first language acquisition, examining in particular development of tense and aspect in children's narratives (see Slobin 1985, Slobin 1987).[8] This book consists of twenty-four pictures which show the story of a boy and a dog who have lost their pet frog, and go on a search for it through the wood; the boy and dog encounter various misadventures in the form of interaction with various forest animals, which fortuitously lead them to the location of their pet frog. The current discussion is based on the first set of data collected from ten adult native speakers' of Japanese.

---

[7] For example, the analysis does not account for the aspectual constraints on the TO construction. He points out that '*If S1 refers to a state, it must be of a short duration.*' But, this is not the major aspectual constraint, as I demonstrate in Section 3.1 with sentences (8) and (9).

[8] This project (Frog Story Project) was directed by Dan I. Slobin and conducted at University of California, Berkeley. I wish to thank Dan I. Slobin and other participants of the project for introducing me to this methodology as well as to this picture book, in his seminar (1985).

Scheme A, which we discussed earlier in Subsection 2.2.1, has proved to be the most frequent among uses of the TO construction in a narrative — at least in telling this story. This story has various discovery scenes; in each scene, the TO construction is used to establish an new setting and to describe the content of the discovery. In each case, S1 brings the subject of the sentence (as well as the audience) to a new viewpoint, by expressing either A) physical movement, physical change, as in (10) [be thrown off of the cliff] and (11) [climbed over the tree]; B) increased perceptual, as in (12) [listened more carefully] and (13) [looked more carefully]; or C) mental or cognitive change, as in (14)[woke up]. In other words, these physical or cognitive changes enable the discovery. S2, on the other hand, describes the state of affairs made perceivable (that is, made visible, audible, sensible, or relevant) in the new setting.

10)*gake no naka wa otosareru* ***to*** *sokoni wa mizuumi ga*
cliff GEN inside TOPIC 'be dropped' TO there TOPIC lake NOM

arimasita
existed

Lit. (When he was dropped off the cliff, there was a lake there.)
"He was thrown off of the cliff into a lake."

11) *ki no mukoo ni nobotte–miru* ***to***
tree GEN 'the other side' DAT climb–try/see TO

hutatu no kaeru ga pyokorito nakayoku narande-imasita
two GEN frog NOM cutely 'was sitting together side by side'

(When he climbed over the tree and looked around, two frogs were sitting there together.)

12) ... *mimi o sumasite-miru* ***to*** *nanika kikoemasu*
ears ACC sharpen-try TO something be heard
Lit. (When he listened more carefully, something can be heard.)
"When he listened more carefully, he could hear something."

13) *yoku miru* ***to*** *kaeru wa ni–hiki de wa naku*
carefully see TO frog TOP two NOT

kodomo ga takusan imasita
children NOM many exist–PAST

Lit. (When he looked more carefully, there were not only two frogs, but also many little frogs.)

14a) *asa* *okite-miru* *to* *kaeru ga* *imasen*
morning wake up-see TO frog NOM exist-NEG

Lit. (When (he) woke up (and see) in the morning, the frog was not there.) => "When he woke up next morning, the frog was gone."

14b) *tugi no hi no asa otokonoko ga okite-miru **to** kaeru ga ita hazu no bin no naka ni wa nanimo imasen*
(When the boy woke up next morning, there was nothing in the jar where he expected to find his frog.)

14c) *asa ni natte boku ga me o samasu **to** kaeru wa dokoka ni itte bin wa karappo desu*
(When the (next) morning came and he woke up, the frog had been gone somewhere and the jar was empty.)

14d) *tugi no asa ni narimasita* (The next morning came.)

*syoonen to inu ga okite-miru **to** ara bin no naka ga karappo desu*
(When the boy and dog woke up, alas ... the jar was empty.)

Among the sentences using the connective-particle TO, sentences (14a) through (14d), describe a scene in which a boy (the main character) wakes up and finds that his frog — who was placed in a jar when the boy went to bed — has disappeared. Since all the native speakers in my study preferred to express this scene using the TO construction, this might be regarded as typical of temporal S1-TO S2 construction. Notice that in all these sentences, the first clause expresses that 'the boy woke up the next morning', which sets up a new temporal space, because the event occurs at one point in a temporal sequence. It also establishes a new cognitive space, within which the state described in the second clause is discovered. The second clause, on the other hand, simply describes that 'the jar was empty'.

Of even greater importance is the fact that this state of the affairs is found and perceived by the subject of the antecedent in a new perceptual/cognitive/temporal setting; yet, unlike in English, such a discovery is presented not as an active/transitive discovery by the agent (such as 'the boy found jar to be empty'), but rather is expressed by simply describing the intransitive state that was found by the agent (i.e., 'the jar was empty). Thus, we see not only that the TO construction tends to have both the properties of switch-reference (from S1 to S2) and low transitivity in the verbal expression of S2, but also that these properties (switch-reference and low-transitivity in S2) are also associated with the aforementioned conceptual scheme of the TO construction.

5.0. Implications

This final section discusses some further implications of this study.

5.1. The clause-linking TO Construction and its relation to the issue of transitivity

First, the properties of the TO construction discussed in this paper relate to the issue of transitivity. We have established that, this construction requires that the second clause be uncontrollable by the speaker or the subject of the first clause; this fact contributes to lowering transitivity in Japanese discourse.

It has been noted that Japanese tends toward lower transitivity, compared with English. This has been discussed in various approaches, including analyses of morpho-syntactic properties and case markings of intransitive and transitive verbs (Jacobsen 1982, 1985; Sugamoto 1982; Teramura 1978), and analyses of fine-grained lexical semantics of verbs by Ikegami (1985). Ikegami (1978, 1981, 1982, 1991), among others, has also investigated the issue of agentivity and transitivity from the point of view of event realization patterns, which Ikegami attributes to the cultural rhetorical patterns. Along a similar line, Ohori (1988) discusses preferred domains of event-coding in narratives.

This study suggests that the Japanese clause–linking mechanisms in general also contribute to lower transitivity in Japanese. The TO clause-linkage discussed here provides one such clear case.

5.2. The clause-linking TO Construction and its relation to crosslinguistic lexicalization patterns

The above issue leads to a second implication in relation to crosslinguistic lexicalization patterns. As Talmy (1985) puts it, different languages package different types of information into single words. In a similar fashion, different languages have different tendencies in the way they package information into a single clause. Let us take another look at sentence (10), shown again below. This sentence can literally be translated as 'When he was dropped off the cliff, there was a lake there', which would be rather unnatural in English; in English one would express the event by a one–clause sentence such as 'He was thrown off of the cliff into a lake.'[9]

10) *gake no* *naka wa* *otosareru* ***to*** *sokoni wa* *mizuumi*
cliff GEN inside TOPIC 'be dropped' WHEN there TOPIC lake
ga *arimasita*
NOM existed
Lit. (When he was dropped off the cliff, there was a lake there.)

'He was <u>thrown off of</u> the cliff <u>into</u> a lake.'

---

[9] This English sentence is taken from another set of Frog Story data elicited from English native speakers.

15) *kokkyoo no nagai tonneru o nukeru* ***TO*** *yukiguni de atta.*
country–border GEN long tunnel ACC pass WHEN snow–country
Lit. (When (the train) left the long tunnel at the border, there was a snow country there.)

'The train came out of the long tunnel into the snow country.'

Example (10) is analogous to sentences shown in (15). The Japanese sentence is the first sentence of the well–known novel, *Yukiguni* 'Snow Country', by Yasunari Kawabata. The English translation, 'The train came out of the long tunnel into the snow country,' is the one given by the American Japanologist, E.G. Seidensticker.[10] What Ikegami (1991) claims by appealing to this case is the contrast that English prefers to represent an event in terms of a change in locus of a particular agent, whereas Japanese prefers to represent an event as a whole in terms of a change in state.[11] His point, regarding the event representation patterns, is important and well-taken. Yet, in order to examine this contrast, we cannot dismiss the specific semantic properties of the TO construction that make it possible to represent the event in the manner Ikegami discusses. Although the envisionment evoked by the mono-clausal English sentence is very different from the bi-clausal Japanese sentence, English speakers often describe the scenes of this sort in one clause, because in English it is possible to represent both terminals of a journey with a single verb phrase. In Japanese, this is not preferred, especially when the journey passes through a certain boundary. Yet, as if to make up for the difficulty, it has special clause-linkage mechanisms such as the TO construction explored in this paper.

5.3. Similar clause-linking constructions in Japanese

While this study focuses on the temporal use of the TO construction, there are other clause-linking grammatical constructions in Japanese which are used in the way quite similar to the TO construction discussed here. In particular, the TARA temporal construction used in modern Japanese informal conversation[12], and the BA construction (with IZEN-form of verbs) in classical Japanese have semantic/syntactic properties and a conceptual scheme analogous to those of the TO construction. Therefore, to large extent my analysis also applies to these other clause-linking mechanisms in Japanese, although further careful case studies of TARA and BA must clarify the subtle differences as well as similarities.

---

10 I am indebted to Ikegami for drawing my attention to this case.

11 To support this generalization, Ikegami, in the rest of the paper, discusses the contrastive ways in which an individuum, a human being, and a human being as agent are represented in English and Japanese.

12 See Iwasaki (1988) for an extensive study of the TARA linkage.

6.0 Conclusions

This study has shown that the TO construction carries with it highly specialized idiomatic meanings, supporting that this construction is a 'formal encoding idiom', in the sense of Fillmore, Kay, & O'Connor (1988).

The proposed canonical conceptual scheme underlying its uses — where the first clause establishes the setting for a cognitive change while the second clause describes the content of the discovery — accounts for the other semantic properties associated with the TO construction, such as the uncontrollability of S2 and aspectual constraints. In addition, grammatical properties (such as switch reference and grammatical aspectual markings which can appear in this construction) can better be treated as syntactic correlates of the above semantic constraints. These properties of the TO construction are consistent with the more general typological characteristics of Japanese, including its lower transitivity, event representation pattern, and lexicalization pattern.

References

Fillmore, Charles J. 1985. Syntactic Intrusions and the Notion of Grammatical Construction. In Proceedings of the 11th Annual Meeting of the Berkeley Linguistics Society. 73-86. Berkeley: Berkeley Linguistics Society.

Fillmore, Charles J. 1988. The mechanisms of Construction Grammar. In Proceedings of the 14th Annual Meeting of the Berkeley Linguistics Society. 73-86. Berkeley: Berkeley Linguistics Society.

Fillmore, Charles J., Kay, Paul, & O'Connor, Mary Catherine. 1988. Regularity and idiomaticity in English grammar: the case of *let alone*. Language, 64(3), 501-538.

Fujii, Seiko Yamaguchi. 1990. Clause-connectives in Japanese and English and their development in foreign language learning: the case of conditionals. A Qualifying Paper for Ph.D. University of California at Berkeley.

Fujii, Seiko Yamaguchi. 1991. Frame-setting constructions in Japanese: When conditionals interact with temporals. A Paper presented at the Second International Cognitive Linguistics Conference, University of California at Santa Cruz.

Ikegami, Yoshihiko. 1978. How Universal is a Localist Hypothesis? A Linguistic Contribution to the Study of 'Semantic Styles' of Language. In R Faucett, & M. A. K. Halliday (Eds.), Semiotics of Culture and Langauge. 49-79. London: Frances Pinter Publishers.

Ikegami, Yoshihiko. 1981. SURU to NARU no Gengogaku [Linguistics of DOING and BECOMING]. Tokyo: Taishuukan.

Ikegami, Yoshihiko. 1982. Hyoogen Koozoo no Hikaku: SURU-teki na gengo to NARU-teki na gengo [Contrast of Linguistic Representation Types: 'DO-language' and 'BECOME-language']. In Tetsuya Kunihiro (Ed.), Nichieigo-hikaku-kooza : Hassoo to Hyoogen [Japanese-English Comparative Grammar]. 286-326. Tokyo: Taishuukan.

Ikegami, Yoshihiko. 1985. 'Activity'-'Accomplishment'-'Achievement': A Language That Can't Say 'I Burned it, But It Didn't Burn' And One That Can. In Adam Makkai, & Alan K. Melby (Eds.), Linguistics and Philosophy: Essays in Honor of Rules S. Wells. 265-304. Amsterdam/Philadelphia: John Benjamins Publishing Company.

Ikegami, Yoshihiko. 1991. 'DO-language' and 'BECOME-language': Two Contrasting Types of Linguistic Representation. In Yoshihiko Ikegami (Ed.), The Empire of Signs: Semiotic Essays on Japanese Culture. 286-326. Amsterdam/Philadelphia: John Benjamins Publishing Company.

Iwasaki, Shoichi. 1988. A Study of Speaker's Perspective in Japanese Discourse. Ph.D. Dissertation. University of California at Los Angeles.

Jacobsen, Wesley. 1982. Transitivity in the Japanese Verbal System. Indiana: Indiana University Linguistics Club.

Jacobsen, Wesley. 1985. Morphosyntactic Transitivity and Semantic Markedness. In CLS 21: Papers from the Parasession on Causatives and Agentivity. Chicago: Chicago Linguistics Society.

Kuno, Susumu 1973. The Structure of the Japanese Language. Boston: MIT Press.

Myhill, John & Junko Hibiya. 1988. The discourse function of clause-chaining. In Haiman, John & Thompson, Sandra. A. (Eds), Clause Combining in Grammar and Discourse. 71-100. Amsterdam/Philadelphia: John Benjamins Publishing Company.

Ohori, Toshio. 1988. Transitivity and the Encoding of Narrative Events in the Process-oriented Language: A Case from Japanese. In J Emonds, P.J. Mistry, V. Samiian, & L. Thornburg (Eds.), Proceedings of the Western Conference on Linguistics. 211-222.

Slobin, Dan I. 1987. Thinking for speaking. Proceedings of the 13th Annual Meeting of Berkeley Linguistic Society. 435-445.

Slobin, Dan.I. 1985. Crosslinguistic developmental study of temporality in narrative. Ms. University of California, Berkeley.

Sugamoto, Nobuko. 1982. Transitivity and Objecthood in Japanese. In Paul J. Hopper, & Sandra A. Thompson (Eds.), Syntax and Semantics, Vol 15: Studies in transitivity. New York: Academic Press.

Talmy, Leonard. 1985. Lexicalization Patterns: Semantic Structure in Lexical Forms. In Timothy Shopen (Ed.), Language Typology and Syntactic Description, Vol 3 (Grammatical Categories and the Lexicon). Cambridge: Cambridge University Press.

Teramura, Hideo 1980. Nihongo no bunpoo (ge) [Grammar of Japanese (Vol. 2)]. Kokuritu kokugo kenkyuusho.

Teramura, Hideo. 1978. 'NARU' hyoogen to 'SURU hyoogen: Nichiei 'tai' hyoogen no hikaku. In Nihongo To Nihongo-kyooiku [Japanese and Japanese Language Education]. Tokyo: Kokuritu Kokugo Kenkyuusho.

Toyoda, Toyoko 1979. Hakken no *to* [*to* of Discovery]. Nihongokyooiku [Japanese Language Teaching] No. 36: 91-105.

Functional Transfer in the History of Japanese Language

SHOICHI IWASAKI
University of California at Los Angeles

0. Introduction

In both Old and Modern Japanese narrative texts two distinct types of declarative sentences can be found: one is the familiar type for narration and the other, as is often claimed, is for "explanation" for another part of a discourse. The distinction, which was made in the verb morphology in Old Japanese, was obliterated in the process of language change. However, the language successfully found a way to preserve this discourse-functional distinction by marking sentences in a different manner. This diachronic process is referred to here as a FUNCTIONAL TRANSFER.

In Section 1, I examine the discourse-functional distinction made by the two types of declarative sentences in Old and Modern Japanese. In Section 2, I argue that one type of declarative sentence presents a proposition as "illocution-less" or NONCHALLENGEABLE (Givón 1982) and that the EXPLANATORY FLAVOR of this type of sentence is a consequence of the dependent nature of such sentences in discourse. I conclude the paper by suggesting that the functional transfer was necessary in the history of Japanese because of the important divisions of labor assumed by the two types of sentences in discourse.

The following diagram summarizes the sentence types which are involved in the functional transfer between Old Japanese and Modern Japanese.

	Old Japanese ===>	Modern Japanese
[+illocution] (challengeable)	Sentence with Finite Form (e.g., *ari-keri*)	Sentence with Bare Form (e.g., *atta*)
[-illocution] (nonchallengeable)	Sentence with Attributive Form (e.g., *ari-keru*)	Sentence with Nominalized Form (e.g., *atta no da*)

[Table 1]

1. Functional transfer of the distinction between narration and explanation

Arlotto (1972:149) describes "conservative change" as a change "in which a grammatical notion or category continues to exist, but the means to express it (its marker) has changed". For example, Latin marks case in the nominal ending. However, this ending distinction was lost in the development of Romance languages from Latin; but the case distinction is still maintained through the rigid word order in modern Romance languages. The functional transfer we will investigate in this paper is similar to this type of language change, although it took place in a domain larger than a single sentence and involves the functional notion of "grounding" in discourse organization.

I will now present and discuss the two types of declaratives in Old Japanese and Modern Japanese in turn.

1.1. Old Japanese

In the texts written in Old Japanese, especially late Old Japanese (twelfth century), declarative sentences may end either with the finite form of inflectional words such as verbs and auxiliary verbs or with the attributive form of such words.[1] This formal distinction is often said to reflect the discourse-functional difference of narration (foreground) and explanation (background). That is, a sentence tends to end with the attributive form when it gives explanation to information given in some other parts in discourse (cf. Koike 1967, Onoe 1982, Yamaguchi 1987, Kobayashi 1987).

This functional distinction is evidenced in the distribution of attributive form ending sentences ("attributive sentences" for short, henceforth) and finite form ending sentences ("finite sentences" henceforth) in narrative texts. Before we discuss such distributional properties of the sentence types, it is helpful to identify them in actual texts. (1-a) and (1-b) below are the first and second sentences of a story from *Konjaku Monogatari* (early twelfth century).

(1) (*Konjaku Monogatari,* vol. 27, narrative 35)
(a) *ima ha mukashi,* _____ *no kuni* _____ *no*
now TOP old times (missing) LK country (missing) LK

kohori ni kiyaudai futari no otoko ari-keri.
district LOC brother two persons LK man exist-AUX:FIN

(b) *tomoni kokoro takekushite omobakari ari-keru.*
both heart courageous:TE thoughtfulness exist-AUX:ATT

(a)A long time ago, there were two brothers in the district of ( ) of the country of ( ).
(b) Both were courageous and thoughtful.

Notice the predicates in sentences (1-a) and (1-b) have the same structure of the verb, *ari-* 'exist', followed by the auxiliary verb of hearsay *ker-*[2]. However, the form of the auxiliary in (1-a) is the finite, *-keri,* while that in (1-b) is the attributive, *-keru.* It should be noted that there is no semantic difference between these two predicates and both report the existence of some entity (i.e., persons and their attributes in the above examples).

Koike (1967:15) argues that a sentence with the attributive form such as (1-b) is used to "describe what kind of a person he/she is", rather than simply to indicate the existence of a person, which is done with the finite sentence such as (1-a). It is necessary, however, to generalize this interpretation to include attributive sentences in other texts. Thus I suggest that this type of predicate shows dependency to a sentence in the surrounding environment which gives rise to such an explanatory flavor. I will give motivation for this hypothesis in Section 2.

The dependency of the attributive form and its explanatory flavor might have evolved gradually through the history of Japanese. This can be adduced in the apparent rewritings of the finite form with the attributive form in different versions of a same story. *Ise Monogatari* (first written around 900 AD), as any other written materials in the ancient times, was copied down by many different hands, and some newer versions contain attributive sentences which replaced finite sentences in older versions. The attributive sentences in a newer version very often give "background" to other parts of a story (Yamaguchi 1987:139-42).

Consider the next passage taken from the fifth episode of *Ise Monogatari*. (Each of the following four segments represents four sentences, some of which are composed of several dependent clauses. Only English translation and the relevant verb forms are given.)

(2) (Ise Monogatari, the fifth episode)
(a) Long ago, there was a man. **ari-keri**

(b) This man secretly frequented (the house of a woman) near Gojo in the eastern part of capital. **iki-keri**

(c) He, since it was a secret affair, could not go through the gate (to enter the compound of the house), so he went inside through the passage which the children had made in the wall.
ariki-keri (in older versions)
kayoi-keru (in newer versions)

(d) Not many people used this passage way, but the man came so frequently, that the owner of the house learned about it and ordered his men to stand watch every night, so although the man went (near the house), he could not see the woman and had to return home.

kaheri-keri

(2-a) opens a story and (2-b) develops it, and (2-d) reports the preclimax for which (2-c) is presented as background. All the sentences are concluded with the finite form in the older version, but in a new version, the attributive form is used for (2-c). Thus, it might be the case that between the time when the older version was composed and the time when the new version was written, the attributive form has acquired a new function of marking a sentence as background.

Both (1) and (2) above suggest the discourse dependency of the attributive sentence with explanatory flavor. It is possible to support this argument with more general patterns which such sentences show in discourse. First, the attributive sentence does not usually appear in discourse initially. For example, only two out of twenty three attributive sentences in the introductory section of *Konjaku Monogatari* are found to be opening sentences like (1-a) and (2-a) (Koike 1967:14). This implies inability of attributive sentence to create discourse environment due to its dependent nature.

This restriction, however, is ineffective when an opening sentence is strongly dependent on the immediately following sentence. This is the second fact suggestive of the dependent nature of attributive sentences. In such works as *Ise Monogatari*, the attributive sentence often appears in discourse initially describing the background incident or the circumstance in which poetry is composed (Yamaguchi 1987:135-8). The verb 'reported' in the following excerpt from the eleventh episode appeared in the attributive form, and this sentence describes the background of the poem which follows.

(3) (*Ise Monogatari*; eleventh episode)

mukashi wotoko azuma he yuki-keru ni tomodachi-domo ni
old times man east DIR go-AUX CONJ friend-PL DAT

michi yori ihi-okose-keru
road ABL say-stand-AUX:ATT

There was a man who went to the East a long time ago, and he reported to his friends during his journey. (A poem follows, which asks the poet's friends not to forget about him until they meet again.)

Finally the attributive sentence appears often in answer to a question (Koike 1967:18-9, Onoe 1982:11). This fact does not concern the use of attributive sentences in narratives directly, but it strongly suggests the discourse dependent nature of this type of sentence. The following is from *Genji Monogatari* (1002 AD).

(4) (*Genji Monogatari; Ukifune*)

(a) "*sono kaherigoto ha ikayau-ni shite idashi-tsuru.*"
that reply TOP how do:TE take out-AUX:ATT

(b) "*sore ha mi-tamae-zu. kotokata yori*
that TOP see-HUM-NEG other side ABL

idashi-haberi-ni-keru."
take out-POL-AUX-AUX:ATT

(a) How did he hand the reply to her?
(b) I didn't see that. He handed it to her somewhere else.

(4-a) is a question presented with the finite form and (4-b) is the answer in the attributive form.

The ongoing observations on the distribution of attributive sentences lead to a conclusion that such sentences are not fully independent in discourse but depend on some other part for the purpose of giving background information to what is laid out in the finite sentence as if to support it from the side line. I will defer discussion about how such division of labor has come about in the two types of sentences until we see the same situation in Modern Japanese.

1.2. Modern Japanese

The distinction made for declarative sentences in the verb form in Old Japanese was no longer sustained via morphological features due to the merger of the finite form (e.g., *keri)* to the attributive form (e.g., *keru*) in Middle Japanese (thirteenth through late sixteenth century). That is, all declarative sentences now end in the attributive form. Nevertheless the discourse-functional distinction made through these lost morphological forms was transferred successfully to the next stage of Japanese language (after the seventeenth century through the present) via the new structural contrast between the bare predicate sentence (e.g., *iku*) and the nominalized predicate sentence with the formal noun *no/-n* or *wake* followed by a predicate formative word such as *da* or *desu* (e.g., *iku-no da)*[3].

While the sentence ending in the nominalized form of inflectional words, as in the case of *no da*, is often characterized as having an explanatory flavor (Alfonso 1966, Kuno 1973, Yoshida 1988), or more generally a nature of "expressing the background for some facts" (Tanomura 1990), the sentence ending in the bare (non-nominalized) form does not. This characteristic of the nominalized predicate is a consequence of, again, its discourse-dependent nature.

Since there has been much discussion on this point in the literature, we will only consider one passage taken from a short story of black humor by Hoshi Shin'ichi to show the functional distinction between the two types of declaratives in Modern Japanese. In this story Mr. K was taken hostage by a hired gun man and taken to his wife's room where the gun man was instructed to execute him. When the gun man opened the door, Mr. K saw something unexpected. (5-a) and (5-b) appear in this sequence.

(5) (*Osekkai-na kamigami* by Hoshi Shin'ichi 1979)

(a) *sono toki, omoigakenai, K-shi ni-totte mattaku omoi mo*
that time unexpectedly Mr. K for utterly thought even

yoranakatta jitai ga tenkai-shita.
lean:NEG:PAST incident NOM develop-PRED:PAST

(b) *atta koto mo nai wakai otoko ga*
meet:PAST NML even exist:NEG young man NOM

heya no naka ni ita no da.
room LK inside LOC exist:PAST SE PRED

(a) At this time, something unexpected, a situation which Mr. K had never dreamed of developed (in front of his eyes).
(b) There was a man whom he had never seen before in the (wife's) room.

The first sentence is concluded with the bare predicate, *tenkai-shita* '(a scene) developed' and the second with the nominalized predicate, *ita no da* '(a man) was there'. The function of the second sentence is obvious. It "explains" the unexpected situation mentioned in (5-a). This effect of explanatory flavor and the discourse coherence between the two sentences becomes lost if the bare predicate is used in (5-2) instead of the nominalized predicate. This again is a consequence of the nominalized predicate sentence being dependent on another sentence in the discourse context.[4]

We have observed that the two types of declarative sentences in Modern Japanese contrast with each other in their discourse functions. Also we saw the discourse dependent nature of the nominalized predicate.

This discourse dependency is often interpreted as explanatory flavor just as the discourse dependent attributive sentence is interpreted in Old Japanese.[5]

2. The "illocution-less" declarative sentence

We will make an inquiry in this section as to how the discourse-functional distinction is made and successfully transferred between Old and Modern Japanese. Our examination will be based on the structural analysis of the attributive sentence in Old Japanese and the nominalized predicate sentence in Modern Japanese. Although the explanatory nature of these sentences is often discussed, examinations of their structural properties is rare (but see Onoe 1982, Iwasaki 1985, 1990). However, an understanding of the structural identity between the two sentence types across time is crucial to our understanding of how the explanatory effect comes about through them, and as a consequence how the transfer was successful.

We saw in the previous section that the attributive sentence in Old Japanese and the nominalized predicate sentence in Modern Japanese have discourse dependency. The reliance on the discourse environment of this type of declarative sentence is created, I will argue, through its nonchallengeable nature. Givón (1982) describes how a proposition is not challengeable discourse-pragmatically if the speaker assumes it to be familiar to, likely to be believed by, accessible to, or within the reach of, the hearer on whatever grounds (p.100). Challengeability of a proposition has relevance in grammatical structure. The speaker presents a proposition in a restricted relative clause when he/she has a reason to believe that it is nonchallengeable. Thus the speaker of (6) puts forth the proposition in the relative clause ("I had never seen a/the man") as if it is not likely to be challenged. This can be contrasted with the proposition presented with the main predicate ("A man came into my office"), which is more prone to a challenge (Givón 1982:101).

(6) A man I had never seen before came into my office and ...

To put it differently, a speech-act, or illocution, of assertion is associated with the main predicate proposition but it is lacking in the proposition expressed in the relative clause.

We should now note that the attributive sentence in Old Japanese and nominalized predicate in Modern Japanese have a grammatical structure parallel to a relative clause in the respective historical stages of Japanese language. (7) and (8) below are relative clause constructions in Old Japanese. Notice that the modifying parts are marked with the attributive form.

(7) (*Konjaku Monogatari*)

kore michino-okuno-kami Sadamori to
this (name) QT

ihi-keru *tsuhamono no* *son* *nari*
call-REC:ATT soldier LK grand child PRED

This is a grandson of the soldier named Michino-okuno-kami Sadamori.

(8) (*Konjaku Monogatari*)
onna *no* *itari-keru* *tokoro ni* *oshiirite ...*
woman LK stay-REC:ATT place LOC enter:TE

(He) forced his way into the room where the woman was and ...

In (7) the soldier is relativized by the clause, "(who) is called Michino-okuno-kami Sadamori," and in (8) the place is relativised by the clause "(where) the woman stayed". These relativizing clauses are nonchallengeable according to Givón as we saw earlier. To put it differently, these relativizing clauses with attributive form lack an illocutionary force of assertion. When the same form is used at the end of a sentence, the sentence naturally lacks illocution.

Thus the difference between the two sentences we saw at the outset of this paper can be now stated as follows. The sentence with the finite form (e.g., (1-a)) asserts the existence of two brothers while the one with the attributive form (e.g., (1-b)) does not have such illocution. A sentence without illocutionary force is somewhat deficient. This deficiency brings about reliance on the complete sentence with full illocution in the surrounding discourse environment. Thus (1-b) (i.e., the "fact that the two brothers are courageous and thoughtful"), depends on, and must be understood with respect to, (1-a).[6]

This is the source of the explanatory flavor interpretation of attributive sentences. However, it should be noted that there is no strict rule of dependency interpretation. A sentence with the attributive ending only signals that it be interpreted with another part of the surrounding discourse, and an explanatory interpretation is just one such interpretation.

In Modern Japanese there is also a clear structural similarity between the nominalized sentence and the relative clause. (9) below, taken from an earlier example (5), has a relative clause construction while (10) is a constructed nominalized sentence.

(9) *omoi* *mo* *yoranakatta* *jitai*
thought even lean:NEG:PAST incident
an incident which he has never dreamed of

(10) *omoi* *mo* *yoranakatta* *no* *desu*
thought even lean:NEG:PAST SE PRED
He has never dreamed of such an incident.

In the relative clause construction, (9), the noun *jitai* 'incident' is preceded by the verb *yoranakatta* 'did not lean' to form a nominal conjunct, and in the nominalized predicate, (10), the formal noun *no* is used to construct such a conjunct.

I should note here a slight difference between the Old Japanese attributive sentence and Modern Japanese nominalized predicate. The former lacks illocution completely but the latter has illocution in the last element of predicate formative *da/desu.*[7] Still, the nominalized predicate is a way to deprive assertion from the main proposition of a sentence. Thus, for example, the difference between (11) and (12) below is that assertion is directed towards the proposition, "(he) went" in (11), while no assertion is operating on it in (12).

(11) *itta.*
go:PAST
He went.

(12) *itta no da.*
go:PAST SE PRED
He went.

Lack of illocution in the proposition in the nominalized predicate may be adduced also in the following facts. First, the position before the formal noun *no* cannot contain the politeness marking, which, like illocution, hinges upon the speaker-hearer relation (Iwasaki to appear).[8]

Second, it is impossible to nominalize verbs with clear illocution. (13) is ungrammatical because the verb form indicates explicit imperative illocution.

(13) **hayaku okiro no.*
immediately get up:IMP SE
Get up now!

Third, there is a difference in acceptability of nominalization of declarative sentences. Most verbs can appear either with the bare or nominalized predicate depending on the discourse demand. Thus both (14) and (15) are easily acceptable.

(14) *koko wa yoku ame ga furimasu*
here TOP frequently rain NOM fall:POL:NONPAST
It rains here a lot.

(15) *koko wa yoku ame ga furu-n desu.*
here TOP frequently rain NOM fall-SE PRED:POL:NONPAST
It rains here a lot.

However some verbs such as below are not suitable for nominalization.

(16) *onegai desu.* *tanomimasu/* *tanomu no desu
favor PRED beg:POL:NONPAST beg SE PRED
Please. I beg you.

(17) *suimasen.* *ayamarimasu/* *ayamaru no desu
I am sorry. apologize:POL:NONPAST apologize SE PRED
I am sorry. I apologize.

(18) *yoroshiku onegai-shimasu*
well favor-PRED:POL:NONPAST

**yoroshiku onegai-suru* *no desu*
well favor-PRED:POL:NONPAST SE PRED

(lit.) Please treat me nicely. (as a greeting at an initial meeting.)

Ungrammaticality of nominalized versions in the above examples (15) through (18) must be related to the strong illocutionary force associated with these verbs of 'begging, apologizing', and 'requesting'.

To summarize, both attributive sentences and nominalized predicate sentences link up to a clause/sentence which appears in the discourse environment. This is a consequence of presenting a proposition as illocutionless.[9] It is this structurally induced discourse dependency that causes the explanatory force interpretation of this type of sentence.

With a declarative sentence, the speaker states what he believes to be true (cf. Palmer 1986:26). This is a characterization of declarative sentences according to the type of intention the speaker wants to express in it (e.g., statements, questions and commands). Sentences might also be classified according to their text-internal functions (cf. Halliday and Hasan 1976). From this perspective, we might consider the opposing types of sentences in Old Japanese and Modern Japanese as the declarative for used for foregrounding and that used for backgrounding in discourse (cf. Hopper and Thompson 1980), and it is this function which was transferred from the earlier stage of Japanese to the latter.

3. Conclusion

I have suggested in this paper that the attributive sentence in Old Japanese and nominalized predicate in Modern Japanese are a way to present a proposition without illocution. This function is a result of their structural property. This illocutionless nature gives rise to discourse dependency, which is often interpreted as explanation. We must conclude that this function is crucial for text creation in Japanese since it refused obliteration while the language experienced a massive change between Old

Japanese and Modern Japanese including the crucial morphological distinction.

Although there have been many studies on the attributive form of Old Japanese and the nominalized predicate of Modern Japanese independently, no studies have taken both forms within a single scope of investigation. However, such a historical perspective could provide us with a new insight into many aspects of language. I hope this paper has shown that possibility. Since we are endowed with rich linguistic resources from different stages of Japanese language, and have inherited much research on them, we should not ignore such data and wisdom even when we investigate the synchronic phenomenon of the language.

Notes

*I would like to thank Professor Keisuke Onoe of Tokyo University, who was kind enough to discuss the issues presented in this paper with me. I learned much from him about the attributive sentence and the nominalized predicate. If there are any shortcomings in the analysis of these grammatical phenomena, it is certainly due to my own inability.

Note the following abbreviations used in this paper.

ABL ablative	AUX auxiliary	ATT attributive form	CONJ conjunctive
DAT dative	DIR direction	FIN finite form	HON honorific
HUM humble	IMP imperative	LK linker	LOC locative
NEG negative	NML nominalizer	NOM nominative	NONPAST nonpast tense
PAST past tense	PL plural	POL polite	PRED predicate formative
QT quotative	REC recollective	SE sentence extension	
TE te form	TOP topic marker		

[1] The sentence with the attributive form is referred to as *rentai-shuushi bun* in the tradition of Japanese linguistics. This type of sentence is believed to be evolved from a sentence which contains emphatic particles of *zo* and *namu*, or interrogative particles of *ya* or *ka* (i.e., *kakari-joshi*) which require the sentence ending form to be attributive rather than finite. It should also be noted that the attributive ending may be followed by the auxiliary of designation *nari*. There is little semantic, functional difference between the attributive form with *nari* and the one without (McCullough 1988:25).

[2] The auxiliary *ker-* also has the continuative and recollective meanings, but most of the relevant cases for the present discussion have the hearsay meaning.

[3] I only consider *no da* (or its clitic form *-n da*) and *wake da* as the nominalized predicate. There are other sentence types which end with a formal noun with a predicate formative word such as *tokoro da, mono da* and *hazu da*, but they indicate clear aspectual or modal information. *No* does not have any semantic content and *wake* also has very little meaning attached to it when used in actual discourse.

[4] Shimozaki (1981) examines the use of nominalized predicate *no dearu* (a variant of *no da*) in the novels by Mori Ogai and finds this type of sentence appears very often at the end of a paragraph to make a conclusion of what is expressed in the paragraph. This supports the argument that the nominalized predicate has a discourse-dependent nature.

[5] Although I suggest a functional similarity between the Old Japanese attributive sentence and the Modern Japanese nominalized predicate sentence, I do not propose that they are complete equivalents to each other. In other words it is not the case that all attributive sentences can be rendered into the nominalized predicate when translating an Old Japanese text into Modern Japanese. The overall structure of discourse and general clause-combining mechanisms for sentence construction in two stages of Japanese language must be taken into account to explain particular use of this type of sentences.

[6] This reminds us of the tenseless (and illocutionless) *te* form which must always depend on the main clause structurally and semantically.

[7] In this respect, the nominalized sentence is closer to the attributive form followed by the designatory auxiliary *nari* in Old Japanese. (See Note 1.)

Also it should be mentioned that the predicate formative (e.g., *da*) is somewhat deficient when used with the nominalized predicate in spoken discourse. When the predicate formative is used after a true noun, it conjugates fully, but when it is used with the nominalized predicate, its conjugation is restricted to the non-past form and often missing. I argue in Iwasaki (to appear) that the predicate formative is a carrier of deictic information.

[8] In women's speech *no* has been reanalyzed as an interactional (or sentence final) particle. In this use the pre-*no* position allows politeness marking.

(i) *kinoo* *sensee ga* *irasshaimashita no.*
yesterday teacher NOM come:HON:POL:PAST SE
The teacher came yesterday.

This use of *no* is clearly different from the one we are considering here.

[9] There is also a way to deprive or weaken illocutionary force associated with a proposition. They include the use of the concessive conjunction *kedo* or causal conjunction *kara.* They behave similarly to the nominalized predicate in spoken discourse (Iwasaki 1990).

References

Alfonso, Anthony. 1966. Japanese Language patterns, Volumes 1 and 2. Tokyo: Sophia University Press.

Arlotto, Anthony. 1972. Introduction to hitorical linguistics. Washington D.C.: University Press of America.

Givón, Talmy. 1982. Logic vs. pragmatics, with human languages as the rewferee: Toward an empirically viable epistemology. Jounal of Pragmatics. 6.81-133.

Halliday, M. A. K. and Ruqaya Hasan. 1976. Cohesion in English. London: Longmans.

Hopper, Paul and Sandra Thompson. 1980. Transitivity in grammar and discourse. Lg. 56/2.251-299.

Iwasaki, Shoichi. 1985. Cohesion, challengeability, and *-n desu* clauses in spoken discourse. Journal of Asian Culture (UCLA). 9.125-142.

Iwasaki, Shoichi. 1990. Nominalized clauses and cohesion in conversation. Paper delivered at the 1990 AAS Annual Meeting.

Iwasaki, Shoichi. (to appear) Subjectivity in grammar and discourse: theoretical considerations and a case study of Japanese spoken discourse. Amsterdam & Philadelphia: John Benjamins.

Kobayashi, Chigusa. 1987. *Kindai-go no bunpoo: Kamakura-Muromachi jidai go* [Modern Japanese Grammar: The Language of Kamakura and Muromachi] In *Kokubunpoo kooza* 5 ed. by A. Yamaguchi. pp.1-32. Tokyo: Meiji Shoin.

Koike, Kiyoji. 1967. *Rentai-shuushi-hoo no hyoogen-kooka: Konjaku Monogatari, Genji Monogatari o chuushin ni* [The Stylistic effect of attributive sentences]. *Kokugogaku (Gengo to bungei)* 54.9/5.12- 21.

Kuno, Susumu. 1973. The structure of Japanese language. Cambridge: MIT Press.

McCullough, Helen Craig. 1988. *Bungo manual: Selected reference materials for students of classical Japanese.* Ithaca: Cornel University East Asia Program.

Onoe, Keisuke. 1982. *Bun no kihon-koosee - Shiteki tenkai* [Basic sentence structures - their historical development]. ed. by Morioka et al. pp.1-19. Tokyo: Meiji-shoin.

Palmer, F. R., 1986. Mood and modality. Cambridge: Cambridge University Press.

Shimozaki, Minoru. 1981. *'No de aru' ni okeru kessoku-sei no kenkyuu* [A study of cohesion of *no de aru*]. Gengo Kenkyuu 79.130-2.

Tanomura, Tadaharu. 1990. *Gendai Nihongo no bunpoo I - `noda' no imi to yoohoo* [Modern Japanese Grammar I - The meaning and the use of *noda*]. Osaka: Izumi-shoin.

Yamaguchi, Nakami. 1987. *Ise Monogatari no bunpoo* [The Grammar of the Tale of Ise]. In *Kokubunpoo Kooza 4* ed. by A. Yamaguchi. pp.128-159. Tokyo: Meiji-shoin.

Yoshida, S. 1988. *NO DA keishiki no koozoo to hyoogen-kooka* [The structure and expressive effect of the NO DA]. Kokugo Ronsoo. (March) 15.46-55.

Topicality in Korean Conversation: A Conversation Analytic Perspective

KYU-HYUN KIM
University of California at Los Angeles

1. Introduction

In recent years, a number of studies have produced a variety of interesting observations about the functions of the Korean and Japanese topic markers. However, previous studies have focused on semantic and functional characterizations of the Korean and Japanese topic markers based on the examination of isolated sentences, or written or spoken monologic narratives (Kuno 1973, Hinds, Maynard, & Iwasaki 1987, Hwang 1987, Lee 1987). In this respect, in spite of many insightful analyses provided by these studies, no serious attempt has been made to characterize the interactional functions of the topic marker in natural conversation in terms of how it is actually used by speakers of these languages.

In order to complement the previous findings on topicality from an interactional perspective,[1] I attempt to explicate functions of the Korean

[1]This paper builds on Kim (1990a), where I made a preliminary attempt to examine the interactional functions of *nun*.

topic marker *nun/un*[2] in ordinary conversation with special reference to (i) the contexts where *nun* is used in everyday informal interaction, (ii) the interactional motivation underlying the use of *nun*,[3] and (iii) interactional account of thematicity and contrastiveness, which have been noted as two essential properties of topicality. Several contexts where *nun* is frequently found are described in terms of the kind of actions that it performs towards the preceding talk and the interlocutor, as well as with reference to how such actions shape the following course of talk. By attending to the dynamic context-shaped and context-renewing aspect of an action constituted by the use of a linguistic form which is observed through the interlocutor's displayed orientation to the preceding turns and sequences (cf. Goodwin & Heritage 1990), I focus upon the function of *nun* which indexes the speaker's particular STANCE[4] towards the preceding talk, and which sometimes projects an affective domain in the subsequent talk.

2. Methodology and Data

The theoretical framework and methodology for this study is conversation analysis (CA) (Sacks, Schegloff, & Jefferson 1974). The major concerns of this approach are to provide a systematic account of ordinary conversational interaction in such a way that we can account for the actual course which particular episodes of interaction take, capturing the orientation of participants, and to develop a systematic explication of the recurrent practices of talking in natural interaction (Schegloff & Sacks 1973). I take the position that sentences and utterances that speakers produce cannot be fully explicated without looking at the specific interactional contexts where they are employed for particular interactional works, and without explicating the speakers' specific orientation to these contexts where the actions constituted by linguistic forms are situated. Moreover, non-referential, affective information is treated as a significant factor to consider in explicating the interactional function of *nun* (cf. Ochs 1988, Ochs & Schieffelin 1989, Besnier 1990).

---

[2]The Korean topic marker is realized as *nun* after a vowel, and as *un* following a consonant. For the sake of convenience, I will represent the topic marker as *nun* throughout the paper.

[3]This study is particularly intended to complement Lee's (1987) observation that *nun* establishes unchallengeable common grounds whose relevance is taken for granted for the subsequent discourse. While most of my observations are in line with Lee's characterization of the function of *nun*, I concern myself with the explication of the interactional motivation for establishing such an unchallengeable domain through *nun*.

[4]I am using this term in the sense of Biber & Finegan (1989), who define stance as the speaker's attitudes, feelings, judgments, or commitment concerning the propositional content of a message.

The data used are non-elicited, spontaneous conversations among friends. I used audio-taped, face-to-face conversational data.[5] Following the conversation analytic perspective, it is assumed that spontaneous, naturally occurring conversation is the most basic, primordial context of human sociality and language use (Sacks, Schegloff, & Jefferson 1974, Levinson 1983).

3. Interactional functions of *nun*

The examination of conversational data suggests that *nun*-utterances are used in interactional management contexts where the speaker expresses disagreement, or backs down before reasserting his/her point, and in discourse-organizational contexts where the speaker initiates a story, or provides a situational comment.[6] Even though these contexts certainly do not exhaust all of the kinds of contexts where *nun* is frequently found, they represent sequential and action contexts which provide a clue for understanding the basic interactional function of *nun* in a systematic fashion. Each of these interactional contexts is discussed below.

3.1. Interactional management: Oblique countering move

3.1.1. Disagreement

Nun-utterances are frequently found in disagreement contexts, and one such type of context associated with *nun* is related to the traditionally noted function of *nun* that projects a negative domain. Example (1) is a case in point:

(1) (Morning talk)
1 A: khukey colipha -nun -key ani -la:
much assemble-ATTR-NOML:SUB NEG:COP-CONN

[5]In transcribing the data, I basically followed the transcription conventions of conversation analysis introduced in Sacks, Schegloff, & Jefferson (1974). I used double hyphens '- -' to mark an uncompleted utterance in order to distinguish it from the morpheme boundary ('-'). A point of interruption is marked by '//', placed in the interrupted utterance, and/or by '[' between turns. Simultaneous start in overlap is marked by '['. I also use bold type for *nun*-marked referents both in the transcribed Korean data and English glosses.

[6]Interactional management refers to the speaker's dealing with the interlocutor's prompt. Discourse organization refers to the speaker's organization of his own talk. The distinction between the two archetype functions, however, is intended here only for the purpose of highlighting differences between the two at the most global level. As the following discussion will suggest, these two archetype functions are inherently inseparable in spontaneous conversation.

2 (khukey colipha) -nun -key ani -kwu:
much assemble -ATTR-NOML:SUB NEG:COP-CONN

3 kunyang .h iss -nun -ke ilehkey m//wusun yeki twu-kay
simply exist-ATTR-thing like:this what here two-CL

4 pwuti-ela,
attach-INJ
It's not a big deal to assemble it. Not like those that are hard to assemble. You just follow the instructions like "put these two together", like this.

---> 5 B: eng: kleh -telatwu **yocum -ey -n** kulehke-kkaci
I:see like:that-although these:days-LOC-TOP like:that-to
ssa
cheap

---> 6 **-ci -n** anh -ulke -eyyo.
-CONN-TOP NEG-MOD-POL
I see. Even so, it wouldn't be that cheap these days.

7 A: ey? <<--- *Next Turn Repair Initiator (NTRI)*
yes
Huh?

8 B: samsip myes pwul kulehkey ssa -ci anh
thirty how:many dollar like:that cheap-CONN NEG-
-ulke -eyyo.
MOD-POL
For thirty dollars or something, no, it wouldn't be that cheap.

9 A: kulay -yo? sasip o pwul //cwu -kwu sa -ss -na?
like:that-POL forty five dollar give-CONN buy-PST-DUB
Really? Maybe we bought it for forty-five dollars.

---> 10 B: **yocum -un.**
these:days-TOP
*(Not) **these days.***

In the context that precedes this segment of talk, A has been telling H and B that she and her husband bought a very nice computer desk for about thirty-five to forty dollars several months before. From line 1 through line 4, A continues the positive description of the desk in terms of its ease of assembly. In lines 5 and 6, B produces a *nun*-utterance to challenge A by saying that such a nice desk must cost more than thirty-five or forty dollars.[7]

If we focus on this *nun*-utterance, we find that it contains two occurrences of *nun*. One is attached to an adverbial of time *yocum-ey-n* 'these days', which is implicitly contrasted with the past time point when A bought the desk. The *nun*-marked adverbial functions to bring up the present time as a ground for rejecting the interlocutor's statement that she bought the desk at some past time point. One of the interactional consequences of doing so is that B conveys oblique disagreement by showing that A's point would not hold in the present. In this respect, the message of disagreement inferred from the *nun*-utterance is highly oblique. In the second *nun*-marked clause, *nun* is used in the context of negating a point that is directly relevant to the interlocutor's talk, i.e. the low price of the desk. Here, the speaker signals more specifically that he is treating the interlocutor's point as something to be addressed in earnest in the course of projecting his disagreeing position.

From these observations, we can note that the use of *nun* relates the current proposition to the preceding talk in such a way that the speaker shows his counteractive stance specifically towards the point of the interlocutor's talk that the desk is nice and easy to assemble even though it is very cheap. That the use of *nun* is motivated to be responsive to the interlocutor's point in the prior context is supported by an observation that *nun* is present when the speaker is countering the interlocutor, but that it is not used when the speaker is dealing with his own talk. For instance, in example (1), B's *nun*-utterance at lines 5 and 6 is followed by a NEXT TURN REPAIR INITIATOR (NTRI) at line 7, the function of which is to show the interlocutor that there has been trouble in hearing or understanding the interlocutor's utterance in the preceding turn, and prompt the interlocutor to address the trouble (Schegloff, Jefferson, and Sacks 1977). Prodded by A's NTRI, B initiates repair by repeating his trouble source turn in more or less the same form at line 8. What is noteworthy in this respect is that *nun* is absent in the repair turn at line 8 where B re-formulates his own preceding utterance, while it was present in the trouble source turn at lines 6 and 7 where B counters A's point. This observation strongly suggests that the use of *nun* is interactionally motivated to display the speaker's counteractive orientation and responsiveness to the point that the interlocutor made in the preceding talk.

Finally, we also find in example (1) that, while A backs down at line 9, B produces a *nun*-marked phrase, *yocum-un*, again at line 10, which is

[7]Actually, what B does here is to re-initiate disagreement because in an earlier context B already expressed his disagreeing position. However, B's utterance was backgrounded by an utterance from H, another interlocutor who has been treated by A as her major conversation partner.

appended to his repair turn at line 8. This shows B's resuming his counteractive orientation or stance towards A's point after finishing the task of repairing his trouble source turn. Concurrently, the speaker also displays persistent orientation to the interactional need to make his disagreement oblique and implicit by emphasizing one more time that the interlocutor's point is being rejected only with reference to the current time point.

Another type of disagreement context in which *nun*-utterances are found is where the *nun*-marked referent anaphorically refers to a point at issue, and the post-*nun*-utterance provides an assessment of that point. Note the *nun*-utterances at lines 6, 11 and 14 in example (2). I first focus on the *nun*-utterances at lines 6 and 14, which show exactly the same pattern of expressing disagreement:

(2) (Lunch Talk)
1 A: selkeci -to hay-cwu-ci -anh -ayo:, nay-k//a (0.5)
doing:dish-ADD do -give-CONN-NEG-POL I -SUB

2 dishwasher-eyta ta neh -e -noh -umye:n (0.5)
dishwasher-LOC all put:in-CONN-leave-COND

3 turn on the dishwasher. you know. ccak uhha.h// selkeci--
turn on the dishwasher you know ONOM doing:dish
My husband does the dishes, you know. I put everything into the dishwasher, and he turns it on, you know, uhha,h Doing dish-

4 C: ( ).hhh.hhhh

5 C: (ani) ku machankaci ani -a, kulen -ke
well that same NEG-IE like:that-thing

---> 6 **kule -n -ke -n.**
like:that-ATTR-thing-TOP
( ).hhh.hhhh Well, it's the same, isn't it, ***that kind of thing.***

7 (0.8)

8 A: >mwe-ka<.= <<--- *NTRI*
what-SUB
What's the same?

9 C: =waip-to machankaci-ci.
wife-ADD same -COMM
It's the same for the wife. ((meaning "It is just as easy for the wife to turn on the dishwasher"))

10 (0.5)

--> 11 A: ai kuntey **elyewun-ke -n** mwe-nya ha-myen
well but difficult -thing-TOP what-QUES do-COND-
-yo,
POL

12 (.) ta ilehkey ssi -e -kaciku ilehkey ilehkey
all like:this wash-CONN-CONN like:this like:this

13 neh -e -noh -nun -kes //iss -ci -anh -a.
put:in-CONN-leave-ATTR-NOML exist-CONN-NEG-IE
Well, but ***what is difficult*** *is ((lit. "if you ask what is difficult, it is...")) to wash the dishes all like this and put them into the dishwasher, you know.*

--> 14 K: **ku-ke -n-- ku -ke -n** nay-ka ha-nun
that-thing-TOP that-thing-TOP I -SUB do-ATTR

15 il -i -ci -anh -a **ku-ke -n.**
job-COP-CONN-NEG-IE that-thing-TOP
That*'s,* ***that****'s the chore that I usually do, right?* ***that one.***

16 A: ung? <<--- *NTRI*
what
What?

17 K: nay-ka //( ) son -ulo -to hay-cwu -ko, (.)
I -SUB hand-INST-ADD do -give-CONN

18 uh ceki selkeci cal ha-nun salam tto
uh over:there do:dish well do-ATTR person again

19 o -ney.
come-FR
I do the dishes by hand too, (.) uh here comes another person who's good at doing dishes.

In this example, K and A are husband and wife, and C is their mutual friend. This example illustrates an extended disagreement sequence. In line 1 through 3, A talks about how her husband helps her do the dishes, and says that all he does is turn on the dishwasher. In response to this, C, produces a *nun*-utterance in lines 5 and 6, and downgrades A's point by asserting that what A presents as a problem does not apply solely to A, but is equally relevant to her husband. While I will not explicate here the use of the *nun*-marked phrase which is placed in a marked word order, i.e., where it is placed after the verb, we find that C uses *nun* in *kule-n-ke-n* 'that kind of thing' for anaphorically referring to the point about which A expressed her position, and that, through the *nun*-utterance, C expresses disagreement with A by way of assessing the point at issue. The same disagreement mode in which *nun* is used for assessing the interlocutor's point is also found in lines 14 and 15, where K disagrees with his wife.

As in example (1), we can observe the counteractive responsiveness to the interlocutor that *nun* indexes by examining sequential positioning of *nun* in relation to the use of NTRI's. If we first look at the sequential contexts where the *nun*-utterance in lines 5 and 6 are situated, we find that A produces an NTRI *mwe-ka* at line 8,[8] which leads C to specify in what respect the matter being discussed is the same. We can note that the *nun*-marked referent, which was present in C's turn in lines 5 and 6 where he expresses disagreement with A, is no longer present in the repair turn at line 9. The same observation can be made regarding K's *nun*-utterances in lines 14 and 15 where K disagrees with A. Immediately after K's utterances, A produces another NTRI signaling that there has been trouble in hearing or understanding K's preceding utterance, thus prodding K to repair his *nun*-utterance in the trouble source turn in lines 14 and 15. Again, we find that the *nun*-marked referent is not present in K's repair turn. Given that the repair which follows an NTRI is not intended to deal directly with the interlocutor's interactional point, but rather to address the speaker's own trouble source turn, *nun* is not necessary here since, according to the the preceding observations, the function of *nun* is to respond to the interlocutor's utterance in some counteractive ways.

While these two *nun*-utterances illustrate a way of conveying the speaker's position of oblique disagreement by assessing the point concerned, the *nun*-utterance at line 11, which takes the form of what is called a pseudo-cleft, suggests another way of conveying disagreement in which the speaker assesses her internal state, presumably in the most oblique fashion possible. Here the pseudo-cleft with *nun* is produced as A re-asserts her point after C's disagreement in the prior context. In this

[8]Notice that A's NTRI follows a substantial pause at line 7. As many studies about English conversation have observed, pauses often project a DISPREFERRED RESPONSE like disagreement (Pomerantz 1984).

utterance, the *nun*-marked *ket*-clause, *elyewun-ke-n* 'what is difficult', refers to what the speaker generically presents as her first-hand experience about using the dishwasher. This *nun*-marked clause is followed by a specific account for what it is that she finds difficult about using the dishwasher.

The sense of obliqueness with which the speaker counters the interlocutor's point seems to increase further in the case of a pseudo-cleft by virtue of the fact that the speaker is conveying disagreement without referring to the interlocutor's point; what the speaker does is to assess her stance expressed in the utterance-initial *ket*-clause, with her counteractive stance towards the interlocutor being signaled by *nun*. This characteristic of the pseudo-cleft with *nun* may be responsible for the observation that the speaker uses it in order to reassert her previous point which was challenged or rejected by the interlocutor. That is, it seems to be the case that, in order to persuade the interlocutor who rejected the speaker's point in the preceding talk, the speaker may need to be more oblique in reasserting his/her point with a view to converting the interlocutor to his/her side.[9]

---

[9]*Nun*-marked pseudo-clefts are contrasted with *ka*-marked pseudo-clefts in that the latter is usually used in contexts where the speaker initiates extended talk with the interlocutor's attention already being secured. For instance:

(S & H)
1 S: ku salam -to kapcaki nao -n salam -i -ci -yo?
that person-ADD suddenly come:out-ATTR person-COP-COMM-POL
siin.
poet
He is one of those poets who became known suddenly, right? That poet?

----> 2 H: kuntey ku-- **kukes-i wuskinun-kes -i,** (1.0) ku salam -i
by:the:way that--that -SUB funny -thing-SUB that person-SUB
3 kuke-lul yengnam tayhak (.) sinmwun -ey palpyo -lul ha-yess
that -OBJ Youngnam Univ. newspaper-LOC presentation-OBJ do-PST
-tay,
-QUOT
*By the way, **that's, what is funny** is, (1.0) that person published his poem in the newspaper of Youngnam University, they say, and...* ((H continues to talk about the poet and his poem.))

In the context preceding this segment of talk, S and H have talked about a poet who is very popular among young people. In lines 1 and 2, S asks a question about the poet at issue. In response, H produces a pseudo-cleft with *ka* at line 3 as he initiates a story about the poet, with S's attention already being secured. Therefore, while there is a sense in which *nun*-marked and *ka*-marked pseudo-clefts both establish a kind of unchallengeable domain through the *nun*-marked *ket*-clause (cf. Lee 1987), we can see that, in the case of *ka*-marked pseudo-clefts, there is little sense of counteractiveness in relation to the preceding talk.

3.1.2. Backing-off

While I have shown above some contexts where speakers use *nun*-utterances to counter the interlocutor's point, *nun*-utterances are also found in contexts where the speaker backs off in the face of the interlocutor's argument as a way of securing a ground for reasserting his/her point. Example (3) below illustrates such a case. A *nun*-utterance is found at line 7:

(3) (S & H)
1 H: i hyen-swu ssi apeci -nun ka-si -ess -tay?
Lee Hyun-soo Mr. father-TOP go-POL-PST-QUOT"
Has Mr. Hyun-soo Lee's father left?

2 S: onul achim -ey new york-ulo ka-si -ess -tay -yo
today morning-LOC New York-LOC go-HR-PST-QUOT-POL
They say that he left for New York this morning.

3 H: new york -ey nwuku-ka iss -na?
New York-LOC who -SUB exist-DUB
Does he have anyone (he knows) in New York?

4 S: kaynada-ey hyeng -i iss-- sal -koiss -ta
Canada-LOC elder brother-SUB exist-- live-PROG-DEC
-ko
-QUOT

5 kule -te -ntey -yo
do:such-RETRO-CIRCUM-POL
(I heard that) his elder brother is living in Canada.

6 H: hyeng -i ? chin hyeng -i ?
elder brother-SUB? real elder brother-SUB
Elder brother? (you mean) real elder brother?

---> 7 S: ney. **keki -l ka-nunci an ka-nunci-nun** molu
yes there-OBJ go-SUSP NEG go-SUSP -TOP not:know
Yes. I am not sure ***whether he will go there or not.***

8 -keyss-e -yo.
-MOD-IE-POL

9 ((pause))

10 H: Yi seng -in sensaygnim-i (1.5) cenhwa -ha-ess -te
Yi Sung-In teacher -SUB telephone-do-PST-RETRO-
-lakwu
QUOT
(I found) Prof. Sung-In Yi called.

The *nun*-utterance at line 6 illustrates a case where the speaker backs down while being specifically oriented to a perceived interactional move by the interlocutor. This conversation is triggered by H's question at line 1 about Mr. Lee's father's departure, which occurs discourse-initially after a substantial silence. In line 2, S responds by saying that Mr. Lee's father left for New York. After H's follow-up question about relatives in New York, S says that he heard that Mr. Lee's brother is living in Canada. In response, H produces a double NTRI at line 6 by first repeating the term *hyeng* 'an older brother', and then adding a more specific term *chinhyeng* 'a blood elder brother', thus expressing surprise over the statement that Mr. Lee has a blood brother in America. In response, after a brief confirmation, S immediately produces a *nun*-utterance at line 6, in which he expresses his uncertainty as to whether Mr. Lee's father would really visit his son in Canada, and backs down.

What is noteworthy in this example is that the interactional basis for S's backing down lies in addressing the interlocutor's implicit interactional move which he finds he needs to deal with. That is, throughout the segment of talk, S, reporting the newsworthy event that Mr. Lee has a brother in New York, leads H to make an inference that Mr. Lee's father is going stay at Mr. Lee's brother's place in New York. Faced with H's NTRI which prompts him to confirm that Mr. Lee's blood brother is indeed living in New York, S revokes the inference through the *nun*-marked utterance, and absolves himself of further responsibility by backing down in the face of the interlocutor's implicit inferential move. As Lee (1987) notes, there is a sense in which the speaker establishes an unchallengeable domain through a *nun*-marked referent. The preceding observations further suggest that the speaker establishes such a domain in order to counteractively act on what the speaker (and the analyst) perceive(s) as an interactional move by the interlocutor. Display of such a counteractive stance in this case has an interactional consequence of terminating the talk about the matter, thus leading to a topic shift beginning at line 10.

As a whole, the association of *nun* with disagreement and backing-off contexts indicates that the function of *nun* is to display the speaker's counteractive stance towards the interlocutor's point made in the preceding turn. We can say that in such cases the speaker's stance is projected to impinge upon the interlocutor and his/her action, which is constituted by the interlocutor's utterance in the preceding context.[10]

3.2. Discourse-organization: Affect display

3.2.1. Story-telling contexts

While *nun* is used for certain interactional management purposes of dealing with the interlocutor's prompt, it also plays a significant role in discourse organization, though the former is inherently involved in the latter in that the speaker organizes his/her discourse and weaves his discourse into the on-going interaction by way of being attuned to the interlocutor. Example (4) below illustrates a context where a *nun*-utterance is used in a story-telling sequence:

(4) (S & H)

1 S: ay -tul-i (ta kule -ci -yo) ta tachi -myense
child-PL-SUB all do:that-COMM-POL all get:hurt-SIMUL

2 (khu -nun -ke -ci.)
grow -ATTR-NOML:COP-COMM
Children are all like that, they're always getting hurt somehow, it's part of growing up.

3 (2.0)

---> 4 H: kuntey **kay -nun** ttu -e -ka-l -ttay aph -ul
but that:kid-TOP run-CONN-go-ATTR-time front-OBJ

5 an -po -a.
NEG-see-IE
But ***that kid*** *doesn't watch where he's going when he runs.*

[10]In some contexts, *nun* can be used where the speaker pursues co-alignment with the interlocutor. In such a context, the counteractive stance indexed by *nun* is still observed in a highly subtle way, in that full agreement with the interlocutor's point is usually done through a positive assessment where the object of assessment is zero-marked. If *nun* is used in agreement, as in *kukes-un maca* 'That-*nun* is right', it would not mark full agreement, but still indexes the speaker's counteractive attitude in terms of projecting an imminent non-collaboration such as conveyance of non-enthusiastic agreement, proposal of a counter-example, or strategically motivated termination of talk. There are also cases in which the function of *nun* is positively exploited as when the speaker upgrades the degree of assessment (cf. Pomerantz 1984). For instance, one can mark a strong endorsement of the interlocutor's point in the context of providing intensified assessment by adding adverbials like *cengmal* 'really' to a *nun*-utterance in the form of *kukes-un cengmal maca* 'That-*nun* is really right'.

6 S: uhuhuh

7 H: ku k//hun-- kuce ile -kwu,
that big just do:like:this-CONN
That big- he just did something like this,
[
8 S: hahaha

In the context that precedes this conversation, H initiated a story about an accident in which his friend's son bumped his head on a steel chair at school. In lines 1 and 2, S produces an assessment, whereby he downgrades the import of the preceding story rather than taking the upshot. That is, S says that all kids are like that, thus not taking H's story as newsworthy or unique. In response, H produces a *nun*-utterance in lines 4 and 5, where he emphasizes one of the unique characteristics of the kid that he is talking about (*But that kid doesn't watch where he's going when he runs*). Here, H produces the *nun*-utterance to claim the tellability of the story in order to counteractively deal with S's prior trivialization by highlighting a characteristic of the child's running habits. It is noteworthy that H continues his affectively-loaded description of the child's running at line 7.

The function of *nun* which displays the speaker's counteractive stance towards the sequential development in the preceding talk is also observed in example (5), produced about seventy lines following the segment of talk in example (4):

(5) (S & H)
---> 80 H: kulay **wuli halapeci -nun**, (.) nacwung-ey nay-ka
so our grandfather-TOP later -LOC I -SUB
naylyeka
go down

81 -se incey yechayechahayse ilehkey toy
-CONN now for such and such reasons like:this become
-ess
-PST

82 -upnita kle -kwu selmyeng -ul tuli -nikka ku--
-FORM do:like-CONN explanation-OBJ give-CAUS that

83 kulehkey toy -n -ke ani -a, "ku eccetaka
like:that become-ATTR-NOML NEG-IE that how
keki
over:there

84 -ta son -ul neh -ess -ulkka, eccetaka son -ul neh
-LOC hand-OBJ put:in-PST-DUB how hand-OBJ put:in-
-ess
PST

85 -ulkk//a," kyeysok ku cilmun -i -si -e.
-DUB continuously that question-COP-HONOR-IE
*So, **my grandfather**, when I later went to see him and told him that the accident happened for such and such reasons, you know, it was just an accident, but he keeps saying, "How come she put her hand in there? How come she put her hand there in the first place?"*

[
86 S: hhh

87 H: hhh "son neh -un -kel mos po -ko way
hand put:in-ATTR-NOML:OBJ not:able see-CONN why

88 kuke -l y//el-ess -ci?"
that:thing-OBJ open-PST-COMM
hhh "Why did they open the door, didn't they see she had her hand in there?"

[
89 S: hhh

In the context preceding this talk, S produced as a second story one about how his parents-in-law over-react whenever his son falls off his bed, triggered by H's previous story about an accident involving one of his relatives, and the over-reaction of the injured person's mother. In line 80, H produces a *nun*-utterance as he resumes the story about his relative by bringing in a new referent *wuli halapeci* 'my grandfather'. It is important to note here that H produces an episode which relates to his first episode without producing an assessment of S's intervening story, suggesting that *nun* is used where the story boundary is disjunctive. This point is noteworthy because a preliminary observation suggests that *nun* is not used when the speaker tells a second story after providing an assessment of the preceding first story, i.e., when there is a smooth transition from one story to the next through turn-by-turn assessment. Therefore, there is a sense in which the speaker uses a *nun*-utterance to do competitive story-telling,[11]

[11]This aspect of *nun*-utterances is similar to the competitive turn-holding function of LD's in Italian (Duranti & Ochs 1979) and English (Kim 1991b).

which is actually the resumption of a previous story, designed to resemble the beginning of a second story.[12]

While examples (4) and (5) illustrate a context where *nun* serves a sequentially counteractive function, we can also note that *nun* projects an affective domain. In both (4) and (5), *nun*-utterances are followed by a highly affectively-loaded telling of a story. In (4), H's *nun*-utterance, which is appreciated by S through laughter at line 6, is followed by an affectively-loaded description of the way in which the kid runs. In (5), we find that H's extended turn, initiated with the *nun*-utterance, contains direct quotations of his grandfather's reaction, which is responded to by S's laughter at line 86. Following the interlocutor's display of appreciation of the tellability of the story through the laugh token, H repeats the telling of the grandfather's response at lines 87 and 88, again in direct quotation format.

These observations show that the speaker uses *nun* in a sequentially disjunctive way in which he/she displays counteractive stance towards the interlocutor's prior talk in a procedural sense. Display of such a stance towards the preceding talk is accorded interactional relevance by the post-*nun* utterances, which highlight the tellability of the story through an affectively-loaded description including direct quotations and repetition. We can say that the conveyance of affect contributes to asserting the import of the utterance, and consequently justifies the display of counteractive stance by inviting the interlocutor's involvement (Tannen 1989).

3.2.2. Situational comments

Nun-utterances are frequently used in contexts where speakers produce a short comment about a referent or an event. In such contexts, they often convey the speaker's affective disposition in turn-by-turn talk, as in example (6), where the interlocutors are having a TA meeting. In the context that precedes this conversation, one TA asked K, a TA co-ordinator, whether an answer sheet for a lab worksheet is available:

(6) (TA Meeting)
1 K: tuli-lkkey-yo cikum tap.
give-INT -POL now answer
I will give you the answers (for the lab worksheet) now.

[12] In relation to the function of *nun* that displays the speaker's counteractive stance and that marks a sequential disjunction, we can also observe that *nun*-utterances are often preceded by discourse markers (Schiffrin 1987), or turn-initial 'pre-placed appositionals' (Schegloff 1987) such as *kuntey* meaning something like 'well, you know, but...', which often projects that some kind of dispreferred response is in order. These discourse markers seem to aid the disjunction-marking function of *nun* as a precursor of an action that is less than a total agreement.

2 (2.4)

---> 3 H: hangsang **kim cay-ywun ssi-nun** cwunpi -ka toy
always Kim Jae-yun Mr.-TOP preparation-SUB become-
-e
CONN

4 -iss -e ttak (0.5) meli sok -ey ( ) ttak
-exist-IE precisely head inside-LOC precisely
mwe
something

5 -ka nawa hangsang. (kwa--)(h).
-SUB come:out always
Mr. Jae-yun Kim *always has things ready in his mind, always(h).*

6 A: (maynnal-) kulen -ke(h) kat(h)-ci(h).h
everyday like:that-NOML seem -COMM
(Everyday-) he may look like that.hh (=Actually he is not like that.)

In response to the inquiry, K says at line 1 that answer sheets are available, and gives one to the TA who asked the question. In line 3, H, another TA, produces a *nun*-utterance to provide a situational comment referring to K's immediate reaction to the TA's request. We can readily note that this utterance is highly disjunctive with the preceding talk and the on-going TA meeting situation. However, the relevance of its being disjunctive is situationally provided by the interactional import of complimenting the interlocutor in relation to what he just did in the preceding context, i.e. K's having the answer sheet ready at the unexpected prompt from a TA.

Similarly, in example (7), we find a case where the speaker suddenly brings in a new referent through *nun*:

(7) (After Dinner)
((A and R have been talking about A's cushion cover.))
1 R: mantul-e -cwu-ess -na -pwu-ci?
made -CONN-give-PST-DUB-see -COMM
Someone made them for you, right?

2 A: sa -n -ke -eyyo.
buy-ATTR-thing-COP:POL
I bought them.

3 (1.0)

---> 4 A: **se cin-swuk ssi -nun** ttak ichen wen -ey
Suh Jin -sook Miss-TOP exactly two thousand won-LOC

5 mak campa -lul ip -kwu tani
without hesitation campus-OBJ wear-CONN go:around
-te
-RETROS

6 -lakwu -yo (cengmal) na cwuk-keyss -e
-QUOT-POL (r//eally) I kill -MOD -IE
Ms. Jin-sook Suh *bought a jacket made of the same material for 2,000 won, and I saw her wearing it. It's really funny.*
[
7 R: hhh

8 A: wuli cip -eyse pangsek-ulo ssu-nun -ke -l kacta
our place-LOC cushion-INSTR use-ATTR-thing-OBJ with

9 R: hhh.
[
10 A: ca(h)mb(h)a-lwu ip -kwu t(h)an(h)i -nikka.
jacket -INST wear-CONN go:around-CAUS
Because materials that we use for cushion covers she w(h)ears as a ja(h)ck(h)et!

In line 4, speaker A suddenly brings up a new referent with the topic marker in the context where the interlocutors are talking about A's cushion cover, and produces an affectively-loaded utterance by telling of a person who wore a jacket made of the same material as A's cushion cover. Therefore, even though the way in which the speaker brings up the subject of Miss Jinsook Suh is highly disjunctive with the preceding talk, the utterance is contextually accorded relevance by virtue of the interactional import of relating the talk about the cushion cover to the new referent in humorous manner.

We can also observe that these affectively-loaded *nun*-utterances in examples (6) and (7), as well as those in example (5) are all responded to by the interlocutor's laughter or utterances accompanied by laughter, and often are further appended by utterances reformulated with a stronger affective overtone. This observation suggests that the interlocutors are oriented to the speaker's expression of affective stance towards the referent, and to its unique affective import to the on-going conversation. The expression of affect through the *nun*-utterance, which also provides relevance for the *nun*-utterance, does so as the major part of the action of providing a comment (cf. Li, Thompson, & Thompson 1982), as the upshot of a comment often lies in the affective import that it has towards the context of talk and situation.

4. Implications for contrastiveness and thematicity

It is important to note that the speaker's display of counteractive stance leads the interlocutor to make an inferential effort to relate the current utterance to some point against which the speaker has acted counteractively, to the effect that the speaker's counteractive stance is FOREGROUNDED, i.e., brought to the foreground of the hearer's mind (cf. Ochs & Schieffelin 1983).[13] The locally disjunctive nature of foregrounding the speaker's counteractive stance towards the immediately preceding context of talk and action is accorded discoursal/interactional relevance by the presentation of materials which serve as a ground on which such an act of stance-foregrounding is justified (Kim 1991a).[14] In this respect, interlocutors are led to be oriented to the following:

(i) a point against which the speaker foregrounds his/her counteractive stance
(ii) a ground on which foregrounding such a stance is shown to be relevant

The constrastive reading of *nun*, which has been noted to be an important semantic and pragmatic property of topicality (Kuno 1973), seems to be inferred saliently when the interlocutor is substantially oriented to (i), with different degrees of contrastiveness being inferred on the basis of different degrees and combinations of orientation directed to (i) and (ii).[15]

---

[13]Given that, in disagreement or backing-off contexts, *nun* orients the current hearer's attention to his/her own point in the preceding context by way of indexing that the current speaker is displaying counteractive stance towards it, the orientational function of *nun* would be especially effective.

[14]It should be noted that the speaker's counteractive orientation can be directed to his/her own point and create locally motivated cohesive ties in a monologue (cf. Clancy & Downing 1987). In a monologue, the use of *nun* invites the listener to co-participate in the speaker's narrating by triggering the listener's inferential effort to find some ground on which the speaker asserts his/her counteractive stance.

[15]For instance, the disagreement mode of assessment (cf. example (2)) is a case in which (ii) is provided by the post-*nun*-utterance which provides a relevance for the display of counteractive stance in the form of assessing an object at issue, with (i) being inferred from the prior context. On the other hand, the disagreement mode in which the *nun*-marked adverbial projects a negative domain (example (1)) would be a case in which the *nun*-marked adverbial serves as (ii), with (i) being marked by the interlocutor's utterance that the current speaker

The findings in this paper also suggest that thematic reading of *nun* (Kuno 1973) is salient in story-telling or comment-proffering contexts where the interlocutor's attention is mostly oriented to (ii), rather than (i). This observation suggests that a salient affective function of the utterance following *nun* may be associated with a thematic reading. Furthermore, I suspect that, at a more basic level, a salient thematic reading is derived from interactional characteristics of *nun* which evoke the action relevance of the utterance towards the current interaction. For instance, in the story-telling context, the disjunctive use of *nun*, which is based on the display of the speaker's counteractive stance, is not perceived as very disjunctive because *nun* is situated in an action context where speakers produce a series of second stories and assessments often in a competitive manner. As a result, there is little motivation on the part of the interlocutor to make an inferential effort about (i), a point in relation to which the counteractive stance is signaled. Likewise, relevance for the disjunctive use of *nun* in a situational comment is significantly provided by the comment-proffering action *per se* which is situationally relevant. In both cases, what is thus highlighted is the action-relevance of the current *nun*-utterance. The functions of *nun* that project an affective domain and that evoke action-relevance of the current utterance can be treated as being intertwined with each other, because the conveyance of affect constitutes the major, not a subsidiary, part of the story-telling and comment-proffering action in terms of inviting the interlocutor's co-participation and collaboration in talk. The thematic reading associated with *nun*, then, seems to be a discourse message that can be explicated with reference to the constitution of action and indexicalization of affect.

5. Conclusions

As a whole, the function of *nun*-utterances that constitutes an oblique countering move, projects the affective domain, and invokes the action-relevance can be treated either in terms of the discourse strategy of negotiating the display of the counteractive stance indexed by *nun*, or as a part of the counteractive stance-marking function of *nun*. In any case, what is at the core of the function of *nun* can be elaborated as the following. *Nun* clues the interlocutor to the speaker's act of foregrounding his/her counteractive stance towards the preceding talk, and leads him/her to orient himself/herself to the point in relation to which such a stance is displayed as well as to the ground on which such a stance-display is accorded relevance.

---

counters. In this case, the display of counteractive stance is accorded relevance mainly by the sequential positioning of the *nun*-marked adverbial *per se* in relation to the interlocutor's utterance.

One important aspect of this process, which needs to be further examined in future research, is that the speaker gives a very subtle sense in which the *nun*-marked referent is brought in, not by the personal motivation of the speaker, but as is dictated by the development of discourse and interaction in the current participation framework and/or by some prior discoursal/interactional history. In terms of the action constituted by *nun*, this has the interactional consequence of showing that the speaker displays counteractive stance not by his/her own initiation, but because speaker-external discoursal/interactional contexts somehow have led him/her to do so[16]. Moreover, by invoking shared discoursal/interactional history, and by giving the sense in which the speaker picked up the *nun*-marked referent from the shared pool of parallel instances of referents, the use of *nun* creates COLLUSION with the interlocutor (cf. Besnier 1989). This sense is found particularly saliently in contexts where the speaker brings in a referent, either new or given, in order to initiate or shift a topic through a yes-no question (cf. H's utterance at line 1 in example (3)). While this issue needs to be further explicated in future research, the findings in this paper suggest in general that the interactional and non-referential aspect of language use is the essential domain of language that linguists should concern themselves with, and that the various interactional functions of *nun* can be grasped and analyzed in a unified manner only if we attend to the dynamic process through which it is situated in on-going interaction.

References

Besnier, Niko. 1989. Information withholding as a manipulative and collusive strategy in Nukulaelae gossip", Language in Society 18.315-341.

__________. 1990. Language and affect. Annual Review of Anthropology 19.419-451.

Biber, Douglas., & Edward Finegan. 1989. Styles of stance in English: Lexical and grammatical marking of evidentiality and affect. Text 9 (1).93-124.

Clancy Patricia M., and Pamela Downing. 1987. The use of *wa* as a cohesion marker in Japanese oral narratives. Perspectives on topicalization: The case of Japanese *wa*, eds. by John Hinds, Senko K. Maynard, & Shoichi Iwasaki. 3-56. Amsterdam: John Benjamins.

[16]It may be due to this characteristic of *nun* that the use of *nun*, at least partly, contributes to giving the sense of obliqueness in the context of dealing with the interlocutor's prompt, with the speaker's subjective dimension being downgraded in terms of the intention to disagree with the interlocutor.

Duranti Alessandro, and Elinor Ochs. 1979. Left-dislocation in Italian conversation. Discourse and Syntax: Syntax and Semantics 12, ed. by Talmy Givon, 377-416. New York: Academic Press.

Goffman, Erving. 1979. Footing. Semiotica 25.1-29.

Goodwin, Charles, and John Heritage. 1990. Conversation analysis. Annual Review of Anthropology 19.283-307.

Hinds, John, Senko K. Maynard, & Shoichi Iwasaki. 1987. Perspectives on topicalization: The case of Japanese *wa*, Amsterdam: John Benjamins.

Hwang, Shin Ja Joo. 1987. Discourse Features of Korean Narration, Summer Institute of Linguistics, University of Texas at Arlington.

Kim, Kyu-hyun. 1991a. The role of the Korean topic marker in foregrounding speaker stance. Paper presented at the Seventeenth Annual Meeting of the Berkeley Linguistics Society, University of California, Berkeley, California.

____________. 1991b. WH-clefts and left-dislocation in English conversation: Cases of topicalization. Paper presented at the Milwaukee Linguistics Symposium: Word Order in Discourse, University of Wisconsin, Milwaukee, Wisconsin.

Kuno, Susumu. 1973. The structure of the Japanese language. Cambridge: MIT Press.

Lee, Hyo Sang. 1987. Discourse presupposition and the discourse function of the topic marker *nin* in Korean. Indiana University Linguistics Club.

Levinson, Stephen C. 1983. Pragmatics. Cambridge: Cambridge University Press.

Li, Charles N., Sandra A. Thompson, and R. McMillan Thompson. 1982. The discourse motivation for the perfect aspect: the Mandarin particle *le*. Tense and aspect: Between semantics and pragmatics, ed. by Paul J. Hopper, 19-24. Amsterdam: John Benjamins.

Ochs, Elinor. 1988. Culture and language development. Cambridge: Cambridge University Press.

Ochs, Elinor, and Bambi Schieffelin. 1983. Foregrounding referents: a reconsideration of left dislocation in discourse. Acquiring conversational competence, eds. by Elinor Ochs and Bambi Schieffelin, 158-174. London: Routledge.

Ochs, Elinor, and Bambi Schieffelin. 1989. Language has a heart. Text 9 (1).7-25.

Pomerantz, Anita. 1984. Agreeing and disagreeing with assessments: Some features of preferred/dispreferred turn shapes. Structure of social Action: Studies in conversation analysis, eds. by J. M. Atkinson & J. Heritage, 57-101. Cambridge: Cambridge University Press.

Sacks, Harvey, Emanuel A. Schegloff, and Gail Jefferson. 1974. A simplest systematics for the organization of turn-taking for conversation. Language 50.696-735.

Schegloff, Emanuel A. 1987. Recycled turn beginnings: A precise repair mechanism in conversation's turn-taking organization. Talk and social organization, ed. by Graham Button and John R. E. Lee, 70-85. Clevedon: Multilingual Matters.

Schegloff, Emanuel A., Gail Jefferson, and Harvey Sacks. 1977. The preference for self-correction in the organization of repair in conversation. Language 53.361-382.

Schegloff, Emanuel A., and Harvey Sacks. 1973. Opening up closing. Semiotica 8.289-327.

Schiffrin, Deborah. 1987. Discourse markers. Cambridge: Cambridge University Press.

Tannen, Deborah. 1989. Talking voices: Repetition, dialogue, and imagery in conversational discourse. Cambridge: Cambridge University Press.

Linguistic Politeness and Cultural Style: Observations from Japanese

YOSHIKO MATSUMOTO
The Ohio State University

1. Introduction[0]

It is widely known that languages such as Japanese and Korean lexically encode socio-psychological factors which fit under the broad term of politeness. A commonly held view by researchers in pragmatics is that the use of honorific (or politeness) morphemes can be adequately explained in terms of inherent violations of the Gricean MAXIM OF MANNER (especially the sub-maxims `avoid prolixity' and `avoid ambiguity') (e.g. Green 1990), with Brown and Levinson's politeness theory (1978, 1987) explaining the motivation for the violation. Such a view reflects two assumptions: that politeness is to be understood in terms of Gricean CONVERSATIONAL IMPLICATURES, and that

[0]I would like to thank Georgia Green for her discussions and comments on this and my earlier work on politeness, though what appears here does not necessarily reflect her views. My thanks are also due to Richard Janney, the organizer of a lecture series `Politeness Phenomena' held in Innsbruck in May, 1991, and to other participants for their discussions.

politeness phenomena are motivated by the universal `FACE WANTS' described by Brown and Levinson.

In this paper, I will argue that, although an explanation in terms of the above universal principles holds undeniable attractions, it is easy to over-generalize, thus missing language-and culture-specific characteristics that more accurately describe the system of linguistic politeness. In illustrating this point, I will first consider the question of whether the use of honorifics necessarily involves a violation of Gricean maxims, in particular those in the category of Manner, and will ask a related question of whether politeness can be described in terms of `Q-BASED' or `R-BASED' implicatures in the terminology of the neo-Griceans (Horn 1984, inter alia). I will also point out some problems that arise in applying the universal theory of politeness proposed by Brown and Levinson to Japanese politeness phenomena. I will then suggest a view of linguistic politeness as a systematic phenomenon in based on cultural factors, and suggest also that explanations of cross-linguistic politeness phenomena would likely benefit from consideration of what specific linguistic devices are used to convey the intended politeness and how they relate to the cultural factors. Although I do not discuss examples from Korean in this paper, I expect that the phenomena discussed here would be found also in Korean to a much greater extent than, for example, in English. Differences between Korean and Japanese in this regard would be of interest to the study of variations within a similar politeness style.

2. Gricean Manner Maxims and Japanese Honorifics

As is well known, Grice's theory was developed to account for a class of implicatures in ordinary language use that cannot be explained by the logical entailments of propositions. Participants in a conversation, according to Grice, are expected to observe what he called the COOPERATIVE PRINCIPLE, namely, `Make your conversational contribution such as is required, at the stage at which it occurs, by the accepted purpose or direction of the talk exchange in which you are engaged' (Grice 1975). Grice expanded on this principle, positing four categories of Maxims, which he called QUANTITY, QUALITY, RELATION, and MANNER.[1] The first three categories deal solely with

[1]Grice provides the following maxims under the four categories.

QUANTITY:

1. Make your contribution as informative as is required (for the current purposes of the exchange).

2. Do not make your contribution more informative than is required.

QUALITY: Try to make your contribution one that is true

1. Do not say what you believe to be false.

the amount, truthfulness, relevance of the proposition conveyed in an utterance, while the Manner Maxims concerns the way in which a proposition is expressed. Conversational implicatures, in Grice's term, characteristically arise when maxims are FLOUTED, i.e. blatantly not fulfilled. (Grice 1975: 49)[2]

Implicatures of the sort considered by Grice are certainly found in Japanese. What is at issue in this paper, however, is not Grice's theory per se, but whether linguistic politeness phenomena in Japanese can be fully explained in terms of conversational implicature. I argue that expressions of politeness in Japanese, particularly honorifics, are not well accounted for in terms of the proposition conveyed, or in terms of the degree of perspicuity of the utterance, which are the basic concepts relevant to the generation of conversational implicature. It is important to emphasize here that, when I speak of `expressions of politeness', I do not mean superfluous elements to an interactionally neutral expression of propositional content. It is a crucial fact about Japanese that the structure of the language does not allow the neutral expression of a proposition without conveying information about contextual factors; the speaker cannot opt out of choosing some expression that conveys an acknowledgement of the social context.

One simple illustration is how the information that today is Saturday is conveyed.[3] In English one could simply say *Today is Saturday*; in this form, it could be said to any addressee. It could, thus, be said to be interactionally neutral. This is far from the case in Japanese, where no single form could appropriately be said in all situations. Example (1) presents some of the most frequently found versions of *Today is Saturday*.

1a)	*Kyoo wa*	*doyoobi*	*da.*
	today TOPIC	Saturday	COPULA (plain)
	`Today is Saturday.'		

2. Do not say that for which you lack adequate evidence.

RELATION: Be relevant

MANNER: Be perspicuous

1. Avoid obscurity of expression.
2. Avoid ambiguity.
3. Be brief (avoid unnecessary prolixity).
4. Be orderly.

[2]An example given by Grice of a flouting of a maxim for the purpose of making a conversational implicature is a professor's recommendation letter for a philosophy job which reads `Mr. X's command of English is excellent, and his attendance at tutorials has been regular.' By flouting the first maxim of Quantity, the professor is implicating that the applicant is not a good philosopher.

[3]More detailed discussions on this point are given in Matsumoto (1989).

b) *Kyoo wa doyoobi desu.*
COPULA (polite)

c) *Kyoo wa doyoobi degozaimasu.*
COPULA (super polite)

The terms `plain', `polite', and `super polite' in the glosses in example (1) are traditional, but perhaps misleading. (1a) would be chosen when the speaker does not have to acknowledge any interpersonal relationship with the addressee, either because the relationship is intimate, and can be taken for granted, or because the communication is impersonal, such as in expository writing. This form may be perceived as the neutral form, but it is not neutral in the true sense since it is subject to the described conditions of use.

(1b), on the other hand, encodes an acknowledgement of a relationship with the addressee. (1c) expresses a greater degree of deference in the speaker's relation with the addressee and a greater degree of formality in the discourse.

The choice of honorifics (including what may be regularly considered as neutral forms) according to what they communicate about the interpersonal relationship could certainly be described as a choice of the manner in which a proposition is conveyed. What I wish to argue here, however, is that it is not a choice that fits under Grice's Manner Maxim `Be perspicuous', and that the Manner Maxims cannot be altered to cover such choices without considerable revision to Grice's framework.

Grice's maxims in the category of Manner are the supermaxim `Be perspicuous', under which are various sub-maxims, of which he lists `Avoid obscurity of expression', `Avoid ambiguity', `Be brief (avoid unnecessary prolixity)' and `Be orderly'. The fact that these concern how something is said, rather than what is said, may explain their appeal as a basis for politeness theory. One drawback of the Gricean implicature approach to an account of politeness, is that it does not distinguish between the expression of politeness by means of indirectness, hedging, presenting options and so forth, and the obligatory use of honorifics, in which, in the absence of a truly neutral form, some interactionally-loaded lexical or morphological element must be chosen. It should be made clear that I am not suggesting that the politeness effect of, for example, honorific expressions in Japanese cannot be achieved in a language like English, in which interactionally neutral forms are possible, nor that Gricean implicatures are never employed to convey politeness in languages like Japanese. The fact that there is a variety of means for expressing politeness in languages that do not have a system of honorific morphemes has been amply demonstrated, for example by Lakoff (1973, 1975, 1979) and by Brown and Levinson (1978, 1987); moreover, there is no doubt that utterances in Japanese can be polite by virtue of their flouting the Gricean maxims. But I believe that further insights can be found by recognizing at least two ways of achieving linguistic politeness than by lumping them in a single category. We could then consider whether there is a common principle of politeness observable across different means of expressing politeness.

Let us focus on Grice's Manner Maxim: `Be perspicuous' and its implication to Japanese politeness expressions. By way of comparison with the examples considered earlier in (1), suppose that, in response to a question asking what day it is today, the utterance in (2) were elicited.

2)	Kinoo	ga	kinyoobi	de	asita	ga
	yesterday	NOM	Friday	is	tomorrow	NOM

nitiyoobi da *kara*...
Sunday is so
`Yesterday was Friday, and tomorrow is Sunday, so..'

There is no doubt that the utterance in (2) infringes the Manner maxims, in particular the submaxim `Be brief (avoid unnecessary prolixity)'. It could be argued that it also violates the maxims in the category of Quantity, which require that an utterance express as much information as is necessary, and no more. In any event, an utterance such as (2) would cause a conversational implicature, for instance, that the speaker wishes to tease the addressee by pointing out an obvious fact of dates, or, less likely, that the speaker does not know the name of the day between Friday and Sunday. What we see from example (2) is that a violation of the Manner Maxim `Be brief' need not be associated with an implicature that the speaker wishes to make the utterance polite. That does not, of course, preclude violations of Manner Maxims from implicating politeness, but it does show that an account treating politeness in the framework of Grice's Manner Maxims, i.e. an account claiming that politeness including honorific uses are to be understood as types of Manner Maxim flouting, would require a supplementary account of precisely which types of violations of the maxims cause expressions to be considered polite.

It might be argued that, while prolixity may not imply politeness, the converse at least is true; in other words, the greater the degree of politeness, the longer the expression, since something additional is conveyed. An apparent example for this is the subject-honorific verb *mesiagaru* `eat' in (3 a), which is a longer expression than the verb *taberu* `eat' in (3 b). However, an equally long verb *tabeyagaru* `eat', which is in a so-called vulgar form, conveys not politeness but contempt. We cannot, therefore, expect a close correlation between politeness and prolixity at the level of lexical variants.

3a) *mesiagaru*
eat (Subject Honorific)

b) *taberu*
eat

c) *tabeyagaru*
eat (Vulgar)

Similarly at the sentence level, the indirect request in (4a), is LESS polite than the direct request in (4b), although it is both less brief and less direct.

4a) *Kore, motte-kure-nai kasira.*
this hold-give-not I wonder
(lit.)`I wonder if you will give me the favor of holding this.'
`Won't you hold this for me?'

b) *Kore, motte-kudasai.*
this hold-give (Subject Honorific) -IMPERATIVE
(lit.)`Please give me the favor of holding this.'
`Please hold this for me.'

It is not that the Gricean Manner Maxims have no role in linguistic politeness or in honorific expressions, but that they are not sufficient to explain, for instance, why (4b) is more polite than (4a).

Furthermore, it is perfectly possible, as is well recognized, that violations of maxims other than those of Manner could be exploited to make an utterance polite. Suppose, for example, that the inquiry of which day it is were to elicit the response in (5).

5) *Genkoo no simekiri wa mada desu yo.*
manuscript GEN deadline TOP not-yet COP(polite) SFP
`It's not the deadline for the manuscript yet.'

The utterance in (5) can be viewed as violating Grice's maxims of Quantity, in that it does not give enough information to determine the day, and Relation, in that the question did not mention the deadline for the manuscript. These deviations from Grice's maxims can be seen as motivated by some consideration of politeness, in that the speaker tries to be helpful by offering directly the information that he or she believes to underlie the inquiry, but they are not associated with violations of the maxims of Manner.

We have seen in this section that, although honorific expressions may seem to be explicable in terms of Gricean conversational implicatures based on violations of Manner Maxims, such an explanation misses the very characteristics of honorifics in Japanese and would not contribute to the understanding of the nature of politeness phenomena in Japanese.[4]

3. The Neo-Gricean Formulation of Implicatures

Grice's approach to conversational implicature has been streamlined and expanded in scope by Horn (1984), who separates out Grice's maxim of Quality, or the requirement of truthfulness, from the arena of conversational implicatures, and distills the remaining Gricean maxims into two principles, which he terms the `Q-' and `R-principles'. The `Q-PRINCIPLE': `Make your contribution sufficient,' is a lower-bounding principle, while the `R-PRINCIPLE': `Make your contribution necessary,' gives an upper-bound. In this framework, in contrast to Grice's, implicatures arise from the assumption that the principles are observed, rather than from violations of conversational maxims. Thus, for example, *Some of my friends are Buddhists* implicates, in accordance with the Q-principle, that NOT ALL of my friends are Buddhists, while the often-discussed example of an indirect speech act *Can you pass me the salt?* implicates, following the R-principle, that the speaker desires the addressee to pass him the salt.

For Horn, the rules of politeness discussed by R. Lakoff (1973) and the theory of Brown and Levinson (1978) can be recast as upper- and lower-bounding principles governing actions. Thus, Lakoff's rules `Don't impose' and `Give options', or Brown and Levinson's principle of respecting the addressee's `NEGATIVE FACE' are viewed as constraints analogous to his `R-principle', while Lakoff's rule `Be friendly', or Brown and Levinson's principle of respecting the addressee's `POSITIVE FACE' are treated as analogous to the `Q-principle'.

---

[4]Grice distinguishes CONVENTIONAL IMPLICATURE from conversational implicature. When the conventional meaning of the words used determine what is implicated rather than what is SAID (in the strict sense), one speaks of conventional implicature. Levinson (1983) alludes to honorifics as conventional implicatures. I consider this view to be more plausible than the one in terms of conversational implicatures. It is interesting to note, however, that the failure to use an expected honorific expression could be treated as a distinct type of implicature (not mentioned by Grice). For more discussion of such an implicature (INTERACTIONAL IMPLICATURE), see Matsumoto (1989).

Horn's formulation of politeness styles in terms of the polar opposites of `R-based' politeness, or the avoidance of being explicit, and `Q-based' politeness, or the ready communication of one's intentions, is particularly effective in analyzing the sort of communication breakdown reported by Tannen (1975, 1979) in her accounts of the clash between the conversational styles of a speaker who is voluble and talkative and one who is terse and reserved.

It is less clear, however, how such a bi-polar system can accommodate distinct politeness styles such as those suggested in Lakoff (1979) under the headings `Clarity', `Distance', `Deference', and `Camaraderie.' To collapse such distinctions onto the `Q-R' axis seems to diminish their possible explanatory power, and seems to require the assumption that Distance and Deference styles involve avoiding saying too much, an assumption that, in fact, runs counter to claims that politeness results from exploiting the Gricean Manner Maxim, insofar as such claims are based on the association of politeness with prolixity. It is at least not apparent how the quantity of action in the framework of Q- and R-principles should be related to the linguistic realizations of politeness.

4. The Politeness Theory of Brown and Levinson

A comprehensive and detailed framework to account for politeness phenomena was proposed by Brown and Levinson (1978, 1987). Their analyses of politeness do not necessarily adhere to the theory that politeness is explicable in terms of violations of the Manner Maxim, but they consider politeness to be one of the major motivations for deviation from the Gricean maxims. In other words, they focus on one motivation, namely, politeness, for various linguistic expressions, and assume the universality of such a motivation. Their goal was to `show that superficial diversities can emerge from underlying universal principles' (1978:61), and they propose, as the universal principles underlying politeness phenomena, rational strategies oriented towards the `face' of the conversational participants. In their account, `face' comprises two aspects: `negative face', or the want that one's actions be unimpeded by others, and `positive face', or the want that one's wants be desirable to at least some others. They divide politeness strategies into `negative' and `positive' politeness, according to whether they are directed to the addressee's negative or positive face wants.

The basic idea that a universal motivation for linguistic politeness can be founded on the general concept of `face', or `socially-given self-image' is appealing and may well be true. What seems less certain, however, is whether `negative' and `positive' face, as defined by Brown and Levinson, together form the content of `face' in all societies. One indication to the contrary is the existence of deferential expressions in Japanese that nonetheless impose an obligation on the addressee. An example is given in (5).[5]

6) *Doozo yorosiku onegaisimasu.*
please well ask (polite)
(lit.) `I ask you please to take care of me.'

The example in (6) is a commonly-used expression by which the speaker expresses deference to someone to whom he or she has just been introduced. In Brown and Levinson's account, deference is a negative politeness strategy. From that perspective, however, it is odd, at least, that the speech act conveyed by the deferential utterance in (6) is a request, an act that imposes an obligation on the addressee; an act, in other words, that threatens the addressee's `negative face'.

The lack of fit between the theory based on the proposed constituents of `face' and politeness phenomena in Japanese cannot easily be avoided simply by viewing deference in Japanese as a positive politeness strategy. As Brown and Levinson point out, positive politeness is `in many respects normal linguistic behavior between intimates,...' (1978:106). Expressions of deference, however, would usually be inappropriate in conversations between intimates.

The problem revealed by examples such as (6) stems in part from the inclusion under the name `deference' of two quite distinct politeness strategies: one being the recognition and acceptance that the relationship between the speaker and addressee is, in some sense, that of inferior and superior; the other, which we might, following Lakoff (1973, 1975, 1979), distinguish as a strategy of `distance', being the denial of any relationship between speaker and addressee, and the consequent acceptance that the speaker has no right to place demands on the addressee. The degree to which a person may impose on someone towards whom he or she is expected to be deferent will probably depend very much on the particular culture. In Japanese society, one is expected to show deference to others NOT by virtue of attributes they possess as a natural right, such as would be the case in a caste society, but by virtue of the position that they occupy in a social frame or group to which one belongs.[6] In such a society, which is at once egalitarian and conscious of claims of seniority, a requirement of deference does not preclude the right to impose.

---

[5]For more detailed and related discussions, see Matsumoto (1988).

[6]This view of the Japanese society in contrast to others is most clearly articulated by Nakane (1967, 1970).

With regard to honorifics in Japanese, Brown and Levinson make the important point that `they are not arbitrary forms: they originate as productive outputs of face-preserving strategies which become stabilized and change their meaning' (1978:284), and they attribute honorifics to the operation of negative politeness. It is important to note, however, that the origin of such honorific morphemes is based on rank-ordering rather than on freedom from imposition as can be observed in examples such as the polite verb ending *masu* `cause to be, honorably dwell and the first person referential term *watakusi* `slave, servant'.

What I have sketched here is an argument that the politeness theory of Brown and Levinson may fail to be universal not in its generalities, in other words in positing maintenance of `face' as the dynamic governing polite behavior, but in the specific aspects, `positive' and `negative' face, which they propose as the universal components of `face'. To be sure, Brown and Levinson allow for cultural relativity in the weights assigned to such interpersonal factors as social distance and power differentials in the calculation of the degree to which utterances may threaten `face', but I would argue that the theory should allow for variations at the more fundamental level of what constitutes `face' in a particular culture.

5. Linguistic Form and Cultural Style

A universal framework for politeness phenomena can, as I have argued, mask factors that are of central importance in a particular culture. An account of the politeness content of particular linguistic expressions, on the other hand, can bring those culture-specific factors into clear focus.

One example, noted by Mizutani (1979), is the degree to which the choice of an intransitive over a transitive verb in Japanese can be pragmatically loaded. This is illustrated in the contrast between the utterances in (7a) and (7b).

7a) *Kariteita sutoobu ga* *kowarete-simai-masita.*
borrowed heater NOM break(v.i.)-result-PAST (polite)
`The heater that (I) had borrowed broke.'

b) *Kariteita sutoobu o* *kowasite-simai-masita.*
ACC break(v.t.)-result-PAST (polite)
`(I) broke the heater (I) borrowed.'

Mizutani reports that an American graduate student who was staying at a Japanese village was surprised when her utterance of the sentence in (7a) to her landlady was apparently regarded as offensive. As Mizutani explains, that was because the choice of an intransitive verb in (7a) does not convey any sense of the speaker's responsibility. In such an instance, some expression of responsibility, such as in (7b), would be expected.

It could be argued that the interpretation of (7b) as a polite way of reporting the fact that the heater has broken involves a conversational implicature that results from at least a violation of the maxim of Quality. That is, by saying that one broke the heater in a context where one would be assumed not to have intended to break it, one implicates that one is taking responsibility for its breaking. In the corresponding English sentences, on the other hand, the sentence with the transitive verb would not generate such an implicature; it would, more likely, be taken as implying that the speaker had deliberately broken the heater belonging to the addressee.

Such differences in the degree of politeness conveyed or implicated by sentences in one language and their semantic equivalents in another are common, and militate against a universal account of politeness based on Gricean implicatures.[7] I would argue, however, that such differences are systematic, and to some extent predictable from a general description of the interpersonal factors to which speakers of the languages in question are attentive.

Consider, as another example, request forms in English and Japanese. In English, as described in Searle's theory of `indirect speech acts' (1975), one may make a request in the form of a question that asks about the addressee's future action, or ability to perform a certain action; or in the form of an assertion of the speaker's desire that a certain action be performed. The canonical example, as I mentioned earlier, is *Can you pass me the salt?* . Such an indirect speech act is usually more polite than a direct form.

In Japanese, on the other hand, polite requests are typically expressed with the use of verbs of giving and receiving, such as *kudasaru, kureru* , `give', or *morau, itadaku* `receive', which serve as auxiliaries that convey that the action in question would be of benefit to the speaker, and that the speaker would be honored if the addressee were to bestow that benefit. Requests are not made polite in Japanese simply by couching them in the form of another speech act such as a question. This can be explained by saying that the primary face-threat occasioned by a request in Japanese is not simply the imposition on the addressee's freedom of action -- the threat to his `negative face' -- but the imbalance in the rank relation caused by a directive speech act. The primary politeness strategy,

[7]Peter Sells pointed out to me that similar differences can be noticed in the contrast between *can you?/can't you?* and *kudasaimasu ka* `(lit.) will you give me the favor of ...?' /*kudasaimasen ka* `won't you give me the favor of...?' In English, the first is more polite, while in Japanese, the second is more polite.

consequently, must redress the balance in the rank relation by an expression of humility on the part of the one making the request.

Honorific forms, as mentioned in the discussion of the examples in (1), are used in Japanese even in the apparent absence of face-threatening situations. This illustrates the cultural characteristic that the non-acknowledgement of the interpersonal and role relation in the context of a conversation implies a familiarity that cannot be claimed without insult, except among intimates. In this respect, it could be said that all utterances in Japanese are face-threatening, requiring acknowledgement of the interpersonal relation.

These linguistic phenomena I have mentioned illustrate the general tendency of the Japanese politeness style, which we could encapsulate as deference based on the social roles of the interlocutors and referents. The encoding of the acknowledgement of the social and interactional relationship in accordance with this general style is observable in various situations and expressions. Thus, it seems to me that a cross-cultural study of precisely how the notion of `cultural style' is manifested in real discourse situations would be of particular value and would contribute to future studies toward an understanding of the principles underlying politeness, and would in fact be necessary as the basis of any truly universal pragmatic theory of linguistic politeness.

References

Brown, Penelope & Stephen Levinson. 1978. Universals in language usage: politeness phenomena. Questions and politeness, (ed.) E.N. Goody. Cambridge: Cambridge University Press. 56-290.

_______. 1987. Politeness: Some universals in language usage. Cambridge: Cambridge University Press.

Green, Georgia M. 1990. The role of pragmatics in language understanding. New Jersey: Pragmatics & Language Learning, (eds.) L. Bouton & Y. Kachru. Univ. of Illinois. 21-41.

Grice, H. Paul. 1975. Logic and conversation. Syntax and Semantics 3: Speech Acts, (eds.) P. Cole & J. Morgan. New York: Academic Press. 41-58.

Horn, Laurence R. 1984. Toward a new taxonomy for pragmatic inference: Q-based and R-based implicature. Georgetown University Round Table of Language and Linguistics, (ed.) D. Schiffrin. Georgetown: Georgetown University Press. 11-42.

Lakoff, Robin. 1973. The logic of politeness: Or, minding your p's and q's. Papers from the ninth regional meeting of the Chicago Linguistic Society, (eds.) C. Corum et al. 292-305.

_________. 1975. Language and women's place. New York: Harper and Row.

________. 1979. Stylistic strategies within a grammar of style. The Annals of the New York Academy of Science. 53-78.

Levinson, Stephen C. 1983. Pragmatics. Cambridge: Cambridge University Press.

Matsumoto, Yoshiko. 1988. Reexamination of the universality of face: Politeness phenomena in Japanese. Journal of Pragmatics 12. 403-426.

______. 1989. Questions on politeness and conversational universals: Observations from Japanese. Multilingua 8-2/3. 207-221.

_______. 1991. Cultural relativity in theories of politeness: Arguments from Japanese (Or, Being nice without Grice), a paper presented at Lecture Series: Politeness Phenomena at the international conference `New departures in contrastive linguistics' in Innsbruck, Austria.

Mizutani, O. 1979. Nihongo no seitai (Ecology of Japanese). Tokyo: Sootakusya.

Searle, J. 1975. Indirect speech acts, (eds.) P. Cole and J. Morgan. Syntax and Semantics 3: Speech Acts. New York: Academic Press. 59-82.

Idiomatic Conditionals in Japanese

SHIGEKO OKAMOTO
California State University, Fresno

I. Introduction

There are a number of morphosyntactic formulas in Japanese which require reduplication of a verb, adjective, or noun (Okamoto 1990, 1991). This paper examines three verbal reduplicative constructions (VRCs): 1. *V temo V temo* (the *temo* construction), 2. *V/A eba V/A hodo* (the *hodo* construction), and 3. *V/A tara V/A ta de* (the *tara* construction). (*V* stands for verb, and *A* adjective.) By analyzing their similarities and differences with regard to the morphosyntactic, semantic, and pragmatic properties, I will demonstrate that these constructions, though idiomatic, are nevertheless productive, and that they exhibit properties of both unanalyzable lexical items and regular analyzable phrases. These VRCs, I argue, are best accounted for in a nonmodular manner as 'grammatical constructions', as characterized by Fillmore and others (Fillmore, Kay, and O'Conner 1988, Fillmore 1985, Lambrecht 1984).

In the following, I will first describe the semantic and pragmatic properties of these constructions, proceeding then to their morphosyntactic properties.

II. Semantic and Pragmatic Properties

Semantically, all three constructions are noncompositional, that is, they cannot be analyzed according to regular semantic interpretation principles. Their meanings differ from each other as follows:

1. V temo V temo: Literally, *V temo V temo* means 'even if/though V, even if/though V', but the construction as a whole means 'no matter how much/how often . . . V'. For example, *osaetemo osaetemo,* literally 'even if/though (I) suppress (it), even if/though (I) suppress (it)', actually means 'no matter how much (I try to) suppress (it)', as shown in example (1).

(1) <from a book review by Kurimoto Shinichiroo>
hara no soko kara osaetemo osaetemo
stomach Gn bottom from suppress even though suppress even though
osae-kirenai ikari ga komi-agete kite simatta no da.
suppress completely Neg anger SM burst out come Pst
'(lit.) The anger that (I) couldn't suppress completely, no matter how much (I) tried to suppress (it), (it) burst out from the bottom of my stomach.'

2. V/A eba V/A hodo: Literally, *V/A eba V/A hodo* means 'if V/A, to the extent V/A'; as a whole it means 'the more V/A, (the more X)'. For example, *tabereba taberu hodo,* literally 'if (one) eats, to the extent (one) eats', actually means 'the more (one) eats', as shown in example (2).

(2) (Mother to her son:) <attested in conversation>
Tabereba taberu hodo ookiku nareru no yo.
eat if eat extent big can become
'The more (you) eat, the bigger (you) can become.'

3. V/A tara V/A ta de: Literally, *V/A tara V/A ta de* could be interpreted as 'if/when . . . V/A, in (the case that . . .) V/A'. This construction followed by a main clause marks contrastiveness of the condition (P) and sameness of the consequence (Q). That is, it presupposes 'If/When not P, then Q (or similar to Q)' and asserts 'If/When P, also Q'--the intended nuance is a weakened version of 'Even if P'. For example, *itara ita de* may be literally interpreted as 'if (someone) is (there), in (the case someone) is (there)', but as a whole it means '(even) if (someone) is there' with the contrastive nuance mentioned above. Example (3) illustrates the usage.

(3) *Nyooboo ga inakattara komaru kedo, itara ita de mata urusai.*
wife SM be Neg if bothered but be if be also annoying
'If/When (my) wife is not (around), (I)'m bothered, but (even) if/when (she) is, (it) is also annoying.'

Thus all three constructions, like lexical compounds, are semantically unanalyzable. Further, each construction exhibits other semantic and pragmatic idiosyncrasies, as described below:

1. *V temo V temo*: The *temo* construction, like the other two constructions, involves not only the level of propositional content, but also the level of inter-clause linkage. At the level of the proposition, the *temo* construction is used to refer to an action and the manner in which it is performed; more specifically, it indicates that some goal-oriented laborious action is attempted repeatedly or persistently. At the level of clause linkage, it serves as a connective between two propositions, marking the proposition in the *Vtemo V temo* clause as subordinate to the succeeding main proposition and at the same time indicating that the relationship between the two propositions is strongly paradoxical: It violates the normal expectation that by trying an action repeatedly or persistently, one can achieve one's goal. For example, in (1) the reduplicative expression *osaetemo osaetemo* describes a situation in which the writer made repeated attempts to suppress his anger, but, nevertheless, failed to do so. Similar examples are given in (4)-(6).

(4) <from *Asahi* weekly magazine>
Hito ni yotte wa itizi-teki ni harattemo harattemo . . .
person depending on temporarily pay even if pay even if
roon no zandaka ga hueru to yuu zitai mo okiru no da.
loan Gn remainder SM increase situation also occur
'Depending on the person, there are cases in which no matter how much (they) pay (back), the remaining amount of the loan increases.'

(5) (The speaker is describing how difficult it is to get a computer terminal at the LSA Summer Institute.) <attested in conversation>

Mattemo mattemo, minna itido suwattara
wait even if wait even if everyone once sit down when
hanaretakunai tte omouzya nai, ...
leave want Neg Comp think Neg
'No matter how much (I) wait (for a terminal to become available), (I cannot easily get one) because once people sit down (at a terminal), they all think that they do not want to leave, right?'

(6) *Hataraitemo hataraitemo kurasi ga raku ni naranai.*
work even though work even though living SM better become Neg
'No matter how much (I) work, (my) living (condition) does not improve.'

To understand the nature of this reduplicative *temo* construction better, let us compare it with the more commonly used single *temo* construction. The single *temo* construction also expresses paradoxicality, but does not in itself specify the repetitive manner of the action, as the double *temo* construction does. This difference is illustrated in (7) and (7a).

(7) *Kusa o* *tottemo* *tottemo* *mata sugu*
weed OM remove even if remove even if again immediately
haete kuru.
grow come
'No matter how many times (I) remove the weeds, (they) come back again immediately.'

(7a) *Kusa o* *tottemo* *mata sugu*
'Even if (I) remove the weeds, (they) come back again
haete kuru.
immediately.'

As indicated in the above examples, the use of the double *temo* construction is restricted to action verbs that can be performed repeatedly or persistently. The single *temo* construction, on the other hand, has no such restriction. For example, in (8) the double *temo* construction is used inappropriately because an adjective (i.e. a stative verbal) is involved; the single *temo* construction, on the other hand, is fine (8a).

(8) #*Takakutemo* *takakutemo* *kau.*
expensive even if expensive even if buy
'(lit.) Even if (it) is expensive, even if (it) is expensive, (I) will buy (it).'

(8a) *Takakutemo* *kau.*
'Even if (it) is expensive, (I) will buy (it).'

Note that a hightened sense of paradoxicality can also be expressed by the single *temo* construction when accompanied by a universal or 'free choice' quantifier, such as *donna ni* and *ikura* 'no matter how much/many'. This expression with a universal quantifier (e.g. (6a)) and the expression with the reduplicative *temo* construction (e.g. (6)) are near paraphrases. But there is a difference of nuance. The reduplicative construction emphasizes the repetitive or endless nature of the action; the expression with a universal quantifier indicates that the degree of the situation expressed by the *temo* clause may vary from the minimum to the maximum in its possible range.

(6a) *Ikura* *hataraitemo* *kurasi ga raku ni naranai.*
how much work even though living SM better become Neg
'No matter how much (I) work, (my) living (condition) does not improve.'

As we saw earlier, the use of the reduplicative *temo* construction is restricted to action verbs (e.g. (7) and (8)). The use of universal quantifiers, however, has no such restriction, as shown in (8b).

(8b) *Donna ni takakutemo kau.*
how much expensive even if buy
'No matter how expensive (it) is, (I) will buy (it).'

2. *V/A eba V/A hodo*: At the level of propositional content, the *hodo* construction is used to describe a certain action/process/state and the manner in which it may be realized. More specifically, it indicates that the action/process/state may be realized in progressively varying degrees within the possible range. At the level of clause linkage, the *hodo* construction functions as a connective between two propositions, marking the proposition in the *V eba V hodo* clause as subordinate to the proposition in the succeeding main clause and at the same time specifying the proposition in the subordinate clause as the condition for the truth of the proposition in the main clause. Further, as discussed by Fillmore (1987), the *hodo* construction dictates a proportional scalar interpretation of the subordinate and main clauses: that is, the situation in the main clause is interpreted as varying in proportion to the change in the condition specified in the subordinate clause. For example, in (2) (reproduced below) the speaker asserts that eating is a condition for the addressee to become big, and also that the degree of becoming big depends on the degree of eating.

(2) (Mother to her son:) <attested in conversation>
Tabereba taberu hodo ookiku nareru no yo.
eat if eat extent big can become
'The more (you) eat, the bigger (you) can become.'

In (2a), on the other hand, the subordinate clause, containing only a single verb and the connective *reba,* is interpreted as a straightforward conditional clause, having no scalar meaning.

(2a) (Mother to her son:) <attested in conversation>
Tabereba ookiku nareru no yo.
eat if big can become
'If (you) eat, (you) can become big.'

Examples (9)-(11) further illustrate the usage of the *hodo* construction. Note that the construction is not restricted to verbs, but is applicable to adjectives as well, as shown in (11).

(9) <from the short story *Run Run Syookoo-gun* by Hayashi Mariko>
Yoohuku to yuu no wa kaeba kau hodo, manzoku dekinaku
clothes TM buy if buy extent be satisfied can Neg
natte iku.
become
'Clothes, the more (you) buy, the more (you) become unable to be satisfied/(the less satisfied (you) become).

(10) <from the novel *Chookyori Denwa* by Akagawa Jiroo>
Kangaereba Kangaeru hodo, denwa-sitemo muda da to
think if think extent telephone futile
yuu kimoti ga tuyomatta.
feeling SM strong become Pst
'The more (I) thought, the stronger the feeling became--the feeling that it's futile to call (him).'

(11) <from the short story *Hana yori Kekkon Kibi-dango* by Hayashi Mariko>
Kuroo ga ookikereba ookii hodo, koohuku datte ookiku
hardship SM large if large extent happiness also big
naru.
become
'The larger the hardship is, the larger the happiness becomes.'

As the above examples show, the main clause/the consequent often contains a change-of-state verb, such as *naru* 'become' and *tuyomaru* 'become strong'. Even when this is not the case, however, the main verb(al) receives a scalar interpretation.

(12) <from the novel *Hushin no Toki* by Ariyoshi Sawako>
Hayakereba hayai hodo, ii.
early if early extent good
'The sooner the better.'

(13) *Heta de areba aru hodo, rensyuu ga hituyoo da.*
unskillful be if be extent practice SM need
'The more unskillful (you) are, the more practice (you) need.'

For example, in (12) the main clause, if taken alone, literally, means 'it is good'; in (13) the main clause literally means 'you need practice'. But with the *hodo* construction both clauses receive a scalar interpretation.

3. *V/A tara V/A ta de*: At the level of propositional content, the *tara* construction is used to describe a certain action, process, or state (but not its manner). At the level of clause linkage, it functions as a connective between two propositions, marking the proposition in the *V/A tara V/A ta*

de clause as subordinate to the proposition in the succeeding main clause, and also specifying the proposition in the subordinate clause (Q) as the condition/framework for the truth of the proposition in the main clause (P). Further, as mentioned, in using the *tara* construction, the speaker presupposes 'If/When not P, then Q (or similar to Q)', and asserts '(Even) if/when P, also Q'. The use of this construction suggests that the two contrasting conditions/frameworks independently bring about the same or a similar result. For example, observe (3) (reproduced below).

(3) *Nyooboo ga inakattara komaru kedo, itara ita de mata*
wife SM be Neg if bothered but be if be also
urusai.
annoying
'If/When (my) wife is not (around), (I)'m bothered, but (even) if/when (she) is, (it) is also annoying.'

The speaker in (3) first describes the situation in which the absence of the speaker's wife brings about inconvenience for the speaker. Then, the speaker uses the reduplicative expression *itara ita de* to refer to the opposite condition, in which his wife is not absent. By doing so, he indicates that this condition independently brings about the same kind of consequent inconvenience as the opposite condition does. A similar example is given in (14).

(14) (A and B are talking about B's niece, who came to the US from Japan because she had difficulty fitting into Japanese society.)
<attested in conversation>
A: *Moo America ni sumu no.*
now in live
'Is (she) going to live in America from now on (permanently)?'
B: *Uun, Nihon ni kaeru tte. Yappari America wa iya da tte*
no Japan to return say as expected TM dislike say
itteru.
say
'No, (she) says (she) will go back to Japan. (She) says (she) does not like America, as expected.'
A: *Demo, Nihon ni kaettara kaetta de, mata taihen nan zya*
but Japan to return if return again have difficulties
nai no.
Neg
'But, (even) if (she) goes back to Japan, don't you think (she) will again have a hard time?'

By the expression *kaettara kaetta de*, speaker A in (14) is implicitly comparing the results of the two contrastive conditions (i.e. staying in the

US vs. returning to Japan) and suggests that either condition will result in the same kind of situation (i.e. having a hard time).

When the two contrasting conditions/frameworks produce contrasting, rather than similar, consequences, the use of the reduplicative *tara* construction is unacceptable, as shown in (14b). In such a situation the regular single *tara* conditional construction is appropriate, as in (14c).

(14b) A: #*Amerika ni itara* *iroiro* *taihen da* *kedo, Nihon ni*
in stay if various have difficulties but Japan to
kaettara kaetta de, umaku iku daroo.
return if return well go probably
'If (she) stays in the US, (she) will have various difficulties, but (even) if (she) goes back to Japan, (she) will probably do well.'

(14c) A: *Amerika ni itara* *iroiro* *taihen da* *kedo, Nihon ni*
in stay if various have difficulties but Japan to
kaettara umaku iku daroo.
return if well go probably
'If (she) stays in the US, (she) will have various difficulties, but if (she) goes back to Japan, (things) will probably go well.'

Example (15) further illustrates the kind of comparison implicit in the reduplicative *tara* construction.

(15) <from a TV drama>
Baretara bareta de *gomen nasai tte* *atama sagerya*
found out if found out sorry saying apologize if
sumu *koto zya nai desu ka.*
alright Comp Neg
'(Even) if (they) find out (our secret), (we) will apologize saying sorry, then (everything) should be alright, shouldn't (it)?.'

The speaker of (15) implies that if the secret is not found out, it is fine, and asserts that even if it is found out, it will not be a problem, either.

The three constructions examined above have a number of properties in common, one of which is the fact that they all involve both the level of the proposition and that of inter-clause linkage. This property distinguishes them from various other VRCs, such as *V ni V* (the *ni* construction) and *V koto wa V* (the *koto wa* construction). For example, the *ni* construction involves only the level of the proposition (e.g. (16)); and the *koto wa* construction involves the level of the proposition and that of modality (e.g. (17)) (Okamoto 1990).

(16) *Kinoo wa nomi-ni nonda.*
yesterday TM drink drink Pst
'Yesterday, (I) drank to an extreme extent.'

(17) <from a TV drama>
Mita koto wa mita kedo kao wa oboete imasen.
see Pst Comp TM see Pst but face TM remember Neg
'It is true that (I) saw (him), but (I) don't remember (his) face.'

In sum, the analysis of the three constructions in this section shows that each construction bears a unique semantic and pragmatic properties that are unanalyzable by regular compositional semantic interpretation rules, and suggests that it be treated as a whole, like an idiom or a lexical item (i.e. verbal compound).

Note that there are two other constructions that are similar in function to the *tara* construction: *V/A eba V/A ta de* (e.g. (18)) and *V/A nara V/A de* (e.g. (19)).

(18) (talking about a baby) <from a novel *Hushin no Toki* by Ariyoshi Sawako>
Me o samaseba samasita de kawaiku, nereba neta de
wake up when wake up Pst cute sleep when sleep Pst
zitu ni airasikatta.
truly adorable Pst
'When (she/the baby) woke up, (she) was cute; when (she) slept, (she) was (again) truly adorable.'

(19) <from a TV drama>
Iku nara iku de uso wa tuku na.
go if go lie TM tell
'If (you) go (to a disco), don't lie.'

There are differences in matters of detail, however, which call for further study.

III. Morphosyntactic Properties

I now turn to the morphosyntactic (and phonological) properties of the three VRCs. My analysis will demonstrate that despite their semantic-pragmatic non-compositionality, these constructions cannot be considered genuine idioms/lexical items, and that they exhibit both the properties of idioms/lexical items and those of analyzable phrases. To show this, I will examine the following eight properties in each of the three constructions: (1) productivity, (2) morphological elements, (3) pitch pattern, (4) analyzability by regular phrase structure rules, (5) possibility of syntactic intrusion, (6) behavior with regard to tense markers, (7) behavior with regard to the passive morpheme, and (8) behavior with regard to the causative morpheme.

(1) Productivity

Although the three constructions are semantically like idioms, they are all fully productive; that is, their members are not exhaustively listable. In this respect, they behave like regular phrases.

(2) Morphological elements

Morphologically, all three constructions differ from compound verbs, and are similar to analyzable phrases. A compound verb, such as *tobi-tuku* 'jump at', consists of a verb stem (e.g. *tobi* 'jump') followed by another verb (e.g. *tuku* 'stick to'). There is no intervening element between the two verbs. On the other hand, the three VRCs examined here all have (an) extra element(s) beside the two occurrences of the verb: the *temo* construction has the connective particle *temo*; the *hodo* construction the connective particle *eba* and the particle *hodo*; and the *tara* construction the connective particle *tara* and the particle *de*.

(3) Pitch pattern

The three constructions also differ from verbal compounds with regard to pitch patterns. In the case of verbal compounds, there is only one accentual peak in each compound, as shown in (20). That is, they have the pitch pattern of lexical items.

(20) *oti-tuku*
fall arrive
'calm down/settle dowm'

Each of the three reduplicative constructions, on the other hand, has two accentual peaks, which is a regular phrase-like property. This is shown in (20a)-(20c) (NB: *nomu* 'drink').

(20a) *non demo non demo*
(20b) *nomeba nomu hodo*
(20c) *nondara nonda de*

(4) Analyzability by regular phrase structure rules

It was mentioned above that the three constructions are fully productive. Yet they cannot be generated by regular phrase structure rules. In other words, they are not fully analyzable in term of regular syntactic categories. All three constructions use reduplication of a verb(al), and the two instances of the verb in each construction are not independent verbs belonging to two separate clauses. Rather, they function like a constituent of a single subordinate clause. As suggested in the earlier discussion, each constructions as a whole acts as if it were of the form 'V+(Adv)+Conj'. With regard to the *temo* construction, for example, it might be argued that one of the two instances of *V temo* can be regarded separately as an adverbial phrase, meaning 'repeatedly' or 'persitently'. This argument, however, is not sustainable: the adverbial function in question is effected only through the reduplication, not by either *V temo* independently. The same principle applies mutatis mutandis to the other two constructions.

(5) Possibility of syntactic intrusion

The unanalyzability of the three constructions discussed in subsection (4) is further supported by the fact that these constructions do not in general allow the syntactic intrusion of a noun phrase or an adverbial phrase. For example, (21) has appropriate word order, with the adverbial *mainiti* preceding the *temo* construction; (21a), on the other hand, is unacceptable because the adverbial is placed within the *temo* construction. Nor is the intrusion of a noun phrase or an adverbial phrase possible in the other two constructions, as shown in the (a) sentences in (22) and (23).

(21) *Mainiti hataraitemo hataraitemo kurasi ga*
every day work even though work even though living SM
raku ni naranai.
better become Neg
'No matter how much (I) work every day , (my) living (condition) does not improve.'

(21a) #*Hataraitemo mainiti hataraitemo kurasi ga*
work even though every day work even though living SM
raku ni naranai.
better become Neg
'No matter how much (I) work every day , (my) living (condition) does not improve.'

(22) *Ano hito wa o-sake o nomeba nomu hodo osyaberi ni*
that person TM sake OM drink if drink extent talkative
naru.
become
'The more sake (he) drinks, the more talkative (he) becomes.'

(22a) #*Ano hito wa nomeba o-sake o nomu hodo osyaberi ni*
that person TM drink if sake OM drink extent talkative
naru.
become
'The more sake (he) drinks, the more talkative (he) becomes.'

(23) *Nihon ni kaettara kaetta de, mata taihen nan zya nai no.*
Japan to return if return again have difficulties Neg
'If (she) goes back to Japan, don't you think (she) will again have a hard time?'

(23a) #Kaettara Nihon ni kaetta de, *mata taihen nan zya nai no.*
return if Japan to return again have difficulties Neg
'If (she) goes back to Japan, don't you think (she) will again have a hard time?'

These facts about syntactic intrusion suggest that the three VRCs are all syntactically integral wholes.

(6) Behavior with regard to tense markers

Each of the three VRCs also behaves as a single unit with regard to tense marker. That is, tense is marked, not in these construction itself, but in the accompanying main clause, so that the interpretation of the construction's tense depends on the tense of the main clause. Compare (4) and (1) for the *temo* construction, (2) and (10) for the *hodo* construction, (3) and (18) for the *tara* construction; within each pair of examples, the former has a present-tense main cluase and the latter a past-tense.

(7) Behavior with regard to the passive morpheme

With regard to the passive morpheme *(r)are*, on the other hand, the three constructions do not behave as syntactically integral wholes. That is, the passive morpheme *(r)are* is applied, not to the construction as a whole, but individually to both instances of the verb, as shown in (24)-(26).

(24) *Kare wa kaigi de tatak-are-temo tatak-are-*
he TM meeting at criticize Pass even though criticize Pass
temo, zenzen ki ni site inai yoo da.
even though at all be concerned Neg seem
'No matter how much he is criticized at meetings, he does not seem to care.'

(25) *Kare wa kaigi de tatak-are-reba tatak-areru hodo*
he TM meeting at criticize Pass if criticize Pass extent
tuyoku naru.
strong becomes
'The more he is criticized at meetings, the stronger he becomes.'

(26) *Kaigi de tatak-are-tara tatak-areta de, ii keeken ni*
meeting at criticize Pass if criticize Pass good experience
naru daroo.
become probably
'If (I) get criticized at the meeting, (it) will (also) be a good experience (for me).'

The behavior of the three constructions with regard to the passive morpheme differs from that of verbal compounds, in which the passive morpheme is applied to the compound as a whole, as shown in (27).

(27) *Kodomo ni tobi-tuk-areta.*
child by jump stick Pass Pst
'(I) was jumped at by the child.'

8) Behavior with regard to the causative morpheme *(s)ase*

With regard to the causative morpheme *(s)ase*, the three constructions behave in the same manner as they do with regard to the passive morpheme. That is, the causative morpheme must be applied to both instances of the verb in the construction, as shown in (28)-(30).

(28) *Hasir-ase temo hasir-ase temo, kiroku wa onazi datta.*
run Caus even though run Caus even though record TM same Pst
'No matter how much (I) made (him) run, the record was the same.'

(29) *Hasir-asereba hasir-aseru hodo, hayaku natta.*
run Caus if run Caus extent fast become Pst
'The more (I) made (him) run, the faster (he) became.'

(30) *Hasir-ase-tara hasir-aseta de mondai daroo.*
run Caus if run Casus problem probably
'If (I) made (him) run, (that) would (also) be problematic.'

This behavior differs from that of verbal compounds, in which the causative morpheme is applied to the compound as a whole, as in (31).

(31) *Taroo o oti-tuk-ase-ta*
OM fall stick Caus Pst
'(I) made Taroo calm down.'

The morphosyntactic (and phonological) properties of the three VRCs described above can be summarized as follows: (1) All three constructions show properties of analyzable phrases with regard to productivity, morphological elements, pitch patterns, the passive mopheme, and the causative morpheme. (2) All three constructions show properties of unanalyzable words with regard to analyzability by regular phrase structure rules, the possibility of syntactic intrusion, and tense markers. The morphosyntactic properties of the three VRCs thus suggest that these constructions are neither genuine idioms/lexical items nor fully analyzable phrases. Rather, they have an intermediate status.

IV. Conclusion

I have analyzed three VRCs in Japanese with regard to their semantic, pragmatic, and morphosyntactic properties. The noncompositionality of their semantic and pragmatic properties suggests that the three constructions be treated as idioms/lexical items. On the other hand, the morphosyntactic properties suggest that these constructions are neither genuine idioms/lexical items nor fully analyzable phrases. Rather, they have an intermediate status. These results thus support the view that productivity and idiomaticity in language are not necessarily mutually exclusive. Further, this study has demonstrated that the three VRCs cannot be fully accounted for in a modular fashion, by separating syntax from semantics/ pragmatics. I argue that these VRCs, along with numerous other idiomatic constructions, are best described as 'grammatical constructions'-- as integral morphosyntactic patterns bearing unique semantic and pragmatic properties.

References

Fillmore, Charles. 1985. Syntactic intrusions and the notion of grammatical construction. BLS 11. 73-86.

Fillmore, Charles. 1989. "*Seisei-koozoo bunpoo*" *ni yoru Nihongo no bunseki ichi-shian.* (An analysis of Japanese based on 'Construction Grammar'.) *Nihongo-gaku no shintenkai.* (New development in Japanese Linguistics.) Tokyo: Kuroshiro Shuppan.

Fillmore, Charles, Paul Kay, and Mary C. O'Connor. 1988. Regularity and idiomaticity in grammatical constructions: The case of *let alone.* Lg. 64. 501-538.

Lambrecht, Knud. 1984. Formulaicity, frame semantics, and pragmatics in German binominal expressions. Lg. 60. 753-796.

Okamoto, Shigeko. 1990. Reduplicated verbs in Japanese as grammatical constructions. BLS 16.

Okamoto, Shigeko. 1991. Nominal 'tautologies' in Japanese: *X wa X*, *X ga X*, and *X mo X*. BLS 17.

Cognition, Affect, and Topicality of the Causal Particle -Nikka in Korean

SUNG-OCK S. SOHN
University of California at Los Angeles

1. Introduction

This paper attempts to explore semantic-pragmatic functions of the causal particle *-nikka* in Korean from the perspective that the linguistic coding of the causality interacts with the way we conceive a situation in our knowledge system and the way we use the conceived situation for our own affective purposes. The function of *-nikka* will be compared and contrasted with that of *-ese*.[1] Both *-nikka* and *-ese* are acceptable as answers to why questions, as illustrated below.

(1) (A Teacher asks a student why he was late for a class.)
Teacher: ne, way nuc-ess-ni?
you why late-Past-Q
'Why were you late (for class)?'

Student: (a) pi-ka wa-se nuc-ess-eyo.
rain-Nom come- late-Past-Dec
'I was late because it is raining.'

--> (b) pi-ka o-*nikka* nuc-ess-eyo.
'(You know/I believe) I was late because it is raining.'

In the above examples both clause-*nikka* and clause-*ese* indicate the cause of being late. Their semantic and affective (emotive) functions are, however, different, as English glosses indicate: while *-ese* states neutral information, *-nikka* highlights the speaker's assertive/emphatic attitude, thus implying 'Don't you know that it is raining? That is why I am late.'

In addition to the causality, *-nikka* can be used for setting up a temporal domain with the sense of 'discovery/realization' (cf. Lukoff & Nam 1982). For instance,

(2) a. pakk-ul po-*nikka* pi-ka o-ko iss-ess-eyo.
outside-Acc see rain-Nom come-Prog-Past-Dec
'When I saw outside, (I found) it was raining.'

b. kay-nun pes-*unikka*, acwu mala-ss-te-la.
she-Top take off very skinny-Perf-Retro-Dec
'When she took off her clothes, I saw that she is very skinny.'

In (2a) and (2b), there is no causal relation between the events in *-nikka* clause and in the main clause. The clause-*nikka* in (2a) simply serves to provide a temporal background for the accidental discovery of 'raining'. What construal mechanism makes it possible to use the causal particle for temporality in Korean?

This paper attempts to provide a unified semantic account for the temporal and causal functions of the particle *-nikka* by proposing that the two functions of *-nikka* are a manifestation of one's 'phenomenal knowledge' about the world (cf. Goldsmith and Woisetschlaeger 1982). The notion of the phenomenal knowledge which stands in contrast with the 'structural knowledge' will be elaborated in section 2.1.

A second purpose of this paper is to show the affective and topic function of *-nikka*. The particle *-nikka* is concerned with the causals subjectively perceived by the speaker and hence marks the speaker's 'affective disposition' (cf. Besnier 1990, Ochs 1988). In discourse, the entity of clause-*nikka* refers back to a prior proposition, marking its entity as the common ground for the speaker and the interlocutor. This use of *-nikka* elicits some common properties with topics. The topic functions of *-nikka* will be supported by the following features of *-nikka*: 1) definiteness, 2) discourse-dependent, 3) domain setting, 4) morphological marking, and 5) point of view.

2. Causality and Temporality

2.1 Causality

The causal function of *-nikka* has often been discussed in contrast with *-ese.* (cf. Lee 1988, Nam & Lukoff 1982, Ree 1977, etc.). In causal expressions, *-nikka* has broader range of functions than that of *-ese*. While *-nikka* may occur in any type of causals such as speech-acts (i.e. 'persuading others and controlling others' behavior' (Kyratzis *et al* 1990)), evidential causals as well as in real-world causality (i.e. content-level), the occurrence of *-ese* is mostly restricted to the types of real-world causality.[2] This is illustrated below.

(3) pi-ka o-*nikka* /**ase* naka-ci ma.(Speech-acts causal)
rain-NOM come-because go out-COMP not-Pol-Dec
'Don't go outside because it is raining.'

(4) pi-ka o-*nikka* /*ase* chwup-ta.(Content-level causal)
cold-Dec
'It is cold because it is raining.'

(5) onul Suni-ka hakkyo-ey an o-assu-*nikka* /**ase* aphun key
today Suni-Nom school-to not come past-because sick Comp
thullimeps-ta. (Epistemic/Evidential causal)
sure -DEC
'Suni must be sick, because she didn't come to school today.'

The speech act-level causals as in (3) above refer to the causals which involve 'interpersonal functions' (request, command, suggestive, etc.). The second type of causals, i.e., content-level causals, involve the 'real-world causality' as exemplified in (4). Finally, epistemic/evidential causals describe a speaker's evidence for a conclusion drawn in a main clause. For example, the *-nikka* clause in (5) presents the speaker's evidence for making the judgement (i.e. 'Suni must be sick.'). While *-nikka* may occur in any type of causals such as speech act-level, content-level, and epistemic causals, the occurrence of *-ese* is mostly limited to the content-level causals (i.e. real-world causality). The semantic functions of *-nikka* and *-ese* in content-level causals, however, are not quite identical as shown in (1). Are there any implications of one's knowledge of the world (that is, the way the speaker conceptualizes the causal link between events) for the functional difference between *-nikka* and *-ese*?

I propose, applying the dual types of knowledge in Goldsmith & Woisetschlaeger (1982, henceforth G & W), that the choice of *-nikka* and *-ese* is based on the speaker's different perception of the world. With the assumption that a semantic description is a reflection of how a speaker conceives and structures a situtation in a particular manner (cf. Langacker 1985), we can expect that the same conceived situation can be described in different ways. According to G & W (1982), one might view events or a situation in the world in terms of a dual typology of knowledge mode--1) 'by describing what things happen in the world' (phenomenal knowledge) or 2) 'by describing how the world is made that such things may happen in it' (structural knowledge) (G & W 1982). The structural description 'specifies the structure of the universe, not merely its observed constituents.' In contrast, the phenomenal description of a world is directly associated with a speaker's observation. That is, it describes a particular event as it is viewed from the observer's point of view.[3]

The structural vs. phenomenal knowledge can be applied to the two types of causals in Korean. Namely, a causal connection between events can be described in either of two ways: 1) A speaker can link a causal relation of two events as being inherent and universal, which reflects the speaker's knowledge of a structural property of the causal relation. Or 2) a speaker can describe the relationship between the same two events based on his own subjective judgement/perception (phenomenal knowledge). One does not require a direct personal experience for the structural description of causals. On the other hand, the phenomenal description of a causal relation is a manifestation of individuals' observation, which expresses a speaker's own point of view. Thus, the latter type of causal is often brought up by a speaker's own personal need for argumentation and justification.

-Nikka is associated with 'phenomenal knowledge' whereby the causal relation encoded by *-nikka* is based on a speaker's 'eyewitness account'. The speaker of *-nikka* actively participates in creating a causal link between events by drawing upon his/her own observation. Hence, *-nikka* involves a speaker's subjective attitude whereby the speaker's own point of view plays a central role in creating the causality. On the other hand, *-ese* is associated with the knowledge of the structure of the world, which exists independently from the speaker's direct experience or observation. Hence, *-ese* is frequently used for a logical progression of events or impersonalized factual information rather than representing a speaker's point of view. This contrast between *-ese* and *-nikka* is supported by the following example.

(6) olaykanman-ey masi-*nikka* /**ese* maiss-ta.
a long time-for drink is tasty-Dec
'It's very tasty because I haven't drunk it in a long while.'

The occurrence of *-ese* in (6) is not allowed, because the logical connection between S1 (the first clause) and S2 (the second clause) does not require a structural knowledge. Rather, the connection in (6) is brought about by the speaker's direct perceptual experience. This accounts for the reason why the causal connection between *-nikka* and the main clause events is often tentative (cf. Lee 1988) and may not be valid to the interlocutor.

The proposal that *-nikka* and *-ese* are associated with phenomenal and structural knowledge, respectively, can account for the functional differences between the two particles presented in (3)-(5). Consider, first of all, speech-acts causals where, of the two forms, only *-nikka* is acceptable. Let us reconsider (3), which is renumbered as (7).

(7) pi-ka o-*nikka* /*ase nakaci ma.
'Don't go outside because it is raining.'

There is no real-world connection between the event of raining and the command of 'don't go outside.' The proposition of S1-*nikka* serves to justify/assert why the speaker makes the command. The causal link between the two propositions is thus not structural, but is created on the basis of a speaker's own observation (phenomenal knowledge). For speech-acts causals, pragmatic and interpersonal functions such as persuading, requesting, and controlling others' behavior are heightened. Hence, the causal link in speech-acts is motivated by a speaker's own subjective view. The use of *-ese* in (7) will not accomplish such a function, because *-ese* is linked with a structural property of the causal link.

For epistemic causals, a pattern similar to speech-acts causals is observed whereby a speaker heavily relies on his/her own subjective judgement for making an inference.[4] The unacceptability of *-ese* in the following examples is accounted for in light of this.

(8) Suni-ka hakkyo-ey an wa-*se/ss-*unikka*
Nom school-to not come
aphun-key thullim eps-ta.
sick-Comp must be-Dec
'Suni must be sick, because she didn't come to school.'

(9) papo-ka ani-*nikka* /**ese* ne-to kuken al-keya.
idiot-Nom not you-also that know-will
'You would know it, because you are not stupid.'

The mode of knowledge involved in the epistemic causal is phenomenal in that the evidence which plays a crucial role in making an inference is acquired from the speaker's own observation or belief (i.e. phenomenal knowledge). This knowledge is a part of the speaker. That is, the speaker is the one who makes the causal links on the evidence presented in the *-nikka* clause. The frequent use of *-nikka* in describing speaker's prediction/presumption, conjecture, belief, arguments, or justification in the conclusion expressed in a final clause (i.e. for epistemic causals) can be accounted for by the phenomenal nature of *-nikka.*

2.2 Temporality

The phenomenal vs. structural knowledge can further explain the temporal function of *-nikka.*[5] Our knowledge of the phenomenal nature of the world comes through our own encounter/perception with particular events. A speaker acquires a phenomenal knowledge by observing or discovering something based on perceptual evidence. Since *-nikka* is associated with speaker's direct observation (i.e. phenomenal knowledge), it can be used for describing what a speaker has discovered/realized. Consider the following examples.

(10) a. pakk-ul po-*nikka* pi-ka o-ko iss-ess-ta.
outside-Acc see-when rain-Nom come-Prog-Past-Dec
'When I saw outside, (I found) it was raining.'

b. cinanoh-ko sayngkakha-*nikka*
pass-Conj think
ku-nun kathun kwa namhaksayng-i-ess-ta.
he-Top same dept. male student-be-past-Dec
'When I thought later, (I realized that) he was my classmate.'

c. mwul-i yengto-ka toy-*nikka* el-ess-ta
water-Nom zero degree-Nom become freeze-Past-Dec
i. 'The water became frozen when it became zero degrees.'
ii. 'The water became frozen because it became zero degrees.'

Note that in the above examples (10a) and (10b), *-nikka* is interpreted temporally ('when'). In (10a) the event of watching outside does not cause 'raining', and thus there is no causal relation between S1 and S2. In (10b), clause-*nikka* indirectly provides a reasoning process of how the speaker has come up with the realization that he was the former classmate. The function of *-nikka* in (10c) can be ambiguous between temporal and causal interpretations. What is common among the examples in (10) is that the *-nikka* marked entity involves the speaker's direct observation or perception and that it provides a temporal setting for discovery of S2 content (accidental discovery). The temporal function of *-nikka* is attributed to the phenomenal nature of the knowledge wherein the speaker's 'eyewitness' account of the events is conveyed (cf. Miyakawa & Nakamura 1991, Nam & Lukoff 1982). This knowledge (i.e. phenomenal) may evoke a causal link under certain contexts, as we have seen in previous examples (3), (4), and

(5), or may be ambiguous as in (10c), or may simply be a description of what a speaker has observed without implying a causality as in (10a).[6]

At any rate, the role of phenomenal knowledge in manifesting temporality and/or causality of *-nikka* is evident. The analysis proposed here provides not only a unified account of the two functions of *-nikka* but also provides a simple treatment for the various characterizations of the two causal particles *-nikka* and *-ese* (cf. performative analysis (Ree 1977), 'tentative'(*-nikka*) vs. 'definite'(*-ese*) (Lee 1987), (Nam & Lukoff 1982), etc.).

Thus far, I have shown that the temporal and causal functions of *-nikka* are brought about by the phenomenal nature of *-nikka*. I have also shown that the functional difference between *-nikka* and *-ese* follows from the dual type of knowledge: while the speaker of *-nikka* makes use of his/her own observation for the causal connection (i.e. phenomenal knowledge), the speaker of *-ese* relies on structural knowledge, independently acquired from his/her direct experience.

3. Interpersonal functions

3.1 Affective function

The causality encoded by *-nikka* has affective impact, wherein affect refers to expression of speaker's personal attitude including emotions, feelings, moods, and general disposition (cf. Besnier 1990, Biber & Finegan 1989, Ochs 1988). *-Nikka* marks phenomenal knowledge and at the same time it indexes a speaker's overtly expressed personal, subjective affect (attitude) toward the proposition it is attached to. The affect marked *-nikka* stands in contrast with depersonalized *-ese*. Compare the following sentences. (1a) and (1b) are repeated below.

(1) (a) pi-ka wa-se nuc-ess-eyo.
'I was late since it is raining.'
(b) pi-ka o-*nikka* nuc-ess-eyo.
'(You know/I believe) I was late because it is raining'

In the above examples, both *-nikka* and *-ese* can be used to indicate the cause of being late. However, there is difference in terms of their affective functions: while the *-ese* marked entity expresses the cause being objective and impersonal (neutral, depersonalized statement), the clause-*nikka* encodes a speaker's emphatic attitude (for justification). Thus, by employing *-nikka*, the speaker in (1b) implicitly conveys the message that 'Aren't you aware of the fact that it is raining and that it can cause being late for a class?.' Due to the affect function (i.e. an emphatic/assertive attitude of the speaker), *-nikka* can evoke an impolite attitude.[7] In fact, the use of

-nikka in a context like (1) sounds rude because the speaker of (1b) focuses on justifying his being late instead of offering an apology. For this reason, the use of *-nikka* is not appropriate in situations where politeness is called for, as illustrated in (11).

(11) a. nuc-*ese*/**unikka* mianha-pnita.
late sorry-Dec
'I am sorry that I am late.'

b. mos towa tulye-*se*/**nikka* mianha-pnita.
not able to help sorry-Dec
'I am sorry that I cannot help you.'

c. pappa-*se*/**nikka* iman sillyeyha-pnita.
busy now excuse-Dec
'Excuse me that (because) I am busy.'

The affect function of *-nikka* may also account for the frequent use of *-nikka* in speech-acts causals. A speaker in speech-acts causals, may wish to intensify his/her justification for the act, or to indicate to the hearer which speech act is being performed (Ochs 1989). *-Nikka* is employed to mark a speaker's intensified affect to the proposition it is attached to. In contrast, *-ese* marked entity does not exhibit speaker's intensified affect. Rather, the clause-*ese* serves to provide neutral information, thus denoting inherent and objective causality.

In addition to speech-acts, *-nikka* is often used for argumentation and justification (cf. Nam & Lukoff 1982), as exemplified in the following example.

(12) (A talk among friends)
While watching a scene on TV where Koreans eat lots of eggs for breakfast, A mentions that Koreans don't pay much attention to cholesterol. The following dialogue takes place afterwards.

B: kulayto hankwuk salam-tul koki kathun ke-n
but Korean people-PL meat someting like that-Top
manhi an mek-canh-a.
much not eat-Neg-Dec
'But, Koreans don't eat lots of meat.'

--> A: pissa-*nikka* an mek-ci.
expensive not eat-Dec
'They don't eat it because it is expensive.'

The speaker A chose to use *-nikka* instead of *-ese*. By employing *-nikka*, the speaker A emphasizes 'Meat is very expensive in Korea. That's why they don't eat lots of meat.' Thus, beyond conveying 'referential information', by choosing *-nikka* the speaker tries to dissuade B from the original position. This affective orientation, encoded by *-nikka* serves as critical cues to the interlocuter as to how that interlocutor should interpret and respond to the predication communication (Ochs & Schieffelin 1989).

3.2 Topic function

We have seen that the particle *-nikka* marks the causal link as phenomenal and may evoke at the same time an affect/attitude of speaker's emphatic (overtly expressed) response. In the discourse, the proposition of *-nikka* clauses constitues a discourse topic in that the proposition is known or knownable by the interlocutor (cf. Ochs and Schiefflin 1976). In other words, by using *-nikka*, the speaker draws on background knowledge which is identifiable from the interlocutor's register. The interlocutor's shared knowledge (linguistic or nonlinguistic materials) plays an important role in creating the causal link encoded by *-nikka*. Consider the following example in which the speaker (A) is wondering why the car runs well.[8]

(13) A: i cha-ka ecey-pota cal nakanta. way kuleh-ci?
this car-Nom yesterday-than well run why that-Q
'This car runs more smoothly than yesterday. Why is that?'

--> B: eyngin-ul sonpo-ass-*unikka* kulehci.
engine-Acc tune up-past-because is so
'(You know) It is because the engine is tuned up.'

The speaker (B) indicates that the interlocutor should know, and yet does not realize the causal chain (between the car's running well and tuning up). Thus, by using *-nikka*, (B) establishes a context that the interlocutor can identify from his knowledge. Although Lee (1988) does not associate the function of *-nikka* with topicality, it is evident that *-nikka* is used to signal a speaker's belief that the cause/reason expressed by *-nikka* is known or knowable to the interlocutor (i.e. 'given information' in Chafe 1976).

Evidence for the topic function of *-nikka* is provided by the following features of *-nikka*: 1) definiteness, 2) discourse-dependent, 3) domain setting (cf. Chafe 1976:50-51, Li & Thompson 1976), 4) morphological marking, and 5) point of view.

3.2.1 Definiteness

One of the characteristics of topics is that they are definite (Chafe 1976, Li and Thompson 1976). A speaker assumes that the referent he is talking about is identifiable from the hearer's knowledge. In Korean, the NP topic marker *-nun* is used to mark information which the speaker assumes to be part of the hearer's register. Thus, *-nun* does not occur with information seeking *wh*-words. Similarly, the information introduced by *-nikka* is definite. This is evidenced by the fact that *-nikka*, unlike *-ese*, cannot occur simultaneously with *wh*-words within a clause. Consider the following examples.

(14) a. nwu-ka chwuwe-se mwun-ul tat-ass-ni?
who-Nom cold door-Acc close-Past-Q
'Who was cold and hence closed the door?'

b. *nwu-ka chwuwu-*nikka* mwun-ul tat-ass-ni?
(is O.K. only when nwuka is interpreted as 'someone'.)
'Did someone close the door because it is cold?'

(15) a. mwuel mek-*ese* pay-ka pwulu-ni?
what eat stomach full-Q
'What did you eat that you became full?'

b. *mwuel mek-(ess)*unikka* pay-ka pwulu-ni?
'Did you become full because you ate what?'

(16) a. encey ka-se cikum o-ni?
when go now come-Q
'When did you go that you return now?'

b. *encey ka-(ss)*unikka* cikum o-ni?

(17) a. eti-eyse nol-ase os-i telep-ni?
where-at play clothes dirty-Q
'Where did you play that your clothes are dirty?'

b. *eti-eyse no-*nikka* os-i telep-ni?

The ungrammaticality of (14b)-(17b) above is explained by the same principle that NP topics cannnot occur with wh-words. That is, the content of *-nikka* clauses must be identifiable from the interlocutor's knowledge. In contrast, the proposition of *-ese* clause can mark new information.

3.2.2 Discourse-dependent

The second piece of evidence for the topic function of *-nikka* is provided by the use of *-nikka* as a sentence-final particle. *-Nikka* as a sentence-final particle is placed at the end of a sentence and functions to reassert the speaker's prior statements, proposals, or commands, roughly equivalent to English phrases 'You know' or 'I (already) told you'. For example, in (18) below, the kid keeps asking his dad's plan of going to the beach. The dad uses *-nikka* to reassure the kid of his plan.

(18) A: appa, cengmal kanunke-ya?
dad surely go-Q
'Dady, are you sure we are going to (the beach)?'

--> B: ung. kan-ta-*nikka.*
yes go-Dec-NIKKA
'Yes, we are going (I already told you so.).'

The discourse role of *-nikka* in (18) is to recapitulate previously mentioned information and to bring it back into focus[9], hence marking the the entity of clause-*nikka* as the 'center of attention' (cf. Li & Thompson 1976:464). The definiteness of *-nikka* clauses is established through prior mention in the discourse. It is for this reason that the use of *-nikka* is contextually constrained when the proposition of *-nikka* is not drawn from a preceding discourse. An example is taken from a written narrative (Simchung's story). (19) is the beginning of the folk tale.[10]

(19) men yeysnal pata pwulkyel soli-ka sachel tullyeonun
long time ago sea wave sound-Nom always be heard
cokumahan maul-ey Sim ilanun yeyppun sonye-ka salko
small village-at Sim be called pretty girl-Nom live
iss-ess-ta. Simchung-uy apeci-nun aph-ul mos po-nun
Prog-Past-Dec Gen dad-Top front-Acc not see-Comp
cangnim-i-ess-ta. maul-eysenun ku-lul Sim pongsa-lako
blind-be-past-Dec village-at he-Acc blind-Quot
pulle-ss-ta.
call-past-Dec

--> [Sim pongsa-nun yangpan cip cason-i-ese/**nikka*
blind man-Top noble family descendent-be-ESE/*NIKKA
salam-tul-i pwulewuehay-ss-ta.]
people-Pl-Nom envy-Past-Dec

"In a small village, where a sound of ocean far away and long ago can be heard through four seasons, there lived a pretty girl named Sim Chung. Sim Chung's father was a blind person who couldn't see ahead of him. So, in the village people called him Mr. Blind man Sim.

[Since the blind man Sim was a descendent of a noble family, others had envied him.]"

In the above underlined part, *-nikka* is not acceptable for indicating the reason why the village people envied Mr. Sim. *-Nikka* clauses, like NP topics, are presupposed parts of their sentences. The unacceptablity of *-nikka* in (19) is due to the presuppositional characteristics of *-nikka*. That is, the information 'Mr Sim is a descendent of a noble family.' is introduced into the story for the first time. In contrast, *-ese* clause is not presupposed since its entity is not necessarily shared by the speaker and the hearer.

3.2.3. Domain setting

According to Chafe (1976:50-51), a topic in topic prominent languages (e.g. Chinese, Japanese, and Korean) are not necessarily what the sentences are about (cf. Kuno 1973), but it 'sets a spatial, temporal, or individual framework within which the main predication holds.' For instance, a temporal adverbial 'Tuesday' as in "Tuesday I went to the dentist." is somewhat similar to the Chinese style topic. *-Nikka* clauses, like NP topics, constitute the framework which has been selected for what is going to be said. In (20), a doctor is talking about his experience with a patient who complained that the result of a plastic surgery turned out to be worse than before. Notice that the discourse role of *-nikka* in (20) is to link the preceding clause with the clause to which it is attached and to set a domain which the following clause comments on.

(20)	kulelli-ka	eps-nuntey kulemyense		
	that-Nom	cannot-and saying		
	sacin-ul	yelsimhi chass-ass-eyo.		
	photo-Acc	intently look for-past-Dec		
-->	[sacin-ul	chac-ko po-*nikka*],		
	photo-Acc	find-and see-when		
	swuswul cen	pota	koyngcanghi	cohaci-ess-nuntey.
	operation before	than	very	improve-past-and

"While thinking 'that (*looking worse than before the operation*) can't be', I intently looked for her pre-surgery photo. [When I found that photo], I discovered that the result of the surgery was actually a dramatic improvement."

The content of clause-*nikka* [When I found that photo] in (20) sets a temporal domain within which the following clause holds. The function of *-nikka* as 'domain setting' precludes the occurrence of *-nikka* in an indefinite proposition, as demonstrated by earlier examples (14)-(17).

3.2.4 Morphological marking

Morphological evidence independently supports the topic function of *-nikka* whereby the topic marker *nun* follows *nikka*, thus forming the structure of **'[clause-*nikka* -*nun*] [clause]'**. In colloquial Korean, *nikka-n* (or *nikka-nun*) is used more frequently than the form without the topic marker. For instance,

(21) cip-ey ka-nikka-nun phyenci-ka wa iss-te-la.
home-to go letter-Nom come Perf-Retro-Dec
'When I went home, I found a letter.'

In (21) the NP topic marker *-nun* occurs at the end of the *-nikka* clause and manifests a strong topicality whereby the proposition of *-nikka* sets a framework for the rest of the sentence.

3.2.5 Point of view

Finally, *-nikka* clauses share characteristics of topics in that the speaker of *-nikka* describes a causal relation from the speaker's point of view. According to Kuno (1976), it is easier for the speaker to 'empathize' (i.e. to express the speaker's own point of view) with a definite referent than with an indefinite object. The referent of a topic NP is the individual with whom the speaker is empathizing (cf. Chafe 1976:54-55). Similarly, we have seen that the causality of *-nikka* is brought about by the speaker's own viewpoint (i.e. phenomenal knowledge). If the speaker's viewpoint plays an active role in creating the causality, it makes sense that the speaker of *-nikka* empathizes with the proposition that is identifiable in the interlocutor's knowledge than with the material that is unidentifiable.

4. Conclusion

In short, I have shown that *-nikka* clauses share significant characteristics of topics. Evidence from semantic, morphological, and discoursal features of *-nikka* indicates a striking similarity between NP topics (marked by *-nun*) and *-nikka* clauses. Like NP topics, the proposition of a *-nikka* clause is definite, discourse-dependent, presupposed, and sets a domain for the following predication. Moreover, *-nikka* signals a speaker's affective disposition in that it indexes the speaker's assertive and emphatic attitude toward the propositional content it is attached to.[12]

The topic function of *-nikka* clause is not accidental but based on the fundamental use of *-nikka*. The functional role of *-nikka* is to mark a causal relation as phenomenal description directly associated with a speaker's own perception. The temporal and causal functions of *-nikka* which may appear to be unrelated and separate, are in fact adjoined as the result of the phenomenal nature of human cognition.

Notes

*I thank Noriko Akatsuka and Young-Ki Kim for their insightful comments. Of course, I am responsible for any errors.

1. The functions of the two particles *-nikka* and *-ese* are very similar to those of *-kara* and *-node* in Japanese, repectively. However, unlike *-kara*, *-ese* in Korean has a temporal meaning as well as a causality.

2. The distinction among the three types of causals is based on Kyratzis, Guo, and Ervin-Tripp (1990). Causal expressions can be divided into three types: 1) Speech act-level causal, 2) Content-level causal, and 3) Epistemic causals, as illustrated by (a) (b), and (c), respectively.

a. Don't go outside because it is raining. (Speech-act)
b. It is cold because it is raining. (Content-level)
c. Suni must be sick, because she didn't come to school today. (Epistemic))

3. See Miyakawa & Nakamura (1991) for a similar approach to Japanese *node* and *kara*.

4. This can be supported by the fact that epistemic causals often occur with modals such as *'thullim epsta* 'must be', *-keyss* 'probably', *-ul kes-i-* 'probably', etc.

5. Note that *-ese* can be also used to mark a temporal sequence of events. But, unlike *-nikka* , there is no 'discovery/realization' interpretation for *-ese*, as in (i) below.

(i) hakkyo-ey ka-se chinkwu-lul manna-ss-eyo.
school-to go-and then friend-Acc meet-past-Dec
I went to school and then met a friend (there).

6. It is also to be noted that *-nikka* as a temporal interpretation is often found in the pattern perceptive verb + e/a + po-*nikka* 'When I tried doing..., I found/discoverd that.....'.

7. The impoliteness of *-nikka* has been mentioned in Ree (1977) and Nam & Lukoff (1982).

8. The example is taken from Lee (1988). Note that the topic function of *-nikka* becomes clear when compared with *-ese*. Suppose that the speaker (B) in (13) chose to use *-ese*, instead of *-nikka* as in (i) below.

(i) B: engin-ul sonpo-ase kulay.
engine-Acc tune up that
'It is because the engine is tuned up.'

The speaker in (i) implicitly states that he does not expect the interlocutor to be aware of the causal connection between 'the engine's being tuned up' and 'the car's running well'.

9. This function is also related to definiteness of *-nikka* . Note that the form without *-nikka* does not convey any reassertive message, as shown below.

(i) ung. ka-nta.
Yes. go-Dec
'Yes. we are going.' (New information)

10. The story is taken from Korean text (Yonsei University Press).

11. - clauses are not the only adverbial clauses which occur with the topic marker. There is a group of adverbial clauses which can occur with *-nun* and marks a strong topicality. See Sohn (forthcoming) for means to indicate the topic of a sentence.

12. Another factor that interacts with the topic function of *-nikka* is its role as a stance-marker. By stance, I follow Ochs's (1989) notion, 'the overt expression of attitude, feelings, judgement, or committment concerning the propostional content of message.' We can characterize the affective function of *-nikka* as a foregrounded speaker stance. The foregrounded speaker stance, contrasted with a backgrounding stance, conveys 'the speaker's affective disposition and hence marks the current utterance as the one in which the speaker's personal, subjective response is overtly expressed' (cf. Kim 1991). The topicality of *-nikka* is associated with a speaker foregrounded stance, as Kim (1991) proposed that the Korean topic marker (*-nun*) should be characterized as a stance-marker. Both *-nikka* and *-nun* marked entity can be characterized as a marker of foregrounded speaker stance.

References

Besnier, Niko. 1990. "Language and Affect." Annual Review of Anthropology. Vol. 19.

Biber, D. and E. Finegan. 1989. "Styles of Stance in English: Lexical & grammatical marking of evidentiality & affect." Text 9(1), 93-124.

Chafe, W. L. 1976. "Giveness, contrastiveness, definiteness, subjects, topics, and point of view." In Subject and Topic, Li & Thompson (ed.) (1976:27-55).

Goldsmith, J. & Woisetschlaeger, E. 1982. "The logic of the English progressive." Linguistic Inquiry. 13:79-90.

Kim, Kyu-hyun. 1991. "The Role of Korean Topic marker in Foregrounding Speaker Stance." Paper presented at BLS 17.

Kuno, S. 1973. The Structure of the Japanese Language. Cambridge: MIT Press.

_____. 1976. "Subject, Theme, and the Speaker's Empathy." In Subject and Topic. Li & Thompson (ed.) (1976:419-444)

Kyratzis, A., J. Guo, and S. Ervin-Tripp. 1990. "Pragmatic Convention influencing Children's Use of Causal Constructions in natural Discourse." BLS. 16:205-214.

Langacker, R. 1985. "Observations and Speculations on Subjectivity." In Haiman, J. (ed.) Iconicity in Syntax: Philadelphia: John Benjamins Publishing Co. 109-150.

Lee, Keedong. 1988. A Korean Grammar. Ms.

Li, C. and S. Thompson. 1976. "Subject and Topic: A new typology of language." Subject and Topic. New York: Academic Press. 457-489.

Miyakawa, S. & Nakamura, M. 1991. "The logic of *kara* and *node* in Japanese." Interdisciplinary Approaches to Language. ed. Carol Georgopoulos & Roberta Ishihara. Kluwer Academic Press. 435-448.

Lukoff, F and K. Nam. 1982. "*-nikka* and *-ese* as logical streams." Syntax and Semantics in Korean. (Ed.) Ko & Nam. Tap Press. 1-27.

Ochs, E. 1988. Cultures & language developing. Cambridge: Cambridge University Press.

Ochs, E. and B. Schieffelin. 1976. "Topic as a discourse notion." in Subject and Topic. (ed. Li & Thompson) 337-384.

_____. 1989. "Language has a heart."Text. 9: 7-25.

Ree, Joe J. 1977. "A Reanalysis of (u)ni and (e)se". Papers in Korean Linguistics. (Ed. Chin-W. Kim) 177-184.

Sohn, Ho-min. (forthcoming). The Language of Korea. Croom.

The Korean Modal Marker Keyss as a Marker of Affect: An Interactional Perspective

KYUNG-HEE SUH AND KYU-HYUN KIM
University of California at Los Angeles

1. Introduction

Recently, some attention has been paid to how the speaker's attitude is encoded in language, especially with reference to the role of AFFECT[1] in language. This is quite revolutionary considering that mainstream linguists define the referential meaning of language as their main area of inquiry, with the referential meaning being considered the most representative language behavior. The focus on referential meaning has been questioned by many scholars who point out that linguistic meaning can be broken down into three sub-components such as descriptive meaning (frequently termed referential meaning or propositional meaning), social meaning, and expressive meaning (Lyons 1977). Alternatively, these three meanings are labeled as the ideational, the interpersonal and the textual in Halliday's functional model (1976).

In their seminal paper, Ochs and Schieffelin (1989) bring into relief the

[1]The term AFFECT is taken to refer to feelings, moods, dispositions, and attitudes associated with persons and /or situations. (Ochs and Schieffelin, 1989)

affective function of language with regard to the notion of SOCIAL REFERENCING.[2] They point out the importance of social referencing in language use and language acquisition:

> 'Just as interactants use facial expressions to signal how they feel about entities, speakers use language for the same purpose. Moreover, just as interactants seek out affective information from one another's faces, so they seek out affective information from one another's language' (Ochs & Schieffelin 1989:9).

They further propose that:

1. There are linguistic features that speakers use to index affect to the interlocutors or propositions;
2. Others use these features as a basis for organizing their interactional moves, i.e. for constructing their own subsequent feelings, moods, dispositions and attitudes towards some uncertain information.

With this theoretical background, this paper draws upon a previous study of *keyss* and *(u)lkes* (K.-H. Suh & K.-H. Kim 1991), where the EPISTEMIC STANCE indexed by the Korean modal *keyss* and its periphrastic form *(u)lkes* are found to interface with AFFECTIVE STANCE.[3]

In this regard, this study aims to explore the interactional functions of the Korean modal particle *keyss,* with special reference to its affect-displaying function in interactional contexts. While this marker has been traditionally viewed as expressing modality or future tense similar to the English modal auxiliary *will*, this paper attempts to show that the meaning and function of *keyss* can be grasped in a unified manner by looking at its affective meaning negotiated in spontaneous conversational contexts.

The questions addressed in this paper are: (1) In what way does the speaker express affect using *keyss*? (2) How are affective expressions involving *keyss* constrained by a sequential organization of affect across turns and speakers? And in relation to these questions, (3) How is the affect-displaying function sequentially related to the constitution of action enactment?

---

[2]The notion of SOCIAL REFERENCING has been considered in studies of the social development of children. For instance, infants as early as 6 months of age were noted to begin to monitor the facial expressions of significant others (Ochs & Schieffelin 1989). Ochs & Schieffelin (1989:8) point out, 'this type of monitoring and understanding of another's affective displays continues beyond the period of infancy and is crucial to the child's social and cognitive development'.

[3]Following Ochs (1990), EPISTEMIC STANCE refers to participants' beliefs or knowledge vis-a-vis some proposition. AFFECTIVE STANCE refers to feelings, moods, and attitudes of participants toward some proposition.

2. Background

While the modal *keyss*, along with its periphrastic form, *(u)lkes* were classified as future tense markers (K.-M. Hong 1947 etc.) in traditional grammar, there has been a recent tendency to treat these forms in terms of modality, i.e. the speaker's volition and conjecture (J.-S. Suh 1977, C.-S. Shin 1972 etc.), with the future meaning being demoted to a secondary position. While we basically accept this observation that these forms are modal particles, it should be noted that the observation is mainly based on analyses of these forms at the sentential level which rely on the researcher's intuitive judgment of made-up sentences or dialogues (K.-Y. Lee 1977, K.-C. Sung 1979, J.-S. Suh 1977, 1978 etc). These studies mainly concern themselves with the analysis of *keyss*, often in relation to its periphrastic form *(u)lkes*, in terms of the source of evidence on which the speaker's epistemic judgment is based, the degree of certainty thereof (J.-S. Suh 1977 1978, K.-Y. Lee 1977), whether the source of evidence is provided by speaker's current experience or past experience (K.-C. Sung 1979), or any combination of the three. Few studies have analyzed these two forms in terms of their affective meaning or their interactional function in authentic conversational contexts.

As we suggested in K.-H. Suh & K.-H. Kim (1991), the functions of *keyss* can be better elucidated by examining them in terms of the speaker's affective stance which is interfaced with the epistemic stance. We claimed that attention should be paid to actual interactional contexts and that the functions of these epistemic markers cannot be fully accounted for without looking at the non-referential, expressive meanings of language and their correlation with activity types, which are important facets of language use that have been neglected and underestimated in mainstream linguistics. In this respect, we have shown that the subjective and objective epistemic stance indexed by the Korean modal *keyss* and its periphrastic form *(u)lkes* can be elaborated respectively as the speaker's INVOLVING STANCE and DISTANCING STANCE[4], which represent affective meaning interfaced

---

[4]In discussing differences between English *will* and *be going to*, Gee and Savasir (1985) make a distinction between the speaker's stance of INVOLVEMENT and DETACHMENT, which are shown to be indexed by *will* and *be going to* respectively. They argue that each verb reflects different activity types, i.e. UNDERTAKING reflected by *will*, and PLANNING by *be going to*. The activity type of undertaking constituted by *will*-utterances refers to 'the phenomenon when the speaker in some way commits herself to sustaining a cooperative activity with her interlocutor, with her on-going or subsequent actions' (1985:151). On the other hand, Planning refers to 'part of a larger activity-type which functions to project events in accordance with some kind of sequential ordering structure' (1985:156). They suggest that the activity frames of undertaking and planning involve different kinds of speaker stance, i.e. interpersonal involving stance for undertaking (constituted by *will*) and distancing stance for planning (constituted by *be going to*). In our earlier study (K.-H. Suh & K.-H. Kim 1991), we argued that this distinction between the two kinds of speaker stance is highly relevant to the

with epistemic meaning. In the same vein, K.-H. Suh (1991) notes that *keyss* marks the speaker's emotional commitment to the person(s) or proposition(s) by indexing sympathy to the preceding turns, by giving sympathy to oneself or by providing supportive feedback to the interlocutor.

On the basis of these observations, this study aims to describe the ways in which the marker *keyss* serves as an AFFECT KEY (Hymes 1974, Gumperz 1977, Ochs and Schieffelin 1989) in casual conversation with special reference to a sequential organization of affect (i.e. sympathy) across turns and speakers.

3. Data and Methodology

The theoretical framework adopted in this study represents a combination of conversation analysis (Sacks, Schegloff, & Jefferson 1974) and an ethnographically oriented socio-cultural approach to language (Ochs & Schieffelin 1989, Ochs 1988, 1990). Unlike previous studies which mainly examine the use of *keyss* at the sentence level and which use introspective data (J.-S. Suh 1977, 1978, K.-C. Sung 1979), this study examines naturally occurring conversation, and looks at the constitutive role of language in the construction of interactional works and actions that are performed by the interactants.

The data examined in this study are several audio taped face-to-face conversations in Korean, which amount to approximately 6 hours. The subject group consists of UCLA graduate students and their families who have lived in the United States no more than 4 years. They are all in their late 20's and early 30's. All the data have been transcribed according to the transcription conventions introduced in Sacks, Schegloff, & Jefferson (1974).

The assumption underlying the theme of this study is that conversational discourse is the primordial context of language use and human sociality (Sacks, Schegloff, & Jefferson 1974), with the context being viewed not merely as the setting that statically surrounds an utterance but the social and psychological worlds where the interlocutors interact at a given moment. (Ochs 1979).

---

distinction between Korean *keyss* and *(u)lkes*; the subjective and objective epistemic state indexed by *keyss* and *(u)lkes* are interfaced with involving stance and distancing stance respectively. The former indexes a highly affectively-loaded collaborative response to the interlocutor's turn, and/or a more immediate action-relevance while the latter indexes the speaker's detached attitude towards the interlocutor or towards the proposition in such a way that the speaker provides factual information that interlocutor seeks, with the subjective dimension being downgraded.

4. Analysis: *keyss* as a sympathy marker

In this section, we will examine conversation data to see how *keyss* is used as an affect key. Following Ochs and Schieffelin (1989:15), affect keys are defined as linguistic features that intensify or specify affect. Given this definition, we propose that *keyss* functions as an affect key which indexes sympathy to a person or situation. In other words, by using *keyss*, the speaker provides affective information about a situation being talked about in a highly collaborative manner, which may in turn additionally help to key how the speaker feels about the situation, and then clues the addressee to the appropriate response in the next turn.

4.1. *keyss* in the context of complaints/self-deprecations

Keyss often occurs in the contexts of complaints and self-deprecations. The speaker's affective stance, defined as the speaker's involving stance in our previous study (K.-H. Suh & K.-H. Kim 1991), subsumes the expression of a felt sense of jointness and cooperativeness, empathy, and negotiatory stance towards the interlocutor (cf. Gee & Savasir 1985, Chafe 1982, Tannen 1982). One context where *keyss* is used for marking the speaker's involvement is where the speaker produces a complaint with a view to eliciting some sort of commiseration from the interlocutor. In example (1), for instance, we can see how *keyss* marks the interpersonal involvement such that the speaker empathizes with the interlocutor in response to his complaint:

(1) (After Dinner)
((K, who is not wearing his glasses, has talked to his friend C about how he broke his glasses.))

1 K: ku taysin hakkyo -eyse cip -ey o -myen amwu
that instead of school -LOC home-LOC come-COND any
kes
thing

2 -to mos ha-e chayk-to mos
-ADD NEG(IMPOS) do-IE book -ADD NEG(IMPOS)
ilk -ko
read -CONN

3 tibi-to mos po -ko : :
TV-ADD NEG(IMPOS) watch-CONN
Instead, once I come from school, I can't do anything. I can't read a book nor watch TV.

---> 4 C: kkway taptapha -si -**keyss** -ta
considerably uncomfortable-HON-MOD -DEC
You must feel very uncomfortable.

In the context that precedes this segment of talk, K, who is extremely near-sighted, said that he had broken his glasses. From line 1 to line 3, K complains about his inconveniences. Upon hearing that, C produces a *keyss*-utterance in line 4 to empathize with K's unfortunate situation. In this case, showing sympathy to the addressee with the *keyss* marked utterance helps to create an emotional tie such as intimacy between the speaker and addressee. This example demonstrates one way in which the speaker uses *keyss* to index his/her sympathy towards the interlocutor's predicament by collaboratively attempting to be attuned to the interlocutor's situation.

Another context where *keyss* is often used is that of self-effacement or self-deprecation. In this context, the speaker shows sympathy to him/herself, or his/her situation. What should be noted in this case is that the turn containing the self-effacement/self-deprecation constrains the following turns, where the desired response is produced by prefacing either agreement or disagreement. Example (2), for instance, shows how *keyss* is used to display sympathy for the speaker himself, and in turn to elicit sympathy from the interlocutors. Here *keyss* utterances are found in lines 7 and 12.

(2) (Going to a conference)
((Four graduate students are chatting after lunch. K has brought up L's (a fellow graduate student and friend) going to a conference.))

1 J: onul po -nikka kekcengtoy -nunci sasayk -i
today see -CAUS worry -CONJ desperate look-NOM

2 toy -kaciko handout -to acik an mantul -ko
become-CONN handout -ADD yet NEG make -CONN
mwe=
what
When I saw him (L) today, he seemed very worried (about the conference). I noticed the anxiety on his face. And (he said) he hasn't made the handout yet

3 C: =eti -lay -ni?
where -QUOT-INTERR
(Have you heard about) where (the conference is to be held)?

4 K: Texas -uy El Paso kat -untey,
Texas -GEN El Paso seem -CIRCUM,
I think it's in El Paso, Texas

5 (.)

6 C: uh koyngcanghi cal toy -ney cengmal kulay
EXCLA very much well become-FR really like:that
-to
-though

---> 7 term-paper -to mos ssu **-keyss**
term-paper -ADD NEG (IMPOT) write-MOD
-nuntey ((laughing))
-CIRCUM

8 ettehkey kulehkey
how in that way
Wow, he is doing such a wonderful job, though. How come (he is doing so well) when I can't even write a term-paper.

9 ((pause))

10 K: klen -kes -un yakkwa -ci classmate-ka
such -thing-TOP nothing -COMM classmate-NOM

11 ywuswuhan journal -ey mak publish-lul
prestigious journal -LOC very much publish-ACC
That's nothing. (Imagine) that your classmate is publishing (quite often) in prestigious journals -
[
12 S: publish-lul ha-myen
publish-ACC do-COND

---> 13 sinkyengcilna-a cwuk-**keyss**-e
upset -CONN die -MOD -IE
The thought of them publishing their papers drives me crazy.
[
14 K: ha -koiss -nuntey mos ha-koiss
do-PROG -CIRCUM NEG (IMPOT) do-PROG

15 -umyen =
-COND
if I'm unable to publish (my paper) while my classmates are publishing (theirs)

16 S: =ywu: swuhan journal ( ) twu kay ssik
prestigious journal two thing each
mak
without any hesitation
in prestigious journals, (they are publishing not just one) but two.

In this conversation, four graduate students are chatting after lunch. In the context that precedes this segment of talk, K has talked about L, who is scheduled to read a paper at a conference. In lines 1 and 2, J says that L seems to be very worried about the conference. After some exchange of talk about where the conference is being held, C expresses his frustration in lines 6, 7 and 8 by saying that he cannot even write a term paper whereas L is going to a conference. Notice the use of *keyss* in this utterance, where it appears with the impotential negative marker *mos* 'cannot' in line 7, thus adding the sense of helplessness to the propositional content in the sense of *I cannot do so.*

It is important to note that the *keyss*-utterance in line 7 in turn helps to influence the affective frame for subsequent turns. In response to C's self-deprecation, K downgrades C's point by producing *klen-kes-un yakkwa-ci* 'that's nothing' in line 10, and goes on to talk about his more serious situation, where his classmates are even publishing their papers in prestigious journals. It is to be noted that K's direct rejection of C's self-deprecation is done to support C through the presentation of a more serious situation which K is facing. K's disagreement in this context counts as a PREFERRED RESPONSE to the interlocutor's self-effacement or self-deprecation, which is also observed in English conversation as Pomerantz (1984) shows. That is, in response to C's self-deprecation, K goes one step further to attempt to attenuate the seriousness of C's situation by proposing that C's just uttered self-deprecating comments are less negative or less serious than the situation he finds himself in. We can say that this is one way of showing commiseration with another, the theme of which is cogently expressed by a Korean proverb saying that misery is the best company.

In the subsequent context, another interlocutor, S, interrupts K's utterance and collaboratively completes it in line 12, while K completes his own utterance in lines 13 and 14. By doing so, S, along with K, contributes to showing sympathy to C, and at the same time gives sympathy to herself through the *keyss* marked utterance, *cwuk-keyss-e* '(what a pity) I would die' in the context of expressing self-deprecation. Actually, expressions such as *cwuk-keyss-ta* 'I would die'/'It drives me crazy' or *michi-keyss-ta* 'I'm going crazy' are frequently used in ordinary Korean conversation, often accompanied by an exclamation. These idiomatic *keyss* utterances clue the hearer to the speaker's affective orientation toward the preceding or subsequent talk.

In passing, it is to be noted that such a sympathy-giving function is also discussed by Ochs (1986, 1988), who looks at the linguistic expression of affect in Samoan. We find that the use of Korean *keyss* is similar to the use of the sympathy-marked first person pronoun (*ta ita* 'poor me') in Samoan in the sense that both forms are used to convey sympathy to the referent and to elicit sympathy from the interlocutor. In relation to this finding, Ochs further notes that the use of these affective expressions are constrained by a sequential organization of affect across turns and speakers, and she suggests, 'a narrator will use one or more affect features that indicate the attitude or feelings of the narrator toward the events discussed. These features clue the addressee as to the appropriate feedback response' (Ochs, 1988:175-6). This observation seems to be relevant to our discussion of the Korean sympathy marker *keyss,* which also displays the speaker's affective disposition in such a way that it is constrained across turns and speakers.

4.2. *Keyss* as a boundary marker

In this section, we turn to a context where *keyss* functions to mark a boundary in talk, which is also constituted by its sympathy-giving function. As we discussed in K.-H. Suh & K.-H. Kim (1991), one characteristic of the involving stance indexed by *keyss* is that *keyss* has a tendency to implicate a high degree of action fulfillment or action enactment, particularly when it is used with an action verb accompanied by a first person subject in a declarative sentence or by a second person subject in an interrogative sentence. Furthermore, we pointed out that the interpersonally involving stance indexed by *keyss* can be observed in the context where the use of *keyss* often performs the act of offering/promising, or a compliance to a suggestion. For instance, in our data, we found that *keyss* is used to ask about the hearer's intention, and at the same time, to express the speaker's intention to offer something, thus performing the speech act of offering, as in *kwail tu-si-keyss-eyo?*, meaning 'Would you like to have some fruit?'. *Keyss* is also used in the context where the speaker engages in the event immediately after or contemporaneously with the moment of speech, as when the speaker utters *cca -se te mos mek-keyss-ta* 'I can't eat any more because it's too salty', as he/she actually stops eating. We suggested that this enactment function of *keyss* derives from the speaker's signaling of involving stance in terms of involving the interlocutor in the current interactional state with regard to some kind of consequent action break. This is also observed in a situation where the speaker interrupts an on-going interaction, and projects a new action through a *keyss*-utterance. For instance, when a presider or MC announces the beginning of a meeting, he/she will say, *cikum hoyey-lul sicak ha-keyss-supnita*, meaning 'Now, we will start the meeting' as a way of getting attention from people who are engaged in chatting with each other, and at the same time, as a way of excusing him/herself for the sudden interruption. In this case, the utterance concurrently projects a new action.

In such contexts, we find a sense that, when the speaker immediately interrupts or initiates an action while giving an account of doing so, or projecting such an account for some newly-enacted action, he/she asks for the interlocutor's adjustment to the interactionally disjunctive act. In terms of the collaborative support-giving and sympathy-giving function of *keyss*, this is a case in which the use of *keyss* elicits the interlocutor's co-alignment with an action break or an initiation of a new interactional state. The speaker's volition or intention marked by this form is closely associated with the creation of the sense of jointness and the interlocutor's co-participation in a sudden shift in an interactional dimension, hence requesting the interlocutor's orientation to the speaker's causing a sudden action break. In this respect, we can say that *keyss* indexes affect in such a way that it 'serves as a boundary marker that initiates or terminates events with a certain affective tone' as Ochs & Schieffelin (1989) observe where the sympathy marked first person pronoun in Samoan often prefaces a story.

Following this line of argument, we will discuss example (3) to see how the *keyss* utterance in line 10 marks a sudden break from the on-going talk, and how the speaker negotiates a ground for causing such an interruption through extended talk. In the context that precedes this segment, four graduate students have been talking about their research. H, who has several dissertation topics in mind, has talked about the difficulty he has in selecting a topic, and L, who has almost finished his dissertation, advises H not to try to pick just one topic, but to conduct a less thorough research on all the three topics which H has worked on so far. The excerpt starts with H's agreement to L's suggestion.

(3) (North-Campus Chat)

1 H: kulehke ha -lye -ko ha-ko -sip -ss -nuntey
in that way do-INT-CONN do-CONN-like -ANT-CIRCUM
I intended to, I mean I really want to do it that way -

2 L: cokum yap -key shallowhakey chapter
a little superficially-CONN in a shallow manner chapter
hana ssik
one each

3 nemki-e kulem te swip-ci mwe ( ) kule -myen
pass -IE then more easy -COMM what do:that-COND

4 introduction hako chapter ssu -nun ke -ci
introduction and chapter write-ATTR thing-COMM
chapter twu
chapter two

5 kay tak nao -ntako
CL exactly come:out-QUOT
Just conduct your research not in depth - less in depth so that you can complete at least some chapters (with the research you have already done). After doing that, (I'm sure) it gets easier, right? (if you do so) you can definitely finish the introduction and a chapter. That makes exactly two chapters!

6 H: good idea ((laughing))
good idea
That's a good idea.

7 L: kulenikka in-depth-lo ha-lye -myen han-i
so in-depth-INSTR do-INT-COND limit-NOM
eps
not exist-

8 -ko
-CONN
So if you try to do your research in depth, there will be no end in sight.

9 H: han-i eps -ci -yo hana hana-ka ta
limit-NOM not exist-COMM-IE each each -NOM all
dissertation
dissertation

10 topic-i -te -lakwu -yo wancenhi
topic-be-RETRO-QUOT-POL completely
(I agree) it'll take forever. I mean each of the three topics can be a candidate for a dissertation.

((There is some overlap in talk between K and S))

--> 11 H: pick-up ha-le ka -ya **-keyss** -ta ((standing up))
pick-up do-PURP go -NECESS-MOD -IND
I have to go and pick up (my daughter)

12 K: Ah
EXCL
I see (who you are going to pick up)

13 H: Ai, i ke mwe hangsang achim -ey -to mal
EXCL this thing what always morning-LOC-ADD talk-
-i
COP

14 -ci, Sukyungi hakkyo teylye-ta cwu-nulako
-COMM Sukyungi school take -INTER give-ACCO
keki -nun
there-TOP

15 cikak -i -lanun -kes -i, cikakha-myen kyocang
being:late-COP-QUOT -thing-NOM be:late -CONN dean
sungin
excuse

16 -ul pat-aya toy -e=
-ACC get-NECESS become-IE
Shoot, (it's a bit of pain) to take Sukyung to school every morning. Because if students are late for school, they have to be excused by the dean.

17 K: =ung
oh
oh
[
18 S: emena
EXCL
really?

19 H: kule-nikka yetel-si isip pwun -kkaci teyli-e
like:that-CAUS 8 -hour 20 minute-by take -CONN
-ta
-INTERR

20 cwu-ko kkok ( ) tases si samsip pwun kkaci
give-CONN exactly 5 o'clock 30 minute by
pickup-ul
pickup-ACC

21 ha-llye -nikka i -ke cakku
do-INT-CAUS this-thing again and again
Therefore, since I have to take her to school by 8:20 sharp and then pick her up by 5:30 sharp, what a bother! - day after day -

22 K: hakkyo-ka eti -i -ntey -yo ?
school -NOM where-COP-CIRCUM-POL
Where is her school?

23 H: keki VONS twi -ey =
there VONS behind-LOC
Over there behind VONS market

24 K: =ung
yes
I see

25 ( )

26 H: keki salam -i mayi -e iss -unikka
there person-NOM be:bound-CONN exist-CAUS
Since I have been tied down to that tight schedule

27 S: kuleh-ci -yo
that -COMM-POL
That's right (I understand how you feel)

28 H: kipwun-i an coh -a = ((laughing))
feeling -NOM NEG good-IE
I don't feel good.

---> 29 K: =kuleh-**keyss** -ney
that -MOD -FR
(I guess) that's the case.

30 H: ce ka-po -l kkey -yo. taum -ey po -ayo. ((leaving))
I go-see-INT -POL next time-LOC see -POL
I'm gonna leave now. See you later

31 K: ney. ahnyenghe ka-sey -yo.
yes comfortably to-HONOR-POL
O.K. Good-bye.

In line 11, H, who has been talking about his dissertation topic, suddenly expresses his intention to leave, using the *keyss* utterance as he stands up to leave. Notice that in the subsequent context, H produces extended talk in the course of further explaining why he is departing rather abruptly, thus excusing himself for terminating the current conversation. We find that in line 11, H causes an interruption of the on-going interaction in a way to apologize for bringing up a sudden action break as if to say *I'm sorry, but I have to say this or do this.* In this regard, we can say that H's *keyss*-utterance in line 11 allows H to excuse himself and elicits the interlocutor's sympathy towards causing such an action break.

In the subsequent talk, K acknowledges H's situation with an exclamatory expression *Ah* in line 12. This particle corresponds to what Heritage (1984) calls a CHANGE-OF-STATE TOKEN like English *Oh*. By producing this exclamation marker, K displays that he accepts H's sudden break from the on-going interaction as something that deserves his own interactional as well as cognitive adjustment. After getting feedback from the interlocutors, H continues to provide further explanation about his situation in which he has to pick up his daughter by a certain time. This talk is again collaboratively responded to by K and S in lines 17 and 18, and also later by K in line 24, and by S in line 27. In line 28, H finally relates the preceding, extended account of his situation to his personal emotional state, by saying *kipwun-i an coh-a* 'I don't feel good about it'. This utterance is immediately responded to by K's *keyss*-utterance in line 29, which is latched onto H's preceding turn, as the equal sign indicates in lines 28 and 29.

In relation to our preceding discussion, this *keyss*-utterance provides a striking case where the speaker provides sympathy towards the interlocutor and the interlocutor's situation. That is, what K does here through the *keyss*-utterance is to express full sympathy towards H and H's situation, exactly at the point where H vented his feeling in line 28. In passing, we can also note that H's utterance is accompanied by his own laughter, which is produced side by side with K's *keyss*-utterance in line 29. As laughter is often produced in a context where the speaker moves out of an extended turn by way of negotiating a high degree of mutual orientation to the talk (cf. Jefferson, 1978), we can see that K provides sympathy towards H through the *keyss*-utterance exactly at such a point, where H invites such an orientation from the interlocutors. In line 30, H produces the first pair part of the leave-taking adjacency pair, which is responded to by the interlocutors' second pair part in line 31, and the parting sequence is finally completed.

To summarize our discussion, H uses the *keyss*-utterance to express self-sympathy to the speaker himself, and sets up an affective frame for the subsequent proposition in line 11. In line 29, the full endorsement is reached with the *keyss*-utterance by K, whereby K shows concern and sympathy for H's situation with an upgraded affective tone. It is after getting this sympathy-loaded response from K that H fulfills his intention to leave, which was expressed earlier in line 11. Therefore, we find a sense in which the *keyss*-utterance in line 11 projects an extended pre-departing sequence by way of negotiating the interactional ground on which the action break with the on-going talk and the initiation of a new action is licensed by simultaneously expressing and evoking sympathy.

5. Conclusion

Throughout this study, we have defined the Korean modal *keyss* as an affect key which indexes sympathy to a person or situation. The speaker uses *keyss* as a way of displaying sympathy for oneself or others and, additionally, to elicit sympathy from the interlocutors.

A primary context where *keyss* is frequently found in the conversation data collected is that of self-deprecations, self-effacement or complaints. The display of sympathy in these contexts is shown to help define these acts and to provide an affective orientation for the following talk. In this sense, *keyss* is often used to mark an episode boundary by either initiating or terminating events with a tone of sympathy. Subsequent to the display of the prior speaker's sympathy to him/herself or a proposition, the preferred response is often found to be prefaced by an agreement or disagreement.

The current study is presented as an initiating effort to provide a handle for additional future research that takes the interactional perspective with reference to the constitutive role of language. There should be further attempts to explore how a particular linguistic form, *keyss*, serves as a resource for a range of social meanings, and how these social meanings are constitutively related to each other, i.e., how the expression of sympathy marked by *keyss*, which interfaces with subjective epistemic expression (K.-H. Suh & K.-H. Kim 1991), can be explicated in terms of positive politeness or face (Brown & Levinson 1987), and how they help to constitute the socio-cultural ideology of the Korean community (cf. Ochs 1990, Clancy 1986). Consideration of non-referential, affective meaning would be extremely important in pursuing these issues because, as is pointed out by Ochs & Schieffelin (1989:22), 'Language has a heart as well as a mind of its own'.

References

Brown, Penelope, and Stephen C. Levinson. 1987. Politeness: Some Universals of Language Usage. Cambridge: Cambridge University Press.

Chafe, Wallace. 1982. Integration and Involvement in speaking, writing, and oral literature. Spoken and Written Language: Exploring Orality and Literacy, ed. by D. Tannen, 35 - 53. Norwood, NJ: Ablex.

Clancy, Patricia. 1986. The acquisition of communicative style in Japanese. Language Socialization across cultures, eds. by B.B. Shieffelin and E. Ochs, 213-50. New York: Cambridge University Press. 213-50.

Gee, Julie, and Iskender Savasir. 1985. On the use of will and gonna: Toward a description of activity-types for child language. Discourse Processes 8, 143-175.

Gumperz, John. J. 1977. Sociolinguistic knowledge in conversational inference. Georgetown University Round Table on Languages and Linguistics, ed. by M. Saville-Troike, 191-212. Washington, D.C.: Georgetown University Press.

Halliday, M. A. K. 1973. Explorations in the Functions of Language. London: Edward Arnold.

Heritage, John. 1984. A change-of-state token and aspects of its sequential placement. Structure of Social Action: Studies in Conversational Analysis, eds. by J. M. Atkinson & J. Heritage (eds.) Cambridge: Cambridge University Press.

Hong, Ki-Moon. 1947. Cosene mwunpep yenkwu (Study of Korean Grammar). Seoul: Seoul Sinmwunsa.

Hymes, Dell. 1974. Foundations in Sociolinguistics: an ethnographic approach. Philadelphia: University of Pennsylvania Press.

Jefferson, Gail. 1978. Sequential aspects of story-telling in conversation. Studies in the Organization of Conversational Interaction, ed. by J. N. Schenkein. 219-48. New York: Academic Press.

Lee, Ki-Yong. 1977. cimcakuy ttus: *keyss* kwa *(u)lkes* ul cwungsimulo (Meaning of prediction with reference to *keyss* and *(u)lkes*). Hapdong yenkwu palphyo nonmwun yeci II, Hankul Hakhoy.

Lyons, John. 1977. Semantics. Vol. 1. Cambridge: Cambridge University Press.

Ochs, Elinor. 1979. Introduction: what child language can contribute to pragmatics. Development Pragmatics, eds. by E. Ochs & B. B. Schieffelin, 1-17. New York: Academic Press.

_________. 1986. From feeling to grammar: a Samoan case study. Language Socialization across cultures, eds. by B. B. Shieffelin & E. Ochs, 213-50. New York: Cambridge University Press.

_________. 1988. Culture and Language Development: language acquisition and language socialization in Samoan village. Cambridge: Cambridge University Press.

_________. 1990. Indexicality and Socialization. Cultural Psychology: The Chicago Symposia, ed. by Stigler et al., 286-308. Cambridge: Cambridge University Press.

Ochs, Elinor, and Bambi Schieffelin. 1989. Language has a heart. Text 9-1, 7-25

Pomerantz, Anita. 1985. Agreeing and disagreeing with assessments; some features of preferred/dispreferred turn shapes. Structure of Social Action: Studies in Conversation Analysis, eds. by J. M. Atkinson & J. Heritage, 57-101. Cambridge: Cambridge Univ. Press.

Sacks, Harvey, Emanuel A. Schegloff, and Gail Jefferson. 1974. A simplest systematics for the organization of turn-taking for conversation. Language 50, 696-735.

Shin, Chang-Soon. 1972. Hyenday hankwukeuy yongen poco ekan *keyss* uy uymiwa yongpep (Meaning and use of modern Korean auxiliary marker *keyss*). Hyenday kwukmwunpep (Grammar of Modern Korean). Kyeymyeng University Press.

Suh, Jung-Soo. 1977. *keyss* ey kwanhaye (On *keyss*), Mal (Language) 2, 63-87.

___________. 1978. *(u)lkes* ey kwanhaye (On *(u)lkes*), Kwukehak (Korean Language Study) 6, 85-110.

Suh, Kyung-Hee. 1991. The Korean Modal *keyss* as a marker of affect. Ph.D qualifying paper. Applied Linguistics, UCLA

Suh, Kyung-Hee, and Kyu-hyun Kim. 1991. The Korean modal markers *keyss* and *(u)lkes:* An interactional perspective. Paper presented at Harvard Workshop on Korean Linguistics, Harvard University, Mass.

Sung, Ki-Chul. 1979. *keyss* kwa *(u)lkes* uy uymipikyo (Semantic differences between *keyss* and *(u)lkes*). Seoul National University.

Tannen, Deborah. 1982. Oral and literate strategies in spoken and written narratives. Language 58, 1-21

Part II

Phonology

The Phonological Word in Korean

EUNJOO HAN
Stanford University

1. Introduction

In this paper, I would like to argue for the existence of a specific prosodic domain in Korean, which I propose to refer to as the phonological word. The discussion will start with an attempt to define the domain of the phonological rule of Neutralization, and it will be shown that this domain is not isomorphic to any morpho-syntactic constituent; consequently it must be defined in terms of a prosodic constituent, namely the phonological word. The argument will be supported by the presence of other phonological phenomena that are bounded by exactly the same domain or refer to it in their proper characterization.

2. Neutralization

I would like to thank Young-mee Yu Cho, Sharon Inkelas, Paul Kiparsky, Bill Poser and Peter Sells for their helpful comments.

2.1. The domain of Neutralization

I will begin with questioning what the domain of Neutralization is.[1] As is well-known, Neutralization in Korean is a rule which changes all labial and velar stops to homorganic plain stops and all coronal obstruents plus *h*, to *t* in the syllable coda position. This is illustrated in (1).

(1)	a.	p,	p',	p^h	→	[p]
	b.	t,	t',	t^h		
		s,	s'		→	[t]
		c,	c'	c^h		
		h				
	c.	k,	k',	k^h	→	[k]

(2) lists some words that are subject to Neutralization.

(2)	a.	sup^h	→	sup	'forest'
	b.	mit^h	→	mit	'bottom'
	c.	pis	→	pit	'comb'
	d.	is'-	→	it-	'to exist'
	e.	pic	→	pit	'debt'
	f.	pic^h	→	pit	'light'
	g.	tah-	→	tat-	'to arrive'
	h.	pak'	→	pak	'outside'
	i.	$puək^h$	→	puək	'kitchen'

Such a neutralization is characterized as delinking of the features in the laryngeal tier, the continuant feature and the feature [−anterior] as argued in Sohn (1987) and Cho (1990). As Neutralization is sensitive to the syllable structure, it is closely related to lexical syllabification.[2]

Let us now turn to the issue of what the domain of Neutralization is. The following examples show that Neutralization does not apply to stem-final consonants of nouns and verbs when they are followed by inflectional suffixes. Thus, Neutralization does not seem to apply in the stem cycle.

---

[1] Throughout this paper, the domain of a phonological rule means the domain by which the application of the rule is bounded.

[2] In Korean, both lexical syllabification and postlexical syllabification are needed. The former is bounded in the word level and interacts closely with word-level rules such as Neutralization or Consonant Cluster Simplification whereas the latter applies freely across words in a very large domain. Hence, as will be shown later, the domain of Neutralization or Consonant Cluster Simplification coincides with the domain of lexical syllabification.

(3)	a.	[[k'oc^h] i] 'flower' Nom.	→	[k'oc^{h}i] 'flower (Nom.)'
	b.	[[pak'] e] 'outside' Loc.	→	[pak'e] 'outside'
	c.	[[is'] ə] 'to exist' Cont.	→	[is'ə] 'exist (Cont.)'
	d.	[[put^h] ɨmyən] 'to stick' Cond.	→	[put^{h}ɨmyən] 'stick (Cond.)'

On the other hand, the final consonants of nouns *mulɨp*^{h} 'knee' and *k'oc*^{h} 'flower' are neutralized to plain stops in the following examples.

(4) a. nə mulɨp^h ap^{h}ɨ-ni?
you knee be painful-QUE 'Are your knees hurt?'
[nə murɨb ap^{h}ɨ ni] *[nə murɨp^{h}ap^{h}ɨ ni?]

b. i k'oc^h an-a!
this flower hold-IMP 'Hold these flowers!'
[i k'od ana] *[i k'oc^h ana]

In (4), the conversion of *p* (< *p*^{h}) to *b* and *t* (< *c*^{h}) to *d* is due to a separate postlexical rule, Intersonorant Voicing, which changes plain stops into corresponding voiced stops between sonorants. Considering (3) and (4), one might conclude that the application of Neutralization is bounded within a morphological word.[3] However, the compound words in (5) show that this is incorrect.

(5)	a.	[[p^{h}at^h][al]] 'red bean''grain'	→	[p^{h}adal] *[p^{h}at^{h}al] 'a grain of red bean'
	b.	[[cəc][əmi]] 'milk''mother'	→	[cədəmi] *[cəjəmi] 'wet nurse'
	c.	[[ap^h][ap^h]] 'front''front'	→	[abap] *[ap^{h}ap] 'individualy'

These examples show that each member of a compound forms a separate domain with regard to Neutralization. In other words, at the moment when Neutralization applies, the final consonant of the left member of a compound

[3] Cho and Sells (1991) claim that nominal case markers in Korean as well as verbal suffixes are lexically attached.

is in the syllable-coda position, even though postlexically such a stem-final consonant is resyllabified as the onset to the first syllable of the right member.

Case-inflected compounds, as demonstrated in (6), raise another problem in determining the domain in which Neutralization is bounded.

(6)	a.	[[[ap^h][ap^h]] i]	→	[abap^{h}i]
		'front' 'front' Adv.		'individually'
	b.	[[[kət^h][os]] ɨl]	→	[kədosɨl]
		'surface''clothes' Acc.		'outer clothes (Acc.)'

Note that in case-inflected compounds, the final consonant of the right member is not neutralized whereas that of the left member is. This fact indicates that compounds with suffixes form two domains with regard to Neutralization such that one domain consists of the left member of a compound and the other domain the right member plus the following suffixes. Here we see a clear case of a bracketing paradox – in which phonological structure and morphological/semantic bracketing disgree. The appropriate bracketing for phonology requires that the right member of a compound cohere more closely to the suffix rather than the left member. In contrast, the bracketing required by morphology/semantics is as shown in the left column of (6).

Let us now consider how prefixes behave with respect to Neutralization. As far as prefixes are concerned, however, it is not so simple to decide whether they form the same domain with the following stems or they themselves constitute separate domains for the following reasons. First, as Korean is a heavily suffixing language, there is a relatively small number of prefixes. Secondly, we can posit *t* as an underlying representation for the prefix-final consonant of almost all the prefixes that end in an obstruent even though they have orthographically *th, c,* or *s*, such as *cit-* 'indiscriminately', *hæt-* 'new', *pit-* 'aslant' or *sut-* 'pure'.

In this paper I assume that while there is no prefix that ends in *s* underlyingly, there are some prefixes that end in t^h or *c*, on the grounds that they are related to lexical words. (7) are some examples of such prefixes and the lexical words related to them.

(7)	hot^h-	'single'	hot^h(n.)	'single'
	kyət^h-	'side'	kyət^h(n.)	'side'
	mac-	'facing'	macu (adv.)	'face-to-face'
	nɨc-	'late'	nɨc- (v.)	'to be late'

Under this assumption, (8) shows that prefixes constitute independent domains on their own.

(8)	a.	[nɨc [yəlɨm]]	→	[nɨdyərɨm] *[nɨjərɨm]
		'late' 'summer'		'late summer'
	b.	[hotʰ [os]]	→	[hodot] *[hotʰot]
		'single' 'clothes'		'unlined clothes'

Accordingly, in a word that contains both a prefix and a suffix, two domains will be found, the prefix and the stem plus the suffix. To take an example, [[hotʰ [os]] i] 'unlined clothes (Nom.)' surfaces as [hodosi]. In this respect, prefixes appear to behave like words. Actually, similarities between prefixes and words have been observed in various languages (Booij and Rubach 1984, Nespor and Vogel 1986). It is therefore not surprising that these two types of elements have the same phonological status in some languages.[4]

2.2. The Phonological Word

To sum up what has been discussed so far, the domain of Neutralization includes a stem plus any adjacent suffixes. A prefix and the following stem and the two members of a compound constitute two separate domains. Such a domain, which is smaller than the morphological word, is not isomorphic to any morpho-syntactic constituent. This leads us to resorting to a prosodic constituent in defining the domain of Neutralization. I propose that the domain defined for Neutralization be referred to as the phonological word.

Selkirk (1986), Selkirk and Tateishi (1988), Cohn (1989) and Selkirk and Shen (1990) argue that prosodic domains are defined by reference to 'ends'. That is, the basic hypothesis of this 'end-based' theory is that phonological domains are demarcated by the right or left end of certain morph-syntactic constituents. According to the analysis given above, the phonological word in Korean is the domain demarcated by left edges of prefixes or stems and can be specified by the mapping parameter as illustrated below.

(9) Korean Phonological Word Parameter

Phonological Word: $\{\text{Left}, X_{lex}\}$

where X_{lex} stands for lexical item

With the phonological word in Korean as defined above, it turns out to be of the same type as the phonological word in Hungarian. Nespor

[4] It has been reported that in some languages prefixes behave like phrases phonologically. Based on the peculiar tone patterns of certain Japanese prefixes, Poser (1990) argues that these prefixes, which he refers to as Aoyagi prefixes, typically belong to a separate minor phrase from the stem to which they attach.

and Vogel (1986) claim that the phonological word in Hungarian, which is the domain of Vowel Harmony and Palatalization, includes a stem plus any linearly adjacent string of suffixes. The two members of a compound thus form two different phonological words. In addition the category of elements often referred to as preverbs, which they refer to simply as prefixes also form independent phonological words. Similarly, defining the domain of application of Intervocalic Voicing of *s* in Italian, Nespor (1984) argues that the phonological word in Italian, which consists of an underived stem plus its suffixes and certain prefixes, is smaller than the morphological word.

3. Other Phenomena that Refer to the Phonological Word

It has been argued that the prosodic theory is able to account for the clustering behavior of phonological rules by positing a small set of prosodic domains (Nespor and Vogel 1986, Inkelas 1989). In other words, once prosodic domains are introduced as formal entities in the grammar, there must be phonological rules that have the same prosodic domains as their domain of application. Thus the existence of the phonological word as a phonological entity in Korean would be supported if there are some other phonological phenomena whose domain of application is the phonological word as well. In what follows, I will show that besides Neutralization, two other phonological phenomena, Palatalization and Consonant Cluster Simplification, are bounded by the phonological word and one other phenomenon, *n*- Insertion, refers to the constituent phonological word in its proper formulation. Moreover, it will be shown that the phonological word serves as the host in the affixation of particles to verbal forms.

3.1. Palatalization

Korean Palatalization is a well-known phonological phenomenon for its "derived environment" behavior.[5] The rule changes *t* to *c* and t^h to c^h before *i* or *y*, but only when the target and the trigger are in different morphemes. Thus, morpheme-internal *ti*, t^hi sequences are not converted to *ci*, c^hi as in *mati* [madi] (*[maji]) 'knot' or *pət^hi-* [pət^hi-] (*[pəc^hi-]) 'to withstand'. As illustrated in (10), however, the rule applies between stems and suffixes.

---

[5] Kiparsky (in press) presents a new analysis for ***non-derived environment blocking*** in general as well as Korean Palatalization, arguing that ***non-derived environment blocking*** can be reduced to the application of structure-building rules to underspecified representations. In his paper, a unified account is given for both "lexical" and "postlexical" palatalization in Korean and the different outcome of lexical and postlexical palatalization of *t* and t^h is attributed to a word-level Affrication rule that specifies the [−Anterior, +High] obstruent stops as [+Delayed Release]. Although his analysis is compelling, I will deal with only "lexical" palatalization in this paper since this paper does not concern the analysis of palatalization itself. If his analysis were adopted, the term Palatalization would be replaced by Affrication.

(10)	a.	[[mat] i-] 'eldest' Cop.	[maji-] 'to be the eldest'
	b.	[[pat^h] i] 'field' Nom.	[pac^{h}i] 'field (Nom.)'
	c.	[[kut] i] 'to be firm' Adv.	[kuji] 'stubbornly'
	d.	[[kət] hi-] 'to collect' Pass.	[kəc^{h}i-] 'to be collected'

It has been said that the sensitivity to a morpheme boundary of Palatalization indicates that it is a lexical rule (Ahn 1985, Sohn 1987). Palatalization, however, does not apply in every morphologically derived environment. Consider the examples in (11), where morpheme-final *t* or t^h does not get palatalized in spite of the presence of the potential trigger *i* in the following morpheme.

(11)	a.	[[pat^h][ilaŋ]] 'field' 'ridge'	[padiraŋ] (or [panniraŋ]) *[pajiraŋ] 'the ridge of a field'
	b.	[hot^h [ipul]] 'single''comforter'	[hodibul] (or [honnibul]) *[hojibul] 'unlined comforter'
	c.	[nɨc [yəlɨm]] 'late' 'summer'	[nɨdyərɨm] (or [nɨnnyərɨm]) *[nɨjyərɨm] 'late summer'

Thus, Palatalization does not apply across a prefix and the following stem or two members of a compound; rather it is confined to the very domain that has been defined as the phonological word in the preceding section – a prefix or a stem plus any adjacent suffixes.

3.2. Consonant Cluster Simplification

In this subsection, I will discuss so-called Consonant Cluster Simplification by which segments not integrated into the syllable are erased. While the maximal syllable template of Korean is CGVC, certain morphemes have an underlying consonant cluster in the final position. (12) is a list of the possible underlying clusters.

(12)	ps	lk
	lm	lp
	ks	lp^h
	nc	nh
	lt^h	lh

As only one consonant is allowed in the coda position in Korean, underlying clusters are reduced to one consonant when it is impossible for both consonants to be syllabified, that is, word-finally or preconsonantally. Which of the two consonants is realized as the coda on surface varies depending on speakers and dialects. Just like Neutralization, Consonant Cluster Simplification closely interacts with lexical syllabification and it is usually assumed that both the consonants are syllabified when the following morpheme begins with a vowel. Relevant examples are listed in (13). In (13)a, the final consonant is simply erased whereas in (13)b, the final consonant is syllabified as the onset to the following syllable.

(13)	a.	[[kaps] kwa]	[kapk'wa]
		‘price’ ‘and’	‘price and’
		[[anc] ki]	[ank'i]
		‘to sit’ Nominal.	‘sitting’
	b.	[[kaps] i]	[kaps'i]
		‘price’ Nom.	‘price (Nom.)’
		[[anc] a]	[anja]
		‘to sit’ Cont.	‘sit (Cont.)’

Yet it is not always the case that both members of a consonant cluster are syllabified prevocalically in a word. (14) demonstrates that the final cluster of the lefthand stem of a compound gets reduced despite the fact that the following stem begins with a vowel. Thus Consonant Cluster Simplification applies in the final position of the lefthand stem in compounds.

(14)	a.	[[[kaps][əps]] ə]	[kabəps'ə] *[kaps'əps'ə]
		‘price’ ‘not to have’ Cont.	‘be worthless (Cont.)’
	b.	[[[nəks][ilh]] ɨn]	[nəgirɨn] (or [neŋnirɨn]) *[nəks'irɨn]
		‘spirit’‘to lose’ Past Mod.	‘be absent-minded’

It is impossible to apply the same test to the juncture of a prefix and a stem since there is no prefix that contains a consonant cluster in the final position. Nevertheless, it would not be far-fetched to say that a prefix does not form the same domain as the following stem with regard to Consonant Cluster Simplification. Given these facts, I conclude that Consonant Cluster Simplification, a sort of Stray Erasure, is bounded by the same domain as Neutralization, namely the phonological word.

3.3. *n*-Insertion

There is an $n/\emptyset$ alternation stem-initially in certain environments.

(15) a.	[[cip][il]] 'house''work' [[path][ilaŋ]] 'field''ridge' [[sæk][yuli]] 'color''glass' [[khoŋ][yəs]] 'bean''candy'	[cimnil] (or [cibil]) 'house work' [panniraŋ] (or [padiraŋ]) 'the ridge of a field' [sæŋnyuri] (or [sægyuri]) 'colored glass' [khoŋnyət] (or [khoŋyət]) 'bean candy'
b.	[cit [iki-]] 'indiscriminately''to mash' [hoth [ipul]] 'single''comforter' [tət [yaŋmal]] 'extra''socks'	[cinnigi-] 'to mash' [honnibul] (or [hodibul]) 'unlined comforter' [tənnyaŋmal] (or [tədyaŋmal]) 'oversocks'

As shown above, *n*, which is not present in a bare stem, optionally appears before a stem when the stem begins with *i* or *y* and, at the same time, it is preceded by another stem or a prefix. This $n/\emptyset$ alternation has been analyzed as *n*-Insertion (Choi 1955, Huh 1965) or *n*-Deletion. Those who have argued for *n*-Deletion have proposed that the stems in question have an initial *n* underlyingly, which is deleted in the word-initial position (Ahn 1985, Sohn 1987). They have postulated, for example, underlying /nil/ and /nyuli/ for the stems *il* 'work' and *yuli* 'glass' and claimed that the initial *n* is retained in compounding and prefixation since it is not placed in the word-initial position in these cases.

In this paper I will take the position that *n* is not present underlyingly but inserted later. The argument against the *n*-Deletion approach is that *n* is never present when the preceding stem ends in a vowel.

(16)	[il] 'work' [[noŋsa][il]] 'farming''work' [yəs] 'candy' [[k'æ][yəs]] 'sesame''candy'	[il] *[nil] [noŋsail] *[noŋsanil] 'farm work' [yət] *[nyət] [kæyət] *[k'ænyət] 'sesame candy'

Furthermore, there is a variation between a form with *n* and a form without *n* in some words even when the preceding stem ends in a consonant, as shown in the variants [panniraŋ]/[padiraŋ] in (15). Under the *n*-Deletion approach, these facts would be stated in the way that *n* is obligatorily deleted word-initially and after a vowel but optionally deleted after a consonant. On the other hand, on the hypothesis that those stems do not have *n* in the underlying representation, the regularity could be described more simply; *n* is optionally inserted before stems with initial *i* when they are preceded by a consonant.

Let us now focus on the appropriate morphological structure in which *n* is inserted. As stated above, it is inserted before a stem when the stem is preceded by a prefix or another stem. To translate it into prosodic terms, *n* is inserted at the juncture of two phonological words. However, *n* is not inserted at every juncture of two phonological words; there must also be a domain larger than the phonological word, within which *n*-Insertion is bounded. I will not pursue the issue of defining that domain in this paper. Given this caveat, *n*-Insertion can be formulated as a domain-juncture rule (in the sense of Selkirk 1980) as in (17).[6]

(17)

n-Insertion

$\emptyset \rightarrow n$ / [...[...C]$_\omega$ _ [i ...]$_\omega$ ...]

Thus *n*-Insertion must crucially refer to the phonological word in its proper formulation, providing an additional evidence for the argument that the phonological word is needed as a phonological entity in Korean.

3.4. Phonological Constraint on the Particle Attachment

Cho (1991) and Sells and Cho (1991) note that the attachment of particles (also known as delimiters eg. *-to* 'also, even', *-man* 'only', the topic marker *-(n)ɨn*, *-(i)lato* 'even' and the plural marker *-tɨl*) to a verbal form is constrained by the phonological length of the verbal form as demonstrated by the examples in (18).

(18) a. cap-a-to cu-se-yo.
hold-COMP-also give-HON-VE
'Please also hold (it).'

b. *ca-to(<ca-a-to) cu-se-yo.
sleep-COMP-also give-HON-VE
'Please sleep also.'

[6] Even though there is no evidence for determining whether *n* is inserted in the initial position of the second phonological word, in the final position of the first phonological word or between two phonological words, I assume that it is inserted between two phonological words.

The condition is that the verbal form must be at least disyllabic in order for a particle to attach.[7] (18)b is ill-formed since *-to* is attached to a monosyllabic host *ca,* which is contracted from *ca-a*. The fact that the constraint is only on the affixation of particles but not on the specific phonological sequence *cato* is evident from (19), which contrasts with (18)b.

(19) ca-to(<ca-ato) kwæncʰanh-ayo.
sleep-although all right-VE
'Even if you sleep, it's all right.'

The same phonological sequence *ca-to* is well-formed in (19) where *to* is not a particle but a part of the concessive ending *-ato*.

Given that the constraint pertains to the phonological length of the "host", let us now consider what constituent can serve as the "host" for particle attachment. Look at the following examples.

(20) a. *tolaka-nɨn(<tolaka-a-nɨn) po-as'-əyo.
go back-COMP-TOP try-PAST-VE
'(I) tried going back.'

b. tolatani-ə-nɨn po-as'-əyo.
wander around-COMP-TOP try-PAST-VE
'(I) tried wandering around.'

c. *yətpwa-nɨn(<yətpo-a-nɨn) tu-əs'-əyo.
peep-COMP-TOP put-PAST-VE
'(I) peeped (for future use).'

d. yəttɨl-ə-nɨn tu-əs'-əyo.
eavesdrop-COMP-TOP put-PAST-VE
'(I) eavesdropped (for future use).'

Note that (20)a and (20)c are ill-formed despite the fact that the verbal forms to which particles are attached are polysyllabic. How can these counterexamples be handled? Looking into those verbal forms, we can find out a common property among them. Those verbal forms are morphologically complex – *tolaka-* is a compound verb with the structure [[[tol] a][ka-]] and *yətpo-* consists of a prefix *yət* 'secretly' and a verb stem *po-* 'to see'. Thus

[7] This constraint does not seem to hold in some dialects such as the Kyengsang dialect where monosyllabic verb stem can be combined with the particles in question as in *mək-to mos ha-ko* ('cannot even eat and'). Also some speakers of the standard dialect find the attachment of *-man* to be less constrained than that of the other particles.

these examples indicate that a prefix or a lefthand stem of a compound does not contribute to the length of the verbal form as the "host" of a particle. Given this fact, it appears that the host in affixing particles to a verbal form must be defined as a prosodic constituent – here the constituent phonological word is invoked again. Then the condition could be stated such that in order for a particle to attach to a verbal form, the phonological word preceding the particle must be at least disyllabic.

4. Conclusion

In sum, I have argued that the phonological word in Korean is a necessary constituent to characterize various phonological phenomena properly. The application of some phonological rules such as Neutralization or Palatalization is bounded by the phonological word and *n*-Insertion applies at the juncture of two phonological words. In addition, the phonological word serves as the host in the attachment of particles to a verbal form.

The definition of the phonological word in Korean specifies left edges of prefixes and stems and therefore refers to morphological structure in an asymmetric way; any string of suffixes is included in one phonological word with the preceding stem while prefixes form a phonological word on their own.

The basic theoretical result of this paper is an argument for prosodic theory in general and, in particular, for the existence of sublexical prosodic constituents.

References

Ahn, S.-C. 1985. *The Interplay of Phonology and Morphology in Korean.* Doctoral dissertation, University of Illinois at Urbana-Champaign.

Booij, G. 1984. Coordination Reduction in Complex Words: a case for Prosodic Phonology. In H. vander Hulst and N. Smith (eds.), *Advances in Non-linear Phonology*, 143-160. Dordrecht: Foris.

Booij, G. and J. Rubach. 1984. Morphological and Prosodic Domains in Lexical Phonology. *Phonology Yearbook* 1, 1-27.

Booij, G. and J. Rubach. 1987. Postcyclic versus Postlexical Rules in Lexical Phonology. *Linguistic Inquiry* 18, 1-44.

Cho, Y.-M. 1991. A Phonological Constraint on the Attachment of Particles in Korean. Paper presented at the 4th Harvard Workshop on Korean Linguistics, Harvard, July 1991. To appear in the Proceedings.

Cho, Y.-M. and P. Sells. 1991. A Lexical Account of Phrasal Suffixes in Korean. Ms. Stanford University.

Choi, H.-B. 1955. *Uli Malbon [Our Grammar]*. Seoul: Cengumsa.

Cohn, A. 1989. Stress in Indonesian and Bracketing Paradoxes. *NLLT* 7, 167-216.

Huh, W. 1965. *Kuko Umunhak [Korean Phonology]*. Seoul: Cengumsa.

Inkelas, S. 1989. *Prosodic Constituency in the Lexicon*. Doctoral dissertation, Stanford University.

Kiparsky, P. in press. Blocking in Non-Derived Environments. In E. Kaisse ans S. Hargus (eds.), *Studies in Lexical Phonology*. New York: Academic Press.

Nespor, M. 1984. The Phonological Word in Italian. In H. van der Hulst and N. Smith (eds.), *Advances in Non-linear Phonology*, 193-204. Dordrecht: Foris.

Nespor, N. and I. Vogel. 1986. *Prosodic Phonology*. Dordrecht: Foris.

Poser, W. J. 1990. Word-Internal Phrase Boundary in Japanese. In S. Inkelas and D. Zec (eds.), *The Phonology-Syntax Connection*, 278-287. Stanford: CSLI.

Selkirk, E. 1980. Prosodic Domains in Phonology: Sanskrit Revisited. In M. Aronoff and M.-L. Kean (eds.) *Juncture*, 107-129. Saratoga: Anma Libri.

Selkirk, E. 1986. On Derived Domains in Sentence Phonology. *Phonology Yearbook* 3, 371-405.

Selkirk, E. and K. Tateishi. 1988. Constraints on Minor Phrase Formation in Japanese. *CLS* 24.

Selkirk, E. and T. Shen. 1990. Prosodic Domains in Shanghai Chinese. In S. Inkelas and D. Zec (eds.), *The Phonology-Syntax Connection*, 313-337. Stanford: CSLI.

Sells, P. and Y.-M. Cho. 1991. On the Distribution of X^0 Elements in Korean. Paper presented at the Santa Cruz Workshop on Korean Syntax and Semantics.

Sohn, H.-S. 1987. *Underspecification in Korean Phonology*. Doctoral dissertation, University of Illinois at Urbana-Champaign.

Prosodic Approach on Korean Partial Reduplication

JONGHO JUN
University of California at Los Angeles

1. Introduction

The development of reduplication theory has focused on defining the location and vocabulary of the conditions governing the process. Marantz (1982) claims that reduplication is best analyzed as the affixation of a CV-skeletal morpheme to a stem, as opposed to a transformational approach which would generate many types of morphological rules not instantiated in natural language:

(1) a. $C_1 V_1 \; C_2 V_2 \; + \; V_2 C_2 \; V_1 C_1$
b. C V C V
1 2 3 4 --> 4, 3, 2, 1, 1, 2, 3, 4

However, Marantz's analysis is also subject to the same argument as the transformational one. Any CV sequence in the Marantzian framework can be a well-formed reduplicative affix, even though the class of reduplicative affixes in natural language is restricted.

Recent research by McCarthy and Prince (1986, 1988) and Steriade (1988) has departed from segmentalism where a CV or X skeleton is assumed as a reduplicative affix. Instead, these researchers propose that reduplicative affixal templates be expressed in prosodic terms (e.g. syllable, core syllable, foot, minimal word).[1] Thus, the restriction on the reduplicative affix of natural language comes from the prosodic terms which define the affixal template.

Most recently, within the framework of prosodic morphology, McCarthy and Prince (1990) propose a theory of prosodic circumscription. According to the theory of prosodic circumscription, morphological operations including reduplication, which usually operate on a base defined in morphological terms, may need a further delineation of the base subject to prosodic conditions.

---

[1] Steriade's use of template is a bit different from that of others. According to her theory, the template consists of two conditions, one of which is a condition on prosodic weight of the reduplicative affix.

Thus, from Marantz (1982) through McCarthy and Prince (1986, 1988) and Steriade (1988) to McCarthy and Prince (1990), the focus has been changed in the two subparts of conditions governing reduplication: the location has been extended from the affix to the stem as well, and the vocabulary has been changed from segment to prosodic constituent.

Partial reduplication (henceforth, PR) in Korean has been analyzed as a simple suffixation process of a syllable with the final consonant melody rendered extrasyllabic by McCarthy and Prince (1986). However, in this paper, by introducing new observations not dealt with in previous analyses, I will show that McCarthy and Prince's analysis of Korean PR is not general enough. Furthermore, adopting the theory of prosodic circumscription (McCarthy and Prince 1990), I will argue that Korean PR falls out from a more general morphological process subject to a prosodic condition on the metrical weight of surface forms. More specifically, Korean PR will be derived by imposing a surface prosodic condition on the output of the reduplication operation with prosodic circumscription. In so doing, I will show that Korean PR is an unusual case in which a morpheme consists of matching a template against the prosodic structure of the derived output, including the stem and the affix.

In summary, Korean PR consists of two steps; 1) reduplication with phonological circumscription and 2) prosodic surface constraints. The organization of this paper is as follows: In section 2, based on the discussion of fortisity and aspiration, I will argue that Korean fortis and aspirated consonants are geminates. This will be followed by the formulation of Korean foot structure. In section 3, I will discuss observations related to PR. I will then present my arguments against McCarthy and Prince's (1986) analysis, offering an alternative approach. In section 4, I will sum up my analysis.

2. Preliminaries

2.1. Korean geminate fortis and aspirated consonants

In many respects, fortis and aspirated consonants in Korean behave differently from the lenis consonants. First, fortis and aspirated consonants are not allowed in coda position. Second, the lenis consonants /p, t, k, c/ become voiced between sonorant segments as in (2), whereas neither aspirated nor fortis segments undergo this voicing rule.

(2) lenis --> [+voice] / [+sonorant] ___ [+sonorant]
Thus, /k,t,p,c/ become [g,d,b,j] respectively in the above environment.[2]

Third, unlike lenis consonants, it is not clear whether aspirated and fortis consonants are syllabified as onsets of the following syllable or as codas of the preceding syllable. Huh (1965:209) states that fortis and aspirated consonants seem to be ambisyllabic.[3]

As Martin (1951), Kim (1986) and Kim (1989) have indicated, these observations suggest strongly that the lenis : fortis distinction is actually one between simplex and geminate consonants. This is supported by phonetic experimental studies which show that Korean fortis and aspirated consonants are of longer duration than lenis consonants.

Let us see how this proposal can provide a general account of three observations mentioned before. The fact that fortis or aspirated consonants are not allowed in the coda position can be accounted for by the principle, which is general in Korean, that restricts a coda in Korean syllable

---

[2] /j/ indicates voiced counterpart of /c/. But, except here, /j/ always indicates a glide in this paper.

[3] Huh(1965:209) says that there is an impression that a fortis or aspirated consonant is ambi-syllabic between vowels. Nevertheless, he regards it as an onset only for the pattern congruity.

structure to a single segment. Secondly, geminates do not become voiced intervocalically in any language known to us. Consequently, we would not expect the aspirated and fortis consonants to do so in Korean.[4] Finally, the observation that fortis and aspirated consonants seem to be ambisyllabic falls out directly from the proposal.

There are yet further arguments that support the hypothesis that Korean fortis and aspirated obstruents are geminates. Let us consider first the diverse surface realizations of /h/ in Korean, which were already discussed by Kim (1989). A lenis consonant becomes aspirated as in (3i-ii) or fortis as in (3iii) in the same environment as a sonorant geminates as in (3iv) (Korean sonorant segments do not have a fortis counterpart.):

(3) Base	Surface	
(i) /nah+ko/	[nak^{h}o]	'bear' + verbal connective ending for conjunction
(ii) /kop.ha.ki/	[kop^{h}a.ki]	'multiplication'
(iii) /nah+sɨp/	[nassɨp]	'bear' + verbal ending for humbling
(iv) /nah+nɨn/	[nannɨn]	'bear' + verbal connective ending for present progressive

Aspirated consonants [k^h] and [p^h] in (3i-ii) are derived by merger of /h/ and an adjacent stop, each of which has its own timing unit, whereas fortis consonant [ss] and geminate consonant [nn] are derived by an association of an adjacent consonant to the unassociated timing unit after /h/ deletion. As a result, those aspirated and fortis consonants retain two timing units like geminate consonants.[5] (See Kim 1989 for a detailed analysis)

Another argument concerns the historical development of fortis and aspirated consonants in Korean. According to Huh (1965), consonant clusters were allowed in Korean until the sixteenth century. In addition, each constituent in a cluster had its own phonetic value. As the language changed, the outer constituents in the clusters assimilated to the inner most consonant, which was eventually changed into its fortis counterpart as below.

(4)	around the 16th century		
(i) ptɨs	--->	ttɨs	'meaning'
(ii) psi	--->	ssi	'seed'
(iii) pstɛ	--->	ttɛ	'time'

A similar pattern of historical development for some aspirated consonants in Modern Korean is shown below.

(5)			
(i) amh.tak	--->	am.t^{h}ak	'hen'
(ii) salh.ko.ki	--->	sal.k^{h}o.ki	'fresh'
(iii) coh.pap	--->	cop^{h}ap	'boiled rice with millet'

This shows that some fortis and aspirated consonants in Modern Korean were produced by the historical merger of lenis consonants.

---

[4] The above two arguments in favor of (8) were already discussed in Kim (1986).

[5] Consequently, all the lenis and sonorant consonants of Korean except /ŋ/ can be geminates: geminates of obstruents are realized as fortis; or aspirated in case they retain aspiration.

Another important argument concerns consonantal alternations in Korean onomatopoetic and mimetic words (which will be discussed in detail in section 3). Onomatopoetic and mimetic words with fortis or aspirated onsets tend to have different connotations from ones with lenis onsets. For example, /piŋ.piŋ/ is a mimetic word denoting the manner in which a top spins. In contrast, /p^hiŋ.p^hiŋ/ and /ppiŋ.ppiŋ/ denote faster, more intense, spinning. The interesting case is where the fortis counterpart of a consonant does not exist. /l/ in Korean does not have fortis/aspirated counterparts. Nevertheless, we can derive the same connotations by making /l/ geminate as below:

(6) a.loŋ a.loŋ 'mottled' ---> alloŋ alloŋ 'densely mottled'

This suggests that fortis and aspirated consonants have the same morphological and phonological status as geminates.

We are now in a position to observe how geminate fortis and aspirated consonants are syllabified. Following the principles of moraic phonology (Hyman 1985; Hayes 1989), I assume that Korean geminates bear an underlying mora. In other words, geminates always bear a mora. Lenis consonants do not bear a mora unless assigned one by a rule supplying "weight by position".[6] This underlying mora can explain the diverse behavior of aspirated and fortis consonants depending on the position in syllable structure and adjacent segments.

First, when geminate consonants occur word-initially or following another consonant, they are associated to a syllable node directly, which will produce a syllable preceded by an underlying mora. If they occur intervocalically, their underlying moras spread to the previous syllable rendering it heavy.[7] This can account for ambisyllabicity of intervocalic aspirated and fortis consonants. In contrast, when they occur word-finally or preceding another consonant, they can not be associated to an onset since there is no available onset position. Furthermore, they already retain an underlying mora, which will block the mora assignment by "weight by position". Thus, geminate consonants behave like their lenis counterparts in the coda position. This provides a more general account of the fact that is explained by the coda condition which restricts a coda in Korean syllable structure to a single segment.

In this section, I argued that Korean fortis and aspirated consonants are geminates, and then discussed their behavior in syllable structure under the framework of moraic phonology.

2.2. Foot structure

It is generally held that Korean is not a stress language. The morphological and phonological role of Korean stress is minimal compared to true stress languages such as English. It is not considered distinctive. Nevertheless, it exists phonetically and its distribution is predictable. It

6 (Hayes 1989:258)

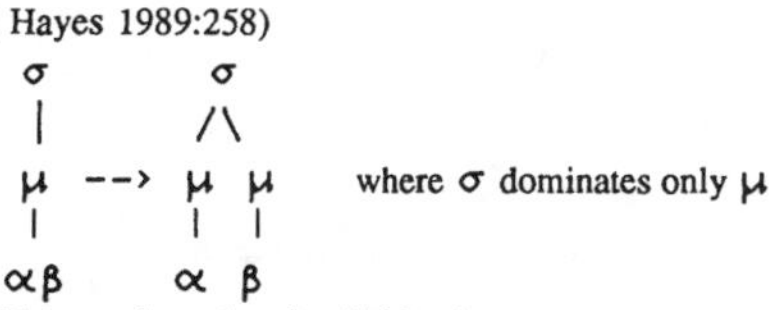

This renders closed syllables heavy.

7 There is a fact which supports this. In Korean, [l] and [r] are allophones for /l/. [l] occurs syllable-finally as opposed to [r] occurring syllable-initially. But, when two /l/'s occur in sequence, i.e., a coda and an onset of the following syllable, it is pronounced as long [l] rather than a sequence [lr]. This can fall out from the assumption that geminate /l/ is ambisyllabic.

seems then, that as in most stress languages, syllable structure is primary and stress is a redundant feature ancillary to it. Previous analyses of Korean stress support this.

Lee (1974) argues that, in Korean, stress position within a word is basically dependent on the vowel length and its syllable structure. To support this argument, he presents the following observations.

(7) stress falls on
 (i) a syllable with a long vowel if there is a long vowel.[8]
 (ii) Else, the second syllable when the syllable is (C)V + CV(C)
  first syllable when the syllable is (C)VC + CV(C)

If we represent a long vowel as two V's, the above observation can be reduced to the following: a stress falls only on heavy syllables (i.e., (C)VV(C) and (C)VC). A similar statement is found in Korean stress rule that Lee (1987) formalized as follows :

(8) (i) If the first syllable is heavy (i.e., (C)VV(C) or (C)VC), a stress falls on it.
 (ii) If the first syllable is light (i.e., (C)V), a stress falls on the following syllable.

No rules for longer words can be found in Lee (1987) or in Lee (1974). However, interestingly, Lee (1987:39) says that when a word begins with two light syllables, it is hard to decide which syllable a stress falls on. Thus, as in (7), this ends up with the same generalization that only a heavy syllable is a canonical locus for stress.

Now, I will propose the following Korean foot structure, which is compatible with the above discussion:

(9) Korean foot structure
 (i) right headed (ii) unbounded (iii) quantity-sensitive

Therefore, no matter how many light syllables precede a heavy syllable, they form a single foot with the heavy syllable. An additional statement is necessary for an aspirated and fortis onset with an underlying mora.

(10) A foot can be preceded by an optional stray mora.

In the version of moraic theory I adopt here, its assignment is illustrated in the following manner:

(11) (i) /ot/ 'clothes'

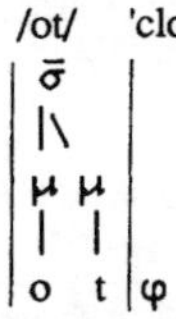

(ii) /kkok/ 'exactly'

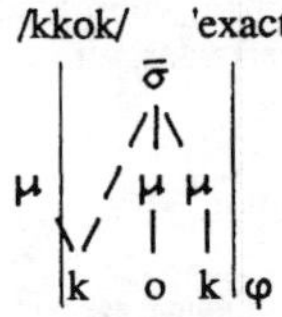

[8] In Korean, long vowels usually occur in the first syllable. Therefore, multiple occurrence of the long vowel will never happen.
Cook (1990) has also argued for an intrinsic relationship between vowel length and stress, but he (personal communication) denied the stress of the (C)VC type syllable.

(iii) /a.til/ 'son'

(iv) /copʰap/ 'boiled millet'

Notice the extrametrical mora of a fortis consonant in (ii) and the association to the first syllable of the underlying mora for an aspirated consonant in (iv).

2.3. **Partial Extension of onomatopoetic and mimetic words**

Korean onomatopoetic and mimetic words can have different connotations through PR (applicable only to onomatopoetic words) or suffixation of a semantically-null syllable (applicable to both onomatopoetic and mimetic words).

(12) a. PR

Base	PR	
(i) tuŋ	tu.tuŋ	with a tum
(ii) ppaŋ	ppa.paŋ	bang
(iii) ppi:	ppi.pi:	beep
(iv) kʰwaŋ	kʰwa.kwaŋ	bombing
(v) cu.luk	cu.lu.luk	dribbling
(vi) wa.cak	wa.ca.cak	munching

b.Suffixation

Base	Suffixation	
(i) cal.pʰak	cal.pʰa-tak	squelching
(ii) cʰal.kʰak	cʰal.kʰa-tak	with a snap
(iii) tal.pak	tal.pa-tak	with splashes
(iv) cil.pək	cil.pə-tək	with squishing noises
(v) ccəl.kkək	ccəl.kkə-tək	with a snap
(vi) cʰəl.kʰək	cʰəl.kʰə-tək	rattling
(vii) cʰal.kʰaŋ	cʰal.kʰa-taŋ	with a snap, click
(viii) cʰəl.kʰəŋ	cʰəl.kʰə-təŋ	with a snap
(ix) kkom.cil	kkom.ci-lak	budging
(x) pu.sil	pu.si-lək	rustlingly
(xi) ceŋ.kɨl	ceŋ.kɨ-laŋ	clanking
(xii) kɨn.til	kɨn.ti-ləŋ	dangling
(xiii) kko.kis	kko.ki-cak	wrinkling

To clarify the semantics associated with forms generated by PR or suffixation, we need to compare PR with total reduplication (henceforth, TR). TR forms denote repetition, as opposed to base forms which denote nonrepetitive sounds, actions or movements. For instance, while an onomatopoetic word /kʰwaŋ/ denotes a single occurrence of bombing and /kʰwaŋ.kʰwaŋ/ its multiple occurrences, PR form /kʰwa.kwaŋ/ is used when the bombing it refers to has longer duration.[9] The similar semantic contrast can be found among words generated by suffixation of a semantically null syllable. An onomatopoetic word /cʰal.kʰa.tak/ refers to a sound slightly longer than the base word /cʰal.kʰak/. Similarly, while a mimetic word /kkom.cil/ refers to one occurrence of a slight movement, a suffixed word /kkom.ci.rak/ refers to slower instance of the same movement.

In summary, PR and suffixation belong to the same morphological category denoting lengthening or temporal extension, which I will refer to as partial extension of onomatopoetic and mimetic words. This category does not, however, involve connotations associated with repetition. In the following section, we will discuss more details on phonological behavior of partial extension.

3. Partial Reduplication

I will now introduce phonological data relevant to PR of Korean onomatopoetic forms, and then provide a generalized analysis to account for this as well as the suffixation case.

3.1. Data[10]

In this section, I will introduce the data, and also provide a superficial characterization of them to be reanalyzed. The data of Korean PR are classified into two groups, i.e. one derived from monosyllabic base words and one from disyllabic base words. Let us first consider the former group.

PR of monosyllabic bases can be further divided into three subparts based on the onset of base words - lenis, fortis, and aspirated onset. First, PR of monosyllabic words with lenis onset is characterized by the reduplication of the base without coda:

(13)

Base	PR	
(i) sak	sa-sa-k	crisp
(ii) tuŋ	tu-tuŋ	with a tum
(iii) cik	ci-cik	slidingly
(iv) cak	ca-cak	tearing

PR of monosyllabic bases with fortis and aspirated onsets involves the loss of fortisity and aspiration on the second syllable:

(14)

Base	PR	
(i) ppaŋ	ppa-pa-ŋ	bang, bombing
(ii) ttak	tta-ta-k	bumps
(iii) ttaŋ	tta-ta-ŋ	bang
(iv) ppi:	ppi-pi:	beep
(v) tʰaŋ	tʰa-ta-ŋ	bang
(vi) pʰaŋ	pʰa-pa-ŋ	bombing sound
(vii) cʰaŋ	cʰa-ca-ŋ	sound of hitting sword
(viii) tʰuŋ	tʰu-tu-ŋ	with a boom
(ix) tʰuk	tʰu-tu-k	tapping

9 /kʰwa.kwaŋ/ can also refer to a quick sequence of multiple bombings. I think that this can be subsumed under more general usage of PR, i.e., denoting a connotation of lengthening.

10 From Nam (1990), You (1991) and You (1985).

If we assume that the reduplicative affix, which is a partial or full copy of the stem, is more likely to be changed than the stem, then the syllable which loses fortisity or aspiration would be identified as the copied one.

Consider now PR of disyllabic bases.

(15) Base	PR	
(i) tta.lɨŋ	tta.lɨ-lɨ-ŋ	sound of bike horn
(ii) ppu.tɨk	ppu.tɨ-tɨ-k	sound of grinding one's teeth
(iii) cu.luk	cu.lu-lu-k	spattering of tear, dribbling
(iv) a.sak	a.sa-sa-k	crunching
(v) u.cik	u.ci-ci-k	cracking: sputtering
(vi) wa.cak	wa.ca-ca-k	munching
(vii) ppi.tɨk	ppi.tɨ-tɨ-k	with a creaking sound
(viii)ɨ.tɨŋ	ɨ.tɨ-tɨ-ŋ	bickering
(ix) o.tok	o.to-to-k	with a clatter
(x) u.tuk	u.tu-tu-k	with a clatter
(xi) cci.lɨk	cci.lɨ-lɨ-k	with a slurp
(xii) cci.lɨŋ	cci.lɨ-lɨ-ŋ	sound of a bell
(xiii) ho.lok	ho.lo-lo-k	flapping
(xiv) kki.luk	kki.lu-lu-k	honking
(xv) ppa.kak	ppa.ka-ka-k	cracking

As in (15), the pattern of PR of disyllabic bases is characterized by reduplication of the second syllable without the coda. The process is exactly the same as that of monosyllabic bases if we consider only the second syllable, which is always heavy. Thus, both cases can be reduced to reduplication of a heavy syllable without the coda.

Finally, there remains a unique type of PR which we have to consider. All the words allowing PR can also undergo multiple PR as illustrated below.

(16) Base	Multiple partial reduplication
(a) sak	sa-sa-sa-...-sak
(b) cu.luk	cu.lu-lu-lu-...-luk
(c) ppaŋ	ppa-pa-pa-...-paŋ
(d) t^haŋ	t^ha-ta-ta-...-taŋ

The same semantic relation between the base and the single partial reduplicated form can be extended to between the base and the multiple PR form. Thus, 'ppaŋ' indicates the sound of a single pistol shot as opposed to 'ppa-pa-pa-...-paŋ' denoting the repetitive sound of a machine gun.

Now, from the consideration of all the above data of Korean PR, including multiple PR, three important generalization appears. First, regardless of the type of PR, all the output words retain only a single foot since they have a single heavy syllable on their right edge. Interestingly, in the case of PR of monosyllabic bases with a fortis and an aspirated onset, the loss of fortisity and aspiration in the second syllable of the output serves to uphold this generalization. Second, all the input words retain a single foot only, too. Monosyllabic stems consist of a single heavy syllable only and disyllabic stems consist of a light syllable and a following heavy syllable. Third, the process of PR can be characterized as reduplication of a havy syllable without the coda. Based on these observations, I will provide an analysis of Korean PR in the following section.

3.2. Analysis

In this section, I first will argue that McCarthy and Prince (1986)'s approach is incompatible with the facts of Korean PR given in section 3.1., and show that it is not general enough. I will then propose a metrical constraint for Korean PR to encompass all those facts.

3.2.1. Against extrametrical coda

McCarthy and Prince (1986:54) analyzed Korean PR as a simple suffixation process of a syllable, with the final consonant melody rendered extrasyllabic. Their analysis can be illustrated as follows:

```
(17) Base 'cu.luk'    PR 'cu.lu-lu-k'    'dribbling'
     Base                          cu.lu(k)
     copying and template          σ  σ    σ
     applying                      /| /|   /|
                                   cu lu. cu lu  (k)
     Stray Erasure                 cu.lu.lu.k
```

The same process can be applied to PR of monosyllabic bases:

```
(18) Base 'sak'    PR 'sa.sak'    'crisp'
     Base                          sa (k)
     copying and template          σ  σ
     applying                      Λ  Λ
                                   sa  sa  (k)
     Stray Erasure (vacuously      sa.sa.k
     applied)
```

However, their analysis does not seem to hold for the rest of phonological and morphological facts we have discussed in previous sections.

Let us start with PR of bases with fortis or aspirated onsets. As is shown in (14), it is characterized as the loss of fortisity and aspiration. How would McCarthy and Prince deal with this? They might adopt lenis prespecification a la McCarthy and Prince (1986)?[11] But, it would not be a nice solution because prespecification is a sort of stipulation, which is usually called on as a last resort. We may now slightly revise their analysis to incorporate PR of bases with fortis or aspirated onset. Let us redefine a suffixal template for Korean PR as a light syllable, not just a syllable, making the final mora extrametrical, not final consonant. There then would be no difference in the analysis of PR of disyllabic bases:

---

[11] To account for this lenis prespecification, Nam (1990) assumes the following template for Korean PR:

```
  σ
 /|
 c v
 |
[lenis]
```

(19) Base 'cu.luk'   PR 'cu.lu-lu-k'   'dribbling'

```
Base                          σ   σ
                              /|  /|
                              /μ  / μ(μ)
                              / | / | |
                              c u l u k
copying and template (σ)      σ   σ       σ
applying                      /|  /|      /|
                              /μ  /μ      / μ (μ)
                              / | / |     /  |  |
                              c u l u c u l  u  k
Stray Erasure                 cu.lu.lu.k
```

With this revision, we can keep McCarthy and Prince's analysis for the PR of bases with fortis or aspirated onsets as indicated in (20):

(20) Base /ppaŋ /   PR /pa.paŋ /   'bang'

```
Base                            σ
                                /|
                              μ / μ(μ)
                              \/  | |
                               p  a ŋ
copying and template (σ)        σ    σ
applying                        /|   /|
                              μ /μ  / μ (μ)
                              \/ |  / |  |
                               p a  p a  ŋ
Stray Erasure (vacuously      ppa.paŋ
applied)
```

This revision can also deal with PR of words with long vowels such as /ppi.pi:/ of /ppi:/ 'beep' in the same way as words with fortis or aspirated onsets. Without any revision of this kind, it would be derived by regarding the half of a long vowel as an extrametrical coda, which is implausible. It seems now that some minor revision can save McCarthy and Prince's analysis for Korean PR.

However, most importantly, suffixation, which is an allomorph of partial extension, provides an evidence against McCarthy and Prince's analysis. Recall that in addition to PR, suffixation of a semantically-null syllable can indicate the connotation of temporal extension. As can be observed from (12b) of section 2, suffixation involves deletion of the stem final coda.

Since suffixation and PR belong to the same morphological category, we expect that they show the same derivational process. However, if, following McCarthy and Prince (1986), we assume extrametricality of the stem final coda (or mora) for PR, there would be two different derivational processes, i.e., extrametricality and deletion of stem final codas (or moras), for the same morphological category: partial extension. Thus, I conclude that McCarthy and Prince's analysis is not general enough.

One might try to analyze suffixation of a semantically null syllable under the framework of McCarthy and Prince (1986). Suffixation would then involve extrametricality , not deletion, of the stem final coda as indicated in the following sample derivation:

(21) Base /cal.p^hak/ Output 'cal.p^ha.tak'

Base	cal.p^ha (k)
Suffixation of /ta/	cal.p^ha - ta -(k)
Output	cal.p^ha.tak

In (21), the suffix for partial extension is /ta/, and the stem final coda /k/ is extrametrical. The coda extrametricality proposal successfully derives the desired output /cal.p^ha.tak/ from the input /cal.p^hak/. For this proposal to work, the stem final coda must be the same as the word final coda of the suffixed word, which is always velar, i.e., /k/ or /ŋ/, since according to the proposal assuming coda extrametricality, they are one and the same segment. Thus, if there exist suffixed words whose stem does not end with /k/ or /ŋ/, it would be proved that coda extrametricality proposal cannot hold for the suffixation case. Notice that suffixed words in (12ix-xiii) are counter examples because their word final codas are /l/ or /s/. Thus, coda extrametricality proposal cannot be compatible with the suffixation case.

To summarize this section, I have shown that even a major revision cannot save McCarthy and Prince's (1986) analysis for Korean PR. In the following section, I will provide an analysis of Korean PR by applying the coda deletion hypothesis.

3.2.2. MWC

I will now introduce my own analysis which I believe, covers both PR and suffixation. In (22) are words chosen from the data in previous sections. We can compare not only suffixation and PR, but also between the input and the output of both processes.

(22) Base	Suffixation	Base	PR
(i) c^hal.k^hak	c^hal.k^ha-tak	(i) k^hwaŋ	k^hwa.kwaŋ
(ii) ccəl.kkək	ccəl.kkə-tək	(ii) tuŋ	tu.tuŋ
(iii) c^hal.k^haŋ	c^hal.k^ha-taŋ	(iii) ppaŋ	ppa.paŋ
(iv) c^həl.k^həŋ	c^həl.k^hə-təŋ	(iv) ppi:	ppi.pi:
(v) kkom.cil	kkom.ci-lak	(v) cu.luk	cu.lu.luk
(vi) kko.kis	kko.ki-cak	(vi) cu.luk	cu.lu.lu.luk

As we already observed from the data of PR in section 3.1., the number of feet in the input and that in the output are same. From this observation, it falls out that both processes are subject to the same metrical constraint, which I formulate as follows:

(23) Metrical Weight Consistency (MWC)
The foot number of the output to partial extension must be identical to that of the input.

Given (23), the derivation of suffixation will be illustrated by (24).

(24) Base /cal.p^hak/ Output /cal.p^ha.tak/

Base	cal.p^hak
Suffixation	cal.p^hak + tak
MWC	cal.p^ha.tak

In the last step of the derivation, deletion of the stem final coda results the same foot number as the input. If we apply the same process to PR, the derivation in (25) result.

(25) Base /cu.ruk/ Output /cu.lu.luk/

Base	cu.luk
Suffixation	cu.luk + luk
MWC	cu.lu.luk

Again, the stem final coda deletes, obeying MWC. This deletion produces the derived output /cu.lu.luk/. Thus, words of PR and suffixation can be derived in the same way.

However, one might wonder why we may not delete any other coda. Specifically, in (24), one might think that the MWC may trigger the deletion of the coda of the first syllable or final syllable. First of all, it is not plausible to delete the coda of the final syllable, which is a suffix. In doing so, the final foot, consisting of one light syllable, will be degenerate, but it will still be a foot, thus violating MWC.

How about the other option? If we delete the first coda as in (26), the output abides by MWC.

(26) Base /cal.p^{h}ak/ Desired output /cal.p^{h}a.tak/

Base	cal.p^{h}ak
Suffixation	cal.p^{h}ak + tak
MWC	*ca.p^{h}ak.tak

In summary, foot restructuring for MWC can apply either as in (27i) covering (26) or as in (27ii) covering (25).

(27) [cal.p^{h}ak] + tak
 (i) [F1 F2] + F3 ==> F2' + F3
 (ii) F1 [F2 + F3] ==> F1 + F3'

In (27i), the first foot, F1, forms the new foot F2' with the second foot, F2. In (27ii), the second foot, F2, forms the new foot, F3', with the third foot, F3.

However, under the assumption that the foot restructuring is a cyclic rule, the option (i) will violate the Strict Cycle Condition:

(28) Strict Cycle Condition (SCC)[12]
 a. Cyclic rules apply only to derived representations.
 b. Def.: A representation φ is derived w.r.t. rule R in cycle j iff φ meets the structural analysis of R by virtue of a combination of morphemes introduced in cycle j or the application of a phonological rule in cycle j.

This violation occurs in (27i) because foot restructuring applies to the non-derived environment; the output of a previous cycle, i.e. [cal.p^{h}ak]. In contrast, in (27ii) the foot restructuring applies to the derived environment. Consequently, (27ii) is the only foot restructuring process which obeys SCC.

In this section, I have argued that since PR and suffixation belong to the same morphological category, the same derivational process applies in PR and in suffixation. The specific analysis for

12 This proposal was made by Mascaró (1976) and extended to prosodic phenomena by Kiparsky (1982).

the various types of PR will be postponed until I analyze the following observations of the previous section:

(29) (i) Only onomatopoetic words with a single foot can undergo PR
(ii) PR process consists of the reduplication of a heavy syllable of the stem.

I will now analyze (29), which are the first two steps of Korean PR, in terms of prosodic circumscription (McCarthy and Prince 1990). Korean PR shows suppletive allomorphy. The allomorph categorized as PR can be applied to onomatopoetic words with a single foot. The other allomorph, categorized as suffixation, is limited by the Elsewhere Condition. Thus, the whole process is as follows:

(30) If the base contains a single foot, then a reduplication process consisting of selecting and reduplicating a heavy syllable applies.
Else, suffixation of a semantically-null syllable applies.
Finally, the output of both reduplication and suffixation is subject to MWC

Thus, Korean PR consists of two steps; 1) reduplication with phonological circumscription and 2) prosodic surface constraint MWC. This can be illustrated in the following sample derivation:

(31)

base — 1 foot

applying reduplication — 2 feet

applying MWC

output — 1 foot

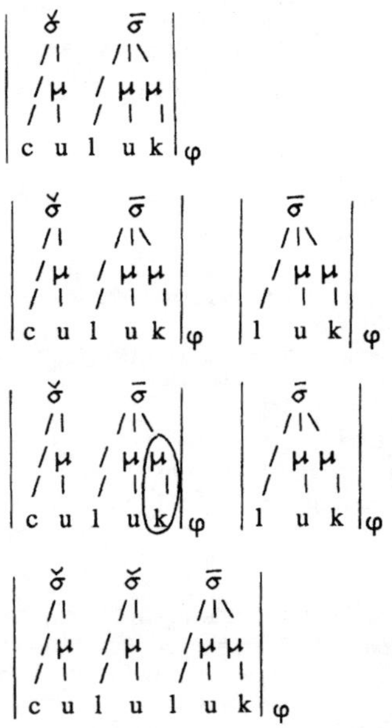

Notice that we start with a single foot and end with a single foot. Stem final coda deletion enables this.

One might wonder why the process of PR is divided into two steps. This question arises because, if we incorporate MWC into the definition of the reduplication operation, we do not have to posit two steps. However, MWC is a more general constraint which is independent of reduplication proper. More specifically, MWC is called on not for PR, but for partial extension of onomatopoetic and mimetic words. Therefore, since both PR and suffixation are subject to MWC, the separation of the MWC from the reduplication process is preferred.

We have just considered the derivation of PR of disyllabic bases. Now, we are in a position to provide the complete analysis for other types of Korean PR.

First, monosyllabic bases always consist of a single foot. Thus, prosodic circumscription is vacuous and so the the process of PR would be straightforward. But, PR of bases with fortis and aspirated onsets is a little complicated. Like monosyllabic words with a lenis onset, they consist of a single foot, and so prosodic circumscription is vacuous. But, there is a difference in applying MWC.

(32)

Base (ppaŋ) — 1 foot

reduplication (ppaŋ.ppaŋ) — 2 feet

MWC

Output — 1 foot; cf. base word 'ppaŋ' which is 1 foot

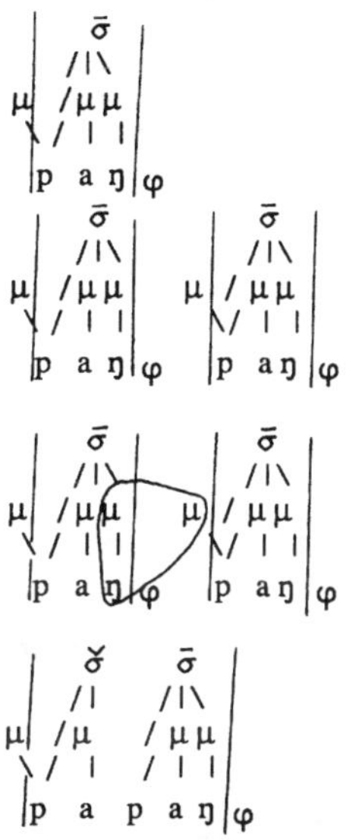

Notice that if only the coda of the first syllable is deleted, a stray mora of the second syllable will be associated to the first syllable, making its output two feet, thus violating the MWC:

(33) ppappaŋ — 2 feet

The PR of words with an aspirated onset is analogous to the above case except that whenever a stray mora is deleted, aspiration is also deleted (which comes from the well-formedness condition of Korean aspirated consonants).

Second, let us consider the suffixation case taking the stem /cil.pək/. Since it is two feet, it will be subject to the Elsewhere Condition, i.e. suffixation. Its derivation is as follows:

(34) base — 2 feet

S(uffixation) — 3 feet

MWC

output — 2 feet

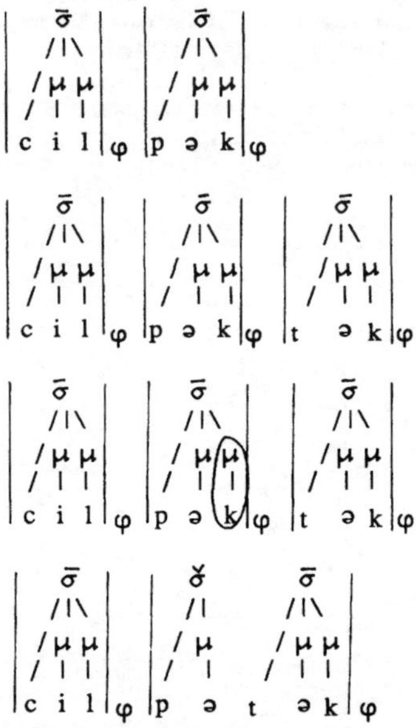

Third, to provide a natural account for multiple PR, we should ask the following question? How does Korean, where multiple PR is possible, differ from Ilokano or X-language where multiple PR is impossible? The only noticeable difference is the nature of the prosodic template - an unbounded foot in Korean vs. a bi-moraic, or monosyllabic foot or sub-foot in other languages. Thus, the following corollary follows:

(35) There is no independent parameter involving the number of applications of PR

This enables us to iteratively apply the reduplication operation without any limitation.

Finally, there remains another kind of Korean PR, i.e. PR of trisyllabic bases, which seems to be problematic for my analysis.

(36)

Base	PR	
kkwa.taŋ.t^{h}aŋ	kkwa.ta-ta-ŋ.t^{h}aŋ	the sound of some one
	*kkwa.taŋ.t^{h}a-ta-ŋ	falling down
wa.caŋ.c^{h}aŋ	wa.ca-ca-ŋ.c^{h}aŋ	with a crash
	*wa.caŋ.c^{h}a-ja-ŋ	

u.taŋ.t^haŋ	u.ta-ta-ŋ.t^haŋ *u.taŋ.t^ha-ta-ŋ	with a bang
wa.taŋ.t^haŋ	wa.ta-ta-ŋ.t^haŋ *wa.taŋ.t^ha-ta-ŋ	clattering

PR of trisyllabic bases can be characterized by reduplication of the second syllable minus the coda, as in PR of disyllabic bases. However, two problematic points must be noted. First, the base has more than one foot. Thus, it is not eligible for PR. Secondly, only the first heavy syllable can undergo PR; the last heavy syllable is not allowed to undergo PR.

However, we need to consider that all trisyllabic words are bi-morphemic. For instance, /kkwa.taŋ.t^haŋ/ is a compound of /kkwa.taŋ/ with the same meaning as /kkwa.taŋ.t^haŋ/ and /t^haŋ/ 'with a clash'. Here, /t^haŋ/ seems to have an emphatic meaning only. If we limit our concern to a semantic head, i.e., first two syllables, the above reduplication process is no longer exceptional.

I will now adopt the head operation for reduplication which is due to Aronoff (1988):

(37) F is a head operation if F(Y) = Z, and W = XY (where Y is the head of W) together imply that F(W) = X + F(Y) = X + Z.

If we follow the above formulation, the derivation of PR of trisyllabic bases is:

(38) F(kkwa.taŋ) = kkwa.ta.taŋ (F = reduplication + MWC)
W = kkwa.taŋ .t^haŋ (/kkwa.taŋ/ is the head of W)
F (W) = F (kkwa.taŋ) + t^haŋ
= kkwa.ta.taŋ + t^haŋ
= kkwa.ta.taŋ.t^haŋ

Consequently, by adopting head operation, we can account for two problems noticed in PR of trisyllabic base words: the base has more than one foot and only the first heavy syllable (which is a part of semantic head) can undergo PR.

4. Conclusion

After providing an in-depth discussion of Korean syllable and foot structure, I have introduced the observations of Korean PR. I have then argued that in explaining the observations, McCarthy and Prince's (1986) analysis is not general enough, mainly because it cannot cover suffixation, which belongs to the same morphological category, Partial Extension, with PR.

I have provided a generalized account for Korean PR and suffixation by proposing a prosodic constraint, the MWC, on the output to partial extension. Furthermore, by adopting prosodic circumscription (McCarthy and Prince 1990), I have explained the suppletive allomorphy of PR and suffixation, and also generalized PR of various types of syllablic bases.

Finally, I have analyzed PR of trisyllabic base words, which is apparent counter example, by assuming that Korean PR is a head operation.

References

Aronoff, Mark. 1988. Head Operations and Strata in Reduplication: A Linear Treatment. In *Yearbook of Morphology 1*

Cook, E. D. 1990. Length, Accent and Phonological Phrase. In Fred Lukoff (ed.) *Journal of the International Circle of Korean Linguistics vol. 6*
Hayes, Bruce. 1989. Compensatory lengthening in Moraic theory. In *Linguistic Inquiry 20*
Huh, Woong. 1965. *Kuke Umwunhak (Korean phonology)*. Seoul: Cengkumsa
Hyman, Larry. 1985. *A theory of phonological weight*. Dordrecht: Foris
Kim, Jong-mi. 1986. *Phonology and Syntax of Korean Morphology*. Ph. D dissertation, USC, Los Angeles, California
Kim, Sun-hee. 1989. "the behavior of /h/ in Korean", in Kuno et al. (eds.) *Harvard Studies in Korean Linguistics III*, Seoul: Hanshin
Kiparsky, Paul. 1982. "From Cyclic Phonology to Lexical Phonology", in Harry van der Hulst and Norval Smith (eds.) *The structure of phonological representations (part I)*. Foris
Lee, Hoyoung. 1987. *Study on modern Korean accent* MA thesis. Seoul National University, Seoul
Lee, Hyunbok. 1974. Rhythm and intonation of Seoul language *Language Research 10.2*. Seoul National University, Seoul
Marantz, Alec. 1982. Re reduplication. In *Linguistic Inquiry 13*.
Martin, Samuel. 1951. Korean Phonemics, *Language 27.4*.
Mascaró, J. 1976. *Catalan Phonology and the Phonological Cycle*. Ph.D. dissertation, M.I.T. Reproduced by the Indiana University Linguistics Club.
McCarthy, J. and A. Prince. 1986. Prosodic Morphology. ms, University of Massachusetts, Amherst, and Brandeis University.
1988. Quantitative transfer in Reduplicative andTemplatic morphology. ms. Umass., Amherst
1990. Foot and Word in Prosodic Morphology: The Arabic Broken Plural. In *Natural language and Linguistic theory 8*
Nam, Seungho 1990. Copying Domain Constraint in Reduplication -- with special reference to Korean. ms, UCLA, Los Angeles, California
Steriade, Donca. 1988. Reduplication and Syllable Transfer in Sanskrit and Elsewhere. In *Phonology Yearbook*
You, Jaewon. 1985. *A Reverse Dictionary of Modern Korean*, Seoul: Chengumsa
You, Seokhoon. 1991. Expressives and Ideophones in Korean. to appear in Working papers in Linguistics, Dept. of Linguistics, University of Hawaii

Prosodic Word-Level Rules in Korean

ONGMI KANG
University of Washington

0. Introduction

The existence of word-internal prosodic constituents has been reported by Inkelas (1989, to appear), Cohn (1989), Rice (to appear), Nespor and Vogel (1986), Hannahs (1991), Kang (1991a) and others. A current issue in Prosodic Phonology is how to derive word-internal prosodic constituents and whether to extend the Prosodic Hierarchy (Selkirk 1986, Selkirk and Shen 1988; Nespor and Vogel 1986; Hayes 1989) in the lexicon. Along these lines, several proposals have been made; Cohn (1989) and Rice (to appear) claim to extend Selkirk's End-Based Theory.

In this paper I will provide further arguments for this approach based on several rules in Korean. I will first show that in Korean word-internal phonological domains are predictable, supporting Selkirk (1986), Selkirk and Shen (1988), Cohn (1989), and Rice (to appear), contrary to Inkelas (1989, to appear). Secondly, modifying Selkirk's analysis (Selkirk 1986; Selkirk and Shen 1988), which claims that the syntax-phonology mapping applies postlexically, I argue that prosodic word formation in Korean must be basically lexical, supporting Inkelas (1989, to appear). Thirdly, the current proposal is an improved analysis of Korean. Especially, Coda Neutralization, once analyzed as a multi-domain rule (both lexical and postlexical) within standard Lexical Phonology by Ahn (1985) will be reanalyzed as a prosodic word-level rule.

---

[0] This is a revised version of the paper presented at the 2nd Japanese/Korean Linguistics Conference, which was later presented at NELS 22 held at the University of Delaware in October, 1991. I would like to thank Eunjoo Han, S.J. Hannahs, Junko Itô, Jongho Jun, Eunsoo Kim, Hyunsoon Kim, Young-Key Kim-Renaud, Jerzy Rubach, Elisabeth Selkirk, David Silva, and Irene Vogel for their valuable criticisms and encouragement on the earlier version of this paper. I especially thank Ellen Kaisse and Sharon Hargus for their help in writing this paper.

The organization of this paper is as follows. In § 1 the theoretical background will be introduced. In § 2 I will propose a rule for the construction of the Prosodic Word in Korean. In § 3 I show how the several rules in Korean are bounded by the prosodic domain, 'the prosodic word'.

1. Theoretical Background

1.1. Syllable Structure and Syllabification

In this section I introduce the syllable structure of Korean and the Syllable Structure Algorithm. Note that Korean syllable structure maximally allows one consonant either in the onset or in the coda, or in both. Syllable structure is assigned by the following Syllable Structure Algorithm (SSA):

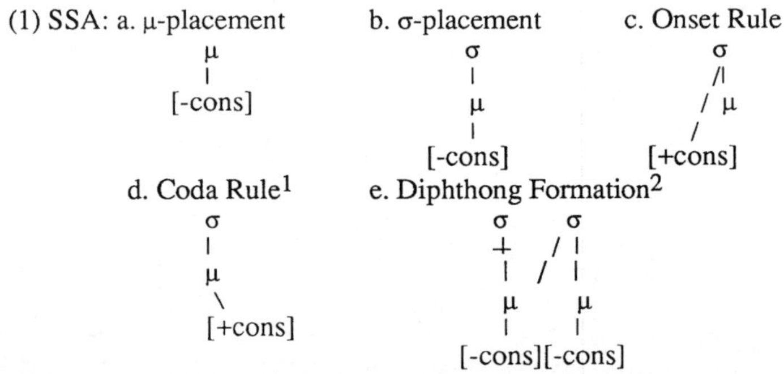

Following the Continuous Syllabification Hypothesis (Selkirk 1978; Halle and Vergnaud 1978; McCarthy 1979; Clements and Keyser 1983; Rubach and Booij 1988), syllabification applies continuously throughout the lexical and postlexical components, bounded by prosodic domains.

As a result of Bracket Erasure at the end of the lexical component, the Onset Rule has the power to resyllabify codas from the preceding syllable to the onset of the following one across ω's within a prosodic phrase (ϕ), as shown in (2):[3]

(2) kot oseyo --> ω(kot) ω(oseyo) --> ϕ(ko.do.se.yo)
soon come "Please come soon" Onset Rule & voicing

Therefore, resyllabification, once regarded as a separate syllabification process, is simply the Onset Rule reapplying in the postlexical component.

---

[1] Jun (1991) has a different analysis from mine in that a consonant in the coda is given a mora forming a heavy syllable. This observation is drawn from partial reduplication of onomatopoetic vocabulary in Korean.

[2] Diphthongs in Korean have the underlying representation of a sequence of two vowels. Diphthong formation operates by delinking the σ of the first [-cons] and relinking the μ to the preceding σ, as shown in (1e).

[3] In subsequent sections parenthesis ( ) will be used to denote prosodic constituents.

1.2. Other Assumptions

Other theoretical assumptions adopted in this paper will be summarized in this section. Firstly, with respect to the interaction between morphology and phonology in Lexical Phonology, I adopt the Non-Interactive Model (Halle and Vergnaud 1987; Halle and Kenstowicz 1989; Sproat 1985; Odden to appear) where all morphology precedes all phonology. I follow the assumption that derivational morphology and compounding are done in the lexicon (Kiparsky 1982, Mohanan 1986).[4] In the process of derivation, unlabelled brackets are labelled according to Feature Percolation Conventions (Lieber 1980). On the other hand, functional categories (Agreement, Tense marker, Aspect marker, Mood marker, and complementizer) are projected at D-structure in the syntax as functional heads (X^{o}s), but the sequence of a lexical head V/Adj and functional categorial suffixes are agglutinated at S-structure through rightward head-movement (Chomsky 1988).[5] Secondly, Bracket Erasure (Pesetsky 1979; Kiparsky 1982; Mohanan 1986) applies to the output of the morphological component in the lexicon, erasing all internal brackets. Thus, the internal structure of words is invisible to the syntax; this is called the strong interpretation of Bracket Erasure.[6] Thirdly, Prosodic Licensing (Itô 1986, 1991; Goldsmith 1990) plays a key role in the current analysis.

2. Constraints on Deriving Prosodic Words in Korean

The Prosodic Hierarchy Theory claims that prosodic structure projected from syntactic structure serves as the domain of phonological rules. As an alternative to previous non-prosodic analyses, I propose a prosodic analysis for the domain of several rules in Korean. As constraints on deriving prosodic constituents in Korean, I adopt Selkirk's End-Based Theory (Selkirk 1986; Selkirk and Shen 1988) and the Prosodic Structure Wellformedness Constraint (Selkirk 1981, 1984; Hayes 1989; Nespor and Vogel 1986). Selkirk argues that the syntax-phonology mapping has to be parameterized depending on the grammar of an individual language, as stated in (3):

(3) **The Syntax-Phonology Mapping**

For each category C^n of the prosodic structure of a language there is a two-part parameter of the form C^n:
{Right/Left; X^m}
where X^m is a category type in the X-bar hierarchy.

A syntactic structure-prosodic structure pair satisfies the set of syntax-phonology parameters for a language iff the Right (or Left) end of each constituent of type X^m in syntactic structure coincides with the edge of constituent(s) of type C^n in prosodic structure.

---

4 However, there are other positions on morphology. Fabb (1984) and others have argued that compounding is done "in the syntax". Furthermore, Sproat (1985) and Lieber (1991) claim that all morphology is done "in the syntax".

5 Adjectives in Korean are sometimes classified as descriptive verbs or adjectival verbs, because they behave similar to verbs (action verbs). Adjectives as well as verbs have to be inflected by mood, aspect, and tense suffixes.

6 Sproat (to appear) claims that some phonetic implementation rules, considered to be postlexical, may make reference to word-internal structure, such as compounding. This is a problem for the strong interpretation of bracket erasure.

The basic idea in (3) is that a prosodic constituent is delimited by two parameters, directionality and a level on the X' hierarchy: right or left ends of X^{max} (the Prosodic Phrase) or X^{o} (the Prosodic Word). The four logical possibilities are in (4):[7]

(4) (i) $]_{X^m} = C^n$ (ii) $_{X^m}[= C^n$

a. $]_{X^o}$ --> $)_\omega$ $_{X^o}[$ --> $_\omega($

b. $]_{X^{max}}$ --> $)_\phi$ $_{X^{max}}[$ --> $_\phi($

The projection of prosodic constituents, ω or φ, from syntactic structure is cross-categorial. But only the lexical categories (N, V, A, Adv, etc) can form prosodic constituents. However, the mapping rule in (3) alone cannot exhaustively predict the location of the prosodic constituents of a sentence. Thus, each prosodic constituent is further conditioned by a universal well-formedness constraint, the Prosodic Structure Wellformedness Constraint (i.e., Strict Layer Hypothesis):

Keeping the two constraints in mind, let us turn to Korean. At first glance, for Korean, as a head-final language, the left-end parameter in (4.ii) seems appropriate. The $_{XP}[$ setting derives the prosodic phrase correctly. An intriguing question in Prosodic Phonology is at what level prosodic words are formed in the grammar. Selkirk's original idea was that prosodification applies postsyntactically after Bracket Erasure (Mohanan 1986). Thus, the $_{X^o}[$ setting derives only a single ω at most, due to Bracket Erasure at the end of the lexical component. However, morphologically complex words exhibit different behavior with resespect to the prosodic word in several languages; in Hungarian and Italian (Nespor and Vogel 1986;Vogel 1990), Indonesian (Cohn 1989), and Korean (Han 1991; Kang 1991a), each member of a compound forms a separate ω as does a prefix in Polish (Booij and Rubach 1984, 1990), French (Hannahs 1991), and Korean (Han 1991; Kang 1991a).

Zec (to appear) claims that ω's may be derived lexically or postlexically across languages. In this paper I claim that prosodic word formation (henceforth PWF) should apply lexically for complex words in Korean, Hungarian and others, where all internal structure is visible in the lexicon.[8] If prosodic word formation is lexical, a bracket $_{X^o}[$ would coincide with a ω(. Then, each member of a compound as well as a prefix in a prefix + stem combination is assigned a ω. Thus, in Korean, ω's can be derived by extending Selkirk's (1986, 1988) $_{Xo}[$ setting within the word, as in (5):

(5) **Korean Prosodic Word Rule** (KPWR: lexical)[9]

$_{Xo}[$ --> ω[(X is a lexical category)

---

[7] Usually the right-end or left-end parameters correspond to head-initial or head-final languages, respectively. However, this is not always true. Two dialects of Chinese, Xiamen (Chen 1987) and Shanghai (Shen and Selkirk 1990) have identical syntactic structure, but have different settings; Xiamen for the right-end setting; Shanghai for the left-end setting.

[8] See Kang (1991b & (forthcoming)) for the parameter for prosodic word formation. This follows from the relative ordering of Bracket Erasure with respect to PWF, which is parameterized according to languages. That means that Selkirk's X^o setting in (4) precedes Bracket Erasure in some languages but follows it in others (Greek (Nespor and Vogel 1986); Shanghai Chinese (Selkirk and Shen 1988)).

[9] Han (1991) has a similar idea, suggesting that the prosodic word in Korean coincides with either the left-end of a stem or the left-end of a prefix.

Note that (5) is very much in accord with Prosodic Minimality (McCarthy and Prince 1986, 1990) in that both predict that only lexical categories can form ω's. Since only lexical categories (N, V, Adj, Adv...) map into ω's in the lexicon, prosodically dependent elements are incorporated into a preceding ω, as shown in (6):[10]

(6) **Stray Adjunction/Incorporation**
ω is left-headed, with leftward adjunction of stray material
i) lexical adjunction: derivational suffixes
ii) postlexical adjunction: functional categorial suffixes, clitics

Adjunction of phonologically dependent elements to the preceding ω is a direct consequence of Prosodic Licensing (Itô 1986, 1991). Derivational suffixes will be incorporated into the preceding ω's lexically. Then the lexically created ω is also present postlexically where the functional categorial suffixes or clitics are available in the syntax. This supports the claim that ω is visible both in and out of the lexicon (Booij and Rubach 1987; Inkelas and Zec 1988). Clitics and functional categorial suffixes are cliticized to the preceding ω postlexically.[11] The prosodic category of the host remains intact throughout cliticization.

Keeping (5) and (6) in mind, let us see how the lexical PWF derives the prosodic domain for syllabification and Coda Neutralization:

(7) i) Morphological Structure			ii) Phonological Structure		
a) Prefixation	:	[təs $_N$[os] 'outer' 'cloth'			
b) Percolation	:	$_N$[təs $_N$[os]]	a) PWF (lexical):		ω(təs) ω(os)
c) BEC	:	$_N$[təsos]	b) Syll.& CN	:	ω(təs) ω(os) |/ \/ σ σ ω(tət̲)ω(ot̲)
			c) Resyll.	:	ϕ(tə.t̲ot)
			d) Voicing	:	ϕ(tə.d̲ot)

If PWF applies before Bracket Erasure, as in (7.ii.a), we can correctly derive two ω's. Bracket Erasure at the end of the lexical component would not affect the derived ω's, since they are in different planes. Within each ω, syllabification and Coda Neutralization apply. This means we have to know the domain of the ω before we construct syllables, since syllabification is bounded by the ω.

PWF in Korean is thus lexical. However, PWF must also apply postlexically. Determiners (i.e., functional category), such as quantifiers and numerals situated to the left of a content word will leave the lexicon without any prosodic specifications:

---

[10] Yip (in personal communication) has pointed out to me that instead of postulating lexical vs. postlexical adjunction, we can generalize it in the following way: adjunction applies whenever things are available.

[11] As observed in other languages, clitics show considerable syntactic freedom about what they attach to, and this is also true in Korean. In addition, clitics (topic marker, delimiter, conjunction) in Korean can attach to material already containing clitics. See Zwicky (1991) for the common types of clitics and also Choe (1991) and Cho and Sells (1991) for the distribution of clitics in Korean. Delimiters can attach either to nouns or to postpositions in Korean.

(8)
```
                 φ
                 |   \
   (ω=)          ?        ω (lexical)
                 |         |
            NP[Det         N
```

The noun in (8) becomes a ω by the KPWR (5) in the lexicon. In the syntax, the string determiner + noun forms a prosodic phrase (φ) by the $_{XP}[$ setting. Note that the Prosodic Structure Wellformedness Constraint implicitly requires that an utterance be exhaustively parsed into a hierarchy of prosodic constituents. Thus, the determiner in (8) is prosodified as a ω postlexically. Notice that adjunction of the determiner to the following ω is blocked, since the direction of adjunction in (6) is leftward. To sum up, the Korean Prosodic Word Rule in (5) and the Prosodic Structure Wellformedness Constraint are required to derive the word-internal prosodic constituent in Korean.

Next, let us compare the present proposal with Inkelas' (1989, to appear) Prosodic Lexical Phonology. To derive prosodic constituents, the following Prosodic Constituent Formation Algorithm (henceforth PCF) was proposed:[12]

(9) Prosodic Constituent Formation (Inkelas: to appear)

m-structure	p-structure		m-structure	p-structure
$< X >_i$	$[X]_{i-1}$	-->	$< X >_i$	$[X]_i$

Prosodic constituents are formed on the basis of morphological constituents, as in (9). A new prosodic constituent is derived whenever a prosodically bound morpheme is attached, producing the effect of cyclicity. In Inkelas' framework, suffixes will be listed with prosodic as well as morphological subcategorization in the lexicon. But, there is a restriction on the base in that PCF only applies to well-formed morphological constituents, (derived or free) stems. Therefore, bound roots never precede the PCF but acquire the prosodic feature specifications (α/β) by affixation.

Since the default PCF (9) can not apply in morphologically complex words, where each stem of a compound as well as a prefix in a prefix + stem combination corresponds to a distinct prosodic constituent, Inkelas provides a special algorithm for compounds, as in (10), for languages in which the two constituents of a compound form separate ω's:

(10) PCF for compounds

m-structure		m-structure	p-structure
$< X_i >_m ... < X_n >_m$	-->	$< X_i .. X_n >_m$	$[X_i]_p .. [X_n]_p$

As for prefixes in Korean, another rule is needed. Therefore, in addition to the regular PCF (9), we need two more rules for Korean in Inkelas' analysis: one for prefixes, as in (11a), and the other for compounds, as in (11b):

(11) a. təs 'outer' : $[\_\_\ _m[\quad]]$ --> ω(təs) ω( )
     b. $[\ _m[\quad]\ _m[\quad]]$ --> ω( ) ω( )

It appears that Inkelas' algorithm is much more complicated than the Selkirkian approach adopted in this paper and for Korean, at least, this extra power is not

---

[12] Angled brackets indicate morphological constituency and square brackets, prosodic constituency. M-structure refers to morphological constituency and p-structure refers to the domain of phonological rules (see Inkelas (to appear)).

warranted as phonological boundaries in Korean are predictable. In the following section, I will discuss how the current proposal correctly predicts the domain of several rules in Korean.

3. Prosodic Word-Level Rules

In this section, I introduce five rules in Korean which must refer to a word-internal prosodic constituent (i.e., the prosodic word) and show the present prosodic analysis is superior to non-prosodic Lexical Phonology in defining the domain of these rules.

3.1. The Onset Rule and Coda Neutralization

In this section I will show how Ahn's (1985) level ordered analysis fails to explain mismatches between prosodic structure and morphological structure. Instead, I claim that syllabification and Coda Neutralization (henceforth CN) are in fact prosodically conditioned rules, bounded by the ω.

In Korean the three-way laryngeal contrast of lax, aspirated and tense consonants in the onset position is simplified to lax stops in the coda, as in (12):

(12) Coda Neutralization (CN)

p,	p',	p^h	]σ	-->	p
t,	t',	t^h	]σ		
s,	s',	s^h	]σ	-->	t
č,	č',	$č^h$	]σ		
k,	k',	k^h	]σ	-->	k

In Korean all consonants are underlyingly voiceless, but intervocalically they surface as voiced within the ϕ.[13]

Let us first consider the cases where the Onset Rule in (1c) applies:

(13) Bound Root + Derivational suffix[14]

a. $_N$[$_V$[kip^h] i] --> ω(ki.p^hi), *ω(kip.i) --> *ω(ki.bi)
'deep' -Nomi 'depth'

b. $_{Adv}$[$_V$[kat^h] i] --> ω(ka.$č^h$i), *ω(kat.i) --> *ω(ka.di)
'alike' -Advi 'together'

c. $_V$[$_V$[$_V$[nop^h] i] ta] --> ω(no.p^hi.da),
'high' Caus-Dec *ω(nop.i.ta) --> *ω(no.bi.da)

(14) Noun + case marker

a. $_N$[$_N$[os] i] 'cloth' -Nom --> ω(o.si)
b. $_N$[$_N$[os] il] 'cloth'-Acc --> ω(o.sil)

(15) Verb root + functional suffix

a. $_V$[$_V$[$_V$[k'oč] as'] ta] --> ω(k'o.ǰat.t'a),
'to arrange' Past Dec *ω(k'ot.at.t'a) --> *ω(k'o.dat.t'a)

---

13 Critically only lax consonants in Korean undergo Voicing.

14 In this paper the following abbreviations are used: Nomi (nominalizer), Advi (adverbializer), Nom (nominative case marker), Acc (accusative case marker), Past (past tense marker), Dec (declarative ending), and Cau (causative suffix).

b. V[V[V[k'ək'] əs'] ta] --> ω(k'ə.k' ət. t'a),
'to cut' Past Dec *ω(k'ək.ət.t'a) --> *ω(k'ə.gət.t'a)

In (13a) the bound root-final consonant p^h is syllabified to the onset of the vowel-initial suffix *-i*. The noun stem-final *s* in (14a) surfaces as the onset of the following vowel-initial nominative case marker *-i,* and the verb-root final *č* in (15a) is also realized as the onset of the vowel-initial past tense morpheme *-as'*.

Contrary to (13)-(15), the following shows where the Onset Rule in (1c) is blocked. If not syllabified as an onset, target consonants undergo CN:

(16) Compound (stem + stem)

a. N[N[čəč] N[əmi]] -->	ω(čət) ω(əmi) -->	φ(čə.də.mi)
'milk' 'mother'	'nursing mother'	*φ(čə.ǰə.mi)
b. N[N[puək^h] N[an]] -->	ω(pu.ək) ω(an) -->	φ(pu.ə.gan)
'kitchen' 'inside'	'inside of kitchen'	*φ(puə.k^{h}an)
c. V[N[təs] V[əpsta]] -->	ω(tət) ω(əp.t'a) -->	φ(tə.dəp.t'a)
'a short time' 'not exist'	'transient'	*φ(tə.səp.t'a)

(17) Compound + Derivational suffix

a. Adv[N[N[ap^h] N[ap^h]] i] -->	ω(ap) ω(a.p^{h}i) -->	φ(a.ba.p^{h}i)
'front' 'front'-Advi	'to each person'	*φ(a.p^{h}a.p^{h}i)
b. Adv[N[N[nat^h] N[nat^h]] i] -->	ω(nat) ω(na.č^{h}i) -->	φ(nan.na.č^{h}i)
'piece' 'piece' Advi	'thoroughly'	

(18) Prefix + Stem[15]

a. N[təs N[os]] -->	ω(tət) ω(ot) -->	φ(tə.dot),
'outer' 'cloth'	'outer cloth'	*φ(tə.sot)
b. N[has N[os]] -->	ω(hat) ω(ot),	*φ(ha.sot)
'wadded' 'cloth'	'wadded cloth'	
c. V[ničV[olita]] -->	ω(nit) ω(o.ri.ta) -->	φ(ni.do.ri.da)
'late' 'bloom'	'bloom late'	*φ(ni.ǰo.ri.da)
d. N[sus N[imsik]] -->	ω(sut) ω(imsik) -->	φ(su.dim.sik)
'untouched' 'meal'	'untouched meal'	*φ(su.sim.sik)

The examples in (17) are crucial ones which show the mismatches between prosodic structure and morphological structure for the domain of the Onset rule and CN. In (17a) the adverbial suffix *-i*, which has scope over the whole compound *ap^{h}ap^h*, is grouped with the second stem for the domain of the lexical Onset Rule, where the compound-final p^h is syllabified as the onset of the following syllable of suffix *-i*. On the other hand, the first stem-final consonant p^h does not surface as the onset of the following syllable across compound-internal boundaries, but gets neutralized to *p*. This suggests that each member of a compound forms a separate prosodic constituent for the domain of the Onset Rule and CN. By the same token, in (18) each prefix constitutes a prosodic unit independent of the stem for the domain of CN. If either compound in (16)-(17) or prefix + stem in (18) were a single prosodic constituent, the Onset Rule would apply across compound-internal boundaries or prefix-stem boundaries, which is not correct here.

[15] Prefixes in Korean are not independent syntactic words, since they do not stand in isolation. Therefore, they are bound morphemes.

Therefore, (16)-(18) motivate a prosodic constituent within words rather than one which is coextensive with a morphological constituent for the following reasons: i) both prefixes and suffixes are bound morphemes but they show an asymmetry with respect to the prosodic constituent to which they belong, as shown by the domains of the Onset Rule and CN; ii) a stem and a prefix are different from each other in morphological category, but they form separate prosodic constituents with respect to these rules.

CN has been analyzed as a syllable-sensitive rule by Kim-Renaud (1974:116) and Chung (1985). Kim-Renaud names the above process 'Obstruent Unreleasing' in syllable final position as a syllable-boundary phenomenon. It occurs before a consonant, a phrase boundary or a compound boundary. The compound boundary (¢) can be reinterpreted as ω in the current analysis. Next, let us review how CN was analyzed within standard Lexical Phonology. Ahn (1985) claims that the lexicon in Korean is composed of four levels, as represented in (19):[16]

(19) Level 1 : subcompounding --> *t*-epenthesis
Level 2 : cocompounding
Level 3 : derivation --> *t*-palatalization
Level 4 : inflection & case marking--> Predicate Tensing & *t*-pal.

Ahn assumes that syllabification and resyllabification apply cyclically both in the lexical and postlexical components after every morphological operation. Also, he analyzes CN as a multi-domain rule (both lexical and postlexical). First, let us look at an example of the lexical CN in (20) (Ahn 1985:172):

(20) $_N[_N[$ os $]$ $_N[$ an̩ $]]$	:	subcompounding (level 1)
'cloth' 'inside'		
[ot] [an]	:	CN
[o.tan]	:	resyllabification
[o.dan]	:	Voicing (post-lexical)

As shown in (20), the first stem-final *s* of the compound is neutralized to *t* when it is followed by a vowel-initial stem in level 1. Based on the fact that CN precedes the postlexical rule of Voicing, Ahn concludes CN occurs either at level 1 or 2 as a lexical rule. On the other hand, Ahn defines the CN occurring in (21) as postlexical, which shows a mismatch between the prosodic structure and morphological structure: in terms of morphological structure the suffix *-i* is affixed after the compound *nat^h-nat^h*; in terms of prosodic structure, the first stem of the compound is in a prosodic constituent for the domain of CN, and the second stem and the following suffix is in another prosodic constituent for the domain of the Onset Rule:

(21) $_{Adv}[_N[_N[nat^h]$ $_N[nat^h]]$ i] --> [nannač^hi]
'piece' 'piece' -Advi 'throroughly'

lexical	a. [[nat] [nat^h]]	:	level 2 co-com. & syll.
	b. [[nat^hnat^h] i]	:	level 3 derivation & (CN is blocked)
	c. [nat^hnač^hi]	:	t-palatalization
postlexical	d. [natnač^hi]	:	CN
	e. [nannač^hi]	:	Nasal Assimilation

---

16 For a detailed analysis of problems with Ahn's Lexical Phonology, see Park (1990).

Ahn posits the ad-hoc and unusal condition that consonants do not undergo level 3 application of CN in (21b) (cf. (22b)) if followed by a vowel-initial word at either level 3 or 4, while they do when followed by a consonant. The postlexicality of CN in (21d) results from its ordering after the cyclic rule *t*-palatalization. Notice that he also assumes that CN precedes Nasal Assimilation.[17] For if CN had applied cyclically in level 2, the following would be expected:

(22)				
lexical	a	[[nat^h] [nat^h]	:	level 2 cocompound
		[[nat] [nat]]	:	CN
	b.	[[natnat] i]	:	level 3 derivation
		[natnači]	:	t-palatalization
postlexical	c.	[nannači]	:	Nasal Assimilation
	d.	*[nannaǰi]	:	Voicing

If so, each stem-final *t*^{h} of the compound in (22a) would be neutralized to *t* in level 2. The problem arises when, in level 3, the neutralized compound-final *t* is followed by the suffix *-i*, causing *t* to undergo *t*-palatalization, as shown in (22b), and subsequently voicing postlexically, as in (22d), which is incorrect. To derive the correct output, Ahn concludes that CN in (21) applies postlexically after *t*-palatalization. However, is level ordering between *t*-palatalization and CN necessary? For the derived adverb *nat*^{h}*-nat*^{h}*-i*, the prosodic structures for CN and the lexical syllabifiction are (nat^h) and (nat^{h}i), which does not correspond to their morphological structure. Furthermore, application of CN at levels 1, 3, 4 and postlexically constitutes a violation of the Continuous Stratum Hypothesis (Mohanan 1986), which was reported by Sohn (1986), Park (1990) and Kang (1991a). Considering the fact that the determiner-final consonant *č*^{h} always gets neutralized before it precedes the postlexical resyllabification as in (23a), Ahn's motivation for CN as a postlexical rule does not hold:

(23) a. $_{NP}$[$_{Det}$[myəč^h] $_N$[ai]] --> ω(myət) ω(ai) --> ϕ(myə.da.i)
'several' 'child' *ϕ(myə.č^{h}a.i)

b. $_N$[$_N$[myəč^h] i] --> ω(myəč^{h}i)
'several' Nom

Therefore, I conclude that CN cannot be postlexical.

First, I claim that before we construct syllables, we have to know the ω, since syllabification is delimited by the ω. Secondly, the leftward adjunction in (6) plays a key role in explaining the blocking of several rules. Let us see how the current prosodic analysis dispenses with Ahn's (1985) level ordering problem between *t*-palatalization and CN, as shown in (24):

```
(24) Adv[N[N[natʰ] N[natʰ]]i]                 (25) N[N[os] i]
        'piece' 'piece' Advi                          'cloth' Nom
a) KPWR  : ω(n  a tʰ) ω( n  a tʰ) i            a) KPWR    :  ω(o s) i
b) Adjun : ω(n  a tʰ) ω( n  a tʰ i)            b) Adjunc. :  ω(o s i)
c) syll  :     \|/.        \|  \|              c) syll.   :    | \|
                σ           σ   σ                               σ σ
d) CN    : ω(nat)         _____                d) CN      :  _____
```

---

[17] Any consonant occurring at the coda must undergo neutralization. For example, $_{Adv}$[$_N$[$_N$[pak'] $_N$[pak']] i] is pronounced as (pak.p'a.k'i).

e) t-pal	:	____ ω(na.č^{h}i)	e) output	:	(o.si)
f) NA	:	ϕ(nan.na.č^{h}i)			
g)output	:	(nan.na.č^{h}i)			

By the KPWR (5), we derive two ω's here, ω(nat^{h}) and ω(nat^{h}). The adverbial suffix *-i* is adjoined to the second ω by lexical adjunction, as shown in (24b). Lexical syllabification applies within each ω. In the first ω, the first stem-final t^h undergoes CN, as shown in (24d). Within the second ω, the stem-final t^h is realized as the onset of the following vowel-initial suffix *-i*, further undergoing *t*-palatalization, as shown in (24e). The crucial point here is CN applies to the consonant in the coda position and *t*-palatalization, in the onset position; they are in complementary distribution. Therefore, Ahn's argument for CN as a multi-domain rule no longer holds, instead, it is simply a ω-level rule. Also, in (25) the noun *os* forms a ω by the KPWR (5) and the following case marker *-i* is incorporated to the preceding ω postlexically, as shown in (25b). Therefore, lexical syllabification and CN are delimited by the ω.

3.2 t-palatalization

T-palatalization in Korean is analyzed as a lexical rule (Ahn 1985 and others) in which a stem-final alveolar *t*, t^h become *č*, $\check{c}^h$ when followed by a suffix beginning with a high front vowel *i*, as shown in (27)-(28). T-palatalization only applies to morphologically derived forms (Kiparsky 1973). It is blocked across compound-internal boundaries, prefix+stem, or word-boundaries, as shown in (29):

(26) within nonderived words: NA
a. N[mati] 'knob' --> ω(ma.di), *ω(ma.ǰi)
b. N[panti] 'firefly' --> ω(pan.di), *ω(pan.ǰi)
c. Adv[əti] 'where' --> ω(ə.di), *ω(ə.ǰi)

(27) between root+suffix or stem +clitic
a. N[[mat] i] --> ω(ma.či) --> ω(ma.ǰi)
'old' 'person' 'the oldest'
b. V[V[V[put^{h}] i] ta] --> ω(pu.č^{h}i.da)
'to attach' Cau-Dec
c. Adv[A[kat^{h}] i] --> ω(ka.č^{h}i)
'same' Advi
d. N[N[pat^{h}] i] --> ω(pa.č^{h}i)
'field' Nom
e. N[N[pat^{h}] ilaŋ] --> ω(pa.č^{h}iraŋ)
'field' and

(28) between root + suffix within a compound
a. N[N[hæ] N[V[tot] i]] --> ω(hæ) ω(do.či) --> ϕ(hæ.do.ǰi)
'sun' 'to rise'-Nomi 'sunrising'
b. N[N[mul] N[V[pat]i]] --> ω(mul) ω(pači) --> ϕ(mul.ba.ǰi)
'water' 'to hold'-Nomi 'drain pipe'
c. N[N[p'i] N[V[put^{h}]i]] --> ω(p'i) ω(puč^{h}i) --> ϕ(p'i.bu.č^{h}i)
'blood' 'to attach-Nomi 'family members in a direct line'
d. N[N[V[V[put^{h}]i]m] N[səŋ]] --> ω(puč^{h}im) ω(səŋ) --> ϕ(pu.č^{h}im.s'əŋ)
'to attach'-Caus-Nomi 'nature' 'sociability'

(29) t-palatalization : NA

a. $_N$[$_N$[pat^h] $_N$[ilaŋ]] --> ω(pat) ω(i.raŋ) --> ϕ(pa.di.raŋ),
'field' 'ridge' 'the ridge of a field' *ϕ(pa.ǰi.raŋ)

b. $_N$[$_N$[hot^h [ipul]] --> ω(hot) ω(ipul) --> ϕ(ho.di.bul),
'single' 'comforter' 'unlined comforter' *ϕ(ho.ǰi.bul)

c. $_{PP}$[$_{AdP}$[kot] $_{PP}$[$_{NP}$[ili- $_P$[lo]]] --> ω(kot) ω(iriro) --> ϕ(ko.di.ri.ro),
'soon' 'here' 'to' '(He will) come to here soon.'*ϕ(ko.ǰi.ri.ro)

T-palatalization applies within each part of a compound if it is derived, as in (28). If either the compound (29a) or the prefix+stem (29b) were a single prosodic constituent, *t*-palatalization would apply there. Therefore, the examples in (29) also indicate that there should be a word-internal prosodic constituent for the domain of t-palatalization.

T-palatalization is a domain span rule, formulated as in (30):

(30) t, t^h --> č, č^h / ω(...___ i ...)ω

However, (30) must still be restricted to morphologically derived forms by some version of the ***Strict Cycle Condition*** (Mascaró 1978; Kiparsky 1985).

3.3. Stray Erasure

Underlyingly tautomorphemic consonant clusters C_iC_j in Korean are either simplified or surface as heterosyllabic due to Korean syllable structure, as shown in (31) and (34):

(31) C_iC_j#

a. $_N$[kaps] 'price' --> ω(kap)

b. $_N$[nəks] 'spirit' --> ω(nək)

(32) C_iC_j + C

a. $_N$[$_N$[kaps] kwa] --> ω(kap.k'wa)
'price' and

b. $_N$[$_N$[nəks] to] --> ω(nək.t'o)
'spirit' too

(33) C_iC_j + V

a. $_N$[$_N$[kaps]i] --> ω(kap.s'i)
'price' Nom

b. $_N$[$_N$[nəks] il] --> ω(nək.s'il)
'spirit' Acc

(34) C_iC_j] [V

a. $_N$[$_N$[kaps] $_N$[əč^{h}i]] --> ω(kap) ω(əč^{h}i) --> ϕ(ka.bə.č^{h}i)
'price' 'value' 'value' *ϕ(kap.s'ə.č^{h}i)

b. $_N$[$_N$[č^{h}æk]$_N$[kaps]i] --> ω(č^{h}æk)ω(kap.s'i) --> ϕ(č^{h}æk.k'ap.s'i)
'book' 'price' Nom

When the tautomorphemic consonant cluster C_iC_j appears word-finally in (31), the C_i adjacent to the nucleus is syllabified as a coda and then the C_j is deleted. When C_iC_j is followed by a consonant-initial suffix in (32) forming a triconsonantal cluster, the C_j is also deleted. However, where C_iC_j is followed by a vowel-initial suffix in (33), C_i closes the preceding syllable by the Coda Rule and C_j begins the following syllable by the Onset Rule. In contrast to (33), in (34a) where the first stem ends with the cluster *ps*, the *s* cannot be syllabified onto the onset of the vowel-initial syllable ə of the second stem, but is deleted. If (34a) were a single prosodic constituent, *ps* would be fully syllabified, which derives the wrong output *(kap.s'ə.č^{h}i). The application of Stray Erasure within the compound in (34a) also supports our claim that each stem of a compound constitutes a ω.

This phenomenon was analyzed as Consonant Cluster Simplification (henceforth CCS) by Kim-Renaud (1974), Chung (1980), and Ahn (1985). Following Steriade (1982), I claim that CCS is a result of Stray Erasure, not a separate rule (see Itô 1986).

Thus, stray erasure in Korean is bounded by ω, which is illustrated in (36):

(35) $_{N}$[$_{N}$[kaps] i]
'price' Nom

a) KPWR	:	ω(k a ps) i
b) Adjun.	:	ω(k a ps i)
c) syll.	:	|/ | σ σ
d)	:	ω(kap.si)
e) POT	:	ω(kap.s'i)

(36) $_{N}$[$_{N}$[kaps]$_{N}$[əč^{h}i]]
'price' 'value'

a) KPWR	:	ω(k a p s) ω(ə č^{h} i)
b) syll.	:	|/ σ | | σ σ
c) SE	:	s --> ø
d)	:	ω(kap) ω(ə.č^{h}i)
e) resyll.	:	ϕ(ka.pə.č^{h}i)
f) voicing	:	ϕ(ka.bə.č^{h}i)

In (35) the noun *kaps* forms a ω by the KPWR (5) and the following case marker is adjoined to the ω postlexically. Then within the ω, tautomorphemic consonant cluster *ps* are fully syllabified, and *p* is realized as the coda of the preceding syllable; *s* surfaces as the onset of the following vowel-initial syllable *-i*. In (36), the compound projects two ω's by the PWFR (5). Since the Korean syllable structure allows maximally one consonant either in the coda and in the onset, within the first ω, *p* is syllabified as a coda and then *s* is erased by the Stray Erasure Convention. If stray erasure is delayed until the postlexical level, *s* may be syllabified to the onset of the syllable-initial ə, producing the wrong output *(kap.s'ə.č^{h}i). This indicates that the domain of stray erasure in Korean should be ω. Therefore, I claim that extraprosodicity turns off at the prosodic word-level in Korean.[18]

3.4. l-deletion

Korean has underlying tautomorphemic *l*-C clusters, and an *l*-deletion rule to simplify them. In this section I will discuss only how this applies to nouns. The domain of *l*-deletion is similar to Stray Erasure discussed in 3.3. Then, let us consider the examples in (37)-(40):

---

[18] Itô claims that all autosegmental materials must be licensed at the word-level. Along these lines, Itô (1986), Borowsky (1986), and Goldsmith (1990) propose that if consonants are not licensed at the word-level, they will not proceed to the postlexical phonology but erased by the Stray Erasure Convention. However, Rice (1988) argues that for the domain of syllabification in Turkish and Slave extraprosodicity continues to operate postlexically.

(37) *l* C_i
a. [talk]$_N$ 'chicken' --> ω(tak)
b. [hilk]$_N$ 'soil' --> ω(hik)

(38) *l* $C_i + C_j$
a. $_N[_N[$talk] to] --> ω(tak.t'o)
'chicken' 'too'
b. $_N[_N[$salm] kwa] --> ω(sam.gwa)
'life' 'and'

(39) *l* C_i + V
a. $_N[_N[$salm] i] --> ω(sal.mi)
'life' 'Nom'
b. $_N[_N[$talk] in] --> ω(tal.gin)
'chicken' Top

(40) *l* C_i] [V
a. $_N[_N[$talk] $_N[$əmi]] --> ω(tak) ω(əmi) --> ϕ(ta.gə.mi)
'chicken' 'mother' 'mother chicken' *ϕ(tal.gə.mi)
b. $_N[_N[$hilk] $_N[$akuŋi]] --> ω(hik) ω(akuŋi) --> ϕ(hi.ga.guŋ.i)
'soil' 'furnace' 'soil furnace' *ϕ(hil.ga.guŋ.i)

Contrary to our expectation, an *l* which is adjacent to the nucleus is deleted so that the following consonant is syllabified as the coda, as shown in (37) and (38). In (39) when *lk* is followed by a vowel-initial suffix, they are both fully syllabified. However, in (40) where the *lk* appear compound-internally, *l* cannot be syllabified but is deleted. The compound-internal *l*-deletion also motivates the prosodic constituent within words.

L-deletion was once analyzed as a special case of Consonant Cluster Simplification (Kim-Renaud 1974; Chung 1980). But I will analyze it as a separate rule. As a ω–bounded rule, *l*-deletion is also a domain span rule, as shown in (41):

(41) *l* --> ø / (...__ C' ...)ω (C': unsyllabified C)

L-deletion has to precede the Coda Rule in (1d). Let us look at *l*-deletion within a compound, as in (42):

(42) $_N[_N[$talk] $_N[$əmi]] --> ω(tak) ω(əmi) --> ϕ(ta.gə.mi)

```
a) KPWR        : ω(t  a lk)  ω(ə  m  i )
b) Onset Rule  :    \ |         |   \ |
                     σ          σ    σ
c) l-deletion  :       l --> ø
d) Coda Rule   : ω(t a k)  ω(ə  m i)
                    \ | /     |  \ |
                      σ       σ   σ
```

By the KPWR in (5) we derive two ω's; within the first ω, *l* is deleted, which confirms our rule (41).

However, when *lk* are followed by a vowel-initial suffix, *lk* are fully syllablified, as shown in (43):

```
(43) N[N[talk] i]     -->  ω(tal.gi)
a) KPWR             :  ω(talk) i
b) adjunction       :  ω(talki)
c) Onset Rule       :  ω(t  a l  k  i)
                           \|    \|
                           σ     σ
d) l-deletion       :  ________
e) Coda Rule        :  ω(t  a l  k  i)
                           \|/   \|
                           σ     σ
f) Voicing          :  ω(tal.gi)
```

By the KPWR in (5), the noun projects a ω and the suffix is adjoined to the preceding ω. Then, within ω, *l* is syllabified as the coda of the first syllable and *k*, as the onset of the second syllable. So, the structural description for *l*-deletion is not met within ω.

4. Conclusions

In this paper I have proposed the Korean Prosodic Word Rule, which derives the domain of syllabification, Coda Neutralization, *t*-palatalization, stray erasure, and *l*-deletion. Since those rules are bounded by the prosodic word, we have to know the domain of ω before we construct syllables. Arguing against Ahn's (1985) analysis of CN, I claim that Coda Neutralization is not a multi-domain rule but is a prosodic word-level rule, and ordering relationship between CN and t-palatalization is not necessary .

References

Ahn, Sang-Cheol. 1985. *The Interplay of Phonology and Morphology in Korean.* Ph.D. dissertation, University of Illinis.

Booij, Geert and Jerzy Rubach. 1984. Morphological and Prosodic Domains in Lexical Phonology. *Phonology YearBook.* 1.

Booij, Geert and Jerzy Rubach 1987. Postcyclic versus Postlexical Rules in Lexical Phonology. *Linguistic Inquiry.* 18. 1-44.

Borowsky, Toni 1986. *Topics in the Lexical Phonology of English.* Ph.D. dissertation, University of Massachusetts.

Chen, Matthew 1987. The Syntax of Phonology: Xiamin Tone Sandhi. *Phonology.* 4.

Cho, Young-mee Yu & Peter Sells 1991. A Lexical Account of Phrasal Suffixes in Korean. ms., Stanford University.

Choe, Hee-Rach 1991. The Morphological Status of Nominal "Particles in Korean". paper presented at the Workshop on Korean Syntax and Semantics, Linguistics Institute at University of California Santa Cruz.

Chomsky, Noam 1988. Some Notes on Economy of Derivation and Representation. *MIT Working Papers in Linguistics.* 10.

Cohn, Abigail 1989. Stress in Indonesian and Bracketing Paradoxes, *Natural Language and Linguistic Theory.* 7. 167-216.

Chung, Kook 1980. *Neutralization in Korean: A Functional View.* Ph.D dissertation, University of Texas at Austin.

Clements, G.N. & S.J. Kyser 1983. *CV Phonology: A Generative Theory of the Syllable.* MIT Press, Cambridge, Massachusetts.

Fabb, Nigel 1984. *Syntactic Affixation.* Ph. D. dissertation, MIT.

Goldsmith, John 1990. *Autosegmental and Metrical Phonology*. Basil Blackwell: Cambridge, Massachusetts.

Halle, Morris and Jean-Roger Vergnaud 1987. *An Essay on Stress*. MIT Press.

Halle, Morris and Michael. Kenstowicz 1989. On Cyclic and Noncyclic Stress. ms., MIT.

Han, Eunjoo 1991. The Phonological Word in Korean. paper presented at the 2nd Southern California Japanese/ Korean Linguistics Conference, UC Santa Barbara.

Hannahs, S.J. 1991 *Prosodic Structure and French Morphology*, Ph.D. dissertation, University of Delaware.

Hayes, Bruce 1989. The Prosodic Hierchy in Meter. In P. Kiparsky & G. Youmans eds. *Perspectives on Meter*. New York: Academic Press.

Inkelas, Sharon 1989. *Prosodic Constituency in Prosodic Phonology*. Stanford University, Ph.D. disseration.

Inkelas, Sharon (to appear). Deriving Cyclicity. in Ellen Kaisse and Sharon Hargus eds. *Studies in Lexical Phonology*. New York: Academic Press.

Itô, Junko 1986. *Syllable Theory in Prosodic Phonology*. Ph. D.dissertation, University of Massachusetts.

Itô, Junko 1991. lecture notes, Linguistics Institute, UC Santa Cruz.

Jun, Jongho 1991. Prosodic Approach on Korean Partial Reduplication. To appear in *the Proceedings of the second Southern California Japanese/ Korean Linguistics Conference*.

Kang, Ongmi 1991a. Prosodic Phonology in Korean. ms., University of Washington.

Kang, Ongmi 1991b. Word-Internal Prosodic Words in Korean. To appear in *the Proceedings of NELS* 22.

Kang, Ongmi (forthcoming) *Morphology and Prosodic Phonology in Korean*, Ph.D. dissertation, University of Washington.

Kim-Renaud, Young-Key 1974. *Korean Consonantal Phonology*. Ph.D. dissertataion, University of Hawaii.

Kiparsky, Paul 1982. Lexical Phonology and Morphology. in I.S.Yang ed. *Linguistics in the Morning Calm*. Linguistic Society of Korea, Hanshin, Seoul.

Kiparsky, Paul 1985. Some Consequences of Lexical Phonology. *Phonology Yearbook*. 2. 85-138.

Lieber, Rochelle 1980. *On the Organizati of the Lexicon*. Ph. D. dissertation, MIT.

Lieber, Rochelle (forthcoming). *Deconstructing Morphology: Word Formation in a Government-Binding Syntax*. The University of Chicago Press.

Mascaró, John 1978. *Catalan Phonology and Phonologcal Cycle*. Ph.D. dissertation, MIT.

McCarthy, John 1979. Stress and Syllabification. *Linguistic Inquiry*. 10. 443-466.

McCarthy, John & Alan Prince 1986. Prosodic Morphology. ms., University of Massachusetts, Amherst and Brandeis University.

McCarthy, John & Alan Prince 1990. Foot and Word in Prosodic Morphology: The Arabic Broken Plurals. *Natural Language and Linguistics Theory*. 8. 209-282.

Mohanan, K.P. 1986. *The Theory of Lexical Phonology*, Dordrecht: D. Reidel.

Nespor, Marina and Irene Vogel 1986. *Prosodic Phonology*. Dordrecht: Foris.

Odden, David (to appear). Interaction Between Modules in Lexical Phonology. in Ellen Kaisse and Sharon Hargus, eds. *Studies in Lexical Phonology*, New York: Academic Press.

Park, Duk-Soo 1990 *Lexicon and Syntax in Korean Phonology*. Ph.D. dissertation, University of Hawaii.

Pesetsky, David 1979. Russian Morphology and Lexical Theory. ms., MIT Cambridge, Massachusetts.

Rice, Keren 1988. Predicting Rule Domains in the Phrasal Phonology, Sharon Inkelas and Draga Zec, eds. *The Phonology-Syntax Connection.* 1990. Chicago: University of Chicago Press.

Rice, Keren (to appear). On Deriving Rule Domains: the Athapaskan Case. in the *Proceedings of WCCFL*. 10.

Rubach, Jerzy and Geert E. Booij 1988. Syllable Structure Assignment in Polish. *Vrije Universitet Working Papers in Linguistics*. 32. 1-59, appears in *Phonology*. 7. 1990.

Rubach, Jerzy and Geert E. Booij 1990a. Edge of Constituent Effects in Polish. *Natural Language and Linguistic Theory*. 8: 427-463.

Selkirk, Elisabeth 1978. The Syllable. in van der Hulst and Smith eds., *The Structure of Phonological Representations*. 1982. 337-384.

Selkirk, Elisabeth 1984. *Phonology and Syntax: The Relation Between Sound and Structure*. Cambridge, Massachusetts: MIT Press.

Selkirk, Elisabeth 1986. On Derived Domains in Sentence. *Phonology*. 3.

Selkirk, Elisabeth & Tong Shen 1988. Prosodic Domains in Shanghai Chinese. Sharon Inkelas and Draga Zec, eds. *The Phonology-Syntax Connection* 1990. Chicago: University of Chicago Press.

Shih, Chi-Lin 1985. *The Prosodic Domain of Tone Sandhi in Chinese*. Ph.D. dissertation, University of San Diego.

Sproat, Richard 1985. *On Deriving the Lexicon*. MIT Ph.D. dissertation.

Sproat, Richard (to appear). Looking into Words. in Ellen Kaisse and Sharon Hargus eds. *Studies in Lexical Phonology*. New York: Academic Press.

Steriade, Donka 1982. *Greek Prosodies and the Nature of Syllabification*. Ph.D. dissertation, MIT, Cambridge, Massachusetts.

Vogel, Irene 1990 The Clitic Group in Prosodic Phonology, Mascaró, J. and M. Nespor eds. *Grammars In Progress*, Dordrecht: Foris: 447-454.

Zec, Draga & Sharon Inkelas 1988. Prosodically Constrained Syntax. Sharon Inkelas and Draga Zec eds. *The Phonology-Syntax Connection*. 1990. Chicago: University of Chicago Press.

Zec, Draga (to appear). Rule Domains and Phonological Changes. in Ellen Kaisse and Sharon Hargus eds. *Studies in Lexical Phonology*. New York: Academic Press. .

Zwicky, Arnold 1991 What is a clitic?, paper presented at the Clitics Workshop, Linguistics Institute at University of California Santa Cruz.

A Phonetically Based Analysis of [Voice] and [Fortis] in Korean

DAVID JAMES SILVA
Cornell University

INTRODUCTION

Standard accounts of Korean consonantal phonology (C-W Kim 1965; K-H Kim 1987; Kim-Renaud 1974; Lee 1955; Martin 1974) claim that while Korean distinguishes three types of stop consonants in underlying representation--lax, aspirated, and reinforced--it maintains a four-way distinction on the surface as shown in (1). In surface representations, Korean allows not only for lax, aspirated and reinforced obstruents (all voiceless), but also for so-called voiced lax stops, which arise when an underlying voiceless lax stop sits between two voiced segments within the same PHONOLOGICAL PHRASE (Cho 1987, 1990; Jun 1990; Silva 1989).

(1) Standard Description of Korean Obstruent Types

Underlying	*Surface*	*Example*	*Gloss*
Aspirated	Aspirated (voiceless)	/t^{h}al/ --> [t^{h}al]	'mask'
Reinforced	Reinforced (voiceless)	/t'al/ --> [t'al]	'daughter'
Lax ("initial")	Lax voiceless	/tal/ --> [tal]	'moon'
Lax (intersonorant)	Lax voiced	/i-tal/ --> [idal]	'this moon'

---

*Research for this paper was funded in part by a Fulbright Fellowship administered by the Korean-American Educational Commission. Thanks to all those involved with the Fulbright Program in Korea and to all who have given their time to comment on previous drafts of this work.

However, Silva (1991) reports that the PHONOLOGY-TO-PHONETICS MAPPING of the lax stops is more complicated than that suggested in (1). As discussed below, underlying lax stops have two percepts--voiced and voiceless--but three acoustic realizations: voiceless lightly aspirated [p], voiceless unaspirated [b̥], and voiced unaspirated [b]. This more detailed description of the Korean lax stops calls into question widely-held beliefs regarding both laryngeal features and the rule of stop 'voicing'; in particular one might ask the following:

a. What are the laryngeal features for the underlying and surface representations of Korean lax stops (and Korean consonants in general)?
b. How is the rule of lax stop 'voicing' formalized?

It is the goal of this paper to re-evaluate our understanding of Korean consonantal phonology, particularly with regard to laryngeal features, and move toward an explanation that accurately accounts for the observed patterning of the stop consonants in *both* the phonology and the phonetics.

We begin by outlining some basic facts about Korean phonology that pertain to the issue at hand. Next we consider the phonetic data reported in Silva 1991 which indicate that the primary means of differentiating between "voiced" and "voiceless" lax obstruents appears to be voicing lag (post-release VOICE ONSET TIME or VOT); vocal cord vibration during closure is a secondary, enhancing feature. We then move to a discussion of phonological features and demonstrate that a phonological account for the phonetic data can be handled in terms of two laryngeal features for Korean: [spread glottis] and [fortis]. The feature [voice], it will be argued, is not phonological per se, but phonetic. Finally we turn to the rule of lax stop "voicing" and argue that it is not a phonological assimilation rule (as argued by K-H Kim), but part of a two-part process: 1) a prosodically conditioned aspiration rule and 2) a phonetic rule of VOICING INTERPOLATION.

BACKGROUND

The Korean consonant inventory appears in (2). The lax stops /p, t, k/--the focus of this investigation--appear in the box.

(2)

	labial	alveolar	alv-pal	velar	glottal
lax plosive	p (p)	t (t)	tʃ (c)	k (k)	
aspirated plosive	p^h (ph)	t^h (th)	$tʃ^h$ (ch)	k^h (kh)	
reinforced plosive	p' (pp)	t' (tt)	tʃ' (cc)	k' (kk)	
lax fricative		s (s)			h (h)
reinforced fricative		s' (ss)			
nasal obstruent	m (m)	n (n)		ŋ (ng)	
liquid		l/ɾ (l)			

As is widely assumed in the literature, the lax stops are susceptible to "voicing" when they occur between voiced segments (redundantly, sonorants). Aspirated and reinforced segments, however, are never voiced.

(3)	*citation form*	*'this X'*			*gloss*
	tal	i + tal	-->	[idal]	'moon/month'
	t^hal	i + t^hal	-->	[it^{h}al]	'mask'
	t'al	i + t'al	-->	[it'al]	'daughter'

The so-called voicing rule, however, does not simply operate on all intersonorant lax stops in the post-lexical component of the grammar; rather, it is prosodically conditioned. On the basis of native speaker judgments, it has been discerned that lax obstruent voicing is a domain-span rule (in the sense of Nespor and Vogel 1986), and that the domain of the rule is that of the phonological phrase, or, in the terms used in Silva 1990 (following Selkirk and Tateishi 1988a, 1988b and McCawley 1968) the minor phrase. An example of stop-voicing judgments--as they would appear in the existing literature--is given in (4).

(4)

UR: [$_{\phi}$ [$_{\omega}$ cʰəlsu-ka]] [$_{\phi}$ [$_{\omega}$ pata] [$_{\omega}$ parapwas'ə]]

Minor Phrase Edge ←*voiceless*

Word Edge ←*voiced*

Word Internal ←*voiced*

SR: [$_{\phi}$ [$_{\omega}$ cʰəlsu-ga]] [$_{\phi}$ [$_{\omega}$ pada] [$_{\omega}$ barabwas'ə]]

'Chelsu stared at the ocean'

Lax stops that occur at the edge of a minor phrase are judged "voiceless"; lax stops that are situated elsewhere, however, are judged as "voiced." The "voiced" stops include those that occur at the edge of a phonological word (word edge) and within a phonological word (word internal). Thus we see that the intersonorant lax stop in any one of three prosodic positions falls into one of two perceptual categories, either voiced or voiceless.

THE PHONETIC DATA IN LIGHT OF PROSODIC STRUCTURE

While native-speaker judgments remain a valuable source of information regarding the structure of a particular language, any careful study of phonetic phenomena must go beyond intuitions and examine the physical evidence. With regard to the current study, then, the question to ask is the following: Given an enriched prosodic description of Korean, what are the acoustic characteristics of the lax stops in each position?

In an attempt to address such a question, Silva (1991) reports that there are significant differences among Minor-Phrase-Edge, Word-Edge, and Word-Internal lax stops with regard to three acoustic measures: (1) the duration of vocal cord vibration during stop closure; (2) the degree to which the stop closure is voiced (in terms of a percentage); (3) post-release voice onset time (VOT)--the time period between the release of the stop and the onset of voicing for the following segment. The mean values obtained for each of these three acoustic measures appear in (5).

(5)

	ϕ-Edge	ω-Edge	ω-Internal
Voicing during Closure	10 ms	17 ms	33 ms
% of Closure that is Voiced	23%	36%	77%
Post-Release VOT	60 ms	22 ms	3 ms

These figures reveal several noteworthy trends in the data. First, the numbers suggest that even those segments that are perceived as voiceless--i.e. minor-phrase-edge (ϕ-edge) segments--receive some degree of voicing. Second, the numbers for

VOT exhibit a pattern that is the inverse of that for the voicing data. Here, a longer VOT is associated with a voiceless percept (i.e. a ϕ-edge segment) while shorter VOTs are characteristic of those segments perceived as voiced. Within the "voiced" category, however, there is a significant difference between the VOT for word-edge (ω-edge) segments and word-internal (ω-internal) segments. Clearly, then, each of the prosodic categories plays a role in conditioning the acoustic values for voice and aspiration for the stops. As we have already seen, however, these three acoustic values correspond to only two perceptual values, namely voiced and voiceless. This relationship is schematized in (6).

(6)

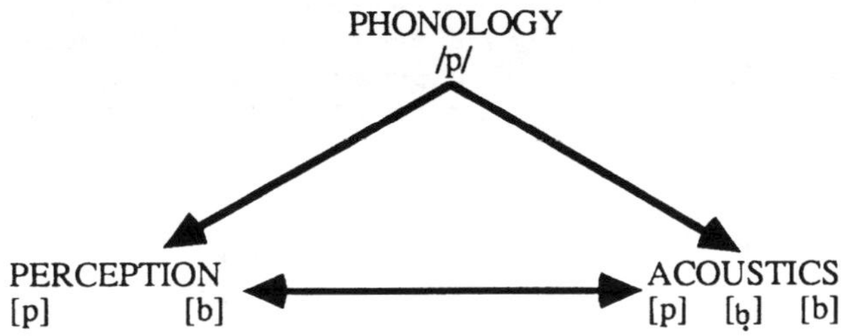

The issue of how to account for the multiple representations of the underlying lax stops--both in terms of acoustics and perception--becomes a matter of concern.

ASSIGNING PHONOLOGICAL FEATURES TO THE KOREAN STOPS

Laryngeal Features and "Articulatory Power"

Given the systematic behavior of the intersonorant lax stops as described above, we can propose the following descriptions for each positional variant. In ϕ-initial position, intersonorant lax stops are voiceless, lightly aspirated segments.[1] Word-edge lax stops are voiceless, relatively unaspirated segments; this description is based on the observation that the word-edge stops are less than 50% voiced during closure and that their VOT values are relatively smaller than those for ϕ-initial stops. Finally, word-internal lax stops are essentially voiced, unaspirated stops. These three positional variants for the lax stops, coupled with surface descriptions for the Korean aspirated and reinforced stops and a 3-feature system for laryngeal specifications (Keating 1984; K–H Kim 1987; Lombardi 1991), yields the table in (7).

(7)

stop-type V--V environment	lax ω-Internal	lax ω-Edge	lax ϕ-Edge	aspirated all	reinforced all
[voice]	yes	no	no	no	no
[spread glottis]	no	no	yes	yes (+)	no
[constricted glottis]	no	no	no	no	yes
	[b]	[b̥]	[p]	[pʰ]	[p']

\/

most accounts (e.g. C-W Kim 1965)
collapse these first two groups;
they are judged as voiced.

---

[1] See also C-W Kim (1965), Martin (1974) among others for a similar description.

Problems arise in using only [voice], [spread] and [constricted] to describe the phonetic realizations of the stops as we can not distinguish between ϕ-edge [p] and aspirated [p^h]: both are characterized by a lack of voicing, a lack of glottal constriction, and the presence of glottal spread. Where they differ in the degree to which the glottis is spread upon release: lax ϕ-edge stops are lightly aspirated while underlying aspirated stops are heavily aspirated. Unfortunately, this observation regarding the relative differences in aspiration can not be adequately described in terms of the system of binary features presented thus far: ϕ-edge [p] and [p^h] remain indistinguishable. How, then, can we account for the observed relative differences?

In addressing this very issue, C-W Kim (1965) proposes the classification for Korean obstruents shown in (8). He accounts for the observed four-way surface distinction in terms of two binary features, [±aspirated] (±glottal spreading).and [±tense], a feature independent of voicing and aspiration. Note that C-W Kim claims that "the tense/lax feature is not an absolute category, but a relative one...," a category that involves relative differences in muscular activity, oral air pressure, and semantics (C-W Kim 1965 (1988: 29-31)).

(8)

		aspirated	
		+	-
tense	+	aspirated /p^h, t^h, c^h, k^h/	reinforced /p', t', c', k'/
	-	lax /p, t, c, k/	"voiced" [b, d, j, g]

Further support for including a "tensity" category in the phonology of Korean (and a number of other languages) comes from Kohler's (1984) cross linguistic study of the fortis/lenis contrast. Kohler claims that in addition to the usual voice and aspiration features, the inventory of phonological features should include a means for capturing differences in articulatory "power" and, turning back to the early work of Trubetzkoy and others, proposes the addition of the feature [±fortis]. This feature, he writes, is one "connected with power in the supraglottal movements and in the air stream, and with tension, especially in the larynx" (p. 168). With regard to Korean, Kohler cites data from a number of instrumental studies (among them Han & Weitzman 1965, 1967, 1970), and claims that Korean makes use of two "laryngeal mechanisms, aspiration and tensing, to differentiate between two fortis stop categories beside a lax one" (p. 161). Thus Kohler advocates a system much like that put forth by C-W Kim, one that includes a power feature ([fortis]) as well as a specification for aspiration. Following this proposal, we can revise (7) by replacing [cg] with [fortis], as in (9); doing so allows us to differentiate between the ϕ-edge lax stop [p] and the aspirated stop [p^h], the former being non-fortis and the latter fortis.

(9)

stop-type	lax	lax	lax	aspirated	reinforced
V--V environment	ω-Internal	ω-Edge	ϕ-Edge	all	all
[voice]	yes	no	no	no	no
[spread glottis]	no	no	yes	yes	no
[fortis]	no	no	no	yes	yes
	[b]	[b̥]	[p]	[p^h]	[p']

The Feature [voice]

Having motivated the need for [spread glottis] and [fortis], what of the feature [voice]? It is clear that in underlying structure, [voice] is predictable in Korean ([α sonorant] --> [α voice]); only on the surface does voicing play a role in the grammar, and a minor one at that, given the fact that acoustic voicing differences do not seem to be perceptually salient. Moreover, the fact that voicing appears to be a gradient value for word-internal and word-edge lax stops, leads us to believe that voicing is not phonological, but phonetic in nature (see Keating 1984, 1988; Cohn 1990). Thus we are left with the following feature system for Korean: [spread glottis] and [fortis] are underlying phonological features while the feature [voice] is phonetic.

(10)	Phonology		Phonetics
	[spread glottis] [fortis]	---->	[voice]

RETHINKING THE RULE OF LAX STOP "VOICING"

To evaluate the system proposed in (10), let us now turn to the rule of "Intervocalic Lax Obstruent Voicing" in Korean as analyzed by K-H Kim (1987). K-H Kim begins by motivating a three-feature system for the laryngeal aspects of Korean and proposes the underlying structures for lax, aspirated, and reinforced stops shown in (11).

(11) • 3 binary laryngeal features: [±spread glottis], [±constricted glottis], [±voice]

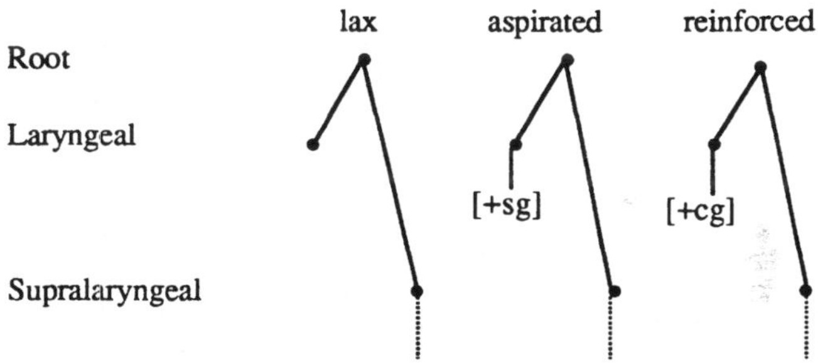

Lax segments have a bare laryngeal node; aspirated segments have a laryngeal node that dominates the feature [+spread glottis]; and reinforced segments have a laryngeal node that dominates the feature [+constricted glottis]. Under this system, lax obstruent voicing is treated as a rule of assimilation by spreading: [+voice] spreads rightward onto an bare laryngeal node, as in (12).

(12)

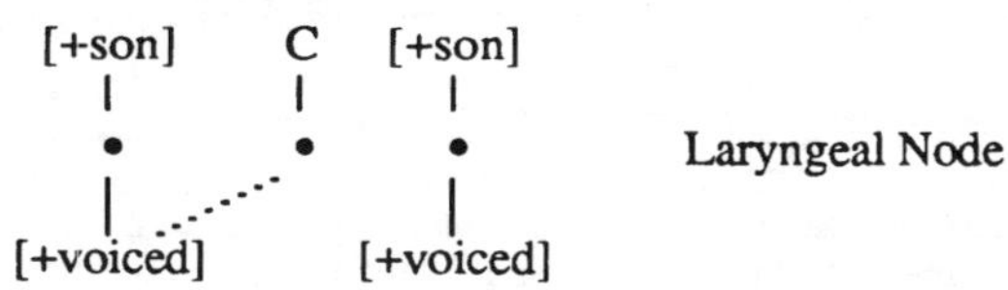

K-H Kim's analysis, though elegant and intuitively appealing, has a number of potential shortcomings, both in light of the phonetic data presented here and on general theoretical grounds. First, his analysis assumes that "voicing" results in categorical (100% voiced) output. The phonetic data suggest otherwise; there is "partial" voicing in many cases. Second, the left-to-right spreading of the rule is arbitrary. As Kim himself notes, other processes in Korean move right-to-left (lateral assimilation) or are mirror image (h-assimilation). Third, the rule misses the generalization that both voicing features are equally important and necessary; hence we are left wondering if the non-spreading feature for [voiced] plays more than a context-providing role. Last, Kim does not address the status of lax stops that do not undergo "voicing" for prosodic reasons; in other words, what happens to the laryngeal node of lax stops in ϕ-edge position?

These four points in mind, let us now turn to an alternative account for obstruent "voicing," one that incorporates the feature system in (9). The relevant laryngeal and manner features for the major non-nasal consonant types in Korean appear in (13). (Here "pl" = plosive; redundant features are given in parentheses.)

(13)

	lax pl	aspir pl	reinf pl	lax /s/	reinf /s/	/h/
[spread glottis]	(-)	+	(-)	(-)	(-)	+
[fortis]	(-)	+	+	(-)	+	(-)
[continuant]	(-)	(-)	(-)	+	+	+

Under such a system, lax oral plosives bear no specifications for laryngeal or manner features; aspirated plosives are designated by [sg] and [fortis]; reinforced plosives are designated by [cg] and [fortis].[2] The resulting feature geometries appear in (14).[3]

(14) • 2 laryngeal features: [spread glottis], [fortis]

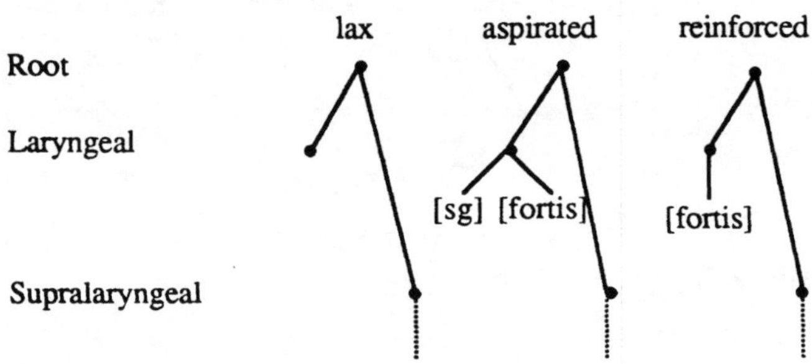

2 Here I follow other sources (e.g., Whitman 1985) and assume that the maximally underspecified consonant in the Korean consonant system is the lax alveolar stop /t/. Under such an assumption, it follows that an aspirated alveolar stop /t^h/ would be represented simply in terms of the feature [spread glottis]. This representation contrasts with the representation for /h/ in (12), which includes not only [spread glottis] but also [continuant].

3 I believe that the placement of [fortis] under the laryngeal node is open to question as it is unclear to me at this time where such a feature might sit in the hierarchy. My hunch is that like [continuant], [fortis] should be considered a "manner" feature and thus sit directly under the root node. For the time being, however, I leave this question to further research and assume the structure in (13).

Accounting for the difference between the ϕ-edge lax stops and their phrase-span (ω-edge, ω-internal) counterparts is then a matter of inserting the feature [spread glottis] at the left of a minor phrase.

(15) Aspiration: Attach [spread glottis] to a bare laryngeal node at the left edge of a minor phrase (ϕ).

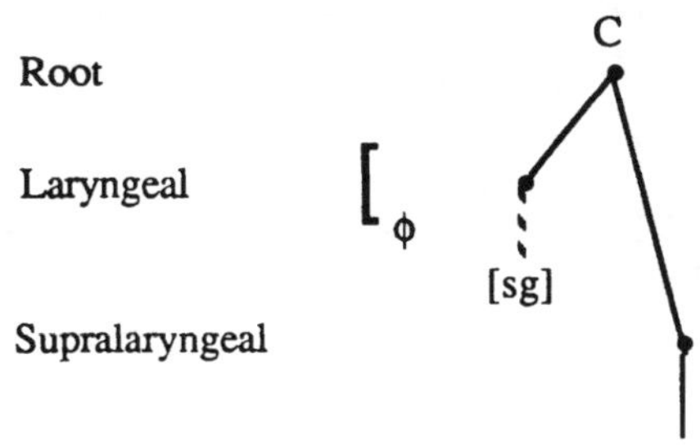

The rule in (15) accounts for the observation that phrase-initial lax stops are lightly aspirated ([spread glottis]) but not as heavily as underlying aspirated stops, which are not only marked [spread glottis] but also [fortis]. This prosodically conditioned aspiration insertion rule of Korean is analogous to the well-known English aspiration rule, the rule whereby phonemically voiceless stops are aspirated in absolute syllable initial position. Both rules target underlying voiceless, unaspirated stops; both rules insert the feature [spread glottis]; and both rules are prosodically conditioned, albeit at different levels of the hierarchy.

Now what of those lax stops that are not situated at the left edge of a minor phrase? Here it is proposed that these stops exit the phonology with no laryngeal specifications and that they acquire such features in the phonetics. In particular, intersonorant lax stops that do not meet the conditions for the rule in (15) may acquire voicing by means of phonetic interpolation (16). The [voiced] specifications on either side of the lax stop act as endpoints for the linear (i.e. temporal) instantiation of vocal cord vibration, an operation that, as Kohler points out, is "regulated passively" in Korean; "... voicing only continues during a stop closure as long as the articulatory context allows a pressure drop across the glottis"(p. 162). The lack of laryngeal specifications for the phrase-internal lax stops provide such an "articulatory context"; the vocal folds are in neutral position and thereby amenable to vibration. As a matter of contrast, consider the status of intersonorant stops with laryngeal specifications: is voicing interpolation possible in these cases? No. A [spread glottis] specification would preclude voicing, given that the vocal folds are not sufficiently adducted. A [fortis] specification would likewise preclude voicing as the high degree of glottal resistance (Rg) would inhibit a drop in glottal pressure (Ug).[4]

[4] Interestingly enough, the analysis presented here fits well with Kim-Renaud's (1974) proposal that consonantal processes are subject to the "metaforces" of strengthening and weakening, the former taking place at constituent boundaries and the latter occurring elsewhere.

(16) [voice] is variably interpolated across laryngeally unspecified (i.e. lax) stops

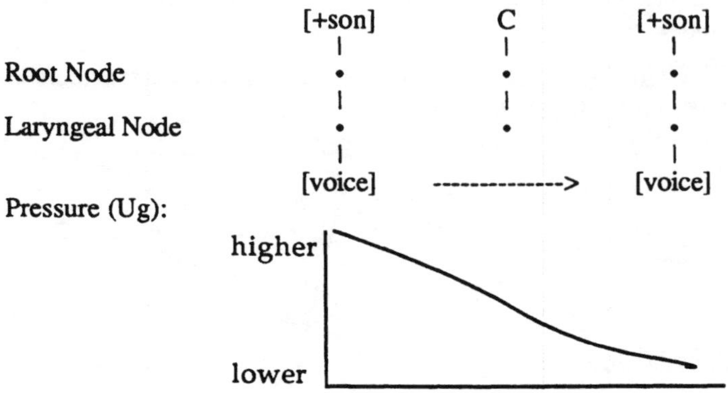

Before closing this discussion, let us consider the derivation given in figure 17. Here, three lax stops each sit in a different prosodic position: /p/ is at ϕ-edge; /k/ is at ω-edge; /t/ is ω-internal. In underlying representation (UR), none bear laryngeal features. Aspiration insertion (AI) then applies to the bilabial, inserting the feature [spread glottis]. In the phonetics, voicing interpolation (VI) allows for variable voicing of the velar and alveolar. The phonetic realization (PR) provided is the canonical form, with a voiceless unaspirated velar at word-edge position and a more fully voiced alveolar word internally. (In denoting the variable voicing, I follow the convention adopted in the sociolinguistic literature and enclose the feature in parentheses.)

(17)	$[_\phi\ [_\omega$	pusan-e] $[_\omega$	ka	ta]]	
UR:		ø	ø	ø	
AI:		[sg]	--	--	
VI:		--	(vc)	(vc)	
PR:	[	pusane	g̊a	da	]

Gloss: '(e) goes to Pusan'

CONCLUSION

This paper is a move towards better understanding the laryngeal behavior of the Korean lax stops, with special attention to their prosodically conditioned allophones. Under the assumption that phonological feature specifications should, to a great extent, mirror phonetic reality, it has been argued that the underlying inventory of Korean stops--lax, aspirated, and reinforced--can be accounted for in terms of two privative features: one for glottal width ([spread glottis]) and the other for "articulatory power" ([fortis]). Under such a system, lax stops are unmarked for laryngeal features; aspirated stops are marked [spread glottis, fortis]; and reinforced stops are marked [fortis]. In accounting for the observed allophony of the lax stops in each of three prosodic environments--phrase edge, word-edge, and word-internal--two rules are proposed. The first is a phonological rule that inserts [spread glottis] onto a bare laryngeal node at that left edge of a minor phrase (figure 15). The second is a phonetic rule that interpolates the feature [voice] through a laryngeally unmarked segment when it is flanked by two voiced segments (16).

In closing, I would note that while the Korean data appear to be successfully accounted for by the proposal developed here, it is also true that they would submit to alternative analyses. A framework adopted here, one in which the link between phonological features and phonetic realizations is assumed to be very direct, has received much scrutiny over the years and, in many cases, has been overcome by alternative programs that allow for a more abstract phonology. In such cases, however, it sometimes follows that the analyses account for only what is phonological in a language and do not cover allomorphy or phonetics. For example, in her work on laryngeal features, Lombardi (1991) deals primarily with phonological abstraction, leaving questions of phonetic detail unanswered. Keating (1984, 1988), however, has moved towards reconciling phonological abstraction with phonetic reality in terms of phonology-to-phonetics mapping algorithms. While these alternative analyses are not discussed here (cf. Silva forthcoming), they--as well as the type of the analysis presented herein--remain to be more fully explored in the context of prosodically conditioned allomorphy such as that exhibited by Korean.

REFERENCES

Cho, Young-Mee Yu. 1987. Phrasal Phonology of Korean. *Harvard Studies in Korean Linguistics* II, ed. by S. Kuno et al. Cambridge, MA: Harvard University, Department of Linguistics.

-----. 1990. Syntax and phrasing in Korean. *The Phonology-Syntax Connection*, ed. by S. Inkelas and D. Zec, 47-62. Chicago: University of Chicago Press.

Cohn, Abigail C. 1990. *Phonetic and Phonological Rules of Nasalization*. (UCLA Working Papers in Phonetics 76.)

Dart, Sarah N. 1987. An aerodynamic study of Korean stop consonants: Measurements and modeling. *JASA* S1, 1.138-147

Davis, Katharine. 1991. *Phonetic and Phonological Contrasts in the Acquisition of VOT*. Doctoral dissertation, Cornell University.

Halle, Morris and K. Stevens. 1971. A note on laryngeal features. *MIT Research Laboratory of Electronics Quarterly Progress Report* 101.198-213.

Han, Mieko S. and Raymond S. Weitzman. 1965. *Acoustic Characteristics of Korean Stop Consonants*. (Studies in the Phonology of Asian Languages III.) Acoustic Phonetics Research Laboratories, University of Southern California. Department of Naval Research Technical Report, NR 049-183, Nonr 228(28).

-----. 1967. *Acoustic Features in the Manner-Differentiation of Korean Stop Consonants*. (Studies in the Phonology of Asian Languages V.) Acoustic Phonetics Research Laboratories, University of Southern California. Department of Naval Research Technical Report, NR 049-183, Nonr 228(28).

-----. 1970. Acoustic features of Korean /P,T,K/, /p,t,k/ and /p^h,t^h,k^h/. *Phonetica* 2.112-128.

Jun, S-A. 1990. The prosodic structure of Korean--in terms of voicing. *ICKL 7: Papers from the Seventh International Conference on Korean Linguistics*, edited by E-J Baek. Seoul: International Circle of Korean Linguistics and Osaka University of Economics and Law.

Kang, O. 1990. A prosodic hierarchy analysis of aspiration and consonant mutation in Korean. *ICKL 7: Papers from the Seventh International Conference on Korean Linguistics*, edited by E-J Baek. Seoul: International Circle of Korean Linguistics and Osaka University of Economics and Law.

Keating, Patricia A. 1984. Phonetic and phonological representation of stop consonant voicing. *Language* 60, 2.286-319.

-----. 1988. The phonology-phonetics interface. *Linguistic Theory: Foundations* (Linguistics: The Cambridge Survey I), ed. by Frederick J. Newmeyer, 281-302. Cambridge, UK: Cambridge University Press.

Kim, Chin-Wu. 1965. On the autonomy of the tensity feature in stop classification. *Word* 21.339-359. (Reprinted in Kim C-W. 1988. *Sojourns on Language*. Seoul: Pagoda Publishing Co.)

Kim, Kee-Ho. 1987. *The Phonological Representation of Distinctive Features: Korean Consonantal Phonology*. Doctoral dissertation, University of Iowa. (Published by Hanshin Publishing Co., Seoul.)

Kim-Renaud, Young-Key. 1974. *Korean Consonantal Phonology*. Doctoral Dissertation, University of Hawaii.

Kohler, Klaus J. 1984. Phonetic explanation in phonology: the feature fortis/lenis. *Phonetica* 41.150-174.

Lee, C-H. 1955. *Practical Korean Grammar*. Seattle, WA: University of Washington Press.

Lombardi, Linda. 1991. *Laryngeal Features and Laryngeal Neutralization*. PhD Dissertation, University of Massachusetts at Amherst.

Martin, Samuel E. 1974. *Korean Reference Grammar*. Unpublished manuscript, Yale University.

McCawley, James. 1968. *The Phonological Component of a Grammar of Japanese*. The Hague: Mouton.

Nespor, Marina and Irene Vogel. 1986. *Prosodic Phonology*. Dordrecht: Foris Publications.

Ramstedt, G.J. 1939. *A Korean Grammar*. Helsinki: Suomalaisen Kirjallisuuden Seuran Kirjapainon Oy.

Selkirk, Elisabeth O. and Koichi Tateishi. 1988a. Syntax and phonological phrasing in Japanese. *Essays in Honor of S. Y. Kuroda*, ed. by C. Georgopoulos and R. Ishihara. Dordrecht: Reidel.

-------. 1988b. Constraints on minor phrase formation in Japanese. *Proceedings of CLS* 24, 316-336.

Silva, David J. forthcoming. *The Phonetics and Phonology of Lax Stop Voicing in Korean*. Doctoral dissertation, Cornell University.

--------. 1991. A prosody-based analysis of lax stop voicing in Korean. Paper presented at the Fourth Harvard Workshop on Korean Linguistics. (To appear in *Harvard Studies in Korean Linguistics* IV, ed. by S. Kuno et al. Cambridge, MA: Harvard University, Department of Linguistics.)

--------. 1990. A comparison of Korean and Japanese pitch-accent from a prosodic perspective. *Japanese/Korean Linguistics*, ed. by H. Hoji, 205-218.

--------. 1989. Korean obstruent voicing: Investigations into prosodic structuring. *Harvard Studies in Korean Linguistics* III, ed. by S. Kuno et al. Cambridge, MA: Harvard University, Department of Linguistics.

Sohn, H-S. 1987. *Underspecification in Korean Phonology*. PhD dissertation, University of Illinois.

Whitman, John. 1985. Korean Clusters. *Harvard Studies in Korean Linguistics*, ed. by S. Kuno et al. Cambridge, MA: Harvard University, Department of Linguistics.

Part III

Psycholinguistics and Language Acquisition

Conditionality and Deontic Modality in Japanese and Korean: Evidence from the Emergence of Conditionals

NORIKO AKATSUKA AND PATRICIA M. CLANCY
University of California at Los Angeles and University of California at Santa Barbara

1. Introduction

Conditional sentences have been a central concern in the study of reasoning in the fields of linguistics, psychology and philosophy. Under the influence of formal logic, conditional sentences have typically been analyzed in terms of the domain of truth and inference. Our research (Akatsuka 1985, 1986, 1991), on the other hand, has shown that natural language conditionals are also important devices for encoding the speaker's affect, with the relevant notions being the desirability/undesirability of the action, state or event in question, rather than the logician's notion of true vs. false. This view of conditionals, we believe, gives new insight into the use and function of natural language conditionals, and also sheds light on an interesting puzzle in language acquisition.

A consistent finding in acquisition research has been that conditional sentences emerge late in the course of development of complex sentences. Bowerman (1986), based on the available cross-linguistic data, concludes that children typically begin to produce explicitly marked conditional sentences in the second half of their third year. Reilly (1986) reports the appearance of conditionals as early as 2 1/2 years of age in English.

Conditionals also emerge late in the developmental sequence of complex sentence types Clancy, Jacobsen and Silva (1976), using data from English, Italian, German and Turkish, found that conditional sentences emerged after several other types of links between sentences, including coordination, antithesis, sequence and causality. In English, Bloom, Lahey, Hood, Lifter, and Fiess (1980) found that sentences with if were acquired at about 3 years of age, usually after sentences with the connectives and, and then, then, because and usually when.

One explanation that has been proposed for the lateness of conditionals is that they are beyond the conceptual grasp of very young children. Thus, for example, following Slobin's (1973) proposal that the emergence of semantic intentions exhibits a universal, cognitively-based order of development across languages, Clancy et al. (1976) concluded that the place of conditionality in the emergence of notions underlying conjunction has a cognitive basis.

In this light, certain acquisition findings from Japanese are rather startling. Children acquiring Japanese may begin to use conditional sentences even before 2 years of age; Okubo (1967), for example, has reported that her daughter's first conditionals appeared when she was only 1 year, 10 months old. Furthermore, Japanese conditionals may also emerge at an earlier stage in the course of development of complex sentences. Okubo (1967) and Clancy (1985) report that conditionals appear after the first conjunction -te, which means 'and, and then, and so', before the use of connectives such as kara 'because' and kedo 'but'. This early emergence of conditionals in Japanese, which we will confirm for Korean as well, raises the question of what it is that makes conditional sentences more accessible to very young children acquiring these languages.

In this paper, we discuss some preliminary findings from an ongoing pilot study of the acquisition of conditional sentences in Japanese and Korean. First, we consider the range of meanings expressed by conditional sentences in these two languages. Next, we turn to the frequency and functions served by the conditional sentences we found in our data and their order of emergence in the children's speech. Finally, we present a hypothetical sequence of development for conditionals in Japanese and Korean, based on our findings to date.

2. Conditionality and deontic modality

The key to the early emergence of conditionals in Japanese and Korean lies, we believe, in the range of meanings expressed by Japanese and Korean conditionals, which incorporates the semantic domain typically referred to as DEONTIC MODALITY, including notions expressed in English by modals, e.g. should, must and may. In Japanese and Korean, conditional sentences express these notions in the following form: **IF you do it, it's GOOD/BAD**. An interesting case, for example, is that of wishes/hopes, which in Japanese and Korean are usually expressed in the form of conditionals. While in English, speakers say, I hope/wish you can/could come, in Japanese and Korean conditional sentences such as the following are used:

(1) J: Anata mo ik-e- tara, ii n dakedo.
you also go can if good NOM[1] though
K: Ne to ka-l suiss-umyen, coh- ul theyntey.
you also go ATT can if good ATT though
(Lit.) 'If you can/could go, it will/would be good.' (='I hope you can go/I wish you could go.')

Suggestions and advice are also expressed in this way:

(2) Japanese: Koo shi-tara ii.
this way do if is good
Korean: Ilehkey ha-myen tway.
this way do if go well
(Lit.) 'If you do it this way, it is good.' (='You should do it this way.')

A final class of conditionals lacking English counterparts are permission/obligation conditionals:

(3) Japanese: Tabe- cha[2]/tara dame.
eat CON+TOP/if no good
Korean: Mek-umyen an-tway.
eat if NEG go well
(Lit.) 'If you eat it, it's no good'.
(='You may/must not eat it.')

Thus in Japanese and Korean, conditional sentences have been grammaticized as the typical way of expressing a range of notions in the semantic domain of deontic modality. The affective implications of this semantic domain, namely, the speaker's evaluation of the event or situation in question as good or bad, are encoded explicitly. In English, the

---

[1]The following abbreviations are used in this paper:

ATT	Attributive	NEG	Negative
COP	Copula	NOM	Nominalizer
CON	Connective	PRT	Pragmatic Particle
DIM	Diminutive	SUB	Subject Marker
NEC	Necessitative	TOP	Topic Marker

[2]In standard Japanese, -cha (the contracted form of the connective -te suffix plus the topic marker wa) is typically used in this construction. Kansai dialect does not have this form, and uses only the conditional -tara.

corresponding meanings are conveyed in other ways, usually by modals.

Turning to language acquisition, it is apparent that the range of meanings conveyed in Japanese and Korean by deontic conditionals is crucial in early caregiver-child interactions. Young children are expected to carry out adult wishes, they frequently need adult instructions and advice to carry out tasks successfully, they are not allowed to perform many activities without adult permission, and they are obliged to do what adults tell them to do. Motivated by the observation that deontic conditionals can be found quite early in Japanese acquisition (Clancy 1985), our research takes as its starting point the hypothesis that the clearly encoded affective nature of deontic conditionals in Japanese and Korean may facilitate their early mastery. Once Japanese and Korean children have acquired deontic conditionals, it may be easier for them to break into the full range of conditional meanings at an earlier stage than it is for children acquiring languages in which conditionals do not convey deontic modality.

3. Frequency, forms and functions of conditionals

Our data base consists of conversational interactions collected from three Japanese and two Korean children, who were tape-recorded with their caregivers, usually their mothers. Table 1 summarizes this data base, showing the language, gender and age (years;months) of each child, the number of sessions recorded, and the total number of conditional sentences produced by the child and his/her caregivers. These sentences include all of the children's conditionals, as well as all conditional sentences addressed to the children by members of their immediate families: father, mother, and siblings.

As Table 1 shows, conditional sentences were quite frequent in the speech addressed to the children, and were produced by four of the five children.

Language	Child	Age	Number of 1-hr. Sessions	Number of Cond.Sentences Adult	Child
Japanese	Y (m)	1;11-2;4	12	279	25
Japanese	M (f)	2;1 -2;3	3	89	8
Japanese	MK (m)	2;4 -2;5	2	32	0
Korean	H (f)	1;10-2;10	24	167	173
Korean	W (f)	1;8 -2;8	24	161	121

Table 1. Subjects and data.

Table 2 lists the forms of deontic conditionals we found in the data, along with one or more of the most frequent functions served by each form. The deontic conditionals in these caregiver-child interactions took the range of available grammatical forms in Japanese and Korean, and served a variety of pragmatic functions in the domain of deontic modality, including suggestions, imperatives, instructions on how to perform specific activities, permission seeking and granting, prohibition, and generic statements about socially appropriate behavior and physical reality. The first form in Table 2 consists of a single clause with the conditional suffix on the predicate; this form was used to make suggestions. The next three sets of forms have predicates expressing a positive evaluation in the second clause. In Japanese, this is the adjective ii 'is good', in Korean it is the verb toyta (inflected, tway) 'to become/be realized', in these constructions 'to go well/work out'. Deontic conditionals with positive evaluations in the second clause mean approximately 'If you do it, it's good', that is, 'You should/may/must do it', and 'If you don't do it, it's good', or 'You should/may/must not do it.'

The fifth set of forms in Table 2 includes deontic conditionals with negative evaluations in the second, consequent clause meaning 'unacceptable', 'unworkable', or 'impossible': dame/ikenai in Japanese, antway in Korean. These deontic conditionals mean approximately, 'If you do it, it's no good', that is, 'You shouldn't/mustn't do it', and are typically used to tell the addressee to stop doing what s/he is doing or about to do, and to make generic claims about what should not be done.

The final group of deontic conditionals in Table 2 is used to say what must be done. In Japanese, this is accomplished with the double negative construction naku-cha/ya ikenai 'If you don't do it, it's no good', from which the second clause is frequently omitted. In Korean, the necessitative (NEC) suffix -ya 'must' (Lee 1991:123), which has no Japanese counterpart, is used; again, the second clause is frequently omitted.

JAPANESE Forms	Functions	**KOREAN** Forms
V-tara/eba if	suggestion	V-(u)myen if
'If (you) do (it)?' (= 'Will you do it?')		
V-tara ii if good	suggestion imperative	V-(u)myen tway if go well
V-eba ii if good	instruction	
'If (you) do (it), (it) is good/all right.' (= 'You may/should/must do it.')		

Japanese	Function	Korean
V-te[3] ii	permission	V-e tway
CON good	instruction	CON go well
V-temo[4] ii	imperative	V-eto tway
even if good		even if go well
'Even if (you) do (it), (it) is good/all right.' (= 'You may/should do it.')		
V-naku-te ii	prohibition	
NEG CON good	instruction	
V-naku-temo ii	general rule	an-V-eto tway
NEG even if good		NEG even if go well
'Even if (you) don't do (it), (it) is good/all right.' (= 'You don't have to do it.')		
V-tara dame/ikenai		
if no good	prohibition	
V to dame/ikenai	instruction	V-(u)myen an-tway
if no good	refusal	if NEG go well
V-cha dame/ikenai	general rule	
CON+TOP no good		
'If (you) do (it), (it) is no good.' (= 'You shouldn't/mustn't do it.')		
V-naku-ya (dame/ikenai)	imperative	V-e-ya (tway)
NEG if no good	instruction	CON-NEC go well
V-naku-cha (dame/ikenai)	general rule	
NEG CON+TOP no good		
'If (you) do not do (it), (it) is no good.' (= 'You should/must do it.')		

Table 2. Forms and functions of deontic conditionals.

Table 3 presents the non-deontic conditionals in our data, along with some of their more frequent functions. These conditionals, which take a wide variety of predicates in the second clause, are commonly found in other languages; here we will call them TYPICAL CONDITIONALS.

---

[3]The connective (CON) suffix -te is the non-finite, linking form of the verb in Japanese; the Korean counterpart is -e (-a when the last vowel of the verb stem is o or a).

[4]In Japanese, -temo, the -te form of the verb plus mo 'also, even', is typically analysed as the concessive conditional; -eto is the Korean counterpart, with the connective form -e plus to 'also, even'. These forms are glossed 'even if' in this paper.

JAPANESE Forms		Functions	**KOREAN** Forms
V-tara			
if		warning	
V-naku-ya		instruction	
NEG if		explanation	
V(-nai) to	V(-nai)	threat	(an-)V-(u)myen (an-)V
NEG if		narrative	NEG if NEG
V(-nai) nara		prediction	
NEG if			
'If S1, S2.'			

Table 3. Typical conditionals.

Like deontic conditionals, the typical conditionals served a variety of functions, and were used for a number of affectively loaded speech acts, such as warnings and threats.

Both the range of conditional forms that appear in our data and their high frequency are quite different, we suspect, from what is to be found in the speech addressed to and produced by children who are only two years old acquiring languages that lack deontic conditionals. Table 4 gives the relative frequencies of deontic conditionals versus typical conditionals in the speech of the children and their caregivers.

	JAPANESE			KOREAN	
	Y	M	MK	H	W
Deontic					
Adult	.70 (195)	.75 (67)	.47 (15)	.74 (124)	.52 (83)
Child	.80 (20)	.75 (6)	-- (0)	.95 (164)	.39 (47)
Typical					
Adult	.30 (84)	.25 (22)	.53 (17)	.26 (43)	.48 (78)
Child	.20 (5)	.25 (2)	-- (0)	.05 (9)	.61 (74)

Table 4. Percentages of deontic and typical conditionals.

As Table 4 shows, the caregivers of Y, M and H produced a majority of deontic conditionals, and the children followed suit, producing 75-95% deontic conditionals. Two caregivers showed a different pattern: the mothers of MK and W had approximately equal ratios of deontic to typical conditionals. Although in his two recording sessions MK used no conditional sentences, W showed a surprising reversal of the usual frequencies, with the majority of her conditional sentences being typical rather than deontic conditionals.

4. Developmental sequences

To understand the place of deontic conditionals in the acquisition process, it is necessary to look at the actual sequence of development followed by each child. Tables 5-8 below give the developmental sequences in which conditionals were produced by the four children who used conditional sentences. On the left side, the child's age is given in years and months, followed by the first appearance of each new conditional form in Tables 2-3 that was produced by that child. Once a particular form appeared, it typically continued to occur in the following transcripts. To the right of the form is given the function of the first recorded usage, followed in parentheses by the major functions served by that form in later transcripts.

Table 5 presents the sequence in which conditional sentences emerged in the speech of the Japanese child for whom we have the most data, collected over a total of six months. As the table shows, Y's earliest conditional sentences were of the deontic type, as in example (4), with the predicate of the second clause being either dame 'no good' or ii 'good'. Conditionals with other predicates in the second clause did not begin to appear until two months later, and continued to be quite rare, while deontic conditionals were more frequent to the end of the recorded sequence of development. Example (5) is Y's first non-deontic conditional sentence, a concessive with -temo; he and his mother were imagining a big snowstorm, and Y said, Fut-temo daijoobu 'Even if (snow) falls, daijoobu', which here means 'safe, all right'. One month later, in example (6), Y produced his first typical conditional in which the second clause expressed a negative consequence, namely, the arrival of an ambulance or police car. Thus during this period in Y's speech, the forms -tara and -temo appeared in typical conditionals, following the emergence of deontic conditionals.

1;11	V-cha dame	general rule (prohibition, instruction, imperative)

(4) (Y and his mother are looking at a vase of flowers.)
Y: Koko wa koko wa tot- cha dame ne.
here TOP here TOP take CON+TOP no good PRT
'If you take from here, it's no good.'

2;1	V-te ii	permission (instruction)
	V-tara dame	instruction
	V-eba	suggestion, temporal[5]
	V-temo V	concessive

(5) (Y and his mother were talking about snow)
Y: Fut- temo daijoobu.
fall even if all right
'Even if (snow) falls, it's all right.'

2;2	V-tara V	general rule

(6) (Y looking at storybook with two deer fighting.)
Y: Kenka shi-tara, pipo pipo.
fight do if sound of siren
'If you fight, (a police car/ambulance will come.)'

2;4	V-temo ii	permission

Table 5. Japanese: Y's developmental sequence

Turning to the other Japanese child, M, again the earliest conditionals are deontic, as Table 6 shows. Example (7), M's first recorded conditional, is a permission-granting deontic with ii 'good' in the second clause. Two months later, after more deontic conditionals emerge, M produced her only typical conditional, the concessive in example (8). Although the data from this child are sparse, it is clear that she, like Y, began using deontic before typical conditionals.

2;1	V-te ii	permission

[5]In both Japanese and Korean, the conditional suffixes are also used to express temporality. Although we do not consider temporal uses here, Y and H each used the conditional suffix temporally once, in what may have been a fixed formula: oniichan nar-eba 'when I become older brother' (Y: 2;1) and khe-myen 'when I grow up' (H: 2;9). In both cases the consequent was that the child would be able to go to school. Only W used the conditional suffix productively for temporal meanings, beginning with khe-myen 'when I grow up' at 2;3, but soon moving on to other uses.

(7) (M and her mother are playing hostess/guest, and M is serving imaginary food.)
Mother: Kore tabe -te ii?
this eat CON good
'Is it all right if I eat this?'
Child: Tabe -te ii.
eat CON good
'It's all right if you eat it.'

2;1	V-tara	suggestion
2;3	V-temo ii	permission
	V-temo V	concessive

(8) (M tries to ride on a toy, which the Research Assistant fears will break.)
RA: Koware-nai kanaa, not-tara?
break not PRT ride if
'Won't it break, if you ride on it?'
M: Not- temo kowae-nai. (=kowarenai)
ride even if break not
'Even if I ride on it, it won't break.'

Table 6. Japanese: M's developmental sequence

Tables 7-8 present the developmental sequences for the two Korean children, for whom more detailed information is available, covering an entire year. As Table 7 shows, H followed the pattern familiar from the Japanese children. After two months in which she produced no conditionals, H began producing deontic conditionals with both positive and negative consequent clauses, using tway and antway, respectively, as in examples (9) and (10). The earliest functions of her deontic conditionals were prohibition, permission and suggestion; during the course of the year, H developed an extensive repertoire of deontic forms and functions. H's first conditional with a predicate other than toyta in the second clause (example 11) appeared only one month after the appearance of deontic conditionals, but was ungrammatical. H produced this sentence by copying the initial conditional clause from her mother's utterance, and then adding anhay 'I won't do it'. From then on, H made occasional attempts at typical conditionals, for example, repeating ones produced by the prior speaker, and using and misusing fixed formulaic expressions with -(u)myen. H's only typical conditional that was not formulaic, imitative or temporal was not comprehensible to her adult addressee. Thus throughout the year, H's use of typical conditionals remained marginal, and her data provide a clear case of early acquisition of deontic, compared with typical, conditionals.

1;10 --

2;0 V-(u)myen antway — prohibition, permission (general rule, instruction, refusal, imperative)

(9) (H is sitting on the table).
Ike anc-umyen an -tway.
this sit if NEG go well
'If you sit on this, it's no good.'

V-eya tway — suggestion (instruction, offer, demand, general rule, opinion, request, permission)

(10) (Her mother asked H to sing a song.)
Enni hay-ya tway.
older sister do NEC go well
'If sister does it, it's good.'

2;1 *V-(u)myen V promise (formulaic, temporal)

(11) (H brings some pieces of paper)
M: Ccic-umyen an-tway.
tear if NEG go well
'If you tear them, it's no good.'
H: *Ccic-umyen an-hay.
tear if NEG do
(Lit.) 'If I tear them, I won't do it.'
(= 'I won't tear them'.)

2;6 V-(u)myen tway — instruction (prohibition, general rule, opinion)
V-eto tway — permission, instruction, opinion

(12) (H is asking her father where to put her cup.)
Yeki nwa- nwa-to tway?
here put leave even if go well
'If I put it here, is it all right?'

2;8 an-V-eto tway — prohibition, refusal

2;9 V-eya — instruction, imperative, general rule (suggestion)
V-e antway — general rule
V-(u)myen — suggestion, imperative (instruction)

Table 7. Korean: H's developmental sequence

As noted above, only one child in our sample who produced conditionals was exposed to equal frequencies of deontic and typical conditionals, the Korean child W. Table 8 presents the sequence of development followed by this child.

1;8 --
2;0 V-(u)myen antway — instruction (permission, prohibition)
V-(u)myen V — general rule (warning, prediction, request, hypothetical, instruction, imperative, temporal, criticism, explanation, threat)

(13) (W has been trying to make a toy ship stand up, and her mother goes to get a basin of water.)
M: Ike mwul eyta twu-myen ttuntay.
this water in put if floats
'If you put it in water, it floats.'
W: Mwul ey twu-myen,
water in put if
'If you put it in water,'
RA: Ung.
yes
'Uh-huh.'
W: ike neme-ka.
this fall go
'this will fall over.'

2;1 V-eya — instruction
V-eya tway — warning (instruction, opinion, necessity, imperative)
V-(u)myen V

(14) (W is jumping off a chair.)
Ilehkey ha-myen W-i ka tachye-cye.
like this do if W DIM SUB hurt become
'If I do this, I'll get hurt'.

2;3 V-(u)myen V — temporal
V-(u)myen tway — permission (instruction)
2;4 V-eto tway — opinion (permission)
2;6 V-(u)myen — instruction

Table 8. Korean: W's developmental sequence.

As Table 8 shows, like H, W produced no conditionals until she was 2 years old. Then she produced both deontic conditionals with antway and her first typical conditionals, including example (13). Starting in the next month, at 2;1 years, W began producing typical conditional sentences in a single utterance, as in example (14). For 7 months, W used deontic and typical conditionals with equal frequency, but by the last two months of the study, more the 75% of her conditionals were typical conditionals. Thus the pattern of development for W is simultaneous emergence of deontic and typical conditionals.

5. A hypothetical sequence of development

Returning now to our original hypothesis, our data do provide support for the idea that deontic conditionals in Japanese and Korean are often the starting point for the acquisition of conditionality. Three of the four children clearly began by producing deontic conditionals, in which a state or action is characterized as good/bad, before moving on to other types of consequent clauses. No child acquired typical conditionals first, and only one child, W, showed simultaneous emergence of the two types of conditionals. Based on the data available so far, we propose the following preliminary interpretation of conditional acquisition in Japanese and Korean.

First, the child learns the words that appear in the consequent clause of deontic conditionals: in Japanese, ii 'good' and dame 'bad', in Korean tway and antway. On this foundation, the child then begins to understand adult conditionals expressing deontic modality, in which the description of a situation or action is given with a conditional inflection on the verb, followed by the familiar evaluative term. The fact that caregivers frequently use deontic conditionals in situations in which the child is not actually performing the action in question conveys the hypotheticality of the action and the contingency of the positive or negative evaluation that it would evoke. And since many of the deontic conditionals involve general rules concerning approved and disapproved behavior, the strong implication of genericity is also present. Thus the conceptual foundations of conditionality are inherent in these early deontic conditionals.

In the next stage, the crucial link between deontic and typical conditionals occurs, as the child realizes that the terms 'good' and 'bad' can be replaced in the conditional construction by predicates that refer to specific consequences that are good or bad. This link is facilitated by the fact that even typical conditionals as they are used in adult-child discourse generally have an affective base, in that the content of the consequent clause is underlyingly either desirable or undesirable from the perspective of the speaker. For example, returning to example (5) in Y's developmental sequence (Table 4), Fut-temo daijoobu 'Even if (snow) falls, it's all right', it is clear that the form daijoobu, although not grammaticized in the conditional construction like ii 'good', conveys a very similar positive evaluation, although it is more specific, here implying safe and secure. And in example (6), the consequent pipo pipo (sound of siren) can be seen as replacing the original dame 'bad' with a specific negative outcome, rather than merely a general negative evaluation. In fact, in all the above examples, the consequent clause is either good (e.g. having one's toy intact in (8), having a toy boat float successfully in (13), or else is bad (as in needing an ambulance or police car in example (6) or getting hurt in (14). This affective link between the simpler, overtly affective deontic conditionals and the less obviously affective typical conditionals may provide a crucial developmental connection between the two types of conditionals.

The child's recognition of this link is probably facilitated by the nature of the discourse contexts in which deontic and typical conditionals occur. The examples given in (15) below demonstrate this relationship between the two types of conditionals in discourse.

(15) J: (M at 2;2 is instructed by her mother on how to strike a toy hammer and ring game)
Mo sukoshi ushiro ika-nak -ya dame yo.
even a little back go NEG if no good PRT
Yari-nikui deshoo.
do hard COP:presumptive
(Lit.) 'If you don't go a little farther back, it's no good. It will be hard to do.'

K: (H at 2;0 is playing with her doll, and has covered the doll's face with a blanket; her mother corrects her.)
Baby elkwul ha-myen an-tway. Elkwul ha-myen
baby face do if NEG go well face do if
swum i makhi-canha.
breath SUB be stopped-tag
(Lit.) 'If you do the baby's face, it doesn't work. If you do her face, she'll suffocate.'

In these examples, the adult first gives a deontic conditional, then follows it with a specification of why the action in question has just been evaluated negatively. Thus the child is exposed to typical conditionals in a way that highlights their semantic and structural relationship with deontic conditionals.

For children like W, who are exposed frequently to both types of conditionals in their caregivers' speech, establishing this link may take place extremely quickly, so that the two types of conditionals appear simultaneously in production. Probably it is more common for a couple of months to elapse (as with the Japanese children Y and M) before typical conditionals appear. The Korean child H, who did not actually seem to master typical conditionals during the year, may be an extreme case, perhaps reflecting the continuing low frequency of typical conditionals in her input.

6. Conclusions

In conclusion, the acquisition data we have examined thus far provides support for our hypothesis that conditionals expressing deontic modality are developmentally prior in Japanese and Korean, and may help facilitate the early acquisition of typical conditionals. Deontic conditionals are extremely frequent and emotionally charged, occurring in the crucial speech acts of permission, prohibition, instructions, and imperatives. They are also apparently cognitively accessible; the contingent relationship between positive/negative evaluations and approved/disapproved behaviors is surely well within the grasp of children at 2 years of age.

In fact, Bowerman (1986) has argued quite convincingly, based on data from English and other languages, that children show a grasp of the notions involved in conditionality long before the appearance of the first conditionals in languages that exhibit late conditional acquisition. In her data Bowerman found a variety of linguistic means used to express causal contingency, hypotheticality, genericity and inferential reasoning at or before 2 years of age. For example, sentences such as I wish me have an airplane successfully express hypotheticality, while utterances like Hold a handle, puppy go wuff-wuff (in describing a toy) effectively convey causal contingency. Thus there is independent reason to believe that conditionality per se is not beyond the cognitive capacity of very young children.

The combination of high input frequency, clearly encoded affective meaning, and cognitive accessibility found in Japanese and Korean deontic conditionals may be responsible for the precocious emergence of conditional sentences in these languages. The grammaticization of crucial speech acts such as probitions and instructions in deontic conditionals in these languages, we hypothesize, provides Japanese and Korean children with the basis for analyzing and acquiring typical conditionals at an earlier stage than children learning languages in which conditionals do not express deontic modality. Clearly, much further research on a larger sample of Japanese and Korean children, as well as a comparative analysis of conditional data from a language such as English, is necessary to determine the generality of the hypothetical developmental sequence presented here and the validity of our interpretation of it. This research is currently in progress.

Our findings thus far, however, already provide support for our larger claim that many instances of natural language conditionals belong to the domain of affect rather than logic, and rest on the notions of desirable/undesirable rather than true/false. In the use of conditional sentences to express deontic modality, Japanese and Korean clearly demonstrate that natural language conditionals are important devices for encoding the speaker's affect. By highlighting the affective nature of conditional sentences, Japanese and Korean not only provide linguists with valuable evidence for a fuller understanding of conditionality, but also provide acquisition researchers with the opportunity to observe the true potential of young children to acquire conditionality at a very early age.

References

Akatsuka, N. 1985. Conditionals and epistemic scale. Language 61. 625-39.

Akatsuka, N. 1986. Conditionals are discourse-bound. On conditionals, ed. by E.C. Traugott, A. ter Meulen, J.S. Reilly, and C.A. Ferguson, 333-372. New York: Cambridge University Press.

Akatsuka, N. 1991. Affect and Japanese conditionals. Asian discourse and grammar (Santa Barbara Papers in Linguistics, Vol. 3), ed. by P. Clancy and S. Thompson, 1-8.

Bowerman, M. 1986. First steps in acquiring conditionals. On conditionals.

Bloom, L., Lahey, M., Hood, L., Lifter, K. & Fiess, K. 1980. Complex sentences: acquisition of syntactic connectives and the semantic relations they encode. Journal of Child Language 7.235-61.

Clancy, P.M. 1985. The acquisition of Japanese. The crosslinguistic study of language acquisition: Vol. 1 The data, ed. by D.I. Slobin, 373-524. Hillsdale, NJ: Erlbaum.

Clancy, P.M., Jacobsen, T., & Silva, M. 1976. The acquisition of conjunction: a cross-linguistic study. Papers and Reports in Child Language Development (Stanford University) 12.71-80.

Lee, Hyo-Sang. 1991. Tense, aspect and modality: A discourse-pragmatic analysis of verbal affixes in Korean from a typological perspective. Unpublished doctoral dissertation, UCLA.

Okubo, A. 1967. Yooji gengo no hattatsu. Tokyo: Tokyodoo, 1967.

Reilly, J.S. 1986. The acquisition of temporals and conditionals. On conditionals.

Slobin, D.I. 1973. Cognitive prerequisites for the development of grammar. In C.A. Ferguson & D.I. Slobin (eds.), Studies of child language development, 175-208. New York: Holt, Rinehart & Winston.

Word Order vs. Word Class: Portmanteau Sentences in Bilinguals

SHOJI AZUMA
University of Utah

1. Introduction

In bilingual speech communities, it is often observed that bilingual speakers spontaneously alternate two languages, that is, they switch linguistic codes or perform so-called code-switching. If the switch from one language to the other occurs between sentences, it is called intersentential code-switching. If the switch occurs within a sentence, it is called intrasentential code-switching. Observe the following Spanish/English inter- and intra-sentential code-switching examples:

(1) Intersentential code-switching
The three old ones spoke nothing but Spanish.
Nothing but Spanish.
No hablaban ingles .
not speak 3 PL IMPF English
' . . . They did not speak English.' (Gumperz 1982)

(2) Intrasentential code-switching
No van a *bring it up in the meeting* .
not are going to
'They're not going to bring it up in the meeting.'
(Pfaff 1979)

Weinreich (1955: 73) states that bilinguals fluent in both languages switch intersententially, not intrasententially.

> The ideal bilingual switches from one language to the other according to appropriate changes in the speech situation (interlocutors, topics, etc.), but not in an unchanged speech situation, and certainly not within a single sentence. (emphasis added)

However, contrary to Weinreich's observation, it is well attested that fluent bilinguals switch intrasententially as well, and it is a laymen's mistake to regard code-switching, especially intrasentential code-switching, as a sign of deficiency in one of the two languages (Poplack 1980, Appel and Muysken 1987). It is interesting to note that Weinreich's attitude still exists among those who believe that intrasentential code-switching is something that should be avoided (Milroy 1987). In reality, intrasentential code-switching requires a large degree of linguistic competence in both languages. Poplack (1980: 615) states, 'precisely those switch types which have traditionally been considered most deviant by investigators and educators, those which occur within a single sentence, are the ones which require the most skill.'

Traditionally, there have been two areas of focus regarding code-switching research. The first area includes socio and psychological views that bilingual speakers gain a conversational effect by code-switching. This area of research has produced sociolinguistic notions such as 'they-code' vs. 'we-code' in Gumperz (1982) or 'marked' vs. 'unmarked' switching in Scotton (1983).

The second area of research includes purely linguistic notions such as linguistic constraints that limit switching patterns. The view of most linguists in this area of research is that code-switching, especially intrasentential code-switching, is not a random alternation of two languages, but a systematic rule-governed speech behavior (but see Lance 1975 for a contrary position). If this is the case, there might be cross-linguistically valid constraints on code-switching. Despite the efforts made by many researchers, currently this view remains unpersuasive as represented by the following statement made by Bokamba (1987: 48).

> The postulation of syntactic constraints, regardless of the scope of their validity (e.g., language-specific or putative universal), is not only misguided but also unwanted at this stage of the research.

This paper argues that purely linguistic constraints on intrasentential code-switching deserves continued scholarly investigation. Specifically, I will argue that a linguistic constraint based on word class distinction (i.e., open vs. closed class) exists. I will present portmanteau sentences from Japanese/English as evidence for the word class constraint. Portmanteau sentences exhibit an interesting type of intrasentential switching; a constituent in one language is used as an intrasentential bridge to the other language.

The paper is organized as follows: Section 2 discusses the equivalence of structure constraint (Poplack 1980) which is based on the word order difference between two languages. Numerous counter-examples to the constraint will be presented. Section 3 introduces the word class as the pivotal notion in searching for a linguistic constraint. Section 4 demonstrates, by using portmanteau sentences, that the word class, not the word order, is indeed the relevant notion. Finally, section 5 suggests that studies on code-switching can offer interesting implications for understanding natural language processing.

2. Word order: equivalence constraint

In an effort to find linguistic constraints in intrasentential code-switching, researchers have noted that the relative word order of the two languages involved has something to do with a constraint.[1] This view was formulated by Poplack (1980: 586) as the equivalence of structure constraint:

> Code-switching tends to occur at a point in discourse where juxtaposition of L1 and L2 elements does not violate a syntactic rule of either language, i.e., at points around which the surface structures of the two languages map onto each other.

Figure 1 illustrates where possible switching may occur according to the equivalence constraint.

Figure 1.

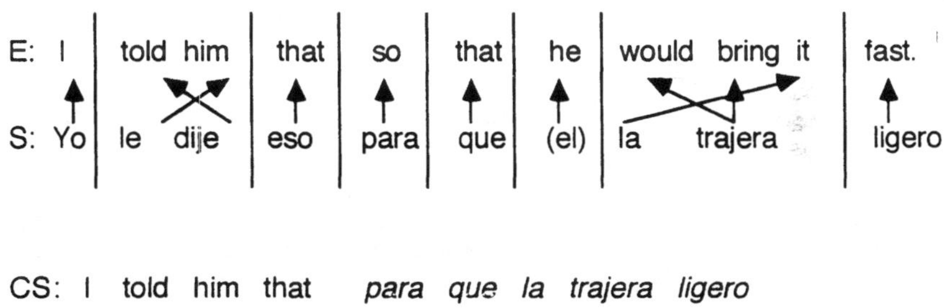

In Figure 1, the equivalence constraint predicts that a switch could occur at any syntactic boundary represented by columns. Switching is facilitated by the fact that the two languages share the relative order of their constituents. For example, English *that* and *so* occupy the same slots as their Spanish counterparts *eso* and *pa ra* respectively, thus the syntactic boundary between *that* and *so* can be a switching site. Indeed such a switch was reported in natural speech as the sentence in Figure 1 illustrates. If the relative word order is not shared by the two languages, the equivalence constraint predicts that no switching will occur. For example, in Spanish a pronominal object precedes a verb whereas in English an object follows a verb. Thus, no switching would occur between a verb and a pronominal object. Switching patterns in (3) have never been reported in natural speech.

(3)
  (a) * dije *him*

  (b) * told *le*

Although the equivalence constraint seems persuasive, its formulation was based solely on Spanish/English, syntactically similar languages. If the equivalence constraint is to be universal, it must be rigorously tested using various language pairs. To date, studies on syntactically divergent language pairs suggest that the equivalence constraint does not hold true (Bentahila and Davies 1983, Nishimura 1985, Berk-Seligson 1986). Observe the following examples from Japanese/English code-switching data.

(4) All over the place *datta* *no yo*
were TAG
'(They) were all over the place, you know.'
(Nishimura 1985)

(5) But she's not going for grade or anything, she is our age

dakara
because
'But she's not going for grade or anything because she is our age.' (Azuma 1991)

In (4) the verb *datta* 'were' terminates the sentence while its counterpart *were* does not terminate the sentence. In other words, the relative word order is not shared by the two languages, yet the switching in (4) is reported. The switching example in (5) also illustrates the violation of the equivalence constraint. In Japanese the subordinate conjunction *dakara* closes the conjoined clause in Japanese, whereas it always initiates the conjoined clause in English. Thus, the word order is not shared by the two languages. The equivalence constraint wrongly predicts no switching.

Japanese/English is not the only language pair that violates the equivalence constraint; examples are abundant in other language pairs as well. Observe the following sentences.

(6) Marathi/English
kahi *chairs* war
some on
"on some chairs" (Joshi 1985)

(7) Hebrew/English
Salesmen *dynamiyim* can make a lot of money
dynamic
"Dynamic salesmen can make a lot of money."
(Doron 1983)

(8) French/Arabic
c°est le seul *ustard*
it is the only teacher
"it is the only teacher." (Bentahila & Davies 1983)

In (6), Marathi has a postnominal adjective, whereas English has a prenominal adjective. The relative word order inside such a noun phrase is not shared, yet switching occurs as (6) illustrates. The Hebrew/English example in (7) as well as the French/Arabic example in (8) exhibit the same situation. The relative word order is not shared, yet switching occurs. The equivalence constraint wrongly predicts no switching in such cases.

An examination of the equivalence constraint as demonstrated in (6)-(8) suggests that the constraint is not cross-linguistically valid.[2] In the next section, I will argue that a constraint exists as to the nature of the switched item itself, rather than the item's relative linear location.

3. Word class

Several linguists have suggested the relevance of word class in investigating linguistic constraints on code-switching. For example, in his study of Marathi/English code-switching, Joshi (1985) observed that all code-switched items were open class, and that closed class items did not switch. Similar observations were made by Hasselmo (1980) (Swedish/English), Kamwangamalu (1989) (Bantu languages/French), and Petersen (1989) (Danish/English). Observe the following Japanese/English examples in (9)-(10) in which switched items are in the open class, but not the closed class.

(9) Japanese/English
Midori nanka *move*-shinakute yokatta
-do NEG
"Midori didn't have to move." (Nishimura 1985)

(10) Japanese/English
Boston ni *hit*-shita toki ga
to -do PAST time NOM
"The time when (we) hit Boston..." (Nishimura 1985)

In (9) and (10), the Japanese helping verb *suru* 'do' can create a new verb with a noun from another language. The helping verb carries information such as tense and aspect. Note that the switched item is a noun which is a open class item. Closed class items such as a tense morpheme never switch into the other language. Marathi, which also has a helping verb, exhibits a similar switching pattern. Observe the Marathi/English example in (11).

(11) Marathi/English
Mula khurcya *paint*-kartat.
boys chairs -do (+TENSE)
'Boys painted the chair.' (Joshi 1985)

The switched item *paint* is an open class item and there is no switching of a closed class item. Next, observe the English/German example in (12).

(12) English/German
They are *stimm*-ing.
tune
'They are tuning (instruments).' (Leopold 1954)

The switched word *stimm* 'tune' is a verb stem, which is an open class item. Interestingly, the progressive closed class morpheme *ing* is not switched along with *stimm* and it stays in English. Next observe the Korean/English example in (13).

(13) Korean/English
Second group-ul ceyil cohahay
-ACC best like
'I like second group best.' (Park, et al. 1989)

The open class item *second group* is switched into English, but the case marker *ul*, which is a closed class item, stays in Korean. Next observe the Hebrew/Spanish example in (14).

(14) Hebrew/Spanish
Ze lo maanyen oti a*konsezas* haele.
'That's not interesting to me, those folktales.' [gloss not available]
(Berk-Seligson 1986)

All of the above examples from various language pairs support the validity of the following claim: open class items participate in switching, but closed class items do not. This claim can be called the 'word class constraint.'

Given that the equivalence constraint is not applicable cross-linguistically, the word class constraint emerges as a possible universal constraint on code-switching. However, caution is necessary. Although examples violating the equivalence constraint are abundant in the literature, as illustrated in section 2, the word class constraint examples in (9)-(14) do not discount the equivalence constraint. The equivalence constraint correctly predicts the examples in (9)-(14) as acceptable, just as the word class constraint does. Because all switching instances in (9)-(14) are at the sites where two languages have the same word order, either constraint predicts the switching as acceptable. In order to prove the claim that the word class, not the word order, is the vital notion, we need test sentences where the two notions give us different predictions. In the next section, I will introduce test sentences, namely portmanteau sentences, and argue for the word class constraint.

4. Word class vs. word order: portmanteau sentences

A portmanteau sentence is a sentence which has a hybrid structure from two sentences in different languages. In this type of sentence, a constituent in one language is shared as a constituent in another language. Observe the following portmanteau sentence.

(15) If it goes three rounds *datta ra ne.*
was if TAG
'if it goes three rounds.'

The speaker started her sentence with the English word order (Conj. + V), then suddenly switched into Japanese word order (V + Conj.), incorporating the English noun phrase 'three rounds' into the following Japanese syntax. In other words, one shared constituent 'three rounds' was used as a bridge from English to Japanese. Schematic illustration of the portmanteau sentence in (15) is found in Figure 2.

Figure 2 Portmanteau sentence:
Compare (15). The underlined part is shared by the two languages.

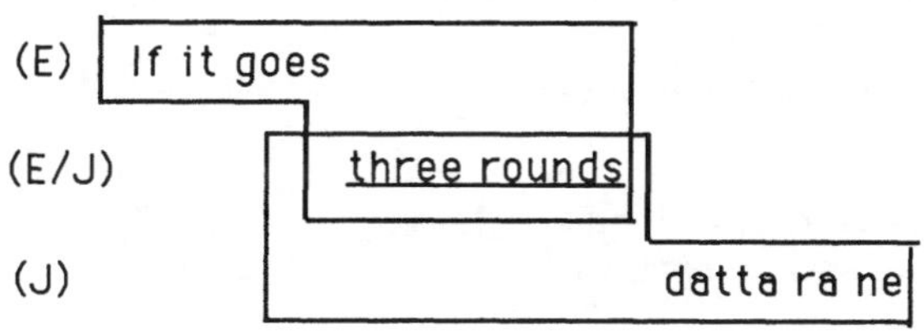

Although this type of hybrid sentence does not occur with high frequency, it is a fairly common type of switching in natural speech. Observe the following examples from Nishimura (1985).

(16) You pull this much *tsukau desho.*
use will

(17) There 's children *iru* *yo.*
exist TAG

(18) We bought two pounds *gurai* *kattekita* *no*
about bought TAG
(Nishimura 1985)

In (16), an English sentence *you pull this much* is followed by a Japanese sentence *tsukau desho*, using *this much* as a shared element. This is possible because English has V+O order while Japanese has O+V order. In (17), the English sentence is followed by the Japanese sentence incorporating the English word *children* as a member of the Japanese sentence. Neither grammar of the two languages is violated. In (18), again, the English sentence is followed by the Japanese sentence incorporating *two pounds* as a member of the Japanese sentence. This is possible because Japanese has a postposition such as *gurai*, which follows a noun phrase in a prepositional phrase.

All portmanteau sentences, as in (15)-(18), share common characteristics. First, all of them take advantage of the relative word order difference in two languages. That is, a switch occurs where the word order is different (e.g., postposition vs preposition). Second, and more interestingly, the bridge, the element shared by the two languages, is always an open class item (mostly noun/nominal). In other words, there are no reports of portmanteau sentences employing a closed class item as a bridge, although this is logically possible. This nature of the portmanteau sentence gives us a test base for deciding whether the word order or word class is relevant in code-switching. If the word class constraint were not a relevant notion, then we would expect closed class items just as open class items to serve as a bridge in portmanteau sentences. For example, a postposition in Japanese could logically serve as a bridge for switching into English because the postposition could be used as a preposition in English. The same logic pertains to complementizers, which appear at the end of subordinate clauses in Japanese while they are a pre-clausal element in English. The situation is similar with respect to subordinating conjunctions. Observe the invented examples in (19)-(22), which are all judged unacceptable by my informants.

(19) * Kinoo tomodachi kara *my friend I heard the news.*
yesterday friend from
'Yesterday from my friend I heard the news.'

(20) * Uchi no yatsu to *my wife I went to see the movie.*
house GEN person with
'With my wife I went to see the movie.'

(21) * Sensoo ga owatta to *war was over is true.*
war NOM over COMP
'That war was over is true.'

(22) * Aitsu ga kuru nara *he comes I won't go.*
he NOM come if
'If he comes I won't go.'

In (19) and (20), the prepositions *kara* 'from' and *to* 'with' serve as the bridge from Japanese to English, and their positions are appropriate within both the Japanese and English parts. Likewise in (21), the complementizer *to* 'that' serves as the bridge, and its position is appropriate in both the Japanese and English segments. In (22), the subordinate conjunction *nara* 'if' is the bridge, and its position is appropriate for both the Japanese and English sections. Yet, examples such as (19)-(22) have neither been attested in natural speech data nor judged as acceptable by bilingual informants.

To summarize, portmanteau sentences such as (15)-(18), in which open class items serve as the shared bridge between two languages, are attested in natural speech. In contrast, examples such as (19)-(22), in which closed class items serve as the shared bridge, are neither attested nor judged grammatical when constructed. These facts strongly suggest that the relevant notion regarding code-switching is the word class rather than the word order. In the following section, I will discuss what this conclusion implies in our natural language processing.

5. Implication of the word class constraint

The dichotomy of open vs. closed class items has been a longstanding issue in various fields of linguistics. For example, language acquisition studies show that children acquire open class items before function words. Brown (1973) describes the very early stage of children's speech as 'telegraphic' in which open class items appear frequently, but not closed class items. Research on aphasia suggests that Broca's apahsics show difficulty in processing closed class items but not open class items (e.g. Zurif 1980). Speech error studies show that open class items participate in errors but not closed class items in so-called 'morpheme stranding errors' (e.g. Garrett 1975).

These speech performance data including the present code-switching study suggest that there are different modes of lexical organization for open and closed class items. Open class items are stored and accessed distinctively from closed class items. More specifically, there may be two stages in speech processing; the frame stage where closed class items are activated and the content stage where open class items are activated. In this two stage processing model, a possible procedure for generating portmanteau sentences can be described as follows. Speakers build a syntactic frame first. After building the frame, the content stage follows where open class items are inserted into the frame. During the utterance of a sentence in L1, when speakers reach a content word, which can also serve as a content word in L2, speakers can build a frame in L2. In the new L2 frame, the content word from L1 can legitimately be inserted. Speakers can continue working on the L2 frame until the end of the utterance. In this way, a portmanteau sentence is generated. On the other hand, closed class items could not play the same role as open class items because closed class items are intrinsic members of the frame. If speakers began to build a new L2 frame during their initial L1 utterance, they could do so, but they would have to use closed class items from L2, not L1. As a result, the invented examples in (19)-(22) can be improved to the point of acceptability by repeating the L1 closed class bridge in L2, thus building the switched portions' frame entirely with L2 function words. Such sentences are no longer portmanteau. For example, observe (23), which is an improved version of (22).

(23) Aitsu ga kuru nara *if he comes I won't go.*
he NOM come if
'If he comes I won't go.'

This line of analysis would suggest that verbs can not serve as bridges for switching in portmanteau sentences if accompanied by closed class morphemes, such as inflections. Indeed, this prediction is borne out. In Japanese/English code-switching, I did not find any portmanteau sentences of this type (see also Nishimura 1985). In Japanese/English code-switching, only Japanese nouns serve as bridges -- never verbs.

An outstanding characteristic of portmanteau sentences, that is, that open class but not closed class items may serve as bridges for switching, not only lends support to the word class constraint on code-switching, but sheds new light on our understanding of natural language processing.

Notes:

1. The free morpheme constraint (Poplack 1980), claimed to be universal, was excluded from this paper. For the discussion of the free morpheme constraint, see Azuma (1990, 1991).

2. Despite the amounting evidence against the equivalence constraint, Poplack and her associates (Sankoff, Poplack, and Vanniarajan 1990) stand by their constraint. Their notion of 'nonce loan' is not clearly defined, thus it is difficult to make a fair assessment of their claim. For further discussion, see Eliasson (1990).and Myers-Scotton (1990).

References:

Appel, Rene, and Peter Muysken. 1987. Language contact and bilingualism. London: Edward Arnold.

Azuma, Shoji. 1990. Frame-content hypothesis and code-switching. Eibungaku 66. 25-34. Waseda University, Tokyo.

__________. 1991. Processing and intrasentential code-switching. Doctoral dissertation. University of Texas at Austin.

Bentahila, Abdelali, and Eirlys Davies. 1983. The syntax of Arabic-French code-switching. Lingua 59. 301-30.

Berk-Seligson, Susan. 1986. Linguistic constraint on intrasentential code-switching: a study of Spanish/ Hebrew bilingualism. Language in Society 15. 313-48.

Bokamba, Eyamba. 1987. Are there syntactic constraints on code-mixing? Variation in Language: NWAV-XV at Stanford, ed. by K. Denning, S. Inkelas, F. McNair-Knox, and J. Rickford. Departmen of Linguistics. Stanford University.

Doron, Edit. 1983. On a formal model of code-switching. University of Texas Linguistic Forum 22. 35-59.

Eliasson, Stig. 1989. English-Maori language contact: code-switching and the free-morpheme constraint. Reports from Uppsala University Department of Linguistics 18. 1-28.

Garrett, Merrill. 1975. The analysis of sentence production. The psychology of learning and motivation, ed. by Gordon Bower. New York: Academic Press.

Gumperz, John. 1982. Conversational code-switching. Discourse strategies, ed. by John Gumperz. New York: Cambridge University Press.

Hasselmo, Nils. 1980. Some problems in immigrant bilingualism: quantitative and qualitative constraints. Journal of Intercultural Studies 15-29.

Joshi, Aravind. 1985. Processing of sentences with intrasentential code switching. Natural Language parsing, ed. by David. Dowty, Lauri Karttunen, and Arnold Zwicky, 190-205. New York: Cambridge University Press.

Kamangamalu, Nkonko. 1989. Some morphosyntactic aspects of French/English-Bantu code-mixing: evidence for universal constraints. CLS 25. 157-70.

Leopold, William. 1954. A child's learning of two languages. Fifth Annual Georgetown University Round Table on Language and Linguistics. Washington, DC: Georgetown University Press.

Milroy, Lesley. 1987. Observing and analyzing natural language. Oxford: Basil Blackwell.

Myers-Scotton, Carol. 1990. Accounting for structure in Swahili/English codeswitching. Working papers in Kiswahili 9. State University of Gent.

Nishimura, Miwa. 1985. Intrasentential codeswitching in Japanese and English. Doctoral dissertation. University of Pennsylvania.

Park, Jun-Eon, Rudolph C. Troike, and Park Mun. 1989. A preliminary study of constraints in Korean-English Code-switching. Paper presented at UCLA Second Language Research Forum.

Petersen, Jenifer. 1988. Word-internal code-switching constraints in a bilingual child's grammar. Linguistics 26, 479-493.

Pfaff, Carol. 1979. Constraint on language mixing: intrasentential code-switching and borrowing in Spanish/English. Language 55. 291-316.

Poplack, Shana. 1980. 'Sometimes I'll start a sentence in Spanish *y termino en espanol*': toward a typology of code-switching. Linguistics 18. 581-618.

Sankoff, David, Shana Poplack, and Swathi Vanniarajan. 1990. The case of the nonce loan in Tamil. Language Variation and Change 2. 71-101.

Scotton, Carol. 1983. The negotiation of identities in conversation: a theory of markedness and code choice. International Journal of the Sociology of Language 44. 115-36.

Weinreich, Urel. 1955. Language in contact. The Hague: Mouton.

Zurif, Edgar. 1980. Language mechanisms: a neuropsychological perspective. American Scientist 68. 305-12.

Development of Locative Case Markers in Korean

SOONJA CHOI

In the last few decades, research of language acquisition has focused on discovering rules of children's grammar, and the extent to which the rules are innate or learned. In the 60's, influenced by Chomsky's work on syntax, researchers' endeavors have been to determine innate syntactic rules in young children. Indeed, studies on the syntactic development of negation and question in English showed strong support for Chomsky's transformational grammar (1965) as an explanation for children's syntactic development (Bellugi 1967, Brown & Bellugi 1964). However, in the early 70's, as researchers began to conduct cross-linguistic comparisons, arguments for innate syntactic structure as the sole explanation for children's language development became less convincing. In particular, Bowerman's cross-linguistic study (1973) of the development of syntax in English- and Finnish-speaking children showed little evidence for a universal innate syntactic structure. Instead, Bowerman's data showed considerable semantic similarities in the children's grammars. For example, children across languages express similar semantic concepts such as agent, object, and action in their grammars. In part as an alternative to Chomskian proposals, Bowerman (1973), therefore, suggested that the basic mechanisms for learning the grammar of a language were universal semantic concepts rather than innate syntactic rules.

As language acquisition research developed toward understanding its semantic bases, researchers paid much attention to Piaget's work (1954) on children's cognitive development. According to Piaget, a critical foundation for language learning is laid during the sensorimotor period of development, as children build up an understanding of such basic notions as object permanence, agency and causality, and spatial relations. In line with this view, theorists of language acquisition have hypothesized that the human cognitive/perceptual apparatus both universally shapes language structure and guides language acquisition (Clark 1977, Johnston & Slobin 1979). At the same period, Slobin's (1973) extensive cross-linguistic studies on the acquisition of morphology suggested universal cognitive operating principles as mechanisms for learning a language: Children use a set of cognitively-driven operating principles (e.g., Pay attention to the end of words.) in acquiring the relations between meaning and form.

The emphasis on discovery of semantic universals lead to several cross-linguistic investigations of language acquisition in the 80's, and recent studies have proposed specific claims about how language acquisition takes place from this perspective. This paper will be concerned with three kinds of claims. First, language bioprogram hypothesis by Bickerton (1984, 1989) says that children are born with a specific semantically-driven innate mechanism. Specifically, Bickerton claims that distinctions between stative and process verbs, and between punctual and nonpunctual verbs are semantic primitives, and that they are biologically programmed in the human brain. In other words, these distinctions form part of the innate mechanisms specific to language acquisition. Evidence for this claim comes from Bickerton's reinterpretation of child language data in Brown's study (1973) and from Creole grammars. In Brown's study, English-speaking children never overgeneralize progressive *-ing* to stative verbs, and in several Creole grammars, the two types of distinctions are consistently made.

Another type of theory in the direction of nativistic view is Pinker's (1984, 1989) semantic bootstrapping theory which attempts to connect semantic and syntactic knowledge in children. In this theory, children have innate semantic concepts like agent and patient, and as they experience regularities (e.g., word order, case endings) between a semantic category, say agent, and a syntactic rule, say before the verb, children map the agent role to subject position by innate linking rules. Pinker (1984) claims that the innate knowledge of agent and patient is strongest for canonical verbs like *hit* and *break*, and that these roles should be correctly linked to syntactic rules from early on in children's grammar.

A quite different approach and yet similar to the above in that it seeks universality is the cognitive prerequisite view which gives much weight on cognitive preparedness for learning a language. According to this view, cognitive/perceptual apparatus both universally shapes language structure and guides language acquisition, i.e., the child's language development follows the child's cognitive development. As the child begins to produce words, she would acquire relatively early the words or morphemes that map onto their preestablished cognitive concepts (e.g., agent, location, aspect), but would acquire late those grammatical aspects that are cognitively developed later (e.g., time, number). Slobin's (1985) study analyzed children's grammar with this approach. Based on an extensive amount of cross-linguistic data, Slobin has argued for a number of universal cognitive mechanisms, called Basic Child Grammar, that initiate the child's acquisition of grammar. For example, the event in which an agent 'manipulates' an object and brings about a change of state in the object (e.g., *break*) is cognitively salient to children, and children mark this in their grammar from early on. This is demonstrated by children's early acquisition of accusative marker (or ergative marker in an ergative language) across languages.

Recent studies, however, have cast some doubts about the strong version of the views that semantic categories are ready made to be mapped onto linguistic forms. A preliminary reason for doubt is the existence of significant cross-linguistic differences in the way form and meaning are mapped across languages. Language specific mapping between form and meaning has rarely been taken into account in acquisition studies, even in studies that are explicitly cross-linguistic, since the goal of cross-linguistic comparisons has usually been to determine how timing of acquisition is affected by the use of different formal devices for expressing the same meaning. For example, locative morphemes in various languages have simply been equated, with their "translation equivalents" in English. However, Choi and Bowerman (1992) have recently shown evidence that the semantic categories of locative morphemes between Korean and English are significantly different and that children are sensitive to language-specific categories from one word stage. Also, contrary to Pinker's claim that children have innate linking rules, Bowerman (1990) has shown that children make errors in linking thematic roles to syntactic functions, and that linking regularities are learned on the basis of specific linguistic experience.

To get a clearer picture of what is innate and what is learned, we need much more cross-linguistic data than are available now. The present paper examines the acquisition of locative case markers in young Korean children with this goal in mind.

Korean locative case markers expressing goal, location, and source make several distinctions about semantic and syntactic properties of certain elements in the clause: animate vs. inanimate nouns, stative vs. process verbs, and intransitive vs. transitive verbs. These distinctions must be made in order to use the locative markers appropriately. In this study, we will trace the development of these markers to see how children come to distinguish these categories. It will be shown that the forms are acquired in a piecemeal fashion at the beginning and are later generalized, suggesting that the grammar underlying the markers are at least in part learned. Furthermore, some of the distinctions became productive only after a reorganization period. Before we look at children's data, we will examine the adult system of locative case markers.

Locative Case Marking System in Korean

In this paper, we will discuss four locative case markers in Korean: -EY, -EYTA, -HANTHEY, -EYSE. Their thematic functions are as follows:

Morpheme	Thematic functions
-EY	Goal, Location.
-HANTHEY	Goal, Location (= entails Possession), Indirect Object.
-EYTA	Goal.
-EYSE	Source, Location.

Examples from 1a to 4b below illustrate these functions. For example, -EY expresses Goal as in 1a.

1a. John-i hakkyo-EY ka-n-ta. (-EY: Goal)
John-Sub school-TO go-Prs-Dec
'John goes to school.'

-EY also expresses static location with the verb -ISSTA 'to be located' as in 1b.

1b. John-i hakkyo-EY iss-ta. (-EY: Location)
John-Sub school-AT be-Dec.
'John is at school.'

-HANTHEY expresses goal as in 2a, and location or possession in the case of 2b. -HANTHEY is also used for the indirect object which marks goal of the verb, as shown in 2c. This use of
-HANTHEY contrasts with -(L)UL which marks the direct object, or theme/patient function.

2a. Aki-ka emma-HANTHEY ka-n-ta. (-HANTHEY: Goal)
Baby-Sub mommy-TO go-Prs-Dec.
'The baby goes to mommy.'

2b. John-HANTHEY hyeng-i iss-ta. (-HANTHEY: Location/ Possession)
John-AT/TO older brother-Sub be-Dec.
'John has an older brother.'

2c. EMMA-HANTHEY senmwul-ul cwu-n-ta. (-HANTHEY: Goal (Indirect Object))
MOMMY-TO present-Obj. give-Prs-Dec.
'(Somebody) Gives Mommy a present'.

-EYTA also expresses goal as in 3a.

3a. Aka-ka cup-EYTA uyu-lul pwu-ess-ta. (-EYTA: Goal)
Baby-Sub cup-TO milk-Obj pour-Past-Dec.
'The baby poured milk into the cup.'

-EYSE, on the other hand, expresses source as in 4a, and also location of an activity as in 4b.

4a. John-i hakkyo-EYSE tolawa-ss-ta. (-EYSE: Source)
John-Sub school-FROM return-Past-Dec.
'John returned from school.'

4b. John-i hakkyo-EYSE kongpwu ha-n-ta. (-EYSE: Location)
John-Sub school-AT study do-Prs-Dec.
'John is studying at school.'

As it is apparent from the above examples, several forms are used for the same function. For example, three forms, -EY, -HANTHEY, and -EYTA are all used to express goal meaning. Also, both -EY and -EYSE refer to location. However, a closer look at these forms shows that each represents a specific semantic or syntactic category related to the noun they are suffixed to or to the main verb of the clause.

Let's look at these distinctions. First, as shown in 5, the two case markers for goal, -EY and -HANTHEY, make a distinction between animacy and inanimacy of the noun: -EY is used when the goal argument is an inanimate object, whereas -HANTHEY is used when it is an animate being.[1] This inanimacy vs. animacy distinction is obligatory, i.e., violation of this distinction would result in ungrammaticality, as shown in 5.

5. -EY vs. -HANTHEY: inanimate vs. animate noun.

HAKKYO-EY/*-HANTHEY kata, SCHOOL-TO go, 'go to school',
EMMA-HANTHEY/*-EY kata, MOMMY-TO go, 'go to mommy'.

Second, as shown in 6, the distinction between -EY and -EYTA--both express goal-- involves difference in transitivity: -EY is used with intransitive motion verbs, i.e., when an agent spontaneously moves toward a particular place. For example, -EY is used when somebody 'goes up on the table'. On the other hand, -EYTA is used with transitive motion verbs. That is, -EYTA is often used, when an agent causes an entity to move from one place to another, e.g., when an agent 'puts a cup on the table.' However, the use of -EYTA is optional, and -EY is the unmarked form as the latter can be used for both types, as shown in 6.

6. -EY vs. -EYTA: intransitive motion verb vs. transitive motion verbs. (This distinction is optional.)

table-EY/*-EYTA OLLA KATA, table-TO ASCEND GO,
'go up on the table',
table-EYTA/-EY cup-ul NOHTA, table-TO cup-DO PUT-ON,
'put the cup on the table'.

Third, in expressing the location of an event (i.e. the event occurs at a stationary location (without involving change of places)), an obligatory distinction is made between stative verbs and activity/process verbs. For stative verbs, -EY is used, whereas for activity/process verbs, -EYSE is used, as shown in 7.

7. -EY vs. -EYSE: stative vs. activity/process verbs.

hakkyo-EY/*-EYSE ISSTA,	school-AT BE-LOCATED, 'be at school',
hakkyo-EYSE/*-EY NOLTA,	school-AT PLAY, 'play at school'.

The stative verbs in Korean are restricted to a small set of verbs which denote spatial motions:

ISSTA 'to be located', SWUMTA 'to hide', NAMTA 'to remain', SOKHATA 'to belong', and all posture verbs, e.g., ANCTA 'to sit', SETA 'to stand', KITAYTA 'to lean', NWUPTA 'to lie down'.

These verbs are stative in that they do not take the progressive form -KO ISSTA '-ing', whereas activity/process verbs do (Kim 1990). As shown in 7, these stative verbs in Korean are distinguished from activity/process verbs in that the goal argument of the stative verbs take the -EY marker, whereas that of the activity/ process verbs take -EYSE. The category of stative verbs in Korean differs from English at least in two aspects: In contrast with Korean, posture verbs in English such as *sit*, *stand*, are NOT considered to be stative verbs (i.e., they can take the progressive form *-ing* as in 'I am sitting down'.). Also note that stative verbs in English include psych verbs like *love*, and *need*, whereas the stative verbs in Korean are restricted to spatial verbs (perhaps with the exception of SOKHATA).[2]

To summarize, several semantic/syntactic distinctions are made with locative case markers in Korean: animate vs. inanimate noun, transitive (caused) vs. intransitive (spontaneous) motion verbs, and stative vs. process/activity verbs. For example, when -EY expresses goal, it contrasts with -HANTHEY and -EYTA, in that it is used with an animate goal argument with an intransitive verb. When -EY expresses location, it occurs with stative verbs.

Development of Locative Markers in Korean Children

In many languages, the distinctions discussed above are also made grammatically, although the morphological rules are, of course, language-specific. Several acquisition researchers have examined children's development of these distinctions in different languages and made specific claims:

(1) Animate vs. inanimate noun: Based on cross-linguistic studies, Slobin (1985) has argued that children do not make this distinction in their grammar at an early period even when the language makes such distinction grammatically. Slobin therefore claims that the animacy vs. inanimacy distinction is not part of cognitive predisposition in children.

(2) Transitive vs. intransitive verb: Rispoli (1987) has observed that Japanese children rarely make errors on this distinction from an early period in their spontaneous speech. Naigles' (1990) experimental study with transitive and intransitive argument structures has also shown that the distinction is made early and is used productively in English-speaking children.

(3) Stative vs. process verb: Bickerton (1984) has argued that this distinction is innate in children. This is based on his study of creole grammars in which the distinction between stative and process verbs is fundamental and is consistently made.

Korean provides a good test case for these claims because its locative case marking system makes these distinctions grammatically. If a particular distinction is salient and cognitively or biologically predisposed, we would expect that Korean children will use the related locative markers appropriately with a variety of nouns and verbs from early on. On the other hand, if the distinction is learned through linguistic experiences, we might see a period which reveals children's attempts to figure out the rules underlying the markers.

The data to be analyzed are shown in Table 1. Five children were observed by three different researchers. The data of the first and the last child were collected by the author, PL by Youngjoo Kim, and HS and WJ by Pat Clancy.[3]

Name	Ages	Recording intervals
TJ	2;2-4;8	2-3 weeks
PL	1;8-3;0	4 weeks
HS	2;0-2;10	2 weeks
WJ	1;8-2;8	2 weeks
SB	2;10-4;0	4 weeks

Table 1. Spontaneous Data of five Korean children.

Among the five children, we will focus on TJ's data because they cover the longest period of development, and because, the author is quite familiar with the data. Developmental patterns will be analyzed for all children except SB (the last child in Table 1), since the first recording of SB did not occur until 2;10 when he was already producing all four markers.

The four locative forms were developed in the following sequence: -EY was acquired first by all children, and then -EYTA was typically acquired within one or two months. A few months later, -EYSE and -HANTHEY were acquired around the same time. This order of acquisition is consistent with the findings that children express goal of motion before location of an event. For example, Clancy (1985) reports that Japanese children acquire the marker for Goal ('ni') before the marker for location of an activity ('de'). However, -HANTHEY which expresses goal was acquired relatively late. This may be due to the plurifunctional nature of -HANTHEY: it expresses location, possession, and indirect object.

-EY > -EYTA > -EYSE, -HANTHEY

Figure 1. Average order of acquisition of locative case markers.

First, let's look at the early development of these markers. Concerning -EY, the children initially used the locative marker correctly with a restricted set of verbs: In TJ's case, -EY was mostly used to express goal with two verbs, KATA 'to go' and OTA 'to come'. -EY was much less frequently used to express location at this early stage. When it expressed location, however, the stative verb ISSTA 'to be located' was typically used. Examples are shown from 8 through 11 below. (Examples are shown along with the child's age (years; months) at which period a particular utterance was made. In parentheses, the most crucial elements for understanding the children's grammar are translated into English, e.g., verb in the case of -EY.)

8. TJ (2;2): appa hakkyo-EY kassta. (to go)
9. TJ (2;7): cip-EY wasse. (to come)
10. WJ (1;8): pwuek-EY kasse. (to go)
11. WJ (2;1): cip-EY isse. (to be located)

When -EYTA emerged, it contrasted with -EY correctly. That is, -EYTA was always used with transitive verbs denoting agentive caused motion. For example, -EYTA was most frequently used with the transitive verb NOHTA 'to put an object on a surface' as shown in Example 12. Two other transitive verbs frequently used with -EYTA were NEHTA 'to put an object in a container' and the all-purpose transitive verb HATA 'to do something'. The children made only occasional errors on the distinction between -EY and -EYTA during the development period studied.[4] This is consistent with Rispoli's finding (1987) that Japanese children distinguish between transitive and intransitive verbs from early on. Also, Choi and Bowerman's study (1992) on the Korean spatial transitive and intransitive verbs shows that Korean children do not overgeneralize transitive verbs, such as KKITA 'put an object tightly onto/into something', to intransitive situations, i.e. an agent spontaneously moves from one place to another. In the present study of locative markers, it should be recalled that the -EYTA case marking for caused movement is optional, i.e., it is grammatical to use -EY for both spontaneous and caused motions. Nevertheless, the children acquired -EYTA early, and used it for caused motions only. This suggests that the spontaneous vs. caused motion distinction is salient to very young children.

12. HS (1;11): yeki-(EY)TA nwa. (to put)
13. WJ (1;9): cecpyeng-EYTA pwue. (to pour)

Let's now turn to the acquisition of -EY vs. -HANTHEY. The present data show evidence that the distinction is clearly grasped by children learning Korean from the beginning: The children produced -EY first with inanimate nouns only, and when they acquired -HANTHEY, they used it only with animate nouns, typically human (see 14-16 for examples). At the beginning, the nouns were restricted to CIP 'house' or HAKKYO 'school' for -EY, and EMMA 'mommy' for -HANTHEY. Later, the distinction became more productive, and it was consistently observed throughout the developmental period.[5]

14. TJ (2;11): nwukwu-HANTHEY ka? ('go to who?')
15. PL (2;2): emma-HANTHEY nalla kaca? ('let's fly to Mommy')
16. HS (2;5): na-HANTHEY cwe. ('give (something) to me')

This is contrary to Slobin's argument (1985) that the distinction between animacy and inanimacy is acquired late in the child's language development, and is not part of a universally shared set of nonlinguistic concepts. According to Slogin, the animate vs. inanimate distinction is language-specific, and is 'not a notion that children readily attend to in establishing mapping for functors.' (Slobin 1985: 1186) However, it is important to note that such claim is based on languages where the animate vs. inanimate distinction is typically combined with gender and number distinction in a complex way (e.g., in Polish, the animate vs. inanimate distinction is made for masculine singular in accusative case). Furthermore, in these languages, the distinction is not always obligatory. In contrast, the distinction between animacy and inanimacy in Korean is systematic, morphologically transparent, and obligatory. The present data, therefore, suggest that children attend to language-specific semantic categories from early on, particularly when the language makes a morphologically clear and obligatory distinction between two categories.

So far, we have seen two kinds of distinction both of which were appropriately made by Korean children: animate vs. inanimate nouns, and transitive vs. intransitive verbs. Interestingly, the two types of categories seem to be closely related in sentence construction: In spontaneous motion, expressed by an intransitive verb, the entity that moves is typically an animate being as 'John' in 'John ran to the store.' On the other hand, in caused motion expressed by a transitive verb, the entity moved is typically an inanimate noun as 'the cup' in 'John put the cup on the table.' It is possible, therefore, that in Korean, the early distinction between animacy vs. inanimacy enables the early differentiation between transitive and intransitive sentences. Rispoli's studies (1987, 1989) of Japanese children are insightful in this regard. Rispoli (1987) reports that Japanese children predominantly use intransitive sentences when an animate being undergoes a change of location. Conversely, Japanese children predominantly use transitive sentences when the entity moved is inanimate. Furthermore, Rispoli (1989) has found that such pattern is modeled in Japanese caregiver sentences. A similar case may be posited for Korean. That is, caregivers' language-specific input may enhance an early distinction between animate and inanimate nouns in children's speech and this relates to the early differentiation between transitive and intransitive verbs.

Let's now turn to the marker -EYSE. The locative marker for activity/process verbs, -EYSE, was initially used correctly with a few activity verbs, as shown in 17 and 18.

17. SB (2;11): nay-ka hakkyo-EYSE mantulesse. (to make)
18. HS (2;3): pang-EYSE haysse. (to do something)

However, children soon began to make a number of errors with -EY and -EYSE, as shown in examples 19 through 38. Recall that -EY is used for stative verbs and -EYSE is used for process/activity verbs. Children made errors by using -EYSE with stative verbs, as shown in Examples 19-27. It is striking to note that several children used -EYSE with the most prototypical stative verb ISSTA 'to be located'. TJ also used -EYSE with the stative verb, EPTA 'not-be' (the negative form of ISSTA), and HS used -EY with a posture verb NWUPTA 'to lie down'. The children also made errors in the reverse direction: the children used -EY with process/ activity verbs, such as *play*, or *clean*. Some examples are shown from 28-38 below.

Examples of errors

A. -EYSE substituted for -EY.
(-EYSE is inappropriately used with stative verbs.)

19. TJ (3;1): chimtay-*eyse swumesse. (to hide)
20. TJ (3;5): yeki-*(ey)se swumesse thokki-ka. (to hide)
21. TJ (3;6): Mr. Bump yeki-*(ey)se epsse. (not-be located)
22. TJ (3;8): os-un Tops-*eyse epsci. (not-be located)
(Tops= a supermarket)
23. TJ (3;10): cip-*eyse issci. (to be located)
24. SB (2;10): kyohwey-*eyse ike isse. (to be located)
25. HS (2;8): chimtay-*eyse nwue. (to lie down)
26. HS (2;8): Baby yeki-*(ey)se nwupca. (to lie down)
27. WJ (2;1): echung-*eyse issci. (to be located)

B. -EY substituted for -EYSE.
(-EY is inappropriately used with process verbs.)

28. TJ (3;2): cip-*ey theyleybi pwa. (to see)
29. TJ (3;2): chyeta poko isse, changmwun-*ey. (to look)
30. TJ (3;3): eti-*ey cwukesse? (to die)
31. TJ (3;5): ichung-*ey chengso-hay. (to clean)
32. SB (2;11): canti-*ey campwu-hay. (to jump)
33. PL (2;3): ike yeki kesil-*ey chikwa hanun keya. (to play dentist)
34. WJ (2;0): PL-cip-*ey ike kacko nolketun. (to play)
35. WJ (2;2): appa pang-*ey nolassketun. (to play)
36. WJ (2;2): Baby acwumma cip-*ey [pota][6]. (to see)
37. WJ (2;3): na ce pang-*ey [cata]. (to sleep)
38. WJ (2;6): cip-*ey mwe hana? (to do)

These errors suggest that the stative vs. process verb distinction is not clearly established at this developmental stage. Recall that the children initially used the case marker
-EY correctly for prototypical stative verbs, ISSTA (cf. Example 11). Also, during the first few months, children used -EYSE correctly with a few activity/process verbs such as MANTULTA 'to make', and HATA 'to do' (cf. Examples 17-18).

In examining children's errors of the four locative markers, another type of errors was striking, namely that of -HANTHEY. As noted above, -HANTHEY is used with indirect objects (typically animate beings), for example with verbs, e.g., *give* and *send*. During this developmental period, the children made a number of errors, using -HANTHEY for patient/theme role where the direct object marker -(L)UL would be appropriate. Examples are shown from 39 to 50. Particularly interesting errors are those uses of -HANTHEY with prototypical transitive verbs such as *hit*, *eat*, and *bite*. The actions referred to by these verbs result in a clear change of state, and yet, the children in the study marked the patient of the verb with the indirect object marker.

C. -HANTHEY substituted for -(L)UL.
(-HANTHEY is inappropriately used for direct objects.)

39. TJ (3;6): nwukwu-*hanthey [ttaylita]? (to hit)
40. TJ (3;6): mwune-ka Mr. Bump-*hanthey meknuntay. (to eat)
41. TJ (3;6): yay-*hanthey [meke]. (to eat)
42. TJ (3;6): Lalary-*hanthey [ttaylita]. (to hit)
43. TJ (3;6): mengmeng-ika yay-*hanthey ttalaka. (to follow)
44. TJ (3;8): HJ-ka Lalary-*hanthey yeki mwulesse. (to bite)
45. TJ (4;7): emma-*hanthey manasse. (to meet)
46. PL (2;6): hon naysse yay-*hanthey. (to scold)
47. PL (3;0): swukyuni-*hanthey ilekhey kkok kkianasse. (to hug)
48. HS (2;5): nay-ka yoke-*hanthey haysse. (to do something.)
49. HS (2;8): pise, acwumma-*hanthey. (to comb)
50. WJ (2;6): cow-*hanthey man/(self-corrected) cow-lul mannasse. (to meet)

To summarize so far, the children initially made correct distinctions for all four locative markers with a restricted set of verbs or nouns.

However, their later developmental patterns show that the four markers did not go through the same acquisition path: Whereas the animacy vs. inanimacy distinction and the transitive vs. intransitive distinction continued to be almost error-free, the stative vs. activity/process verb distinctions, and the direct and indirect object distinctions went through error periods. As discussed above, the transitive/intransitive distinction and the animacy/inanimacy distinction may be related, so that the saliency of one distinction may reinforce the other.

What do the errors mean?

Let's focus now on the errors related to Examples from 19 through 50. What do these errors mean? First of all, the error period for the two types of distinction mentioned above (-EY vs. -EYSE and -HANTHEY vs. -(L)UL) started after a few months of correct usage. As Table 2 shows, depending on the child, the amount of time it took to produce all four forms varied from two to nine months. However, all four children were similar in that their error period started about three months after the production of all four markers. Also, note that the error period lasted about three to six months, and after that, only occasional errors were detected. Thus, the data show a U-shaped learning pattern, which has been reported in Bowerman's studies (1981, 1982) on English-speaking children's acquisition of syntax and word meaning. Following Bowerman's explanation (1981, 1982), the processes or rules by which Korean children learn the two types of distinctions (stative vs. activity/process verb, and the direct and indirect object distinction) seem to differ from the adult rules, and during the error period, certain types of reorganization takes place before assimilating the adult rules.

Child	Study period	Onset of case marking	Production of all four markers	Frequent error period
TJ	2;2-4;8	2;2	2;11	3;0-3;6
PL	1;8-3;0	1;8	2;2	2;3-2;6
HS	2;0-2;10	1;11	2;3	2;5-2;8
WJ	1;8-2;8	1;8	1;10	2;1-2;6

Table 2. Error periods in the four Korean children.

One clue to explaining the error data is that the reorganization period began as the children increased rapidly the number of verb types. For example, in TJ's case, the number of verb types during the initial correct stage was restricted to one or two verbs for each marker adding up to seven in total for the four markers:

with -EY: KATA 'to go', OTA 'to come', ISSTA 'to be located';
with -EYSE: CATA 'to sleep';
with -EYTA: NOHTA 'to put something on', NEHTA 'to put something in';
with -HANTHEY: KATA 'to go', CWUTA 'to give'.

However, during the error period, the number of verb types increased to 53 in TJ's speech. This suggests that, during the initial correct stage, the child is acquiring the case marker in a piecemeal fashion, associating each marker with individual verbs or nouns. During the error period, more general underlying rules seem to be formulating as the child deals with many different verbs. In the case of -EY and -EYSE, it seems that as the verb types increase in her lexicon, TJ discovers that both -EY and -EYSE share the function of expressing stationary location of an event. As she sees this shared property of -EY and -EYSE, she uses both markers interchangeably for location and does not yet differentiate between stative and activity/process verbs. As a result, errors occur, e.g., use of -EYSE with a stative verb ISSTA. Errors may also arise because the actions of some verbs like POTA 'to see' and CATA 'to sleep' that take -EYSE (therefore conventionally considered to be activity verbs) are only indirectly dynamic in the sense that there is no visible activity going on in the context. Korean children have to learn that -EY is restricted to only those verbs which express location with physical existence verbs like ISSTA 'to be locate', NAMTA 'to remain', SWUMTA 'to hide', EPTA 'not-be', and to posture verbs.

In the case of the errors with -HANTHEY, children initially seem to restrict -HANTHEY to animate goals, and -(L)UL to inanimate patients, and as long as they keep the two markers separate in this way, they produce correct forms. However, as children become able to process a large number of verbs and nouns, they produce sentences that have animate as well as inanimate patients. Using the animacy vs. inanimacy distinction that they have developed, children may continue to use -HANTHEY to animate nouns, even when they are direct objects, i.e., patients (cf. example 40 above). This results in errors. Furthermore, as it is well known, the degree of affectedness or change of state does not always work in determining whether the argument is direct or indirect object. For example, in John-i Mary-lul ttala kanta 'John is following Mary', there is no obvious affectedness in the patient 'Mary'. However, the direct object marker -(L)UL is used in Korean (cf. example 43 above). Korean children have to learn that -HANTHEY is often used as a formal dimension for dative or goal role determined by language-specific verb argument structure. What these error data suggest is that the distinction between stative vs. process/activity verbs is language-specific and that children learn the system through language-specific input. The present data suggest, then, the nativistic views presented in Bickerton's language bioprogram hypothesis (1984) and Pinker's innate linking rule hypothesis (1984) are too strong. Contrary to their claims, the grammatical distinction between stative and process/activity verbs and the argument structure are learned over time with a period of errors and reorganization.

Conclusion

In summary, the present study has shown that the appropriate usage of four locative case markers in Korean requires several types of semantic/syntactic distinctions. Korean children acquire the locative case markers between their second and third years. The present analysis of the development of the locative markers in five Korean children suggests that children initially acquire these markers in a piecemeal fashion with a small number of verbs or nouns. That is, at the beginning, children seem to select the correct morpheme on the basis of individual verbs or nouns that they are familiar with. As they move into a productive period, they go through a reorganization period before the final correct stage. The reorganization period was observed particularly in relation to the distinctions between stative and process/activity verbs, and between direct and indirect objects. The errors made during the reorganization period could be explained in terms of children's generalizations made through their linguistic experiences. The study, thus, suggests that children are sensitive to language-specific input from early on, and that they develop much of their grammar on the basis of the language they hear in their environment.

Notes

[1]-EYKEY is also possible with animate nouns, but -HANTHEY is more colloquial, and children acquire -HANTHEY much earlier than -EYKEY.

[2]It is interesting to note that stative verbs in Chinese also include posture verbs as in Korean (Li 1989).

[3]I would like to thank Young-joo Kim and Pat Clancy for allowing me to analyze their data.

[4]The children made a few errors at a later stage, however, since they were proportionately much less than the errors we'll be concerned in this paper, we will not discuss them here.

[5]Of all the instances of -HANTHEY in all four children, only three errors have been detected.

[6]Verbs in [ ] are implied from the preceding utterance in the discourse.

References

Bellugi, Ursula. 1967. A transformational analysis of the development of negation. Doctoral dissertation. Harvard University.

Bickerton, Derek. 1984. The language bioprogram hypothesis. The Behavioral and Brain Sciences. 7.173-188.

________. 1989. The child, the bioprogram and the input data: A commentary on Cziko. First Language. 9.33-37.

Brown, Roger and Ursula Bellugi. 1964. Three processes in the child's acquisition of syntax. New directions in the study of language. ed. by E.H. Lenneberg. Cambridge, MA: MIT Press.

Bowerman, Melissa. 1973. Early syntactic development: A cross-linguistic study with special reference to Finnish. England: Cambridge University Press.

________. 1981. Beyond communicative adequacy: From piecemeal knowledge to an integrated system in the child's acquisition of language. Papers and Reports on Child Language Development. 20.1-24.

________. 1982. Reorganizational processes in language development. The state of the art in language acquisition, ed. by L. Gleitman and E. Wanner. Cambridge, English: Cambridge University Press.

________. 1990. Mapping thematic roles onto syntactic functions: are children helped by innate linking rules? Linguistics. 28.1253-1289.

Brown, Roger. 1973. A first language: the early stages. Boston, MA: Harvard University Press.

Choi, Soonja and Melissa Bowerman. 1992. Learning to express Motion events in English and Korean: The influence of language-specific lexicalization patterns. Cognition. 41.83-121.

Chomsky, Noam. 1965. Aspects of the theory of syntax. Cambridge, MA: MIT Press.

Clancy, Patricia. 1985. The acquisition of Japanese. Crosslinguistic study of language acquisition, Vol. 1, ed. by D. I. Slobin, 373-524. Hillsdale, NJ: Lawrence Erlbaum Associates.

Clark, Herbert H. 1973. Space, time, semantics, and the child. Cognitive development and the acquisition of language, ed. by T.E. Moore, 27-64. New York: Academic Press.

Johnston, Judith and Dan I. Slobin. 1979. The development of locative expressions in English, Italian, Serbo-Croatian, and Turkish. Journal of Child Language. 16.531-547.

Kim, Young-joo. 1990. The syntax and semantics of Korean case: The interaction between lexical and syntactic levels of representation. Doctoral dissertation. Harvard University.

Li, Ping. 1989. Aspect and Aktionsart in Child Mandarin. Doctoral Dissertation, University of Leiden.

Naigles, Letitia. 1990. Children use syntax to learn verb meanings. Journal of Child Language. 17.357-374.

Piaget, Jean. 1954. The construction of reality in the child. New York: Basic Books.

Pinker, Steven. 1984. Language learnability and language development. Cambridge, MA: Harvard University Press.

________. 1989. Learnability and cognition: The acquisition of argument structure. Cambridge, MA: MIT Press.

Rispoli, Matthew. 1987. The acquisition of the transitive and intransitive action verb categories in Japanese. First Language, 7.183-200.

________. 1989. Encounters with Japanese verbs: Caregiver sentences and the categorization of transitive and intransitive action verbs. First Language. 9.57-80.

Slobin, Dan I. 1973. Cognitive prerequisites for the development of grammar. Studies of child language development, ed by C. A. Ferguson and D. I. Slobin. New York: Holt.

________. 1985. Crosslinguistic evidence for the language-making capacity. The crosslinguistic study of language acquisition, Vol. 2, ed. by D.I. Slobin, 1157-1256. Hillsdale, NJ: Lawrence Erlbaum Associates.

The Organization of the Korean Syllable: Experimental Evidence

BRUCE L. DERWING, YEO BOM YOON, AND SOOK WHAN CHO

University of Alberta, Canada and Sogang University, Korea

1. BACKGROUND

The experimental phonological investigation of syllable structure was pioneered by Treiman (1983, 1986, etc.), who used a variety of string manipulation tasks (notably word-blending) to determine whether such hypothesized units as the onset, rime or coda were viable for English. Dow (1987, 1989, etc.) continued this work, using primarily a unit-substitution (and deletion) task. Taken together, this research lent support to the idea that English syllables have an onset+rime or right-branching structure.[2] Treiman has also been prominently involved in the experimental exploration of syllable boundaries in English, using both (oral) string-inversion and (written) slash-insertion tasks (Treiman and Danis 1988). A chief purpose of the present study was to extend or adapt the methodologies developed in these English language investigations to other languages of diverse types, in order to explore the question of the universal generality of the findings.

For a variety of both practical and theoretical reasons, four languages were selected for the initial phases of this investigation, including Arabic, Blackfoot and Taiwanese, as well as Korean. Data collection attempts were subsequently made in Ilan, Taiwan (for Taiwanese), in Cairo, Egypt (for Arabic), and in Lethbridge, Alberta, Canada (for Blackfoot), in each case employing the same unit-substitution (US) and string-

---

[1] The research reported here was supported by research grants from the Social Sciences and Humanities Research Council of Canada (Nos. 410-88-0266, 410-91-0249), awarded to the first author. The authors also wish to thank G.E. Wiebe for her technical assistance.

[2] More recent work has suggested an alternative interpretation that is less hard and fast (see Derwing & Nearey 1991).

inversion (SI) tasks that had worked particularly well for English. These initial attempts were disappointing, however, as our pilot subjects in all three locales had great difficulties with both techniques, failing either to understand the tasks at all, even after multiple promptings, or yielding data that were chaotic and uninterpretable. Before we even attempted to explore the Korean case, therefore, it had already become clear that some new or at least greatly modified techniques were going to have to be developed if the project was to progress any further.

2. THE EXPERIMENTAL ASSESSMENT OF SYLLABLE CONSTITUENTS

The purpose of the US task, as noted above, was to yield information about the full range of hypothesized intra- or sub-syllabic units (see Dow & Derwing 1989 for a convenient summary). However, among the various hypothesized constituent elements of syllables, the onset and the rime have a particularly important status, both from the standpoint of empirical support and theoretical prominence. (Some claims have been advanced, in fact, that these two categories might even be universal.) If it was impractical at this stage to collect good information about all of the various sub-components of syllables, therefore, an alternative that might clarify the primary intrasyllabic break point was the next most appealing prospect.

From this perspective, Treiman's word-blending task was an attractive possibility, since it had also been successfully employed in English for this purpose. From a purely practical standpoint, however, this task also shared a common handicap with the more ambitious US technique, in that both were production tasks that required the eliciting of individual responses from individual subjects, at considerable cost in time and effort for subjects and experimenters alike. In order to expedite the data-collection process, we decided to try a forced-choice version of this task that could be group administered.

2.1. The Forced-Choice Word-Blending Task.

Two versions of this task were developed and were validated for English, as illustrated below. In both cases, the main question of interest concerned the relationship of a vowel nucleus to an adjacent consonant or consonants: was the nucleus linked with a following coda consonant or cluster to form a rime-like unit (as confirmed by the English results), or did the nucleus instead join with a preceding onset consonant or cluster to form a BODY?[3] To help answer this question for Korean, a series of mono-syllabic real words were presented as input and two or more first-order blends were offered for selection as output, one set based on a primary break occurring before the vowels (the onset-rime or 'On + Ri' blends) and the other based on a primary break after it (the body-coda or 'Bo + Co' blends).

2.1.1. Four-Choice version (Written Choices Only)

In this version of the test, which was the first one we tried with Korean, subjects heard a pair of input words and were asked to choose which of the four blends they preferred, selecting from a set of written responses. Four examples from an English form of this test are indicated below. For convenience, the two On + Ri blends are underlined, with the Bo + Co blends left unmarked.

[3] There seems to be no standard term for a unit of this kind, and in previous work Derwing (Derwing, Dow & Nearey 1987, 1988; Dow & Derwing 1989) has used the term HEAD to characterize such an onset-nucleus combination. In the interest of terminological uniformity, however, the term BODY is adopted here from Vennemann (1988). It should be noted, however, that Vennemann uses the term ONSET in a different sense than the standard one employed here.

1.PACK + DOG → (a) POG (b) DACK (c) PAG (d) DOCK

2.GOOSE + SHADE → (a) GADE (b) GUDE (c) SHOOSE (d) SHACE

3.BOOT + COVE → (a) BOOVE (b) BOVE (c) COOT (d) COAT

4.POUND + JOIST → (a) JOINED (b) POUST (c) JOUND (d) POIST

One advantage of this four-choice version of the test is that it permits the very rapid collection of a large body of data, since the test cannot only be group administered, but all four possibilities are handled at once for each input word-pair, yielding a relatively large amount of data from a relatively short test - a particularly valuable feature for pilot work. However, this form of the test also suffers from some potentially serious defects related to problems of control: (1) it places a relatively high burden on short-term memory, possibly biasing the results in favor of early or late responses; (2) it confounds directionality of blending with structural blend-type; and so (3) it rather arbitrarily forces subjects to choose between two blends of the same structural type. As with any other forced-choice variant of this task, care must also be taken to control for the possible effects of real word meaning and frequency, when real words appear as answer choices (cf. choices 1(d), 3(c), 3(d), and 4(a) above).

2.1.2. Two-Choice Version (Oral or Written Choices)

In order to better control some of the extraneous factors introduced in the four-choice version of this task, a comparable two-choice version was also developed. In this version, the four possible first-order blends of each input word-pair are scattered over four different test items, randomly distributed throughout the test, as illustrated by the four examples provided below:

1.(a)	SMORG	+ BLAND	→	SMAND	(= On + Ri)
(b)	SMORG	+ BLAND	→	SMOND	(= Bo + Co)
2.(a)	BLAND	+ SMORG	→	BLAIRG	(= Bo + Co)
(b)	BLAND	+ SMORG	→	BLORG	(= On + Ri)
3.(a)	SMORG	+ BLAND	→	SMAND	(= On + Ri)
(b)	SMORG	+ BLAND	→	BLORG	(= On + Ri
4.(a)	BLAND	+ SMORG	→	SMOND	(= Bo + Co)
(b)	BLAND	+ SMORG	→	BLAIRG	(= Bo + Co)

Directionality effects are controlled here by presenting the input words in both orders, allowing all structurally diverse responses (as in items 1 and 2 above) to be composed of the first part of the first input word and the second part of the second. Order of choice biases are also controlled for by presenting each blending type both as an '(a)' choice and as a '(b)' choice, on different items (cf. 1(a) vs. 2(b), which are the two On + Ri blends). Note that two other items are also included, based on the same input word-pair, that allow for no principled choice based on structural type (i.e., both are On + Ri blends as in item 3 above, or both Bo + Co blends as in 4; these items provide a useful standard of comparison for the structurally diverse items, as well as permitting the assessment of the effects, if any, of ancillary factors, such as directionality and response order). One consequent disadvantage of this approach, however, is that it results in a test that is longer (in this case four times longer) than its corresponding four-choice counterpart would be, but the corresponding increase in control seemed worth this sacrifice. Moreover, this form of the test also greatly reduced the short-term memory effects noted in connection with the four-choice version, allowing for the possibility of purely oral as well as written responses.

When presented to English subjects, both versions of this test confirmed Treiman's result, by showing a general preference for onset-rime over body-coda type blends, though, as expected, this result was clearer using the two-choice rather than the four-choice version of this task. (A single choice 'Yes/No' version has also been tried; see Derwing and Wiebe forthcoming for details).

2.2. Application to Korean

The Korean language was of much interest to this line of investigation, as there were reasons to believe that syllables in this language reflected a body-coda or 'left-branching' structure rather than the onset-rime or 'right-branching' organization of English (i.e., unlike English, vowel nuclei in Korean seem to adhere more closely to preceding consonants than to following ones). Native speakers have reported this to be the case on the basis of their own intuitions, and Youn (1990) conducted an informal word-blend production task whose results were claimed to support this analysis. Cheun (1980) also observes that when parts of words are deleted in fast speech, the deleted elements are usually a syllable-initial CV, rather than a syllable final VC (e.g, CASUPSE → CAPSE by the loss of the body element SU). In addition, Kim-Renaud (1986) reports on a Korean secret language in which the string NOSA is inserted after the first CV in a phonological phrase, again attesting to the special status of CV as a unit. A key aspect of the present investigation, therefore, was to extend the forced-choice word-blending task to this language, in the hope of firming up these intriguing preliminary suggestions.

2.2.1. Results from the Four-Choice Version

A four-choice version of this task was first presented to Korean subjects in April of 1991, much in the way of a pilot investigation.[4] Subjects were 79 undergraduate students registered in an English course at Sogang University in Seoul. One Korean example from this test is illustrated here, with the two On + Ri choices underlined as in the previous examples: KANG + SEM → (a) KAM (b) SENG (c) <u>KEM</u> (d) <u>SANG</u>. The full test contained 13 such items in all, with every attempt made to control for the problematic factors discussed in section 2.2. above (the 13 word-pairs used on this test are marked with (a) in the Appendix). Answer sheets contained the four alternative blends for each input pair, randomly ordered and written out in standard Korean orthography so that subjects could circle their single, most preferred choice for each item. As shown in Figure 1a below, an overall analysis of On + Ri vs. Bo + Co choices throughout the test revealed an approximate 2:1 preference in favor of the latter, which was a highly significant result ($t(78)=5.67$ for subjects; $t(12)=5.58$ for items; $p<.0001$ for both). This supported our preliminary expectations, but as a double check we also proceeded to a longer but better-controlled two-choice version of the test.

2.2.2. Results from the Two-Choice Version

The two-choice version of the forced-choice word-blending task was carried out in Seoul in June of 1991. Two sample test items from this test are illustrated below:

1. (a) SEM + THONG → <u>SONG</u>   2. (a) THONG + SEM → THOM
   (b) SEM + THONG → SENG   (b) THONG + SEM → <u>THEM</u>

[4] Thanks are due here to Mr. S.K. Cho, who not only offered the students in his class as experimental subjects, but who also assisted in the tabulation of the responses.

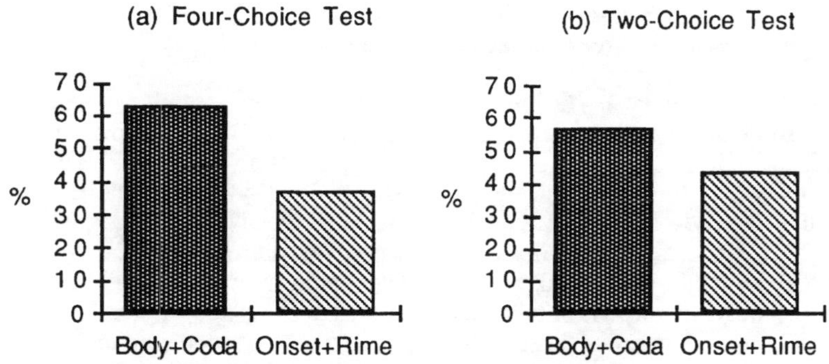

Figure 1. Blend-Type Preference

Subjects were 80 students registered in an undergraduate English class at Sogang University, all different from the ones tested previously.[5] About a third of the word-pairs used on this version of the test were also changed, in order to eliminate cases of blends that yielded a real Korean word in one condition but a nonsense word in the other.[6] The end result was a test of 48 items, half of which were of the contrastive types illustrated in (1) and (2) above; 12 of these yielded blends that were both real words (as in 1ab above) and the others yielded double nonsense or non-word blends (as in 2ab above; the 12 word-pairs used in the two-choice version of the test are marked with (b) in the Appendix). As shown in Figure 1b above, the results showed a somewhat diminished but still clear preference in favor of Bo + Co blends ($t(79)=3.35$ for subjects; $t(23)=3.51$ for items; $p<.01$ for both). Interestingly, this result remained significant regardless of the choice order (choice '(a)' vs. choice '(b)') and for both real and nonsense blends. (Some differences emerged for real vs. nonsense words if the two blending types were of the 'no choice' variety, but this difference was significant only in the case where both choices were of the Bo + Co type.)

Based on these data, the conclusion seems warranted that Korean vowels are indeed more closely linked to preceding consonants than to succeeding ones, a result that is consistent with a left-branching model of the syllable. This is precisely the opposite result to that found for an onset-rime language like English and constitutes a direct challenge to the notion of a universal right-branching approach to syllable structure.

3. THE EXPERIMENTAL ASSESSMENT OF SYLLABLE BOUNDARIES

As already noted in section 1 above, much as in the case of Dow's US task, some practical difficulties were encountered in our attempts to extend to other languages the oral SI task that Treiman & Danis used to assess syllable boundaries in English. A new oral technique, called the 'pause-break' task, was thus developed on rough analogy

[5] We thank Professor C.J. Kwon for kindly allowing us to use her class for twenty minutes, in order to conduct this experiment. Answer sheets contained written responses as before.

[6] This was because our pilot study on English had revealed the distinction between onset-rime and body-coda blends was blurred in the condition when one of the words was real and the other nonsense, evidently reflecting a bias towards or away from the real words (see Derwing and Wiebe in preparation for details).

with Treiman's written slash-insertion task. In this new task subjects are asked to choose which of two or three alternative 'breakings' of a word sounded the 'most natural.'

3.1. The 'Pause-Break' Technique

To illustrate this technique with the English word MELON, the following three alternatives might be offered (where ... indicates the location of the pause): (a) ME...LON (where /l/ is treated as the onset of the second syllable), (b) MEL...ON (where /l/ is the coda of the first syllable), or (c) MEL...LON (where /l/ is ambisyllabic). In an extensive pilot study, this task was presented to 95 undergraduate students, all native English speakers with little or no prior exposure to linguistics or phonetics. The main purpose of this pilot study was to evaluate whether the earlier Treiman-Danis results, using more difficult production tasks, could be replicated, and, as shown in Derwing (in press), the answer was resoundingly in the affirmative. This new task has thus been adopted for testing or re-testing in most of the languages in the project, though only the Korean results, of course, will be presented here.

3.2. Syllable Boundaries in Korean

In the Korean (hangul) writing system, letters are used for individual segments and written from left to right, much as in English, but, by utilizing the vertical dimension, as well, these letters are also grouped into syllable-like bundles. The hangul spelling of each Korean word thus makes a commitment as to the location of a syllable-like boundary which every literate speaker presumably knows. The purpose of the present investigation, therefore, was to establish whether any general preference could be found that was independent of these orthographic norms.

In principle, we saw three possible ways to investigate this. One obvious course of action would be to carry out the study among illiterate speakers, who would not know the orthographic norms. This effort is planned but has not yet been implemented, as the location of a suitable subject pool of this kind presents certain practical difficulties. A second approach, which involved the use of nonsense words, was implemented later, as discussed in section 3.2.3 below. The approach first adopted, therefore, was to focus the investigation on homophones having a variable placement of the orthographic syllable boundary, depending on the morphological structure and/or meaning of the words involved, and to control for the effect of spelling through differences in presentation mode.

3.2.1. Testing Ambiguous and Unambiguous Orthographic Strings

As an example of one of the homophones just discussed, consider the (transliterated) phonemic string MILI in standard Korean. Though consistently pronounced [miɾi] (the medial consonant is articulated as a flap), two different words are involved, and these are sharply differentiated in the spelling: one, spelled MI/LI (a slash is used in the transliteration here to show the location of the break between the two syllable-like hangul 'packages') has the meaning 'in advance', while the other, spelled MIL/I, means 'wheat' (with the nominative suffix /-i/ attached). For subjects in our 'meaning' group, who were given the glosses of the Korean words along with the oral stimuli, we expected a more-or-less slavish conformity to these orthographic norms in deciding on the preferred position of the pause-break. For our other group, however, who were not given the meanings but merely the articulated strings, we were curious to see what alternative strategy might be used to make a choice in such cases: would they choose randomly, or perhaps on the basis of word frequency (i.e., deciding by reference to the spelling of the word most commonly associated with each string), or might they, as we hoped, decide on some general phonological basis, independent of meaning or spelling?

The first round of Korean data was collected in October 1990 in Seoul, when two groups totaling 117 subjects were presented with six items similar to the one above, as well as a number of supplementary items selected to test cases mostly involving intervocalic tense consonants or consonant clusters. All subjects were undergraduate students in the Department of English at Sogang University, the great majority of whom grew up in the general Seoul area. The 30 words shown in Table 1 were presented in a single random order, with two choices of break position provided: choice (a) always placed the pause immediately before the second vowel of the word (i.e., in each case the consonant or entire cluster was treated as first-syllable coda) and choice (b) always placed the pause either before a single intervocalic consonant or between an intervocalic cluster (i.e., it treated the only or last consonant involved as a second-syllable onset), as illustated below for the strings MILI and KWUKSWU:

1. MILI	2. KWUKSWU[7]
(a) MIL . . . I	(a) KWUKS . . . WU
(b) MI . . . LI	(b) KWUK . . . SWU

The one exception to this involved the sequence PY (as in I/PYENG 'this bottle' and IP/YENG 'going to the army'), where the choices were (a) I ... PYENG and (b) IP ... YENG, to parallel the spellings.

The results in Table 1 can be briefly summarized as follows:[8] (A1) The clearest cases involved single consonants that are restricted phonotactically to word- and syllable-initial position, such as the /c/ in SA-/CANG (100%), or to syllable-final position, such as the /ŋ/ in PANG-/I (also 100%).[9] (A2) The results were also very clear for consonant clusters, where the preferred break position was between them. This result was virtually unanimous if this break corresponded with the spelling, as in CHENG-/SO (99%) and KWUK-/SWU (98%), and remained the majority view even when the orthography put the break after the second consonant, e.g. PWUL-K/E (74%; i.e., 26% preferred the segmentation PWULK-E) and KAP-S/I (68%).[10] (A3) For tense consonants (written as geminates in this particular transliteration scheme) the results were also fairly clear, with the preferred break once again after the vowel in spelling-supported cases, e.g. A-/PPA (99%) and KA-/CCA (79%), but with a major shift to the spelling break if it occurred after the consonant, e.g. MWU-KK/E (45%) and KA-SS/E (32%). Note that this effect is purely orthographic, as the tense

[7] In the Yale romanization scheme used here to transliterate Korean spellings, the sequence WU is used for the vowel /u/ and U alone for its unrounded counterpart /ɨ/. Phonemically, this word is /kuksu/.

[8] As before, a slash is used in this table to show the position of the break-points in the standard spelling, while a hyphen is used to show the pause-break position that is scored. (If both positions coincide, the composite symbol -/ is used.) Of the two scores shown in parentheses after each item, the first represents the proportion of subjects who broke the words at the hyphen under the 'no meaning' or 'ambiguous string' condition, while the second relates to the other presentation condition, when the meanings were all supplied.

[9] Since the results for the orthographically non-ambiguous strings were in general little affected by supplying their meanings, only those for the 'no meaning' condition are discussed for these items.

[10] Even this partial shift to the spelling-break position is notable, as none of these consonant clusters occur in word- or syllable-final position in speech and had to be rather artificially articulated there in this experiment. (See Derwing 1992 for a general discussion of the problem of orthographic influence.)

consonants (like /c/ above) are also restricted phonotactically to syllable-initial position.

A. Words with Unambiguous Spellings
1. Words with Medial Plain Consonants/Positional Constraints

SA-/CANG 'boss'	(1.00/1.00)	PANG-/I 'room (nom.)'	(1.00/.97)

2. Words with Medial Consonant Clusters

CHENG-/SO 'cleaning'	(.99/.99)	PWUL-K/E 'red'	(.74/.92)
SIM-/CI 'wick'	(.99/1.00)	KAP-S/I 'price (nom.)'	(.66/.75)
KWUK-/SWU 'noodle'	(.98/1.00)	SAK-S/I 'wage (nom.)'	(.58/.57)
NAM-/CA 'man'	(.97/1.00)	SAL-M/I 'living (nom.)'	(.52/.72)

3. Words with Medial Tense Consonants

A-/PPA 'daddy'	(.99/.97)	MWU-KK/E 'bundling'	(.45/.88)
KA-/CCA 'fake'	(.79/.92)	KA-SS/E 'went'	(.32/.70)

B. Ambiguous Strings
1. Words Disambiguated under 'Meaning' Condition

MI-/LI 'in advance'	(.91/.95)	MI-L/I 'wheat' (nom.)'	(.91/.27)
A-/NI 'not'	(.83/1.00)	A-N/I 'inside (nom.)'	(.81/.20)
I-/MOKI 'this mosquito'	(.89/.94)	I-M/OKI (nonsense word)	(not tested)
I-/PYENG 'this bottle'	(.66/.97)	I-P/YENG 'going to army'	(.45/.25)
CE-/KE 'that'	(.55/.95)	CE-K/E 'little'	(.55/.63)
SO-/KA 'cow'	(.53/.97)	SO-K/A 'being cheated'	(.52/.25)
IMO-/KI 'this mosquito'	(.60/1.00)	IMO-K/I 'attention (nom.)'	(not tested)
KO-/KI 'meat'	(.90/1.00)	KO-K/I 'music piece (nom.)'	(.87/.25)

2. Words Treated as Unambiguous under Both Conditions

AN-/CA 'not sleeping'	(not tested)	AN-C/A 'sitting'	(.74/1.00)
KI-/LI 'perpetually'	(not tested)	KI-L/I 'length'	(.48/.54)

Note: The first number in each pair represents the 'no meaning' condition and the second number the 'meaning' condition.

Table 1
Results of First Pause-Break Study

Finally, however, (B1) in the crucial orthographically ambiguous strings, the effect of presentation mode is evident, as illustrated by the results for the string MILI previously discussed: under Condition 1 (i.e., without benefit of glosses), the segmentation MI-LI was preferred by 91% of the subjects for both the word spelled MI/LI and the word spelled MIL/I; under Condition 2, however, (i.e., when glosses were supplied), the preference for MI-LI varied sharply from 95% for MI/LI to 27%

for MIL/I (i.e., under the 'meaning' condition, 73% of the subjects preferred the segmentation MIL-I for this word, in conformity with the spelling). The fact that over 90% preferred the segmentation MI-LI in the neutral condition, however - and over a quarter of the subjects persisted in this, even when they were aware that the spelling dictated otherwise - strongly suggests a phonological preference for open syllables (i.e., for single intervocalic consonants to be treated as syllable onsets, rather than as codas).[11]

One other potentially interesting facet of these results is that the magnitude of the effect seems to vary here as a function of the consonant involved: about a 91% preconsonantal break preference with L, down to 84% with N and M, and only about 55% for K, averaging over the five items CE/KE, CEK/E, SO/KA, SOK/A and IMO/KI.[12] This result was initially intriguing in the light of findings from other studies that the tendency of consonants to 'stick to' adjacent vowels seemed to vary as a function of the place of that consonant on the so-called 'sonority' or (inversely) 'strength' hierarchies (see Derwing and Nearey 1991 for further discussion).

3.2.2. Testing for Frequency Effects

The purpose of our next test was to try and assess the true character of the apparent effect of consonant-type on the results for the ambiguous strings: was this indeed another example of the 'vowel stickiness' phenomenon alluded to, or perhaps merely an artifact of word/spelling frequency? In other words, since only a handful of ambiguous strings were actually tested here, it is quite possible that spelling might be indirectly responsible for these results. All that would be required would be for subjects to associate each unglossed string with its most frequent or common meaning and associated spelling, and then to solve the 'pause-break' problem on the basis of that. Thus, if the word MI/LI were much more common than the word spelled MIL/I, and the same for A/NI 'not' compared with AN/I 'inside (nom.)', but with little difference in the case of words like CE/KE 'that' vs. CEK/E 'little', etc., these facts alone might readily explain the results we obtained. (Note that in fn.12 that we have already tried to exploit a possibility of this kind in our attempt to account for the outlier results for the string KOKI, in comparison to those for the other strings with medial K.)

Unfortunately, none of us knew of any published word frequency count in Korean that we could use to check this possibility out. Instead we designed a small word-frequency experiment of our own for the 23 different strings that we had used in the first pause-break study. In brief, we presented these strings under the 'no meaning' condition to the same group of 82 subjects who took the four-choice version of the WB experiment described in section 2.2.1 above. Rather than requiring these subjects to choose between two break positions, however, we asked them instead to write down, in standard orthography, any words they could think of that sounded like what they had heard. For the 14 unambiguous strings, of course, we generally got the spellings for the

[11] Note also in B2 that the results for the words ANC/A 'sitting' and KIL/I 'length' or 'road (nom.)' do not conform with those for the other ambiguous strings, despite the existence of words spelled AN/CA 'not sleeping' and KI/LI 'perpetually' (neither of the latter were tested here). Instead, the results for ANC/A strongly parallel those for the non-ambiguous string PWULK/E (see A2 in Table 1), no doubt due to the positional constraint on /c/ already noted. We have no parallel explanation for the KIL/I results, however, which show a roughly 50-50 split under both presentation conditions, which is a radically different result than for the word MIL/I.

[12] The average value for K increases sharply to 65% if the results for KO/KI and KOK/I are also figured in, but in both of the latter cases the frequency effect of the very common word KO/KI 'meat' can be readily seen to have influenced the results in the 'no meaning' condition.

words presented. For the remaining 9 strings, however, which were the ambiguous ones of interest, we sometimes got one of the two alternative possibilities and sometimes the other, and most often both.[13] We then used these data to calculate an informal relative frequency estimate as follows: a given meaning was taken to be the most frequently associated for that string if either (1) it appeared alone as the only response or (2) if it appeared as the first of the two spellings given. Thus, for the string MILI, we found the spelling MI/LI listed alone 53 times and MI/LI listed before MIL/I another 24 times, but in no case was MIL/I listed either alone or before MI/LI. From this we concluded that the word MI/LI was overwhelmingly more likely to be associated with the string MILI than was the word MIL/I (by a total margin of 77 to 0 in this particular case; see fn. 13 for an explanation of the missing scores). The results for the each of the nine ambiguous strings are summarized in Table 2 below, with percentages of the total number of responses shown in parentheses:

MI/LI	77 (96%)	MIL/I	0 (0%)
A/NI	64 (79%)	AN/I	15 (19%)
KO/KI	54 (67%)	KOK/I	0 (0%)
CE/KE	60 (74%)	CEK/E	17 (21%)
SO/KA	58 (72%)	SOK/A	14 (17%)
IMO/KI	48 (33%)	IMOK/I	48 (59%)
I/PYENG	3 (4%)	IP/YENG	60 (75%)
AN/CA[14]	11 (14%)	ANC/A	67 (83%)
KI/LI[14]	24 (30%)	KIL/I	56 (69%)

Table 2
Relative Frequency Estimates for Ambiguous Strings

As is evident from these results, in the critical first six examples involving the medial L, N and K, the relative frequencies all favor the spellings that parallel the preferred preconsonantal break positions, and by roughly the same margins (96% here vs. 91% in Table 1 for L, 79% vs. 82% for N, and 62% vs. 65% for K [see fn. 12]), leading to the conclusion that frequency effects might well have been responsible for the entire pattern of results we found with the ambiguous items on the first PB task.

3.2.3. Testing Real vs. Nonsense Strings

In view of the development just noted, which detracts significantly from the conclusion that a purely phonological basis for syllable division has been identified for Korean, a different approach to the spelling-interference problem was called for. Still lacking ready access to a suitable pool of illiterate subjects, the approach we tried next was the second one outlined in section 3.2 above, namely, to expand the PB test to a good-sized sample of nonsense strings (for which no spelling preferences are

[13] There were also a few unexpected 'other' spellings, which generally seemed to reflect a mishearing of the strings involved. The only large numbers of such spellings involved the strings KOKI (about a third of the subjects apparently heard this string as KOK/WI 'sublimeness'), IPYENG (21% heard this as one of ten different alternatives, such as the nonsense strings I/PPYENG or IP/NYEM, or the words IP/PYENG 'mouth-disease', IS/PYENG 'tooth-disease', I/NYEM 'ism', etc.), and SOKA (11% heard this as SO/KAM 'feeling', SO/KANG 'lull' or as the nonsense strings SOK/AK or KO/KAM). There was an average of about 3% extraneous responses on the remaining items.

[14] Not tested in the first PB task.

presumably available), as well as an expanded sample of real, ambiguous strings.

As indicated by the words provided in the three tables below, our new test contained 42 ambiguous items, distributed as follows: 9 strings (6 real and 3 nonsense) with medial /l/, 9 strings (5 real and 4 nonsense) with medial nasals, 6 strings with medial fricatives (4 real and 2 nonsense) and 15 with stops (6 real and 9 nonsense), plus 2 items with a medial stop + Y combination (1 real and 1 nonsense) and, as a check on reliability, a repeat of the ambiguous string ANCA. In addition, 18 real, unambiguous strings were also included, yielding a total test of 60 items. These items were randomly ordered and then presented to a total of 101 subjects in both forward (n=60) and reverse (n=41) orders, using the 'no meaning' presentation condition throughout, and with the same two pause-break choices and orders as outlined for the previous experiment.[15] The results are summarized in Tables 3A through 3C.[16]

A. Real Ambiguous Words and Nonsense Strings		**S1/Co**	**S2/On**
1. Liquids (flaps)	**Average /l/**	**.34**	**.66**
a. Real Words	**Average Real /l/**	**.38**	**.62**
(1) MILI 'in advance' or 'wheat (nom.)'		.16	.84
(2) KILI 'perpetually' or 'road (nom.)'		.57	.43
(3) TALI 'bridge' or 'moon (nom.)'		.37	.63
(4) KALA 'go (imp.)' or 'change-by'		.45	.55
(5) TTALA 'follow-by' or 'pour-by'		.16	.84
(6) KKULE 'turn off-in order to' or 'pull (imp.)'		.58	.42
b. Nonsense	**Average Nonsense /l/**	**.25**	**.75**
(1) TALO		.33	.67
(2) NWULWU		.18	.82
(3) SOLWU		.25	.75
2. Nasals	**Average Nasals**	**.41**	**.59**
a. Real Words	**Average Real Nasals**	**.40**	**.60**
(1) ANI 'not' or 'inside (nom.)'		.30	.70
(2) PHANI 'sell (interr.)' or 'record (nom.)'		.67	.33
(3) CHANEY 'kick (ind.)' or 'side dish (loc.)'		.21	.79
(4) KIMI 'feeling' or 'seaweed (nom.)'		.21	.79
(5) TAMA 'beads' or 'put in-by'		.60	.40
b. Nonsense	**Average Nonsense Nasals**	**.42**	**.58**
(1) ENI		.26	.74
(2) TUNO		.47	.53
(3) NEMI		.46	.54
(4) HEMO		.49	.51

Table 3A
Results of Second Pause-Break Study
(Liquids and Nasals)

[15] Thanks to Mr. S.K. Cho for the use of three of his classes and to Mr. Y.C. Song for presenting the stimuli to two of them.

[16] The heading S1/Co stands for 'first-syllable codas' and the scores represent those cases where the pause-break occurred after a single C or both C's of a cluster; the scores under the heading S2/On represent those cases where the pause-break occurred before a single C or between the two C's of a cluster, producing single 'second-syllable onsets'. (PY and KY clusters are treated somewhat differently, as explained in fn. 17.)

		S1/Co	S2/On
3. Fricatives	**Average Fricatives**	**.22**	**.78**
a. Real Words	**Average Real Fricatives**	**.20**	**.80**
(1) PISE 'secretary' or 'comb hair (imp.)'		.18	.82
(2) KASI 'fishbone' or 'hat (nom.)'		.29	.71
(3) KISEY 'energy' or 'collar' (loc.)'		.20	.80
(4) CISI 'instruction' or 'behavior (nom.)'		.15	.85
b. Nonsense	**Average Nonsense Fricatives**	**.23**	**.77**
(1) TESU		.24	.76
(2) TWUSSI		.23	.77
4. Stops	**Average Stops**	**.33**	**.67**
a. Real Words	**Average Real Stops**	**.37**	**.63**
(1) SOKA 'cow (nom.)' or 'being cheated'		.47	.53
(2) YAKI 'stimulate' or 'medicine (nom.)'		.52	.48
(3) MACE 'even' or 'hit (ind.)'		.27	.73
(4) NACI 'be produced (ind.)' or 'daytime (nom.)'		.39	.61
(5) KIPHI 'run away' or 'depth'		.36	.64
(6) NOPHA 'worry' or 'be high (ind.)'		.32	.68
b. Nonsense	**Average Nonsense Stops**	**.28**	**.72**
(1) CWUPA		.42	.58
(2) TWUKWU		.14	.86
(3) LWUCA		.07	.93
(4) WUPHA		.16	.84
(5) SWUKHA		.40	.60
(6) WUCHI		.22	.78
(7) CIPPI		.57	.43
(8) NWUKKI		.32	.68
(9) PACCWU		.27	.73
5. Single Segments	**Average Single Segments**	**.33**	**.67**
a. Real Words	**Average Real Single Segments**	**.35**	**.65**
b. Nonsense	**Ave Nonsense Single Segments**	**.30**	**.70**
6. Clusters			
a. Real Words			
(1) ANCA 'sitting' or 'not sleeping'		.34	.66
(2) IPYENG 'this bottle' or 'going to the army'		.29[17]	.71
b. Nonsense			
(1) IKYONG		.34[17]	.66

Table 3B
Results of Second Pause-Break Study
(Fricatives and Stops)

[17] For PY and KY clusters the S1/Co scores actually represent cases where the pause break occurred before the entire cluster, rather than after it; the S2/On scores still represent a break between the C's, as with all the other clusters.

B. Real Unambiguous Words		**S1/Co**	**S2/On**
1. Single Segments	**Average Single Segments**	**.32**	**.68**
a. Spelling Break before C	**Average Preconsonant**	**.13**	**.87**
1) PHI/LI 'flute'		.24	.76
(2) SO/LA 'shell'		.34	.66
(3) SO/MO 'consumption'		.05	.95
(4) SA/CHANG 'boss'		.02	.98
(5) A/PPA 'daddy'		.02	.98
(6) KA/CCA 'fake'		.12	.88
b. Spelling Break after C	**Average Postconsonant**	**.59**	**.41**
(1) SEYM/I 'counting (nom.)'		.61	.39
(2) PANG/I 'bread'		.87	.13
(3) KASS/E 'went' '		.42	.58
(4) MWUKK/E 'bundling'		.48	.52
2. Clusters	**Average Clusters**	**.19**	**.81**
a. Spelling Break between CC	**Average Intercluster**	**.03**	**.97**
(1) KWUK/SWU 'noodle'		.02	.98
(2) CHENG/SO 'cleaning'		.04	.96
(3) NAM/CA 'man'		.04	.96
(4) SIM/CI 'wick'		.02	.98
b. Spelling Break after CC	**Average Postcluster**	**.35**	**.65**
(1) SALM/I 'living (nom.)'		.35	.65
(2) PWULK/E 'red (ind.)'		.42	.58
(3) KAPS/I 'price (nom.)'		.36	.64
(4) SAKS/I 'wage (nom.)'		.30	.70

Table 3C
Results of Second Pause-Break Study
(Real Unambiguous Words)

The real words in this expanded study show some of the same frequency effects that were noticed in the first study, as illustrated once again by MILI vs. KILI. (Note that the 84% vs. 43% preference for the onset treatment found here is very close to the 91% vs. 48% differential we found previously for these two strings under the 'no meaning' condition.). A couple of other such examples are ANI (70%) vs. PHANI (33%) and KIMI (79%) vs. TAMA (40%). For all of this, the overall means for single intervocalic consonants for the real words do not differ substantially from those for the nonsense strings (65% vs. 70%). Nonetheless, despite the occasional unexplained anomaly even in the latter set (see the results for CWUPA, SWUKHA and especially CIPPI on Table 3B, for example), the results for the nonsense words present the most consistent pattern and undoubtedly provide our best guide to a purely phonological syllabification strategy. As before, the general preference for an onset and cluster-splitting strategy is strongly supported, as the overall nonsense mean for S2/On breaks is about 68%, a highly significant result ($t(100)=9.76$ for subjects; $t(18)=4.97$ for items; $p<.0001$ for both).

So what about the effect of consonant-type, which seemed to be a spurious finding from our first test? As indicated in Tables 3A and 3B above, the nonsense means for the four major C-type categories represented are as follows:

Liquids	.75
Nasals	.58
Fricatives	.77
Stops	.71

While t-tests show that there is a highly significant difference here between the liquids and the nasals for subjects ($t(100)=5.61$, $p<.0001$), there is none between the liquids, fricatives or stops, so the full hierarchy seems to break down. It is worth noting, however, that the 'liquids' in this case are always intervocalic, where they are realized phonetically in Korean as flaps, a segment-type whose place on the sonority/strength scale is problematic. These data suggest, in fact, that flaps pattern more like obstruents than sonorants, as represented here by the nasals, which clearly behave quite differently from all of the others.

Finally, it is of some interest to look at the clusters PY and KY, which are the only two tested that may serve as syllable onsets (cf. the words PYENGWEN 'hospital' and KYOCANG 'principal'). Contrary to the predictions of the maximal onset principle (e.g., Selkirk 1982), our subjects preferred to break between these clusters, too, by a roughly 2:1 margin, both in the case of the nonsense string IKYONG (66%) and the real word IPYENG (71%). The significance of this last result is considerably weakened, however, by the fact that IP/YENG is by far the most common interpretation of the real word string, as already noted in section 3.2.2 above. Thus the only clean evidence we have here that bears (in this case negatively) on the maximal onset notion is based on the single nonsense string IKYONG, which may be atypical, so any conclusion reached will be tentative at best and further testing on this point is definitely indicated.

Overall, however, this second PB study seems to have provided sufficient data to support the conclusion that the preferred intersyllabic break point for Korean, uninfluenced by the spelling, generally occurs between two consonants in a CC cluster, but before a single intervocalic consonant, thereby confirming the obligatory onset notion.

4. CONCLUSIONS

Our attempt to expand the experimental exploration of syllable structure to languages beyond English has been slowed by the fact that new experimental techniques have had to be developed in nearly all cases. Nevertheless, the following preliminary results can now be reported for Korean on the basis of our new WB and PB tasks: (1) Korean syllables appear to be of the left-branching or body+coda type, challenging the universality of a general onset-rime strategy; and (2) Korean speakers show a decided preference to divide V-/C/V and V/C-/C/V sequences at the positions marked by hyphens, even though their orthography permits syllable-like breaks at all five of the positions marked by slashes. This provides important support for the general notion of obligatory onsets, though not for the maximal onset principle.

References

Cheun, Sang Buom. 1980. Lapsus linguaeuy umwunloncek haysek (A phonological interpretation of lapsus linguae). Ene (Language), Vol. 5, No. 2, 15-32. Korean Linguistics Society: Seoul.

Derwing, Bruce L. In press. A 'pause-break' task for eliciting syllable boundary judgments from literate and illiterate speakers: initial results for five diverse languages. To appear in Lg and Speech.

Derwing, Bruce L. 1992. Orthographic aspects of linguistic competence. Linguistic aspects of literacy, ed. by P. Downing, S. Lima and M. Noonan, 193-210. Amsterdam: John Benjamins.

Derwing, Bruce L., Dow, Maureen L. and Nearey, Terrance M. 1987. Experimental evidence for phonological units. Proceedings of the XIth International Congress of Phonetic Sciences, Vol. II, 249-252. Tallinn, Estonia.

Derwing, Bruce L., Dow, Maureen L. and Nearey, Terrance M. 1988. Experimenting with syllable structure. ESCOL '88, ed. by J. Powers and K. de Jong, 83-94. Columbus, OH: The Ohio State University.

Derwing, Bruce L. and Nearey, Terrance M. 1991. The 'vowel-stickiness' phenomenon: three sources of experimental evidence. Proceedings of the XIIth International Congress of Phonetic Sciences, Vol. III, 210-213. Aix-en-Provence, France.

Derwing, Bruce L. and Wiebe, Grace E. In preparation. Three versions of a forced-choice word-blending task: validation for English.

Dow, Maureen L. 1987. On the psychological reality of sub-syllabic units. Ph.D. dissertation, University of Alberta, Edmonton.

Dow, Maureen L. and Derwing, Bruce L. 1989. Experimental evidence for syllable-internal structure. Linguistic categorization, ed. by R. Corrigan, F. Eckman and M. Noonan, 81-92. New York: John Benjamins.

Kim-Renaud, Young-Key. 1986. The syllable in Korean phonology. Study in Korean linguistics, ed. by Y-K. Kim-Renaud, 31-44. Seoul: Hanshin.

Selkirk, Elizabeth O. 1982. The syllable. The structure of phonological representations, Part II, ed. by H. van der Hulst and N. Smith, 337-383. Dordrecht: Foris.

Treiman, Rebecca. 1983. The structure of spoken syllables: evidence from novel word games. Cognition 15.49-74.

Treiman, Rebecca. 1986. The division between onsets and rimes in English syllables. Journal of Memory and Language 25.476-491.

Treiman, Rebecca and Danis, Caroline. 1988. Syllabification of invervocalic consonants. Journal of Memory and Cognition 27.87-104.

Vennemann, Theo. 1988. Preference laws for syllable structure and the explanation of sound change. Berlin: Mouton de Gruyter.

Youn, Yeo Bum [= Yoon, Yeo Bom]. 1990. Arguments against the universality of the onset/rime division. Sogang Working Papers in Linguistics 4.93-104.

Appendix 1
Word-Pairs Used in the Word-Blend Experiments

1. KANG 'river' - SEM 'island' (a,b)
2. NAL 'day' - SOM 'cotton' (a)
3. SWUPH 'forest - CEM 'dot' (a)
4. CAL'well' - KIM 'seaweed' (a)
5. SAM 'three' - KIL 'road' (a,b)
6. SWUS 'male' - HIM 'power' (a,b)
7. PHATH 'red-bean' - CENG 'chisel' (a,b)
8. THONG 'pail' - SEM 'island' (a,b)
9. TACH 'anchor' - KKWUM 'dream' (a,b)
10. TALK 'rooster'- KETH 'surface' (a,b)
11. KAM 'persimmon' - HOK'swelling' (a)
12. TON 'money' - SWUL 'wine'(a,b)
13. TUNG 'back'- SOTH 'kettle' (a,b)
14. CHES 'beginning' - KKUTH 'end'(b)
15. HULK 'soil' - SOT.H 'kettle' (b)
16. CEM 'dot' - SWUPH 'forest' (b)

Note: Pairs marked (a) were used on the four-choice version and those marked (b) were used on the two-choice version.

The Acquisition of the Japanese Subject Marker Ga and its Theoretical Implications

PATRICIA MAYES AND TSUYOSHI ONO
University of California at Santa Barbara

1. Introduction

In this paper, we investigate the acquisition of the subject marker ga in Japanese by examining some longitudinal data from one child.[2] The results of the study will be used to evaluate several recent theories concerning the acquisition of syntactic categories such as "subject" and "direct object".

Initially, we would like to briefly summarize three of these theories in which the major point of contention is the extent to which two possible factors, innate acquisition mechanisms and adult input, play a role in acquisition. First, Pinker (1984; 1989) believes that a large part of the acquisition of syntactic

---

[1]We would first like to thank Junya Noji and Kazue Noji for their monumental records of language development. We would also like to thank Hiromi Morikawa for letting us use her computerized version of Noji's data as well as her consistent help in using it. Without these people's work and/or generosity, we could not have written this paper. We would like thank Wally Chafe, Pat Clancy, Marja-Liisa Helasvuo, Hajime Hoji, Toshi Nakayama, Clifton Pye, Sandy Thompson, Shigeo Tonoike, Akira Yamamoto, as well as many others for their help and/or comments on earlier versions of this paper. We were not always able to incorporate the suggestions made by these people.

[2]For this paper, we will only be concerned with instances of ga which, according to Kuno (1973), can be analyzed as marking the subject. We will follow Kuno in assuming that ga is a subject marker. Instances in which ga is used to mark an object have thus been excluded from this analysis.

categories is performed by innate mechanisms. Specifically, he proposes a model of "semantic bootstrapping" in which children initially use a set of innate ("linking") rules to map syntactic categories onto semantic categories. Mapping is based on syntactic and semantic hierarchies in that agent maps onto subject, and patient maps onto direct object, etc. A prediction that follows from this theory is that the child initially begins marking subjects of highly transitive clauses because they are the best examples of agents. Using this mechanism, the child then associates input subjects with universal properties of subjects which are also assumed to be innate. In Pinker's theory, input does not have as a large role in the formation of syntactic categories as it does in other theories, its main role being to provide a starting point for the linking rules.

The second theory is that of Slobin (1985), who has suggested that children start with a set of general conceptual categories which are used in the construction of syntactic categories. For example, initially, the child notices agents in active transitive events because they are perceptually salient participants; then s/he forms a linguistic category for agent. The syntactic category "subject" is then acquired by extending this initial category to include other members (e.g. agents of less prototypical transitive events, experiencers, etc.). Slobin suggests that since only certain notions ever receive grammatical marking cross-linguistically, they constitute a "privileged" set of conceptual categories. Thus, in Slobin's model, the child's preexisting conceptual categories play a major role in the construction of syntactic categories. Input provides the linguistic marking onto which the conceptual categories are mapped, and later, input is used to modify and refine those categories into the specific categories that are appropriate for the target language.

The third major theory has been proposed by Bowerman (1976; 1982; 1985; 1990). Bowerman agrees with Slobin's contention that conceptual categories play an important role in the construction of syntactic categories, but she places a greater emphasis on the role of adult input, arguing against the idea that there is a tightly fixed set of "privileged" conceptual categories. Instead, she argues in favor of conceptual freedom, suggesting that which categories a child forms may, in fact, be molded by the input. Bowerman points out that different children may use different strategies to construct syntactic categories and suggests that some children may initially begin forming these categories using a word-by-word strategy and later generalize to more inclusive categories.

In her most recent study, Bowerman (1990) attempted to test the predictions made by Pinker's theory, using English data from her two children. She found that the children produced more ordering errors (e.g. OV and VS) in utterances involving prototypical transitive verbs than in less transitive clauses. These results are contrary to expectations based on Pinker's theory (and also Slobin's). These theories would predict that prototypical transitive clauses would be the first to be acquired, and fewer errors would be made in production of these clauses than would be made with less transitive clauses. Additional support for this interpretation is provided by Pye's (1990) cross-linguistic comparison of the acquisition of case marking in nominative-accusative and ergative-absolutive languages (see also Schieffelin 1985). He found that both systems were acquired with equal ease and that there was no tendency to overextend case marking based on semantic roles as might be predicted by Pinker's theory. Since children make few errors acquiring either system, he contends that they must be learning how to use the case marking based on distribution in the input, rather than on semantic bootstrapping. As we will see, our Japanese data also show that ga was used to mark subjects of intransitive clauses before it was used to mark subjects of transitive clauses, and this order of acquisition reflects the distribution of ga with these clause types in the adult input.

2. Data

The data used in the present study were collected from a Japanese boy named Sumihare, a first-born child in a middle-class family. His language and the adult input were recorded with contextual information almost daily by his parents from the day of birth to his seventh birthday in a diary which is published as Noji (1973-1977). For her dissertation, Morikawa (1989) computerized some of these data, along with information such as the predicate type, missing case particle (see below), and the Japanese gloss for any idiosyncrasies in the child's language. She was kind enough to allow us to use this computerized database. The portion we have used in the present study covers a seven-month period, from ages 1;11-2;5.

3. Methods

Recent studies (Silverstein 1976; Dixon 1979; Du Bois 1985; 1987; Durie 1988; Comrie 1989; Fox and Thompson 1990) have suggested that we can gain further understanding of linguistic structure by examining the distribution of arguments with different predicate types. In addition, Iwasaki (1985) and Suzuki and Ono (1991) have found that, in adult Japanese discourse, ga is used more often with subjects of intransitive verbs than with subjects of transitive verbs. Thus in this paper, we have chosen to examine the distribution of ga with subjects of different types of predicates in order to determine if our data are consistent with the claim that distribution in the adult input is a major factor influencing the acquisition of syntactic categories.

It has been noted by some researchers that ga is occasionally omitted in naturally occurring adult discourse, and we found this to be true of our data as well. We classified each occurrence of ga and each ellipsis of ga in the possible positions based on the type of predicate with which it occurred. We used a modified version of Dixon's (1979) classification system to categorize subjects. Thus subjects of intransitive verbs were classified as S; subjects of transitive verbs were classified as A; subjects of adjectival predicates were classified as Sa; and subjects of nominal predicates were classified as Sn. (1) through (4) are typical examples of these four types:[3]

```
(1) S:  Kazubochan ga otta  ne                    [2;1]
        Kazubochan ga exist PR
        'Kazubochan was there'
```

[3]The material in the parentheses was not expressed by Sumihare, but supplied by Morikawa based on Noji's notes. The number in the square brackets indicates the age of Sumihare at the time of utterance.

```
(2) A:  Benjo     (o)  tonton  shita  ne  boku ga  [2;0]
        bathroom  ACC  fix     did    PR  I    ga
        'I fixed the bathroom'

(3) Sa: Akachan ga  samui                          [2;1]
        baby    ga  cold
        'The child is cold'

(4) Sn: Koko ga  tonneru (da) zo                   [2;5]
        here ga  tunnel   COP PR
        'Here is a tunnel'
```

The increase in the use of ga with the four different types of noun phrases (S, A, Sa, and Sn) was then examined month by month.

In some cases in which the particle was omitted, it would be possible to choose between two or three particles and still produce a syntactically correct clause. The most notable case is a choice between ga and the topic marker wa. In these cases, the missing particles were either filled in by Morikawa (1989) or the second author. (5) is a typical example of a choice between wa and ga:

```
(5) Buranko (wa | ga)  nai        ne               [2;1]
    swing    TOP  ga   not exist  PR
    'There is no swing (here)'
```

In this example, ga was chosen because wa would imply that there is no swing here, but there are other things. This is clearly not what was implied in the context in which this utterance was made.

There were also some cases in which the predicate was not overtly expressed but was recoverable from the context. Many of these were already provided either by Noji or by Morikawa. There were a few cases where the second author of the present paper filled in the predicate based on the contextual notes of Noji.

When two or more verbs are concatenated and used as the predicate (i.e. a serial verb construction), the verb which functions as the main verb was considered to be the predicate.

Finally, Sumihare's rote imitations were eliminated by Morikawa when she computerized the data and thus did not enter into the present analysis.

4. Results

Next, we will present the results of the quantitative analysis. Consider Table 1. In this table, the top row indicates the types of NPs used with different predicate types. The first column shows the age, broken down by month. The column labeled ga indicates the number of ga-marked NPs, and the column labeled (ga) indicates the number of NPs which could have been marked by ga but were not. The percentage is the ratio of the ga-marked NPs among NPs for which ga-marking is possible. Below, we will use FREQUENCY to refer to the number of overt ga and CONSISTENCY to refer to the percentage of overt ga in the possible positions.

Table 1
Occurrence of ga with Different Types of NPs

	S (intrans subj)			A (trans subj)			Sa (subj pred adj)			Sn (subj pred N)		
Age	ga	(ga)	%	ga	(ga)	%	ga	(ga)	%	ga	(ga)	%
1;11	8	127	5.9	1	8	11.1	0	13	0.0	0	0	-
2;0	15	77	16.3	1	8	11.1	0	5	0.0	0	0	-
2;1	44	142	23.7	15	28	34.9	1	7	12.5	0	0	-
2;2	121	223	35.2	25	37	40.3	6	15	28.6	0	0	-
2;3	90	72	55.6	12	14	46.2	6	6	50.0	0	0	-
2;4	100	66	60.2	14	5	73.7	5	12	29.4	0	0	-
2;5	150	49	75.4	27	6	81.8	6	7	46.2	1	1	50.0
Total	528	757	41.1	95	106	47.3	24	65	27.0	1	1	50.0

Table 1 shows several interesting patterns. First, if you examine the ga and percentage columns of the table vertically from age 1;11 to 2;5, it is apparent that both the frequency and the consistency of ga-marking in Sumihare's language increased gradually over the seven-month period.[4] This indicates that the acquisition of the subject marker in Japanese is not accomplished in an instantaneous way, but involves a period of learning.

Second, there appears to be a hierarchical pattern in the order of the acquisition of ga with regard to the different types of NPs. Although S and A show a similar increase in terms of consistency, the frequency of instances may suggest that S began to be marked by ga a little earlier than A. This may be more clearly observed by examining the frequency of ga-marking at ages 1;11 and 2;0 in the table. While the frequency of ga-marked S gradually increased (from 8 to 15) during these periods, only one A was marked in each period. The first steady increase in frequency of A marking began at age 2;1. Sa was initially marked by ga at 2;1, and there was a gradual increase in the consistency with which it was

[4]Since Noji's data are from a longitudinal study which recorded the child's language in a diary style, in a strict sense the frequency is not directly comparable month to month. However, one may still be able to observe some meaningful patterns in frequency partly because of the vastness of this database.

marked (12.5% at 2;1, 28.6% at 2;2, and 50% at 2;3). Sn was expressed and marked by ga for the first and only time at age 2;5. These observations may suggest a hierarchical order of emergence in the acquisition of ga with the different types of NPs:[5]

(6) S > A > Sa > Sn

Third, one may notice that the hierarchical pattern discussed also holds in terms of frequency, not just order of emergence. As the total numbers in the bottom row of Table 1 show, the four types of subjects can be aligned in a similar hierarchy which, this time, indicates the frequency of ga-marking (S: 528, A: 95, Sa: 24, Sn: 1).

5. Discussion

5.1. The Theories of Pinker and Slobin

The results of our study do not support the theories of either Pinker (1984; 1989) or Slobin (1985). Recall that Pinker hypothesizes that the syntactic category "subject" is initially learned by a "semantic bootstrapping" mechanism. In essence, this hypothesis claims that children use "the agentive argument of active action predicates" to form their first rules concerning which entities should be labeled as subjects (Pinker 1984:44). What this implies is that the child should initially begin marking subjects of highly transitive verbs because they are the best examples of agents. Slobin (1985) also contends that the child maps a "manipulative activity scene" onto linguistic segments; thus the first evidence of this strategy we would expect to see is the marking of agents and patients in highly transitive clauses. Thus, though Pinker and Slobin have very different theoretical orientations, each of their theories seems to predict that agents of prototypical transitive clauses should be the first to show ga-marking. However, as we have shown, this is not what happened when Sumihare acquired ga. Rather, he began by marking S NPs most often and later extended his use of ga to other types of NPs. In addition, the S clauses in which he used ga were often clauses with existential verbs, and thus agentless (example (1) has the existential verb oru). We also found that when Sumihare first began marking A NPs, the distribution of ga-marked A NPs and unmarked A NPs appeared to be random. In other words, clauses with highly transitive verbs did not favor ga-marking of the subject, and clauses with less transitive verbs did not favor unmarked subjects.

Another prediction that may follow from Pinker's theory is that the child would attain 100% subject marking at some stage because s/he would attempt to regularize subject marking after learning what to place in the syntactic category. However, as we have seen, Sumihare never used ga in 100% of the possible positions. Thus our results do not seem to support the theories of either Pinker or Slobin.

---

[5]Morikawa (1989:77) concluded that ga-marking of S, A, and Sa NPs all had "roughly comparable patterns of increase" (though she did notice that marking of Sa was somewhat delayed). Apparently, the reason she did not notice any difference in the patterns for S and A is because she examined the data over several three-month periods, rather than month by month. Based on a closer examination of the data, we obtained the present hierarchy.

5.2. Bowerman's Theory

On the other hand, our results are consistent with Bowerman's theory which emphasizes the important role of adult input.

Recall that in terms of both order of emergence and overall frequency, ga-marking followed the hierarchy presented in (6). Interestingly, when we examined the adult input, we found a strikingly similar pattern in the frequency of ga-marking among different subject types. Table 2 is based on the adult input during a period which includes the seven-month period which we investigated. It is based on several tables from Morikawa's dissertation; thus she had already determined which particle would be appropriate in the cases in which they were omitted.

Table 2
Occurrence of ga with Different Types of NPs in the Input
(Adapted from Morikawa 1989)

	S (intrans subj)			A (trans subj)			Sa (subj pred N)		
Period	ga	(ga)	%	ga	(ga)	%	ga	(ga)	%
1;11-2;7	377	77	83.0	62	17	78.5	25	13	65.8

As can be seen, ga-marked S is much more frequent than ga-marked A, and ga-marked A is more frequent than ga-marked Sa (377 vs. 62 vs. 25). We also found that the use of ga-marked Sn is extremely rare in the adult input. Thus we find exactly the same pattern in the child's production and the adult input in terms of frequency. It may also be noticed that the same hierarchy holds for the consistency of ga-marking in the input. S is more consistently marked by ga than A, and A is more consistently marked by ga than Sa (83.0% vs 78.5% vs 65.8%). These striking similarities between the child's production and the adult input suggest that the adult input had a strong influence on the acquisition of ga.

Comparing Tables 1 and 2, we find that Sumihare's consistency of ga-marking with S and A reached near the adult levels by age 2;5.[6] Once he had attained the adult level, he never extended his use of ga beyond this level. The fact that Sumihare does not ever extend his use of ga beyond this level to 100%, but stops at roughly 80%, may also indicate the importance of the distribution in the input for the acquisition of ga. In other words, Sumihare's sensitivity to the input can be demonstrated by the fact that the input level is his target level. We have seen that the child's acquisition of ga reflects the frequency and consistency of ga-marking in the input. These results are clearly consistent with Bowerman's theory.

---

[6]This point was originally made by Morikawa (1989).

6. Conclusion

To sum up, our study has cast doubt on Pinker's (1984; 1989) theory in which innate mechanisms are the primary force influencing the acquisition of syntactic categories. They have also cast doubt on Slobin's (1985) theory in which a certain "privileged set" of conceptual categories plays the major role in the construction of syntactic categories.

On the other hand, Bowerman suggests that though the child has a predisposition for forming conceptual categories, the particular set of categories is more flexible than in Slobin's theory. Further, the syntactic categories used in the particular language that the child is acquiring will influence which conceptual categories s/he constructs. Our findings are consistent with Bowerman's theory in that there was no evidence that the child had a preexisting category for agent; rather, he followed the pattern presented in the adult input when deciding what to mark with ga.

List of Abbreviations

ACC	Accusative particle
COP	Copula
PR	Pragmatic particle
TOP	Topic particle

References

Bowerman, Melissa. 1976. Semantic factors in the acquisition of rules for word use and sentence construction. Normal and deficient child language, ed. by D. M. Morehead and A. E. Morehead, 99-179. Baltimore: University Park Press.

Bowerman, Melissa. 1982. Reorganizational process in lexical and syntactic development. Language acquisition: The state of the art, ed. by E. Wanner and L. R. Gleitman, 319-46. Cambridge: Cambridge University Press.

Bowerman, Melissa. 1985. What shapes children's grammars? The crosslinguistic study of language acquisition: Vol. 2: Theoretical issues, ed. by D. I. Slobin, 1257-319. Hillsdale, NJ: Lawrence Erlbaum.

Bowerman, Melissa. 1990. Mapping thematic roles onto syntactic functions: Are children helped by innate linking rules? Linguistics. 28.1253-89.

Comrie, Bernard. 1989. Language universals and linguistic typology. Second edition. Chicago: Chicago University Press.

Dixon, Robert M. W. 1979. Ergativity. Lg. 55.59-138.

Du Bois, John W. 1985. Competing motivations. Iconicity in syntax, ed. by J. Haiman, 343-65. Amsterdam: John Benjamins.

Du Bois, John W. 1987. The discourse basis of ergativity. Lg. 63.805-55.

Durie, Mark. 1988. Preferred argument structure in an active language: Argument against the category 'intransitive subject'. Lingua. 74.1-25.

Fox, Barbara A. and Sandra A. Thompson. 1990. A discourse explanation of the grammar of relative clauses in English conversation. Lg. 66.297-316.

Iwasaki, Shoichi. 1985. The "given A constraint" and the Japanese particle ga. Proceedings of the first annual meeting of the Pacific Linguistics Conference, ed. by S. DeLancey and R. S. Tomlin, 152-67. Eugene, OR: Department of Linguistics, University of Oregon.

Kuno, Susumu. 1973. The structure of the Japanese language. Cambridge, MA: MIT Press.

Morikawa, Hiromi. 1989. Acquisition of case marking and predicate-argument structures in Japanese: A longitudinal study of language acquisition mechanisms. Doctoral dissertation, University of Kansas.

Noji, Junya. 1973-1977. Yojiki no gengo seikatsu no jittai [Language use in childhood]. Vols. 1-4. Hiroshima: Bunka Hyoron.

Pinker, Steve. 1984. Language learnability and language development. Cambridge, MA: Harvard University Press.

Pinker, Steve. 1989. Learnability and cognition: The acquisition of argument structure. Cambridge, MA: MIT Press.

Pye, Clifton. 1990. The acquisition of ergative languages. Linguistics. 28.1291-330.

Schieffelin, Bambi B. 1985. The acquisition of Kaluli. The crosslinguistic study of language acquisition: Vol. 1: Theoretical issues, ed. by D. I. Slobin, 525-93. Hillsdale, NJ: Lawrence Erlbaum.

Silverstein, Michael. 1976. Hierarchy of features and ergativity. Grammatical categories in Australian languages, ed. by R. M. W. Dixon, 112-71. New York: Humanities Press.

Slobin, Dan I. 1985. Crosslinguistic evidence for the language-making capacity. The crosslinguistic study of language acquisition: Vol. 2: Theoretical issues, ed. by D. I. Slobin, 1157-256. Hillsdale, NJ: Lawrence Erlbaum.

Suzuki, Ryoko. and Tsuyoshi Ono. 1991. Japanese ga, spotlighting, and intransitives in spoken narratives. Santa Barbara papers in linguistics: Vol. 3: Asian discourse and grammar, ed. by P. M. Clancy and S. A. Thompson, 144-52. Santa Barbara, CA: Department of Linguistics, University of California Santa Barbara.

Processing of Japanese Relative Clause Constructions

HIROKO YAMASHITA, LAURIE STOWE, AND MINEHARU NAKAYAMA

The Ohio State University and The University of Groningen

0. Introduction

The processing of the Japanese language has attracted much attention recently in both experimental and theoretical psycholinguistics (e.g., Frazier and Rayner 1988; Mazuka and Lust 1988; Horii 1990; Mazuka 1991; Nakayama 1990; 1991a,b; Inoue 1991; Inoue and Fodor 1991; Sakamoto 1991a,b). This paper discusses two issues in the processing of the Japanese language. The general question is to what extent the processing of Japanese, an SOV, left-branching language with relatively free occurrence of empty categories, is different from the processing of English, an SVO, right-branching language in which empty categories are much more restricted. More specifically, we will examine (1) whether verb information is used in Japanese in a similar way to English and (2) how empty categories are processed in Japanese. Especially, we will investigate if there is any processing cost involved in processing empty categories. These questions will be answered as we discuss an experiment contrasting two types of relative clause constructions: the GAPLESS relative clause construction and the REGULAR relative clause construction. The Regular relative clause construction is the one with a gap (or an empty category) in the relative clause, which is coindexed with a head noun. This is shown in (1a). A Gapless relative construction is one in which there is no gap in the clause and all the arguments of the verb occur within the relative clause (cf. Teramura 1976; Matsumoto 1988). This is shown in (1b).

(1) a.[$_{NP}$[kodomo-ga EC_i katta] $okasi_i$]
child-nom bought candy
'the candy that the child bought'

b.[NP[kodomo-ga okasi-o katta] oturi]
child-nom candy-acc bought change
'the money left after the child bought candy'

These two types of relative clause constructions were contrasted in an experiment employing a word-by-word reading task. The results of the experiment suggest that verb information in Japanese is used in the same manner as in English, in the sense that it is used immediately to determine the preceding syntactic structure and affects the processing of the following structure. The results also reveal that the processing of an empty category has a cost in Japanese.

The organization of the paper is as follows. In section one, some syntactic differences between Japanese and English will be briefly summarized. In section two, we will review the previous experimental studies on the use of verb information and the processing of empty categories, and then we will address some questions on the processing of the Japanese language. The experiment will be discussed in section three. Section four will present the experimental results.

1. Some Syntactic Differences between English and Japanese

There are three major types of syntactic differences between English and Japanese: word order, phrase structure branching directions, and occurrence of empty categories. In this section, we will provide a brief summary of syntactic differences between the two languages.

1.1. Word-order

The basic word order Japanese is SOV, whereas English is an SVO language. In a transitive sentence in Japanese, both subject and object precede the transitive verb. This is shown in (2a). In English, the subject precedes the verb and the object follows the verb, as sentence (2b) demonstrates.

(2) a. John-ga hon-o katta.
John-nom book-acc bought
S O V
'John bought a book.'

b. John bought a book.
S V O

1.2. Branching Directions

The second difference is the direction of phrase structure branching, which depends on the position of the phrasal head in each language. While English is a right-branching language, Japanese is a left-branching language. The effects of this difference are clearly apparent in the relative clause construction, which is shown below.

(3) a.

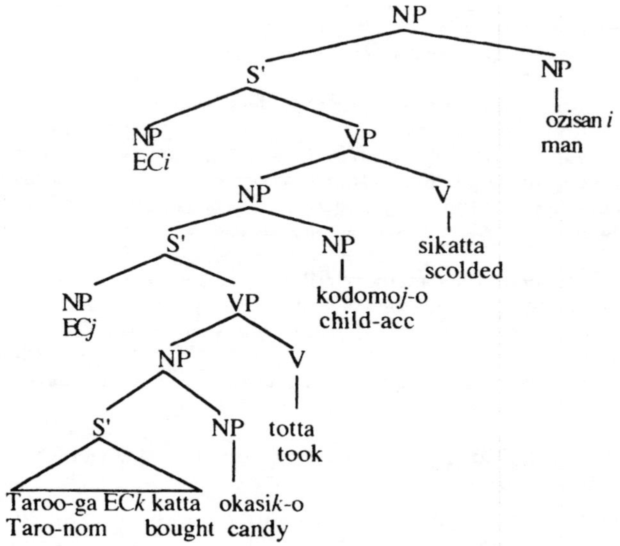

[[EC_i [[EC_j [[Taroo-ga EC_k katta]okasi$_k$-o] totta] kodomo$_j$-o] sikatta]ozisan$_i$]
Taro-nom bought candy-acc took child -acc scolded man

b.

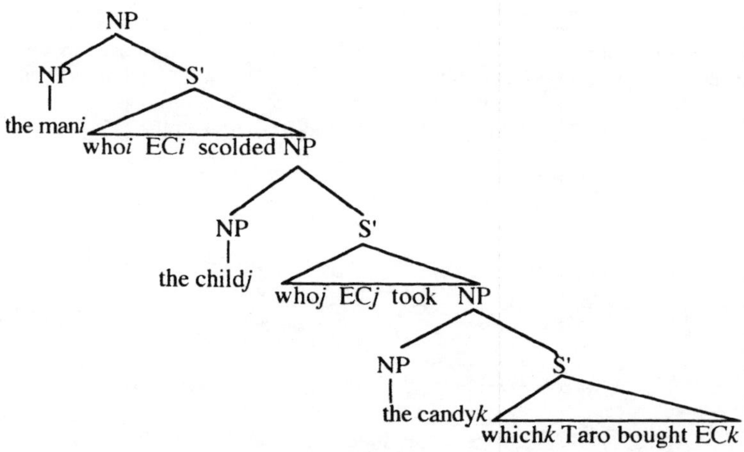

[The man$_i$ [who$_i$ [EC_i scolded the child$_j$ [who$_j$ [EC_j took the candy$_k$ [which$_k$ [Taroo bought EC_k]]]]]]]...
'The man who scolded the child who took the candy which Taro bought'

When relative clauses in Japanese are embedded recursively, the structure branches out to the left (cf. Kuno 1973), as shown in (3a). English, on the other hand, branches out rightward as the embedding deepens. This is demonstrated in (3b).

1.3. Occurrences of Empty Categories

The third difference between English and Japanese is that Japanese allows the occurrence of empty (phonologically null) pronouns, which is a type of empty category, in a tensed clause (cf. Perlmutter 1972, Huang 1984, Hoji 1985, but cf. Hasegawa 1984). This is shown in (4).

(4) a. Taroo-ga hon-o katta.
Taro-nom book-acc bought
'Taro bought a book.'

b. Taroo-ga EC katta.
Taro-nom bought
'Taro bought EC.'

c. EC hon-o katta.
book-acc bought
'EC bought a book.'

d. EC EC katta.
bought
'EC bought EC.'

Sentence (4b) has an empty object while (4c) contains an empty subject. In sentence (4d), both subject and object are phonologically null. The presence of either an empty subject or object, or both, does not make these sentences ungrammatical. This phenomenon is not unique to simple sentences. Empty categories may also occur in tensed subordinate clauses, as well as in relative clauses. This is shown below.

(5) a. Taro-wa [EC tumaranai kara] sanpo-ni itta.
Taro-top bored because for-a-walk went
'Taro went for a walk because (he) was bored.'

b. Taro-ga [Hanako-ga EC miru maeni] gakko-e itta.
Taro-nom Hanako-nom see before school to went
'Taro went to school before Hanako saw EC.'

(6) a. [[seito-ga EC_i katta] hon_i]
student-nom bought book
'the book that the student bought'

b. [[EC EC_i katta] hon_i]
bought book
'the book that EC bought'

c. [[EC_i hon-o katta] $seito_i$]
book-acc bought student
'the student that bought a book'

d. [[EC_i EC katta] $seito_i$]
bought student

'the student that bought EC'

The sentences in (5) demonstrate that empty categories may occur in subordinate clauses. The examples in (6) show that empty categories occur in relative clause.[2]

In English, on the other hand, an empty pronoun cannot appear. This is shown in (7)-(9).

(7) a. Taro bought a book.
b.*Taro bought EC.
c. *EC bought a book.
d. *EC bought EC.

(8) a. *Taro went for a walk [because EC was bored]
b. *Taro went to school [before Mary saw EC]

(9) a. [the book$_i$ [that a student bought EC$_i$]]
b. *[the book$_i$ [that EC bought EC$_i$]]
c. [the student$_i$ [that EC$_i$ bought a book]]
d. *[the student$_i$ [that EC bought EC$_i$]]

As shown in (7) and (8), empty pronouns may not occur in tensed clauses in English, whether it is a simple or subordinate clause. The examples in (9) show that an empty category in a relative clause makes the relative clause construction ill-formed unless it is coindexed with the head noun (i.e., it is created by syntactic movement).

In the above,we have discussed three syntactic properties of English and Japanese: word-order, branching direction, and empty pronouns in a tensed clause. Given these differences, we want to know whether the two languages are processed by the same processing mechanisms.

2.0. Previous Studies on Verb information and the Processing of ECs

In this section, a brief review of previous studies on the use of verb information in processing English will be presented. This will be followed by a summary of previous studies on the processing of empty categories in Japanese.

2.1. Verb Information

A number of studies report that verb information such as subcategorization and thematic structure affects processing (e.g. Clifton, Frazier, and Connine 1984; Tanenhaus, Garnsey and Boland 1991; Mitchell 1987, 1989; Shapiro, Zurif and Grimshaw 1989; Stowe 1989; Boland and Tanenhaus 1991; Cupples and Stowe 1991, Stowe, Tanenhaus and Carlson in press). Clifton, Frazier, and Connine (1984) demonstrate that people find sentences easier if the preferred subcategorization frame is congruent with what follows the verb. The sentences they use contain a verb which can be used either transitively or intransitively, with a preference for one over the other. Each verb is put into either a transitive or an intransitive environment, as shown below.

(10) 'read'-- preferred as a transitive verb
a. The baby sitter read the story to the sick child. (used as a transitive verb)
b. The baby sitter read to the sick child. (used as an intransitive verb)

(11) 'sing'-- preferred as an intransitive verb
a. The baby sitter sang to the sick child. (used as an intransitive verb)
b. The baby sitter sang the song to the sick child. (used as a transitive verb)

In the (a) versions of (10) and (11), the verb is used according to its preferred subcategorization frame, while the less preferred version is used in the (b) versions. Clifton, Frazier, and Connine found that response times in making a lexical decision at the first word after the verb were shorter in (a) sentences than (b). In other words, processing was easier if the verb was used in the preferred subcategorization. This suggests that verb information is used either to project syntactic structure or used to check the structure rapidly when the structure is assembled.[3] The fact that verb preference takes effect by the first word after the verb indicates that verb information is utilized immediately.[4]

2.2. Possible Role of Verb Information in Processing Japanese

We are interested in the question of to what extent verb information is used in the same way in Japanese as in English. This is particularly intriguing since Japanese verbs come at the end of the clause, following their arguments rather than preceding them as in English. It appears that in processing English, the verb signals the parser to expect certain preferred complements rather than other possible complements. This is not normally possible in Japanese. However, we can use relative clauses to look at the role of verb information in Japanese.

The relative clause in Japanese shown in (12) is identical to a simple sentence with an empty category, as shown in (13).

(12) a. [$_{NP}$[$_S$ kodomo-ga EC_i katta] $okasi_i$]
child-nom bought candy
'the candy that the child bought'
b. [$_{NP}$[$_S$ EC_i okasi-o katta] $kodomo_i$]
candy-acc bought child
'the child who bought candy'

(13) a. [$_S$ kodomo-ga EC katta]
child-nom bought
'The child bought EC.'
b. [$_S$ EC okasi-o katta]
candy-acc bought
'EC bought candy.'

Since neither a syntactic nor a morphological cue is available to distinguish a relative clause from a simple sentence, it is not possible for the parser to identify the relative clause as such until the head NP appears. In other words, a string of words is ambiguous between a simple sentence and complex NP analysis until the information after the verb becomes available.

However, it is possible that information in the relative clause, especially verb information, can be used by the parser to make a tentative decision about the type of construction involved. For instance, if the verb expects certain arguments which are not present in the clause, the parser may prefer the relative clause analysis over the simple analysis, in which the argument must be an empty pronoun. This is intuitively plausible since one of the typical relative clause constructions contains a "gap" or an empty category in the relative clause. On the other hand, if all the expected arguments are overtly present, the reader might choose a simple clause analysis rather than the relative clause construction. The current experiment investigates this possibility.

2.3. Previous Studies on Processing ECs in Japanese

As shown earlier, Japanese is different from English in the sense that it allows relatively free occurrence of empty pronouns. Mazuka (1991) claims that inserting and interpreting empty categories in Japanese do not cause processing difficulties.

(14) Yuuzin-ga [EC mootyoo -de nyuuin site ita] toki mimai-ni kite kureta.
friend-nom appendicitis with was hospitalized when visit came for me
'When (I) was hospitalized with appendicitis, a friend came to visit me.'

Sentence (14) has an empty pronoun as the subject of the temporal adjunct clause. Mazuka observes no effect of processing the empty pronoun on overall reading time per character in this type of sentence, compared to a control sentence. From this observation, she concludes that the postulation of empty categories in Japanese is cost-free.

However, the results showing the same overall reading times do not actually prove that the postulation of empty categories is cost-free. Reading time per character compares the overall reading times of a particular sentence type. Although the reading time per character is put in terms of the mean time to read the characters in the sentence, it does not actually directly reflect local reading times. Therefore, it is possible that reading times actually increase and decrease locally, but somehow the local change is canceled out later. If there is an increase in local reading time while processing sentences with empty categories, it can be claimed that the postulation of empty categories is not cost-free in Japanese. Therefore, the nature and the cost of postulating an empty category calls for further investigation.

3.0. Experiment

3.1. Two Types of Relative Clause Constructions in Japanese

In order to investigate the use of verb information and the cost of processing empty categories in Japanese, two types of relative clause constructions are compared. The commoner type is the Regular relative clause shown in (1a), repeated here as (15).[5]

(15) [[kodomo-ga EC_i katta] okasii]
children-nom bought candy
'the candy that the children bought'

The head of the relative clause is coindexed with an empty category in the relative clause and takes that role in the semantic interpretation of the relative clause.

The other type is the Gapless relative clause shown in (1b), which is repeated here as (16).

(16) [[kodomo-ga okasi-o katta] oturi]
children-nom candy-acc bought change
'the money left after the child bought candy'

In (16), both the <Agent> 'children' and the <Theme> 'candy' are inside the relative clause. This type of relative clause occurs quite frequently in both written and spoken language. The head noun in the Gapless relative sentences used in the experiment is a noun describing the consequence of the action described in the relative clause (cf. Matsumoto 1988). When the head noun is a consequence, the relative clause verb is in the perfective form. If the verb is imperfective, a systematic ambiguity between habitual or future action is introduced. We wished to avoid introducing this irrelevant factor into the experiment.

The difference between (15) and (16) lies in the number of arguments that appear within the relative clause and how the semantic relationship between the relative clause and the head noun is established. Gapless relatives such as (16) have all the arguments inside. Regular relatives such as (15) have, theoretically, at least one empty category. The head noun of the Regular relative is coindexed with the empty category in the relative clause.

Comparing these two relative constructions, two things can be investigated. First, suppose that Japanese readers use verb information in the same manner as in English. Japanese readers use verb information to either expect the forthcoming structure or check the structure with the information as soon as it becomes available. This means that when readers see the verb, they check the number of overt arguments that have been presented so far and postulate empty categories if needed. In this case, if postulating an empty category has a cost, we expect a difference in reading times between the two relative constructions at the verb presentation, with the Regular relative taking longer than the Gapless relative.

Suppose that the simple clause analysis is preferred over the relative clause analysis when there is no missing argument in a sentence, because the relative clause analysis requires building more nodes than the simple clause analysis. If Japanese readers use verb information to project or filter upcoming structure, as soon as the readers see the transitive verb *katta* 'bought' in the Gapless construction (16), they learn that the expected arguments, bearing <Agent> and <Theme> theta roles, have both appeared. Therefore, they would not expect a relative clause construction as strongly as a simple clause. Consequently, when the readers see the head noun, they should be surprised to see the noun there. This should result in an increase in reading times. In the case of the Regular relative construction, the readers notice that one of the arguments is phonologically null. This indicates a possibility of a Regular relative construction. In this case, the preference for a simple clause may be overridden; at least the readers should not be as strongly committed to a simple clause analysis as in the case of the Gapless relatives. Our hypothesis on the reading times at the head noun is summarized below.

(17) Hypothesis: Japanese readers use verb information in processing. Using this information, readers choose a certain syntactic structure according to the preferred subcategorization.

Prediction: Reading times are longer at the head noun in Gapless relative clauses than in Regular relative clauses.

Second, the cost related to processing an empty category may be tested by these two relative constructions. If we hypothesize that postulating an empty category does require a processing effort, we should see an increase in reading times immediately after the gap is identified. Thus we should see increased reading times at the verb in the Regular relative clause.

(18) Hypothesis: Postulating an empty category is costly.

Prediction: The reading times at the verb in Regular relatives should be longer than those at the verb in Gapless relatives, since an empty category must be postulated at this point.

On the other hand, if postulating an empty category is cost-free, as claimed by Mazuka (1991), we should not see any difference in local reading times at the verb between the Gapless and Regular relative constructions.

3.2. Test Sentences

For the experiment, twelve sets of two matched sentences were constructed. Both constructions were identical wherever possible. A typical pair of experimental sentences is as shown below.

(19)

	subj		adv
Yokohama-de[[	**kodomo-ga**		**nessinni**
Yokohama-at	children-nom		ardently

	obj		V head noun
(GAPLESS)	**sisyuu-o**		**utta] okane]-ga**
	anthology-acc		sold money-nom
	PP		V head noun
(REGULAR)	**mati-de**	**ECi**	**utta] sisyuui]-ga**
	town-at		sold anthology-nom

temporal adj	matrix V
hookago	**kaisyuu-sareta.**
after school	was collected

'In Yokohama, (GAPLESS)the money from the children's selling of anthologies
(REGULAR) the anthologies (which) the children sold in town

was (were) collected after school.'

Both constructions begin with a postpositional phrase. The postpositional phrase is to avoid subjects' reading without making sense of the area of interest.[6] Inside both relative clauses, there is a subject with <Agent> theta-role. The Gapless relative differs from the Regular relative at the fourth word. At this point, the Gapless relative has an object, which has the <Theme> theta-role. In the Regular relative clause, the <Theme> argument is an empty category, which has the effect of shortening the clause. Thus a locative PP was put in to equalize the number of overt words and the length of the sentences. The verb in the relative clause is the same for both constructions. All of them are transitive verbs. At the relative head, the two constructions differ again. As mentioned earlier, the Gapless relative clause is followed by a noun that describes a consequence. The Regular relative clause has a head that is coindexed with the null argument in the relative clause.

If our hypothesis is correct and readers use verb information immediately, we should see that reading times at the head noun in Gapless relatives is longer than the Regular relatives. Also, if the postulation of an empty category is costly, we should see reading times in Regular relatives are longer at the verb than in Gapless relatives.

3.3. Experimental Design and Procedure

For the experiment, two lists of experimental materials were created and given to two groups of subjects. In each list, there were 6 Gapless relative and 6 Regular relative sentences. There were 78 filler sentences. The filler sentences included sentences with and without empty categories. Some fillers were grammatical but incomplete. The sentences were presented to the subjects using a word-by-word, self-paced reading presentation, which was controlled by HyperCard on a Macintosh SE. Each word appeared in a rectangular window at the center of the screen. In presenting the words, Kanji, Hiragana, and Katakana characters were appropriately used.

Both test sentences and fillers contained no punctuation. Since there was no overt marker of the end of the sentence, subjects could take either the simple clause analysis or the relative clause analysis at the verb. At the end of each sentence, a probe word was presented. Readers had to decide if it was contained in the sentence they just read. This probe word was also presented in the center of the screen and it was clearly marked as a probe word. This task was used to keep the subjects' attention on processing, as well as indicating the end of a sentence. All 12 target sentences and 13 filler sentences were followed by a simple wh-question such as 'what did the children sell?'. This also kept the subject's attention on reading for comprehension.

Fifty native speakers of Japanese between age 19 and 33 from Columbus, Ohio, participated in the experiment. They were paid for their participation. They all had normal or corrected normal vision, and had education beyond a high school diploma in Japan. Each list was presented to twenty-five subjects. Subjects were told that the lengths of the sentences varied, and that there were some grammatical but incomplete sentences. They were also told that there was no punctuation, and the only way to know where the sentence ended was by the presentation of the probe word. Before the test session, there was a practice session. The practice material contained ten sentences, in which all the test sentence types were introduced.

4. Results and Discussion

4.1. Results of the Experiment

The results of those who scored 85% correct or above for the entire test materials were considered appropriate for the analysis. Since nobody scored lower than 85% correct, everyone's reading and response times were analyzed using ANOVA. Only the response times obtained in the correct YES responses were used for the probe. Within-sentence reading times were all included in the analysis whether they responded correctly to the probe or not. Times greater than 3.5 x Standard Deviation plus his or her own mean time for an individual subject were replaced by 3.5 SD plus the mean time. Figure 1 and Table 1 below containa summary of the results.

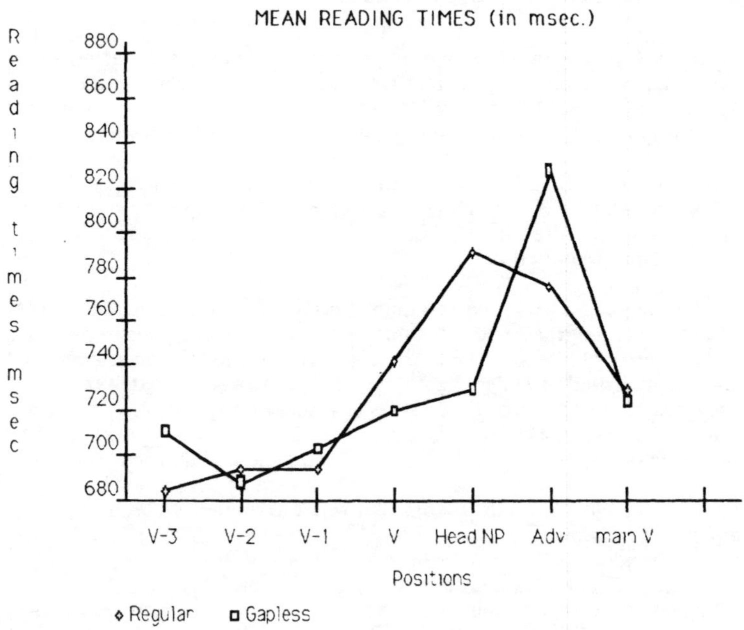

FIG. 1. MEAN READING TIMES (in msec.) FOR SENTENCE POSITIONS

	REGION								
TYPE	RELATIVE CLAUSE				HEAD	VP		PROBE	OVERALL
GAPLESS	subj	adv	obj	rel V	(conseq)	temporal	V		
	711	688	703	720	730	828	724	1391	729
REGULAR	subj	adv	PP	rel V	(obj)	temporal	V		
	685	693	693	742	791	776	729	1423	730
difference	26	-5	10	-22	-61	52	-5	-32	-1

TABLE 1. MEAN READING TIMES (in msec.) FOR SELECTED POSITIONS IN TARGET SENTENCES

Just as reported by Mazuka, overall reading times for sentences with and without an empty category do not differ. However, the two constructions show local differences. Increased RTs were observed at the head NP of the Regular relative clause, compared to the Gapless relative clause. Subjects took 61 milliseconds longer to read the head noun of the Regular relative. This difference was significant for both subjects and items ($F1(1,48)=8.6$, $p<.01$; $F2(1,10)=5.97$, $p<.04$). At the next word, a temporal adjunct, increased RTs were observed in Gapless relative clauses. Subjects took 52 msec. longer, on the average, than in the Regular relative clauses. This increase was significant for subjects ($F1(1,48)=6.57$, $p<.01$) and nearly significant in the item analysis ($F2(1,10)=4.69$, $p<.06$). There was no significant difference at any other point in the sentence. There was also no significant difference in time or accuracy for identifying the probe word.

4.2 Discussion

These results show that verb information and the number of overt arguments, make a difference in the way that the two relative constructions are processed. This is shown in that the two types of relative clause showed increases in reading times at completely different words.

The reading times at the temporal adjunct in the Gapless relatives were longer than in the Regular relatives. Notice that this is the effect that we predicted at the head noun. However, it is known that increased RTs in response to a stimuli can be reflected one word later in a self-paced reading task (Cupples and Stowe 1991). Therefore, it is reasonable to assume that the increased reading time at the temporal adjunct in the Gapless relative clause reflects a difficulty with the head noun, since there is no other plausible source for the difference. This indicates that readers were more strongly committed to a simple clause analysis when reading the Gapless relative construction. The relative ease of dealing with the head noun in the Regular relatives indicates that the readers were not as surprised by the head noun as in the Gapless relative clause. In other words, the presence of an empty category, made obvious by the use of verb information, kept readers from choosing the simplex clause analysis.

It was found that the RTs at the relative head were longer for the Regular relatives than for the Gapless relatives. This is the effect that we predicted at the verb, if postulating an empty category is costly. However, the effect was reflected one word later, as with the previous difference. The increased reading times at the head noun mean that postulating and processing an empty category was difficult. This is evidence against the claim made by Mazuka (1991). This is interesting since Japanese is a language in which empty categories appear relatively freely. Nevertheless, they are not necessarily easy to process.

It is also important to point out that the increased RTs in the Regular relatives were observed immediately after the verb. This indicates that the postulation of the empty category was reasonably immediate, which is consistent with the findings in English (Clifton, Frazier and Connine 1984; Tanenhaus, Garnsey and Boland 1991; Boland and Tanenhaus 1991; Stowe, Tanenhaus and Carlson in press). The empty category was postulated as soon as verb information became available. The finding suggests that the use of verb information in Japanese is similar to English in the sense that it is utilized immediately and affects the readers' expectation as to what will follow it.

5. Conclusion

The present study investigated the use of verb information and the processing of an empty category. We have found that Japanese readers utilize verb information similarly to English readers, despite the syntactic differences in the two languages. In processing Japanese relative clauses, readers utilized verb information as to whether or not all the arguments of the verb were overtly present and immediately choose a certain syntactic structure. We have also found that there was some processing cost involved in processing empty categories in Japanese, despite the relative frequency with which they occur.

Notes

[1] The first author is affiliated with the Department of East Asian Languages and Literatures, The Ohio State University, and the second author is affiliated with the Department of Linguistics, The University of Groningen. The third author is affiliated with the Department of East Asian Languages and Literatures and the Center for Cognitive Science, The Ohio State University. We would like to thank the participants of the conference for their comments. All shortcomings are, of course, ours. This research was supported by a grant from the College of Humanities, The Ohio State University, to the third author.

[2] Theoretically, the status of the phonologically null argument in the relative clause may not be identical to the empty categories shown in (4). The status of phonologically null arguments in the Japanese tensed clause has been controversial. While it is claimed by Perlmutter (1972) that null arguments at both subject and object positions in Japanese relative clauses are empty pronouns, Hasegawa (1984-5) claims that the null arguments at the object position is a variable bound by the empty operator (see also Huang 1984, Hoji 1985). In this paper, the "gap" in the Regular relative clause in Japanese is referred to as the empty category (EC), without committing to a particular theory.

[3] The precise role of verb information in processing is still controversial. While Mitchell (1987, 1989) claims that verb information filters out implausible constructions slightly after the verb occurs ("Checking"), Ford et al. (1982) claim

that subcategorization directs building of the forthcoming syntactic structure. However, in either case, if an unlikely structure occurs, increased difficulty is predicted.

[4] See also Frazier, Clifton and Randall (1983), Tanenhaus, Garnsey and Boland (1991) and Boland and Tanenhaus (1991) for detailed discussion of the point at which verb information is utilized and the type of verb information used in English.

[5] The term "relative clause" in Gapless relative clause is conventional, to match Regular relative clause, and is not intended to claim that there is any clear syntactic parallelism between these two constructions (cf. Matsumoto 1988). See Saito (1985), Murasugi (1991) and Yamashita (1991) for detailed discussions of the structure of these constructions.

[6] There is a potential tendency for subjects in a self-paced reading to read the first few words without completely processing syntactically or semantically, as they can rely on their memory to complete the processing later. Thus the first few words' reading times may not reflect processing differences which are actually present.

REFERENCES

Boland, Julie and Michael Tanenhaus. 1991. The role of lexical representations in sentence processing. In G.B. Simpson (ed.), Understanding Word and Sentence, North-Holland: Elsevier Science Publishers B.V.

Clifton, Charles Jr., Lyn Frazier, and Cynthia Connine. 1984. Lexical expectations in sentence comprehension. Journal of Verbal Learning and Verbal Behavior 23. 696-708.

Cupples, Linda and Laurie Stowe. 1991. Thematic structure and the disambiguation of reduced relative clauses. ms. Macquarie University and The Ohio State University.

Frazier, Lyn, Charles Clifton Jr., and Janet Randall. 1983. Filling gaps: Decision principles and structure in sentence comprehension. Cognition 13. 187-222.

Frazier, Lyn, and Keith Rayner. 1988. Parameterizing the language processing system: Left- vs. right- branching within and across languages. Explaining Language Universals ed. by J.A.Hawkins, 247-279. Basil Blackwell.

Ford, Marilyn, Joan Bresnan, and Ronald M. Kaplan. 1982. A competence-based theory of syntactic closure. The Mental Representation of Grammatical Relations. ed. by J.W. Bresnan, Cambridge, MA: MIT Press.

Hasegawa, Nobuko. 1984-5. On the so-called "zero pronouns" in Japanese. The Linguistic Review 4. 289-341.

Hoji, Hajime. 1985. Logical Form Constraints and Configurational Structures in Japanese. Doctoral dissertation, University of Whashington.

Horii, Kasumi. 1990. Ga/no Conversion and Japanese Sentence Processing. MA Thesis, The Ohio State University.

Huang, James C-T. 1984. On the distribution and reference of empty pronouns.

Linguistic Inquiry 15. 531-74.

Inoue, Atsu. 1991. A Comparative Study of Parsing in English and Japanese. Doctoral dissertation, University of Connecticut.

Inoue, Atsu and Janet Fodor. 1991. Information-paced parsing of Japanese. Paper presented at International Symposium on Japanese Syntactic Processing, Duke University.

Kuno, Susumu. 1973. The Structure of the Japanese Language. Cambridge, MA: MIT Press.

Matsumoto, Yoshiko. 1988. Grammar and Semantics of Adnominal Clauses in Japanese. Doctoral dissertation, University of California, Berkeley.

Mazuka, Reiko. 1991. Processing of empty categories in Japanese. Journal of Psycholinguistic Research 20-3. 215-232.

Mazuka, Reiko and Barbara Lust. 1988. Why is Japanese not difficult to process?: A proposal to integrate parameter setting in Universal Grammar and parsing. Proceeding of NELS 16, ed. by Blevins & J.Carter, 333-356.

Mitchell, Don C. 1987. Lexical guidance in human parsing: Locus and processing characteristics. Attention and Performance XII, ed. by M. Coltheart, Hillsdale, NJ: Lawrence Erlbaum Associates Inc.

Mitchell, Don C. 1989. Verb-guidance and other lexical effects in parsing. Parsing and Interpretation, ed. by G. Altmann, 1232-154. East Sussex, U.K.: Lawrence Erlbaum Associates Inc.

Murasugi, Keiko. 1991. Noun Phrases in Japanese and English. Doctoral dissertation, University of Connecticut.

Nakayama, Mineharu. 1990. Accessibility to the antecedent in Japanese sentence processing. ms. The Ohio State University.

Nakayama, Mineharu. 1991a. Japanese motion verbs and probe recognition. Paper presented at Fourth Annual CUNY Conference on Human Sentence Processing, University of Rochester.

Nakayama, Mineharu. 1991b. Scrambling and probe recognition. Paper presented at International Symposium of Japanese Syntactic Processing, Duke University.

Perlmutter, David M. 1972. Evidence for shadow pronouns in French relativization. The Chicago Which Hunt, ed. by P.M. Paranteau, et al. 73-105. Chicago: Chicago Linguistic Society.

Saito, Mamoru. 1985. Some Asymmetries in Japanese and Their Theoretical Implications. Doctoral dissertation, MIT.

Sakamoto, Tsutomu. 1991a. Processing Empty Subjects in Japanese: Implications for the Transparency Hypothesis. Doctoral dissertation, City University of New York.

Sakamoto, Tsutomu. 1991b. Processing of empty subjects in Japanese. Paper presented at International Symposium of Japanese Syntactic Processing, Duke University.

Shapiro, Levin, Edgar Zurif and Jane Grimshaw. 1987. Sentence processing and the mental representation of verbs. Cognition 27. 219-46.

Stowe, Laurie. 1989. Thematic structures and sentence comprehension. Linguistic Structure in Language Processing, ed. by Greg Carlson and Michael Tanenhaus, 319-358. Netherlands: Kluwer Academic Press.

Stowe, Laurie, Michael Tanenhaus, and Greg Carlson. in press. Filling gaps on-line: Use of lexical and semantic information in sentence processing. Language Speech 34.

Tanenhaus, Michael, Susan Garnsey, and Julie Boland. 1991. Combinatory lexical information and language comprehension. Cognitive Models of Speech Processing: Psycholinguistic and Computational Perspectives, ed.by G. Altmann. Cambridge, MA: MIT Press.

Teramura, Hideo. 1975-78. Rentai-syuusyoku no sintakusu to imi (Syntax and semantics of noun modification) Nos. 1-4. Nihongo Nihonbunka (The Japanese Language and Culture). 4-7 Osaka Gaikokugo Daigaku. 71-119, 29-78, 1-35, 1-24.

Yamashita, Hiroko. 1991. On the status of a gap in the complex noun phrases. ms. The Ohio State University.

Part IV

Syntax and Semantics

Indefinite Wh Pronouns and the Morpheme Mo in Japanese

RURIKO KAWASHIMA
Cornell University

I. INTRODUCTION

In Japanese, an indefinite WH pronoun which lacks its own fixed quantificational force comes to acquire different quantificational forces as well as different syntactic functions by interacting with postpositional morphemes such as *mo* and *ka*.[1] This paper discusses the combination of indefinite WH pronouns and emphatic *mo* and their quantificational force, [2] focusing on WH/*mo* licensed by negation, i.e. Negative Polarity Items (NPIs). Empirical data suggest that when this combination appears with negation, it has an existential reading while it has a universal reading in non-negative contexts.[3] I will provide a uniform account for the existence of different

[1]*Ka* appears with indefinite WHs. It also functions as a question marker as well as a disjunction marker 'or.'

[2]I will use WH/*mo* to refer to Negative Polarity Items (NPIs) such as *nani-mo* 'anyone' and *dare-mo* 'anyone' as well as discontinuous WH and *mo* association unless otherwise specified.

[3]Of course, this generalization is too brief. Some type of WH and *mo* combinations such as WH...*te-mo* 'WH-*ever*' construction always takes wide scope. The point here is merely that there is a case in which the combination of WH and *mo* has to be interpreted as existential, as we

quantificational forces associated with WH/*mo*, by appealing to a particular function of *mo*.

Previous analyses (Nishigauchi (1987) and Ohno (1983)) treat *mo* solely as a universal quantifier. Hasegawa (1986) and Fujita (1991), among others, argue that WH/*mo* in some case is an existential NPI. Under previous analyses, it is not clear how the different quantificational forces associated with WH/*mo* can be explained in a uniform way.

I will propose that both the existential and universal quantificational forces associated with WH/*mo* come from the same function of *mo*. By establishing the similarity between *mo* and English *any*, I will argue that the function of *mo* is to expand the domain of quantification and that the apparent difference in quantificational force comes from the interaction between the function of *mo* and the local environment.

At the end of this paper, I will briefly discuss the syntactic licensing conditions for NPIs in Japanese. Following Rizzi's (1991, LSA Lectures) Neg Criterion, I argue that NPIs are licensed by NEG^0 through Spec-head agreement at LF. The occurrence of NPIs separated from negation by a clausal boundary is then explained in terms of [±irrealis] specification of the complementizer.

II. *MO* IS LIKE *ANY*

A. English *Any*

Any in English is said to have two usages: one is as an NPI and the other is 'free choice (FC).' These are illustrated in (1) and (2) respectively.

1) Mary didn't see any student (existential under negation)

2) Any student can solve that problem (universal)

Previous analyses treat NPI *any* as existential and FC *any* as universal. Kadmon and Landman (1990, 1991) give a uniform analysis of these two usages of *any*. They propose that *any* in both usages should be analyzed like an indefinite NP. The apparent differences in quantificational force shown in (1) and (2) can be explained by viewing '*any* NP' as an indefinite NP in the case of NPI *any* and as an indefinite NP with generic interpretation in the case of FC *any*. As an indefinite NP, '*any* NP' picks up its quantificational force in the

---

see below.

I am grateful to H. Hoji, H. Kitahara, Y. Ohno, B. Partee, S. Tonoike, and L. Rizzi for their comments on earlier version of this paper. I am especially indebted to F. Landman and J. Whitman for all their help and suggestions.

local environment[4]. In either case, *any* conveys "reduced tolerance of exceptions" along a contextual dimension. Furthermore, the meaning of *any* is widening and its function is strengthening. The definitions Kadmon and Landman use are the following.

3) a. Widening -- In an NP of the form *any CN*, *any* widens the interpretation of the common noun phrase (CN) along a contextual dimension. (K & L, 1991, p. 15)

b. Strengthening -- *Any* is licensed only if the widening that it induces creates a stronger statement, i.e., only if
the statement on the wide interpretation -->
the statement on the narrow interpretation (Ibid, p. 29)

In other words, when the interpretation of a sentence in which *any* induces a widening effect entails the interpretation of the sentence without the widening effect of *any,* then *any* is licensed.

To see more exactly how this works, let us look at some examples. The following is an example of FC *any.*

4) a. A: An owl hunts mice
B: A sick one doesn't, right?
A: Any owl hunts mice

b. Wide: An owl, healthy one or sick one, hunts mice
--> Narrow: A healthy owl hunts mice

The second speaker confirms if the first speaker means 'an owl' to be 'a healthy one.' The first speaker answers with *any* to widen the domain of quantification along the dimension 'healthy vs. sick.' As shown in (4b), the strengthening entailment goes through, thus, *any* is allowed in (4).

Now, what about NPI *any*? (5a) is licensed because the widened interpretation along the dimension 'cooking vs. other' entails the interpretation of the sentence without the effect of *any.*

5) a. I don't have any potatoes
b. Wide: We don't have potatoes, cooking or other
--> Narrow: We don't have cooking potatoes (Ibid, p. 29)

On the other hand, in (6), *any* is not licensed because the wide interpretation of the sentence does not entail the narrow interpretation as shown in (6b).

6) a. *I have any potatoes
b. Wide: We have potatoes of SOME kind (cooking or other)

---

[4]This is based on the analysis of indefinite NPs given by Heim (1982).

-/->Narrow: We have cooking potatoes (Ibid, p. 30)

Thus, Kadmon and Landman's analysis accounts for both NPI and FC usages of *any* very nicely. Under the view that *any* NP is an indefinite NP and that *any* widens and strengthens the statement it occurs in, it follows that it carries the different quantificational forces depending on the environment it appears in.

Let us turn to the Japanese data and see how *mo* can be analyzed in a similar fashion.

B. Japanese *MO*

1. NPI

NPIs WH/*mo* can appear both in subject and object position in Japanese, as shown in (7). Japanese uses Nom-Acc Case markers to indicate the structural relation between an argument and a predicate; however, note that in the case of NPIs, neither the Nominative Case marker (*-ga*) nor Accusative Case marker (*-o*) appears with NPIs.

7) a. dare-mo ko-na-katta
who-MO come-NEG-PERF
'No one came'

b. Mary-wa nani-mo tabe-na-katta
-TOP what-MO eat-NEG-PERF
'Mary didn't eat anything.'

Furthermore, WH/*mo* cannot occur with an affirmative predicate:

8) a. *dare-mo ki-ta
who-MO come-PERF
'(intended) Everyone came.'

b. *Mary-wa nani-mo tabe-ta[5]

[5] If *mo* had exactly the properties of *any*, we should expect a Japanese counterpart of FC *any* and (8a, b) would be such examples. However, these examples are not acceptable (note that they are non-accented, as we discuss later). In a generic context, when WH is accented and its restriction NP is present, an FC-type universal interpretation is possible (Bold letters indicate the accent):

Kodomo-wa**DA**re-mo ninzin-ga kirai-da
children-TOP who-MO carrot-NOM hate-COPUL
'Any child hates carrots.'

-TOP what-MO eat-PERF
'(intended) Mary ate anything/everything.'

WH-phrases do not have to be directly suffixed with *mo:* discontinuous association of WH and *mo* is also possible. The following example involves WH inside the complement clause of a negated matrix verb.

9) Watasi-wa [dare-ga nani-o si-ta to]-mo
I-TOP who-NOM what-ACC do-PERF COMP-MO
omow-ana-katta
think-NEG-PERF
'I didn't think that anyone did anything.'

In (9), *mo* does not directly attach to WH, but rather to the complementizer *to.* Other possible contexts for discontinuous association include WH contained inside a complex NP whose head is suffixed with *mo,* as well as concessive sentences ending in *-te-mo* '-ing-MO.'

2. Problems with the View that Mo *Is a Universal Quantifier*

Nishigauchi (1987) argues that *mo* unselectively binds WH-phrases and that it gives them the interpretation of universal quantifiers. This view that *mo* is a universal quantifier must claim that the logical representation of NPIs WH/*mo* would always have to take wide scope over negation. However, this view is problematic, as we see below. On the other hand, if we allow WH/*mo* to have narrow scope when it appears with negation, that would mean that *mo* is ambiguous between a universal and existential interpretation, which is also not a desirable direction to take, either.

3. Mo *as a Domain Expander*

To resolve the above problems, I propose the following:

10) *Mo* expands the domain of quantification
It does not have its own quantificational force but is sensitive to the context it occurs in and strengthens the statement (like *any*).

This is to say that the universal quantification and existential quantification associated with WH/*mo* result in fact from the interaction of the function of *mo* and the environment in which *mo* occurs.[6]

[6]This way of viewing WH/*mo* can easily be extended to the other occurrence of *mo,* in which it is combined with NPs to give the meaning 'also' or 'even' in English.

Mary-mo ki-ta

a. Mo *Shows Widening and Strengthening Effects*

The first argument comes from the same kind of widening and strengthening effects that we saw for English *any* in sentences in which WH/*mo* occurs. The following example of discontinuous association of WH/*mo* in the form WH-Noun-*mo* shows this similarity. *Dono*-N-*mo* '*which/each*-N-*mo*'[7] behaves like FC *any*.

11) A: Gakusei-wa zikyuu sen-en desu
student-TOP pay-per-hour thousand-yen COPUL
'A student gets paid a thousand yen per hour.'
B: Keiken-no ar-u gakusei-wa?
experience-GEN exist-IMP student-TOP
'What about students who have experience?'
A: **Dono**-gakusei-**mo** onazi desu
which-student-MO same COPUL
'Any student gets the same.'

(11')
Wide: Students get paid a thousand yen whether they have experience or not.
--> Narrow: Students who have experience get paid a thousand yen.

Imagine a situation where <u>B</u> is a student who is interested in a part-time job that he found in the newspaper. He calls up the company and asks for more information. After the first utterance of speaker <u>A</u>, who is a manager of the company, <u>B</u> inquires if 'a student' includes 'a student who has experience.' <u>A</u>'s response with 'WH-student-*mo*' is now widened to include students who have experience as well as students who have no experience. The quantificational domain is widened along the dimension of 'students with experience vs. students with no experience' and the wide interpretation entails the narrow interpretation as given above. This shows that WH/*mo* has the same function that *any* has.

-MO come-PAST
'Mary also came/Even Mary came.'

This is explained if we consider the intrinsic effect that *mo* has; namely, strengthening. By strengthening the statement that Mary came, it implies that the incident of Mary's coming is the least expected thing to happen. The fact that *mo* can function as 'also' and 'even,' which are considered to be focus markers in English, is consistent with the appearance of *mo* as NPI which is also associated with focus.

[7] Hasegawa (1986) claims that the form WH-N-*mo* is an Affirmative Polarity Item (API) which appears outside the scope of negation when it occurs with negation.

b. De Re and De Dicto Contrast

The second argument is that a *de dicto* reading for WH/*mo* is possible in the following sentence.

12) Mary-wa [donna-unikoon-mo mituke-tai to]
    -TOP which-unicorn-MO find-want COMP
    omow-ana-katta[8]
    think-NEG-PERF
    'Mary didn't want to find any unicorn.'

The view that *mo* is solely a universal quantifier would require *donna*-N-*mo* to have scope outside of the scope of negation, incorrectly predicting the existence of the *de re* reading for 'unicorns.' The conclusion from this is that we must allow *donna*-N-*mo* in (12) to stay in the scope of negation to correctly derive the *de dicto*.[9]

c. Accent: FC and NPI Counterparts

The third argument is that the stress difference between NPI *any* and FC *any* seems to parallel the accentuation that Japanese uses for negation vs. non-negation contexts. Depending on the accent difference, we get WH/*mo* in the negative context as well as the affirmative context. It seems that the accent plays an important role in determining the scope interaction with respect to negation.

A non-accented alternant is used in negative contexts while its accented counterpart is used in non-negative contexts. We will represent the non-accented WH/*mo, dare-mo* 'anyone' as in (13a) and the accented one as in (13b).

13) a. NPI as dare-mo
    b. FC as **DA**re-mo[10]

---

[8] *Donna* is an emphatic form of *dono* 'which.'

[9] Ladusaw (1980) points out similar facts concerning English.

[10] This does not directly extend to the other occurrence of the accented WH-*mo* where WH-*mo* is marked by the nominative case marker *-ga,* which may have a universal interpretation.

DAre-mo-ga ki-ta
who-MO-NOM come-PERF
'Everyone came.'

The presence of nominative case outside WH/*mo* suggests that the function of *mo* is not in effect at least in the root clause level. Further investigation is called for along this line; however, I will not go into this here.

The capitalized bold letters are used to indicate where the accent falls in (13b).
Examples of NPI and FC WH/*mo* are the following:

14) a. Watasi-wa dare-ni-mo tegami-o kak-ana-katta
I-TOP who-to-MO letter-ACC write-NEG-PERF
'I didn't write a letter to anyone.'

b. Watasi-wa **DA**re-ni-mo tegami-o kai-ta
I-TOP who-to-MO letter-ACC write-PERF
'I wrote a letter to anyone (everyone).'

If *mo* simply were a universal quantifier, we would not need to differentiate both cases with the accent. In both cases, they would have to take scope over negation. If we take the view that *mo* is polarity sensitive, we can capture this contrast. With negation as in (14a) WH/*mo* is existential while in (14b) it is universal.[11, 12]

d. Scope Interaction with Negation

The next argument concerns the scope interaction of WH/*mo* with negation.

With negation, WH/*mo* does not have a partial negation reading even with WH/*mo* in object position. However, since $\neg\exists$ and $\forall\neg$ are indistinguishable, the view that takes *mo* as a universal quantifier would say that in both cases above WH/*mo* takes wide scope over negation. Thus, in order to see a real scope interaction, we need to look for a scope island.

The scope island we will look at is the negative imperative. Ladusaw (1980) uses negative imperatives to argue that *any* in the following sentence is existential, following Schmerling's analysis (1978) of negative imperatives, where she argues that negation has to take wide scope.

---

[11] I assume without providing any argument that universal quantificational force is given by an invisible operator, perhaps an invisible adverb of quantification in the sense of Heim (1982), but not by *mo* itself. The exact identity of this operator is beyond the scope of this paper.

[12] When *mo* directly attaches to a numeral quantifier, we can also observe scope interaction. In the following sentences, the absence of accent signals that the item is in the scope of negation while the presence of accent signals that the item is outside of the scope. This corresponds to the scope interaction between *even* and *not* in English translations.

a. sen-en-mo haraw-anakute-sum-da
thousand-yen-MO pay-NEG-finish-PERF
'I didn't have to pay even a thousand yen.'

b. **SE**n-en-mo haraw-anakute-sum-da
'Even thousand yen, I didn't have to pay.'

I thank Shigeo Tonoike for bringing my attention to this.

15) a. *Don't somebody open a window
b. Don't everybody open a window
c. %Don't nobody open a window
d. Don't anybody open a window (Ladusaw, 1980; p. 72)

Given that quantified NPs cannot escape from the scope of negation in negative imperatives, Ladusaw argues that if *anybody* in (15d) were universal, we would need to allow it to move out of the scope of negation in negative imperatives.

Following the same reasoning, if the negative imperative is a scope island and WH/*mo* in the negative imperative has a complete negation reading, it cannot involve universal quantification, given that no quantified NP can move out of the scope island.

The first thing that we must determine is whether the negative imperative is a scope island in Japanese or not. The contrast between the following sentences shows that the universal quantifier *zenbu* 'all' is ambiguous in a declarative sentence as in (16), while it only has a partially negated reading in the negative imperative as in (17).

16) a. zenbu si-na-katta
all do-NEG-PERF
b. 'For all x, I didn't do x.'
c. 'It is not the case that I did all x.'

17) zenbu suru-na
all do-NEG
'Don't do all the things.'

This shows that in Japanese also the negative imperative is a scope island. When we substitute *zenbu* with WH/*mo*, the result is that the sentence is not ambiguous as shown in (18):

18) dare-mo kuru-na
who-MO come-NEG
'Don't anyone come.'

This is not expected if WH/*mo* is a universal quantifier. We would expect it to behave like *zenbu:* we should have a partial negation reading. This shows that *dare-mo* in (18) cannot involve universal quantification, given that the negative imperative is a scope island in Japanese out of which no quantified NP can be raised.

Interestingly, *dono*-N-*mo* shows the same result.

19) dono-tegami-mo yomu-na
each-letter-MO read-NEG
'Don't read any letter.'

These results argue strongly against the view that treats *mo* as a universal quantifier.[13]

4. Donkey Anaphora

One of the motivations for analyzing *mo* as a universal quantifier has been to explain its presence in donkey sentences (Nishigauchi, 1987).

20) [NP[Dono-hon-o kat-ta] gakusei]-mo sore-o yon-da
which-book-ACC buy-PERF student-MO it-ACC read-PERF
'Every/Any student who bought a book reads it.'

We need a universal quantifier binding both the WH inside the complex NP and the pronoun outside of it in order to account for their binding relation.

Since *mo* does not have its own quantificational force, we need something else. I assume that the WH/*mo* sequence receives its force of universal quantification from an invisible operator outside the sequence, such as the generic operator proposed by Kadmon and Landman (1991).[14, 15]

To conclude, we have discussed the function of *mo* compared with *any* in English. We have shown that *mo* cannot be simply a universal quantifier. Rather, it receives its quantificational force relative to the context it appears in, contributing its widening effect.

III. SYNTAX OF NPI LICENSING

A. WH-*mo*[16]

I assume, following Fujita (1991), that NPIs in Japanese are floating

---

[13] Note also that NPI and *dono*-N-*mo* can co-occur under the scope of negation as is predicted.

dare-mo kinoo-no paatii-de dono-gakusei-mo
who-MO yesterday-GEN party-at each-student-MO
mi-na-katta
see-NEG-PERF
'No one saw any student at the party yesterday.'

In the above case, we can consider both occurrences of *mo* as NPIs under the scope of negation.

[14] Although I will not go into this, this idea has some support. The complex NP in donkey sentences seems to have a conditional flavor; i.e. 'if you are a student and you bought a book, you read it.' Thus, it may be that the same kind of universal operator is present in (20).

[15] The relative clause construction of this type involves a proportion problem pointed out by Ohno (1991). I do not have anything to say about this but I believe that the particular property associated with *mo* which I am discussing in this paper should be extended to this usage as well.

[16] I use WH-*mo* to specifically refer to NPIs *dare-mo* 'anyone' and *nani-mo* 'anything.'

quantifiers which are base-generated in an A'-position.[17] Following Rizzi (LSA lectures, 1991), WH-*mo* is licensed by NEG^0 as a NEG Operator through Spec-head agreement at LF.[18] See Kawashima (forthcoming) for more details.

B. Discontinuous WH and *mo* association

a. [+irrealis] specification and NPI in clausal complements

Although the basic function of *mo,* its domain-expanding function, is the same for both NPIs and discontinuous WH and *mo* association, the [+irrealis] specification of the clause containing NPI (indefinite WH in the case of Japanese) is crucial for NPI licensing.

This [±irrealis] specification accounts for the presence of NPI in the complement clauses of negated factive verbs. In English, NPI is allowed in the complement clause just in case the factive presupposition associated with it is cancelled (Kadmon & Landman, 1991).

21) I didn't know that Mary put anything in that cup.

22) a. I didn't discover that there was a problem
b. I didn't confirm that there was a problem

---

[17]In order to argue for the FQ status of NPI, Fujita points out its ability to co-occur with the coindexed NP and its similarity to numeral FQs in terms of scope interaction with other quantified noun phrases which are in A-positions. However, numeral FQs and NPI WH/*mo* do not always behave the same way. For example, numeral FQs in Japanese in general are conjoinable depending on the syntactic position they occupy but NPIs can never be conjoined nor can they occur inside NPs.

a.* [gakusei-ga dare-mo to sensei-ga dare-mo]
student-NOM who-MO and teacher-NOM who-MO
ko-na-katta
come-NEG-PERF
'(Intended) No students and no teachers came.'

b. [gakusei-ga san-nin to sensei-ga yo-nin]
student-NOM 3-CL and teacher-NOM 4-CL
ki-ta
come-PERF
'Three students and four teachers came.'

I take this to show the adverbial nature of NPIs. However, this is not to say that numeral FQs are never adverbial. It is possible that they can be adverbial depending on the syntactic position they occupy. More research is called for to determine what exact syntactic positions they occupy.

[18]Takahashi (1989) also argues that NPIs in Japanese move to the Spec of NegP at LF.

c. I didn't regret that there was a problem (the presupposition is not cancelled)

23) a. I didn't discover that there was any problem
b. I didn't confirm that there was any problem
c. *I didn't regret that there was any problem

In (22a) and (22b), the factive presupposition can be cancelled, so the NPI is allowed inside the complement clause as in (23a) and (23b). On the other hand, *regret,* even when negated, does not cancel the factive presupposition of its complement clause; thus, the NPI is not licensed. If we assume that the factive presupposition associates with a [-irrealis] specification, NPI is allowed only when its [-irrealis] specification is cancelled.[19]

Japanese data also support this line of analysis. As we have seen, the long-distance licensing of NPIs in English would be a discontinuous association between WH and *mo* across a *to* complement clause in the case of Japanese. An interesting difference between English and Japanese is that Japanese uses a different complementizer for a proposition with a factive presupposition. These two kinds of complementizers are given in (24):

24) a. *to* -- introduces complement clauses of verbs of saying, believing, thinking, and so on.
b. *koto* -- complement clauses with factive presupposition (with perfective tense on a verb inside)[20]

Non-factive verbs like *omow* 'think' can take the *to* complementizer with *mo* attaching to it, which marks the complement clause under the scope of negation.

25) Mary-ga [John-ga dare-o mi-ta to]-mo
-NOM -NOM who-ACC see-PERF COMP
omow-ana-katta (koto)
think-NEG-PERF (the fact)
'Mary didn't think that John saw anyone.'

---

[19]In Laka's (1990) system, a [+NEG] Comp plays an important role in licensing NPIs directly inside complement clauses. [+NEG] Comp, like [+WH] Comp, is selected by matrix verbs such as *doubt, deny,* and so on, and negated verbs such as *not think.* One problem with this approach is that her system would allow NPI in the complement clause of *not regret,* since the verb *regret* is negated. Another is that we would have to state NPI licensing as taking place both under [NEG] Comp and [WH] Comp. On the other hand, [+irrealis] will cover both environments.

[20]*Koto* is also used for complement clauses of control verbs.

Are NPIs licensed in the complement clauses of factive verbs? Let us look at a relevant example where the complement clause is introduced by *koto*.[21]

26) John-ga [Mary-ga dare-o sasot-ta koto]-mo
-NOM -NOM who-ACC invite-PERF KOTO-MO
sir-ana-katta (koto)
know-NEG-PERF (the fact)
Universal reading: 'John didn't know that Mary invited all the people (contextually determined given set).'
NPI reading (disallowed): 'John didn't know that Mary invited anyone.'

As we see from the translation of the sentence above, the WH/*mo* is interpreted as universal but not existential. This suggests that WH/*mo* as NPI is not licensed in the complement clause of negated factive verbs, headed by the *koto* complementizer. *Koto,* since it retains the factive presupposition of the complement clause, makes the complement clause opaque for the association between WH inside the lower clause and negation in the higher clause. In our terms, the factive presupposition associated with the *koto* complement clause corresponds to a [-irrealis] specification. Since this specification can never be cancelled in the case of *koto,* it is predicted that the NPI is never licensed inside the clause headed by the *koto* complementizer. In the case of English, NPIs are licensed in the complement clauses of factive verbs just in case the [-irrealis] specification of the complementizer is cancelled.[22]

b. Discontinuous WH and **mo** *licensing*

Although I cannot fully defend my proposal here, a summary of licensing related movement is briefly sketched as follows: First, WH moves to the Spec of the phrase headed by *mo* at LF. Note that possible barriers to this movement are the clauses headed by a complementizer with [-irrealis] specification such as clauses with a factive presupposition, *to* clauses which receive [-irrealis] by default, and so on. Second, the whole clause containing WH moves to the closest licenser.[23]

[21]In fact, negated factive verbs subcategorize for the *koto* complementizer.

[22]One other possibility, which may be interesting to pursue, is to assign scope to the [±irrealis] specification: In this approach, we assume that [+/-irrealis] specifications correspond to narrow and wide scope respectively. For example, if a given clause has a [-irrealis] specification, it will be assigned wide scope, so an indefinite WH pronoun inside the clause cannot be under the scope of a licenser such as negation in the matrix clause.

[23]This proposal corresponds to Rizzi's (1991) two separate criteria for WH and NPI Operators.

IV. CONCLUSION

In this paper, I have attempted to give a unified account for different quantificational forces associated with WH and *mo* by appealing to the similarity between *any* and *mo*. Although more specifics have to be worked out, the general direction taken in this paper seems to hold: namely, *mo* does not have its own quantificational force but its widening function interacting with the local environment.

Japanese is a language where the same item, namely indefinite WH, functions as NPI Operator as well as WH operator with different morphemes.

References

Fujita, Naoya. 1991. Negative Polarity Items and Floating Quantifiers in Japanese. Unpublished ms., University of Rochester.

Hasegawa, Nobuko 1986. Polarity Neutralization: INFL Movement and The Immediate Scope of Negation. Unpublished ms.

Heim, Irene 1982. The Semantics of Definite and Indefinite Noun Phrases. Doctoral dissertation. University of Massachusetts, Amherst.

——— 1984. A Note on Negative Polarity and Downward Entailingness. Proceedings of NELS, XIV, pp. 98-107.

Kadmon, Nirit and Fred Landman. 1990. Polarity Sensitive 'any' and Free Choice 'any.' Proceedings of Seventh Amsterdam Colloquium (forthcoming).

——— 1991. ANY I, ANY II. Unpublished ms., Tel Aviv University; Cornell University.

Kawashima, Ruriko. Syntax of Indefinite WHs and Morpheme *mo*. (forthcoming).

Kuroda, Sige-Yuki. 1965. Generative Grammatical Studies in the Japanese Language. Doctoral dissertation, MIT. Published in 1979 in Jorge Hankamer (ed.), Outstanding Dissertation in Linguistics. New York and London: Garland Pub.

Ladusaw, William. 1980. Polarity Sensitibity as Inherent Scope Relations. New York: Garland Pub.

Laka, Itziar. 1990. Negation in Syntax: On the Nature of Functional Categories and Projections. Doctoral dissertation, MIT.

Nishigauchi, Taisuke. 1987. Quantification in the Theory of Grammar. Studies in Linguistics and Philosophy. Dordrecht, Netherland; Boston: Kluwer Academic Publishers.

Ohno, Yutaka 1983. On the Form and Function of Quantifier Rule in Japanese. B.A. thesis, Sophia University.

——— 1991. Arguments against unselective binding in Korean. Harvard Studies in Korean Linguistics (forthcoming).

Progovac, Ljiljana. 1991. "Non-Negative Polarity Licensing Must Involve COMP." Unpublished ms.

Rizzi, Luigi. 1991. Lectures at LSA Summer Institute of Linguistics, Santa Cruz, CA.

Schmerling, Susan. 1978. Toward a Theory of English Imperatives. Unpublished ms., University of Texas at Austin.

Takahashi, Daiko. 1989. Locality in Syntax. Masters Thesis, Tohoku University.

Scrambling and Scope in Japanese

MASANORI NAKAMURA
McGill University

Scrambling and Scope in Japanese[0]

Masanori Nakamura
McGill University

0. Introduction

It has been noted in the literature (Hoji (1985, 1986) among others) that in Japanese scrambling of a quantificational phrase (henceforth QP) over another one induces scope ambiguity. Although (2a), the Japanese counterpart of the ambiguous English (1), is unambiguous, its scrambled version (2b) is ambiguous like (1):[1,2]

(1) Someone loves everyone.

(2) a. Dareka -ga daremo -o aisiteiru (koto)
someone-NOM everyone-ACC love fact
'Someone loves everyone.'

b. Daremo -o$_i$ dareka -ga $\underline{t}_i$ aisiteiru (koto)
everyone-ACC someone-NOM love fact
'Everyone$_i$, someone loves $\underline{t}_i$.'

The purpose of this paper is to discuss what scope interpretation in Japanese, which is affected by scrambling, can say about a theory of scope. In Section 1, I briefly review Aoun and Li (1989).[3] Section 2 considers the

---

[0] I am very grateful to Mark Baker, Lisa Travis, and Mihoko Zushi for their valuable suggestions on this paper. All remaining inadequacies are of course my own.

[1] *Koto* 'fact' is added to the end of the sentence to avoid the unnaturalness which stems from the lack of a topic in the matrix sentence. I ignore *koto* in the translations.

[2] In this paper, I assume following Saito (1985) and Hoji (1985) that scrambling in Japanese is an adjunction operation (but see Mahajan (1990)).

[3] May's (1977, 1985) analyses are not discussed here. Suffice it to say that within his

scope of a '*wh*-phrase' and a standard QP. There, it is shown that given LF reconstruction (Saito (1990)), the scope of scrambled QPs in Japanese can be correctly represented by the Scope Principle. It is also shown that the Minimal Binding Requirement follows from the Empty Category Principle (ECP) which utilizes a modified version of Rizzi's (1990) Relativized Minimality. Section 3 deals with NP-movement in Japanese and *Wh*-movement in English. Drawing on Kim (1991), I suggest that the Scope Principle can explain these cases without any modification. I also support the generalized Scope Principle of Ernst (1991).

1. Aoun and Li (1989)

Aoun and Li (1989) argue that the scope of QPs in English and Chinese can be explained by the two requirements in (3) and (4):

(3) Minimal Binding Requirement (MBR)
Variables must be bound by the most local potential antecedent (A'-binder).

(4) The Scope Principle (SP)
A quantifier A has scope over a quantifier B in case A c-commands a member of the chain containing B.

'Potential antecedent (A'-binder)' is defined as follows:

(5) A qualifies as a potential A'-binder for B iff A c-commands B, A is in an A'-position, and coindexing of (A,B) would not violate any grammatical principle.[4]

Aoun and Li suggest that either of the definitions of 'c-command' in (6) may be adopted for their purposes:

(6) a. A c-commands B if A and B do not dominate each other and the first branching node dominating A also dominates B.
b. A c-commands B if A and B do not dominate each other and the first maximal node dominating A also dominates B.

---

framework the difference in scope interpretation between (1) and (2a) cannot be accounted for. See Hoji (1985, sec.5.2) and Kim (1991).

4 This definition is meant to make the MBR apply to variables bound by *wh*-operators. For example:

(i) what$_i$ did everyone$_j$ x_j buy x_i

Aoun and Li assume that variables coindexed with *wh*-operators are R-expressions. Under this assumption, in (i) *everyone* is not a potential antecedent for x_i since the coindexation of the latter with the former will result in a violation of Condition C of the Binding Theory, namely, x_i will be A-bound by x_j.

As for variables coindexed with standard QPs, Aoun and Li assume that they are not subject to Condition C.

Quantifier Raising (QR) adjoins QPs to either IP or VP at LF (see May (1985) for details and the possibility of NP-adjunction).

Let us assume that English has Subject Raising, i.e., subjects are generated within VP and then raised to SPEC of IP (cf. Kitagawa (1986), Kuroda (1988) among others). Let us further assume, as Aoun and Li do for Chinese, that in Japanese this raising operation is not available.[5] Following Nakayama and Koizumi (1991), I presume that subjects in Japanese are generated outside VP.

The MBR coupled with this assumption will give (1) and (2a) the LF representations in (7) and (8) respectively:[6]

(7) $[_{IP}$ someone$_i$ $[_{IP}$ $\underline{x}_i$ $[_{VP}$ everyone$_j$ $[_{VP}$ $\underline{t}_i$ loves $\underline{x}_j]]]]$
(8) $[_{IP}$ dareka$_i$-ga $[_{IP}$ $\underline{x}_i$ $[_{VP}$ daremo$_j$-o $[_{VP}$ $\underline{x}_j$ aisiteiru$]]]]$

In (7) *someone* c-commands and thus may take scope over *everyone*. In addition, *everyone* c-commands a member of the chain containing *someone*, that is, $\underline{t}_i$. Therefore, *everyone* may have scope over *someone* by virtue of the SP. In (8) *dareka* 'someone' c-commands and thus takes scope over *daremo* 'everyone'. *Daremo* cannot have wide scope since it does not c-command a member of the chain containing *dareka*. The scope contrast follows.

Before we proceed, I would like to make the notion of chain explicit. I assume that a chain is defined as follows (cf. Chomsky (1986b), Rizzi (1990:92)):

(9) $(a_1,...,a_n)$ is a chain if n=1 or if, for $1 \leq i < n$,
a_i antecedent-governs a_{i+1}.

What (9) means is that an unmoved element counts as a one-membered chain and that a moved element and its trace or traces form a chain only if antecedent government holds between them. The definition of antecedent government is provided below (Rizzi (1990:6)):[7]

---

[5] Aoun and Li suggest that the lack of Subject Raising in Chinese may be traced back to the degenerate nature of INFL or the ability of SPEC of IP and VP to be assigned Case and a θ-role.

[6] Saito (1990) shows that an A'-position cannot be equated with an operator position. Partly following Taraldsen (1986), let us adopt the definition of a variable in (i):

(i) X is a variable iff X is locally bound by an operator at LF.

[7] Here 'c-command' is defined as in (6a). I will adopt Cinque's (1990:42) definition of barrier (see Cinque (1990, ch.1) for motivation for (i)):

(i) Every maximal projection that fails to be directly selected by a category nondistinct from [+V] is a barrier for government.

Relativized Minimality will be introduced in Section 2.

(10) Antecedent Government: X antecedent-governs Y iff
(i) X and Y are coindexed
(ii) X c-commands Y
(iii) no barrier intervenes
(iv) Relativized Minimality is respected

Let us put (2b) aside for a moment. I will come back to it in the next section.

2. Scrambling and Scope of a *Wh*-QP and a QP

Now, let us turn to the scope of a '*wh*-phrase' and a QP in Japanese. Consider the examples in (11), which are taken from Hoji (1985) with a slight modification:[8]

(11) a. *Daremo -ga sorezore nani-o kaimasita ka?
everyone -NOM each what-ACC bought Q
'Everyone each bought what?'
b. Nani-o$_i$ daremo -ga sorezore t_i kaimasita ka?
what-ACC everyone-NOM each bought Q
'What$_i$, everyone each bought t_i?'
c. Dare-ga daremo -o sorezore syootaisimasita ka?
who -NOM everyone-ACC each invited Q
'Who invited everyone each?'
d. Daremo -o$_i$ sorezore dare-ga t_i syootaisimasita ka?
everyone-ACC each who-NOM invited Q
'Everyone each$_i$, who invited t_i?'

Hoji's (1985) generalizations about these kinds of examples are given in (12):

(12) a. *QP-ga [$_{VP}$ WH-o V] Q
-NOM -ACC
b. WH$_i$-o QP-ga [$_{VP}$ t_i V] Q (WH taking wide scope)
c. WH-ga [$_{VP}$ QP-o V] Q (WH taking wide scope)
d. QP$_i$-o WH-ga [$_{VP}$ t_i V] Q (WH taking wide scope)

(12a) is ungrammatical. (12b-d) are grammatical but unambiguous, the '*wh*-phrase' taking wide scope over the standard QP.

Here I make the two assumptions in (13):

(13) (i) '*wh*-phrases' in Japanese are syntactically standard QPs and are subject to QR (Kim (1989))[9]

---

[8] In (11c,d), *sorezore* 'each' is added to the original sentences to make them parallel to (11a,b). *Sorezore* forces the non-group reading on *daremo* 'everyone'. For discussion of the ungrammaticality of (11a), see Hoji (1986).

[9] Kim (1989) claims that '*wh*-phrases' in Korean are standard QPs, too. As long as his data are concerned, Korean patterns fully with Japanese in terms of scope interpretation.

(13) (ii) *wh*-QPs must be licensed by the feature [+Q] (= +Quantificational) in COMP under government at LF (cf. Nishigauchi (1990))[10]

Following Kim (1989), I distinguish '*wh*-phrases' in Japanese from those in languages like English by calling the former *wh*-QPs.

Let us first consider the possible (but ill-formed) LF representations of (12a) in (14):

(14) a. *$[_{IP}$ WH-o$_j$ $[_{IP}$ QP-ga$_i$ $[_{IP}$ x$_i$ $[_{VP}$ x$_j$ V]]]] Q
b. *$[_{IP}$ QP-ga$_i$ $[_{IP}$ WH-o$_j$ $[_{IP}$ x$_i$ $[_{VP}$ x$_j$ V]]]] Q
c. *$[_{IP}$ QP-ga$_i$ $[_{IP}$ x$_i$ $[_{VP}$ WH-o$_j$ $[_{VP}$ x$_j$ V]]]] Q

(14a,b) violate the MBR. However, nothing seems to rule out (14c), given the assumptions I have made so far. Thus, constraining LF representations by the MBR is in fact insufficient. What we need is a more general constraint which prohibits (14c).

It is certainly desirable to derive the MBR from some principle of grammar. As a matter of fact, Aoun and Li suggest two possibilities; one is to derive the MBR from Relativized Minimality (henceforth RM) proposed by Rizzi (1990), the other is to integrate the MBR into the Binding Theory.

Why is (14c) ill-formed? Its structure is given in (15):

(15)
```
            * /\
            IP   C[+Q]
            /\
   [+Q] QPi  IP
              /\
            xi   VP
                 /\
             WHj   VP
                   /\
                 xj  V
```

I would like to suggest that in structures like (15), government of the *wh*-QP by the [+Q] in COMP is blocked by the intervening [+Q] the standard QP contains. This is a situation where a minimality requirement is imposed on government by a licensing feature. Following Chomsky (1986a), let us assume the Principle of Full Interpretation:

---

[10] For 'government' in (13ii), I will assume (i), where 'c-command' is defined as in (6b):

(i) Feature Government: X feature: governs Y iff
(i) X c-commands Y
(ii) Relativized Minimality is respected

I will assume further that *wh*-QPs can take scope over the c-command ((6a)) domain of the [+Q] COMP which licenses them.

(16) <u>Principle of Full Interpretation (FI)</u>
Every element at PF and LF must receive an appropriate interpretation or must be licensed.

(14c) is ultimately excluded as a violation of the FI.

Note that scope relations among QPs are (partially) determined by antecedent government (see (4) and (9)). Then, it would be natural to think that antecedent government also plays a role in locality in QR. It would be theoretically desirable that the same principle, RM in particular, constrains scope phenomena in general. Note also that the ill-formedness of (14c) cannot be explained by an approach which utilizes the notion of binding. Therefore, I advocate the idea to derive the MBR from the ECP. I will adopt the 'conjunctive' ECP in (17) (see (10)):

(17) ECP: A nonpronominal empty category must be
(i) properly head-governed
(ii) antecedent-governed.[11]

For present purposes, the clause (i) is orthogonal (see Cinque (1990), Rizzi (1990)). I assume without discussion that traces can satisfy the ECP at any level of representation (S-structure or LF) (cf. Lasnik and Saito (1984), Chomsky (1989)).

Rizzi's (1990) formulation of RM is provided in (18):

(18) Relativized Minimality: X a-governs Y only if there is no Z such that
(i) Z is a base-generated position
(ii) Z is a-GT compatible with Y
(iii) Z c-commands Y and does not c-command X.[12]

Intuitively, RM says that government of Y by X is blocked by intervening Z only if Z is a potential governor of the same kind as X for Y (see Rizzi (1990, ch.1) for details).

In order to subsume the MBR under RM, the latter must be made sensitive to adjoined positions created by QR. Thus, we propose to eliminate (18i), as in (19):[13]

---

[11] Traces of *wh*-elements that are D-linked (discourse-linked) in the sense of Pesetsky (1987) are exempt from (17ii). They can meet the 'identification' requirement through binding. See Cinque (1990, ch.1).

[12] Here 'c-command' is defined as in (6a). Incidentally, Rizzi (1990:112, fn.4), commenting on head government, tentatively assumes that 'c-command' must be defined as in (6a) for functional heads and as in (6b) for lexical heads.

[13] One may well ask what motivated Rizzi to include (18i) in his RM. A relevant pair of examples is the following:

(i) a. *It is [for this reason]$_i$ [$_{CP}$ no one$_j$ that [$_{IP}$ x_j believes [that Bill was fired x_i]]]
b. It is [for this reason]$_i$ [$_{CP}$ that [$_{IP}$ everyone$_j$ [$_{IP}$ x_j believes [that Bill was fired x_i]]]]

Rizzi assumes that negative operators like *no one* move to SPEC of CP at LF, whereas operators like *everyone* simply QR. In the *no one* sentence, the lower construal of the adverbial phrase is impossible, though the higher one is possible. The *everyone* sentence is ambiguous. (ia,b) are the LFs for the lower construal. According to RM in (18), antecedent

(19) Relativized Minimality: X α-governs Y only if there is no Z such that
(i) Z is α-GT compatible with Y
(ii) Z c-commands Y and does not c-command X.

'α-Government Theory compatible (α-GT compatible)' can be characterized as in (20) (adapted from Rizzi (1990)):

(20) Government Theory Compatibility:
An element Z is α-GT compatible with Y only if the conditions for the appropriate subcase of government are met (the relevant property of the governor) while the substantive condition on Z as a governor need not be (actual coindexation for antecedent government).

(20) differs from Rizzi's original statement in that it makes no reference to syntactic positions of governors. Instead, it makes use of the property of governors.[14] For instance, the relevant property of operators, I suggest, is operatorhood.[15]

Given (19), (20), and the assumption that a *wh*-QP and a standard QP are GT-compatible with each other (see (13i)), the ill-formedness of (12a) can be accounted for: variables must be antecedent-governed by the closest potential governor (cases like (14a,b)); government by a licensing feature is blocked by an intervening feature of the same kind (cases like (14b,c)).[16]

Now, let us turn to (12b-d). It may seem that in (12b) the S-structure

---

government by an element in an A'-position will never be blocked by an adjoined element. The contrast in (i) thus follows.

What Rizzi does not notice, however, is that his RM wrongly rules out even the higher construal of (ia), as is illustrated in (ii):

(ii) *It is [for this reason]$_i$ [$_{CP}$ no one$_j$ that [$_{IP}$ x_i [$_{IP}$ x_j believes [that Bill was fired]]]]

With (19) and (20), examples like (i) can be handled. Let us assume that QPs, negative or non-negative, are subject to QR. Let us further assume that negative operators but not standard QPs are GT-compatible with adverbials, though it is far from clear to me what nature of negative operators and adverbials is relevant for GT-compatibility. Then, the LFs for the *no one* sentence would be as follows:

(iii) a. *It is [for this reason]$_i$ [$_{CP}$ that [$_{IP}$ no one$_j$ [$_{IP}$ x_j believes [that Bill was fired x_i]]]]
b. It is [for this reason]$_i$ [$_{CP}$ that [$_{IP}$ x_i [$_{IP}$ no one$_j$ [$_{IP}$ x_j believes [that Bill was fired]]]]

(iiia) violates RM because government of x_i by the focused element is disrupted by intervening *no one*. (iiib) is well-formed since it observes RM. Government by an adverbial will not be blocked by a standard QP like *everyone*. This is why (ib) is fine. Notice that postulation of null operators in cleft constructions along the lines of Chomsky (1977) will not help Rizzi. In short, examples like these in fact do not justify (18i) and are at least consistent with the present analysis.

14 See Baker and Hale (1990) where it is argued that RM must be made sensitive to the difference between lexical and functional categories.

15 For the purpose of RM, at least three types of operators must be recognized; (i) standard QPs, (ii) negative or adverbial elements (see note 13), and (iii) *wh*-operators (see Section 4). It may be worth pointing out that operatorhood also plays a part in the SP (see (36) below).

16 Thus, (14b) doubly violates the ECP and the FI. The same remark applies to (23b) and (30b) below.

trace is not antecedent-governed because of the intervening QP. But that is not the case. Notice that neither the QP nor the scrambled *wh*-QP has yet acquired operatorhood at S-structure: Saito (1990) shows convincingly that scrambling in Japanese does not establish operator-variable relations. Therefore, S-structures like (12b) are in effect 'invisible' to RM. Given Saito's (1990) claim, scrambled QPs as well as non-scrambled QPs are subject to QR. (21) is a well-formed LF of (12b) (in the representations that follow, the elements associated with a line form a chain):

(21) $[_{IP}$ WH$_i$-o $[_{IP}$ $\underline{x}_i$ $[_{IP}$ QP-ga$_j$ $[_{IP}$ $\underline{x}_j$ $[_{VP}$ $\underline{t}_i$ V$]]]]]$ Q

In (21) the link between $\underline{x}_i$ and $\underline{t}_i$ is 'broken' since antecedent government does not hold between the two due to the presence of the intervening variable $\underline{x}_j$. This is an instance where variables enter into RM. There is nothing wrong with $\underline{t}_i$ because it has already satisfied the ECP at S-structure. According to the SP, (21) represents the interpretation on which the *wh*-QP takes wide scope, a right result. The LF of (12c) is the following:

(22) $[_{IP}$ WH-ga$_i$ $[_{IP}$ $\underline{x}_i$ $[_{VP}$ QP-o$_j$ $[_{VP}$ $\underline{x}_j$ V$]]]]$ Q

(22) in which the *wh*-QP has scope over the QP correctly represents the interpretation of (12c). In (12d) the S-structure trace, like that in (12a), satisfies the ECP. The (ill-formed) LFs of (12d) are as follows:

(23) a. *$[_{IP}$ WH-ga$_i$ $[_{IP}$ QP$_j$-o $[_{IP}$ $\underline{x}_j$ $[_{IP}$ $\underline{x}_i$ $[_{VP}$ $\underline{t}_j$ V$]]]]]$ Q
b. *$[_{IP}$ QP$_i$-o $[_{IP}$ WH-ga$_j$ $[_{IP}$ $\underline{x}_i$ $[_{IP}$ $\underline{x}_j$ $[_{VP}$ $\underline{t}_i$ V$]]]]]$ Q
c. *$[_{IP}$ QP$_i$-o $[_{IP}$ $\underline{x}_i$ $[_{IP}$ WH-ga$_j$ $[_{IP}$ $\underline{x}_j$ $[_{VP}$ $\underline{t}_i$ V$]]]]]$ Q

(23a,b) are cases of an ECP violation; in (23a) antecedent government of $\underline{x}_i$ by the *wh*-QP is disrupted by the QP, whereas in (23b) $\underline{x}_i$ cannot be antecedent-governed by the QP due to the presence of the *wh*-QP. (23c) is not allowed because the QP bars government of the *wh*-QP by the [+Q] in COMP.

Then, why is (12d) grammatical at all? Let us assume with Saito (1990) that scrambling in Japanese can be undone at LF. Given this assumption, (12d) has the LF in (22), which represents the correct interpretation. Notice that when reconstruction takes place in (12b), the resultant LFs are all ill-formed, as in (14).

Next, let us consider (2b). Its unreconstructed LF is (24):

(24) $[_{IP}$ daremo-o$_i$ $[_{IP}$ $\underline{x}_i$ $[_{IP}$ dareka$_j$-ga $[_{IP}$ $\underline{x}_j$ $[_{VP}$ $\underline{t}_i$ aisiteiru$]]]]]$

This LF represents the interpretation on which *daremo* takes scope over *dareka*. When the scrambled QP is put back to its original position, the LF of (2b) will be identical to (8) in which *dareka* takes wide scope. Therefore,

(2b) is ambiguous.[17]

Summarizing, the above examination of the scope of a *wh*-QP and a QP in Japanese has led us to propose that (i) Rizzi's (1990) RM should be further relativized, (ii) the MBR should be subsumed under the ECP, and (iii) the scope of scrambled QPs in Japanese can be accounted for by the SP together with LF reconstruction.[18]

---

[17] Hoji (1985:248) presents (i) to explain the contrast in (2):

(i) at LF $*QP_i \; QP_j \; \underline{t}_j \; \underline{t}_i$ where each member c-commands the member to its right

Within his framework based on May (1977) and Lasnik and Saito (1984), however, some cases of 'long distance' and multiple scrambling are problematic for (i) (see Hoji (1985:299, fn.25). The analysis developed here can account for such cases as well as VP-internal scrambling (see Aoun and Li (1989) for double object and dative constructions).

[18] I am arguing against Katada's (1991) claim in (i):

(i) Reconstruction is a general property of nonoperators.

(i) is meant to explain the low acceptability of examples like (iib) where the scrambled element is *zibun*, an operator (see Katada (1991)):

(ii) a. John$_i$-ga zibun?$_i$-o semeta (koto)
-NOM self -ACC blamed fact
'John blamed self.'

b. Zibun???$_i$-o [John$_i$-ga $\underline{t}$ semeta] (koto)
self -ACC -NOM blamed fact
'Self, John blamed $\underline{t}$.'

But notice that scrambling of operators can be A-movement:

(iii) a. ?*[Otagai$_i$ -no sensei] -ga [futari-no gakusei]$_i$-o
each other-GEN teacher-NOM two -GEN student -ACC
(sorezore) hihansita (koto)
each criticized fact
'Each other's$_i$ teachers criticized two students$_i$.'

b. ?[Futari-no gakusei]$_i$-o (sorezore) [$_{IP}$ [otagai$_i$ -no
two -GEN student -ACC each each other-GEN
sensei] -ga $\underline{t}$ hihansita] (koto)
teacher-NOM criticized fact
'Two students$_i$, each other's$_i$ teachers criticized $\underline{t}$.'

The grammaticality of (iiib) must be due to the presence of an antecedent in an A-position binding the anaphor *otagai* 'each other' (see Mahajan (1990:25-30) for additional data from Hindi which illustrate that scrambling of QPs can be A-movement). In the absence of contradictory data, I would like to put forth the following hypothesis (see Saito (1990) for the argument that 'long distance' scrambling cannot be A-movement):

(iv) Clause-internal scrambling of operators is to an A-position.

If (iv) is correct, (iib) is ruled out at S-structure as a violation of Condition C of the Binding Theory (cf. Chomsky (1981, 1986a)).

3. The Scope Principle

3.1. NP-Movement in Japanese

It has been argued that Japanese has NP-movement (see Hoji et al. (1989) and the references cited therein). Let us ask if the SP is empirically valid in NP-movement cases as well. Consider (25) and (26) (the latter is from Hoji et al. (1989)):

(25) Daremo -ga$_i$ dareka -ni t_i nagur-are-ta.
everyone-NOM someone by was hit
'Everyone was hit by someone.'

(26) Dareka -ga$_i$ subeteno heya-ni t_i hair-ta.
someone-NOM every room entered
'Someone entered every room.'

(25) involves passivization, while (26) is an ergative construction. Both of them are ambiguous.[19] The LF of (25) is the following:

(27) [$_{IP}$ daremo-ga$_i$ [$_{IP}$ x_i [$_{VP}$ dareka$_j$ [$_{VP}$ [$_{PP}$ x_j-ni] t_i nagurareta]]]]

In (27) the link between x_i and t_i is not disrupted because the variable of the agentive QP x_j does not intervene between them; x_j is inside the PP (postpositional phrase) (see (19ii)). (27) represents ambiguity since the higher QP c-commands the lower QP and the latter c-commands t_i, the tail of the chain containing the former.

Now, consider the passive sentences in (28) which involve a *wh*-QP and a QP:[20]

---

[19] Hoji et al. (1989, fn.12) note that 'the Japanese passive does not seem to induce scope ambiguity between the preposed subject and the agentive NP, unlike Chinese'. Thus for them, (25) should be unambiguous. But I find it ambiguous. They discuss the following passive sentence:

(i) Dareka -ga$_i$ subeteno hito -ni t_i syookais-rare-ta.
someone-NOM every person-DAT was introduced
'Someone was introduced to everyone.'

I agree that (i) is ambiguous and that if we take *subeteno hito* 'everyone' as an agentive NP (*-ni* can be used either as the dative marker or 'by'), (i) is not ambiguous, *dareka* 'someone' taking scope over *subeteno hito*. I suggest that the unavailability of the wide scope interpretation of the agentive NP can be attributed to the fact that agentive NPs in Japanese strongly favor group readings (for reasons unknown to me). Observe the ambiguous (ii):

(ii) Dareka -ga$_i$ subeteno hito -ni sorezore t_i syookais-rare-ta.
someone-NOM every person by each was introduced
'Someone was introduced by everyone each.'

In (ii) *sorezore* 'each' is added to guarantee the non-group reading on *subeteno hito* (this technique is due to Hoji (1985)).

[20] Considering the property of the agentive phrase mentioned in the preceding note, I use

(28) a. *Daremo -ga$_i$ sorezore [$_{VP}$ dare-ni t_i sikar-are-ta] no?
everyone-NOM each who by was scolded Q
'Everyone each was scolded by whom?'

b. Dare-ni$_j$ daremo -ga$_i$ sorezore [$_{VP}$ t_j t_i sikar-are-ta] no?
who by everyone-NOM each was scolded Q
'[By whom]$_i$, everyone each was scolded t_i?'

c. Dare-ga$_i$ [$_{VP}$ daremo -ni sorezore t_i sikar-are-ta] no?
who -NOM everyone by each was scolded Q
'Who was scolded by everyone each?'

d. Daremo -ni$_j$ sorezore dare-ga$_i$ [$_{VP}$ t_j t_i sikar-are-ta] no?
everyone by each who-NOM was scolded Q
'[By everyone each]$_i$, who was scolded t_i?'

The S-structure configurations in these examples are given in (29):

(29) a. *QP-ga$_i$ [$_{VP}$ WH-ni t_i V] Q
-NOM by

b. WH-ni$_j$ QP-ga$_i$ [$_{VP}$ t_j t_i V] Q (WH taking wide scope)

c. WH-ga$_i$ [$_{VP}$ QP-ni t_i V] Q (ambiguous)

d. QP-ni$_j$ WH-ga$_i$ [$_{VP}$ t_j t_i V] Q (ambiguous)

(29a) is ungrammatical. (29b), derived from (29a) by scrambling the *wh*-QP, is rendered grammatical but is unambiguous, the *wh*-QP taking wide scope. (29c) is ambiguous. (29d) derived from (29c) is also ambiguous.

The scope interpretations observed in (29) are exactly what is predicted by the SP, RM, and the assumption that scrambling can be undone at LF. (29a) is ruled out in the same way as (12a). Its LF representations are provided in (30):

(30) a. *[$_{IP}$ WH$_j$ [$_{IP}$ QP-ga$_i$ [$_{IP}$ x_i [$_{VP}$ [$_{PP}$ x_j-ni] t_i V]]]] Q

b. *[$_{IP}$ QP-ga$_i$ [$_{IP}$ WH$_j$ [$_{IP}$ x_i [$_{VP}$ [$_{PP}$ x_j-ni] t_i V]]]] Q

c. *[$_{IP}$ QP-ga$_i$ [$_{IP}$ x_i [$_{VP}$ WH$_j$ [$_{VP}$ [$_{PP}$ x_j-ni] t_i V]]]] Q

(30a,b) violate the ECP, whereas (30c) violates the FI. The LF representations of (29b-d) are (31-33) respectively:

(31) [$_{IP}$ WH$_k$ [$_{IP}$ [$_{PP}$ x_k-ni]$_j$ [$_{IP}$ QP-ga$_i$ [$_{IP}$ x_i [$_{VP}$ t_j t_i V]]]]] Q

(32) [$_{IP}$ WH-ga$_i$ [$_{IP}$ x_i [$_{VP}$ QP$_j$ [$_{VP}$ [$_{PP}$ x_j-ni] t_i V]]]] Q

(33) *[$_{IP}$ QP$_k$ [$_{IP}$ [$_{PP}$ x_k-ni]$_j$ [$_{IP}$ WH-ga$_i$ [$_{IP}$ x_i [$_{VP}$ t_j t_i V]]]]] Q

---

sorezore in (28).

In (31) the *wh*-QP takes wide scope. When (29b) undergoes reconstruction, it will have illegitimate LFs in (30). Thus, it is unambiguous. (29c) is ambiguous since in (32), the *wh*-QP c-commands the QP and the latter in turn c-commands t_i, a member of the chain headed by the former. Although (33), where the *wh*-QP is not governed by the [+Q] in COMP, is ill-formed, (29d) will have the LF in (32) when reconstruction of the scrambled element occurs. Thus, (29d) is ambiguous.

In brief, the scope interaction in Japanese sentences involving NP-movement is amenable to the SP and the analysis developed above.

3.2. *Wh*-Movement in English

We have looked at scrambling and NP-movement. Let us finally consider a third kind of syntactic movement, namely, *Wh*-movement.

May (1985) recognizes a contrast in scope interaction in pairs like (34):

(34) a. What did everyone bring?
b. Who brought everything?

(34a), with a QP in subject position and a *wh*-trace in object position, is ambiguous, whereas (34b), with a QP in object position and a *wh*-trace in subject position, is unambiguous.

I assume with Saito (1990) that *Wh*-movement cannot be undone at LF because it establishes operator-variable relations unlike scrambling in Japanese. The LFs of (34a,b) would be (35a,b) respectively:[21]

(35) a. $[_{CP}$ what$_i$ did $[_{IP}$ everyone$_j$ $[_{IP}$ x_j $[_{VP}$ t_j bring $x_i]]]]$

b. $[_{CP}$ who$_i$ $[_{IP}$ x_i $[_{VP}$ everything$_j$ $[_{VP}$ t_i brought $x_j]]]]$

Let us make the reasonable assumption that a 'true' *wh*-phrase and a standard QP are not GT-compatible with each other. Then, government by *wh*-phrases like *what* and *who* as opposed to *wh*-QPs in Japanese will not be blocked by standard QPs like *everyone* and *everything*.[22] The ambiguity of (35a) is expected by the SP; the IP-adjoined QP c-commands x_i, a member of the chain headed by the *wh*-phrase. The unambiguity of (35b), however, is not expected. The question is: should the SP in (4) be revised so that it can cope with (34b)?

---

[21] Recall that I am assuming Cinque's (1990) barrier system, not Chomsky's (1986b). Hence, VP-adjunction of *wh*-operators is unnecessary.

[22] Thus, we can dispense with (5) and Aoun and Li's (1989) somewhat ad hoc assumption mentioned in note 4 that variables bound by *wh*-operators are subject to Condition C but those bound by standard QPs are not.

My answer to this question is negative. Tacit in the previous discussion (and in Aoun and Li (1989) and Ernst (1991)) is the assumption that the SP applies at LF. I assume along the lines proposed by Kim (1991) that S-structure does contribute to the determination of scope interpretation. To be more specific, let us assume the following:

(36) The SP applies at every level of representation where either A or B bears its operatorhood.

Given (36), the SP applies at S-structure (as well as at LF) in the case of *Wh*-movement. Furthermore, let us assume with Kim (1991) that (37) is correct:

(37) A scope relation must be maintained throughout the derivation.[23]

Consider the S-structure representations of (34a,b):

(38) a. $[_{CP}$ what$_i$ did $[_{IP}$ everyone $[_{VP}$ $\underline{t}_j$ bring $\underline{x}_i]]]$

b. $[_{CP}$ who$_i$ $[_{IP}$ $\underline{x}_i$ $[_{VP}$ $\underline{t}_i$ brought everything$]]]$

The SP assigns (38a) the scope relation whereby either the *wh*-phrase or the QP has wider scope. On the other hand, it assigns (38b) the scope relation whereby only the *wh*-phrase takes scope over the QP. With this in mind, let us go back to the LFs in (35). In light of (37), (35a) is well-formed, but (35b) is not; the scope relation is not changed in (35a) but it is in (35b). The SP allows the QP in (35b) to have wide scope with respect to the *wh*-phrase. The correct LF of (34b) would then be the following (I adopt the Larson-style layered VP (see Larson (1988), Sportiche (1990), and also Travis (1991))):

(39) $[_{CP}$ who$_i$ $[_{IP}$ $\underline{x}_i$ $[_{VP1}$ $\underline{t}_i$ brought $[_{VP2}$ everything$_j$ $[_{VP2}$ $\underline{t}_V$ $\underline{x}_j]]]]]$

(39) successfully represents the unambiguous interpretation of (34b). Notice that (36) does not affect the above explanation of the Japanese examples since they do not contain operators which acquire operatorhood at S-structure.

To sum up, the SP can account for *Wh*-movement cases without modification if we incorporate Kim's (1991) insight into the present analysis.[24]

---

[23] It is reasonable to regard (37) as an instantiation of the principle of Relation Preservation advanced by Watanabe (1991):

(i) <u>Relation Preservation</u>
A relation established at a certain point in the derivation must be maintained throughout.

[24] The SP can be extended to the scope interactions between a *wh*-phrase and a QP other

3.3. The Scope Principle

Ernst (1991:753) proposes the following generalized version of Aoun and Li's (1989) SP:

(40) The Scope Principle
An operator A has scope over an operator B in case
A c-commands a member of the chain containing B.

(40) is intended to cover not only QPs but also nonquantificational operators like adverbs and modals. Ernst suggests that 'c-command' in the SP should be 'strict' c-command given in (6a).

Note that the SP in (40) is fully compatible with the proposals made here. Therefore, I suggest that (4) should in fact be replaced by (40). Following Ernst, I assume that adverbs do not move at LF, thus constituting one-membered chains (see (9)). It would be quite feasible to think that nonquantificational operators acquire their operatorhood at LF (see (36)).

4. Conclusion

In this paper, I have examined Japanese data on the scope of scrambled and non-scrambled QPs, including *wh*-QPs. It has been shown that the scope of scrambled QPs can be explained by the SP combined with LF reconstruction. I have argued that RM of Rizzi (1990) should be further relativized in such a way that it does not refer to the syntactic position of the governor in question. Rather, what seems to be important in formulating RM is the nature of the governor. I have also argued that the MBR derives from the ECP. Finally, I have supported the extend version of the SP in (40).

The differences between English and Japanese in scope interpretation can be boiled down to three differences between the two languages; (i) English has Subject Raising but Japanese does not, (ii) English has 'real' *wh*-phrases, which are subject to *Wh*-movement, but Japanese does not, (iii) Japanese has scrambling, which can be undone at LF, while English does not. These differences, interacting with principles of grammar such as the ECP, the FI, and the SP, manifest themselves as the differences in scope of quantifiers.

A number of questions remain unsolved. For instance, exactly how should we formalize the notion of GT-compatibility; is the SP empirically correct in languages other than English and Japanese; what is the source of the parametric variation in Subject Raising? These questions are left open for future research.

---

than cases like (34). For example, it explains the scope facts of psych-verb constructions (see Kim and Larson (1989)), given the analysis of Belletti and Rizzi (1988). It also explains cases where the *wh*-operator is adverbial, in conjunction with Stroik's (1990) proposal.

REFERENCES

Aoun, J. and Y. Li (1989) Scope and Constituency. *Linguistic Inquiry* 20, 141-172.

Baker, M. and K. Hale (1990) Relativized Minimality and Pronoun Incorporation. *Linguistic Inquiry* 21, 289-297.

Belletti A. and L. Rizzi (1988) Psych-Verbs and T-Theory. *Natural Language and Linguistic Theory* 6, 291-352.

Chomsky, N. (1977) On *Wh*-Movement. In P. Culicover, T. Wasow, and A. Akmajian (eds.) *Formal Syntax*. New York: Academic Press.

Chomsky, N. (1981) *Lectures on Government and Binding*. Dordrecht: Foris Publications.

Chomsky, N. (1986a) *Knowledge of Language: Its Nature, Origins, and Use*. New York: Praeger.

Chomsky, N. (1986b) *Barriers*. Cambridge: MIT Press.

Chomsky, N. (1989) Some Notes on Economy of Derivation and Representation. *MIT Working Papers in Linguistics* 10, 43-74.

Ernst, T. (1991) On the Scope Principle. *Linguistic Inquiry* 22, 750-756.

Hoji, H. (1985) *Logical Form Constraints and Configurational Structures in Japanese*. Ph.D. dissertation, University of Washington, Seatle.

Hoji, H. (1986) Scope Interpretation in Japanese and its Theoretical Implications. In *Proceedings of WCCFL* V. Stanford University, Stanford.

Hoji, H., S. Miyagawa, and H. Tada (1989) NP-Movement in Japanese. ms. USC, OSU, and MIT.

Katada, F. (1991) The LF Representation of Anaphors. *Linguistic Inquiry* 22, 287-313.

Kim, S.-W. (1989) *Wh*-phrases in Korean and Japanese are QPs. *MIT Working Papers in Linguistics* 11, 119-138.

Kim, S.-W. (1991) *Chain Scope and Quantification Structure*. Ph.D. dissertation, Brandeis University, Waltham, MA.

Kim, Y. and R. Larson (1989) Scope Interpretation and the Syntax of Psych-Verbs. *Linguistic Inquiry* 20, 681-688.

Kitagawa, Y. (1986) *Subjects in Japanese and English*. Ph.D. dissertation, University of Massachusetts, Amherst.

Kuroda, S.-Y. (1988) Whether We Agree or not: A Comparative Syntax of English and Japanese. In W. J. Poser (ed.) *Papers from the Second International Workshop on Japanese Syntax*. Stanford: CSLI.

Larson, R. (1988) On the Double Object Construction. *Linguistic Inquiry* 19, 335-392.

Lasnik, H. and M. Saito (1984) On the Nature of Proper Government. *Linguistic Inquiry* 15, 235-289.

Mahajan, A. (1990) *The A/A-bar Distinction and Movement Theory*. Ph.D. Dissertation, MIT, Cambridge, MA.

May, R. (1977) *The Grammar of Quantification*. Ph.D. dissertation, MIT, Cambridge, MA.

May, R. (1985) *Logical Form: Its Structure and Derivation*. Cambridge: MIT Press.

Nakayama, M. and M. Koizumi (1991) Remarks on Japanese Subjects. *Lingua* 85, 303-319.

Nishigauchi, T. (1990) *Quantification in the Theory of Grammar*. Dordrecht: Kluwer Academic Publishers.

Pesetsky, D. (1987) *Wh*-in-Situ: Movement and Unselective Binding. In E. J. Reuland and A. ter Meulen (eds.) *The Representation of (In)definiteness*. Cambridge: MIT Press.

Rizzi, L. (1990) *Relativized Minimality*. Cambridge: MIT Press.

Saito, M. (1985) *Some Asymmetries in Japanese and Their Theoretical Implications*. Ph.D. dissertation, MIT, Cambridge, MA.

Saito, M. (1990) Long Distance Scrambling in Japanese. ms. University of Connecticut, Storrs.

Sportiche, D. (1990) Movement, Agreement and Case. ms. UCLA, Los Angeles.

Stroik, T. (1990) Adverbs as V-Sisters. *Linguistic Inquiry* 21, 654-661.

Taraldsen, T. (1986) *Som* and the Binding Theory. In L. Hellan and K. K. Christensen (eds.) *Topics in Scandinavian Syntax*. Dordrecht: Kluwer Academic Publishers.

Travis, L. (1991) Inner Aspect and the Structure of VP. ms. McGill University.

Watanabe, A. (1991) Wh-in-Situ, Subjacency, and Chain Formation. Generals Paper, MIT, Cambridge, MA.

A Note on So-Called "Donkey Sentences" in Japanese: A Preliminary Study

SHIN WATANABE
University of Southern California

A Note on So-called "Donkey Sentences" in Japanese: A Preliminary Study*
Shin Watanabe
University of Southern California

1. Introduction

Since Geach (1962), it has been widely known that the donkey sentence in (1) is problematic with respect to the structural relation between the pronoun it and a donkey:

(1) Every farmer [who owns a donkey$_i$] beats it$_i$. (Geach (1962))

A major problem involved in this sentence is that it is in violation of a well-known syntactic constraint in (2):

(2) Quantified NPs can have anaphoric relations only with pronouns (or anaphors) in their c-command syntactic domain.
(cf. Reinhart (1983; 122))

In (1), the existential quantifier a donkey fails to c-command it, even though they are coreferential.

Nishigauchi (1990; Chapter 6) reports that certain constructions in Japanese exhibit a similar "donkey" problem. The following are some typical examples of such constructions, which I call Nishigauchi-type donkey sentences[1]:

(3) a. [Dono ronbun$_i$ -o kaita] gakusei -mo sore$_i$-o syuppanshita.
wh article A wrote student Q it A published
(For every x, for every y, x is an article, y is a student that wrote y, y published x.)
b.??[Dono ronbun$_i$ -o kaita] gakusei -ka-ga NELS-ni sono$_i$
wh article A wrote student Q N to its
abusutorakuto -o okutta (koto)
abstract A sent
(There is some x and y, x is an article and y is a student that wrote x, such that y sent x's abstract to NELS.)
c. [Dono ronbun$_i$ -o kaita] gakusei-demo sore$_i$-o
wh article A wrote student Q it A
syuppandekita (koto) .
publish-could
(For every x, for every y, x is an article, y is a student that wrote x, y could publish x.)

It is evident that the syntactic constraint in (2) is violated in these sentences. For example, in (3a), the quantified expression dono ronbun (wh + article) and the pronoun sore are coreferential despite the fact that the former fails to c-command the latter. In this respect, these sentences share a property with the sentence in (1), which is a typical example of a donkey sentence in English.

The aim of this paper is to suggest the following; (i) Neale and Ludlow's treatment of donkey pronouns (Neale (1990), Ludlow (1990)) enables us to dispense with Haik's (1984) theory of INDIRECT BINDING in explaining a certain structural restriction on donkey sentences both in English and Japanese (section 3), (ii) Nishigauchi's (1990) treatment of donkey sentences involves some inadequacies concerning its factual claim and its theoretical predictions (section 4).

As for (i), in particular, I will suggest, following Neale (1990) and Ludlow (1990), that a donkey pronoun is an E-type pronoun, which is interpreted as a (definite) description at LF. Furthermore, I will claim that the definite description associated with a donkey pronoun contains a variable which purports to be bound by a binder outside of the description.

As for (ii), I will point out some aspects of Nishigauchi's treatment of donkey sentences in Japanese which seem to me to be incorrect. In the first place, I will point out that one of his factual claims is wrong. In the second place, it will be discussed that his claim that a quantificational particle functions as an unselective binder in Nishigauchi-type donkey sentences (see the following section) cannot be maintained. The conclusion I will reach there is that such constructions do not correspond to donkey sentences in English like that in (1). Furthermore I will present other types of donkey sentences which do go along with donkey sentences in English with regard to the relevant respects.

2. The Structure of Nishigauchi's (1990) Donkey Sentences

In this section, I will briefly summarize the structural composition of Nishigauchi-type donkey sentences exemplified in (3) above. The basic structure of such constructions is schematically shown in (4) :

(4) $[_{NP}$ $[_{S}$ ... $\underline{wh}_i$ ...] N] - mo / ka / demo ... $Pronoun_i$ ...

In (4), a wh-phrase is located inside of the relative clause and it is coreferential with a pronoun outside of the relative clause. Following Kuroda (1965) and Nishigauchi (1990), I suppose that a wh-phrase in Japanese is not originally equipped with any quantificational force and it can be identified as an expression associated with a certain quantificaitonal force only when it finds a quantificational particle like mo (=also), ka (= or), demo (= even) somewhere higher at the S-structure. In (4), in particular, the wh-phrase gets its quantificational force by a particle attached to the head of the relative clause.

Although I will not give any concrete examples because of the space limitation, rough meanings of " wh + Q " sequences are described below:

(5) a. Wh + mo = a universal quantifier
b. Wh + demo = "free-choice" any
c. Wh + ka = an existential quantifier
(For examples, see Kuroda (1965; chapter 3), Nishigauchi (1990))

As shown, the quantificational particles, mo, ka, demo together with a wh-expression create a universal quantifier, an existential quantifier and a free choice any, respectively. In (4), a wh-phrase and a quantificational particle are discontinuously combined and the combination as a whole behaves like a single quantifier. As to the question of how remote the wh-phrase could be from the quantificaitonal particle, let us simply posit that the association of the quantificational particle and the wh-phrase is obtained as long as the former c-commands the latter and a wh-island does not intervene between them. [2]

3. A C-command Restriction between a Donkey Pronoun and the Relative Clause Containing its Antecedent

In this section, I will discuss a c-command requirement in donkey sentences and suggest a possibility that a donkey pronoun be rendered as a description at the level of semantic interpretation, namely LF.

Let us begin by considering the following example :

(6) [Dono $gakusei_i$ -o nagutta] yakuza -mo atode $soitu_i$ -no
wh student A hit gangster Q later the-guy G
ryoosin -ni ayamatta.
parents D apologized
(For every x, for every y, if x is a student and y is a gangster and y hit x, y apologized to x' parents.)

Recall that the sentence in (6), which is in the form of Nishigauchi-type donkey sentence, is problematic, since dono gakusei (= wh + student), the quantified antecedent of soitsu, fails to c-command the pronoun. Although a strict c-command relation is not required between dono gakusei and soitu, it is not the case that the donkey pronoun can just occur anywhere. As correctly pointed out by Haik (1984) for English donkey sentences (her examples will be given below), that a donkey pronoun must be c-commanded by the noun phrase containing its antecedent in it. In (6), this c-command requirement is satisfied, since the donkey pronoun soitsu is c-commanded by the subject noun phrase involving its antecedent. If the c-command relation fails to obtain, ungrammaticality results :

(7) *Soitu$_i$ -no ryoosin -ga [dono gakusei$_i$ -o nagutta] yakuza-
the guy G parents N wh student A hit gangster
mo nikunda.
Q hated
(For every x, for every y, if x is a student and y is a gangster and y hit x, x' parents hated y.)

The ill-formedness of this sentence is due to the fact that the donkey pronoun soitu is not c-commanded by the noun phrase containing its antecedent in it, namely [dono gakusee -o nagutta] yakuza - mo .

As suggested above, Haik (1984) reports a similar c-command restriction in English. Her examples are as follows :

(8) a. [Every farmer who owns a donkey$_i$] beats it$_i$.
b*Every farmer who owns a donkey$_i$ came, and Mary bought it$_i$.
(slightly changed)

Here, again, a strict c-command relation must hold between the donkey pronoun it and the noun phrase containing its antecedent. It is obvious that this requirement is satisfied in (8a), and, therefore, the sentence is grammatical. If the structural relation does not hold between the relevant two elements, ungrammaticality results as in (8b).

Haik (1984) proposes a somewhat stipulative notion called INDIRECT BINDING to account for the contrast in (8) among other phenomena. The following set of (rather abbreviated) definitions illustrate the essence of her framework:

(9) a. SCOPE INDEXING :
(i) If NP_i is to be interpreted as in the scope of NP_j, then append /j to the index of NP_i ... (= (45a) ; 197)
(ii) NP_i ---> $NP_{i(j)}$ iff NP_i has scope over NP_j. (= (59) ; 203)
b. INDIRECT BINDING : Pronoun $_{i/j}$ must be c-commanded by $NP_{j(i)}$.
(cf. (61b) ; 203)

As is revealed by (9b), the relation of indirect binding is determined in terms of scope indices. Roughly speaking, the scope indexing captures the relation of take scope over in the following fashion: if a noun phrase NP_i takes scope over another noun phrase NP_j, the former and the latter get represented as $NP_{i(j)}$ and $NP_{j/i}$, respectively.

Along these lines, the well-formed sentence given in (8a) and the ill-formed one in (8b) are associated with the following S-structure representations, (10a) and (10b), respectively :

(10) a. [$NP_{1(2)}$ Every farmer [who [S $t_{1(2)}$ owns [$_{2/1}$ a donkey]]]] beats it $_{2/1}$.
b. [$NP_{1(2)}$ Every farmer [who [S $t_{1(2)}$ owns [$_{2/1}$ a donkey]]]] came, and Mary bought it $_{2/1}$.

Given that, in a relative clause, the wh - trace has the same referential index as the whole NP. In (10a), a donkey is in the scope of every farmer. Then we scope-index a donkey as $NP_{2/1}$. This automatically rewrites the donkey pronoun it as $it_{2/1}$, since it is coindexed with the indefinite description. Furthermore, the wh-trace inside the relative clause is marked with $t_{1(2)}$ in conjunction with the whole noun phrase. In this structure, the relation of indirect binding successfully obtains; the donkey pronoun $it_{2/1}$ is c-commanded (namely, indirectly-bound) by the subject noun phrase with the index of 1(2) Therefore the structure is well-formed. On the other hand, in (10b), this c-command requirement cannot be fulfilled, since the noun phrase [$NP_{1(2)}$ Every farmer ...] fails to c-command the donkey pronoun. Therefore the S-structure is in violation of (9b), and, hence, ill-formed.

Though she can account for the contrast in (8), Haik must have recourse to the notions of SCOPE INDEXING and INDIRECT BINDING, which have not yet been theoretically established in the overall framework of the transformational grammar.

Now I would like to seek an alternative analysis which enables us to dispense with such stipulations in order to account for (8). In particular, I suggest, following Neale (1990) and Ludlow (1990), that unbound anaphoric pronouns like donkey pronouns might stand proxy for definite descriptions. The following is the analysis to be pursued:

(11) (Based on (P5), Neale (1990; 182))
If x is a pronoun that is anaphoric on, but not c-commanded by, a quantifier, x is an E-type pronoun which is interpreted as a definite description .
(see also Evans (1977), Parsons (1978), Cooper (1979) and Davies (1981), among others).

Simply put, I assume that a donkey pronoun is an E-type pronoun, which refers back to a certain description and the descriptive contents of which are recovered by a certain algorithm at LF from the description to which the pronoun refers .

Along these lines, consider the donkey sentences in (8) again, which are repeated in (12):

(12) a. [Every farmer who owns a donkey$_i$] beats it$_i$.
b.*Every farmer who owns a donkey$_i$ came, and Mary bought it$_i$.

Notice that both in (12a) and (12b), the donkey pronoun it is anaphoric on, but not c-commanded by, the existential quantifier a donkey. Hence this pronoun is regarded as an E-type pronoun. As is suggested, an E-type pronoun refers back to a certain description, and, then, it is accordingly rendered as a definite description at LF possibly by some copying rule with reference to the description. Putting aside the technical details of such a process [3], the renderings in (13a) and (13b) seem to be the most suitable interpretations of (12a) and (12b), respectively, as is indicated in Neale (1990) : [4]

(13) a. [Every farmer$_i$ who owns a donkey] $_i$ beats the donkey(s) that **he**$_i$ owns.
b.*[Every farmer $_j$ who owns a donkey] $_i$ came , and Mary bought the donkey that **he**$_i$ owns

In these renderings, I suppose, following Neale (1990) and Ludlow (1990), that the donkey pronouns in the examples in (12) are interpreted as definite descriptions. Notice that these descriptions are supposed to contain a pronoun he in them, which is a variable to be bound by the noun phrase " every farmer who owns a donkey ".

Given this interpretation of donkey pronouns, the explanation of the contrast in (13) (therefore, that in (12)) turns out to be rather straightforward. Namely the representation in (13a) is well-formed, since the variable he is successfully bound by its binder every farmer who owns a donkey. On the other hand, the semantic interpretation in (13b) is ill-formed, since the variable remains unbound. We can thus account for the c-command restriction under consideration without recourse to a stipulation like INDIRECT BINDING, and, in this very respect, the present treatment of donkey pronouns seems to be superior to Haik's (1984) analysis.

In the light of this "description" analysis of donkey pronouns, let us turn to the Japanese examples in (6) and (7) above. In both examples, the donkey pronoun soitsu is anaphoric on, but not c-commanded by, dono gakusee (wh + student), which is a quantifier. Therefore, according to the statement in (11), the donkey pronoun soitsu is regarded as an E-type pronoun, and, hence, it refers to a previous description, thereby recovering its descriptive contents at the level of LF. Although I continue to put aside the theoretical characterization of the semantic recovery of donkey pronouns again, we can easily come up with the following interpretations, which seems to be best suited for the examples :

(14) ((14a) and (14b) correspond to (6) and (7), respectively.)
a. [Dono gakusei$_i$ -o nagutta] yakuza$_j$ -mo atode **soitu$_j$** -ga
wh student A hit gangster Q later the-guy N
nagutta gakusee no ryoosin -ni ayamatta.
hit student G parents D apologized
b. *[**Soitu$_j$**-ga nagutta] gakusei-no ryoosin -ga [dono gakusee $_i$-o
the-guy N hit student G parents N wh student A
nagutta] yakuza$_j$- mo nikunda.
hit gangster Q hated

In these renderings, the donkey pronoun soitu is interpreted as the description [soitsu$_j$-ga nagutta] gakusei. As in the English cases in (13), this description contains a variable soitu, which must be bound by the quantificational expression [dono gakusei $_i$-o nagutta] yakuza$_j$- mo. Now the contrast between (14a) and (14b) (hence, the contrast between (6) and (7)) can be accounted for as follows. In (14a), the variable soitsu is c-commanded by the noun phrase, and, therefore, the example is grammatical. On the contrary, in (14b), the variable soitu fails to be c-commanded by its quantified antecedent. Then the semantic rendering, which involves an unbound variable (namely, soitu), turns out to be ill-formed.

In Watanabe (1992), where I presented a detailed discussion of this "description"-analysis of donkey pronouns, it was argued that the view pursued here is independently supported by a property of the so-called "so"-series demonstratives in Japanese. It is well-known that the language has an articulated system of demonstratives called "ko - so - a - do" paradigm. Although I cannot present a detailed argument because of the space limitation, I suggested there that the "so"-series and "a"- series demonstratives have the following properties in their non-deictic use:

(15) a. An a - series demonstrative is an R - expression.
b. A so - series demonstrative is purely anaphoric to a certain description.

In (15a), I suppose that a-series demonstratives are R - expressions, and, therefore, they are objects of singular reference, like names, which refer to certain objects in the real world.

Now recall the argument that a donkey pronoun like soitu in a (Nishigauchi-type) donkey sentence refers back to a previous description, and, thereby recovering its descriptive contents. Given the statement in (15b), this nature of the donkey pronoun of "referring back to a description" turns out to be nothing surprising. Since the donkey pronoun like soitu belongs to the so-series of demonstrative paradigm, it can naturally refers to a description as its general property. Furthermore, the following ill-formed sentence seems to be suggestive for the present context :

(16) [dono gakusei$_i$ - o nagutta] yakuza - mo aitu$_i$ -no oya -ni
wh student A hit gangster Q the-guy G parents D
ayamatta.
apologized
(For every x, for every y, if x is a student, y is a gangster, y apologized to x' parents.)

This sentence involves an a - series demonstrative aitu , but otherwise it is exactly the same as the sentence in (6). Given (15a), the ungrammaticality of this example seems rather straightforward; it is ill-formed, since aitu cannot refer to a description.

4. Critical Comments on Nishigauchi (1990)

In this section, I am going to point out two inadequacies found in Nishigauchi (1990), which is the first comprehensive study of donkey sentences in Japanese. I will claim that unlike his conjecture, Nishigauchi-type donkey sentences do not go along with English donkey sentences on some syntactic and semantic grounds and that we have to take into account other types of donkey sentences, which I term Watanabe-type donkey sentences, to seek correspondence concerning the relevant aspects. While the remarks made below are rather descriptive, they are, nonetheless, extremely important. Any theory of donkey sentences must be based on appropriate observations, and the issue under discussion is one of the most unknown aspects of the Japanese syntax. The clarification of the relevant data as presented in this section, therefore, is intended to provide a significant foundation for future theoretical characterization of donkey sentences in the language.

4.1. On a C-command Restriction inside of the Relative Clause in a Donkey Sentence

Consider the following contrast discussed by Haik (1984) :

(17) (Based on (79) , Haik (1984; 210))
a. Every farmer who kicked a donkey$_i$ hated it$_i$.
b. *Every farmer who a donkey$_i$ kicked hated it$_i$.

(17a), but not (17b), is well-formed, on their intended readings; i.e., the indefinite description a donkey can be in the scope of the universal quantifer every farmer in the former example, but not in the latter. Notice that (17b) is acceptable if we conceive of a donkey taking a wide scope with respect to every farmer, as illustrated below:

(18) $[\exists x : \text{Donkey}(x)]\ [\forall y : \text{Farmer}(y)\ \&\ \text{Kicked}(x, y)]\ \text{Hated}(y, x)$

This reading does not concern us here, needless to say.

Now let us ask ourselves from which grammatical factor the contrast in (17) results? As for this matter, I am in full agreement with Haik

(1984), who says that a structural difference in the relative clauses is responsible for the contrast:

(19) the S-structure representations of (17a) and (17b)
a. [Every person [$_{S'}$ who$_1$ [$_S$ t_1 kicked a donkey$_2$]]] hated it$_2$.
b.*[Every person$_1$ [$_{S'}$ who$_1$ [$_S$ a donkey$_2$ kicked t_1]]] hated it$_2$.

What is observed in these structures is that t_1 c-commands a donkey in (19a), but not in (19b). Then let us suppose, following Haik (1984), that in order for an indefinite description a donkey to have a narrow scope with respect to every person, it must be c-commanded by a trace of an operator who$_1$ which is coindexed with the universal quantifier under the relation of predication [5].

Nishigauchi (1990) claims to have observed that a similar c-command requirement can be found in Nishigauchi-type donkey sentences. Consider the following examples:

(20) (= (34) and (38), Nishigauchi (1990; pp. 219-221), judgements are his.)
a. [e_i dono ronbun$_j$ -o kaita] hito$_i$-mo sore$_j$-o LI-ni okutta.
wh article A wrote person Q it A D sent
(For every x, for every y, if x is a person and y is an article and x wrote y, x sent y to LI.)
b. * [dono ronbun$_j$-ga e_i hihansita] hito$_i$ -mo sore$_j$-o musisita.
wh article N criticized person Q it A ignored
(For every x, for every y, if x is an article and y is a person that x criticized, y ignored x.)

He argues that in (20) the wh-phrase dono ronbun (= wh + man) must be c-commanded by an empty category e_i, just as the indefinite description a donkey must be c-commanded by the trace t_1 in (19).

Though I admit that (20b) is less acceptable than (20a), I am reluctant to admit that the former is totally ungrammatical. Rather I would like to claim that this sentence is grammatical[6]. This claim is motivated by the following examples:

(21) a. [Dono ronbun$_i$-ga e_j hihansita] hito$_j$-mo saibansyo-ni sono$_i$
wh article N criticized person Q court D its
sakusya-o uttaeta.
author A sued
(For every x, for every y, x is an article, y is a person, x criticized y, y sued x's author.)
b. [Dono otoko$_i$ -ga e_j koe-o-kaketa] onna$_j$ -mo suguni
wh man N invited woman Q immediately
soittu$_i$ -no sasoi -ni nottekita.
the-guy G invitation D accepted
(For every x, for every y, x is a man, y is a woman, x invited y, y accepted x's invitation immediately.)

In the sentences in (21), the gap $\underline{e}_j$ fails to c-command the wh-phrases involved. If Nishigauchi's claim were correct, all of these examples should be ungrammatical. But actually these sentences are acceptable. Therefore it seems to me that his claim concerning the contrast in (20) cannot be so maintained.

Having observed that Haik's c-command restriction under discussion does not apply to Nishigauchi-type donkey sentences, the following question arises ; do Japanese donkey sentences entirely lack the c-command requirement of the sort ? The answer seems negative. Rather I would like to suggest that other types of donkey sentences in the language do exhibit a c-command requirement similar to the one discussed by Haik (1984). Consider the following examples:

(22) a. [e_i gakusei$_j$ -o ketobashita] yakuza$_i$ -ga minna
student A kicked gangster N all
sono gakusei$_j$ -ni kokusosareta.
the- student by was-sued
(For every x, for every y, x is a student, y is a gangster that kicked y, y was sued by x.)

b.*? [Yakuza$_j$-ga e_i ketobasita] gakusei$_i$ -ga minna soitu$_j$ -o
gangster N kicked student N all the-guy A
kokusosita.
sued
(For every x, for every y, x is a gangster, y is a student that x kicked, y sue x.)

(23) a. [e_i Mary-ni hon$_j$-o ageta] subeteno otoko$_i$ -ga sugu-ni
D book A gave every man N immediate
sore$_j$-o kanozyo-kara torikaesita.
it A her from got-back
(For every x, for every y, x is a book, y is a man that gave x to Mary, y got back x from Mary immediately.)

b.*[Otoko$_j$-ga Mary-ni e_i ageta] subeteno hon$_i$-ga sono otoko$_j$ -o
man N D gave every book N the man A
hihansiteita.
criticized
(For every x, for every y, x is a man, y is a book that x gave to Mary, y criticized x.)

(24) a. [e_i zyosigakusei$_j$ -to deetosita] dono otoko$_i$-mo sono ko$_j$ -ni
schoolgirl with dated wh man Q the girl D
kisusita.
kissed
(For every x, for every y, x is a schoolgirl, y is a man that dated x, y kissed x.)

b.* [Zyosigakusei$_j$-ga e_i deetosita] dono otoko$_i$-mo sono ko$_j$ -ni
schoolgirl N dated wh man Q the girl D
kisusita.
kissed
(For every x, for every y, x is a schoolgirl, y is a man that dated x, y kissed x.)

In (22) - (24), the (a)examples are well-formed, while the (b)examples are not. This strongly suggests that Haik's c-command restriction is also relevant for Japanese donkey sentences. For example, the contrast in (22) would simply follow, if we suppose that the gap e_i must c-command the indefinite description gakusei just as the trace t_1 ought to c-command a donkey in (19). Therefore, even though his factual claim is mistaken, Nishigauchi (1990) is entirely correct in saying that Haik's c-command requirement is also relevant for donkey sentences in Japanese.

Summerizing, I have argued the following in this subsection ; (i) contrary to Nishigauchi's (1990) conjecture, Haik's c-command restriction is not observable in Nishigauchi-type donkey sentences, and (ii) other types of donkey sentences rather than Nishigauchi's are actually subject to Haik's restriction. As a final remark of this subsection, let me show the structures of the donkey sentences (like those in (22) - (24)) to which Haik's c-command condition applies. For the purpose of exposition and for want of a better term, I call such constructions Watanabe-type donkey sentences.

(25) Watanabe-type donkey sentences
a. [$_{NP}$ [$_S$ ... INP$_i$ ...] N] FQ ... Pronoun$_i$ ... (see (22))
b. [$_{NP}$ [$_S$ ... INP$_i$ ...] QD - N] ... Pronoun$_i$ ... (see (23))
c. [$_{NP}$ [$_S$ ... INP$_i$ ...] dono- N] -mo ... Pronoun$_i$ ... (see (24))

In all of the structures above, an indefinite noun phrase (abbreviated as INP) is contained in the relative clauses and it is coindexed with a pronoun outside of the relative clauses. In (25a), a floating quantifier (like minna in (22)) is present which modifies the head of the relative clause. In (25b), the head of the relative clause goes with a quantified determiner (like subeteno in (23)). In (25c), the head of the relative clause has the wh-determiner dono which is universally quantified by the quantificaitonal particle mo.

4.2. Against Unselective Binding

In this subsection, I will present an argument against Nishigauchi's (1990) claim that a quantificational particle functions as an unselective binder (in the sense of Heim (1982)) in his donkey sentences in Japanese.

Based on Lewis' (1976) idea, Heim (1982) argues that an indefinite NP is not equipped with any quantificational force by itself, and essentially serves as a free variable in a logical representation. The quantificational force of an indefinite NP is then determined by an expression that c-commands it in a larger domain (such as an adverb of quantification or a quantified expression). Along the lines, consider the following sentence:

(26) Every man who owns a donkey$_i$ beats it$_i$.

In this example, the indefinite NP a donkey has no quantificational force and its quantificational force is supplied by the c-commanding universal quantifier every man. This process is actually considered to work in the form of unselective binding at LF, as shown in (27) :

(27) [∀ <x, y>: man (x) & Donkey (y) & Own (x, y)] (beat (x ,y))

In (27), which is a rendering of (26), "∀" stands for a universal quantifier which unselectively binds two variables, namely "x" and "y". As a consequence, this unselective binder quantifies over a pair (or a "case", in the sense of Lewis (1976)) <x, y> which meets the conditions expressed by the restrictive term. Therefore the truth of (27), namely (26), requires that every pair of "a man" and "a donkey" united under the relation of "ownership" must stand in the relation of "the former beating the latter".

Nishigauchi (1990) argues that Haik's unselective binding approach can be extended to semantic interpretation of his donkey sentences in Japanese. Consider the following sentence, which is in the format of Nushigauchi-type donkey sentence:

(28) [Dono ronbun $_i$ -o yonda] gakusee -mo sono$_i$- sakusya o
wh paper A read student Q the author A
hihansita
criticized
(For every x, for every y, x is a paper that y read, y criticized x's author.)

As discussed in section 2 above, a wh-phrase in Japanese does not originally have any quantificational force and it can be associated with such force just in case it is c-commanded by a quantificational particle. With respect to the nature of lacking a quantificational force, a wh-phrase in the language can be correlated with Heim's interpretation of indefinite noun phrases in English. Based on this, Nishigauchi supposes that mo in (28) is a universal quantifier which binds multiple occurrences of wh-phrases. Along the lines, (28) is associated with the following logical form:

(29) [∀ < x, y > : paper (x) & student (y) & Read (y, x)] (y criticized x's author)

In (29), the quantificational particle mo is rendered as a universal quantifier which unselectively binds multiple variables x and y. Therefore the truth of (29) requires that every pair of a student$_i$ and a paper that he$_i$ read must satisfy the proposition of the student criticized the paper's author.

As noted first by Ohno (1989) (furthermore see Ohno (1991) for a relevant argument in Korean), a serious problem arises; the sentence in (28) and the logical form in (29), which is meant to be a rendering of the sentence, are not truth-functionally equivalent. To see the semantic disparity between the two, imagine the following situation; there are four papers each of which was read by two students and only one student out of the two students that read each paper criticized its author. For the expositional purpose, let me show this situation schematically as follows:

(30) Paper 1 ----- **Student 1** ----- Student 2
Paper 2 ----- **Student 3** ----- Student 4
Paper 3 ----- **Student 5** ----- Student 6
Paper 4 ----- **Student 7** ----- Student 8

In (30), suppose that only the students written in boldface letters, i.e., { Student 1, Student 3, Student 5, Student 7 }, criticized the authors of the papers that they read. In this situation, the logical form in (29) is false, since only a half of the relevant pairs can satisfy the proposition denoted by the nuclear scope of the formula. On the other hand, the sentence in (28) seems to be true in this scenario. Roughly put, this observation suggests that (28) should be associated with the following logical form rather than with (29):

(31) $[\,A\,x: \text{paper}\,(x)\,]\ [\,\exists\, y: \text{student}\,(y)\ \&\ \text{Read}\,(y, x)\,]$ (y criticized x's author)

In this logical form, the argument of the particle mo, namely, gakusee (= student) is rendered as an existential quantifier rather than a universal quantifier, as opposed to the conjecture of Nishigauchi (1990) .

We have observed so far that unlike a donkey sentence in English like that in (26), the semantics of Nishigauchi-type donkey sentences cannot be rendered using unselective quantification. Again, in addition to the discussion in the previous subsection, this strongly indicates that Nishigauchi-type donkey sentences do not correspond to donkey sentences in English (in terms of semantics at this time, though).

In this context, recall the argument in 4.1. that Nishigauchi-type donkey sentences do not go along with donkey sentences in English with respect to Heik's c-command restriction. Furthermore I argued there that it are Watanabe-type donkey sentences, not Nishigauchi-type ones, that share a relevant property with donkey sentences in English.

Then it seems rather natural for us to predict that Watanabe-type donkey sentences behave on a par with donkey sentences in English on the semantic grounds under consideration. Actually this prediction appears to be borne out. Consider the following sentences:

(32) a. [Ronbun $_i$ -o yonda] gakusee - ga minna sono$_i$- sakusya o
paper A read student N all its author A
hihansita.
criticized

b. [Ronbun $_i$ -o yonda] subeteno gakusee -ga sono$_i$- sakusya o
paper A read every student N its author A
hihansita.
criticized

c. [Ronbun $_i$ -o yonda] dono gakusee -mo sono$_i$- sakusya o
paper A read wh student Q its author A
hihansita
criticized

The sentences in (32) are all in the formats of Watanabe-type donkey sentences ((32a) = (25a), (32b) = (25b), (32c) = (25c), see the structures in (25) above). Remarkably, these examples are false in the situation given in (30) above. Furthermore in order for these examples to be true, it is required that if a student read a paper, he must have criticized the paper(s) that he read without an exception. Thus, the data in (32) turn out be true in the following:

(33) Paper 1 ----- **Student 1**
----- **Student 2**
Paper 2 ----- **Student 3**
----- **Student 4**
Paper 3 ----- **Student 5**
----- **Student 6**
Paper 4 ----- **Student 7**
----- **Student 8**

As in (30), there are four papers each of which was read by two students. However, unlike (30), all of the students, { Student 1, Student 2, Student 3, Student 4, Student 5, Student 6, Student 7, Student 8 }, are supposed to commit themselves to the action of criticism.

This simple observation suggests that the sentences in (32), which are Watanabe-type donkey sentences, can be rendered using unselective quantification as in (29), which is recapitulated in (34):

(34) [$\forall$ < x, y > : paper (x) & student (y) & Read (y, x)] (y criticized x's author)

Noting that the donkey sentence in (26) is succesfully interpreted by unselective quantification, the current observation indicates that a Watanabe-type, but not Nishigauchi-type, donkey sentence, directly corresponds to a donkey sentence in English with respect to semantic interpretation.

5. Concluding Remarks

Summarizing, the following were discussed in this paper. In the first place, I argued, following Neale (1990) and Ludlow (1990), that a donkey pronoun is rendered as a description at the level of LF. Furthermore it was agrued that with the analysis we can dispense with Haik's (1984)

INDIRECT BINDING to explain a c-command restriction in donkey sentences. In the second place, I criticized Nishigauchi's (1990) treatment of donkey sentences both on syntactic and semantic grounds. As the results of the discussion, I concluded that Nishigauchi-type donkey sentences do not manifest properties found in donkey sentences in English and that we ought to take into accout Watanabe-type donkey sentences in order to seek correspondence of such constructions between the languages with regard to the respects we discussed.

* This paper is an extremely shortened version of my generals paper submitted to USC, which happens to have the same title as the present paper. An earlier version of this paper was reported at the Southern California Japanese / Korean Linguistics Conference, which was held on September 6 - 8 ' 91 at UC Santa Barbara. I would like to thank Hajime Hoji for his invaluable comments and generous help. I am also indebted to Kaoru Horie, Yoshihisa Kitagawa, S. - Y. Kuroda, Yutaka Ohno, Barry Shein, Noriko Yoshimura and Maria-Luisa Zubizarreta for their comments. All remaining errors are my own, needless to say.

Footnotes

1 : Nishigauchi (1986a) himself does not discuss examples like (1b) and (1c) in which the head of a relative clause is followed by ka or demo. Some speakers of Japanese might say that (1b) is somewhat marginal. I am in full agreement with this intuition of native speakers. Though it varies with many factors, the acceptability of the example seems to be significantly improved by restricting the range of quantification. Consider the following :

(i) ?[Kono-nakano dono $ronbun_i$ -o kaita] gakusee -ka-ga
among these wh article A wrote student Q N
NELS-ni $sono_i$ abusutorakuto-o okutta (koto)
to its abstract A sent
(There is some x and y, x is an article and y is a student that wrote x, such that y sent x's abstract to NELS.)

This sentence is exactly the same as (3b) except that it involves a modifier kono-nakano (= among these), which has a function to restrict the range of quantification of dono ronbun (wh + article). Based on this observation, let us simply suppose that (3b) is essentially grammatical.

2 : Furthermore, Nishigauchi (1990) argues that a wh-phrase gets raised and governed by a quantificational particle at LF. For details, see chapter 6 of his work.

3 : Needless to say, in order for this claim to be substantiated, the theoretical characterization of this "copying" rule is necessary. Unfortunately, I cannot go into the details of this issue because of the space limitation (for an idea, see Neale (1990)).

4 : These "LF-representations" are very rough and intuitive. As commonly executed in the LF-semantics, we can formally rewrite (13a), for example, in the language of first order logic as follows :

(i) [∀x: man (x) & [∃y: donkey (y)](Own (x, y)][the z : donkey (z) & Owns (x, z)] (beat (x, z))

For more details, see Neale (1990) and Ludlow (1990). Also the readers are referred to these papers for a potential problem of this analysis related to "uniqueness implication" of a definite description.

5: Although it is of great significance, I will not touch on the issue of why a donkey must be c-commanded by t_1 in (19) because of the space limitation. See Watanabe (1992) for a tentative analysis.

6: It seems to me that the anomaly of (20b) is due to the fact that the pronoun sore is ambiguous. On one hand, the pronoun could refer back to dono ronbun as intended. On the other hand, it can also stand for variant events in which " a paper criticized a person". It seems to me that the latter reading is prefered. Maybe this reading on the pronoun is likely to suppress the former one, even though the both readings are equally viable.

7: For related discussion of proportion problems, see Partee (1984), Kadmon (1987), Berman (1987), among others.

References

Barwise, Jon, and Robin Cooper. 1981. Generalized Quantifiers and Natural Language. Linguistics and Philosophy, 4.

Berman, Steven. 1987. Situation-Based Semantics for Adverbs of Quantification, WCCFL 6.

Cooper, Robin. 1979. The interpretation of pronouns. Syntax and Semantics 10 --- Selections from the Third Groningen Round Table, by F. Henry and H Schnelle eds.

Evans, Gareth. 1977a. Pronouns, Quantifiers, Relative Clauses. Canadian Journal of Philosophy 7, pp.467- 536.

------------1977b. Pronouns, Quantifiers, Relative Clauses: Appendix. Canadian Journal of Philosophy 7, pp.777-797.

------------1980. Pronouns. Linguistic Inquiry 11, pp. 337-362.

Geach, P. 1962. Reference and Generality. Cornell University Press, Ithaca and London.

Haik. Isabelle. 1984. Indirect Binding. Linguistic Inquiry 15, pp. 185-223.

Heim, Irene. 1982. The Semantics of Definite and Indefinite Noun Phrases. Doctoral dissertation, University of Massachusetts, Amherst.

----------- 1990. E-type Pronouns and Donkey Anaphora. Linguistics and Philosophy 13. 2.

Hoji, Hajime. 1985. Logical Form Constraints and Configurational Structures in Japanese. Doctoral dissertation, University of Washington.

----------- forthcoming. Theories of Anaphora and Aspects of Japanese Syntax. Cambridge, MIT Press.

Kadmon, Nirit. 1987. Unique and Non-unique Reference and Asymmetric Quantification. Doctoral dissertation, University of Massachusettes.

Kamp, Hans. 1981. A Theory of Truth and Semantic Interpretation. Truth Interpretation and Information, by Groenendijk et al eds, Dordrecht : Foris.

Kang, M. Y. 1988. Topics in Korean Syntax. Doctoral dissertation, MIT, Cambridge.

Kuroda, Shigeyuki. 1965. Generative Grammatical Studies in the Japanese Language. Doctoral dissertation, MIT.

Ludlow, Peter. 1990. Conditionals, Events and Discourse Pronouns. ms. SUNY at Stony Brook.

----------------1991. Conditionals, Events, and Unbound Pronouns. a talk delivered at USC, on Oct 23, 1991

Lewis, D. 1976. Adverbs of Quantification. Formal Semantics of Natural Language, by E. Keenan ed, Cambridge University Press.

Mikami, Akira. 1970. Bunpo Syooronsyuu (= Collection of Short Essays on Grammar). Kurosio Syuppan, Tokyo, Japan.

Neale, Stephen. 1990. Descriptions. Cambridge: MIT Press.

Nishigauchi, Taisuke. 1990. Quantification in the Theory of Grammar. Kluwer Academic Publishers.

Ohno, Yutaka. 1989. Mo. Papers in Quantification, NSF, Grant BNS 8719999, University of Massachusettes, Amherst.

--------- 1991. Argument against unselective binding in Korean. Harvard Studies in Korean Linguistics IV, eds. by Susumu Kuno et al. Hanshin Publishing Co., Seoul,

Parsons, Terence. 1978. Pronouns as paraphrases. ms. University of Massachusetts, Amherst.

Partee, Barbara. 1984. Nominal and Temporal Anaphora. Linguistics and Philosophy 7, pp. 243 - 286.

Saito, Mamoru. and Hajime Hoji. 1983. Weak Crossover and Move-alpha in Japanese. Natural Language & Linguistics Theory 1, pp. 245-259.

Watanabe, Shin . 1991. Mo: Around its Syntax and Semantics, ms. USC.

--------------- 1992. A Note on So-called "Donkey Sentences " in Japanese : A Preliminary Study, ms. USC.

Part V

Syntax and Morphology

Inalienable-Type Multiple Accusative Constructions in Korean and Japanese

DONG-IN CHO
University of Southern California

Inalienable-Type Multiple Accusative Constructions in Korean and Japanese*

Dong-In Cho
University of Southern California

0. Introduction[1]

This paper is concerned with the Inalienable-type (IA-type) of Multiple Accusative Constructions (henceforth, MAC) in Korean and Japanese in relation to verb movement. This paper claims that the IA-type of MAC in Korean and Japanese can be traced back to the presence of verb movement in

---

*This version is a revised version of a paper presented at the Southern California Japanese/Korean Linguistics Conference held at UCSB in September 1991. I am indebted to Joseph Aoun, Hajime Hoji, and Audrey Li for their valuable comments and suggestions on an earlier version of this paper. I have also benefited from discussions with Jong Whan Chang, Kyung Seun Chang, Daeho Chung, Abdessalam Elomari, Jeong-Shik Lee, Myung-Kwan Park, Shin Watanabe, John Whitman, and Jong-Yurl Yoon. Many thanks also go to Hiroshi Aoyagi, Ho Han, Jongho Jun, and Maki Watanabe for their native speaker's judgments, and Robert Belvin and Heewon Kim for their proofreading of the paper. All responsibility for errors remains my own.

[1]In glosses, I follow the romanization system of Yale. The following abbreviations are used in glossing the data:

ACC: Accusative Case Marker	DAT: Dative Case Marker
DEC: Declarative Sentence Ending	GEN: Genitive Case Marker
IND: Indicative Morpheme	NOM: Nominative Case Marker
NZ: Nominalizer	PASS: Passive Morpheme
PAST: Past Morpheme	Q: Question Ending

these languages.[2] In Korean both the possessor and inalienable NP's (IA-NP) can have an Accusative Case marker. Given the assumption that Case assigner and assignee have a one-to-one relationship, the existence of MAC in Korean might be surprising. To treat this problem, various proposals have been made, e.g., one-to-many relationships between Case assigner and assignee (Kang 1986). Another is that the seeming Accusative Case marker *ul/lul* may not always be a true Case marker; only one Accusative is structurally assigned, while the others might be a realization of something other than Accusative Case (Yoon 1989; Kim 1989). This paper claims that both the Possessor NP and IA-NP are assigned structural Accusative Case directly by a verb, assuming that the trace of a verb can assign Case.

This paper is organized as follows. Section one discusses the previous studies of the IA-type of MAC in Korean. Section two examines the theta-role assignment of Accusative NP's in MAC. Section three provides evidence supporting verb movement in Korean. Section four examines cross-linguistic evidence supporting the claim that the trace of a verb assigns Case. Section five concludes the paper.

1. Previous Studies of the IA-Type of MAC

In the IA-type of MAC, both the possessor NP and IA NP have an Accusative Case marker as seen in (1a) and (2a).[3]

(1) a. Mary-ka John-ul tali-lul cha-ess-ta (Korean)
Mary-NOM John-ACC leg-ACC kick-PAST-DEC
b. Mary-ka John-uy tali-lul cha-ess-ta
Mary-NOM John-GEN leg-ACC kick-PAST-DEC
'Lit. Mary kicked John's leg.'

(2) a. ?/??Mary-ga John-o asi-o ketta (Japanese)
Mary-NOM John-ACC leg-ACC kicked
b. Mary-ga John-no asi-o ketta
Mary-NOM John-GEN leg-ACC kicked
'Lit. Mary kicked John's leg.'

Every IA-type of MAC has a genitive counterpart as seen in (1b) and (2b). However, the reverse is not always true.[4] Note that while the sentences in

---

[2] I will present Korean data in most of the discussions in this paper, but I believe that the same results hold for Japanese as well.

[3] Most Japanese native speakers find the IA-type of MAC in (2a) marginal. I attribute this to the Double O Constraint (Harada 1973). In (2a), if adverbial phrases intervene between the two Accusative NP's the sentence turns out to be more acceptable, as seen in the following sentence.

(i) Mary-ga John-o kinoo undoozyo-de asi-o ketta. (Japanese)
Mary-NOM John-ACC yesterday playground-at leg-ACC kicked
'Lit. Mary kicked John' leg at the play ground yesterday.'

The higher status of acceptability of (i) than that of (2a) indicates that both the possessor and inalienable NP's are assigned Accusative Case at some level of representation, exhibiting the existence of MAC in this language.

[4] Consider the following pair of sentences:

(1b) and (2b) are ambiguous, i.e., inalienable relationship, or alienable relationship, the sentences in (1a) and (2a) have only one interpretation, namely, the interpretation of 'inalienable relationship'. This type of pairs of sentences has been given in support of the derivational hypothesis; namely, MAC is derived from its genitive counterpart (Choe 1987). In what follows I will examine previous proposals in this connection.

Kim (1989) claims that in the MAC the IA-NP is a predicate of the possessor NP, the IA-NP being in an A'-position. Kim argues that Accusative Case is assigned only to the possessor NP and that the IA-NP, which is in a predication relationship with the possessor NP, gets Accusative case under case agreement with the subject of the predicate. That is, only the subject of the predicate in MAC, namely, the possessor NP, is assigned Accusative case by a Case assigner; namely, the verb. Therefore, in (1a), *John* is the subject of its predicate *tali* 'leg' and that the verb *cha* 'kick' assigns Accusative Case only to *John*, which is subcategorized for by the verb, and *tali* 'leg' gets Accusative case marker under case agreement with *John*.

A question immediately arises as to the A' status of the IA-NP. As noted in the literature (Yoon 1989; Maling and Kim 1990), there is evidence supporting the claim that the verb is subcategorized for the IA-NP; therefore it is in an A-position. Consider the following sentences:

(3) a. Mary-ka John-ul meli-lul cal-ess-ta
Mary-NOM John-ACC hair-ACC cut-PAST-DEC
'Mary cut John's hair'
b. *Mary-ka John-ul cal-ess-ta
Mary-NOM John-ACC cut-PAST-DEC
'Mary cut John'

The minimal difference between (3a) and (3b) is that in (3b) the IA-NP *meli* 'hair' is deleted. The oddity of the sentence (3b) comes from the deletion of this NP. This supports the claim that this NP is subcategorized for; therefore, its being in an A-position. If the IA-NP is subcategorized for, Kim's case agreement hypothesis is weakened, if not invalidated.[5]

(i) Mary-ka [John-uy chayk]-ul chassta
Mary-NOM John-GEN book-ACC kicked 'Mary kicked John's book.'
(ii) *Mary-ka John-ul chayk-ul chassta
Mary-NOM John-ACC book-ACC kicked 'Mary kicked John's book.'
The genitive construction in (i) does not have a MAC counterpart, as the ungrammaticality of the sentence in (ii) indicates. Notice that *John* and *chayk* 'a book' do not constitute the inalienable relationship.

[5]A piece of evidence suggesting that non-subcategorized NP's in Korean receive Case directly from a verb, not by case agreement, can be found in sentences with Duration/Frequency expressions. Consider the following sentence:
(i) Mary-ka twupen-ul o-ess-ta
Mary-NOM twice-ACC came
'Mary came twice'
In (i), the Frequency expression, which is not subcategorized for by the verb, is assigned Accusative Case. If only subcategorized NP's are assigned structural Case and non-subcategorized NP's get Case by case agreement under a predication relationship, there is no way to account for the occurrence of the Accusative Case marking on the Frequency expression in (i).

Another account of the MAC could be that the seeming Accusative case marker on the possessor NP is a focus or emphatic marker. This amounts to saying that the focus or emphatic marker and the Accusative case marker are phonologically identical and that only the IA-NP is assigned Accusative Case. Let us consider the sentences in (1), repeated here as (4):

(4) a. Mary-ka John-ul tali-lul cha-ess-ta
Mary-NOM John-ACC leg-ACC kick-PAST-DEC
b. Mary-ka [John-uy tali]-lul cha-ess-ta
Mary-NOM John-GEN leg-ACC kick-PAST-DEC
'Lit. Mary kicked John's leg.'

This line of explanation claims that in (4a) the possessor *John* is derived from its genitive counterpart in (4b) and becomes a focus with the focus marker *lul* which happens to be identical with the Accusative Case marker *lul*. This amounts to saying that the possessor NP in (4a) is in the derived A'-position. This analysis faces a problem when we consider passivization. Passivization is assumed to be A-to-A movement forced by a Case requirement. That is, the absorption of the Accusative Case assigning ability of a verb forces the object NP to move to the Case position, which is assumed to be an A-position. Consider the following pair of sentences:

(5) a. Mary-ka John-ul phal-ul pwutcap-ess-ta.
Mary-NOM John-ACC arm-ACC grasp-PAST-DEC
'Mary grasped John by the arm.'
b. John-ka Mary-eykey phal - ul pwutcap-hi-ess-ta
John-NOM Mary-by arm-ACC grasp-PASS-PAST-DEC
'John's arm was grasped by Mary.'

If passivization is A-to-A movement, the possessor NP must be in an A-position. Otherwise, the movement would be from A'-to-A position, which is an illicit movement.

Choe (1987) also claims that the Accusative possessor NP is derived from its genitive counterpart. Choe's proposal differs from other derivational hypotheses in that the derivation involves A-to-A movement. This analysis can circumvent the potential problem which one faces with passivization. However, this A-to-A movement is not without problems, either. Consider the following sentences:

(6) a. Mary-ka [$_{NP}$ John-uy tung]-ul ccil-ess-ta
Mary-NOM John-GEN back-ACC stab-PAST-DEC
b. Mary-ka John$_i$-ul [$_{NP}$ t$_i$ tung]-ul ccil-ess-ta
Mary-NOM John-ACC back-ACC stab-PAST-DEC
'Lit. Mary stabbed John' back.'

In (6a), *John* has the Genitive Case marker *uy*. If the Accusative Case marked *John* were derived from its genitive counterpart, the chain might have two Cases: the head having Accusative Case, and the tail Genitive Case. This indicates that the movement analysis may not be correct.[6] Note that this type of movement is different from so-called scrambling in that the scrambled NP has only one Case.[7]

Thus, the case agreement hypothesis and the derivational hypothesis face problems. This being the case, we might suggest that *ul* on both the Possessor NP and IA-NP is a realization of the abstract Accusative Case and that both NP's are base-generated. I will now examine the possibility that the MAC is base-generated. Consider first the following sentences:

(7) a. Mary-ka John-ul tali-lul cha-ess-ta
Mary-NOM John-ACC leg-ACC kick-PAST-DEC
'Mary kicked John's leg.'
b. ?Mary-ka John$_i$-ul [ku$_i$-uy tali]-lul cha-ess-ta
Mary-NOM John-ACC he-GEN leg-ACC kick-PAST-DEC
'Mary kicked John's leg.'
c. John$_i$-ul [Mary-ka [ku$_i$-uy tali]-lul cha-ess-ta]
John-ACC Mary-NOM he-GEN leg-ACC kick-PAST-DEC
'John, Mary kicked his leg.'

Even though there are idiolectal variations, the sentence in (7c) is far more acceptable than (7b) for most of speakers. Note that the sentence in (7b) has the overt Genitive-marked pronoun as a possessor NP. If there were a movement of the possessor NP from the Genitive position to Accusative, the occurrence of the overt pronoun could not be accounted for. However, we need an explanation for the less acceptable status of (7b) in comparison to (7a). The marginal status of (7b) can be attributed to the Avoid Pronoun Principle (Chomsky 1981: 65). Namely, nothing more than is required need be said. This is clearer if we consider the scrambled version of (7b), namely (7c).[8] Note that in (7c) the possessor NP in (7b) has scrambled to the sentence-initial position. The more acceptable status of (7c) compared to (7b) clearly indicates that Avoid Pronoun plays a role in (7b). That is, since in (7b) the possessor and inalienable NP's are strictly adjacent, the appearance of an overt pronoun in the possessor position of the inalienable NP is redundant. If the Accusative possessor NP moves away from the following

---

[6] If we stipulate that the assignment of Genitive Case is optional, this problem does not arise. Then, the question is why only Genitive Case is assigned optionally. An alternative to the optional Case assignment might be the Case stacking hypothesis, as in Yoon and Yoon (1990). Both hypotheses have to answer to the question about how to filter out the illicit multiple Accusative NP's in an alienable relationship. (See footnote 4 for relevant examples)

[7] The scrambled NP maintains its original case marker as seen in the following sentence:

(i) [Mary-ka kay-lul cha-ess-ta]
Mary-NOM dog-ACC kick-PAST-DEC
(ii) kay-lul$_i$ [Mary-ka t_i cha-ess-ta]
dog-ACC Mary-NOM kick-PAST-DEC
'Mary kicked the dog'

In (i), *kay* 'dog' is assigned Accusative Case by *cha* 'kick' and it gets the Accusative Case marker *lul*. Notice that the scrambled NP *dog* maintains its original case marker, namely Accusative, showing that the chain has only one Case.

[8] I thank S. Watanabe, who has pointed out this scrambling fact to me (p.c.) with the Japanese data.

inalienable NP, Avoid Pronoun is less strictly observed, yielding a higher acceptability.

If our analysis is correct, we might expect there to be a pro in the Spec of the inalienable NP, as in the following sentence.

(8) Mary-ka John$_i$-ul [pro$_i$ tali-lul] cha-ess-ta
Mary-NOM John-ACC pro leg-ACC kick-PAST-DEC
'Mary kicked John on the leg.'

I assume that the non-referential noun has an internal possessor theta role to discharge. I further assume that if an item has a theta-role to discharge, it discharges its theta-role any way. This gives an explanation for why the possessor theta-role is realized as pro in the above sentence.

Thus far, we have seen that both possessor NP and IA-NP can be base-generated in A-positions. The following section investigates (i) how both the possessor NP and the IA-NP are assigned Accusative Case and (ii) how both NP's are assigned a thematic role.

2. V'-reanalysis and Compositional Theta-roles

We have seen that the IA-NP is assigned a theta-role by a verb. Then a question arises about how the possessor NP is assigned a theta-role in the Korean and Japanese MAC. I examine two possible answers; namely, V' reanalysis and compositional theta-role assignment, arguing for the latter.

The V' reanalysis is proposed in Larson (1988) for English double object construction. Larson suggests that if a V' constituent has unsaturated internal arguments, then that V' may be reconstrued as V and undergoes V raising. At first sight, this approach seems to give an answer to MAC in Korean. A verb assigns a theta-role to the IA-NP, but this IA-NP has an unsaturated theta-role, namely, the possessor NP. Therefore, the V' containing the IA-NP and the verb are reanalyzed as V, which in turn assigns both a theta-role and Case to the possessor NP. However, the free intervention by an adverbial phrase between the verb and its internal argument (IA-NP here) indicates this is not the case in Korean:

(9) a. Mary-ka John-ul ecey ppaym-ul kalki-ess-ta
Mary-NOM John-ACC yesterday cheek-ACC slap-PAST-DEC
b. Mary-ka John-ul ppaym-ul ecey kalki-ess-ta
Mary-NOM John-ACC cheek-ACC yesterday slap-PAST-DEC
'Mary slapped John's cheek yesterday .'

(10) a. Mary-ka John-ul wuntongcang-eyse ppaym-ul
Mary-NOM John-ACC playground-at cheek-ACC
kalki-ess-ta
slap-PAST-DEC
b. Mary-ka John-ul ppaym-ul wuntongcang-eyse
Mary-NOM John-ACC cheek-ACC playground-at
kalki-ess-ta
slap-PAST-DEC
'Mary slapped John's cheek at the playground.'

As seen in (9) and (10), the sentential adverbial *ecey* 'yesterday' and the argument *wuntongcang-eyse* 'at playground' can freely intervene between the IA-NP *ppaym* 'cheek' and the verb *kalki* 'slap'. According to Van Riemsdijk (1978), reanalysis observes a kind of adjacency requirement two constituents can only be reanalyzed into a single constituent if they are string-adjacent at the relevant level of analysis. If Riemsdijk is correct, the intervention of an adverbial and an argument as in (9b) and (10b) disconfirms the possibility of the reanalysis approach to Korean MAC.

An alternative approach, which I am arguing for in this paper, is that the IA-NP is assigned a theta-role directly from the verb, and that the possessor NP is assigned a theta-role compositionally from the verb and its complement IA-NP. Consider the following pair of sentences:

(11) a. Mary-ka John-ul tali-lul cha-ess-ta
Mary-NOM John-ACC leg-ACC kick-PAST-DEC
'Lit. Mary kicked John's leg.'
b. *Mary-ka John-ul tali-lul po-ess-ta
Mary-NOM John-ACC leg-ACC see-PAST-DEC
'Lit. Mary saw John's leg.'

The grammaticality of (11a) and ungrammaticality of (11b) seem to support the approach of compositional theta-role assignment. In (11a), 'kicking the leg' affects *John* to whom the leg belongs, assigning a theta-role to *John*. Namely, 'affectedness' is involved in the assignment of a theta-role to the possessor NP. Notice that in the ungrammatical sentence in (11b) the 'affectedness' is not involved. Namely, 'seeing the leg' does not affect the possessor *John*.[9] If we assume that body parts have an internal theta-role and that the theta-role has to be realized as a possessor without resorting to affectedness, we face the problem of incorrectly ruling the sentence in (11b) grammatical. Furthermore, we cannot account for the fact the possessor NP is located not in the Genitive subject position, but outside of the genitive construction.

This affectedness hypothesis can be tested in Japanese, which in general does not allow MAC. Consider the following pair of sentences:

[9] In (11b), if *po-ess-ta* 'saw' is replaced by *ccaylie-po-ess-ta* 'looked hard/intently at', this sentence turns out to be acceptable. We can say that *ccaylie* 'hard/intently' increases the affectedness.

(12) a. ?Mary-ga John-o hoho-o nagutta.
Mary-NOM John-ACC cheek-ACC hit
'Lit. Mary hit John's cheek.'
b. *Mary-ga John-o me-o mita.
Mary-NOM John-ACC eye-ACC saw
'Lit. Mary saw John's eyes'

Judgments vary across informants, but the general tendency seems to be that the sentence in (12a) is much better than that in (12b). Notice that this is what the affectedness hypothesis predicts.

On the basis of the compositional affectedness theta-role hypothesis, I propose the following structure for the Korean MAC, which is similar to Larson's structure for the English Double Object Construction: (Irrelevant projections are omitted)

(13)

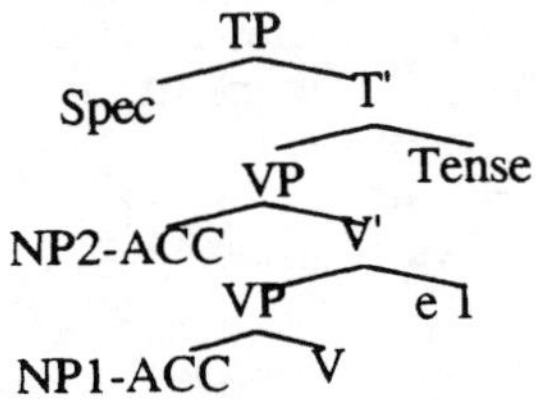

In the structure above, the verb assigns a theta-role to NP1, and the verb and NP2 compositionally assign a theta-role to NP2. Based on this structure, the following sections show how the possessor NP and IA-NP are assigned ACC. Since I argue that verb movement is responsible for the IA-type of MAC in Korean, in the following two sections I provide evidence suggesting that Korean has verb movement and the trace of the verb can assign Case.

3. Verb Movement in Korean

I propose that there is verb movement in Korean and that verb movement is responsible for multiple Accusative Case assignment. In (13), the verb assigns a Case to NP1. When the verb moves up to the position of *e1*, it assigns another Accusative Case to NP2. This amounts to saying that structural Case is assigned at some point between D-structure and S-structure. This hypothesis is crucially based on two assumptions that (a) Korean has verb movement and (b) the trace of a verb can also assign Case. In what follows I provide evidence supporting these claims.

I first examine two types of negation in Korean and argue for the existence of NegP. On the basis of the existence of NegP and ΩP,[10] I substantiate the existence of verb movement in Korean.

[10] ΩP will be discussed in Section 3.2.

3.1 Two Types of Negation

It is well known that Korean has two types of negation (Lee 1970; Oh 1971, among many others), which I call Constituent Negation (the so-called short-form negation; henceforth, C-negation) and Sentential Negation (the so-called long-form negation; henceforth, S-negation). The constituent negative morpheme precedes V^0, while sentential negative morpheme follows VP, having *ci* between the VP and the negation morpheme *an*. The S-negation has what we can call *ha*-support, which is a Korean version of *do*-support. The following two sentences in (14) illustrate C-negation and S-negation, respectively.

(14) a. John-i   an-ka-ess-ta
    John-NOM   not-go-PAST-DEC
    'John did not go'
  b. John-i   ka-ci   an-ha-ess-ta
    John-NOM   go-CI   not-do-PAST-DEC
    'John did not go.'

The Korean C-negation differs from the English C-negation in that it adjoins only to V^0. As the ungrammaticality of the sentence in (15a) indicates, *an* in the C-negation cannot adjoin to VP. The only possible place where it can adjoin is V^o, as seen in (15b).

(15) a. *John-i   an Mary-lul   cha-ess-ta
    John-NOM   not Mary-ACC   kick-PAST-DEC
  b. John-i   Mary-lul   an-cha-ess-ta
    John-NOM   Mary-ACC   not-kick-PAST-DEC
    'John did not kick Mary.'

Positing the two different negations, namely, C-negation and S-negation, has advantages over the hypothesis that these two negations are derived from a single basic form. First of all, it can generate a double negation as in (16), which is the combination of both negations, C- and S-negation.[11]

[11] One question here is whether *ha* in the S-negation can be regarded as a content verb, which has semantic content. However, this might not be the case. Consider the following sentence:
(i) Mary-ka   hakkyo-lul   ka-ci   an-ha-ess-ta
    Mary-NOM   school-ACC   go-CI   not-do-PAST-DEC
    'Mary did not go to school'
(ii) *Mary-ka   hakkyo-lul   ka-ci   an-ka-ess-ta
    Mary-NOM   school-ACC   go-CI   not-go-PAST-DEC
    'Mary did not go to school'
As seen in (ii), the replacement of *ha* in (i) by the content verb *ka* 'go' yields an ungrammatical sentence, indicating that *ha* in (i) is not a content word (cf. Kang 1988).

(16) John-i an-ka-ci an-ha-ess-ta
John-NOM not-go-CI not-do-PAST-DEC
'John did go.'

If both types of negation are derived from the same basic form, the appearance of two *an*'s in a simplex sentence cannot be accounted for.

The second advantage for this differentiation of two types of negation comes from the scope of negation in conjunction structures. The Korean C-negation behaves similarly to the English C-negation in that it negates only the constituent it adjoins to. Consider the following English sentence containing C-negation.

(17) a. Not every student came to school. (not>every)
b. Every student did not come to school (not>every or not<every)

While the scope of S-negation in (17b) is ambiguous, C-negation in (17a) is not. That is, C-negation has scope only over the constituent that it adjoins to. Considering that the English C-negation and S-negation share the same morphology *not*, it is not surprising that Korean also has two types of negation with the same morphology. A conjunction test indeed shows that two *an*'s, namely, C-negation and S-negation behave differently in terms of scope.[12] Consider the following sentences in (18 b, c) with C-negation.

(18) a. John-i [swul-ul masi-ko] [tampay-lul
John-NOM alcohol-ACC drink-and cigarette-ACC
phiwu]- ess-ta
smoke-PAST-DEC
'John drank alcohol and smoked cigarettes'
b. John-i [swul-ul an-masi-ko] [tampay-lul
John-NOM alcohol-ACC not-drink-and cigarette-ACC
phiwu]-ess-ta
smoke-PAST-DEC
'John did not drink alcohol but smoked cigarettes.'
c. John-i [swul-ul masi-ko] [tampay-lul
John-NOM alcohol-ACC drink-and cigarette-ACC
an-phiwu]-ess-ta
not-smoke-PAST-DEC
'John drank alcohol but did not smoke cigarettes.'

The sentences in (18b) and (18c) are negative counterparts of the affirmative counterpart of (18a). The negative sentences have the negative morpheme *an* in the first and second conjuncts, respectively. In (18b) and (18c), *an* in one conjunct does not have scope over the other. This test confirms that C-negation does not constitute an independent syntactic category.

By contrast, S-negation in Korean behaves differently from C-negation in terms of scope. This type of negation in the second conjunct can have scope over the first conjunct, as seen in (19b).

---

[12] See also J.M. Yoon (1989) for a similar test, where the IP conjunction test is employed.

(19) a. John-i [swul-ul masi-ko] [tampay-lul
John-NOM alcohol-ACC drink-and cigarette-ACC
phiwu]- ess-ta
smoke-PAST-DEC
'John drank alcohol and smoked cigarette'

b. John-i [swul-ul masi-ko] [tampay-lul phiwu]-ci
John-NOM alcohol-ACC drink-and cigarette-ACC smoke-NZ
ani-ha-ess-ta
not-do-PAST-DEC
'John did not drink alcohol and smoke cigarettes'
'John drank alcohol but did not smoke cigarettes.'

While C-negation of the counterparts of (19b), namely, (18b) and (18c), cannot negate cross the conjunct in which the negation sits in, S-negation can. This can be attributed to the syntactic status of the S-negation.[13]

Based on the discussions thus far, the following structures can be constructed for the sentence with C-negation and S-negation, as in (20a) and (20b), respectively.[14] (irrelevant nodes are omitted).

(20) a. b.

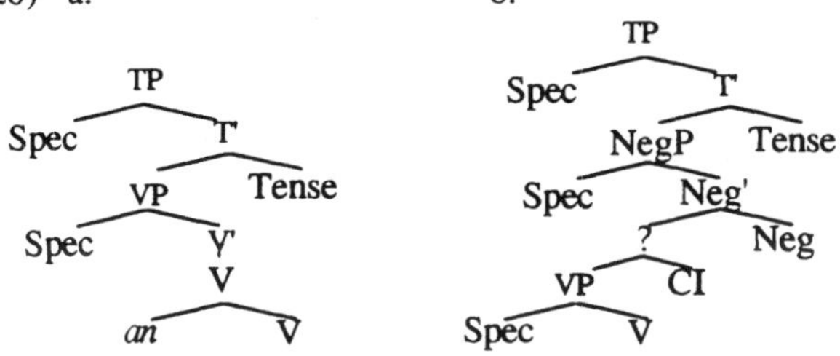

In (20a) the C-negation *an* is generated in the V^o-adjunction position. By contrast, S-negation heads its own projection. On the basis of this NegP, the following section provides evidence supporting the existence of verb movement in Korean.

---

[13] The second reading of (19b) might be problematic to this approach. An alternative to this approach is that in (19b) Neg optionally moves up to C^o. If it moves out of the second conjunct, it has scope over the first conjunct. If it stays in the second conjunct, it has scope only over the second conjunct, resulting in the second reading. This approach raises the following question. That is, if *an* is a bound morpheme, as suggested in No (1988), *an* obligatorily, not optionally, moves up with the verb it attaches to. This approach also leaves a question about why C-Negation *an* in (18c) does not have scope over the first conjunct if *an* can move up to C^o at all. I leave these questions open for a further study.

[14] Yoon (1989), Cho (1991), and Chang (1992) also pursue this line of approach. See also Yoon (1990), where two types of negation are derived from a single D-structure.

3.2. Verb Movement with relation to *Ha* -support

This section examines evidence for the existence of verb movement in Korean,[15] providing theory-external and theory-internal evidence.

In an affirmative sentence, Tense is realized on a verb, indicating that the verb and Tense have somehow amalgamated. If verb movement is blocked, this amalgamation process is blocked; as a result, *ha*-support occurs. This account can substantiate the existence of verb movement. I claim that Delimiters (henceforth, Ω) and Neg (not *ci*) block verb movement. Consider the following pair of sentences:

(21) a. Mary-ka ttena-ess-ta
Mary-Nom leave-PAST-DEC
'Mary left.'
b. Mary-ka ttena-(*ess)-ci ani-ha-ess-ta
Mary-Nom leave-PAST-NZ NEG-do-PAST-DEC
'Mary did not leave.'

In (21a), a verb stem and Tense are amalgamated at S-structure, whereas in the S-negation structure in (21b) they do not. The reason that Tense does not appear on the verb can be attributed to the blocking effect of an intervening head between Tense and the verb. The candidates for the blocking element can be either *ci* or Neg. I claim that Neg blocks verb movement, providing a piece of indirect evidence supporting this claim. The configuration in which blocking takes place is shown below: (irrelevant projections are omitted)

(22)

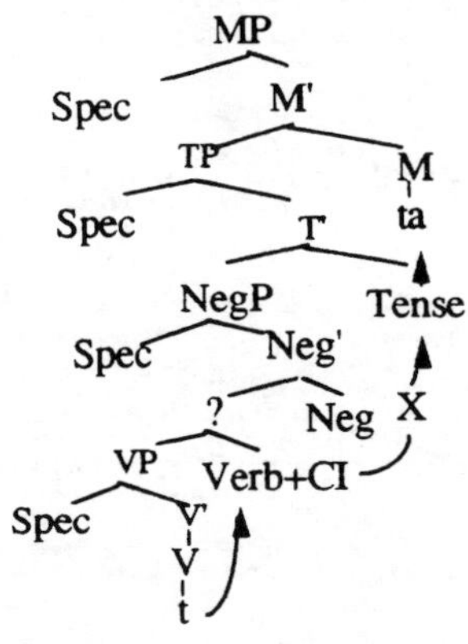

The verb moves up to *ci*, leaving behind a trace.[16] The amalgamated verb+*ci* is blocked to head-move up to Tense by an intervening head Neg.

[15] See also Whitman (1991) for a verb movement analysis for Japanese and Korean.

[16] I assume that the nominalizer *ci* is a base-generated head in a VP adjunct position. This *ci* can have its own project as in Ahn (1991). This paper does not pursue this issue.

That is, since the Neg blocks verb movement to the Tense, *ha*-support occurs to rescue a stranded tense morpheme, as seen in (21b), repeated as (23).[17]

(23) Mary-ka ttena-(*ess)-ci ani-ha-ess-ta
Mary-Nom leave-PAST-NZ NEG-do-PAST-DEC
'Mary did not leave.'

As mentioned above, there are two elements which could conceivably block head-movement of the verb to Tense, namely, *ci* or Neg. The first possibility is that *ci* blocks verb movement. Kang (1988), indeed, suggests that *ci* is a morphological closure; therefore, the verb, which is morphologically closed by *ci*, cannot move further up to Tense.[18] Following Song (1988), I assume that *ki* is an affirmative counterpart of *ci*. That is, *ki* is used in an affirmative sentence, whereas *ci* is used in a negative sentence. If we expect that *ci* blocks verb movement, we may also expect *ki* to have the same blocking effect; namely, verb+*ki* is not expected to have a tense morpheme. This, however, is not borne out. Consider the following pair of sentences:

(24) a. Mary-ka ttena-(*ess)-ci ani-ha-ess-ta
Mary-Nom leave-PAST-NZ NEG-do-PAST-DEC
'Mary did not leave.'

b. Mary-nun [John-i ttena-ess-ki]-lul pala-ess-ta
Mary-TOP John-NOM leave-PAST-NZ-ACC hope-PAST-DEC
'Mary hoped that Mary left.'

As seen in (24a) and (24b), respectively, while *ttena+ci* 'leave+nominalizer' cannot contain Tense, *ttena+ki* 'leave+nominalizer' can.[19] That is, while in (24a) the verb *ttena* 'leave' has not merged with Tense, in (24b) it has merged with the past morpheme *ess*, indicating that *ki* does not bar verb movement. This further indicates that its negative counterpart *ci* does not block verb movement. Thus, the only blocking element for verb movement is Neg.

Alternatively, this *ci* can be taken to be inserted at PF. Even if we assume that *ci* is inserted at PF, the current verb movement analysis is not undermined.

[17] H. Hoji (p.c.) has pointed out to me that Kuroda (1965) briefly mentioned *suru*, which is a Japanese counterpart of *ha*.

[18] See also J.M. Yoon (1989) and K. Park (1990), who suggest that the nominal feature of *ci* blocks verb movement. See also Ahn (1991), who claims that the head *ci* of Aspect Phrase blocks verb movement.

[19] In (24b), I assume that *ki* is generated in a VP adjunction position below TP. Then, a question arises about the array of morphemes. I suggest that the surface order of morphemes does not necessarily reflect the hierarchical order of each projection at D-structure. This can be attributed to a property of the morpheme itself. That is, since *ki* is specified as a suffix in lexicon, it is placed in the word-final position after the head-movement process. Therefore, the occurrence of *ess* before *ki* does not mean that *ki* is outside of TP. See Johnson (1990) and Ahn (1991) for the same line of approach.

However, we face counterexamples to the *ha*-support analysis, if we consider an affirmative sentence which contains a delimiter following *ki*, as observed in Song (1988).[20] The following example shows the point.

(25) Mary-ka kay-lul cha-ki- man / kkaci / to ha-n-ta
Mary-NOM dog-ACC kick-NZ- only / even / also do-IND-DEC
'Mary only / even / also kicks the dog'

Even though this sentence does not have Neg, *ha*-support appears. This contradicts my above analysis about the blocking effect of Neg. I propose that in Korean, Ω heads its own functional projection ΩP, which is located between VP and TP.[21] Therefore, the so-called delimiters like *man* 'only', *kkaci* 'even', *to* 'also', etc. head the ΩP. I further propose that Ω blocks verb movement, as the Neg does. Since Ω blocks the head movement of a verb, *ha*-support occurs as in (25).

A similar analysis can be extended to the sentences, which do not have an overt Neg morpheme. Consider the following sentences.[22, 23]

---

[20] Yang (1972:59) defines delimiters as 'a semantic one which implies that the meaning of the element to which a delimiter is attached is 'delimited and/or specified.' See Yang (1972) for more details.

[21] Since the definition of Ω is closely related to that of delimiters, we need a definition of determiners to define Ω. One may suggest that in Korean the determiners may carry emphatic force. If this is correct, the delimiters can be regarded a realization of abstract emphatic force.

Ω differs from Σ (Laka 1990) in that Ω does not include Neg. As seen in (i), Neg and Ω are not in complementary distribution in Korean.

(i) Mary-ka kay-lul cha-ci- man / kkaci / to ani-ha-n-ta
Mary-NOM dog-ACC kick-NZ- only / even / also not-do-IND-DEC
'Lit. Mary does not only / even / also kick the dog'

In (i), both Ω and Neg appear in a single clause.

[22] Song (1988) takes the sentence in (26c) as grammatical. Most Korean native speakers including myself, however, reject this type of sentence as ungrammatical.

[23] As seen in (26d), the Accusative Case marker *lul* appears after *ki*. One may suggest that the Accusative Case assignment by *ha* 'do' is problematic to my *ha*-support analysis. However, if the auxiliary *have* can assign Accusative Case as Fabb (1984) has suggested, the Case assignment by *ha* 'do' is not that surprising. The real problematic example is the following.

(i) kicha-ka o-ci-ka/lul ani-ha-n-ta
train-NOM come-NZ-NOM/ACC not-do-IND-DEC
'The train does not come.'

Notice that Nominative Case marker *ka* can follow *o-ci* 'come-Nominalizer'. If *ha* assigns only Accusative Case, the appearance of the Nominative Case marker is unexpected. This example indicates that *ha* is somehow related to the main verb *o* 'come', as noted in Kang (1988). Since *o* 'come' in (i) is an ergative verb, Nominative Case is somehow assigned to *o-ci* 'come-Nominalizer'. The following example clearly exhibits that the reflexive Case on *o-ci* is related to main verb *o* 'come'.

(ii) John-i o-ci-*ka/lul ani-ha-n-ta
John-NOM come-NZ-NOM/ACC not-do-IND-DEC
'John does not come.'

Differently from *o* 'come' in (i), the one in (ii) is not used as an ergative verb. The fact that Nominative Case cannot be assigned to *o-ci* in (ii) suggests that *ha* might be a reflexive verb. Unfortunately, the *ha*-support analysis cannot capture this observation. In this paper, I do not pursue this problematic issue any further.

(26) a. Sam-i o-ess-ta
Sam-NOM come-PAST-DEC 'Sam came.'
b. Sam-i o-ess-ni?
Sam-NOM come-PAST-Q 'Did Sam come?'
c. *Sam-i o-ki-lul ha-ess-ta
Sam-NOM come-NZ-ACC do-PAST-DEC 'Sam came.'
d. Sam-i o-ki-lul ha-ess-ni?
Sam-NOM come-NZ-ACC do-PAST-Q 'Did Sam come?'
(I know he didn't come)

In (26a), since there is no intervening functional projection between VP and TP, the verb can head-move to Tense, resulting in a grammatical sentence. Two questions arise about the sentences in (26b) and (26d). The first question is why the sentence in (26b) does not show *ha*-support, as in English interrogative sentences. The second question is why the interrogative sentence in (26d) shows *ha*-support, given that the same interrogative sentence in (26b) does not show *ha*-support. The answer to the first question is related to the hierarchical order of the functional projections. If we assume that the overt Question (Q)-morpheme *ni* generates under the functional head Mood (Ahn & Yoon 1989), this head does not block head movement in the following diagram. (irrelevant projections are omitted)

(27)

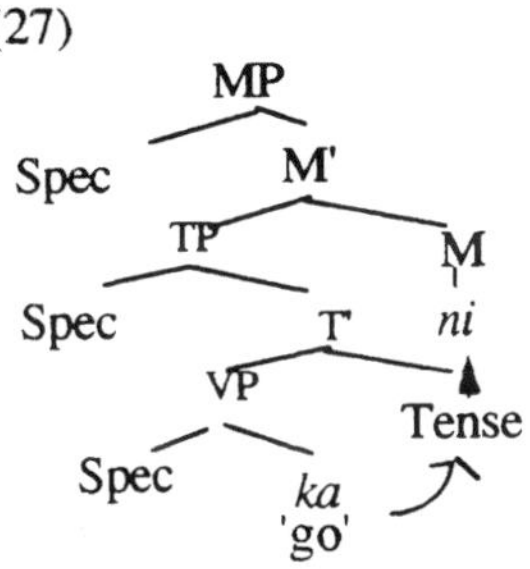

If the head of the MP (*ni* here) does not block verb movement, the occurrence of *ha*-support in (26d) has to be ascribed to some other reason. I propose that in (26d) an invisible functional head Neg blocks verb movement. This is clear if compare the difference in meaning between (26b) and (26d). While the sentence in (26b) is a question about a truth value, the sentence in (26d) has a negative presupposition, as the gloss indicates. This account correctly describes the sentence (26c) as ungrammatical, unlike Song (1988).[24] Since Song (1988) base-generates *ha*, his system incorrectly describes the sentence in (26c) as grammatical. In my account, since this sentence does not have an intervening head between the VP and TP, there is no need for *ha*-support, thus producing a correct sentence.

[24] Even though Kang's (1988) VP-shell hypothesis, in which *ha* generates in a higher V position, can account for the appearance of *ha* without positing *ha*-support, Kang faces the same problem that Song (1988) faces. That is, Kang's VP-shell hypothesis cannot rule (26c) as ungrammatical.

A piece of evidence suggesting that the negativizing *ha* is a kind of *do*-support comes from *ha* contraction. Kim-Renaud (1974; see also Choi 1985) has observed that phonological contraction supports the existence of at least two *ha*'s: the first is the one used in negation; another for verbalizing *ha*. While Neg+negativizing *ha* can have the contracted form, the verbalizing *ha* cannot. The following example shows that negativizing *ha* can be contracted:

(28) ci + ani-ha-ess-ta -> ci anh-ess-ta

This not only shows that there are two different *ha*'s, but also that negativizing *ha* might be generated under a functional head. The same contraction phenomena can be found in the English Aux system. The English Aux located under INFL can be contracted (*hasn't, don't, mustn't*). Similarly, the negativizing *ha* can be regarded as a Korean counterpart of *do* in *do*-support inserted under INFL, as a result of the blocking effect of Neg.

Thus far we have seen that there is verb movement in Korean, as evidenced by the blocking of verb movement by functional heads. The following section examines crosslinguistic data suggesting that the trace of a verb can assign Case.

4. Case Assignment by Verb Trace: Crosslinguistic Evidence

This section examines how verb movement is related to Case assignment and word order. In the preceding section, I have suggested that Case assignment by the trace of a verb is responsible for the MAC in Korean and Japanese. In this section, we will see crosslinguistic evidence supporting this hypothesis. Current Case theory assumes that structural Case is assigned at S-structure, whereas inherent Case is assigned at D-structure (Chomsky 1986b). Crosslinguistic evidence shows that there are two types of languages in terms of Case assignment by the trace of a verb (see also Koopman 1987). I suggest that Korean is a language in which the trace of a verb can assign Case. The following two languages, Icelandic and English, show that the trace of a verb assigns Case.

The following Icelandic data are due to Holmberg (1986:217)

(29) a. Jón ekki keypti bókina
John not bought book
b. Jón $[_{I'}$ keypti$_i$ $[_{VP}$ ekki $[_{VP}$ v_i bókina]]]
John bought not the book
'John did not buy a book.'

In (29a), the verb, *keypti* 'buy', assigns Accusative Case to its complement *bókina* 'book'. In (29b), the verb has moved to pre-Neg position, in which the moved verb cannot govern *bókina* 'book'; therefore, it cannot assign Case to *bókina* 'the book' if structural Case is assigned at S-structure. The only possibility is that the trace of the moved verb V assigns Accusative Case to *bókina* 'the book'.

Another piece of evidence can be found in English. Chomsky (1989) and Lasnik (1990) suggest that English *be* (existential *be*) assigns Case. If this is the case, the grammaticality of (30b) is problematic in that the Case assigner *is* and the Case assignee are not adjacent, as pointed out in Lasnik (1990). (See Stowell: 1981 for adjacency requirement for Case assignment in English)

(30) a. There usually is a man here.
b. There is usually a man here (Lasnik 1990:5)

Sentence (30a) has no problem with the adjacency requirement since the Case assigner *is* and its Case assignee *a man* are adjacent. However, in (30b), the adverbial *usually* intervenes between the Case assigner *is* and its Case assignee *a man*, not satisfying the adjacency requirement. The adjacency requirement between the Case assigner and Case assignee can be evidenced by the ungrammaticality of the following sentence, in which the adverbial *usually* intervenes between the Case assigner and its Case assignee.

(31) a. I usually heard a car (Lasnik 1990:6)
b. * I heard usually a car

In (31a), the Case assigner *heard* and its Case assignee *a car* satisfy the adjacency requirement, yielding the grammatical sentence. In (31b), the adverbial *usually* intervenes between the Case assigner and its Case assignee, resulting in the ungrammatical status.

Now the question is how the grammatical status of (30b) can be accounted for. Recall that in English be/have raises in contrast to other verbs (Pollock 1988; Chomsky 1989). Therefore, the movement of the verb can be expressed as follows:

(32) There is$_i$ usually t$_i$ a man here

If this is the case, the grammaticality of the sentence in (32) can be accounted for in terms of verb movement and the hypothesis that the trace of a verb can assign Case. That is, the trace of the verb *be* assigns Case to its complement, yielding the grammatical sentence. Notice that the trace of the verb and its Case assignee satisfy the adjacency in (32).

5. Concluding Remarks

In conclusion, this paper has tried to provide evidence supporting the existence of verb movement in Korean and that this verb movement is responsible for the MAC. The fact that in Korean both the possessor NP and the IA-NP precede the verb is attributed to the existence of verb movement, together with the hypothesis that the trace of a verb can assign Case. In order to show that Korean has verb movement, this paper has exhibited evidence supporting *ha*-support and that the functional heads, Neg and Ω, block verb movement. This verb movement analysis not only provides an account for the MAC but also solves the problem of overgenerating *ha* -constructions in Song (1988).

This paper, however, leaves some questions open for a further study with regard to scope of negation as noted in footnote 13, and with regard to Case assignment by *ha* 'do' as noted in footnote 23.

REFERENCES

Ahn, Hee-Don & Hang-Jin Yoon. 1989. Functional Categories in Korean. Harvard Studies in Korean Linguistics III. ed. by Kuno et al, 79-88.

Ahn, Hee-Don. 1991. Light Verbs, VP-Movement, Negation and Clausal Architecture in Korean and English. Doctoral dissertation, University of Wisconsin-Madison.

Chang, Kyung Seun. 1992. Negations in Korean. ms. University of Southern California.

Cho, Dong-In. 1991. Functional Projections, Negation, and Verb Movement in Korean. ms. University of Southern California.

Choe, Hyon Sook . 1987. Syntactic Adjunction, A-Chains, and the ECP-Multiple Identical Case Construction in Korean. NELS 17. 100-121.

Choi, Seungja 1985. Explanations of Negation in Korean. Harvard Studies in Korean Linguistics III. ed. by Kuno et al, 124-134.

Chomsky, Noam. 1981. Lectures on Government and Binding. Foris, Dordrecht.

Chomsky, Noam. 1986a. Barriers. MIT Press.

Chomsky, Noam. 1986b. Knowledge of Language: Its Nature, Origin and Use. New York:Praeger.

Chomsky, Noam. 1989. Some Notes on Economy of Derivation and Representation. MIT Working Papers in Linguistics 10.

Fabb, N. 1984. Syntactic Affixation. Doctoral dissertation, MIT.

Harada, S.I. 1973. Counter Equi-NP Deletion. Bulletin of the Research Institute of Logopedics and Phoiatrics 7, 113-48, University of Tokyo.

Holmberg, Anders. 1986. Word Order and Syntactic Features. Doctoral dissertation. University of Stockholm.

Johnson, Kyle. The Syntax of Inflectional Paradigms. ms. University of Wisconsin-Madison.

Kang, Myung Yoon. 1988. Topics in Korean Syntax: Phrase Structure, Variable Binding, Movement. Doctoral dissertation, MIT.

Kang, Young-Se. 1986. Korean Syntax and Universal Grammar. Doctoral dissertation, Harvard University.

Kim, Young-joo. 1989. Inalienable Possession as a Semantic Relationship underlying Predication: the Case of Multiple-Accusative Constructions. Harvard Studies in Korean Linguistics 3. ed. by Kuno et al., 445-467.

Kim-Renaud, Y.-K. 1974. Variation in negation. Language Research 10:1, 1-21. Seoul: Seoul National University. Korea.

Kuroda, Sige-Yuki. 1965. Generative Grammatical Studies in the Japanese Language. Doctoral dissertation, MIT.

Koopman, Hilda. 1987. On the Absence of Case Chains in Bambara. ms. UCLA.

Laka, Miren Itziar. 1990. Negation in Syntax: On the Nature of Functional Categories and Projections. Doctoral dissertation . MIT.

Larson, Richard K. 1988. On the Double Object Construction. LI 19, 335-392.

Lasnik, Howard. 1990. Case and Expletives. ms. University of Connecticut.

Lee, Hong-bae. 1970. A Study of Korean Syntax. Pan Korean Book Corporation. Seoul.

Maling, Joan and Soowon Kim 1990. The Inalienable Possession Construction and Case in Korean. International Korean Linguistics 7. ed. by Eung-Jin Baek, 350-363. University of Toronto Press.

No, Yongkyoon. 1988. Negative Morphemes in Korean: Evidence for a Derivational Treatment. Proceedings of 6th International Conference on Korean Linguistics. ed. by Eung-Jin Baek, 556-567. Seoul:Hanshin Publishing Company.

Oh, C.-K. 1971. On the Negation of Korean. Language Research 7.2.

Pollock, Jean-Yves. 1989. Verb Movement, UG and the Structure of IP. LI 20, 365-424.

Park, Kabyong. 1990. Negation, Verb Movement and Light Verbs in Korean. Papers from the Seventh International Conference on Korean Linguistics. ed. by Eung-Jin Baek, 387-398. University of Toronto Press.

Riemsdijk, H. Van . 1978. A Case Study in Syntactic Markedness, Foris, Dordrecht.

Song, Seok Choong. 1988. Explorations in Korean Syntax and Semantics. Institute of East Asian Studies. University of California, Berkeley.

Stowell, Timothy. 1981. Origin of Phrase Structure. Doctoral dissertation . MIT.

Thompson, Sandra A. 1973. Transitivity and the *ba* Construction in Mandarin Chinese. Journal of Chinese Linguistics 1, 208-221.

Whitman, John. 1991. String Vacuous I to C. Paper presented at GLOW.

Yang, Hyun-Kwon. 1990. Categories and Barriers in Korean. Doctoral Dissertation. The University of Texas at Austin.

Yang, In-Seok. Korean Syntax: Case Markers, Delimiters, Complementation, and Relativization. Seoul: Paekhap Publishing Company.

Yoon, Jeong-Me. 1989. Verb Movement and the Structure of IP in Korean. ms. Cornell University.

Yoon, Jong-Yurl. 1989. On the Multiple 'ka 'and 'lul' Construction. Harvard Studies in Korean Linguistics III, 369-394.

Yoon, Jong-Yurl. 1990. Korean Syntax and Generalized X-bar Theory. Doctoral Dissertation. The University of Texas at Austin.

Yoon, James H-S. 1989. The Grammar of Inalienable Possession Constructions in Korean, Mandarin and French. Harvard Studies in Korean Linguistics III. ed. by Kuno et al, 357-368.

Yoon, James H-S. and Jeong-Me Yoon. 1990. Chain Condition, Ambiguity of Government and Derivational Grammars. NELS 21.

Case-Motivated Movement to Non-Argument Positions: Evidence from Japanese

STANLEY DUBINSKY
University of South Carolina

0. Introduction

The structure of the Japanese potential construction has been debated by generative syntacticians since Kuroda 1965 and Kuno 1973, and has continued to attract attention over the last two decades (e.g. Tonoike 1975-76, Shibatani 1977, Kuroda 1978, Saito 1982, and Takezawa 1987). Of particular concern, is the syntactic status of the nominative objects in (1b) and (1c).

```
(1)  a.  Tomiko ga  [eigo    o   yom] eru.
                Nom  English Acc read able
         'Tomiko can read English.'

     b.  Tomiko ga  eigo    ga  yom-eru.
                Nom English Nom read-able

     c.  Tomiko ni  eigo    ga  yom-eru.
                Dat English Nom read-able

     d. *Tomiko ni  [eigo    o   yom] eru.
                Dat  English Acc read able
```

Modulo theory-particular concerns, various authors have analyzed them as S-structure direct objects that get nominative case via a special rule, while others have taken their case marking as an indication of their true configurational status and claimed them to be S-structure subjects. This paper argues for a derivation that preserves the major insights of both of these approaches. The option promoted here is that the nominative object is at S-structure neither a subject nor an object. It does not remain in situ, but neither does it move to subject position.

1. Analysis

Turning to the clauses in (1), I propose that nominative marking of the embedded object *eigo* in (1b) and (1c) is a consequence of the raising of the embedded verb *yom* to *eru*,[1] and the ensuing adjunction of the object to the lower VP. The structure of potential clauses arises directly from three crucial properties of the potential verb itself.[2] First, the potential predicate *eru* patterns like the Italian 'psych'-verbs *piacere* 'like' and *preoccupare* 'worry' discussed in Belletti and Rizzi 1988, and assigns the θ-roles Experiencer and Theme. Since neither of these θ-roles is 'maximally prominent' in the sense of Grimshaw 1990, neither of them is marked as 'external'.[3] Accordingly, this verb is predicted (by Burzio's 1986 Generalization) not to assign structural accusative case. The second important property of *eru* is that it is an optional trigger of verb raising. This property interacts with its inability to assign structural accusative case, such that if an embedded transitive verb (such as *yom* in (1)) raises to it, *eru* will prevent the lower verb from assigning case to its object. Finally, it is an optional assigner of inherent case to its Experiencer.

There are two possible D-structures for the sentences in (1), which are given in (2).[4]

---

[1]The potential verb is referred to as *eru* for expository ease. Actually, the *eru* form given here is the verb stem *(rar)e* plus the non-perfective aspectual inflection *ru*. The potential stem appears as *rare* when the verb with which it combines ends in a vowel and as *e* otherwise (e.g. *yom-e*[ru] '[is] able to read' and *tabe-rare*[ru] '[is] able to eat').

[2]The verb *eru* is also assumed to be a control verb whose Experiencer controls a 'pro' subject of its complement VP Theme. However, this assumption does not figure quite as prominently in this analysis as do the others, and it is therefore introduced tacitly into the tree structures below.

[3]In Grimshaw 1990, an 'external' argument is one that is determined to be 'maximally prominent' on both a thematic and an aspectual hierarchy. If the Experiencer does not outrank the Theme in both respects, then the verb will have no external argument regardless of the number of argument positions in the VP. This view, which is adopted here, does not require that there be some special position (e.g. Spec/IP) reserved for the external argument, since while every external argument is a subject, not every subject need be an external argument. If a language has unique specifier positions, it is a consequence of the parameterization of its phrase structure and unrelated to argument structure.

[4]Some comment is in order about the tree-structure representations used here. First of all, I am adopting, with certain modification, Fukui's 1986 suggestion that Japanese lacks phrasal projections of functional categories and that its phrasal projections do not have any reserved Specifier position. In this way, the VP generated by a transitive verb and a psych-predicate would be

(2) a. $[_{V+IP}$ Tomiko$_i$ $[_{VP}$ pro$_i$ eigo yom] eru]

b. $[_{V+IP}$ Tomiko-ni$_i$ $[_{VP}$ pro$_i$ eigo yom] eru]

(2a) represents the D-structures of (1a) and (1b), while (2b) illustrates the D-structures of (1c) and (1d). In both cases, *eru* selects an Experiencer *Tomiko* and a VP Theme, and *Tomiko* controls the pro-subject of *yom*. In (2b), but not in (2a), *Tomiko* receives inherent dative case from the verb *eru*.

The derivation of (1a), given in (3), is the most straightforward. In it, the lower V *yom* does not raise and assigns accusative case to its object *eigo*, while Infl assigns nominative case to *Tomiko*. In (4), representing (1b), verb raising is involved. Here, the lower V *yom* raises to *eru*. Recall the premise that the verb *eru* has no external argument, and thereby does not assign structural case. When *yom* raises to *eru*, then, its case assigning properties are 'absorbed', and its object cannot remain inside the VP without violating the Case Filter. There being no empty 'subject' position for this constituent to move to, the embedded object adjoins to the lower VP. Here, the moved object is no longer dominated by VP, and the VP is no longer a barrier to government from outside.[5] In this fashion, it is assigned nominative case under government by the Infl in the higher clause.[6] In (4), both *Tomiko*, the Experiencer NP, and *eigo*, the moved object, are governed by I and assigned nominative case.

---

configurationally identical, with their distinct case-assigning properties being due to the relative prominence of arguments (i.e. external vs. internal) in the sense of Grimshaw 1990 (see the previous footnote). The modification I would suggest is to retain the notion X^{max}, wherein the maximal projection of any V is the node dominating the highest subcategorized argument. This is necessary in order to appropriately identify a node that has been adjoined to and to restrict adjunction itself to the edge of phrases. Actually, it is of little consequence to the analysis whether Infl projects a phrase and then lowers into the VP or whether (as presented here) it is generated as a component of the V+I phrasal head, as long as IPs do not come prepackaged with Specifier positions.

[5]VP is a barrier for some category only if it dominates that category, and the category is dominated by VP only if it is dominated by every segment of VP (cf. May 1985 and Chomsky 1986). The same approach to nominative case marking has been independently proposed in Rizzi 1990 for Locative Inversion Constructions and by Whitman (1991) for presentational *there* constructions.

[6]The assumption that Infl actually assigns case is not terribly crucial to this account. It is crucial, however, for a nominative NP to be at least **governed** by Infl.

(3) –(1a) [$_{V+IP}$ Tomiko$_i$-ga [$_{VP}$ pro$_i$ eigo-o yom] eru]

(4) –(1b) [$_{V+IP}$ Tomiko$_i$-ga [$_{VP}$ eigo$_j$-ga [$_{VP}$ pro$_i$ t_j t_k]] [[yom$_k$]eru]]

The derivation of (1c), given in (5), is similar to that of (1b) with the exception that the Experiencer *Tomiko* receives inherent dative case from *eru*. In (1c), the embedded object must adjoin to VP, because a root clause Infl must assign nominative case to at least one element, and only movement of this object allows Infl to do so.[7] In order for VP-adjunction to be possible, the lower verb **must** raise to *eru* (otherwise, the Chain formed by the moved object and its trace would receive two cases). Example (1d), with presumably the same D-structure as (1c), is ungrammatical (as a root clause) because verb raising does not apply, the object remains in its D-structure position, and no element in the clause receives nominative case.

(5) –(1c) [$_{V+IP}$ Tomiko-ni$_i$ [$_{VP}$ eigo$_j$-ga [$_{VP}$ pro$_i$ t_j t_k]] [[yom$_k$]eru]]

(6) –(1d) *[$_{V+IP}$ Tomiko-ni$_i$ [$_{VP}$ pro$_i$ eigo-o yom] eru]

2. Saito's analysis

Saito's (1982) analysis is an approach which assumes: there to be a uniform rule of nominative case assignment, and that nominative objects are S-structure subjects (or 'subject/focus' in Saito's terms). In this analysis, given in (7), the dative Experiencer is an 'adverbial PP' coindexed with a PRO subject of the clause. The nominative NP is a 'subject/focus' coindexed with an empty category in object position, and receives nominative case as a result of its being a daughter of IP.[8]

---

[7] It is important to note here that (1d) is ungrammatical only as a **root clause**. A common misinterpretation of Shibatani's 1977 article is that all clauses must have at least one nominative element. What Shibatani actually wrote was: '... at the surface level, a **non-embedded** clause of Japanese may have more than one NOM NP, but it requires at least one such NP' (p. 807, emphasis mine). A significant body of work on this issue (including some by this author) has been predicated on the assumption that nominative case must appear in all clauses and, hence, that the dative-accusative pattern in (1d) is ungrammatical in every instance. This is found to be untrue, and analyses which establish a dependency between the assignment of nominative case to the object and the assignment of dative case to the subject turn out to be untenable. This issue will be taken up again in section 3 in a discussion of Takezawa 1987.

[8] The bracketing in (7) is more articulated than Saito's example (52), p. 84, from which this sentence is taken. The additional structure is implied by his discussion and our assumption here that all trees are binary branching.

(7) [$_{IP}$ Taroo$_i$ ni [$_{IP}$ rosiago$_j$ ga [$_{IP}$ PRO$_i$ [e$_j$] hanas-eru]]]
Dat Russian Nom speak-able
'Taro can speak Russian.'

By adopting a position in which the dative PP and the nominative NP are coindexed to argument positions within the embedded clause, Saito can account for the fact that these constituents exhibit subject and object properties, respectively. However, once the move is made to license certain properties via Chain formation, then there is an implicit prediction that a Chain should exhibit all the properties of each its members (i.e., the Chain <Taroo-ni$_i$, PRO$_i$> should exhibit adjunct and subject properties, and the Chain <rosiago$_j$, e$_j$> should possess subject and object properties). The following discussion will show that the nominative Theme is neither a subject nor indexed to a subject position.

2.1 The nominative Theme is not a focus/subject

There are at least two ways in which the nominative Theme fails to behave like a subject/focus: it fails to trigger Subject Honorification and it cannot antecede a reflexive. There is also reason for concluding that it is not immediately dominated by IP: genitive *no* can replace nominative *ga* marking the Theme in contexts where it should be impossible, if there were an IP node between the Experiencer and the Theme.

2.1.1 Subject Honorification

Subject Honorification (SH) is indicated in Japanese by adding an honorific prefix *(g)o-* to the verb stem, and following it (the verb stem) with the dative postposition *ni* and the verb *naru* 'become'. An example is given in (8).

(8) Sensei ga kono hon o o-yomi ni natta koto ...
teacher Nom this book Acc Hon-read Dat became fact
'the fact that the teacher read-[+Hon] this book ...'

This morphology can only be triggered by an appropriate element in subject position. It cannot, for example, be triggered by a direct object, as shown in (9).

(9) *Boku wa sensei o o-mati ni natta.
I Top teacher Acc Hon-wait Dat became
('I waited-[+Hon] for the teacher.')

Shibatani (1977) demonstrated that the dative Experiencer can trigger SH, while the nominative Theme cannot do so. This is shown in (10) and (11).

(10) Sensei ni gakusei ga o-mukae-rare ni naru koto ...
teacher Dat student Nom Hon-greet-able Dat become fact
'The fact that the teacher can-[+Hon] greet the students ...'

(11) *Boku ni sensei ga o-mukae-rare ni naru koto ...
I Dat teacher Nom Hon-greet-able Dat become fact
('The fact that I can-[+Hon] greet the teacher ...')

Now Saito makes it quite clear that (10) does not count as evidence that *sensei-ni* is itself a subject, since it is coindexed with PRO in subject/focus position and that element may serve as the syntactic trigger for SH. That being said, there is now no reason why *sensei-ga* in (11) should not also trigger SH, if it is indeed a subject/focus as Saito claims. The ungrammaticality of (11) thus weighs heavily against his analysis.

2.1.2 Reflexive antecedence

The reflexive element *zibun* is subject oriented, and while not every antecedent of *zibun* is a subject, every subject can antecede *zibun*. With this in mind, Shibatani (1977) shows that nominative objects lack this property and cannot antecede a reflexive. Thus (12) is only acceptable on the interpretation that *zibun* and *Taroo* corefer.[9]

(12) $Taroo_i$ ni $Hanako_j$ ga $zibun_{i/*j}$ no heya kara oidaseru hazu ga
Dat Nom self Gen room from can.evict way Nom
nai.
not.be
'There's no way that $Taroo_i$ can evict $Hanako_j$ from $self's_{i/*j}$ room.'

If *Hanako-ga* is a subject/focus, as Saito claims, then it should certainly be a possible antedent for *zibun*. The fact that it is not argues against a subject/focus analysis of nominative Themes.

2.1.3 *ga-no* conversion and scrambling

It is well known that a *ga*-marked NP may show up with genitive case (*no*-marked) when it occurs in a relative clause or in an NP complement clause headed by *koto* or *no* 'fact, thing' (cf. Harada 1971, Inoue 1976, and Shibatani 1976). The alternation is illustrated in (13) and (14).

---

[9]Shibatani also takes the fact that the dative Experiencer can antecede the reflexive to be evidence that it is a subject. However, while this fact is **consistent** with the claim that dative Experiencers are subjects, it does not motivate such an analysis because there are cases in which a subcategorized dative object may also antecede *zibun*. The following example is taken from Kuno (1972, ex. (117a)).

(i) Sono keiken wa $Mary_i$ ni [$zibun_i$ ga baka dearu koto] o osieta.
that exper. Top Dat self Nom fool is fact Acc taught
'That experience taught $Mary_i$ that $self_i$ is a fool.'

In (i), *Mary* is a *ni*-marked object of the matrix verb *osieta* and corefers with *zibun* (the subject of the clausal-NP complement).

```
(13) [[Keiko ga/no    yonda] hon] ...
              Nom/Gen read    book
     'the book which Keiko read ...'

(14) [[Taroo ga/no    tuita] koto] ...
              Nom/Gen arrived fact
     'the fact that Taro arrived ...'
```

In contrast, the accusative case marker *o* can never be replaced with genitive *no*, as (15) shows.

```
(15)  [[Taroo ga  Keiko ni  hon  o/*no    ataeta] koto] ...
              Nom         Dat book Acc/Gen gave    fact
        'the fact that Taro gave Keiko a book ...'
```

Saito, observing that *ga-no* conversion is possible for nominative Themes, as in (16), claims that this is evidence that they are not in object position.

```
(16)  [[Keiko no  eigo    ga/no    hanas-eru] koto] ...
              Gen English Nom/Gen speak-able fact
       'the fact that Keiko can speak English ...'
```

Whatever the precise account for this phenomenon, he suggests, it is most likely an instance of restructuring in the sense of Huang 1982 and thus sensitive to configurational position rather than mere surface case.[10]

While Saito's point is well-taken, the *ga-no* data actually pose a problem for his analysis. It so happens that when some element is scrambled in front of the subject, *ga-no* conversion is ruled out. Compare (17a) and (17b).

```
(17)  a.  [[IP Taroo ga/no   sono  hon   o   yonda]  koto] ...
                     Nom/Gen that  book Acc read     fact
           'the fact that Taro read that book ...'

      b.  [[IP sono hon  o  [IP Taroo ga/*no  yonda]] koto] ...
               that book Acc          Nom/Gen  read     fact
```

In (17b), the adjunction of *sono hon* in front of the subject renders *ga-no* conversion impossible. Now observe (18).[11]

---

[10]For two possible accounts of this phenomenon, see Bedell 1972 and Fukuda 1989.

[11]Saito (1982) reports (i), where a *no*-marked Theme is preceded by a *ga*-marked Experiencer, to be ungrammatical. However, most speakers with whom we have checked find it to be reasonably acceptable.

```
(i)  [[Keiko ga  eigo    no  hanas-eru] koto] ...
             Nom English Gen speak-able fact
     'the fact that Keiko can speak English ...'
```

```
(18)  [[Keiko ni  eigo    ga/no   hanas-eru] koto] ...
              Dat English Nom/Gen speak-able fact
      'the fact that Keiko can speak English ...'
```

Here, the nominative Theme may be marked with *no*. If the nominative Theme in (18) were a daughter of IP and the dative Experiencer were adjoined to IP in front of it, as Saito proposes, then we would expect *ga-no* conversion to be ruled out. The fact that *no* marking is possible suggests that *eigo* is **not** dominated by an IP adjunction. Note that this fact is perfectly consistent with the VP-adjunction analysis no IP node intervenes between the two constituents.

3. Takezawa's analysis

Takezawa (1987) couples the claim that nominative Themes are S-structure objects with a highly principled approach to the assignment of nominative case. In his account, a potential verb can optionally not assign case to its direct object. Since there is no empty position into which this NP can move to receive case, Infl lowers into the VP, amalgamates with the verb, and assigns nominative case to the object under government. With Infl no longer in IP at S-structure, the subject (i.e. Experiencer) is left ungoverned. The *ni*-marking of this subject is then determined by a 'dummy-P' insertion rule, repeated here in (19).

(19) *Ni* is assigned to the subject if it is not governed.

Takezawa's D- and S-structures for (1c) are given in (20).

(20) =(1c) D-structure: $[_{IP}$ Tomiko $[_{I'}$ $[_{VP}$ eigo yom-e] ru]]
S-structure: $[_{IP}$ Tomiko-ni $[_{I'}$ $[_{VP}$ eigo-ga yom-e-ru]]

In (20), the Infl element *-ru* lowers into the VP, leaving *Tomiko* ungoverned. It assigns nominative case to *eigo* under government, and dative case is inserted on *Tomiko* by rule (19).

To account for (1b), in which both the Experiencer and the Theme have nominative case, Takezawa proposes that Infl can optionally govern back up out of the clause into which it has been lowered. The analysis is given in (21).

(21) =(1b) D-structure: $[_{IP}$ Tomiko $[_{I'}$ $[_{VP}$ eigo yom-e] ru]]
S-structure: $[_{IP}$ Tomiko-ga $[_{I'}$ $[_{[V+I]P}$ eigo-ga yom-e-ru]]

The structure of (21) is essentially the same as (20), with the exception that, after Infl-lowering, Infl and V project a 'doubly-headed' phrase [V+I]P which is 'transparent' to government. This allows Infl to govern and case-mark both NPs in the clause.

3.1 An incorrect prediction

One major problem for Takezawa's analysis is the necessary entailment between the assignment of nominative case to the Theme and *ni* to the

Experiencer. In his account, dative case appears on the Experiencer **only if** Infl assigns case to the Theme. The reason for incorporating this dependency into the analysis is to rule out the ungrammatical dative-accusative pattern seen in (1d).

Now, the ungrammaticality of (1d) conforms to Shibatani's (1978) observation that 'an independent sentence in Japanese requires at least one nominative NP'. What Shibatani was seeking to rule out were root-clause, intransitive potential constructions in which the single argument of the clause has dative case. Example (22) illustrates the point.

```
(22)  a.  Taroo ga  hasir-eru.        b. *Taroo ni  hasir-eru.
                Nom run-able                     Dat run-able
          'Taroo can run.'
```

The ungrammaticality of (22b) appears to confirm Takezawa's claims that: an Experiencer is *ni*-marked only when it is ungoverned, the Experiencer is only ungoverned when Infl has lowered into the VP, and Infl will only lower into the VP when so motivated by the need to assign case to an object. Thus, under the Infl-lowering acccount, (22b) is ill-formed **because** the verb *hasir(u)* 'run' is intransitive.

However, Shibatani's observation has been misinterpreted as meaning that **every** clause in Japanese requires at least one nominative NP. In (23), both embedded intransitive clauses have an Infl element, and at least one of these (the second) is a [+Tense] Infl.[12]

```
(23)  Boku ni  hasir-ete,     kimi ni  hasir-enai     wake    ga  nai.
      I    Dat run-able.and you  Dat run-able.not reason Nom not.be
      'I can run, so there's no reason why you can't (run).'
```

Notice that the Experiencers in both potential clauses, *boku* and *kimi*, are each marked with *ni* and not *ga*. In order to explain the unexpected grammaticality of (23), the Infl-lowering account would have to say that, for embedded clauses, Infl may optionally lower when there is no motivation for it to do so. This weakens the explanatory force of Takezawa's analysis, but does not quite eviscerate it, since such a stipulation **could** be made.

The Infl-lowering account actually does come apart when one finds that the purportedly ungrammatical dative-accusative pattern is grammatical in certain embedded contexts.[13] Observe examples (24) and (25).

---

[12]Example (23), and the stimulus to pursue this line of investigation, was suggested by an anonymous reviewer of this article.

[13]It appears to generally be the case that this pattern is most widely accepted when the matrix clause contains a negation. Note that the verb *roodoku-dekiru* 'can recite' is a suppletive form incorporating the light verb *roodoku-si* 'recite-do' and *(rar)eru* 'able', there being no form **roodoku-*

```
(24)  Aitu      ni  Hanako o   nagur-eru wake ga  nai.
      that.guy Dat        Acc hit-able  way  Nom not.be
      'There's no way that guy can hit Hanako.'

(25)  Taroo ni  konna      si   o   roodoku-dekiru wake ga  nai.
            Dat this.sort poem Acc recite-do.able way  Nom not.be
      'There's no way that Taroo can recite this sort of poem.'
```

Under Takezawa's analysis, *aitu* in (24) should only get dative case if Infl lowers into the VP, leaving it ungoverned. If Infl did lower into the VP, then it should mark *Hanako* with nominative case. In order to subsume these facts, then, the Infl-lowering account would have to allow (i) for Infl to optionally lower into the VP in embedded clauses without motivation, and (ii) for a lowered Infl in an embedded clause to optionally give no sign of having done so (i.e. not assign its case). In the VP-adjunction account, the assignment of dative case to the Experiencer and nominative case to the Theme are **not** causally linked in any way, and the grammaticality of (23-25) is explained as a construction-independent, root/embedded asymmetry.

3.2 Nominative Theme is not an S-structure object

Finding that the **motivation** for Infl-lowering is weakened does not in itself argue that nominative case is not assigned in that fashion. This section will consider some evidence which argues **for** an account in which the Theme is moved (string-vacuously) from its VP-internal position, and **against** one in which it remains in situ and is assigned nominative case by a lowered Infl. *Ga-no* conversion was cited by Saito as one reason for analyzing the nominative Theme as VP-external. Various analyses of this phenomenon, as early as Bedell 1972 and as recently as Fukuda 1989, have all taken *ga-no* conversion to be a case of 'restructure α'. If this view is correct, then NPs which can be marked with *no*, such as subjects and nominative objects, must be configurationally distinct from those which cannot, such as accusative objects. Thus, the Infl-lowering account is at pains to explain why it is that nominative Themes can be marked with *no*, while other accusative objects cannot.

The ellipsis of case-markers in casual speech also argues against a VP-internal analysis of the nominative Theme. As first noted in Kuno 1973, and further explicated in Saito 1985, accusative case may be omitted from objects, while nominative case may not be dropped from subjects.[14]

```
(26)  a.  Dare *(ga) kono hon  o   yonda no?
          who    Nom this book Acc read  Q
          'Who read this book?'
```

---

sir(ar)eru 'can recite'. The case of *dekiru* will be taken up again in section 4.

[14]In these examples, and in others presented here, the potential for particle ellipsis is measured for WH-elements. This is due to the fact that WH-elements are more resistant to such ellipsis and the judgements given by most speakers for them are clearer than for non-WH-elements.

```
     b.  Nani (o)  yondeiru no?
         what  Acc reading  Q
         'What are [you] reading?'
```

Takezawa suggests that case ellipsis is licensed by adjacency to a case-assigner. *Ga* may not be omitted in (26a) because the subject *dare* is not adjacent to Infl. In (26b), *o* may be omitted since *nani* is adjacent to the verb.[15] This approach to case ellipsis receives some attenuated support from the fact that the acceptability of *o*-ellipsis is reduced for some speakers when the object is scrambled away from the verb.

```
(27)  Nani ??(o), Taroo wa  yondeiru no?
      what    Acc        Top reading  Q
      'What is it that Taro is reading?'
```

In (27), the ellipsis of *o* is less acceptable than it is in (26b).[16]

Turning to the ellipsis of the *ga* marking nominative Themes, we encounter widely differing findings in the literature. For instance, Saito (1985, p. 266) claims that 'object *ga*' is not optional, while Takezawa insists that it is.[17] In order to evaluate 'object *ga*' ellipsis accurately, it is first necessary to isolate cases in which the omitted particle could be nothing other than *ga*. We know that the case marking of the Theme can be either accusative or nominative when the Experiencer is marked with *ga* or *wa*. (28b) is only slightly less acceptable than (28a).

```
(28)  a.  Taroo ga  nani-go       ga  yom-eru no?
                Nom what-language Nom read-able
          'What language can Taro read?'

      b.  Taroo ga  nani-go       o   yom-eru no?
                Nom what-language Acc read-able
```

[15]According to Saito, the ellipsis of *o* in (26b) is permissible because accusative case is assigned as abstract case by the verb and the *o* marker is merely the phonological realization of case that is present anyway. Nominative case, he claims, is assigned by *ga* itself, which must therefore be phonologically overt. However, Saito's explanation of (26) appears to be weakened by the fact that a *ga* marking the object of a potential sentence is more readily omitted than one marking a true subject.

[16]There is some debate about whether this is in fact the case. Saito (1985) claims that ellipsis in the example is impossible. An anonymous reviewer of this article found the ellipsis not to be very troublesome, and other native speakers tend to find *o*-ellipsis for scambled objects to be marginal (but not nearly as bad as *ga*-ellipsis from subjects).

[17]In both cases, it should be noted, the empirical claims regarding 'object *ga*' ellipsis seem to be somewhat theory-driven (i.e., the observations crucially meet the predictions of their theoretical account).

```
      c.  Taroo ga  nani-go        yom-eru no?
                Nom what-language read-able
```

Speakers tend to find (28c) as acceptable as any case of *o*-ellipsis, and there is no reason (given the acceptability of (28b)) to think that it is anything else. On the other hand, when the Experiencer (in a root clause) is marked with *ni* or *ni wa*, the Theme may not be marked with *o*, as shown in (29b).

```
(29)  a.  Taroo ni  wa  nani-go       ga  yom-eru no?
                Dat Top what-language Nom read-able
          'What language can Taro read?'

      b. *Taroo ni  wa  nani-go       o   yom-eru no?
                Dat Top what-language Acc read-able
```

The absolute ungrammaticality of (29b) suggests that the omitted particle in (30) could only be *ga*.

```
(30) ??Taroo ni  wa  nani-go       yom-eru no?
             Dat Top what-language read-able
       'What language can Taro read?'
```

Nine of ten native speakers found (30) to be less acceptable than (28c), yet most of those felt that (30) was not as bad as 'subject *ga*' ellipsis of the sort illustrated in (26a).

If Takezawa is correct about case ellipsis being sanctioned by adjacency to a case assigner, then he cannot be right about nominative Themes remaining adjacent to the verb at S-structure. On the other hand, suppose that case ellipsis is most acceptable when a constituent is adjacent to its assigner at both D- and S- structure, less acceptable when adjacent only at S-structure, and unacceptable when not adjacent at any level. In (30), under the VP-adjunction analysis, the object *nani-go* is adjacent to the verb at D-structure, but that element is not its case assigner. By adjoining to VP at S-structure, however, *nani-go* winds up adjacent to the V+I element that assigns it nominative case. (31) represents the S-structure of (30).

(31) -(30) $[_{V+IP}$ Taroo-ni$_i$ $[_{VP}$ nanigo$_j$ $[_{VP}$ pro$_i$ t_j t_k]] [[yom$_k$]eru]]

(32) α is adjacent to β, iff there is a category Γ that immediately dominates α and β.

In (31), the NP *nani-go* is not dominated by VP because it is not dominated by every segment of VP. It is therefore immediately dominated by V+I', which immediately dominates *yomeru*. Hence, *nani-go* and *yomeru* are adjacent by (32). However, this adjacency holds at S-structure alone, resulting in the reduced acceptability of (30).

4. Non-potential constructions - a potential counterexample

Thus far, the analysis has focused primarily on potential constructions formed with the verb *eru*, and on the nominative/accusative alternation on the embedded Theme, with the alternation was attributed to the interaction of optional verb raising and case absorption. Now, the verbs *wakaru* 'understand' and *dekiru* 'be able to do' present the most formidable challenge to the account. Their behavior, typified by *wakaru* in (33), begs an explanation.

```
(33)  a.  Tanaka ni   eigo    ga  wakaru      no?
                 Dat English Nom understand Q
          'Does Tanaka understand English?'

      b.  Tanaka ga   eigo    ga  wakaru      no?
                 Nom English Nom understand Q
          'Is it Tanaka who understands English?'

      c.  Tanaka ga   eigo    o   wakaru      no?
                 Nom English Acc understand Q
          'Is it Tanaka who understands English?'
```

As shown in (33), *wakaru* 'understand' selects an NP Experiencer and an NP Theme and optionally assigns dative case to the Experiencer. However, it can also assign accusative case to an NP Theme. If these verbs are genuinely monomorphemic, then the *ga/o* alternation must be unrelated to that observed in *eru* constructions and this would have to be justified. On the other hand, if the *ga/o* alternation is to be subsumed under the VP-adjunction analysis, then (obviously) the verbs cannot be monomorphemic. I will suppose that *wakaru* and *dekiru* are bimorphemic and can be accomodated by the account given in section 1.

There are two phenomena which independently suggest that *wakaru* incorporates the potential verb *eru*. First, note that a potential predicate may not passivize. (34) is ungrammatical for this reason.

```
(34) *Nihongo  ga   gaikokujin ni-mo    hanas-e-rareru.
      Japanese Nom foreigner  by-also speak-able-Pass
     ('Japanese is able to be spoken by foreigners, too.')
```

With this in mind, observe that *wakaru* may not passivize either.

```
(35)  *Sonna koto  ga  minna ni  wakar-areta.
       such  thing Nom all   Dat understand-Pass.
      ('Such things are understood by everyone.')
```

Now presumably the ungrammaticality of (35) has nothing to do with the meaning of the verb, especially given that a thematically similar verb like *siru* 'know' forms perfectly acceptable passives.

```
(36)  Sonna koto  ga  minna ni  sir-areta.
      such  thing Nom all   Dat know-Pass.
      'Such things are known by everyone.'
```

On the other hand, the ill-formedness of **wakar-areru* is predicted if it underlyingly contains the verb *eru*.

The second motivation is based on a difference between the personal potential verb *eru* and the epistemic potential verb *uru*, pointed out in Tomioka 1990. Tomioka notes that the epistemic potential *uru*, but not *eru*, may be added to a complex verb that already contains *eru*. Thus, (37a) is grammatical, but (37b) is not.

```
(37)  a.  Midori ga  Bartok ga/o    hik-e-uru.
                 Nom        Nom/Acc play-able-possible
          'It is possible that Midori can play Bartok.'

      b. *Midori ga  Bartok ga/o    hik-e-rareru.
                 Nom        Nom/Acc play-able-able
```

Observe now, in (38), that the same contrast is obtains with the verb *wakaru*.

```
(38)  a.  Keiko ga  eigo    ga/o    wakari-uru.
                Nom English Nom/Acc understand-possible
          'It is possible that Keiko understands English.'

      b. *Keiko ga  eigo    ga/o    wakar-eru.
                Nom English Nom/Acc understand-able
         ('Keiko is able to understand English.')
```

The unacceptability of (38b) is quite unexpected, there being no reason why a predicate meaning 'able to understand' should be excluded. Moreover, the Sino-Japanese verb *rikai-suru* 'understand' **can** occur with a potential meaning. In place of (38b), one might say (39).

```
(39)  Keiko ga  eigo    o   rikai-dekiru.
            Nom English Acc understand-able.to.do
      'Keiko is able to understand English.'
```

The difference in grammaticality observed between (38b) and (39) begs an explanation, and the hypothesis that *wakaru* is underlyingly complex provides a quite reasonable one.

5. Conclusion

Although case-motivated adjunction has been adopted here without comment, one might ask what sort of movement we are dealing with. Is VP-adjunction best characterized as NP-movement or Operator movement? Is the VP-adjoined position an A-position or an A'-position? Case-driven movement is usually classified as NP-movement, while movement by adjunction normally falls into the category of A'-movement, and I will continue to assume this characterization here.

Suppose that a position which is not present at D-structure **cannot** be an A-position regardless of any case-related properties it may have (cf. Saito 1989). We would then say that case-motivated VP-adjunction, of the sort proposed here, is an instance of A'-movement (although it need not be considered Operator movement). Characterizing VP-adjunction as A'-movement may have some independent motivation as well. Recall, from section 2.2.1, that the nominative Theme cannot trigger Subject Honorification (SH). If this construction involves subject-subject raising (i.e. movement from an A-position to an A-position) and if the S-structure position of a nominative Theme were characterized as non-A, then its inability to act as a SH trigger would be reducible to a universal principle (proposed by Rizzi 1991) that rules out any movement from A' to A positions.

Case-driven adjunction also completes a paradigm of universal possibilities for movement. It is well-known that Operator movement is of two varieties, substitution and adjunction. WH-movement involves movement to an empty Spec (of CP) position already present in D-structure. Scrambling, on the other hand, involves movement by adjunction (to IP). If the account of nominative Themes provided here is correct, then we may recognize two varieties of case-driven (or NP) movement as well: one by movement to an empty (subject) position, as in the case of unaccusatives and passives, and one by adjunction, as in the case of nominative Themes in Japanese, Locative Inversion in Italian, and Presentational *there* constructions in English.

Acknowledgements

My foremost thanks go out to Masako Atake, who studied with me at The University of Wisconsin - Madison in 1989-90. This article was initially inspired by her interest in the topic and by questions that she raised regarding the correctness of the two principal analyses (Saito's and Takezawa's) that are criticized in the text. I also wish to acknowledge helpful comments from and discussion had with the following individuals: Heedon Ahn, William Davies, Naoya Fujita, Shoko Hamano, Caroline Heycock, Kyle Johnson, Joan Maling, Roger Martin, Kazuhiko Tajima, Satoshi Tomioka, Shigeo Tonoike, John Whitman, as well as three anonymous reviewers for the journal *Natural Language and Linguistic Theory*. Further helpful discussion and insights were provided by audiences at the University of Kansas, the University of South Carolina, and the 1991 Japanese/Korean Linguistics Conference at UC - Santa Barbara. I also extend my thanks to the following individuals at the 1991 LSA Linguistic Institute, who very generously provided native speaker judgements on particularly recalcitrant phenomena: Yoshio Endo, Rika Hayami, Kaoru Horie, Satomi Kajihara, Seiko Ono, Hiroko Yamashita, Satomi Honda, Rieko Ikeda, and Sotaro Kita. All errors and omissions remain the sole responsibility of the author.

References

Bedell, George. 1972. On *no*. UCLA papers in syntax 3: Studies in East Asian syntax, ed. by George Bedell. Los Angeles: UCLA.

Belletti, Adriana, and Luigi Rizzi. 1988. Psych-verbs and θ-theory. NLLT 6.291-352.

Burzio, Luigi. 1986. Italian syntax: A government and binding approach. Dordrecht: D. Reidel.

Chomsky, Noam. 1981. Lectures on government and binding. Dordrecht: Foris.

Chomsky, Noam. 1986. Barriers. Cambridge, MA: MIT Press.

Fukuda, Minoru. 1989. A movement approach to *ga-no* conversion in Japanese. M.A. thesis, University of Illinois, Urbana-Champaign.

Fukui, Naoki. 1986. A theory of category projection and its applications. Doctoral dissertation, MIT.

Fukui, Naoki. 1988. Deriving the differences between English and Japanese: A case study in parametric syntax. English linguistics 5.249-70.

Grimshaw, Jane. 1990. Argument structure. Cambridge, MA: MIT Press.

Harada, S.-I. 1971. *Ga-no* conversion and idiolectal variations in Japanese. Gengo kenkyu 61.25-38. Tokyo: Linguistic Society of Japan.

Huang, C.-T. James. 1982. Logical relations in Chinese and the theory of grammar. Doctoral dissertation, MIT.

Inoue, Kazuko. 1976. Henkei-bunpoo to nihongo ('Transformational grammar and Japanese'). Tokyo: Taisyukan.

Kuno, Susumu. 1973. The structure of the Japanese language. Cambridge, MA: MIT Press.

Kuroda, Shige-Yuki. 1965. Generative grammatical studies in the Japanese language. Doctoral dissertation, MIT.

Kuroda, Shige-Yuki. 1978. Case marking, canonical sentence patterns, and counter-equi in Japanese (A preliminary survey). Problems in Japanese syntax and semantics, ed. by John Hinds and Irwin Howard, 30-51. Tokyo: Kaitakusha.

May, Robert. 1985. Logical form. Cambridge, MA: MIT Press.

Rizzi, Luigi. 1990. Relativized minimality. Cambridge, MA: MIT Press.

Rizzi, Luigi. 1991. Issues in Italian syntax (class notes). LSA Linguistic Institute, UC - Santa Cruz.

Saito, Mamoru. 1982. Case marking in Japanese: A preliminary study. Ms., MIT.

Saito, Mamoru. 1983. Case and government in Japanese. WCCFL 2.247-59.

Saito, Mamoru. 1985. Some asymmetries in Japanese and their theoretical implications. Doctoral dissertation, MIT.

Saito, Mamoru. 1989. Scrambling as semantically vacuous A'-movement. Alternative conceptions of phrase structure, ed. by Mark Baltin and Anthony Kroch, 182-200. Chicago: The University of Chicago Press.

Shibatani, Masayoshi. 1976. Nihongo no bunseki ('Analysis of Japanese'). Tokyo: Taisyukan.

Shibatani, Masayoshi. 1977. Grammatical relations and surface cases. Language 53.789-809.

Shibatani, Masayoshi. 1978. Mikami Akira and the notion of 'subject' in Japanese grammar. Problems in Japanese syntax and semantics, ed. by John Hinds and Irwin Howard, 52-67. Tokyo: Kaitakusha.

Takezawa, Koichi. 1987. A configurational approach to Case-marking in Japanese. Doctoral dissertation, University of Washington, Seattle.

Tomioka, Satoshi. 1990. On Japanese potentials. Ms., University of Wisconsin, Madison.

Tonoike, Shigeo. 1975-76. The Case ordering hypothesis. Papers in Japanese Linguistics 4.191-208.

Whitman, John. 1991. Configurational and relational approaches to Case (class notes). LSA Linguistic Institute, UC - Santa Cruz.

The Role of Pro in the Ni Passive in Japanese

HIROTO HOSHI
University of Connecticut

1. Introduction

Universal Grammar consists of various subsystems, each containing certain principles with a limited degree of parametric variation. In addition, Universal Grammar has certain overriding principles such as the projection principle, the principle of full interpretation (FI), and the principles of licensing (Chomsky 1986). In this paper, I will suggest a generalized version of the projection principle, which incorporates argument θ requirements and adjunct θ requirements in a unified way. By appealing to the generalized version of the projection principle, I will argue for Kuroda's (1979) proposal that the subject position of *ni* passives is uniformly a θ-position while that of *ni yotte* passives is a non-θ position.[0] Then, I will present Saito's (1982) argument for an NP movement analysis of the *ni* direct passive as one potential problem for Kuroda's (1965, 1979) analysis.[1]

[0] Following Kuroda (1979), I call the passive construction with *ni*, the *ni* passive, and the passive construction with *ni yotte*, the *ni yotte* passive. Roughly speaking, *ni* and *ni yotte* both correspond to *by* in English.
[1] Following Howard and Niyekawa-Howard (1976), I adopt the terms direct passive and indirect passive for ease of exposition.

Finally, I will sketch a new analysis of the *ni* direct passive, adopting Saito and Murasugi's (1989) PRO movement analysis of the *be* passive. There, I crucially assume Fukui's (1986) and Fukui and Speas's (1986) proposal that the SPEC position of a lexical category is ungoverned.

In addition to argument θ requirements, there is another kind of θ requirement, which I call an adjunct θ requirement, following Zubizarreta (1982).

(1) a. Voluntarily, John rolled down the hill
b. *Voluntarily, the stone rolled down the hill
(Zubizarreta 1982:43)

(1a) is grammatical. But (1b) is ungrammatical since the adjunct Trequirement imposed by the subject oriented adverb, *voluntarily*, is not satisfied. As is clear, the subject oriented adverb requires that the subject be an agent. In section 2, I will discuss Zubizarreta's (1982) proposal for adjunct θ requirements together with Chomsky's (1981) projection principle. After pointing out the differences between what I call the Jackendoff (1972, 1975) type dialect and the Lasnik and Fiengo (1974) type dialect regarding adjunct θ requirements, and, after discussing potential problems for Zubizarreta's analysis of the relevant examples, I will present an alternative analysis in terms of the generalized projection principle (henceforth the GPP), given in (2).

(2) Generalized Projection Principle (GPP)
All the θ relations are represented at all levels in syntax.

In section 3, I will briefly discuss two traditional analyses of Japanese passives, Kuno's (1973) and Kuroda's (1979).[2] Consider examples of the *ni* passive given in (3).

(3) a. John-ga Mary-ni nagur-are-ta
-nom. -by hit-passive-past
'John$_i$ was affected by Mary's hitting him$_i$'

b. John-ga Mary-ni kodomo-o nagur-are-ta
-nom. -by child-acc. hit-passive-past
'John$_i$ was affected by Mary's hitting a/his$_i$ child'

[2] Kuno (1983, 1986) abandons the analysis proposed in Kuno (1973) and he adopts a uniform analysis of *ni* passives, which is quite similar to Kuroda's (1965, 1979) analysis. However, Kuno (1983, 1986) does not differentiate *ni yotte* passives from *ni* passives in the way Kuroda (1979) does.

c. John-ga   ame-ni hur-are-ta
        -nom. rain-by fall-passive-past
   'John$_i$ was affected by rain's falling (on him$_i$)'

The logical object is the subject of the passive sentence in (3a), which is called a direct passive. There does not seem to be any gap in (3b) and (3c). They are called indirect passives.[3] Kuno (1973) argues for a dichotomy between direct passives and indirect passives. If we interpret Kuno's analysis in modern terms, the subject position of the direct passive is a non–θ position while the subject position of the indirect passive is a θ–position.

Kuroda (1979), on the other hand, argues for the existence of a formally distinct type of passive construction in Japanese, the *ni yotte* passive. Then, he proposes a major dichotomy between the *ni* passive and the *ni yotte* passive.[4] (4a), (4b), and (4c) are instances of *ni yotte* passives.

(4) a. John-ga   Mary-ni yotte   nagur-are-ta
          -nom.   -to due   hit-passive-past
     'John was hit by Mary'

b. John-ga   Mary-ni yotte kodomo-o   nagur-are-ta
        -nom.   -to due   child-acc.   hit-passive-past
   'John's child was hit by Mary'

c. *John-ga   ame-ni   yotte hur-are-ta
        -nom. rain-to   due   fall-passive-past

Observing differences between *ni* passives and *ni yotte* passives, Kuroda (1979) argues that the subject position of *ni* passives is a θ–position while the subject position of *ni yotte* passives is a non–θ position. After illustrating differences between Kuno's analysis and Kuroda's analysis in a little more detail, I will argue for Kuroda's (1979) dichotomy between *ni* passives and *ni yotte* passives with respect to the subject position. The argument crucially relies on the GPP.

In section 4, I will provide further support for Kuroda's (1979) hypothesis by showing that verb phrase idioms cannot be passivized in the case of the *ni* passive but they can be passivized in the case of the *ni yotte* passive.

In section 5, I will discuss Saito's (1982) argument for an NP movement analysis of *ni* direct passives as a potential problem for Kuroda's (1965,

---

3 Kubo (1990) and Terada (1990) argue that the so-called possessor passive exists in Japanese and they argue that there can be an NP trace in passive sentences such as (3b). Even if they are ultimately correct, the argument in this paper is not affected. Thus, I just illustrate Kuno's (1973) and Kuroda's (1965, 1979) analyses. The reader is referred to Hoshi (1991) for a different view of passive sentences such as (3b).

4 Kuno (1973) considers the *ni yotte* passive to be a variant of the direct passive. It is unclear how he would analyze (4b).

1979) analysis. Assuming that Kuroda's and Saito's arguments are both correct, I will suggest a new analysis of *ni* direct passives, adopting Saito and Murasugi's (1989) PRO movement theory. I will crucially rely on Fukui's (1986) and Fukui and Speas's (1986) proposal that the SPEC position of a lexical category is ungoverned.

2. Generalized Projection Principle (GPP)

Chomsky (1981) formulates the projection principle as follows:[5]

(5) $[_\gamma \ldots \alpha \ldots ß \ldots]$
$[_\gamma \ldots ß \ldots \alpha \ldots]$

(6) (i) if ß is an immediate constituent of γ in (5) at L_i, and γ = a', then a θ–marks ß in γ.

(ii) if a selects ß in γ as a lexical property, then aselects ß in γ at L_i.

(iii) if α selects ß in γ at L_i, then α selects ß in γ at L_j.

(Chomsky 1981:38)

Informally speaking, the projection principle states that argument θ relations between a primary predicate and its complement or subject are represented at every syntactic level.

In addition to argument θ requirements, there are other θ requirements, imposed by adjuncts such as subject oriented adverbs. Consider (7a) and (7b).

(7) a. The rock rolled down the hill
b. *Intentionally/Voluntarily, the rock rolled down the hill

(Zubizarreta 1982:43)

The subject oriented adverb in (7b) requires that the subject be an agent. Then, a question naturally arises as to the exact nature of adjunct θ requirements and, in particular, as to the syntactic level(s) at which they are imposed.[6]

Jackendoff (1975) claims that subject oriented adverbs can modify subject NPs in raising and passive constructions; this is exemplified in (8), where, according to Jackendoff (1975), the subject oriented adverb, *intentionally*, can modify the subject NP, *John*.

---

[5] If α directly or indirectly θ–marks ß, then α selects ß. The variables L_i, L_j range over syntactic levels: LF, D-structure, S-structure.

[6] Following Zubizarreta (1982), I shall refer to the θ–roles assigned by lexical heads (N, V, A, P) and VP as argument θ–roles, and to the θ–roles assigned by adjunct predicates such as subject oriented adverbs as adjunct θ–roles.

(8) John intentionally happened to be present when Bill arrived
(Jackendoff 1975:439)

Thus, the intention can be attributed to the surface subject in (8). Assuming that *John* is the subject of the embedded clause at D-structure, i.e., that (8) involves raising, Zubizarreta (1982) proposes the generalization in (9):[7]

(9) The adverb argument relation is established at S-structure and/or LF.(Zubizarreta 1982:42)

Observe that the generalization in (9) entails that adjunct θ requirements are different from argument θ requirements and, in particular, that the former are distinguished from the projection principle.

However, Lasnik and Fiengo (1974) present different grammaticality judgements with respect to examples similar to (8). Compare the judgement given in (10) with the one given in (8).

(10) *John is intentionally certain to win
(Lasnik and Fiengo 1974:574)

According to Lasnik and Fiengo (1974), the subject oriented adverb, *intentionally*, cannot modify the subject NP in (10). It seems then that we are confronted with different dialects, which, for expository convenience, I will call the Jackendoff (1975) type dialect and the Lasnik and Fiengo (1974) type dialect. Zubizarreta's (1982) proposal in (9), then, seems to be correct for the Jackendoff (1975) type dialect; however, Lasnik and Fiengo's (1974) judgement could raise a problem for her analysis.

One way to modify Zubizarreta's (1982) proposal in (9), so that it captures the dialectal difference observed in (8) and (10), would be to parameterize adjunct θ requirements as in (11).

(11) a. Adjunct θ relations are represented at S-structure and/or LF in the Jackendoff (1975) type dialect.
b. Adjunct θ relations are represented at all levels in syntax in the Lasnik and Fiengo (1974) type dialect.

Notice that the proposal in (11) captures the empirical difference between the two dialects. However, (11) does not seem to be a correct approach to

[7] Zubizarreta (1982) actually proposes the generalization given in (9) on the basis of the fact discussed in Jackendoff (1972) that the subject oriented adverb, *intentionally*, can modify the subject NP, *Mary*, in the *be* passive sentence in (i):

(i) Mary intentionally has been seduced by Joe (Jackendoff 1972:82)

See Hoshi (to appear) for a discussion of English passives and related topics.

explain (8) and (10), since we do not expect such a parametric variation appealing to different levels of representation in θ requirements. Furthermore, the difference between (8) and (10) does not seem to be due to dialectal variation after all, since many native speakers of English agree not only with the judgement given by Jackendoff (1975) on (8) but also with the judgement given by Lasnik and Fiengo (1974) on (10). Observe, in addition, that (11b) is quite reminiscent of the projection principle. If so, it would be conceptually more appealing to unify the condition in (11b) with the projection principle, denying the parametric variation as well as the dialectal variation in adjunct θ requirements.[8]

Given these considerations, let us assume a generalized version of the projection principle given in (12), which unifies argument θ requirements and adjunct θ requirements:[9]

(12) Generalized Projection Principle (GPP)
All the θ relations are represented at all levels in syntax.

The question now is how to explain the grammaticality judgement given by Jackendoff (1975) without appealing to Zubizarreta's (1982) generalization in (9). Here, I suggest an alternative analysis focusing on the lexical properties of predicates. Let us suppose that the sentence (8) is assigned a control structure[10] while the sentence (10) is assigned a raising structure. If we assume this, the D-structure representations of (8) and (10) could be as in (13a) and (13b), respectively.[11]

(13) a. John intentionally happened [PRO to be present when Bill arrived]
b. *e* is intentionally certain [John to win]

Given this assumption, we can explain the grammaticality judgements given by Jackendoff (1975) on (8) and by Lasnik and Fiengo (1974) on (10) in terms of the GPP. In (13a), the adjunct θ requirement imposed by *intentionally* is satisfied at D-structure since the subject NP, *John*, is in the matrix subject position at that level; however, in (13b), the adjunct θ requirement imposed by the subject oriented adverb is not satisfied at D-structure since there is no NP in the matrix subject position at that level. Hence, the representation (13b) is straightforwardly ruled out by the GPP.

---

8 This possibility was suggested to me by Mamoru Saito (personal communication).

9 Since adjunct predicates such as subject oriented adverbs behave like secondary predicates with respect to adjunct θ–role assignment, I assume that adjunct θ–role assignment takes place under the government configuration, following Williams (1980).

10 Perlmutter (1970) argues that *begin* can project a control structure as well as a raising structure. The reader is referred to Perlmutter (1970) for a detailed discussion of it.

11 Howard Lasnik and Mamoru Saito (personal communication) independently suggested this possibility to me.

The assumption that the verb, *happen*, can assign a θ–role to a subject NP as in (13a) seems to be quite plausible if we consider the fact that (14) has the interpretation in 1.

(14) John happened into the room
  1. 'John$_i$ arranged it so that he$_i$ came into the room'
  2. 'Events were such that John came into the room'
(Lillo-Martin (personal communication))

Happen in (14) clearly assigns a θ–role to the subject NP, *John*.

Let us consider the sentences (15a) and (15b) (= 8). The only difference between (15a) and (15b) is whether the subject oriented adverb, *intentionally*, is present or not.

(15) a. John happened to be present when Bill arrived
  1.' Events were such that John was present when Bill arrived'
  2.' John$_i$ arranged it so that he$_i$ was present when Bill arrived'

  b. John intentionally happened to be present when Bill arrived
  'John$_i$ intentionally arranged it so that he$_i$ was present when Bill arrived' (=8)

As Mona Anderson (personal communication) points out, (15a) is ambiguous between the interpretation 1 and the interpretation 2. Significantly, (15b) contrasts with (15a) in that it has only one interpretation, which is 'John$_i$ intentionally arranged it so that he$_i$ was present when Bill arrived.' The question to be raised is why (15a) has two different interpretations while (15b) has only one. In fact, this is what the alternative analysis appealing to the GPP can straightforwardly explain with the plausible assumption that, in sentences such as (15a), the verb, *happen*, projects a control structure as well as a raising structure. More specifically, the assumption is the following. If a sentence with *happen* means, 'Events are such that ...', then, it has a D-structure as in (16b), where the matrix subject position is a non–θ position. On the other hand, when a sentence with the verb, *happen*, means '... arrange(s) it so that ...', then, it has a D-structure as in (16a), where the matrix subject position is a θ–position.

(16)a. John happened [PRO to be present when Bill arrived]
  b. *e* happened [John to be present when Bill arrived]

Now, given the assumption above, let us examine the two possible D-structure representations for (15b) given in (17).

(17) a. John intentionally happened [PRO to be present when Bill arrived]
  b. *e* intentionally happened [John to be present when Bill arrived]

As is clear, the GPP is satisfied in (17a), since all the θ relations are represented. However, notice that the adjunct theta requirement is not satisfied in (17b), since there is no matrix subject for the subject oriented adverb, *intentionally*. As a result, (17b) is ruled out by the GPP, and it is correctly predicted that (15b) has only one interpretation: 'John$_i$ intentionally arranged it so that he$_i$ was present when Bill arrived.'

The argument presented above does not falsify the condition in (9) but it might eliminate its motivation. Remember that Zubizarreta (1982) motivates the condition in (9), (= 14a), crucially assuming that sentences such as (8) (= 15b) involve NP movement. To summarize, the discussion in this section suggests that we can eliminate the condition in (9). Furthermore, it suggests that we can maintain the GPP and, at the same time, we can explain the difference between (8) and (10). Given this, I will assume the GPP in the rest of this paper.[12]

3. Support for Kuroda's (1979) Dichotomy

The GPP in (12) together with adjunct predicates such as subject oriented adverbs can help us evaluate two traditional analyses of Japanese passives, Kuno's (1973) and Kuroda's (1965, 1979), with respect to their hypotheses on the subject positions of passive sentences.[13]

---

12 Yoshihisa Kitagawa (personal communication) suggests that there is another way to explain the data shown in this section, without appealing to the GPP. His alternative may be informally stated in the following way: subject oriented advervs are licensed by an agent θ–role of the predicate under the head-government holding between the predicates and those adverbs at LF. If this suggestion is correct, then it may suggest that the licensing condition on adjunct predicates should be subsumed under the principle of full interpretation rather than the projection principle. However, the example given in (i) seems to be a potential problem for Y. Kitagawa's (p. c.) alternative.

(i) Intentionally, John tried PRO to win

It seems that *intentionally* must lower in order to hold the head-government relationship with any predicate assigning an agent θ–role at LF in the case of the example (i). If the lowering of subject oriented adverbs is allowed, and if we assume Y. Kitagawa's (p. c.) alternative, then Lasnik and Fiengo's (1974) example is incorrectly predicted to be grammatical. Consider Lasnik and Fiengo's (1974) example again:

(ii) *John is intentionally certain to win (=9)
(Lasnik and Fiengo 1974:574)

This is because, in (ii), *intentionally* is allowed to lower to the embedded clause and is allowed to hold the head-government relationship with *win*. For this reason, I consider the GPP to be superior to Y. Kitagawa's (p. c.) alternative.

13 See Kuno (1973) and Kuroda (1965, 1979) for the details of their analyses of Japanese passives. I will not discuss their analyses in detail here.

3.1 Kuno's (1973) and Kuroda's (1965, 1979) Analyses

Examine the examples of *ni* passives in (18) again.

(18) a. John-ga Mary-ni nagur-are-ta (=3)
-nom. -by hit-passive-past
'John$_i$ was affected by Mary's hitting him$_i$'

b. John-ga Mary-ni kodomo-o nagur-are-ta
-nom. -by child-acc. hit-passive-past
'John$_i$ was affected by Mary's hitting a/his$_i$ child'

c. John-ga ame-ni hur-are-ta
-nom. rain-by fall-passive-past
'John$_i$ was affected by rain's falling (on him$_i$)'

A simplified representation of Kuno's (1973) structure for the direct passive (18a) is given in (19a). In his analysis, a direct passive sentence has a simplex structure and is derived by NP movement.

(19)a. [$_S$ John$_i$-ga [$_{VP}$ Mary-ni t_i nagur-are-ta]] (Kuno 1973)

Simplified representations of Kuno's (1973) structure for indirect passives (18b) and (18c) are given in (19b) and (19c), respectively. In his analysis, indirect passive sentences have a biclausal structure.

(19) b.[$_S$ John-ga [$_S$ Mary-ni musume-o nagur]-are-ta] (Kuno 1973)
c.[$_S$ John-ga [$_S$ ame-ni hur]-are-ta] (Kuno 1973)

Consider the instances of *ni yotte* passives, which Kuroda (1979) considers to be distinct from *ni* passives.

(20) a. John-ga Mary-ni yotte nagur-are-ta (=4)
-nom. -to due hit-passive-past
'John was hit by Mary'

b. John-ga Mary-ni yotte kodomo-o nagur-are-ta
-nom. -to due child-acc. hit-passive-past
'John's child was hit by Mary'

c. *John-ga ame-ni yotte hur-are-ta
-nom. rain-to due fall-passive-past

According to Kuroda's (1965, 1979) analysis, all instances of *ni* passive have a biclausal structure. Simplified representations of Kuroda's (1965,

1979) structure for the *ni* passive are shown in (21a), (21b), and (21c). Kuroda (1965) argues for a deletion analysis of the *ni* direct passive, which informally states that if the embedded sentence is transitive and the object or the indirect object in the embedded clause is coreferential with the matrix subject, then the object in the embedded clause is deleted. This operation is illustrated in (21a).

(21) a.[$_S$ John$_i$-ga [$_S$ Mary-ni John$_i$ nagur]-are-ta]
↓ (Kuroda 1965, 1979)
ø

However, if there is no object in the embedded clause which is coreferential with the matrix subject, or if the embedded sentence is not transitive, then the deletion operation does not take place. Thus, the indirect passives (18b) and (18c) are generated as in (21b) and (21c).

(21) b. [$_S$ John-ga [$_S$ Mary-ni musume-o nagur]-are-ta]
c. [$_S$ John-ga [$_S$ ame-ni hur]-are-ta] (Kuroda 1965, 1979)

Kuno's (1973) representations for the indirect passives (19b) and (19c) are identical to (21b) and (21c).

For the *ni yotte* passive, Kuroda (1979) argues that it has a simplex structure and it involves NP movement. A simplified representation of Kuroda's (1979) structure for the *ni yotte* passive (20a) is shown in (22).

(22) [$_S$ John$_i$-ga [$_{VP}$ Mary-ni yotte t_i nagur-are-ta]](Kuroda 1979)

Kuno's (1973) representation for the *ni* direct passive (19a) is the same as (22) except for *ni* vs. *ni yotte*.

3.2 The GPP and Two Analyses of Japanese Passives

As is clear, if we interpret Kuroda's (1979) analysis of Japanese passives in modern terms, the subject position of *ni* passives is uniformly a θ–position while that of *ni yotte* passives is a non-θ position. On the other hand, according to Kuno's (1973) analysis, the subject position of direct passives is a non–θ position, while that of indirect passives is a θ–position. If we assume Kuroda's (1979) dichotomy together with the GPP, then it is predicted that the subject oriented adverbs such as *orokanimo* 'stupidly' can modify the subject of the *ni* passive but not the subject of the *ni yotte* passive. On the other hand, if we take Kuno's (1973) analysis together with the GPP, we predict that those subject oriented adverbs can modify the subject NP of indirect passives, but not that of direct passives. Keeping this in mind, let us examine the *ni* passive sentences shown in (23).[14]

(23)
a. daitooryoo-ga orokanimo CIA-ni koros-are-ta
president-nom. stupidly -by kill-passive-past
'Stupidly, the president$_i$ was affected by the CIA's killing him$_i$'
(Kuroda 1979:325)

b. daitooryoo-ga orokanimo CIA-ni hisyo-o koros-are-ta
president-nom. stupidly -by secretary-acc. kill-passive-past
'Stupidly, the president$_i$ was affected by the CIA's killing a/his$_i$ secretary'

c. daitooryoo-ga orokanimo hisyo-ni sin-are-ta
president-nom. stupidly secretary-by die-passive-perfect-past
'Stupidly, the president$_i$ was affected by (his$_i$) secretary's dying'

The subject oriented adverb, *orokanimo*, modifies the subject NP in all the instances of *ni* passives shown in (23a), (23b), and (23c). Contrary to Kuno's (1973) analysis, there is no distinction between direct and indirect passives with respect to the subject oriented adverb's modification of the subject. This strongly supports Kuroda's (1979) analysis of *ni* passives with respect to the subject position, and tells us that the subject position of *ni* passives is uniformly a θ–position. This is so since only a subject NP in a θ–position can satisfy the adjunct θ requirement imposed by the subject oriented adverb.

Let us next consider (24), where instances of *ni yotte* passives with the subject oriented adverb, *orokanimo*, are provided.

(24)
a.??daitooryoo-ga orokanimo CIA-ni yotte koros-are-ta
president-nom. stupidly -to due kill-passive-past
'Stupidly, the president was killed by the CIA'(Kuroda 1979:326)

b.??daitooryoo-ga orokanimo CIA-ni yotte hisyo-o
president-nom. stupidly -to due secretary-acc.

14 (23a) and (24a) are cited from Kuroda (1979) with some modifications just for ease of exposition. (The judgements given in (23) and (24) are mine. Kuroda (1979) marks * for (24a). However, this does not mean that we disagree with each other on the grammaticality judgement. Kuroda (1979) does not grade his grammaticality judgements from *, ?*, ?? to OK.) Kuroda (1979) carefully shows the semantic difference between the *ni* passive and the *ni yotte* passive and explicitly argues that the subject of the *ni* passive is required to be the affectee but there is no such requirement on the subject of the *ni yotte* passive. Furthermore, he proposes his syntactic analysis of each passive construction on the basis of this difference. The purpose of my argument in the text is to solidify his conclusion.

koros-are-ta
kill-passive-past
'Stupidly, the president's secretary was killed by the CIA'

Kuroda's (1979) analysis of *ni yotte* passive is also supported by the data in (24). In the *ni yotte* passives (24a) and (24b), the subject oriented adverb, *orokanimo*, is not allowed to modify the subject NP. If we assume Kuroda's (1979) analysis of *ni yotte* passives, this fact is accounted for by the GPP in a straightforward manner. Since the subject position of a *ni yotte* passive is a non-Tposition, the adjunct θ requirement imposed by the subject oriented adverb cannot be satisfied at D-structure. Hence, both (29a) and (29b) violate the GPP.

To summarize, by making crucial use of the GPP, I presented supporting arguments for Kuroda's (1979) dichotomy with regard to the subject position of Japanese passives: The subject position of the *ni* passive is a θ–position while the subject position of the *ni yotte* passive is a non–θ position.[15]

4. Further Support for Kuroda's (1979) Dichotomy

In this section, I will provide further support for Kuroda's (1979) dichotomy by presenting additional evidence from the passivization of verb phrase idioms.

Kuroda's (1979) hypothesis is confirmed by passivization of verb phrase idioms. Let us examine the instances of *ni* passive given in (25):

(25) a. *chuui-ga John-ni haraw-are-ta
heed-nom. -by pay-passive-past
'Heed$_i$ was affected by John's paying it$_i$'

b. *kechi-ga John-ni tsuker-are-ta
fault-nom. -by attach-passive-past
'Fault$_i$ was affected by John's attaching it$_i$'

Passivization of verb phrase idioms is impossible in *ni* passives as shown in (25a) and (25b).[16] (25a) is grammatical with the irrelevant interpretation: Heed was paid to John. This is also true of (25b). The irrelevant interpretation of (25b) is: Fault was found with John. Notice that the *ni*

---

15 See Hoshi (1991) for more discussion on related topics.

16 Harada (1977) claimed that verb phrase idioms can be passivized in Japanese. On the other hand, Shigeru Miyagawa (personal communication) maintained that verb phrase idioms cannot be passivized in Japanese. This difference seems to come from the fact that they did not distinguish the *ni* passive from the *ni yotte* passive with respect to their passivizability. I argue that Harada's (1977) claim is correct for the *ni yotte* passive, while Miyagawa's (p. c.) claim is correct for the *ni* passive, as will become clear in the text.

phrase can not be interpreted as an agent phrase in both (25a) and (25b). Once we assume that the passive morpheme, *(r)are*, imposes a selectional restriction on the subject NP in *ni* passives, we can explain the ungrammaticality of (25). The noun phrase in the verb phrase idioms *chuui* 'heed' or *keri* 'fault' cannot be an affectee, and, hence, cannot satisfy the selectional restriction imposed by the passive morpheme.

Next, let us examine the *ni yotte* passive sentences in (26).

(26)a. chuui-ga John-ni yotte haraw-are-ta
-nom. -to due pay-passive-past
'Heed was paid by John'

b. kechi-ga John-ni yotte tsuker-are-ta
fault-nom. -to due attach-passive-past
'lit.Fault was attached by John(=The fault was found by John)'

There is a sharp contrast between the *ni* passive and the *ni yotte* passive in the passivizability of verb phrase idioms. The passivization of verb phrase idioms is possible in the case of the *ni yotte* passive. If the passive morpheme, *(r)are*, does not impose any selectional restriction in the *ni yotte* passive, we can correctly explain the grammaticality of (26). Furthermore, the data in (26) constitute strong evidence for Kuroda's (1979) NP movement analysis of the *ni yotte* passive. If we assume that the selectional restriction discussed above is to be explained under the mechanism of θ–role assignment, then the contrast between (25) and (26) confirms Kuroda's dichotomy: The subject position of the *ni* passive is a θ–position but the subject position of the *ni yotte* passive is a non–θ position. The passive morpheme, *(r)are*, assigns a θ–role to the subject NP in the *ni* passive but not in the *ni yotte* passive.

5. A Potential Problem for Kuroda's (1965, 1979) Analysis and a Solution

I have strongly supported Kuroda's (1965, 1979) analysis of Japanese passives, but it might have at least one potential problem concerning the *ni* direct passive. A simplified representation of Kuroda's (1965, 1979) structure for the *ni* direct passive is given in (27a), and simplified representations of his structure for the *ni* indirect passives are given in (27b) and (27c).

(27) a. $John_i$-ga $[_S$ Mary-ni $John_i$-o nagur]-are-ta (=21)
↓
ø

b. John-ga $[_S$ Mary-ni kodomo-o nagur]-are-ta

c. John-ga [$_S$ ame-ni hur]-are-ta(Kuroda 1965, 1979)

If we interpret Kuroda's (1965, 1979) deletion analysis of the *ni* direct passive in modern terms, an empty category should exist in the object or indirect object position in the embedded clause. Then, a question naturally arises with respect to the nature of this empty category.

Saito (1982) argues that the empty category in the *ni* direct passive is an NP trace, and, thus, argues for Kuno's (1973) movement analysis of this type of passive. In order to illustrate Saito's (1982) argument, I need to first discuss Harada's (1973) formulation of the double-*o* constraint given in (28).[17]

(28) [Double-*o* Constraint]

A derivation is marked as ill-formed if it terminates in a surface structure which contains two occurrences of NPs marked with *o* [= accusative case] both of which are immediately dominated by the same VP node.(Harada 1973:138)

Given the double-*o* constraint in (28), we can correctly explain the examples in (29).

(29)

a. Mary-ga John-o/ni aruk-ase-ta
-nom. -acc./dat. walk-causative-past
'Mary made/let John walk'

b. Mary-ga John-*o/ni hon-o yom-ase-ta
-nom. -*acc./dat. book-acc. read-causative-past
'Mary made John read a book'

c. kono hon wa [$_S$ Mary-ga John-*o/ni *e* yom-ase-ta]
this book top. -nom. -*acc./dat. read-causative-past
'This book, Mary made John read it'

In the causative construction, the causee can appear with an accusative case marker, *o*, or a dative case marker, *ni*. Since there is at most only one NP with accusative case in (29a), the double-*o* constraint is irrelevant. Hence, the causee in (29a) can be marked by either accusative case or dative case. However, the double-*o* constraint prevents the causee from being marked with accusative case in (29b) since there is another NP, *hon* 'book', marked with accusative case. Therefore, the causee must be marked with dative case in this example. The double-*o* constraint prevents the causee from being marked with accusative case also in (29c) since the empty category in (29c) is either a trace left behind by the movement of the topic NP, *kono hon* 'this

17 Shibatani (1973) first noticed the existence of this surface structure constraint in Japanese.

book', or a *pro*. Since both of these empty categories require Case (Saito 1985) and since the double-*o* constraint applies even when one of the two accusative NPs is phonologically null (Harada 1973, Poser 1981, Saito 1982), the causee in (29c) cannot be marked with accusative case but it must be marked with dative case.

Then, let us examine the sentence in (30).[18]

(30)
Mary-ga John$_i$-o/ni [PRO$_i$ Tom-ni *e* sikar-are]-sase-ta
-nom. -acc./dat. [-by scold-passive]-causative-past
'Mary made John be scolded by Tom'(Saito 1982:92)

In (30), a direct passive sentence appears as a complement of the causative morpheme, *(s)ase*, and, crucially, the causee, *John*, can take accusative case (as well as dative case). If the empty category in (30) receives abstract accusative Case, then the causee should not be marked with accusative case due to the double-*o* constraint. From this, Saito (1982) draws the conclusion that the empty category is an NP trace, which does not require Case, and he argues that NP movement is involved in the *ni* direct passive.[19] [20]

---

[18] (30) is cited from Saito (1982) with some modifications just for ease of exposition.

[19] As Yasuo Ishii (personal communication) and Hoshi (1991) point out, Saito's (1982) argument is strengthened if we can confirm one of his assumptions, i.e. the existence of an empty category *e* in (30). It is because there is a possibility that there would be no violation of the double-*o* constraint in (30) if there were no empty category in the complement position of *sikar(u)* 'scold'. If this is the case, Saito's (1982) argument does not prove the existence of an NP trace in the *ni* direct passive. However, his argument is justified in the following grammatical sentence:

(i)
John$_i$-ga gakusei$_j$-o [PRO$_j$ Tom-ni *e* san-nin sikar-are]-sase-ta
-nom.student-acc. [-by 3-cl. scold-PASS]-CAUSE-past
'John made three students be scolded by Tom'

The numeral quantifier, *san-nin*, modifies *gakusei*$_j$ 'student' or PRO$_j$. If we adopt Miyagawa's (1988, 1989) theory of numeral quantifiers, this fact cannot be explained unless we assume an empty category, i.e. an NP trace, in the complement position of *sikar(u)* in (i). See Miyagawa (1988, 1989) for a detailed discussion of numeral quantifiers in Japanese.

[20] As Hajime Hoji (personal communication) and Hoshi (1991) point out, the argument in the text does not prove that NP movement is always involved in *ni* direct passives in Japanese. Hence, that argument does not falsify Kitagawa's (1986, 1991) structure for *ni* direct passives given below.

(i) John$_i$-ga [Mary-ni pro$_i$ nagur]-are-ta
-nom. [-by hit]-passive-past
'John$_i$ was affected by Mary's hitting him$_i$'(Kitagawa 1986, 1991)

However, it is not clear to me that Kitagawa's (1986, 1991) representation indeed exists for *ni* direct passives. Consider the example given in (ii). An overt pronoun, *kare* 'he', cannot appear in that type of passive. I owe this observation to Mamoru Saito (personal

Saito's (1982) argument above could raise a potential problem for Kuroda's (1965, 1979) analysis of the *ni* direct passive since it is not clear how an NP trace can be created in the *ni* direct passive in Kuroda's (1965, 1979) analysis. Since both Kuroda's (1965, 1979) and Saito's (1982) proposals seem to be well-founded, I will speculate on a way to reconcile those two proposals, adopting Saito and Murasugi's (1989) PRO movement theory.[21] Crucially, I assume Fukui's (1986) and Fukui and Speas's (1986) proposal shown in (31).[22]

(31) The SPEC position of a lexical category is ungoverned.
(Fukui 1986:110 - 115; Fukui and Speas 1986:148 - 150)

For the *ni* direct passive (32), I suggest the D-structure representation representation (33a) and the S-structure or LF representation (33b).

---

communication).

(ii) *John$_i$-ga Mary-ni kare$_i$-o nagur-are-ta
-nom. -by him$_i$-acc. hit-passive-past
'John$_i$ was affected by Mary's hitting him$_i$'(Saito (p. c.))

21 The crucial proposal that VP internal movement of PRO is involved in the passive construction is adopted from Saito and Murasugi (1989). They motivate the VP internal movement of PRO for *be* passive on the basis of examples such as (i).

(i) a. Chosen by the American people, he was
b. [Chosen t_i by the American people]$_j$, he$_i$ was t_j
(Saito and Murasugi 1989)

(ib) is a widely assumed S-structure representation for (ia). Given Fiengo's (1977) proper binding condition, (ib) should be in violation of that condition at S-structure since the trace left behind by the movement of the NP, *he*, is not bound. However, (ia) is grammatical. In order to solve this problem, Saito and Murasugi (1989) propose the S-structure representation given in (ii).

(ii) [PRO$_i$ chosen t_i by the American people]$_j$, he$_i$ was t_j (S-structure) (Saito and Murasugi 1989)

In (ii), the trace is bound by PRO. Therefore, the representation does not violate the proper binding condition.

However, it should be noted that there is a crucial difference between my analysis of the *ni* direct passive and Saito and Murasugi's (1989) analysis of the *be* passive. In my analysis, the subject NP in the *ni* direct passive is licensed by the θ–role assigned by the passive morpheme, *(r)are*. However, Saito and Murasugi (1989) propose, following a suggestion by David Lebeaux, that the subject NP in the *be* passive (ia) is licensed by predication.

22 Here, I am interpreting Fukui's (1986) and Fukui and Speas's (1986) proposal, adopting 'uniform bar level X' Theory,' according to which the number of bars for the maximal projection is uniform among categories. Fukui (1986) and Fukui and Speas (1986) make their proposal on the basis of 'non-uniform bar level X' Theory.' Nemoto (1992) argues for this proposal, by showing that PRO is in the SPEC position of VP in the complement of the control predicate in Japanese.

(32) John-ga Mary-ni nagur-are-ta (= 4, 20)
-nom. -by hit-passive-past
'John$_i$ was affected by Mary's hitting him$_i$'

(33) a. John [$_{VP}$ Mary PRO nagur] are ta (D-S)

b. John$_i$-ga [$_{VP}$ PRO$_i$ Mary-ni t_i nagur] are ta (S-S or LF)

According to this analysis, the matrix subject is base-generated in the position where it receives a θ–role, as Kuroda (1965, 1979) proposes. The NP trace argued for in Saito (1982), on the other hand, is not due to the NP movement of the subject itself but it is created by the movement of PRO. The PRO is base-generated in the complement position of the embedded verb, and is forced to move from that position into the VP SPEC position in order to satisfy Binding Conditions A and B (Chomsky 1981).[23] According to this analysis, (30), in which the causee is marked with an accusative case, is correctly predicted to be grammatical, since neither the NP trace nor the PRO has accusative Case.

In this paper, I have suggested the generalized projection principle (GPP) given in (12), which incorporates argument θ requirements and adjunct θ requirements in a unified way. By making crucial use of this principle, I have argued for Kuroda's (1979) proposal that the subject position of *ni*

23 Kuno (1973) and N. A. McCawley (1972) independently observed the following fact:

(i) John$_i$-ga Mary$_j$-ni zibun$_{i/*j}$-no uti-de koros-are-ta
-nom. -by self-gen. house-in kill-pass.-past
'John$_i$ was affected by Mary$_j$'s killing him$_i$ in self$_{i/*j}$'s house'

(Kuno 1973:303)

As is shown, *John*$_i$ is the only possible antecedent of the so-called long distance subject oriented anaphor *zibun* in (i). This fact has been a potential problem for Kuroda's (1979) analysis of *ni* direct passives, since *Mary*$_j$ is also in the subject position as *John*$_i$ is in his analysis. Then, let us look at the simplified representation of the analysis proposed in the text:

(ii) John$_i$-ga [$_{VP}$ PRO$_i$ [$_{V'}$ Mary-ni zibun-no uti-de koros]] are ta

Given the assumption that the VP SPEC position counts as the subject position for *zibun*, we can correctly account for the fact above. This is because *John*$_i$ and PRO$_i$ are in the subject position but *Mary*$_j$ is not in (ii). Hence, *zibun* takes either *John*$_i$ or PRO$_i$ as its antecedent. As a result, native speakers of Japanese perceive *John*$_i$ to be the only antecedent of *zibun* in *ni* direct passives such as (i). This argument, in turn, seems to have significant implications: the passive morpheme *(r)are* of *ni* direct passives is a control predicate but it also makes the embedded verb a raising predicate; for this reason, *Mary*$_j$ is demoted in (ii) and PRO$_i$ is allowed to move into the VP SPEC position to satisfy Binding Conditions A and B and is allowed to be controlled there. Then, a problem arises as to how the passive morpheme *(r)are* functions in a dual fashion mentioned above. See Hoshi (1991) for an attempt to solve this problem.

passives is a θ–position while that of *ni yotte* passives is a non–θ position. As further supporting evidence for Kuroda's (1979) θ subject vs. non–θ subject dichotomy, I have shown that verb phrase idioms resist *ni* passivization but they do not resist *ni yotte* passivization. Last, relying on Fukui's (1986) and Fukui and Speas's (1986) proposal, I have suggested a way to reconcile Kuroda's proposal with Saito's (1982) argument for the existence of an NP trace in *ni* direct passives. Specifically, I have proposed that, in the *ni* direct passive, the subject is in a θ–position and an NP trace is created by the movement of PRO, which is triggered by Binding Conditions A and B.[24]

Notes

* This is a shortened version of the paper, "The Generalized Projection Principle and Its Implications for Passive Constructions", which I presented at the Southern California Japanese/Korean Linguistics Conference. The full version of the paper will appear in *Journal of Japanese Linguistics*: Volume 13.

I am very grateful to Mona Anderson, Hajime Hoji, Yoshihisa Kitagawa, S.-Y. Kuroda, Howard Lasnik, Diane Lillo-Martin, Shigeru Miyagawa, and especially to Mamoru Saito for their valuable comments and suggestions. Special thanks go to Jun Abe, Yasuo Ishii, Naoko Nemoto, Javier Ormazabal, and Myriam Uribe-Etxebarria for the discussion which I have had with them. Needless to say, all the shortcomings are mine.

References

Chomsky, Noam. 1981. Lectures on Government and Binding. Dordrecht: Foris.

Chomsky, Noam. 1986. Knowledge of Language: Its Nature, Origins, and Use. New York: Praeger.

Fiengo, Robert. 1977. On Trace Theory. LI. 17.35-61.

Fukui, Naoki. 1986. A Theory of Category Projection and Its Application. Doctoral dissertation. MIT.

Fukui, Naoki and Margaret Speas. (1986) Specifiers and Projection. MIT Working Papers in Linguistics 8, ed. by N. Fukui, T. R. Rapoport, and E. Sagey, 128-172. MIT.

Harada, Shin-Ichi. 1973. Counter Equi NP Deletion. Annual Bulletin 7.113-147. Research Institute of Logopedics and Phoniatrics, University of Tokyo.

[24] The reader is referred to Hoshi (1991) for further discussion and consequences of the proposed analysis.

Harada, Shin-Ichi. 1977. Nihongo ni henkei wa hituyoo da. Gengo 6. 88-95.

Hoshi, Hiroto. 1991. The Role of PRO and Multiple Object Structures in Passive Constructions in Japanese. Ms. University of Connecticut.

Hoshi, Hiroto. to appear. The Generalized Projection Principle and Its Implications for Passive Constructions. Journal of Japanese Linguistics 13.

Howard, Irwin and Agnes M. Niyekawa-Howard. 1976. Passivization. Japanese Generative Grammar: Syntax and Semantics 5, ed. by M. Shibatani, 201-237. New York: Academic Press.

Jackendoff, Ray. 1972. Semantics in Generative Grammar. Cambridge, Massachusetts: MIT Press.

Jackendoff, Ray. 1975. Tough and the Trace Theory of Movement Rule. LI. 6.436-446.

Kitagawa, Yoshihisa. 1986. Subjects in Japanese and English. Doctoral dissertation, University of Massachusetts.

Kitagawa, Yoshihisa. 1991. De-Passivization. Workshop on Japanese Syntax, University of Rochester.

Kubo, Miori. 1990. Japanese Passives. Ms. MIT.

Kuno, Susumu. 1973. The Structure of the Japanese Language. Cambridge, Massachusetts: MIT Press.

Kuno, Susumu. 1983. Shin-Nihon Bunpoo Kenkyuu. Tokyo: Taisyuukan. Kuno, Susumu. 1986. Ukemi Bun-no Imi: Kuroda Setu-no Sai-hihan. Nihongogaku 5.70-87.

Kuroda, Sige-Yuki. 1965. Generative Grammatical Studies in the Japanese Language. Doctoral dissertation, MIT.

Kuroda, Sige-Yuki. 1979. On Japanese Passives. Exploration in Linguistics: Papers in Honor of Kazuko Inoue, ed. by G. Bedell, E. Kobayashi, and M. Muraki, 305-347. Tokyo: Kenkyuusya.

Lasnik, Howard and Robert Fiengo. 1974. Complement Object Deletion. Linguistic Inquiry 5.535-571.

Miyagawa, Shigeru. 1988. Theme Subjects and Numeral Quantifiers. Proceedings of Japanese Syntax Workshop, ed. by W. Tawa and M. Nakayama, 132-167. Connecticut College.

Miyagawa, Shigeru. 1989. Structure and Case Marking in Japanese: Syntax and Semantics 22. New York: Academic Press.

Nemoto, Naoko. 1992. Scrambling and Conditions on A-Movement. WCCFL X.349-359.

Perlmutter, David. 1970. The Two Verbs *Begin*. Readings in English Transformational Grammar, ed. by R. A. Jacobs and P. S. Rosembaum, 107-119, Waltham, Massachusetts: Ginn and Company.

Poser, William. 1981. The 'Double-*o* Constraint': Evidence for a Direct Object Relation in Japanese. Ms. MIT.

Saito, Mamoru. 1982. Case Marking in Japanese: A Preliminary Study. Ms. MIT.

Saito, Mamoru. 1985. Some Asymmetries in Japanese and Their Theoretical Implications. Doctoral dissertation, MIT.

Saito, Mamoru and Keiko Murasugi. 1989. N'-deletion in Japanese and the DP Hypothesis. Annual LSA meeting.

Shibatani, Masayoshi. 1973 Semantics of Japanese Causativization. Foundations of Language 9.327-373.

Terada, Michiko. 1990. Incorporation and Argument Structure in Japanese. Doctoral dissertation, University of Massachusetts.

Williams, Edwin. 1980. Predication. Linguistic Inquiry 11.203-238.

Zubizarreta, Maria Luisa. 1982. On the Relationship of the Lexicon and Syntax. Doctoral dissertation, MIT.

On Certain Differences in Comparative Deletion Between English and Japanese

YASUO ISHII
Keio University

1. Introduction

This paper discusses "comparative deletion" in English and Japanese, as illustrated in (1) and (2).[1]

(1) John bought more books than Mary bought ___
(2) Taroo-wa [Hanako-ga ___ katta yori(-mo)] takusan(-no)
-top -nom bought than many -gen
hon -o katta
book-acc bought
(Taroo bought more books than Hanako bought ___)

Chomsky (1977) argues that comparative deletion in English involves *wh*-movement, or in the current terminology, movement of an operator into COMP (or [Spec, CP]) in the *than*-clause. This movement is unbounded and obeys Subjacency.[2]

---

1 The term "deletion" should not be taken literally here. I use "comparative deletion" only as a descriptive term to refer to the construction in question without any theoretical implication. In fact, an analysis based on empty operator movement, which I employ here, claims that there is no deletion involved in the technical sense of the term. See Bresnan (1975) for an analysis of "comparative deletion" based on deletion.

2 (i) shows that the dependency in comparative deletion is unbounded, and (ii) and (iii) show that it obeys Subjacency. (ii) is a case of the Complex NP Constraint, and (iii) is a

Kikuchi (1989) argues that Japanese comparative deletion is also derived by empty operator movement. He shows, quite convincingly, that the dependency involved in comparative deletion is unbounded, as illustrated in (3), and obeys Subjacency, as in (4) and (5). ((4) illustrates the Complex NP Constraint, and (5) illustrates the adjunct constraint.)

(3) [[[John-ga *e* yonda to] iwareteiru to] minna -ga
-nom read that is said that everyone-nom
omotteiru yori-mo] Mary-wa takusan hon-o yondeita
think than -top many book-acc has read
(*Lit.* Mary has read more books than everyone thinks that it is said that John read)

(4) *[[sono tukue-de e_i *e* yondeita] hito -o_i John-ga
that table-on was reading person-acc -nom
nagutta yori-mo] Paul-wa takusan hon -o yondeita
hit than -top many book-acc has read
(*Lit.* Paul read more books than John hit a person who was reading at the table)

(5) *[[John-ga *e* yondeita tokini] zisin -ga okita
-nom was reading when earthquake-nom happened
yori-mo] Paul-wa harukani takusanno hon-o yondeita
than -top far many book-acc has read
(*Lit.* Paul has read more books than an earthquake happened when John was reading) (Kikuchi 1989)

Thus, comparative deletion in English and Japanese involves empty operator movement. As we will see, however, there are two important differences between English and Japanese comparative deletion. These differences are absent in comparative sentences that do not involve operator-movement (such as *John bought more books than Mary*), and therefore the differences must be closely related to the empty operator movement. On the other hand, it is hard to argue that language-particular properties associated with an invisible element like an empty operator are learned from experience in the course of language acquisition. Therefore, I want to pursue the possibility that these differences come from other more "visible" language-particular properties of the two languages.

---

case of the *wh*-island constraint.

(i) Mary isn't taller than [John believes [that Bill claimed [that she was *e* five years ago]]]

(ii) *Mary isn't taller than [John believes [Bill's claim [that she was *e* five years ago]]]

(iii) *Mary isn't taller than [I wonder [whether she was *e* five years ago]] (cf. Chomsky 1977:87)

See Chomsky (1977, 1980, 1981) and Browning (1987) for further details on *wh*-movement or empty operator movement and a range of constructions which are analyzed as involving *wh*-movement or empty operator movement.

2. Quantifier Float and Comparative Deletion

The first difference between English and Japanese comparative deletion constructions is that the distribution of the gap in comparative deletion is more limited in Japanese. It cannot occur in the subject position of an "individual-level predicate" as in (6), while (7) and (8) with "stage-level predicates" are more acceptable.[3] (Individual-level predicates are those which describe a permanent property of an individual, for example, intelligence. I borrow this terminology from Carlson (1977), Kratzer (1988), and Diesing (1988).)

(6) **The subject of an individual-level predicate:**
?*kono kurasu-dewa ___ eigo -ga umai yori(-mo)
this class -in English-nom good than
takusan-no hito -ga huransugo-ga umai
many -gen people-nom French -nom good
(In this class, more people are good at French than are good at English)

(7) **The subject of a stage-level predicate (transitive):**
(??)kinoo -no kaigi -dewa ___ eigo -o hanasita
yesterday -gen meeting-at English-acc spoke
yori(-mo) takusan-no hito -ga huransugo-o hanasita
than many -gen people-nom French -acc spoke
(At yesterday's meeting, more people spoke French than spoke English)

(8) **The subject of a stage-level predicate (unaccusative):**
___ kinoo kita yori zutto takusan(-no) sensei -ga kyoo kita
yesterday came than much many -gen teacher-nom today came
(A lot more teachers came today than came yesterday)

This kind of restriction does not exist in English. (9), which contains an individual-level predicate, is as acceptable as (10), which contains a stage-level predicate.

(9) More people are good at French than ___ are good at English
(10) More people spoke French today than ___ spoke English yesterday

Also, this restriction is unique to comparative deletion. As shown in (11) and (12), *than* and *yori* in Japanese can take a single NP instead of a clause.

---

3 The facts are more or less simplified here, due to lack of space. For example, there seems to be some contrast in acceptability between (7) and (8) as well. In this paper, however, I only concentrate on the contrast found between the subject of individual-level predicates and the subject of stage-level predicates. See Ishii (1991) for finer-grained descriptions and explanations of contrasts in acceptability among various kinds of noun phrases.

(11) John studied harder than Mary
(12) John-wa Mary-yori issyookenmei benkyoo-sita
-top -than hard studied
(John studied harder than Mary)

This construction, either in English or in Japanese, does not involve empty operator movement. *Than* and *yori* serve as prepositions rather than complementizers.[4] Let us call this construction the "NP-comparative".

Returning to the contrast between stage-level predicates and individual-level predicates, NP-comparatives do not exhibit such contrasts, as shown in (13)-(14).

(13) kono kurasu-wa ano kurasu-yori takusan-no hito -ga
this class -top that class -than many -gen people-nom
huransugo-ga umai (individual-level predicate)
French -nom good
(More people are good at French in this class than in that class)
(14) kono kurasu-wa ano kurasu-yori takusan-no hito -ga
this class -top that class -than many -gen people-nom
huransugo-o hanasita (stage-level predicate)
French -acc spoke
(More people spoke French in this class than in that class)

This suggests that the restriction is closely related to some aspects of operator movement rather than the nature of comparative constructions themselves.

Interestingly, this kind of restriction is also observed with numeral quantifiers. Numeral quantifiers in Japanese cannot "float" out of the subject noun phrase of individual-level predicates, as observed in Tateishi (1989).[5]

(15) ?*gakusei-ga san-nin eigo -ga umai (CL=classifier)
student-nom 3 -CL English-nom good
(Three students are good at English)
(16) gakusei-ga san-nin eigo -o hanasita
student-nom 3-CL English-acc spoke
(Three students spoke English)

---

4 See Hankamer (1973) for discussions of *than* as a preposition.

5 Here, I am neutral as to whether floating quantifiers are transformationally derived or not. I am only using the term "floating" for descriptive purposes without any theoretical implication. See Miyagawa (1989), Ueda (1986), and the references cited there for previous analyses of floating quantifiers in Japanese.

(17) a. san-nin-no gakusei-ga eigo -ga umai
3 -CL -gen student-nom English-nom good
(Three students are good at English)
b. Three students are good at English

In (15), the floating quantifier is linked to the subject of an individual-level predicate, whereas the floating quantifier in (16) is linked to the subject of a stage-level predicate. (17a) indicates that the subject of an individual-level predicate can contain a numeral quantifier, when it is not floated. English expressions like *three students* can also be the subject of an individual-level predicate, as shown in (17b).

As Lasnik and Fiengo (1974) and Carlson (1977) point out, bare plurals (indefinite plural NPs) occurring in the subject position of individual-level predicates have only a generic interpretation and lack an existential interpretation.

(18) Whales are swimming (existential)
(19) Whales are intelligent (generic)

While the subject of individual-level predicates allow only the generic reading, as in (19), the subject of stage-level predicates allow the existential reading as well as the generic reading, as in (20).

(20) a. New books are available at Albion.
b. New books are (usually) available at large bookstores.

This is also the case in Japanese. The stage-level predicate ***aru*** (to exist) in (21) allows its subject to be either existential as in (21a) or generic as in (21b), while the individual-level predicate *takai* (expensive) in (22) allows only the generic reading.

(21) a. atarasii hon -ga Albion-ni aru (koto)
new book-nom -at be fact
(There are new books at the Albion bookstore)
b. atarasii hon -ga (yoku) ookii hon-ya -ni aru (koto)
new book-nom often big bookstore-at be fact
(New books are (usually) at large bookstores)
(22) atarasii hon -ga totemo takai (koto)
new book-nom very high fact
(New books are very expensive)
--does not mean "There are very expensive new books"

When a floating quantifier is linked to the subject of a stage-level predicate, the NP is necessarily understood to be existential.

(23) atarasii hon -ga san-satu ookii hon'ya -ni aru (koto)
new book-nom 3 -CL big bookstore-at be fact
(There are three new books at a large bookstore)
--does not mean "If there are three books, they are at a large bookstore"

Thus, floating quantifiers must be linked to an existential indefinite. Floating quantifiers cannot be linked to the subject of individual-level predicates, because the subject cannot be existential.

Returning to comparative deletion, we can capture the similarities between quantifier float and comparative deletion, if the operator in comparative deletion is a floated quantifier. In comparative deletion, the indefinite NP to be construed with the floating quantifier (as an operator in this case) is an empty indefinite. The existence of such empty indefinites can be supported by examples like (24).

(24) a. John-wa hon -o san-satu katta
-top book-acc 3 -CL bought
(John bought three books)
b. John-wa *e* san-satu katta
-top 3 -CL bought
(John bought three (books, magazines, etc.))

The object position of (24a) is occupied by *hon-o* ("books-acc"), which is understood to be indefinite, and the floating quantifier *san-satu* ("three-CL") is interpreted as linked to this indefinite object. There is no overt phrase occupying the object position of (24b). In this sentence, *san-satu* ("three-CL") can be interpreted as modifying any kind of object as long as it can be counted with this classifier *satu*. This suggests that the object position of (24b) is occupied by an empty indefinite (marked by *e* above), which is interpreted as existential.

I have so far argued that the operator involved in comparative deletion in Japanese is a floating quantifier. The next question to raise is why the comparative operator is (or has to be) a floating quantifier in Japanese.

Let us consider the syntactic category of the empty operator. Since comparative deletion compares quantities, it is not unreasonable to assume that the operator belongs to quantificational expressions. Now let us assume (25).

(25) a. The empty operator in comparative deletion is a QP.
b. What constitutes a QP differs from language to language.

Hence, the empty operator in comparative deletion has whatever properties the QPs in that language have. Let us consider what constitutes a QP in English and Japanese.

Abney (1987) argues that expressions like *many students* in English are QPs, and have the structure as in (26), in which *many* is the head of QP.

(26) $[_{QP}[_{Q}$ many$][_{NP}$ students$]]$ (Abney 1987)

This kind of expression can occur in the subject position of an individual-level predicate as well as of a stage-level predicate, as in (27).

(27) a. Many students are angry (stage-level)
b. Many students are intelligent (individual-level)

In Japanese, on the other hand, expressions like *takusan-no gakusei* (*many students*) in (28) do not belong to QP unlike *many students* in English.

(28) takusan-no gakusei
many -gen student
(many students)

Even if expressions like *takusan-no* ("many/much-gen") belong to Q, *takusan-no gakusei* ("many-gen students") is not a QP, because Japanese is a head-final language, and the Q would have to follow the NP, as pointed out in Murasugi (1991). Instead, however, Japanese has floating quantifiers (quantifiers which are outside of the NP they are linked to), which project QP. Hence, the empty operator is moved from the position of a floating quantifier in Japanese. Thus, children look at what overt expressions can form a QP in the language that they are acquiring in order to determine the type of empty operators that are moved in comparative deletion in that language.

In sum, I have argued that comparative deletion can be universally characterized as movement of a QP operator into [Spec, CP]. In English, this QP operator corresponds to expressions like *many* N and *much* N, while in Japanese, it corresponds to numeral floating quantifiers. Because the operator involved in comparative deletion in Japanese is an (abstract) floating quantifier, it exhibits those properties which are shared by quantifier float. Thus, comparative deletion is degraded when the gap occurs in the subject position of an individual-level predicate. On the other hand, English comparative deletion, not involving quantifier float, does not exhibit such restrictions.

3. Comparative Deletion with Adjectives

A second difference between the two languages is that comparative deletion in Japanese cannot compare adjectives in general as shown in (30).[6]

---

6 There are apparent counterexamples to this generalization, to which I will return in Section 4.

Notice that in all the examples we have seen up to this point, comparison is made by number or quantity, and the quantifier *takusan* ("many/much"), which is not an adjective, is used, as in (29). English, on the other hand, does not have such a restriction. (31) and (32) are equally acceptable.

(29) Taroo -wa [Hanako-ga ___ katta yori(-mo)] takusan(-no)
-top -nom bought than many -gen
kasa -o katta
umbrella-acc bought
(John bought more umbrellas than Mary bought ___)

(30) ?*Taroo-wa [Hanako-ga ___ katta yori(-mo)] nagai kasa -o
-top -nom bought than long umbrella-acc
katta
bought
(John bought a longer umbrella than Mary bought ___)

(31) John bought more umbrellas than Mary bought ___

(32) John bought a longer umbrella than Mary bought ___

Again, this kind of restriction seems to be unique to comparative deletion, and is not observed in NP-comparatives, as can be seen from the acceptable (33).

(33) Taroo-wa Hanako yori(-mo) nagai kasa -o katta
-top than long umbrella-acc bought
(Taroo bought a longer umbrella than Hanako)

I propose that this difference between English and Japanese is related to a more general difference in comparatives between the two languages: English has a special morphology for comparatives, while Japanese does not. In English, comparative adjectives are either suffixed with *-er* or preceded by *more*, while Japanese adjectives show up in the same forms in comparatives as in non-comparative sentences. This is illustrated in (34) and (35).

(34) a. John is tall*er* than Mary
b. John is *more* intelligent than Mary

(35) John-wa Mary-yori kasikoi
-top -than clever
(John is cleverer than Mary)
Cf. John-wa kasikoi
-top clever
(John is clever)

As for English, Abney (1987) argues that comparative and superlative adjectives are quantifiers. As one of his arguments, he observes that comparative and superlative adjectives always appear in the leftmost position among prenominal adjectives, as illustrated below.[7]

(36)			
	a.	a big fancy car	the big fancy car
	b.	*a big fancier car	*the big fanciest car
	c.	a fancier big car	the fanciest big car
			(Abney 1987:340)

The lack of comparative morphology in Japanese suggests that adjectives can never be quantificational in this language. I would like to propose an analysis of comparative deletion in English and Japanese based on this idea. As a first approximation, I claim that the *than*-clause (or *yori*-clause) in comparative deletion requires a "quantificational" expression in the matrix sentence, while the *than*-clause (or *yori*-clause) in NP-comparatives does not. Let us refine this idea further.

As Chomsky (1977, 1980, 1981) and Browning (1987) point out, empty operator movement into [Spec, CP] changes the clause (CP) into a one-place predicate. This predicate is licensed only when it has its "subject". The "subject" must be of an appropriate category, or more precisely, of the same category as the trace of the empty operator. In the case of comparative deletion, I have argued earlier that the operator is a QP. Hence, only a QP can license the predicate CP in comparative deletion. Take (37) as an example. In (37), movement of the operator (indicated by OP) makes the embedded CP a one-place predicate, and the QP projected by *longer* can correctly license the CP predicate.[8]

(37) John bought a $[_{QP}[_{Q}$longer] umbrella] $[_{CP}OP_i$ than [Mary bought t_i]]

Let us turn to Japanese. We have seen that Japanese has no overt comparative morpheme corresponding to *-er/more*. Suppose that Japanese has no covert morpheme for this meaning, either. Then Japanese adjectives can never be (turned into) a Q. Thus, *nagai* ("long/longer") in the ungrammatical example (30) repeated here, cannot project QP, and hence cannot license the predicate CP of the *yori*-clause.

(30) ?*Taroo-wa [Hanako-ga ___ katta yori(-mo)] nagai kasa -o
-top -nom bought than long umbrella-acc
katta
bought
(John bought a longer umbrella than Mary bought ___)

Let us next consider the grammatical (29).

---

7 See Abney (1987:340) and Ishii (1991) for more detailed arguments.

8 For more detailed discussions of the structure in (37) (including the status of the indefinite article *a*), see Ishii (1991).

(29) Taroo -wa [Hanako -ga ___ katta yori(-mo)] takusan(-no)
-top -nom bought than many -gen
kasa -o katta
umbrella -acc bought
(John bought more umbrellas than Mary bought ___)

Here, we have to consider two cases. As indicated by the parentheses, *-no* after *takusan* ("many/much") is optional. If *takusan* is not followed by *-no*, it is a floating quantifier, and is a QP, as I argued earlier. I suggest that the *yori*-clause and the floating quantifier *takusan* make a constituent, as diagrammed in (38). (The larger QP as a whole behaves as a floating quantifier.)

(38)

```
                QP (= floating quantifier)
               /  \
             CP    \
            /  \    \
           /____\   QP
          OP ... yori  |
               (than) takusan
                        (many/much)
```

Hence, the QP *takusan* correctly licenses the CP predicate.

If *takusan* is followed by *-no*, it is not floated and is part of the noun phrase. I propose that the *yori*-clause again makes a constituent with *takusan* ("many/much"). Thus, (29) with *-no* has roughly the structure (39), in which *takusan*, being a QP, licenses the predicate CP.

(39)

```
                 NP
                /   \
               /     \
             QP       N'
            /  \      |
          CP    QP    |
         /  \    |    N
        /____\ takusan-no |
      OP ... yori (many)  hon
           (than)        (book)
```

In conclusion, it is generally the case that comparative deletion is not possible with adjectives in Japanese. I have argued that Japanese has this restriction because (i) Japanese adjectives never become Qs, and (ii) the predicate CP in comparative deletion is only licensed by a quantificational expression, or more precisely, a QP.

Note that (40), in which no operator movement is involved, is acceptable.

(40) John-wa Mary yori [nagai kasa] -o katta
-top than long umbrella-acc bought
(John bought a longer umbrella than Mary)

Since empty operator movement is not involved in NP-comparatives, there is no one-place predicate to be licensed by a QP "subject". Thus, the failure of *nagai kasa* ("long umbrella") to project QP in this sentence does not result in ungrammaticality.

4. Subdeletion in English and Japanese

4.1. Subdeletion in English

There are certain counterexamples to my generalization that comparative deletion in Japanese cannot compare adjectives. (41) is such a case.

(41) Taroo-wa [Hanako-ga ___ kaita yori(-mo)] nagai ronbun-o kaita
-top -nom wrote than long paper -acc wrote
(Taroo wrote a longer paper than Hanako wrote)

This problem cannot be localized to (some properties of) the adjectives and the nouns used for comparison, because the example (42), in which exactly the same adjective and the same noun are used with a different verb, is unacceptable.

(42) *Taroo-wa [Hanako-ga ___ hihansita yori(-mo)] nagai
-top -nom criticized than good
ronbun-o hihansita
paper -acc criticized
(Taroo criticized a longer paper than Hanako criticized)

It seems that verbs that can be used in constructions like (41) are those which are called "verbs of creation".[9] I will show, however, that this kind of counterexample is only apparent, and that we can still maintain the

9 More examples are given below.

(i) Taroo-wa [Hanako-ga ___ tateta yori(-mo)] ii uti -o tateta
-top -nom built than good house-acc built
(Taroo built a better house than Hanako built)

(ii) Taroo-wa [Hanako-ga ___ tukutta yori(-mo)] oisii
-top -nom made than delicious dish
ryoori-o tukutta
dish -acc made
(Taroo made a more delicious dish than Hanako made)

generalization that comparative deletion in Japanese cannot have real adjectives for comparison.

Notice first that a similar restriction is observed in English subdeletion, as pointed out by Pinkham (1985). Subdeletion is illustrated in (43), in which the number of books that John bought is compared with the number of magazines that Mary bought.

(43) John bought more books than Mary bought ___ magazines

Pinkham (1985) observes that not all APs that modify NPs can be compared successfully by subdeletion. Pinkham argues, roughly speaking, that in the grammatical cases of subdeletion, the comparison is understood to be between adverbials.[10] Thus, (44a) can be roughly paraphrased as (44b).

(44) a. They make better police dogs than they make pets
b. They make police dogs better than they make pets

On the other hand, (45a) cannot have such an adverbial reading. Thus, (45a) cannot be paraphrased as (45b).

(45) a. *She bought a prettier dress than she bought a shirt
b. #She bought a dress more prettily than she bought a shirt

Extending Pinkham's insight, I propose that, in grammatical cases, the gap of subdeletion is in fact an adverbial, and that it is not actually a case of subdeletion, but a case of comparative deletion applying to adverbials. The example in (46) has the S-structure in (47), which has two abstract adverbs, one in the matrix clause and the other in the *than*-clause. The one in the matrix clause is indicated by MORE. The one in the *than*-clause is moved to the [Spec, CP] in syntax. Quantifier Raising applies to MORE in (47), yielding (48).

(46) John bought more books than Mary bought ___ magazines
(47) [John bought more$_i$ books MORE$_i$ [OP$_j$ than [Mary bought ___$_j$ magazines t_j]]]
(48) MORE$_i$ [John bought more$_i$ books t_i [OP$_j$ than [Mary bought ___$_j$ magazines t_j]]]

I will propose that in (48), MORE (or the trace of MORE) "unselectively binds" *more* in the matrix clause, and OP (or the trace of OP) "unselectively binds" the underlined part in the *than*-clause.[11]

---

10 Based on this observation, Pinkham (1985) develops an interpretive approach to comparative deletion and subdeletion, which is not taken in my analysis. See Pinkham (1985) for details.

11 In this paper, I will not commit myself as to whether the unselective binding takes

Heim (1982) argues that indefinite NPs are not quantifiers, "but are rather like variables, which may get bound by whatever quantifier is there to bind them." (p.127) For example, *always* binds the two indefinite NPs in (49b). The binder, like *always* in (49), may bind more than one variable, as proposed by Lewis (1975), and is thus said to be "unselective".

(49) a. If a man owns a donkey, he always beats it
b. always_{ij} [if a man_i owns a donkey_j, he_i beats it_j]

Returning to subdeletion in English, I propose along a similar line that *more* in subdeletion has no quantificational force of its own, and simply marks a variable, which is unselectively bound by the abstract adverb. Thus, both MORE and OP (or their traces) in (48) are unselective binders in this analysis. This, in turn, implies that there is no such thing as "subdeletion" in the strict sense, and that grammatical cases are in fact comparative deletion applying to adverbs.

Japanese comparative deletion with adjectives resembles English "subdeletion" in that they are possible only when the predicate is a verb of creation. I pursue a similar line of analysis for grammatical cases of comparative deletion with APs in Japanese. In this case, comparative deletion does not apply to the two APs, but applies to the abstract adverbs which unselectively bind them. The abstract adverbs (MORE and the corresponding empty operator OP) are inherently QPs, being qualified to license the predicate CP. (Recall the arguments in Section 3.) Hence, we can still maintain the generalization that comparative deletion with APs is in general impossible in Japanese.

There is some supporting evidence for an analysis of subdeletion based on unselective binding. Corver (1990) points out that there are cases which contain two gap positions in the subdeletion clause, as in (50).

(50) Santa Claus gave [more girls] [more dolls] than he had given [___ boys] [___ pencils]

(Corver 1990:84)

It is important to note that the corresponding comparative deletion is impossible. That is, multiple application of comparative deletion is not allowed, just as multiple *wh*-movement in syntax is not allowed in English.

(51) *[More men] sold [more apples] than ___ had bought ___

(Corver 1990:85)

(50) has the interpretation (52), according to Von Stechow (1984) and Corver (1990).

---

place from the position which MORE and OP occupy at LF or from the position which they occupy at D-structure. See Ishii (1991) for a related discussion.

(52) The number of girls that Santa Claus gave dolls is greater than the number of boys that he gave pencils; the number of dolls that Santa Claus gave to girls is greater than the number of pencils he gave to boys

In other words, two independent comparisons are made here: one is the comparison of the number of girls (that he gave dolls) and boys (that he gave pencils); the other is the comparison of the number of dolls (that are given to girls) and the number of pencils (that are given to boys). However, I will argue that there is in fact only one comparison being made in this sentence. The matrix clause of this sentence has the logical form (53), where MORE indicates the abstract adverb which unselectively binds the two occurrences of *more*.

(53) MORE_{ij} (Santa Claus gave [more_i girls] [more_j dolls])

In the *than*-clause, there is empty operator movement from the adjunct position, as diagrammed in (54). The operator (or its trace) unselectively binds the determiner positions of *boys* and *pencils*. After it is moved, the operator itself is licensed by MORE in the matrix clause.

(54) OP_{ij} (he had given [$\_\_\__i$ boys] [$\_\_\__j$ pencils] *e*)

An intuitive idea behind this analysis is that the sentence (50) simply compares two actions: "giving of dolls to girls" and "giving of pencils to boys". It says that the former was done more (more exceedingly, for example) than the latter, with respect to both the number of presents and the number of recipients. Thus, comparison is made between adjuncts and not between argument NPs.

I have proposed that real subdeletion does not exist in English, and that grammatical cases of "subdeletion" in English are in fact comparative deletion applying to adverbs. This conclusion is a welcome one. If subdeletion in English were possible, it would involve long-distance movement of the head Q out of QP into [SPEC,CP]. However, as pointed out by Ross (1967), such extraction is not generally possible in English.

(55) a. *[How many] did they eat [___ cookies]?
b. *[How] is she [___ pretty]?

This has been pointed out by Bresnan (1975) and Grimshaw (1987) as a counter-argument for a movement analysis of subdeletion. This will pose no problem for my approach, because "subdeletion" in my analysis involves movement of adverbs, and not extraction of the head Q out of QP.

A second argument for subdeletion as comparative deletion applying to an abstract adverb is based on the following fact pointed out by Pinkham (1985). Bresnan (1973) proposes that comparative clauses are base-generated in a position where they form a constituent with the head (i.e. compared element in the matrix clause), as in (56a), and that the sentence (56b), for example, is derived from (56a) by extraposition of the comparative clause.

(56) a. [More people *than I had invited*] came to the party
b. More people came to the party *than I had invited*
(Pinkham 1985:49)

Pinkham (1985) points out that in the case of subdeletion, extraposition of the comparative clause is obligatory, as we can see from the ungrammaticality of (57a) and (58a).

(57) a. *[More men *than women use Chanel #5*] use Eau Sauvage
b. More men use Eau Sauvage *than women use Chanel #5*
(Pinkham 1985:50)

(58) a. ?*[More passengers *than the airline had issued tickets*] tried to board the plane
b. More passengers tried to board the plane *than the airline had issued tickets*
(Pinkham 1985:50)

This fact suggests that (57b) and (58b) are not derived from (57a) and (58a) by extraposition. According to my analysis of subdeletion, it is an abstract adverb, not *more* in the argument NP, which licenses the empty operator in the *than*-clause. Thus, if the *than*-clause in (57b) should be extraposed from anything, it is from a phrase containing the abstract adverb (MORE), as diagrammed in (59).

(59) More men use Eau Savage [MORE *than women use Chanel #5*]

This explains the ungrammaticality of (57a) as opposed to (56a). In the case of comparative deletion, the phrase containing *more* itself licenses the QP operator in [Spec, CP].

A third argument for an abstract adverb analysis of subdeletion comes from the fact that a phrase containing *more* in subdeletion can never be preposed by *wh*-movement, again as noted by Pinkham (1985). This is shown in (60).

(60) *How many more passengers tried to board the plane *than the airline had issued tickets* (Pinkham 1985:50)

Recall that I argued that *more* in subdeletion does not have a quantificational force of its own, and that it marks a variable bound by an abstract adverb. The abstract adverb is raised by Quantifier Raising in LF and adjoined to IP. When the phrase containing *more* has moved to [SPEC,CP] by *wh*-movement, the *more* as a variable is not c-commanded by the quantifier in the IP-adjoined position, and becomes an unbound variable, as we can see from the structure (61).

(61) $[_{CP}$[How many more$_i$ passengers]$_j$ $[_{IP}$MORE$_i$ [t_j tried to board the plane t_i than ...]]]

In the case of comparative deletion, on the other hand, the *more* phrase itself has a quantificational force of its own. Thus, *wh*-movement of the *more*-phrase will not end up with any unbounded variable. The grammaticality of (62) and (63) confirms this conclusion.

(62) How many more passengers *than the plane could hold* tried to come on board? (Pinkham 1985:50)

(63) How many more passengers tried to come on board *than the plane could hold*?

4.2. Subdeletion in Japanese

I have argued that the operator in Japanese comparative deletion is a floating quantifier, which is associated with an empty indefinite. This predicts that the trace of the operator, since it has the status of a floating quantifier, can be linked to an overt NP. This prediction is in fact borne out as in (64) and (65).

(64) John-wa [OP$_i$[Mary-ga e_i zassi -o katta yori]
 -top -nom magazine-acc bought than
 takusan hon -o katta
 many book-acc bought
 (John bought more books than Mary bought magazines)

(65) [OP$_i$ [e_i gakusei-ga kita yori] takusan sensei -ga kita
 student-nom came than many teachers-nom came
 (More teachers came than students came)

Although (64) and (65) look like cases of subdeletion, they are genuine cases of comparative deletion in my analysis.

5. Concluding Remarks

In this paper, I discussed comparative deletion in English and Japanese. As discussed by Chomsky (1977) for English and by Kikuchi (1989) for Japanese, comparative deletion in both languages can be shown to involve empty operator movement. At the same time, we have observed that these two languages have different properties with respect to comparative deletion.

I have claimed that comparative deletion universally involves movement of a QP operator, but what constitutes a QP is different from language to language. In English, a comparative quantifier/adjective heads a maximal projection QP, taking an NP as its complement. In Japanese, on the other hand, prenominal quantifiers never project QP. Japanese instead has floating quantifiers as QPs, which are available as the operator for comparative deletion. This difference in the content of QP is the basis for the observed differences between English and Japanese with respect to comparative deletion.[12]

I have also shown that the fact that Japanese does not have any special morphology for comparatives plays an important role in deriving the fact that comparison of adjectives is very limited in Japanese comparative deletion. The analysis proposed here has been shown to have some important consequences for the analysis of English comparatives as well, in particular, subdeletion.

Acknowledgements

This is essentially part of Chapter 3 of my 1991 Ph.D. dissertation (University of Connecticut). I thank all the people who gave me helpful comments and suggestions at various stages of the project. I am especially grateful to Howard Lasnik, Mamoru Saito, Diane Lillo-Martin, Noriko Kawasaki, and Robyne Tiedeman. I also benefitted from conversations I had with the audience at the Southern California Japanese/Korean Linguistics Conference held at UC Santa Barbara in September 1991. Thanks are also due to Gayle K. Sato for helping me improve the style of this paper. Remaining errors are, of course, mine. This work was in part supported by a grant from the 1991 Keio Gijuku Academic Development Funds.

References

Abney, Steven. P. 1987. The English noun phrase in its sentential aspect. Doctoral dissertation, MIT.

Bresnan, Joan. 1973. Syntax of the comparative construction in English. LI 4.275-345.

---

12 In my analysis of comparative deletion in Japanese, the operator, being a floating quantifier, does not contain the argument NP in its own projection. This raises an interesting problem with respect to the status of sentences like (4) and (5), where Subjacency is violated. If the operator is an adjunct, these cases will be ECP violations as well. Although theses sentences indeed seem to be worse than mere Subjacency violations, they are still not as bad as standard ECP violations. See Ishii (1991) for further discussion of this issue.

Bresnan, Joan. 1975. Comparative deletion and constraints on transformations. LA 1.25-74.
Browning, Marguerite. 1987. Null operator construction. Doctoral dissertation, MIT.
Carlson, Gregory Norman. 1977. Reference to kinds in English. Doctoral dissertation, University of Massachusetts at Amherst.
Chomsky, Noam. 1977. On wh-movement. Formal syntax, ed. by Peter W. Culicover, Thomas Wasow, and Adrian Akmajian, 71-132. New York: Academic Press.
Chomsky, Noam. 1980. On binding. LI 11.1-46.
Chomsky, Noam. 1981. Lectures on government and binding. Dordrecht: Foris.
Corver, Norbert Ferdinand Marie 1990. The syntax of left branch extractions. Doctoral dissertation, Tilburg University.
Diesing, Molly. 1988. Bare plural subjects and the stage/individual contrast. In Krifka, 107-54.
Krifka, Manfred (ed.) 1988. Genericity in natural language: Proceedings of the 1988 Tübingen Conference. Tübingen: Seminar für natürlich-sprachliche Systeme der Universität Tübingen.
Grimshaw, Jane. 1987. Subdeletion. LI 18.659-669.
Hankamer, Jorge. 1973. Why there are two *than*'s in English. Papers from the Ninth Regional Meeting of the Chicago Linguistic Society, 179-188. Chicago: Chicago Linguistic Society.
Heim, Irene Roswitha. 1982. The semantics of definite and indefinite noun phrases. Doctoral dissertation, University of Massachusetts at Amherst.
Ishii, Yasuo. 1991. Operators and empty categories in Japanese. Doctoral dissertation, University of Connecticut. [To be published, Tokyo: Kurosio Publishers.]
Kikuchi, Akira. 1989. Comparative deletion in Japanese. Yamagata University, MS.
Kratzer, Angelika. 1988. Stage-level and individual-level predicates. In Krifka, 247-84.
Lasnik, Howard, and Robert Fiengo 1974. Complement object deletion. LI 5.535-571.
Lewis, David. 1975. Adverbs of quantification. Formal semantics of natural language, ed. by E. L. Keenan, 3-15. Cambridge: Cambridge University Press.
Miyagawa, Shigeru. 1989. Structure and case marking in Japanese. (Syntax and Semantics, vol.22.) San Diego: Academic Press.
Murasugi, Keiko. 1991. Noun phrases in Japanese and English: A study in syntax, learnability and acquisition. Doctoral dissertation, University of Connecticut.
Pinkham, Jessie, E. 1985. The formation of comparative clauses in French and English. New York: Garland Publishing.

Ross, John Robert. 1967. Constraints on variables in syntax. Doctoral dissertation, MIT.

Stechow, Arnim von 1984. Comparing semantic theories of comparison. Journal of Semantics 3.1-77.

Tateishi, Koichi. 1989. Subjects, SPEC, and DP in Japanese. NELS 19.405-418.

Ueda, Masanobu. 1986. On quantifier float in Japanese. University of Massachusetts Occasional Papers in Linguistics 11.263-309.

Inalienable Possession Constructions in Korean: Scrambling, the Proper Binding Condition, and Case-Percolation*

HISATSUGU KITAHARA
Harvard University

O. Introduction

A canonical example of an Inalienable Possession Construction (henceforth, IAC) is (1).

```
(1)   John-i     Mary-lul     ppyam-ul     ttaelyo-ss-ta
      John-NOM   Mary-ACC     cheek-ACC    hit-PST-IND
      'John hit Mary's cheek.'
```

The relationship between the two accusative NPs is often characterized as a Whole-Part (or Possessor-Possessee) relation. In this paper, we will refer to the possessor NP as the whole-NP and to the possessee NP as the part-NP. One important question raised by IACs is whether multiple complements, the whole-NP *Mary* and the part-NP *ppyam* 'cheek' are arguments of a transitive verb such as *ttaelyo-* 'hit'.

Kim (1989, 1990), assigning the following structure in (2), argues that only the whole-NP is a complement. In her analysis, the whole NP is theta-marked by a verb and the part-NP is a secondary predicate of the whole-NP.

```
(2)          ... VP
                /∴
       whole-NP      V'
                    /∴
             part-NP    V
```

* I would like to thank Samuel D. Epstein, Susumu Kuno, and Joan Maling who have read the earlier version of the paper and made comments. I also thank the following people for comments and discussion, Jun Abe, Hajime Hoji, Ruriko Kawashima, Soo-Yeon Kim, Young-joo Kim, Toshifusa Oka, Hiroaki Tada, Shigeo Tonoike, Akira Watanabe, and John Whitman. All errors are my own.

Yoon (1989, 1990), assuming the structure in (2), argues that only the whole-NP is theta-marked, but in his analysis the whole-NP is theta-marked by V' and the unsaturated theta-grid of the part-NP is discharged by theta-identification (Higginbotham (1985, 1987) and Speas (1990)). Maling and Kim (1992), however, provide two pieces of evidence which suggest that the part-NP is indeed an argument selected and theta-marked by the verb. Consider the following sentences.

```
(3)  a.   Mary-ka     sonthop-ul     kkakka-ess-ta
          Mary-NOM    fingernail-ACC  clip-PST-IND
          'Mary clipped the fingernail(s).'

     b.   *Mary-ka     emeni-lul     kkakka-tuli-ess-ta
           Mary-NOM    mother-ACC    clip-HON-PST-IND
           'Mary clipped her mother.'

     c.   ?Mary-ka  emeni-lul  sonthop-ul
          Mary-NOM mother-ACC fingernail-ACC
          kkakka-tuli-ess-ta
          clip-HON-PST-IND
           'Mary clipped her mother's fingernail(s).'
```

The contrast between (3a) and (3b) shows that a verb *kkakka-* 'clip' selects an argument *sonthop* 'fingernail' but not *emeni* 'mother'. If the theta-marking is responsible for such selectional restrictions, then *sonthop* which is a part-NP in (3c) must be an argument selected and theta-marked by a verb *kkakka-* . Furthermore, consider the following sentences.

```
(4)  a.   Nay-ka     Mary-eykey    cwusa-lul    noh-ass-ta
          I-NOM      Mary-DAT      shot-ACC     give-PST-IND
          'I gave a shot to Mary.'

     b.   *Nay-ka     Mary-eykey    cwusa-ey     noh-ass-ta
           I-NOM      Mary-DAT      shot-DAT     give-PST-IND
          'I gave a shot to Mary.'

     c.   Nay-ka Mary-eykey phal-ey cwusa-lul noh-ass-ta
          I-NOM  Mary-DAT   arm-DAT  shot-ACC give-PST-IND
          'I gave a shot to Mary's arm.'
```

The contrast between (4a) and (4b) shows that a dative Case may be assigned to a goal argument *Mary* but not to a theme argument *cwusa* 'shot'. If we assume that such theta-related argument may be assigned an inherent Case by a verb (Chomsky (1986a)), then there must be theta-marking taking place between a part-NP *phal* 'arm' and a verb *noh* 'give' in (4c) in which the part-NP is assigned a dative Case.

Adopting Maling and Kim's analysis of part-NPs, we will discuss some cases which are problematic to the assumption that a whole-NP is an argument of a verb in IACs. We will propose an analysis in which a whole-NP is theta-marked by a relational nominal, a head of a part-NP. The paper consists of four sections; in section 1, we will consider the constraint on scrambling of a part-NP and the property of empty categories in the projection of a relational nominal; in section 2, we will propose an alternative analysis; in section 3, we will discuss why the head of a part-NP in IACs is limited to a relational nominal; and in section 4, we will suggest how the multiple assignment of Case takes place in IACs.

1. Scrambling and Empty Categories

1.1. Scrambling of a Part-NP

It has been claimed in Yoon (1989, 1990) that a part-NP cannot be scrambled as shown in (5b); however, (5c) shows that such constraint is too restrictive.[1]

```
(5)  a.   Kay-ka     John-ul     son-ul     mul-ess-ta
          dog-NOM    John-ACC    hand-ACC   bite-PST-IND
          'The dog bit John's hand.'

     b.   *Son-ul,   kay-ka      John-ul     mul-ess-ta

     c.   John-ul    son-ul,     kay-ka      mul-ess-ta
```

In (5c), both the whole-NP *John* and the part-NP *son* 'hand' (which do not form a constituent under Yoon's analysis) are scrambled over the subject NP *kay* 'dog'.[2] To distinguish (5b) from (5c), one might propose the following purely descriptive constraint:

(6) A part-NP may be scrambled as long as it is c-commanded by the whole-NP.[3]

Interestingly, however, there is no such constraint on scrambling of a part-NP in the lexical passive corresponding to the sentence in (5b). Consider the following sentences.

```
(7)  a.   John-i     (kay-eykey)   son-ul     mul-li-ess-ta
          John-NOM    dog-DAT      hand-ACC   bite-PASS-PST-IND
          'John was adversely affected by being bit on the
          hand by the dog.'

     b.   Son-ul,    John-i      (kay-eykey)      mul-li-ess-ta
```

Following Kim (1990) and Maling (1989), we assume that lexical passives which exhibit NOM-ACC Case pattern do not involve any syntactic movement which raises object NP to a Case-marked position. Furthermore, adopting the VP-Internal Subject Hypothesis (e.g. Koopman and Sportiche (1991) and Kuroda (1988)), we assume that the subject NP *John* is base-generated in the Spec of VP and receives the theta-role, affected theme from a lexical passive morpheme *li*. The question which we would like

---

1 Following Saito (1985, 1989), we assume that scrambling is an adjunction to IP.

2 Yoon (1989, 1990) crucially assumes that a part-NP base-generated in sister to V is licensed by theta-identification (Higginbotham (1985, 1987)) while a whole-NP base-generated in sister to V' is theta-marked. Yoon further argues that non-theta-marked nominals project only up to the N'-level and tries to derive his observation that a part-NP cannot be scrambled (illustrated in (5b) from the fact that single-bar projections are invisible to Move α (Chomsky (1986b)). However, such an account incorrectly rules out (5c), in which a whole-NP and a part-NP each (since they do not form any constituent in Yoon's analysis) are scrambled over the subject.

3 α c-commands β iff α does not dominate β and the first branching node dominating α dominates β (adopted from Reinhart (1976)).

to ask is what syntactic difference is responsible for the contrast displayed between (5b) and (7b) with respect to scrambling of a part-NP.

It is very undesirable to make the descriptive condition stated in (6) specific to the particular construction, namely IACs, but without such construction-specific condition, it is not clear how the previous analysis predicts the contrast between (5b) and (7b).

Kim (1989, 1990), following Kuno (1973), characterizes the descriptive condition stated in (6) as a prohibition on scrambling of a NP over another when they are assigned the same morphological Case. But she also notes that there are some counterexamples such as (8b).

```
(8)   a.    Mary-ka     John-ul     chayk-ul     cwu-ess-ta
            Mary-NOM    John-ACC    book-ACC     give-PST-IND
            'Mary gave a book to John.'

      b.    Chayk-ul,    Mary-ka     John-ul     cwu-ess-ta
```

The sentence in (8b) is grammatical even though the direct object NP *chayk* 'book' is scrambled over the indirect object NP *John* when both *chayk* and *John* are assigned an accusative Case.

In this paper, we will derive the descriptive condition stated in (6) from an independent principle. Following Tellier (1990), let us assume that relational nominals such as *son* 'hand' require a possessor argument to be syntactically present, in order for such relational nominals to be fully referential. With this assumption, let us reanalyze the structure of the sentences in (5a) and (7a).

(9) a. Kay-ka $John_1$-ul [ec_1 son]-ul mul-ess-ta

b. $John_1$-i (kay-eykey) [ec_1 son]-ul mul-li-ess-ta

If there is no overt possessor NP in the projection of a relational nominal, then there must be some empty categories to satisfy the Projection Principle and the theta-criterion (Chomsky (1981)). In this alternative analysis, we will reduce the contrast between (5b) and (7b) to the difference between the empty categories in (9a) and (9b).

1.2. A Whole-NP and an Empty Category in IACs

In Korean, a pronoun may appear in a position of an obligatorily controlled argument shown in (10) (Borer (1989)).

(10) a. $John_1$-i [ec_1 ttena-lye-ko] nolyekhay-ess-ta
John-NOM leave-will-COMP try-PST-IND
'John tried to leave.'

b. $John_1$-i [ku_1-ka ttena-lye-ko] nolyekhay-ess-ta
John-NOM he-NOM leave-will-COMP try-PST-IND

In IACs, however, an empty category in the projection of a relational nominal which is a part-NP cannot be replaced with a pronoun.[4] Consider the following sentences.

```
(11) a.    Kay-ka     John1-ul     [ec1  son]-ul  mul-ess-ta
           dog-NOM    John-ACC          hand-ACC  bite-PST-IND
           'The dog bit John's hand.'

     b.??/*Kay-ka     John1-ul   [ku1-uy  son]-ul   mul-ess-ta
           dog-NOM    John-ACC   he-GEN hand-ACC bite-PST-IND
```

The contrast between the sentences in (10) and (11) suggests that the property of empty categories in (10) is different from the one in (11). With respect to the property of empty categories, the lexical passives corresponding to the sentences in (11) show the same property of those in the control sentences in (10). Consider the following sentences.

```
(12) a.    John1-i (kay-eykey) [ec1  son]-ul   mul-li-ess-ta
           John-NOM  dog-DAT      hand-ACC bite-PASS-PST-IND
           'John was adversely affected by being bit on the
           hand by the dog.'

     b.    John1-i (kay-eykey) [ku1-uy son]-ul
           John-NOM dog-DAT he-GEN hand-ACC
           mul-li-ess-ta
           bite-PASS-PST-IND
```

The data suggest that the empty category in the projection of the part-NP in IACs is different from the one in the control sentences or the lexical passives.

---

4 There is a compound *kyay* (*ku* 'the' + *ai* 'person') which functions as a pronoun (Cho (1989)). This compound may appear in the position of an empty category in the projection of a relational nominal in IACs, referring to the whole-NP (suggested by Hajime Hoji (p.c.)). Consider the following sentences.

```
(i)   a.   ??Kay-ka     John1-ul     [kyay1-uy  son]-ul    mul-ess-ta
             dog-NOM    John-ACC      he-GEN    hand-ACC   bite-PST-IND
           'The dog bit John's hand.'

      b.   Kay-ka     John1      [kyay1-uy   son]-ul     mul-ess-ta
```

(ia) sounds better than (11b). Furthermore, (ib) in which a Case particle on the whole-NP is dropped, sounds perfect. Here, I do not offer any account for the link between the lack of Case particle and the improvement shown in (i); however, I was informed that such improvement may be limited to the use of *kyay*. Consider the following sentences.

```
(ii)  a. ??/*Kay-ka     John1-ul     [ku1-uy   son]-ul     mul-ess-ta
             dog-NOM    John-ACC      he-GEN   hand-ACC    bite-PST-IND
           'The dog bit John's hand.'

      b. ??/*Kay-ka     John1      [ku1-uy   son]-ul     mul-ess-ta
```

The lack of improvement in (ii) seems to suggest that the structure assigned to the sentences in (ii) may be different from the one assigned to those in (i) (If there is a long pause between *John* and *ku-uy* 'his' in (iib), the sentence seems to be improved; however, such a pause is not required in the grammatical IACs e.g. (1)). In this paper, we will not discuss this possibility.

Korean allows a phonetically null pronoun, namely pro. Given that the empty category in the control sentences is a pro, the appearance of an overt pronoun in the same position is the matter of phonetic realization. Following this assumption, we assume that the empty category in the lexical passives is also a pro; however, we analyze the empty category in IACs as not a pro but a trace created by a movement of a whole-NP. In the next section, following this assumption that an empty category in the projection of a relational nominal, which is a part-NP, in IACs is a trace created by movement of the whole-NP, we will show how our alternative analysis accounts for the contrast between (5b) and (7b).

2. An Alternative Analysis

The alternative analysis treats an empty category in the projection of a relational nominal, a head of the part-NP in IACs, as a trace created by a movement of the whole-NP. Hence, (13a) is derived from (13b).[5]

(13) a. Kay-ka John$_1$-ul [t$_1$ son]-ul mul-ess-ta
dog-NOM John-ACC hand-ACC bite-PST-IND
'The dog bit John's hand.'

b. Kay-ka [John-uy son]-ul mul-ess-ta
dog-NOM John-GEN hand-ACC bite-PST-IND

Following Abney (1987) and Stowell (1989), we adopt the DP Hypothesis and propose the following S-structure for the VP in (13a).

(14)

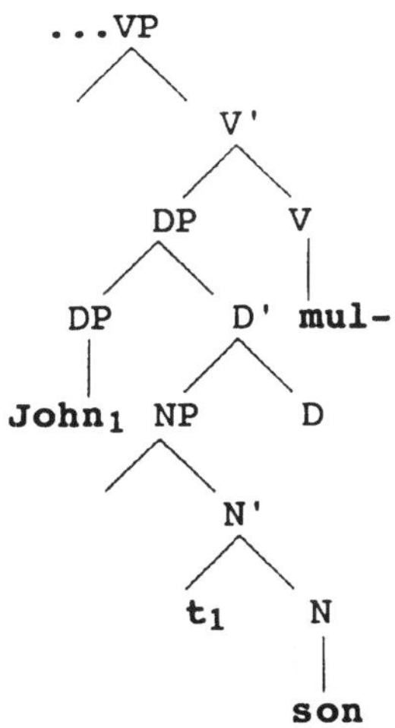

(14) illustrates that the whole-NP *John* is first base-generated as a sister to a relational nominal *son* 'hand', which is a head of the part-NP; then the whole-NP *John* is raised to the Spec of DP, which is the extended maximal projection of a relational nominal *son*

---

5 For some different arguments for the derivational analysis, see Choe (1987).

(Grimshaw (1991)).[6] If further movement takes place, the whole-NP *John* may be scrambled and adjoined to IP, leaving a trace in the Spec of DP.[7]

Let us recall the scrambling sentences in (5), repeated in (14).

(14) a. Kay-ka John-ul son-ul mul-ess-ta
dog-NOM John-ACC hand-ACC bite-PST-IND
'The dog bit John's hand.'

b. *Son-ul, kay-ka John-ul mul-ess-ta

c. John-ul son-ul, kay-ka mul-ess-ta

Although it is not clear whether the NP can be scrambled out of the position sister to D, let us suppose such movement would satisfy the relevant conditions. The alternative analysis then would assign the following structures to the corresponding sentences in (14).[8]

(15) a. $[_{IP}$ Kay-ka $[_{VP}$ $[_{DP}$ **John$_1$**-ul $[_{D'}$ $[_{NP}$ $[_{N'}$ **t_1** son-ul]]]]]-ess-ta]

b. $[_{IP}$ $[_{NP}$ $[_{N'}$ **t_1** son-ul]]$_2$ $[_{IP}$ kay-ka $[_{VP}$ $[_{DP}$ **John$_1$**-ul $[_{D'}$ **t_2**]] mul]-ess-ta]]

c. $[_{IP}$ $[_{DP}$ **John$_1$**-ul $[_{D'}$ $[_{NP}$ $[_{N'}$ **t_1** son-ul]]]]$_2$ $[_{IP}$ kay-ka $[_{VP}$ **t_2** mul]-ess-ta]]

Raising of the whole-NP *John* to the Spec of DP, which is the extended maximal projection of a relational nominal *son* 'hand' takes place in all the structures in (15). In (15b), the maximal projection of a relational nominal *son* (NP) is scrambled out of the DP and adjoined to the IP. In (15c), on the other hand, the extended maximal projection of a relational nominal *son* , the entire DP, is scrambled and adjoined to the IP. For clarification, (16) illustrates the entire derivation of sentence (14b) (assigned the S-structure (15b)):

---

6 In this paper, without further discussion, we assume that raising of a whole-NP to the Spec of DP, the extended maximal projection of a relational nominal is one instantiation of focus movement.

7 We will not discuss the possibility of adjunction to VP as an instantiation of scrambling in the main text. For some discussion, see footnote 10.

8 Following the VP Internal Subject Hypothesis, we assume that the subject is base-generated in the Spec of VP and raised to the Spec of IP. The structures in the main text, however, do not show the trace left in the Spec of VP by such raising, since such trace does not play any role in our analysis of IACs.

(16) a. D-structure:

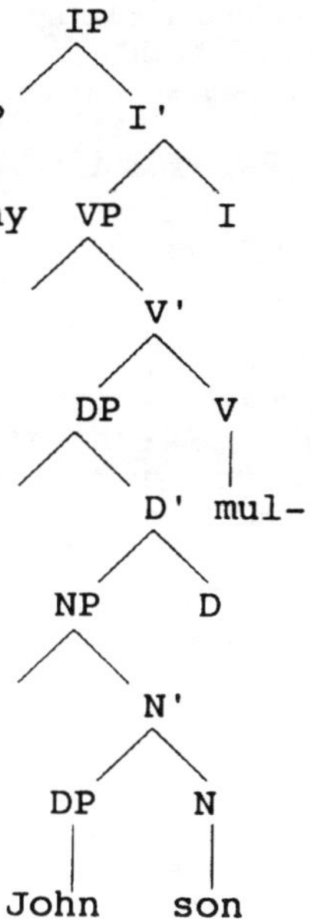

b. Whole-NP raises to the Spec of DP

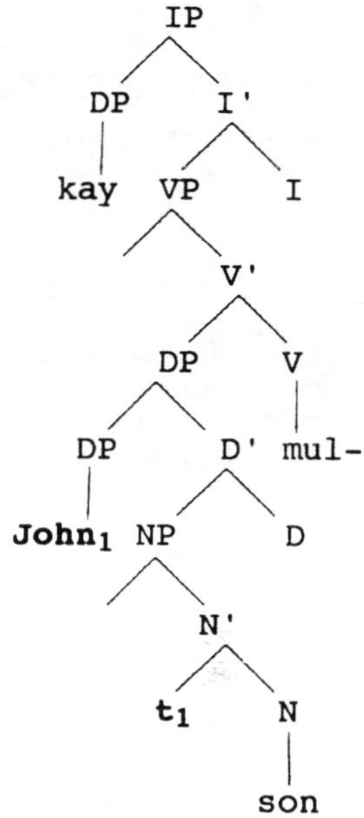

c. NP adjoins to IP

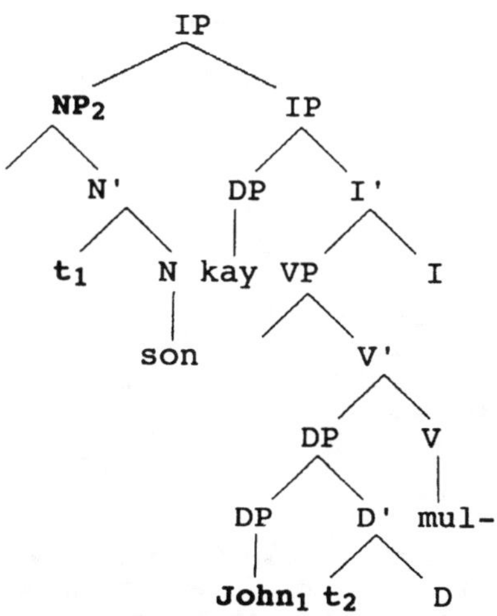

In (16a), the whole-NP *John* is base-generated as a sister to the relational nominal *son* 'hand'. (16b) illustrates raising of the whole-NP to the spec of DP, the extended maximal projection of the relational nominal *son*. Finally, in (16c), the maximal projection of the relational nominal *son* is scrambled out of the DP and adjoined to the IP. Suppose that the two movements, raising of the whole-NP to the Spec of DP and scrambling of the NP out of DP, satisfy the relevant movement conditions. The current theory would still predict that the structure (16c) (= (15b)) violates the Proper Binding Condition (May (1977) and Saito (1985, 1989)) stated in (17).

(17) The Proper Binding Condition[9]

Traces must be bound.

In (16c), the trace $\mathbf{t_1}$ (left in sister to a relational nominal *son* by raising of the whole-NP *John* to the Spec of DP) is not bound ; hence, a violation of the Proper Binding Condition occurs. In (15c), however, the entire DP containing both the trace $\mathbf{t_1}$ and its antecedent $\mathbf{John_1}$ is scrambled and adjoined to the IP. In this structure, the trace $\mathbf{t_1}$ is bound and there is no violation of the Proper Binding Condition.[10]

Let us recall the descriptive condition on scrambling of a part-NP stated in (6).

(6) A part-NP may be scrambled as long as it is c-commanded by the whole-NP.

Under the current analysis, the c-command requirement for a part-NP stated in (6) is derived from the Proper Binding Condition. The part-NP which is the projection of a relational nominal contains the trace of a whole-NP. Hence, whenever the part-NP is scrambled to a position where the whole-NP does not c-command its trace (contained in the Part-NP), the Proper Binding Conditionis violated. The grammatical status of the lexical passive in which the part-NP is scrambled over the whole-NP naturally follows from the assumption that an empty category contained in the part-NP is a pro, not a trace; hence, the Proper Binding Condition is inapplicable.

In the following two sections, we will discuss some consequences of the proposed analysis.

---

9 α is bound by β iff α and β are coindexed and α is c-commanded by β.

10 Suppose that adjunction to VP is allowed as an instantiation of scrambling. The following structures might be assigned to the sentence (14b).

(i) $[_{IP}$ $[_{DP}$ $\mathbf{t'_1}$ $[_{D'}$ $[_{NP}$ $[_{N'}$ $\mathbf{t_1}$ son-ul$]]]]_2$ $[_{IP}$ kay-ka $[_{VP}$ $\mathbf{John_1}$-ul $[_{VP}$ $\mathbf{t_2}$ mul$]]$-ess-ta$]]$

In the structure above, the whole-NP *John* is raised to the Spec of DP and further scrambled out of DP and adjoined to the VP. Then, the entire DP is scrambled and adjoined to the IP. The trace $\mathbf{t_1}$ in sister to a relational nominal *son* 'hand' in (i) is correctly bound by the trace $\mathbf{t'_1}$ left in the Spec of DP; however, the trace $\mathbf{t'_1}$ itself is not bound; hence the Proper Binding Condition would be violated. Thus, even if we assumed that adjunction to VP is an instantiation of scrambling, the Proper Binding Condition would correctly rule out the sentence (14b).

3. Relational Nominals and the Empty Category Principle

In section 1, following Tellier (1990), we have assumed that relational nominals require a possessor argument in order for them to be fully referential. This assumption leads us to hypothesize that a whole-NP is base -generated as a sister to a relational nominal in IACs. In this section, we will consider why a head of a part-NP is limited to a relational nominal under the proposed analysis. Let us first consider the following.

```
(18) a.   John-uy    ppyam
          John-GEN   cheek
          'John's    cheek'

     b.   John-uy    cha
          John-GEN   car
          'John's car'
```

It is important to notice that the role of *John* in (18b) is discourse-dependent whereas the role of *John* in (18a) is not (Anderson (1984)). Hence, (18b) may receive several interpretations whereas (18a) receives only one, as illustrated in (19).[11]

(19) a. *John-uy ppyam* 'John's cheek':
the cheek which is a part of John

b. *John-uy cha* 'John's car':
the car which John owns, used to own, loves, ...

The contrast between (19a) and (19b) is naturally reduced to the difference between the role established in the discourse context and the role assigned by a relational nominal. Let us assume that relational nominals such as *ppyam* 'cheek' are argument-takers whereas concrete nominals such as *cha* 'car' are not. Thus, *John* in (18a) is an argument of a relational nominal *ppyam* whereas *John* in (18b) is not an argument of a concrete nominal *cha*, but an adjunct.

Following these assumptions in the previous discussion, let us consider the contrast shown in (20).

```
(20) a.   John-i     Mary-lul    ppyam-ul     ttaelyo-ss-ta
          John-NOM   Mary-ACC    cheek-ACC    hit-PST-IND
          'John hit Mary's cheek.'
```

---

11 (19a) is structurally ambiguous. Consider the following.

```
(i)  a.   John-uy    ppyam
          John-GEN   cheek
          'John's cheek'

     b.   [John-uy  ppyam]

     c.   [John-uy  [pro  ppyam]]
```

The structure (ib) corresponds to the interpretation 'the cheek which is a part of John' whereas the structure (ic) corresponds to the interpretation 'someone's cheek which John owns, for example for an experiment. The discussion concerns the structure (ib). It is important to note, however, in (ic) a pro, not *John* is the argument of the relational nominal *ppyam.*

b. *John-i Mary-lul cha-lul ttaelyo-ss-ta
John-NOM Mary-ACC car-ACC hit-PST-IND
'John hit Mary's car.'

The contrast in (20) shows that the head of a part-NP in IACs is limited to a relational nominal. Following the assumption that a relational nominal is an argument-taker, we can attribute the contrast to the violation of the Empty Category Principle (ECP) stated in (21) (Chomsky (1981, 1986b)).

(21) The ECP

A non-pronominal empty category must be properly governed.

Consider the following structure.

(22)

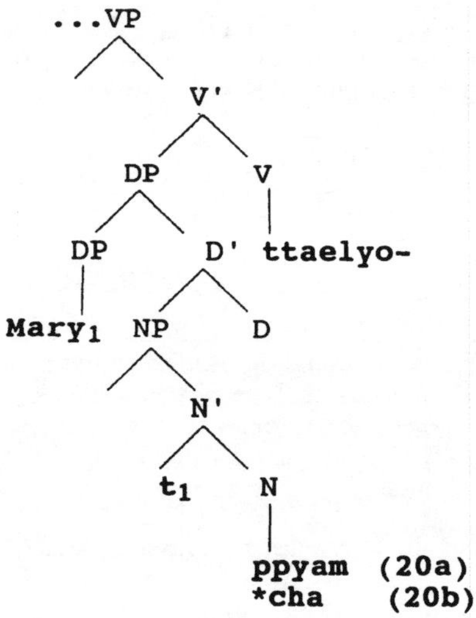

In the structure (22), the whole-NP *Mary* is raised to the Spec of DP, leaving its trace in sister to a head of a relational/concrete nominal.[12] Given that an argument-taking nominal is a θ-assigner, the trace of *Mary* t_1 is θ-governed by a relational nominal *ppyam* 'cheek' in (20a) but not by a concrete nominal *cha* 'car' in (20b). Assuming that a head of DP does not θ-mark its complement NP (Stowell (1989)), NP is a blocking category, and a barrier in the system proposed by Chomsky (1986b).[13]

12 In this paper we do not articulate the position where an adjunct NP is base-generated. In the structure (22), however, the trace of an adjunct NP is represented in sister to a concrete nominal, for the sake of comparison with the trace of an argument NP in sister to a relational nominal.

13 The relevant definitions from the Barriers System are summarized as follows.

(i) The Barriers System (Chomsky (1986b))

Since NP (which is a complement of D) always constitutes a barrier for the categories it dominates, the trace of *Mary* $\mathbf{t_1}$ cannot be antecedent-governed in either (20a) or (20b). Thus, the trace $\mathbf{t_1}$ in (20a) is not antecedent-governed but it is θ-governed; hence, there is no violation of the ECP taking place. However, the trace $\mathbf{t_1}$ in (20b) is neither θ-governed nor antecedent-governed; hence, such an offending trace induces a violation of the ECP.

Following the Barriers System, the current theory correctly predicts the contrast between (20a) and (20b). The contrast is now reduced to the difference between relational and concrete nominals with respect to θ-assigning capacity.

4. Multiple Assignment of Case and Case-Percolation

This section briefly discusses the Case-theoretic problem posed by IACs. We will present an account which is consistent with the analysis proposed in the preceding sections. The direction which we take is to view the assignment of Case in IACs as analogous to that of Exceptional Case-Marking (ECM) constructions. Consider the following sentences.

(23) a. John believes her to be honest.

b. *John believes her is honest.

A certain class of verbs which takes a clausal complement exceptionally assign an accusative Case to the subject NP of the complement clause. Although when and how ECM takes place is not clear, it is important to note that ECM is possible when the complement is infinitival, as illustrated by the contrast between (23a) and (23b). Let us assume that one requirement for ECM is the absence of agreement.

Following the preceding discussion, let us tentatively propose the principle which allows the multiple assignment of Case in IACs.

(24) When there is no agreement enforced by a head H whose projection HP is assigned a Case, the Case feature on HP may percolate into the Spec of HP.
(cf. Tateishi (1988))

In the proposed analysis of IACs, a whole-NP is raised to the Spec of DP which is the extended maximal projection. Given that a head of DP does not enforce any agreement,

---

b. α governs β iff α m-commands β and there is no γ, γ a barrier for β, such that γ excludes α.
c. α θ-governs β iff α is a zero-level category that θ-marks β, and α, β are sisters.
d. α antecedent-governs β iff α governs β and α is coindexed with β.
e. α L-marks β iff α is a lexical category that θ-governs β.
f. γ is a BC for β iff γ is not L-marked and γ dominates β.
g. γ is a barrier for β iff (i) or (ii):
(i) γ immediately dominates δ, δ a BC for β (inheritance)
(ii) γ is a BC for β, γ is not IP (intrinsic)

the principle (24) predicts that when the DP is assigned a Case, such Case feature may percolate into the category in the Spec of the DP.

The Case-realization which we want to capture is as follows (cited from Maling and Kim (1992)).

```
(25) a.    John-i   Mary-eykey phal-ey cwusa-lul  noh-ass-ta
           John-NOM Mary-DAT  arm-DAT shot-ACC give-PST-IND
           'John gave a shot to Mary's arm.'

     b.    John-i   Mary-lul  phal-ey  cwusa-lul noh-ass-ta
           John-NOM Mary-ACC arm-DAT  shot-ACC give-PST-IND

     c.    John-i   Mary-lul  phal-ul  cwusa-lul noh-ass-ta
           John-NOM Mary-ACC arm-ACC  shot-ACC give-PST-IND

     d.    ?John-i   Mary-eykey phal-ul cwusa-lul noh-ass-ta
            John-NOM Mary-DAT arm-ACC shot-ACC give-PST-IND
```

If there were only one Case feature to percolate in the sentences shown in (25), the principle stated in (24) would fail to account for the assignment of distinct Cases to multiple complement of IACs (as illustrated in (25b) and (25d)), just like any of a single-Case spread analysis (Kim (1989, 1990)).[14] However, there is one piece of evidence which suggests that distinct Case features may be assigned to a single argument. Consider the following sentence (cited from Gerdts and Youn (1988)).[15]

```
(26) John-i   Mary-eykey-lul   chayk-ul   cwu-ess-ta
     John-NOM Mary-DAT-ACC     book-ACC   give-PST-IND
     'John gave a book to Mary.'
```

The sentence in (26) shows that if a verb has the capacity to assign two distinct Cases, it may assign such Cases to its single argument. If such assignment of distinct Cases takes place in the sentences in (25), the principle (24) will predict that both a whole-NP and the projection of a relational nominal may have two distinct Case features. The last assumption we need is that Case-realization may be determined by some morphological rule as a free choice. The current theory correctly predicts four possible combinations of Case displayed in (25).[16]

5. Concluding Remarks

We have shown that under the derivational analysis the descriptive condition on scrambling of a part-NP and the requirement of inalienable relation in IACs are both derivable from independently motivated, universal principles, the Proper Binding

---

14 For the detailed discussion on a single-Case spread analysis and its problems, see Maling and Kim (1992).

15 This particular construction is limited to a certain dialect of Korean; but we assume that the assignment of multiple Case features to a single argument takes place in standard Korean and the limited distribution of the realization of multiple Case features is attributed to how the manner of Case-realization is parameterized.

16 If there are three arguments in IACs and two distinct Case features are assigned to each of them, the current theory predicts eight possible combinations of Case-realization. This is precisely what is reported in Maling and Kim (1992).

Condition and the ECP. In the last section, a solution to the Case-theoretic problem of IACs was suggested.

References

Abney, Steven. 1987. The English Noun Phrase in its Sentential Aspect. Doctoral dissertation, MIT.

Anderson, Mona. 1984. Prenominal Genitive NPs. The Linguistic Review 3. 1-24.

Borer, Hagit. 1989. Anaphoric AGR. The Null Subject Parameter, ed. by Osvaldo Jaeggli and Kenneth J. Safir, 69-109. Dordrecht: Kluwer Academic Publisher.

Cho, Sook Whan. 1989. Kyay ('s/he'), Binding, and Logophoricity in Korean. Harvard Studies in Korean Linguistics III, ed. by Susumu Kuno et al, 201-11. Seoul: Hanshin Publishing Company.

Choe, Hyon Sook. 1987. Syntactic Adjunction, A-chain and the ECP: Multiple Identical Case Construction in Korean. Proceedings of NELS 17.

Chomsky, Noam. 1981. Lectures on Government and Binding. Dordrecht: Foris Publications.

Chomsky, Noam. 1986a. Knowledge of Language: Its Nature, Origin, and Use. New York: Praeger.

Chomsky, Noam. 1986b. Barriers. Linguistic Inquiry Monograph 13. Cambridge: The MIT Press.

Gerdts, Donna B. and Cheong Youn. 1988. Korean Constructions: Advancement or Retreat? Proceedings of CLS 24.

Grimshaw, Jane. 1991. Extended Projection. Ms. Brandeis University.

Higginbotham, James. 1985. On Semantics. Linguistic Inquiry 16. 547-594.

Higginbotham, James. 1987. Indefiniteness and Predication. The Representation of (In)definiteness, ed. by Eric J. Reuland and Alice G.B. ter Meulen, 43-70. Cambridge: The MIT Press.

Kim, Young-joo. 1989. Inalienable Possession as a Semantic Relationship Underlying Predication: The Case of Multiple-Accusative Constructions. Harvard Studies in Korean Linguistics III, ed. by Susumu Kuno et al, 445-67. Seoul: Hanshin Publishing Company.

Kim, Young-joo. 1990. The Syntax and Semantics of Korean Case: The Interaction Between Lexical and Syntactic Levels of Representation. Doctoral dissertation. Harvard University.

Koopman, Hilda and Dominique Sportiche. 1991. The Position of Subjects. Lingua 85. 211-258.

Kuno, Susumu. 1973. The Structure of the Japanese Language. Cambridge: The MIT Press.

Kuroda, Shige-Yuki. 1988. Whether We Agree or Not: A Comparative Syntax of English and Japanese. Japanese Syntax, ed. by William J. Poser, 103-43. Stanford: CSLI.

Maling, Joan. 1989. Adverbials and Structural Case in Korean. Harvard Studies in Korean Linguistics III, ed. by Susumu Kuno et al, 297-308. Seoul: Hanshin Publishing Company.

Maling, Joan and Soowon Kim. 1992. Case Assignment in the Inalienable Possession Construction in Korean. Journal of East Asian Linguistics 1.1. 37-68.

May, Robert. 1977. The Grammar of Quantification. Doctoral dissertation. MIT.

Reinhart, Tanya. 1976. The Syntactic Domain of Anaphora. Doctoral dissertation. MIT.

Saito, Mamoru. 1985. Some Asymmetries in Japanese and Their Theoretical Implication. Doctoral dissertation. MIT.
Saito, Mamoru. 1989. Scrambling as Semantically Vacuous A'-Movement. Alternative Conceptions of Phrase Structure, ed. by Mark Baltin and Anthony Kroch, 182-200. Chicago: The University of Chicago Press.
Speas, Margaret. 1990. Phrase Structure in Natural Language. Dordrecht: Kluwer Academic Publishers.
Stowell, Timothy. 1989. Subjects, Specifiers, and X-Bar Theory. Alternative Conceptions of Phrase Structure, ed. by Mark Baltin and Anthony Kroch, 232-62. Chicago: The University of Chicago Press.
Tateishi, Koichi. 1988. On the Universality of X'-Theory: The Case in Japanese. Proceedings of WCCFL 7.
Tellier, Christine. 1990. Underlying Nominals and the Projection Principle: Inherent Possessors. Proceedings of NELS 20.
Yoon, James Hye-Suk. 1989. The Grammar of Inalienable Possession Constructions in Korean, Mandarin and French. Harvard Studies in Korean Linguistics III, ed. by Susumu Kuno et al, 357-81. Seoul: Hanshin Publishing Company.
Yoon, James Hye-Suk. 1990. Theta Theory and the Grammar of Inalienable Possession Constructions. Proceedings of NELS 20.

Modal Phrase and Adjuncts

MASATOSHI KOIZUMI
MIT

Modal Phrase and Adjuncts*
Masatoshi Koizumi
MIT

0. Introduction

Following Whitman (1989), Koizumi (1991) argues that Korean/Japanese-type languages have a MODAL PHRASE (MP) between CP and IP (or TP), as shown in (1b).

(1) a. Kanti-ga Rika-ni nekkuresu-o age-ta *daroo* ne.
-Nom -Dat necklace-Acc give-past probable SP
'Probably, Kanchi gave a necklace to Rika.'

b.
```
                CP
               /  \
                   C'
                  /  \
              MP      C
             /  \     |
                 M'  ne
                /  \
          IP         M
         /  \        |
   NP          I'  daroo
   |          /  \
 Kanti   VP        I
        /  \       |
     NP     V'    ta
     |     /  \
   Rika  NP     V
         |      |
   nekkuresu   age
```

MP is a category headed by a modal element such as *daroo* 'probable/seem', *desyoo* 'probable/seem', *mai* (negative volition), etc. Existence of a maximal projection between CP and IP is confirmed by subsequent work such as Sato-Zhu (1992) and Ueyama (1991).

Assuming the basic correctness of the phrase structure with MP, in this paper I will discuss distributions of clausal adjuncts in Japanese. I will argue that (clausal) adjuncts in Japanese can be divided into three types with respect to their basepositions: i.e. VP-ADJUNCTS, IP-ADJUNCTS, and MP-ADJUNCTS. This amounts to claiming that there is no such a thing as CP-adjunct. A partial list of the three types of clausal adjuncts is given below.

(2) Clausal adjuncts in Japanese

TYPE 1 (VP-adjuncts)		TYPE 2 (IP-adjuncts)		TYPE 3 (MP-adjuncts)	
-nagara	'while'	*-kagiri*	'as long as'	*-kara*	'because'
-tutu	'while'	*-to*	'if'		(circumstantial)
-mae-ni	'before'	*-node*	'because'	*-ga*	'but
-aida-ni	'while'	*-mae*	'before'	*-kedo*	'but'
-toki-ni	'when'	*-aida*	'while'		
-ato-de	'after'	*-toki*	'when'		
		-ato	'after'		
		-sai	'when'		

Clausal adjuncts headed by *nagara* 'while', *maeni* 'before', etc. are AFFILIATED to VP.[1] Those headed by *kagiri* 'as long as', *to* 'if', etc. are affiliated to IP. And those headed by circumstantial *kara* 'because', *kedo* 'but', etc. are affiliated to MP.[2] If it turns out that (2) is basically correct, then that will constitute an indirect support for the phrase structure in (1). In the following, I will present several pieces of evidence for (2).

---

[1] α is affiliated to XP iff α is immediately dominated by a (segment of a) projection of X.

[2] The *kara* clause I am arguing to be Type 3 is a circumstantial *kara* clause, as opposed to a cause/reason *kara* clause. The two types of *kara* clauses are exemplified below.

(i) Circumstantial *kara*

[Kenkyuusitu-no denki-ga kieteiru -kara] Kiyomi-wa moo kaetta daroo.
office -Gen light-Nom off -because -Top already return seem
'Since the light of the her/his office is off, as for Kiyomi, I think, s/he has come home.'

(ii) Cause/reason *kara*

Kiyomi-wa [onaka -ga suita-kara] makudonarudo-ni haitta.
-Top stomach-Nom empty-because McDonald's-Dat entered
'Kiyomi entered McDonald's because s/he got hungry.'

The circumstantial *kara* clause conveys the information based on which the speaker has reached to the conclusion reported in the main clause. That is, the content of the circumstantial *kara* clause is outside the proposition asserted by the sentence. On the other hand, the content of the cause/reason *kara* clause is a part of the proposition asserted by the entire sentence. The latter type of *kara* is most likely Type 2 of my classification. See also Butler (1990), which argues that the cause *kara* is a VP-adjunct (and the reason *kara* is an IP-adjunct).

1. Three Types of Clausal Adjuncts

In this section, I will establish, by using several syntactic tests, that adjuncts of Type 1, Type 2, and Type 3 are affiliated to VP, IP, and MP, respectively.

1.1. *Sae* 'even'

As argued in Kato (1985) and Ogino (1990), a focus particle such as *sae* 'even' sets focus on the maximal projection to which it is attached or on a constituent dominated by this maximal projection.[3] In other words, a constituent in c-commanding domain of *sae* can be focused. In (3a), *sae* attaches to the object, hence the object is focused. More precisely, the sentence has the following set of presuppositions: (i) there are things other than an apple that Kiyomi ate, and (ii) of all the things, an apple is the least expected for Kiyomi to eat.

(3) a. Kiyomi-ga [$_{XP}$ [$_{NP}$ ringo]-*sae*] tabe-ta.
 -Nom apple-even eat-Past
 'Kiyomi ate even an apple.'
 b. Kiyomi-ga [$_{XP}$ [$_{VP}$ ringo-o tabe]-*sae*] si-ta.
 -Nom apple-Acc eat-even do-Past
 'Kiyomi even ate an apple.'

In (3b), *sae* attaches to the VP, hence *sae* c-commands every constituent in the VP as well as the VP itself. As such, the sentence has three possible readings, depending on which of the following three constituents c-commanded by *sae* are to be focused; *ringo* 'an apple', *tabe* 'to eat', or *ringo-o tabe* 'to eat an apple'. The three possible sets of presuppositions are listed below.

(4) a. Focus: [$_{NP}$ ringo] 'apple'
 b. Presupposition:
 (i) There are things other than an apple that Kiyomi ate.
 (ii) Of all the things, an apple is the least expected for Kiyomi to eat.

(5) a. Focus: [$_{V}$ tabe] 'to eat'
 b. Presupposition:
 (i) There are things other than eating that Kiyomi did with the apples.
 (ii) Of all the things Kiyomi did with the apples, eating was the least expected for Kiyomi to do.

---

[3]Other focus particles include *wa* (Topic/Contrastive), *mo* 'also', *dake* 'only', *sika* 'only', etc.

(6) a. Focus: [$_{VP}$ ringo-o tabe] 'to eat an apple'
b. Presupposition:
(i) There are things other than eating apples that Kiyomi did.
(ii) Of all the things Kiyomi did, eating apples was the least expected.

Notice that (3b) does not have a reading in which the subject is focused. This is because the subject NP is outside the c-commanding domain of *sae* attached to the VP (Ogino, 1990) (But see Hasegawa (1989) and Ahn (1991)).

With this in mind, consider the following sentences with a Type 1 adjunct.

(7) a. [$_{T1}$ TV-o mi -nagara] benkyoosi-sae sita.
-Acc watch -while study -even did
'(I) even studied [while watching TV].'
b. Kiyomi-wa [$_{T1}$ zyugyoo-ni iku-mae-ni] wain-o nomi-sae sita.
-Top class-to go-before wine-Acc drink-even did
'Kiyomi even drunk wine before s/he went to a class.'

These sentences have readings, among others, in which the clausal adjunct is within the scopal domain of *sae*. Thus, (7a) can be interpreted as follows: I did several things such as eating pizza while dancing, singing songs while running, etc., and I even studied while watching TV. In this case, the sentence has the following set of focus and presuppositions.

(8) a. Focus: [$_{T1}$ TV-o mi-nagara] benkyoosi 'to study while watching TV'
b. Presupposition:
(i) there are things other than studying while watching TV that I did.
(ii) of all the things I did, studying while watching TV was the least expected.

Similarly, (7b) may have the following set of focus and presuppositions.

(9) a. Focus: [$_{T1}$ zyugyoo-ni iku-mae-ni] sake-o nomi
'to drink wine before going to class'
b. Presupposition:
(i) there are things other than drinking wine before going to class that I did.
(ii) of all the things I did, drinking wine before going to class was the least expected.

This suggests that an adjunct of Type 1 is affiliated to VP rather than to higher nodes such as IP.

On the other hand, neither Type 2 nor Type 3 adjuncts falls into the focus domain of *sae* attached to VP. Thus, in the following sentences, the adjunct clauses are outside the scope of *sae*.

(10) Kiyomi-wa [$_{T2}$ koohii mame-ga nakunar-ana-i -kagiri]
-Top coffee bean-Nom run out-not-NonPast-as long as
kaimono-ni iki-sae si-na-i
shopping-to go-even do-not-NonPast
'Kiyomi doesn't even go shopping unless coffee beans run out.'

(11) [$_{T3}$ Kiyomi-no atama-kara ti-ga deteiru-kara], dooyara
-Gen head-from blood-Nom run out-because probably
Masami-wa (Kiyomi-no) atama-o naguri-sae sita yooda naa.
-Top -Gen head-Acc hit-even did seem SP
'Since Kiyomi's head is bleeding, it seems that Masami even hit her/his (= Kiyomi's) head.'

Since *sae* attached to a VP can set focus on any constituent in the VP, the fact that the *kagiri* -clause and the *kara* -clause cannot be focused in the sentences above implies that these adjuncts are generated in a position higher than VP.

In sum, I have shown that Type 1 but not Type 2 or Type 3 adjuncts are base-generated within VP, as I have suggested in (2).

1.2. Negation

Negation also provides evidence for the trichotomy of adjuncts I am arguing for.

First, consider the following sentences.

(12) a. Kiyomi-wa [$_{T1}$ TV-o mi-nagara] benkyoosi-na-katta.
-Top -Acc watch-while study-not-Past
'Kiyomi doesn't study watching TV.'

b. Kiyomi-wa [$_{T2}$ huttobooru-ga owar-anai-kagiri]
-Top football-Nom finish-not-as long as
benkyoosi-nakat-ta.
study-not -Past
'I didn't study until the football game was over.'

c. [$_{T3}$ Kenkyuusitu-no denki-ga kieteiru-kara]
office -Gen light-Nom off -because
Kiyomi-wa i-na-i daroo.
-Top be-neg-NonPast probable
'Since the light of his office is off, as for Kiyomi, I think, s/he is not (here).'

Among these sentences, only (12a) has the reading in which the clausal adjunct is negated. That is, (12a) may be interpreted as 'Kiyomi studied, but not while watching TV'. However, the clausal adjunct in the other sentences cannot be negated; (12c), for example, does not have the reading 'I think Kiyomi is here, but not because the light of his office is off'. Therefore, the generalization to be drawn is clearly that only Type 1 adjuncts can be negated.

This is naturally accounted for if only Type 1 adjuncts are affiliated to VP. Assuming that Neg is in INFL at S-structure (Hasegawa 1991), Neg and the adjunct in (12a) have the structural relation represented in (13a), and the other two sentences have structures like (13b).

(13) a. $[_{I'}$ $[_{VP}$ **-nagara** (Type 1) . . .] Neg]
b. **-kara** (Type 3) / **-kagiri** (Type 2) $[_{I'}$ $[_{VP}$ . . .] Neg]

In (13a), the adjunct is c-commanded by Neg, hence it can be negated. On the other hand, the adjuncts in (13b), being outside the c-command domain of Neg, cannot be the target of negation.

A negative counterpart of a VP-focused sentence discussed in the preceding section also shows a similar contrast. Generally, what is negated in a negative VP-focused sentence is the entire focused VP, i.e. complement VP of a focus particle such as *wa* (see footnote 3). This is because a focused element tends to be the focus of negation. Thus, in (14), it is *[$_{XP}$ [$_{VP}$ piza-o tabe]-wa]* as a whole that is negated.[4]

(14) Kiyomi-wa $[_{XP}$ $[_{VP}$ piza-o tabe]-wa] si-nakat-ta.
-Top pizza-Acc eat-Top do-not-Past
'Kiyomi didn't do eating pizza, at least.'

When a Type 1 adjunct occurs in a negative VP-focused sentence, it may fall in the scope of negation, as exemplified in (15).

(15) Kiyomi-wa $[_{T1}$ TV-o mi-nagara] benkyoosi-wa si-na-i.
-Top -Acc watch-while study -Top do-not-NonPast.
'Kiyomi doesn't do studying watching TV, at least.'

This shows that the Type 1 adjunct may occur within the VP, and hence it can be within the scope of negation.

On the other hand, neither Type 2 adjuncts nor Type 3 adjuncts can be negated in this construction, as the sentences in (16) show. (16a) does not mean that Kiyomi studies not until the football game is over, nor does (16b) mean that I think Kiyomi is here, but not because the light of his office is off. This implies that the Type 2 adjunct and the Type 3 adjunct are outside the scope of negation in these sentences.

---

[4]With appropriate intonation, (14) may be interpreted in such a way that the *wa* -marked NP, rather than the *wa* -marked VP, is negated. Throughout this paper, I will disregard this interpretation.

(16) a. Kiyomi-wa [$_{T2}$ huttobooru-ga owar-anai -kagiri]
-Top football-Nom finish-not -as long as
benkyoosi-wa si-na-i.
study-Top do-not-NonPast
'Kiyomi won't study until the football game is over.'
b. [$_{T3}$ Kenkyuusitu-no denki-ga kieteiru-kara]
office -Gen light-Nom off -because
Kiyomi-wa i-wa si-na -i daroo.
-Top be-Top do-neg-NonPast probable
'Since the light of her/his office is off, as for Kiyomi, I think, s/he is not (here).'

This is another piece of evidence that adjuncts of Type 2 and Type 3 are generated in a position higher than VP, for the domain of negation in the negative VP-focused sentence is the entire focused VP.

There is another type of negative sentence, in which the entire IP is the focus of negation. A couple of examples of this type are given below.

(17) a. [$_{IP}$ Kiyomi-ga piza-o tabe-ta]-wakede-wa na-i.
-Nom pizza-Acc eat-Past-case-Top not-NonPast
'It is not the case that Kiyomi ate pizza.'
b. Kiyomi$_i$-wa [$_{IP}$ e_i piza-o tabe-ta]-node-wa na-i.
-Top pizza-Acc eat-Past-case-Top not-NonPast
'As for Kiyomi, it is not the case that s/he ate pizza.'

When they occur in this type of sentence, both Type 1 and Type 2 adjunct are included within the scope of negation, as exemplified below.

(18) a. Kiyomi$_i$-wa [e_i [$_{T1}$ TV-o mi-nagara] benkyoosi-ta]
-Top -Acc watch-while study -Past
-wakede-wa na-i.
-case-Top not-NonPast
'As for Kiyomi, it is not the case that s/he studied watching TV.'
b. Kiyomi$_i$-wa [e_i [$_{T2}$ huttobooru-ga owar-anai-kagiri]
-Top football-Nom finish-not-as long as
biiru-o nomi-tuzuke-ru]-wakede-wa na-i.
beer-Acc drink-keep-NonPast-case-Top not-NonPast
'It is not the case that Kiyomi keeps drinking beer until the football game is over.'

Type 3 adjuncts, on the other hand, cannot be included in the focus of negation.

(19) [$_{T3}$ Kenkyuusitu-no denki-ga kieteiru-kara]
office -Gen light-Nom off -because
Kiyomi$_i$-wa [e_i gakkoo-ni kitei -ru]-wakede-wa na-i.
-Top school-to come-NonPast-case-Top not-NonPast
'Since the light of her/his office is off, as for Kiyomi, it is not the case that s/he has come to school.'

The contrast between (18) and (19) thus suggests that clausal adjuncts of Type 1 and 2 are within IP, while those of Type 3 are not.

In sum, examination of negative sentences has revealed (i) that Type 1 adjuncts are base-generated within VP, (ii) that Type 2 adjuncts are affiliated to IP, and (iii) that Type 3 adjuncts are generated in a position higher than IP.

1.3. Pro-IP *Soo*

We have seen that in Japanese, there are three kinds of clausal adjuncts: VP-adjuncts, IP-adjuncts, and adjuncts generated above IP. In this subsection, I will present further evidence for the trichotomy of adjuncts. In particular, I will show that only Type 3 is base-generated outside the IP.

As argued in Koizumi (1991), the proform *soo* may function as a pro-IP. *soo* in (20b) refers to the propositional content of (20a) including Tense (X ate an apple), but excluding Modal. The scope of *soo* is thus IP.[5]

(20) a. Kiyomi-wa [$_{IP}$ eego-ga deki-ru] daroo.
-Nom English-Nom able-NonPast probable
'As for Kiyomi, probably, s/he can speak English.'
b. Masami-mo soo daroo.
-also so probable
'As for Masami, I think so, too. (s/he can speak English)'

Now, it is predicted that, if Type 3 adjuncts are generated above IP, and if adjuncts of Type 1 and Type 2 are generated within IP, as I am arguing, then only Type 3 adjuncts should be able to be outside the scope of *soo*. This in fact is the case.

(21) a. Kiyomi-wa [$_{T1}$ TV-o mi-nagara] benkyoosuru daroo
-Top TV-Acc watch-while study probable
'As for Kiyomi, I think, s/he will study, watching TV.'
b. * Masami-wa [$_{T1}$ razio-o kiki-nagara] soo daroo.
-Top radio-Acc listen-while so probable
'As for Masami, I think so, too, listening to the radio (s/he will study, listening to the radio)'

[5]The subject-like NP in the sentence initial position in (20b) is not a subject, rather it is a sort of topic generated outside the IP. See Koizumi (1991: Chapter III) for details.

(22) a. Kiyomi-wa [$_{T2}$ koohii mame-ga nakunar-ana-i -kagiri]
-Top coffee bean-Nom run out-not-NonPast -as long as
kaimono-ni ik-anai daroo.
shopping-to go-not probable
'As for Kiyomi, I think, s/he won't go shopping unless coffee beans run out.'

b. * Masami-wa [$_{T2}$ orenzi zyuusu-ga nakunaranai-kagiri] soo daroo.
-Top orange juice-Nom run out-not-as long as so probable
'As for Masami, I think so, too, unless orange juice run out. (s/he won't go shopping, either, unless orange juice run out)'

(23) a. [$_{T3}$ Kenkyuusitu-no denki-ga kieteiru-kara]
office -Gen light-Nom off -because
Kiyomi-wa moo kaetta daroo.
-Top already return probable
'Since the light of the her/his office is off, as for Kiyomi, I think, s/he has come home.'

b. [$_{T3}$ Kuruma-ga nai -kara] Masami-mo soo daroo.
car-Nom isn't-because -also so probable
'Since her/his car isn't (in the parking lot), as for Masami, I think so, too. (s/he came home)'

Thus, it can be concluded that the Type 3 adjunct is generated outside IP. This is further supported by the following sentences.

(24) a. Kiyomi-wa [$_{T1}$ TV-o mi -nagara] benkyoosuru daroo
-Top TV-Acc watch-while study probable
'As for Kiyomi, I think, s/he will study, watching TV.'

b. Masami-mo soo daroo.
-also so probable
'As for Masami, I think so, too (s/he will study, watching TV)'

(25) a. Kiyomi-wa [$_{T2}$ koohii mame-ga nakunar-ana-i
-Top coffee bean-Nom run out-not-NonPast
-kagiri] kaimono-ni ik-anai daroo.
-as long as shopping-to go-not probable
'As for Kiyomi, I think, s/he won't go shopping unless coffee beans run out.'

b. Masami-mo soo daroo.
-also so probable
'As for Masami, I think so, too (s/he won't go shopping unless coffee beans run out).'

(26) a. [T3 Kenkyuusitu-no denki-ga kieteiru-kara]
office -Gen light-Nom off -because
Kiyomi-wa moo kaetta daroo.
-Top already return probable
'Since the light of the her/his office is off, as for Kiyomi, I think, s/he has come home.'
b. Masami-mo (tabun) soo daroo.
-also (may be) so probable
'As for Masami, I think so, too (s/he has come home).'

While *soo* in (24b) and (25b) has in its scope the adjuncts in (24a) and (25a), respectively, *soo* in (26b) does not have the adjunct in (26a) in its scope, which implies that Type 3 adjunct cannot be included in the scope of the pro-IP. Thus, I have shown that the basepositions of Type 3 adjuncts are ouside IP.

1.4. Embedding

So far, I have shown that Type 1 adjuncts and Type 2 adjuncts are VP-adjuncts and IP-adjuncts, respectively. I have also suggested that Type 3 adjuncts are generated in a position higher than IP. The question, then, is: Are Type 3 adjuncts MP-adjuncts or CP-adjuncts? I will argue that the Type 3 adjuncts are affiliated to MP. Before doing so, I present an additional piece of evidence for the claim that Type 1 and Type 2 adjuncts are affiliated to VP and IP, respectively.

It is known that some clausal adjuncts such as *nagara* 'while' only allow for members of VP (i.e. a verb stem, and objects, if any) to occur in them. Other adjuncts such as *kagiri* 'as long as' may allow elements dominated by IP (i.e. subject and a Tense marker as well as a verb stem and objects). Still other adjuncts such as *kara* 'because' allow up to members of Modal Phrase (i.e. subject, objects, a verb stem, a Tense marker, and a modal element such as *daroo* 'probable') COMP elements such as Q-morpheme *ka* never occur in clausal adjuncts (cf. Minami, 1974; Sawada, 1983; Koizumi, 1991). This is shown below.

(27) AVP
a. [VP TV-o mi]-nagara benkyoosu-ru.
-Acc watch-while study-NonPast
'(I) study [while watching TV].'
b. * [IP TV-o mi -ru]-nagara benkyoosu-ru.
-Acc watch-NonPast-while study-NonPast
'(I) study [while I watch TV].'

(28) AIP
a. [IP koko-ni i -ru]-kagiri tukamar-anai
here-at stay-NonPast-as long as be arrested-not
'You won't be arrested [as far as you are here].

(28) b. * [$_{MP}$ warui-koto-o su -ru daroo]-kagiri tukamaru
bad-thing-Acc do-NonPast probable-as long as be arrested
'you will be arrested [as far as you seem to do wrong thing].'

(29) AMP
a. [$_{MP}$ kinoo-wa nerarenakat-ta daroo]-kara
yesterday-Top can't sleep-Past probable-because
kyoo-wa yasum -asete-age -yoo.
today-Top take a rest-make-give-let's
'Let's give her/him a day off today [because, I think, s/he couldn't sleep yesterday].'
b. * [$_{CP}$ kinoo-wa nerarenakat-ta ne]-kara kyoo-wa
yesterday-Top can't sleep-Past SP-because today-Top
yasum -oo
take a rest-let's
'Let's have a day off today [because we couldn't sleep yesterday, could we].'

Let's call these three kinds of adjuncts adjuncts of VP (AVP), adjuncts of IP (AIP), and adjuncts of MP (AMP), respectively. Note that these are so named because of their internal selectional restrictions. This classification should not be confused with what is given in (2), which we are arguing for based on the external syntactic distributions. The memberships of AVP, AIP, and AMP are not necessarily identical to those of Type 1, Type 2, and Type 3, respectively.

Since I have argued in the previous subsections that Type 1 adjuncts and Type 2 adjuncts are affiliated to VP and IP, respectively, it is predicted that, among clausal adjuncts, only Type 1 may occur in AVP, and that both Type 1 and Type 2 may appear in AIP. Type 3 adjuncts should not occur either in AVP or in AIP, for they are generated outside IP. The predictions are born out.

(30) a. [$_{AVP}$[$_{T1}$ Sake-o nomi-tutu] syokuzi-o si]-nagara TV-o mita.
rice wine-Acc drink-while meal-Acc do-while -Acc watched
'(I) watched TV [while I dined [drinking rice wine]].
b. * [$_{AVP}$ TV-o [$_{T2}$ onaka-ga suk-anai-kagiri] mi]-nagara
-Acc be hungry -not-as long as watch-while
benkyoosita.
studied
'I studied [while watching TV [as long as I didn't become hungry]].'
c. * [$_{AVP}$TV-o[$_{T3}$syukudai-ga owatta-kara] mi]-nagara
-Acc homework-Nom finished-because watch-while
ohiru-o tabeta
lunch-Acc ate
'I had lunch, [watching TV [because I finished homework]].'

(31) a. [$_{AIP}$[$_{T1}$sake-o nomi-nagara] untensi-nai]-kagiri tukamar-anai
rice wine-Acc drink-while drive-not -as long as be arrested-not
'You won't be arrested [unless you drive [drinking]].'

b. Masami-wa [$_{AIP}$ [$_{T2}$ gakki-matu-ni nar-anai-to]
-Top quarter-end-at become-not-if
benkyoosi-nai]-node seeseki-ga warui.
study-not-because grade-Nom bad
'As for Masami, [since s/he does not study [until the end of quarter comes]], her/his GPA is bad.

c. * [$_{AIP}$ [$_{T3}$ kaze-o hiite iru-ga] sake-o nomu]-to naoru
flue-Acc have-but rice wine-Acc drink-if is cured
'[If I drink wine [although I have flue]], I will be cured.'

(30) shows that only Type 1 adjuncts may occur in AVP, which in turn supports the analysis that Type 1 adjuncts are VP-adjuncts.[6] On the other hand, (31) suggests that adjuncts of Type 1 and Type 2, but not Type 3, appear in AIP. This means that Type 2 adjuncts as well as Type 1 adjuncts are generated under IP. Thus, Type 2 adjuncts are IP adjuncts.

Now, consider the following examples with an AMP.

(32) a. [$_{AMP}$ [$_{T1}$ TV-o mi]-nagara benkyoosita]-kara seeseki-ga
-Acc watch-while studied -because grade-Nom
sagaru daroo.
fall probable
'My grade will probably fall [because I studied, [watching TV]].'

b. [$_{AMP}$ [$_{T2}$ yopparai-unten-o si-nai-kagiri] tukamar-anai
drunk-driving-Acc do-not-as far as be arrested-not
-kara] daizyoobuda
-because be OK
'[Since you won't be arrested [unless you drive dead-drunk]], you don't have to worry.'

c. Kiyomi-wa [$_{AMP}$ [$_{T3}$ Big Bear-ni itta]-ga yasumidatta-kara]
-Top -Dat went-but was closed-because
Kroger-de kaimono-o sita.
-at shopping-Acc did
'[Since, [though s/he went to the Big Bear], it was closed], Kiyomi did shopping at Kroger.'

---

[6](30b,c) could be acceptable if *TV-o* (TV-Acc) is placed immediately before *mi* 'watch'. In that case, however, the sentences have different structures and different interpretations, as given below.

(30b') [$_{T2}$ onaka-ga suk-anai]-kagiri [$_{AVP}$ TV-o mi-nagara] benkyoosita.
be hungry -not -as far as -Acc watch-while studied
'[as far as I didn't become hungry], I studied [while watching TV].'

(30c') [$_{T3}$ syukudai-ga owatta]-kara [$_{AVP}$ TV-o mi-nagara] ohiru-o tabeta.
homework-Nom finished-because -Acc watch-while lunch-Acc ate
'[because I finished homework], I had lunch [watching TV].'

These strings of words are unacceptable with the interpretations in which the Type 2 or Type 3 adjunct is included in the Type 1 adjunct.

These sentences show that all the three types of adjuncts (i.e. Types 1, 2, and 3) are generated under the projection of MP. (32c) in particular suggests that Type 3 adjuncts are MP-adjuncts, for they are outside the IP and within the MP. The following sentence exemplifies the same point.

(33) (Kiyomi had a cancer on his gullet.)
[$_{AMP}$ [$_{T3}$ Hayame-ni syuzutu-o uketa -kara] tasukatta]-ga
in good time operation-Acc underwent-because recovered-but
soodenakereba imagoro sindeita daroo.
otherwise by this time has died probable
'Although s/he recovered as s/he was operated on in good time,
s/he must have been dead, otherwise.'

To summarize this section, I have demonstrated that the clausal adjuncts in Japanese can be classified into three types: VP-adjunct, IP-adjunct, and MP-adjunct. There does not seem to exist such a thing as CP-adjunct.

2. Feature Matching Principle (for Adjuncts)

What we have seen in the previous section can be summarized as follows.

(34) a. Type 1 adjuncts such as *nagara* 'while' are affiliated to VP.
b. Type 2 adjuncts such as *kagiri* 'as long as' are affiliated to IP.
c. Type 3 adjuncts such as *kara* 'because' are affiliated to MP.

If each clausal adjunct is adjoined to a maximal projection, Japanese phrase structure will have the following form.

(35)
```
                 MP
                /  \
   T3-adjunct     MP
                 /  \
                     M'
                    /  \
                 IP     M
                /  \
   T2-adjunct     IP
                 /  \
                     I'
                    /  \
                 VP     I
                /  \
   T1-adjunct     VP
                 /  \
```

This hierarchical relation is also reflected by the natural order of the three types of adjuncts: the most natural order is T3-T2-T1, as exemplified in (36). While (36a), which assumes the T3-T2-T1 order, is perfectly natural, (36b), in which T2 precedes T1, is slightly awkward. (36c) is more awkward, in which the order of adjuncts is T1-T2-T3, the opposite of the most natural T3-T2-T1 order. (36b) and (36c) may be derived by scrambling the adjuncts.[7]

(36) a. Kiyomi-wa [$_{T3}$ arutyuude-wa nai-ga] [$_{T2}$ tokubetuna riyuu-ga
-Top alcoholic-Top not-Nom special reason-Nom
nai-kagiri] [$_{T1}$ sake-o nomi-nagara] syokuzi-o suru.
isn't-as long as wine-Acc drink-while meal-Acc take
'[Although s/he$_i$ is not a alcoholic], Kiyomi$_i$ takes a meal [drinking wine], [unless there is a special reason (not to do so)].'

b. ? Kiyomi-wa [$_{T2}$ tokubetuna riyuu-ga nai -kagiri]
-Top special reason-Nom isn't-as long as
[$_{T3}$ arutyuude-wa nai-ga] [$_{T1}$ sake-o nomi-nagara] syokuzi-o suru.
alcoholic-Top not-Nom wine-Acc drink-while meal-Acc take

c. ?? Kiyomi-wa [$_{T1}$ sake-o nomi-nagara] [$_{T2}$ tokubetuna riyuu-ga
-Top wine-Acc drink-while special reason-Nom
nai-kagiri] [$_{T3}$ arutyuu-de-wa nai-ga] syokuzi-o suru.
isn't-as far as alcoholic-Top not-Nom meal-Acc take

Why should there be a distinction of adjuncts as summarized in (34)? Intuitively speaking, the syntactic hierarchy of adjuncts we have observed is a reflection of semantic hierarchy. Type 1 adjuncts modify what is expressed (or denoted) by VP such as PROCESS (cf. Vendler, 1967; Dowty, 1979; Tenny, 1987, etc.).[8] Type 2 adjuncts modify the content of IP, which might be called EVENT. Type 3 adjuncts are related to MODALITY instead of process or event.

Before formalizing this intuition, let us examine the sentences in (37) below from Travis (1988) to better understand what is meant by process, event, etc. It is well known that a certain group of adverbs such as *quickly* may occur in any of the four positions exemplified in (37) (cf. Jackendoff, 1972, among others).

(37) a. Quickly John will be arrested by the police. (Initial)
b. John quickly will be arrested by the police. (AUX)
c. John will be quickly arrested by the police. (VP-initial)
d. John will be arrested quickly by the police. (VP-final)

Contrary to the widely held view, Travis (1988) points out that (37a,b), on the one hand, and (37c,d), on the other, differ in meaning. In the former sentences, where *quickly* appears in Initial position or AUX position, the

[7]Nakajima (1991) argues that an adjunct movement is subject to a version of Relativised Minimality (cf. Rizzi, 1990). If it is the case, then (36c) might be a Relativised Minimality violation.

[8]Processes 'consist of successive phases following one another in time' (Vender, 1967: 99).

adverb is modifying the **event** of the arrest, while in the latter sentences, where it occurs in VP-initial or VP-final position, the adverb modifies the **process** of the arrest. In other words, in (37a,b) the arrest will happen right away, and in (37c,d) the manner of the arrest will be hurried.

Returning to the distribution of clausal adjuncts, I propose the following: First, a head of a clausal adjunct has the feature given in (38).

(38) Head Features of Adjuncts
Head of Type 1 adjunct: [+process modifier]
Head of Type 2 adjunct: [+event modifier]
Head of Type 3 adjunct: [+modality modifier]

Second, V, I, and M have the following features.

(39) V: [+process]
I: [+event]
M: [+modality]

Finally, the distribution of the clausal adjuncts is (in part) governed by the FEATURE MATCHING PRINCIPLE, given in (40).

(40) Feature Matching Principle (for Adjuncts)
The tail of the chain of an adjunct with [+a modifier] feature must be in a Checking Domain of a head H that has [+a] feature.

Technical details aside, a CHECKING DOMAIN of H is a set of non-complement positions that are immediately dominated by a projection or a segment of a projection of H (cf. Chomsky, class lectures: Fall 1991). Thus, the relation between the three types of adjuncts and their licensers will look like (41).[9]

[9]Not any verb is a process verb, hence not any verb can license a Type 1 adjunct. A non-process verb such as a stative verb has a different head feature, and licenses a different set of VP-adjuncts. Similarly, there are types of EVENTS, each of which appears to license a different set of adjuncts.

```
(41)               MP
                  /  \
     T3-adjunct        MP
     [+modality      /   \
       modifier]           M'
                         /   \
                      IP        M
                     /  \     [+modality]
        T2-adjunct       IP
        [+event         /  \
          modifier]         I'
                           /  \
                        VP      I
                       /  \   [+event]
           T1-adjunct      VP
           [+process      /  \
             modifier]        V'
                             /  \
                                  V
                                [+process]
```

Semantically, a Type 1 adjunct is a function from process to process; a Type 2, from event to event; and a Type 3, from modality to modality.

3. Temporal Adjuncts

This section is concerned with two types of temporal adjuncts; the one with [+process modifier] feature and the one with [+event modifier] feature.

Hoji (1985) argues that clausal temporal adjuncts such as *mae-ni* 'before' and *ato-de* 'after' as in (42) are base-generated between subject and object.

(42) a. Kiyomi-ga [neru-mae-ni] sake-o nonda.
-Nom sleep-before-at wine-Acc drunk
'Kiyomi drunk wine before s/he went to bed.'
b. Kiyomi-ga [hon-o yonda-ato -de] sake-o nonda.
-Nom book-Acc read-after-at wine-Acc drunk
'Kiyomi drunk wine after s/he read a book.'

In our terms, these adjuncts are Type 1. Thus, they can be negated in a negative VP-focused sentence, as shown below.

(43) a. Kiyomi-wa [[ne -ru -mae -ni] sake-o nomi]-wa sinakatta.
-Top sleep-NonPast-before-at wine-Acc drink-Top didn't
'Kiyomi didn't do [drinking wine [before going to bed]].'
b. Kiyomi-wa [[hon-o yon -da -ato -de] sake-o nomi]-wa sinakatta.
-Top book-Acc read-Past-after-at wine-Acc drink-Top didn't
'Kiyomi didn't do [drinking wine [after reading a book]].'

(43a) may be interpreted as 'it is not before going to bed that Kiyomi drunk wine', and (43b) may have the interpretation 'It is not after reading a book that Kiyomi drunk wine.' This implies that these adjuncts are generated within VP, and hence VP-adjuncts (= Type 1).

On the other hand, clausal temporal adjuncts such as *mae* 'before' and *ato* 'after', which are superficially very similar to *mae-ni* 'before' and *ato-de* 'after', are not Type 1: they cannot be negated in a VP-focused sentence. This is shown in (44).

(44) a. Kiyomi-wa [ne -ru -mae] [sake-o nomi]-wa sinakatta.
-Top sleep-NonPast-before wine-Acc drink-Top didn't
'[Before s/he went to bed], Kiyomi didn't do [drinking wine].'
b. Kiyomi-wa [hon-o yon -da -ato] [sake-o nomi]-wa sinakatta.
-Top book-Acc read-Past-after wine-Acc drink-Top didn't
'[After s/he read a book], Kiyomi didn't do [drinking wine].'

In these sentences, the clausal time adverbials are outside the scope of negation, which suggests that they are not Type 1 adjuncts.

The following sentences exemplify the same contrast.

(45) a. Kiyomi-wa [[yama-ni nobotta-toki-ni] sake-o nomi]-wa sinakatta.
-Top mountain-at climbed-time-at wine-Acc drink-Top didn't
'Kiyomi did not [drink sake when s/he climbed the mountain].'
b. Kiyomi-wa [yama-ni nobotta-toki] [sake-o nomi]-wa sinakatta.
-Top mountain-at climbed-time wine-Acc drink-Top didn't
'Kiyomi did not [drink sake when s/he climbed the mountain].'

Toki-ni 'when' in (45a) may be negated, while *toki* 'when' in (45b) cannot.

It is not the case that clausal time adverbial without *-ni/-de* can never be negated. They may be negated in negative sentences of the type exemplified in (17) above, one of which is repeated below.

(46) [$_{IP}$ Kiyomi-ga piza-o tabe-ta]-wakede-wa nai.
-Nom pizza-Acc eat-Past-case-Top not
'It is not the case that Kiyomi ate pizza.'

In this type of sentence, the entire IP may be a scope of negation. Consider now the following examples.

(47) a. Kiyomi-wa [[yama-ni nobotta-toki] sake-o nonda]
-Top mountain-at climbed-when wine-Acc drunk
-wakede-wa nai.
-case-Top not
'It is not the case that Kiyomi drunk wine when s/he climbed the mountain].'
b. Kiyomi-wa [[hon-o yonda-ato] sake-o nonda]-wakede-wa nai
-Top book-Acc read-after wine-Acc drunk-case-Top not
'It is not the case that Kiyomi drunk wine after s/he read a book.'

As shown in the translations, clausal time adverbials in (47) are within the scope of negation, which in turn implies that they are Type 2 adjuncts.

Thus, I have shown that clausal time adverbials with *-ni* or *-de* are of Type 1, and those without them are of Type 2. This means that *mae-ni, ato-de*, etc. have [+process modifier] feature, and *mae, ato*, etc. have [+event modifier] feature. This conclusion is semantically quite natural as well. *Mae-ni* clause in (48a) being a process modifier, the information conveyed by the adjunct is a part of the event, hence it can be new information. On the other hand, *mae* clause in (48b) being an event modifier, the information conveyed by it is not a part of the event itself. It tends to be outside the new information, providing the background information (cf. Jackendoff, 1972).

(48) a. Kiyomi-wa [$_{T1}$ neru-mae-ni] sake-o nonda.
-Top sleep-before-at wine-Acc drunk
'Kiyomi drunk wine before s/he went to bed.'
b. Kiyomi-wa [$_{T2}$ neru-mae] sake-o nonda.
-Top sleep-before wine-Acc drunk
'Kiyomi drunk wine before s/he went to bed.'

I have thus argued that the two types of apparently near-identical clausal time adverbials (i.e. those with *-ni/-de* and those without *-ni/-de*) in fact differ in their nature, as summarized below.[10]

(49) Type 1 temporal adjuncts ([+process modifier]):
mae-ni 'before', *ato-de* 'after', *toki-ni* 'when', etc.
Type 2 temporal adjuncts ([+event modifier]):
mae 'before', *ato* 'after', *toki* 'when', *sai* 'when', etc.

---

[10]It seems that (at least some) syntactic differences between *dooyuu-riyuu-de* 'for what reason' and *naze* 'why' can be reduced to exsistence vs. absence of *-de* . The former, being suffixed with *-de* , is a Type 1 adjunct, and the latter, being without *-de* , is a Type 2 adjunct. Consider the following sentence.

(i) Masami-wa Kiyomi-ni dooyuu-riyuu-de kurasu-o yasum-ase-ta no.
-Top -Dat how-reason-by class-Acc skip-make-Past Q
'For what reason did Masami make/let Kiyomi skip the class?'

This sentence is ambiguous in the interpretation of the wh-adjunct *dooyuu-riyuu-de* 'for what reason'. It may be associated with either *yasum* 'skip' or *(s)ase* 'make/let'. That is, (i) may be interpreted as asking the reason Kiyomi skipped the class, or it may be interpreted as asking the reason of Masami's action. In the former interpretation, the wh-adjunct is affiliated with the VP headed by *yasum* 'skip', while in the latter interpretation it is affiliated with the upper VP whose head is *(s)ase* 'make/let'. (It is known that the same ambiguity arises with other standard VP adverbs such as a manner adverb as well.) On the other hand, the same ambiguity does not arise if you replace *dooyuu-riyuu-de* with *naze* 'why', which is not suffixed with *-de* . (ii) does not have a reading in which the reason of Kiyomi's skipping the class is asking for.

(ii) Masami-wa Kiyomi-ni naze kurasu-o yasum-ase-ta no.
-Top -Dat why class-Acc skip-make-Past Q
'Why did Masami make/let Kiyomi skip the class?'

This is because the sentnece involves only one IP, which is immediately dominating the upper VP headed by *(s)ase* , and the *naze* is affiliated with this IP. (cf. Koizumi, 1991: Chapter V).

4. Conclusion

In this paper, I have discussed the distribution of clausal adjuncts, and argued that there are three types of adjuncts: Type 1, Type 2, and Type 3, affiliated to VP, IP, and MP, respectively. The distribution of these adjuncts is governed by the Feature Matching Principle. If the present analysis is basically correct, then, we can conclude that Japanese has a Modal Phrase as shown in (1), and that there are no CP-adjuncts in Japanese (and possibly in any natural languages).

***Acknowledgment**
In writing this paper, I have benefited from discussions with a number of people. They include Takako Aikawa, Hiroko Yamashita-Butler, Peter Culicover, Shigeru Miyagawa, J.J. Nakayama. I also wish to thank Hajime Hoji: without his council, the focus of the paper would have been a considerably different one.

References

Ahn, Hee-Don. 1991. Light verbs, negation, and VP-movement in Korean and English. Doctoral dissertation, University of Wisconsin.
Dowty, David. 1979. Word meaning and Montague grammar. Dordrecht: Reidel.
Chomsky, Noam. 1986. Knowledge of Language. New York: Praeger.
Hasegawa, Nobuko. 1989. On the VP-internal subject hypothesis. Report of nihongo kyoiku kokusai shinpojumu, eds. by T. Sakamoto and Y. Abe, 249-54. Nagoya Japan: Nanzan University.
————. 1991. Affirmative polarity items and negation in Japanese. Interdisciplinary approaches to language: Essays in honor of S.-Y. Kuroda, eds. C. Georgopoulos and R. Ishihara, 271-86. Dordrecht: Kluwer.
Hoji, Hajime. 1985. Logical Form constraints and configurational structures in Japanese. Doctoral dissertation, University of Washington.
Jackendoff, Ray. 1972. Semantic interpretation in generative grammar. Cambridge, Mass: MIT Press.
Kato, Yasuhiko. 1985. Negative sentences in Japanese. Doctoral dissertation, Sophia University.
Koizumi, Masatoshi. 1991. Syntax of adjuncts and the phrase structure of Japanese. MA thesis, The Ohio State University.
Minami, Fujio. 1974. Gendai nihongo-no kozo. Tokyo: Taishukan.
Nakajima, Takashi. 1991. Licensing adverbs and the minimality effect. ms. Cornell University.
Ogino, Megumi. 1990. An analysis of *sae* . MA thesis, the Ohio State University.
Rizzi, Luigi. 1990. Relativized Minimality. Cambridge, Mass: MIT Press.

Roberts, Ian. 1987. The representation of implicit and dethematized subjects. Dordrecht: Foris.

Sato-Zhu, Eriko. 1992. Topic phrase. (in this volume)

Sawada, Harumi. 1983. S^n sisutemu to nihongo jodosi-no sogo renketsu junjo. Nihongogaku. 2-12.66-80.

Tenny, Carol Lee. 1987. Grammaticalizing Aspect and Affectedness. Doctoral dissertation, MIT.

Travis, Lisa. 1988. Syntax of adjuncts. ms. McGill University.

Ueyama, Ayumi. 1991. On the licensing of functional heads: the WP-analysis of interrogative clauses. ms. Kyoto University of Foreign Languages.

Vendler, Zeno. 1967. Linguistics in Philosophy. Ithaca: Cornell University Press.

Whitman, John. 1989. Topic, modality, and IP structure. ms. Cornell University.

Postverbal Adverbs and Verb Movement in Korean

JAE HONG LEE
Gradute Center, CUNY

POSTVERBAL ADVERBS AND VERB MOVEMENT IN KOREAN[0]

Jae Hong Lee
Graduate Center, CUNY

0. INTRODUCTION

Emonds (1978), Pollock (1989) and Chomsky (1989) have proposed V-to-I RAISING to account for word order variations in SVO languages. Unlike SVO languages, however, V-to-I raising is hard to see in head-final languages like Korean and Japanese, since its result would almost always be string-vacuous. This paper will argue that VERB RAISING can in fact be observed in Korean with a highly restricted class of postverbal adverbs. This supports proposals for Verb Raising in SOV languages that have been made on more theory-internal grounds (Whitman 1991). Unlike Korean, Japanese lacks postverbal adverbials. As a result, the effect of Verb Movement (VM) is not visible in Japanese, for VM will always be a string-vacuous process in this language.

The organization of this paper is as follows. In the first section, two parametric differences will be examined between Korean and Japanese regarding postverbal adverbs and the position of the NEGATIVE MARKER

[0] I am greatly indebted to Robert Fiengo, Richard Kayne, and Richard Larson for discussions and suggestions in developing ideas in this paper. Errors are solely mine.

(NM). In the second section, I propose an IP structure for both Korean and Japanese. In the last section, I will demonstrate how VERB MOVEMENT (VM) derives the correct surface word order in Korean.

1. DIFFERENCES BETWEEN KOREAN AND JAPANESE
1.1. Negative Constructions
1.1.1. Korean Negation

Affirmative sentences in Korean (1a) have two negative counterparts, one in which the negative marker (NM) immediately precedes the main verb (as in (1b): NM-V-AGR-T-C) and the other in which the NM follows the main verb (as in (1c): V-NM-AGR-T-C).[1] Among Korean linguists, the former is often referred to as Type 1 negation, and the latter as Type 2 negation.[2]

(1)a. emeni-kkeyse phyenci-lul ssu-si-n-ta
mom-NOM(HON) letter-ACC write-AGR-PRES-INDIC
'Mother writes a letter.'
b. emeni-kkeyse phyenci-lul *ani* ssu-si-n-ta **(Type 1)**
mom-NOM(HON) letter-ACC NEG write-AGR-PRES-INDIC
c. emeni-kkeyse phyenci-lul ssu-*ci* *ani* **(Type 2)**
mom-NOM(HON) letter-ACC write-NMZ NEG
ha-si-n-ta
DO-AGR-PRES-INDIC
(both (b,c)): 'Mother does not write a letter.'

Type 2 negation has two extra formatives which Type 1 negation lacks: the nominalizing suffix (NMZ) *-ci* and the auxiliary verb *ha*-'do'. The negative sentence always requires *ha-* to be inserted when the NM *ani* follows the main verb *ssu-* 'write' (i.e., Type 2 negation) as in (1c): it never appears when *ani* precedes the main verb (i.e., Type 1 negation, (1b)).

As argued in Lee (to appear), both Type 1 negation (1b) and Type 2 negation (1c) are taken to be instances of sentence negation and have the identical D-structure. This claim is supported by NEGATIVE POLARITY ITEM (NPI) licensing, the scopal ambiguity of an ARGUMENT QUANTIFIER PHRASE (AQP) with respect to both types of negation, and interpretations of negative clauses with a conjunction coordinating two verbs.

---

[1] Imperative sentences and verb of identification *i-* 'be' are apparent exceptions to this generalization. Neither Type 1 nor Type 2 negation is allowed if a verb has its negative counterpart in the lexicon. Some of these examples are: *al-* 'know' vs. *molu-* 'not know', *iss-* 'exist' vs. *eps-* 'not exist'. These exceptional cases will not be discussed in this paper.

[2] Although Korean lacks person, number, and gender agreement, it exhibits a case of honorific agreement (Kitagawa 1986, Choe 1988, Kang 1988). A SUBJECT SSS (a person socially superior to the speaker: Harada 1976, Kitagawa 1986) has to be followed by the honorific morpheme *-si-* immediately after the verb stem in Korean, as the examples in (1) show. The Japanese counterpart to the Korean honorific morpheme is *-are-*.

1.1.2. Japanese Negation

Unlike Korean, Japanese affirmative sentences (2a) have only one negative construction as in (2b).[3]

(2) a. Taroo-no okaasan-ga tegami-o kak-*are*-u
-GEN mother-NON letter-ACC write-AGR-PRES(INDIC)
'Taroo's mother writes a letter.'
b. Taroo-no okaasan-ga tegami-o kak-*are-na*-i
-GEN mother-NON letter-ACC write-AGR-NEG-PRES(INDIC)
'Taroo's mother does not write a letter.'

Japanese negation (2b) and Type 2 Korean negation (1c) are similar in that the NM follows the verb. They are different, however, in the sense that the NM *ani* PRECEDES the honorific morpheme *-si-* in Type 2 Korean negation (V-*NM-AGR*-TENSE), but the Japanese NM *na-* FOLLOWS the honorific morpheme *-are-* (V-*AGR-NM*-TENSE).[4]

1.2. Position of the Negative Marker

Given the order of morphemes observed in sentences (1b,c) and (2b), there are three possibilities as to the position of the NEGP, namely, (3a,b) for Korean Type 1 and Type 2 negation, respectively, and (3c) for Japanese.

(3)

a.	b.	c.
TP	TP	TP
/\	/\	/\
AGRP	AGRP	*NEGP*
/\	/\	/\
VP	*NEGP*	AGRP
/\	/\	/\
NEGP	VP	VP

[3]There is an alternative way to honorify the verb in Japanese:
(i) Taroo-no okaasan-ga tegami-o *o*-kak-*ini nar*-u
-GEN mother-NOM letter-ACC write-AGR-PRE(INDIC)
The honorific morpheme *-ini nar-* consists of the nominalizing suffix *-i*, the dative postposition *ni* and the verb *nar-* 'become', and, therefore, it may have a more complex internal structure than *-are-* shown in (1b) (S. Dubinsky (p.c.)). Since the honorific morpheme *-are-* is similar to the Korean counterpart in its structure, I will be concerned mainly with the *-are-* form.

[4]In addition to differences in the order of morphemes, Japanese negative sentences differ from Type 2 Korean negation in that they do not require *ha* 'do'-insertion. Recall that *ha* should be inserted in Type 2 Korean negation. Although why DO-insertion is called for in negative sentences in some languages (i.e., English and Korean) while it is not in other languages is an important issue, it is beyond the scope of this paper.

A question arises as to whether or not all three structures in (3) are necessary to account for the sentences in (1) and (2). Provided that the subject generated VP-internally surfaces in the SPEC of the AGRP in Korean and Japanese and that NPI's are licensed by a c-commanding NM at S-structure (Reinhart 1976, Laka 1990), representations (3a) and (3b) would never allow NPI's in the subject position, namely, the SPEC of the AGRP.[5] On the other hand, if the NEGP is generated between the AGRP and the TP as in (3c), NPI's are correctly predicted to be licensed in the subject ((4a), (5a)) and object positions ((4b), (5b)) in Japanese and both types of Korean negation.[6]

(4) **KOREAN**: TYPE 1 NEGATION
   a. *amwuto* Chelswu-lul *ani* cohaha-Ø-n-ta
      anybody -ACC NEG like-AGR-PRES-INDIC
      (both (4a, 5a)): 'Nobody likes Chelswu.'
   b. Chelswu-nun onul *amwukesto ani* mek-Ø-ess-ta
      -TOP today anything NEG eat-AGR-PAST-INDIC
      (both (4b, 5b)): 'Chelswu didn't eat anything today.'

(5) **KOREAN**: TYPE 2 NEGATION
   a. *amwuto* Chelswu-lul cohaha-ci *ani* ha-Ø-n-ta
      anybody -ACC like-NMZ NEG DO-AGR-PRES-INDIC
   b. Chelswu-nun onul *amwukesto* mek-ci *ani* ha-Ø-ess-ta
      -TOP today anything eat-NMZ NEG DO-AGR-PAST-INDIC

Based on the argument so far, I propose the IP structure in (6) for Korean and Japanese. Although Korean and Japanese have the same IP structure, they diverge from each other with respect to the status of the NM within the NEGP. That is, the Korean NM *ani* is generated postverbally in

---

[5]Reinhart's definition of c-command (1976):
   X c-commands Y iff
   (i) X does not dominate Y and
   (ii) the first branching node dominating X dominates Y.

[6]Korean (and Japanese as well) allows an NPI to scramble into a position that is not c-commanded by the NEG at S-structure, as illustrated in (i).

(i) *amwu sinye to*$_1$ na-nun [wang-i$_2$ casin-uy$_{1/2}$ apeci-ekey t$_1$
   any maid(DO) I-TOP king-NOM self-GEN father-DAT(IO)

   tolyeponay-ci *ani* ha-Ø-ess-ta-ko] sayngkakha-Ø-n-ta (**KOREAN**)
   send back-NMZ NEG DO-AGR-PAST-INDIC think-AGR-PRES-INDIC
   'I don't think the king$_2$ sent any maid$_1$ back to self's$_{1/2}$ father.'

Unfortunately I do not have an immediate answer to account for the above construction. One possible solution, however, might be that the NPI licensing condition could be slightly modified (in the way Aoun and Li's Scope Principle (1989) is defined) so that an NPI would be licensed if a member of the chain containing that NPI is c-commanded by the NEG. Reconstruction does not seem to be a viable approach to this problem since the fronted NPI direct object *amwu sinye to* 'any maid' must be in an A-position in (i): it can serve as an antecedent for the reflexive contained in the indirect object over which the direct object scrambled. (See Mahajan (1990) for a detailed discussion of A/A-bar distinction.)

the SPEC of the NEGP (See Jung (1990) for more detailed discussion of this issue), while the Japanese NM *na*-heads the NEGP.

(6) **KOREAN/JAPANESE**

```
                         TP
                         /\
                    NEGP
                      /\
               NEG'   ani (KOREAN)
                /\
          AGRP   NEG
           /\     |
          VP      na- (JAPANESE)
```

In the remainder of this article, the following three questions will be explored:

(I) Why is the Korean negative marker generated postverbally?
(II) Why should the Japanese negative marker be treated differently from the Korean one?
(III) What are the consequences of my proposal that the negative marker is generated postverbally in Korean?

The possibility of the Korean NM heading a maximal projection, namely, the NEGP, will not be addressed in this paper. I argued in Lee (1991) that the Korean NM should not be viewed as a head, along the lines of proposals made by Zanuttini (1990) for Piedmontese and Baker (1991) for English, and contra proposals by Pollock (1989) and Chomsky (1989) for English and French.

1.3. Two Types of Adverbs in Korean

To answer Question (I), let us closely examine properties of the Korean NM. There is a highly restricted class of adverbs in Korean that diverges from other adverbs in two important respects. For expository convenience, the former will be referred to as CLASS 1 adverbs and the latter as CLASS 2 adverbs. First, CLASS 2 adverbs like *pelsse* 'already' may occur in various positions as sentences in (7) show.

(7) **KOREAN**: CLASS 2 ADVERB
  a. Chelswu-nun *pelsse* yengekongpwu-lul machi-Ø-ess-ta
     -TOP already English study-ACC finish-AGR-PAST-INDIC
     'Chelswu has already finished (his) English studies.'
  b. *pelsse* Chelswu-nun yengekongpwu-lul machi-Ø-ess-ta
  c. Chelswu-nun yengekongpwu-lul *pelsse* machi-Ø-ess-ta

CLASS 1 adverbs such as *cal* 'often/well' and *mos* 'unable', however, are largely fixed and always IMMEDIATELY followed by a verbal expression, as manifested in (8a). Otherwise, sentences will be ruled out as in (8b-d). The NM *ani* patterns together with *cal* and *mos* with respect to its position of occurrence.

(8) **KOREAN**: CLASS 1 ADVERB
a. Chelswu-nun sayngsenhwoi-lul *cal* mek-Ø-nun-ta
-TOP raw fish -ACC well eat-AGR-PRES-INDIC
'Chelswu eats raw fish well.'
b. **cal* Chelswu-nun sayngsenhwoi-lul mek-Ø-nun-ta
c. *Chelswu-nun *cal* sayngsenhwoi-lul mek-Ø-nun-ta
d. *Chelswu-nun sayngsenhwoi-lul mek *cal* Ø-nun-ta

The second way that CLASS 1 adverbs *cal*, *mos*, and *ani* differ from CLASS 2 adverbs is that the latter may appear in any place marked with # in (9) in the Korean UNERGATIVE NOUN + LIGHT VERB (UN+LV) construction with *ha-* 'do', but CLASS 1 adverbs may occur only between the noun and the light verb *ha-*.

(9) # Subj # *wuntong* # *ha-*
2/*1 2/*1 sports 2/1 LV
(*wuntong ha-*='to do sports,' = 'to exercise')
(1: CLASS 1 Adverbs; 2: CLASS 2 Adverbs)

The pattern displayed in (9) correctly predicts that sentences like those in (10) will be acceptable since *yelsimhi* is a regular adverb.

(10) **KOREAN**: CLASS 2 ADVERB
a. Chelswu-nun cip-eyse *yelsimhi* kongpwuha-Ø-nun-ta
-TOP house-at hard study-AGR-PRES-INDIC
'Chelswu studies hard at home.'
b. Chelswu-nun *yelsimhi* cip-eyse kongpwuha-Ø-nun-ta
c. *yelsimhi* Chelswu-nun cip-eyse kongpwuha-Ø-nun-ta
d. Chelswu-nun cip-eyse kongpwu-lul *yelsimhi* ha-Ø-nun-ta
-TOP house-at study-ACC hard do-AGR-PRES-INDIC

Now, compare examples in (10) with those in (11). CLASS 1 adverbs *cal*, *mos*, and *ani* are not only confined to appearing exclusively in the immediate preverbal position, as illustrated in (8), but in addition, they always have to appear between the noun and the light verb *ha-* in the UN+*ha-* complex verb construction, as in (11d).

(11) **KOREAN**: CLASS 1 ADVERB

a. *Chelswu-nun caki-uy pan-eyse [ceil *ani/cal/mos*]
-TOP self-GEN class-in most not well/unable
kongpwuha-Ø-nun-ta
study-AGR-PRES-INDIC
'Chelswu studies least/best/worst in his class.'

b. *Chelswu-nun [ceil *ani/cal/mos*] caki-uy pan-eyse
kongpwuha-Ø-nun-ta

c. *[ceil *ani/cal/mos*] Chelswu-nun caki-uy pan-eyse
kongpwuha-Ø-nun-ta

d. Chelswu-nun caki-uy pan-eyse kongpwu-lul [ceil *ani/cal/mos*]
-TOP self-GEN class-in study-ACC most not/well/unable
ha-Ø-nun-ta
do-AGR-T-INDIC

Examples (7), (8), (10) and (11) clearly indicate that *cal*, *mos*, and *ani* pattern differently from other adverbs: unlike CLASS 2 adverbs, these three adverbs always have to appear immediately before the verb. If they occur in a verb of UN+*ha*- type, they must surface only between the noun and the verb *ha*-.

Based on these differences between the two classes of adverbs, CLASS 1 adverbs are taken to be generated POSTVERBALLY, whereas CLASS 2 adverbs are generated PREVERBALLY. I adopt Jung's (1990) position that the Korean NM *ani* is generated in the right-branching SPEC of the NEGP. Since I consider all arguments to be initially within the VP, sentences (7a-c) and (10a-d) are derived by scrambling of NP's. Sentences (8b-d) and (11b,c) cannot be derived because scrambling is a leftward movement in Korean (Saito 1987). The unacceptability of (11a) will be addressed in section 3.4.

1.4. Properties of the Japanese Negative Marker *na-*

Question II (i.e., Why should the Japanese negative marker be viewed differently from the Korean one?) can be answered by exploring the properties of the Japanese counterparts to the Korean CLASS 1 adverbs. Unlike Korean, Japanese lacks postverbal adverbs. Japanese has no adverbial equivalent to Korean *mos*. Also *yoku* 'well/often' in Japanese behaves differently from its Korean counterpart *cal*: it may appear in various locations as Korean CLASS 2 adverbs do, as examples in (12) show. Compare sentences in (12) with the Korean counterparts in (8).

(12) a. Taroo-wa sashimi-o *yoku* tabe-Ø-ru **(JAPANESE)**
-TOP raw fish-ACC often/well eat-AGR-PRES(INDIC)
'Taroo eats raw fish well/often.'

b. Taroo-wa *yoku* sashimi-o tabe-Ø-ru

c. *yoku* Taroo-wa sashimi-o tabe-Ø-ru

Another difference between Korean *cal* and Japanese *yoku* is that the latter may PRECEDE an UN+LV construction. Note that Korean *cal* can appear only between the unergative noun and the light verb, as was illustrated in (11).

The Korean NM *ani* is not a bound morpheme. The Japanese NM *na-*, however, is a bound morpheme just as other functional heads (such as tense and agreement morphemes) are. In addition, it inflects precisely in the same manner as adjectivals do. Since all predicative adjectives are heads in Japanese (Kitagawa 1986) and *na-* has adjectival properties, it must be considered a head as well.

These observations lead to the conclusion that unlike the Korean counterpart, the Japanese negative element *na-* heads the NEGP (See Kitagawa (1986) for a similar view). As a result, *na-* will not allow anything to move across it; otherwise, the Head Movement Constraint (HMC) would be violated (Chomsky 1986).

Summarizing, the two types of Korean negation are viewed as instances of sentence negation and derived from the same D-structure. The Korean NM *ani* is generated postverbally in the SPEC of the NEGP while the Japanese counterpart *na-* is the head of the NEGP. The latter conclusion is drawn from word order distribution and morphological considerations.

2. IP STRUCTURE OF KOREAN AND JAPANESE

From the evidence presented in section 1, I propose the IP structure displayed in (13) for Japanese and both types of Korean negation.[7] (Only the relevant segments are represented in (13).)

[7]Following Fukui (1986), Fukui & Speas (1986), Koopman & Sportiche (1988), and Kuroda (1988), the subject is assumed to be base-generated in the SPEC of VP and surfaces as a specifier of AGRP. I claim that the AGR morpheme is realized as a result of SPEC-head agreement in the AGRP.

(13) **(D-STRUCTURE)**

```
                        T'
                       /\
                  NEGP   T
                   /\
              NEG'  ani/mos (KOREAN)
               /\
          AGRP    NEG
           /\      |
         LS  AGR'  na- (JAPANESE)
              /\
            VP  AGR
            /\
          VP   cal (KOREAN)
          /\
      NP1  V'
            /\              (LS: landing site of the subject)
         NP2  V             (NP1:SUBJECT;  NP2:OBJECT)
```

Because of the complementary distribution of *mos* and *ani*, both *mos* and *ani* are generated in the SPEC of the NEGP. Since *cal* may co-occur with and immediately precede either *ani* or *mos*, I argue that it originates lower than *ani* and *mos*, as a VP adjunct.

3. CONSEQUENCES OF THE PROPOSAL

3.1. Verb Movement and AQP in the Subject Position

AQP's in the subject position are scopally ambiguous in Japanese and both types of Korean negation. Hence, two readings are possible for the sentences in (14); one in which the NM *ani* has scope over the AQP *motun salam* 'everyone', and the other in which the AQP has scope over *ani*. Since I adopt the view that both types of Korean negation have the identical D-structure, as discussed in section 1.1.1., the underlying structure of sentences (14a,b) would correspond to (15).[8,9]

---

[8]Han (1987) asserts that Type 1 negation is a case of constituent negation while Type 2 negation is an instance of sentence negation. Thus, sentence (14a) has only the reading where the AQP has wide scope over the NM *ani*, namely, 'Nobody ate the meal.' If this is the case, however, sentences such as (i) should be ruled out as illogical (i.e., *No one sang at the party, but only a few people did.).

(i) **KOREAN: AQP IN THE SUBJECT POSITION**

ecey party-ese *motun salam*-i nolay-lul
yesterday party-LOC all people-NOM song-ACC

ani ha-ko, myech salam-man ha-Ø-ess-ta **(TYPE 1)**
NEG do-but, a few people-only do-AGR-PAST-INDIC
'Everyone didn't sing at yesterday's party;
rather, only a few people did.'

This kind of contradiction, however, is not observed in Korean sentence type (14a). The fact

(14) **KOREAN**

a. *motun* *salam*-i pap-ul *ani* mek-ess-ta **(TYPE 1)**
all person-NOM meal-ACC NEG eat-PAST-INDIC

b. *motun* *salam*-i pap-ul mek-ci *ani* ha-ess-ta **(TYPE 2)**
all person-NOM meal-ACC eat-NMZ NEG DO-PAST-INDIC
(both (a,b)): 'Everyone didn't eat the meal.'

(15) **(D-STRUCTURE)**
KOREAN

```
                                    /\
                                NEGP  T
                                   /\
                             NEG'  ani
                               /\
                       AGRP     NEG
                         /\       |
                   SPEC   AGR'   Ø
                            /\
                        VP     AGR
                        /\       |
                   SPEC   V'  [+HON]
                            /\
                        N'     V
                        /\     |
                   VP     N  ha
                   /\     |
              NP1    V'  -ci
               |     /\
 motun salam   NP2  V
   everyone       |    |
               pap-ul  mek-
            meal-ACC  eat
```

From the base structure in (15), Verb Raising, proposed by Pollock (1989) and Chomsky (1989), will also apply in Korean. The surface structures corresponding to the two types of Korean negation (14a,b) are derived via Verb Movement motivated by a principle called MORPHOLOGICAL CLOSURE (Kang 1988), which requires all the bound morphemes to attach to a base at S-structure (Chomsky 1989, Laka 1990). As shown in (16b), the bound verb stem *mek-* 'eat' merges with the nominalizing suffix *-ci* which is licensed by the NM *ani* and the auxiliary verb *ha-*, forming *mek-ci*, and thus meeting the morphological closure

---

that sentence (i) is NOT semantically "odd" provides evidence for the claim that an AQP is scopally ambiguous in both types of Korean negation.

[9]The nominalizing suffix *-ci*, licensed by the NM *ani* and the auxiliary verb *ha-* 'do' insertion, may be generated as the head of NP in representation (15). If there is no *ha-* generated in a negative sentence, *-ci* is not licensed either, resulting in Type 1 negation.

requirement. The auxiliary verb *ha-*, being a bound morpheme, also has to attach to a morpheme and, therefore, raises to AGR and subsequently to NEG, T, and C across *ani*. This process will yield TYPE 2 negation (14b). When *-ci* is absent as a result of *ha-* not being generated as in (16a), the bound verb stem raises all the way up to C (across *ani* again) where the morphological closure requirement is fulfilled, resulting in TYPE 1 negation (14a).

(16) **KOREAN (S-STRUCTURE)**

a. **(TYPE 1)**

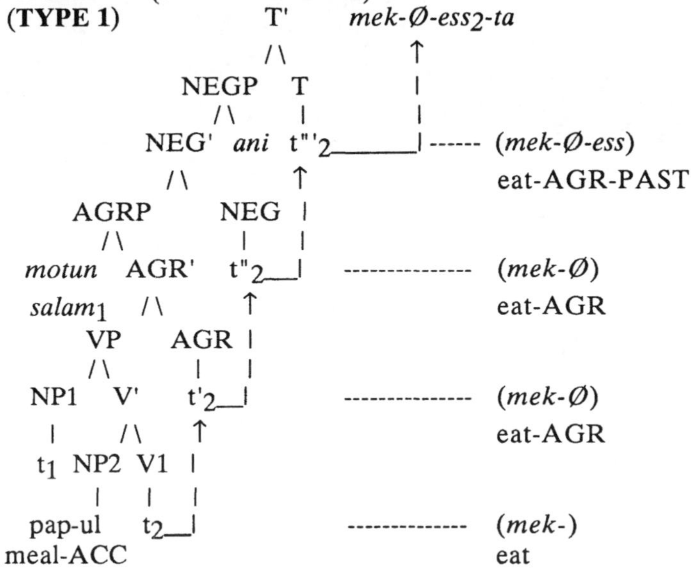

b. **(TYPE 2)**

```
                          T'    ha-Ø-ess3-ta
                         /\          ↑
                    NEGP    T        |
                     /\     |        |
               NEG'  ani  t"'3_______| -- (ha-Ø-ess)
                /\          ↑             DO-AGR-PAST
          AGRP       NEG    |
           /\         |     |
    motun    AGR'   t"3_____|  --------- (ha-Ø)
    salam1    /\      ↑                   DO-AGR
            VP   AGR  |
            /\    |   |
         t'1  V'  t'3_|        ---------- (ha-Ø)
              /\    ↑                     DO
            N'   V  |
            /\   |  |
         VP    N t3_|          ---------- (ha-)
         /\    |                          DO
     NP1  V' mek2-ci           ---------- (mek-ci)
      |   /\ eat-NMZ                      eat-NMZ
     t1 NP2  V  ↑
      |   |  |  |
   pap-ul  t2   |              ---------- (mek-)
   meal-ACC |___|                         eat
```

The subject generated in the SPEC of the VP (lower VP when one exists) raises to the SPEC position of the AGRP through the SPEC of the higher VP (when one exists) to avoid the ECP at S-structure. VPs do not stand as barriers to SUBJECT RAISING since they are L-marked by a lexical item, namely, the verb *mek-* raising to AGR (in TYPE 1 negation) and/or the auxiliary verb *ha-* in AGR (in TYPE 2 negation) (Chomsky 1986:69). L-marking (Chomsky 1986) and/or the Government Transparency Corollary (Baker 1988) will predict that no maximal projection in (16) is a barrier to verb movement. Hence, the ECP is not violated.

Application of the rule of QUANTIFIER RAISING (QR) to both (16a,b) would result in the structure schematically illustrated in (17), where the subject AQP is adjoined to a nonargument maximal projection TP at LF (Chomsky 1986).

(17) **(LF)**

```
                         TP
                         /\
        motun salam1   TP
         'everyone'     /\
                           T'
                           /\
                      NEGP   T
                        /\
                   NEG'  ani
                     /\
              AGRP   NEG
                /\
              x1  AGR'
                    /\
                (VP)  AGR
                  /\
             (t'1)   (V')
                      /\          (x: variable)
                 (N')   (V)       (t: NP trace)
                  /\              (elements in parentheses are
              VP  (N)              unnecessary for (16a))
              /\
            t1  V
```

QR of the AQP from the SPEC of the AGRP must be mediated by intermediate adjunction to the AGRP and subsequently to the NEGP. Intermediate adjunction, along with Chomsky's definition of proper government with the notion of EXCLUSION, would prevent the ECP violation (Chomsky 1986:9) in the QR process in (17).

Two readings are possible in representation (17). The AQP *motun salam* 'everyone' c-commands and thus has scope over the NM *ani*; this generates the reading 'For all x, x did not eat.' In turn, *ani* c-commands members of the chain containing *motun salam*, namely, t_1 (and t'_1) and by THE SCOPE PRINCIPLE of Aoun and Li (1989), has scope over *motun salam*.[10] This generates the reading 'It is not the case that everyone ate.'

Arguments for VM and QR presented in this section also hold for Japanese. The only difference would be that since Japanese lacks postverbal adverbs, the effect of VM would always be string-vacuous. Since the Japanese NM *na-* is argued to be the head of the NEGP, the verb has to move up to COMP through all the functional heads, including NEG,

[10] Aoun and Li (1989) claim that the determination of the scope of quantifier phrases is sensitive to the chain containing the quantifier phrase and the traces with which the quantifier phrase is coindexed. Therefore, they propose the following principle:

The Scope Principle

A quantifier A has scope over a quantifier B in case A c-commands a member of the chain containing B.

resulting in the string of V-AGR-NEG-TENSE(COMP) (i.e., *kak-are-na-i* 'write-AGR-NEG-PRES(INDIC)' as in (2b)). The HMC will prevent the amalgamated [Verb+AGR] from moving across *na-* (Chomsky (1986)). Another reason for [Verb+AGR] not to be able to move across *na-* would be that *na-*, being a predicative affix, must be attached to a predicate. If it is stranded without being merged with a predicate, an ungrammatical sentence would be generated.

3.2. AQP in the Object Position

Both Korean negation types and Japanese negative sentences containing an AQP in the object position ((18a,b) and (18c), respectively) are also correctly predicted to be ambiguous in my proposal.[11]

(18) **KOREAN**

a. Chelswu-nun *motun salam*-ul *ani* manna-ess-ta **(TYPE 1)**
-TOP all person-ACC NEG meet-PAST-INDIC

b. Chelswu-nun *motun salam*-ul manna-ci *ani* ha-ess-ta **(TYPE 2)**
-TOP all person-ACC meet-NMZ NEG DO-PAST-INDIC
(both (a,b)): 'Chelswu didn't meet everyone.'

JAPANESE

c. Taroo-wa *zenin*-ni aw-*ana*-katta
-TOP all person-DAT meet-NEG-PAST(INDIC)
'Taroo didn't meet everyone.'

Since sentences with an AQP in the object position are interpreted in a similar manner to those containing an AQP in the subject position examined in the previous section, they will not be discussed any further.

---

[11]The less preferred interpretation of (18a,b) and (18c) where the negative marker has scope over the AQP is manifested by the logicality of examples in (i) and (ii), respectively:

(i) **KOREAN**
Chelswu-nun *motun salam*-ul
-TOP all people-ACC

ani manna-ko, myech salam-man manna-Ø-ess-ta **(TYPE 1)**
NEG meet-but, a few people-only meet-AGR-PAST-INDIC
'Chelswu didn't meet everyone; rather, (he) met only a few people.'

(ii) **JAPANESE**
Taroo-wa *zenin*-ni aw-*ana*-i-de
-TOP all person-DAT meet-NEG-PRES(IND)-but

ikuninka-take-ni aw-ta
a few people-only-DAT meet-PAST(IND)
'Taroo didn't meet everyone; rather (he) met only a few.'

3.3. Negative Polarity Item Licensing

As mentioned in section 1.2, NPI's are allowed to appear in both subject and object position in Korean and Japanese. On the assumption that NPI's are licensed by a c-commanding NM at S-structure, licensing of NPI's in both the subject and object position can be correctly predicted once representation (13) is adopted.

3.4. Unergative NOUN + ha-

My proposal for Verb Movement in Korean also provides an explanation for what appears to be an unrelated structure, namely, the UN+LV construction which was discussed in section 3. I claim that the noun and the light verb are in a COMPLEMENT-VERB relationship in the UN+LV construction even when the accusative case marker is not present.[12] Therefore, they should be represented as (19a), rather than (19b).

```
(19)  a.    VP                      b.    VP
            /\                            /\
      NP1   V'                      NP1   V'
              /\                            /\
          NP2   V                   NP2         V
           |    |                    |          /\
      kongpwu   ha                  t2 kongpwu2   ha
       'study'  'do'                                    (NP1: SUBJECT)
```

12 As the examples in (i) show, the accusative case marker may or may not appear in the UN+LV construction in Korean and Japanese.

(i) a. John-un nalmata kongpwu(*-lul*) ha-n-ta **(KOREAN)**
-TOP every day study (-ACC) LV-PRES-INDIC
b. John-wa mainichi benkyoo (*-o*) su-ru **(JAPANESE)**
-TOP every day study (-ACC) LV-PRES(INDIC)
(both (a,b)): 'John studies everyday.'

Miyagawa (1991) argues that the noun may incorporate into the light verb and the optional occurrence of incorporation allows the accusative case marker to be absent. However, this kind of case marker deletion is not limited to the UN+LV construction. The nominative marker and other particles are deleted frequently in Korean and Japanese (more prominently in conversation), as illustrated in (iia,b). (Omission site of the case marker or the particle is indicated by Ø.)

(ii) a. ne-Ø chemsim-Ø mek-ess-ni? **(KOREAN)**
you(SUBJ) lunch(OBJ) eat-PAST-Q
'Did you eat lunch.'
b. ne-Ø onul hakkyo-e/Ø ka-ess-ni **(KOREAN)**
you(SUBJ) today school-to/Ø go-PAST-Q
'Did you go to school today?'

Examples such as (iib) pose a problem for Miyagawa's incorporation approach. That is, the subject *ne* 'you' has not incorporated into the verb in (iib), as indicated by the intervening adverbial phrases; nevertheless, the nominative case marker is deleted. I view the UN+LV construction (without the accusative case marker) and examples like (iib) as instances of simple CASE-MARKER SUPPRESSION.

Representation (19a) is supported by data concerning the accusative case marker *-lul* in a negative sentence. That is, *-lul* normally appears between the noun and the light verb *ha-* when the sentence is negated, as shown in (11d) (repeated here as (20a)).

(20) **KOREAN**

a. Chelswu-nun caki-uy pan-eyse kongpwu-*lul* ceil *ani*
-TOP self-GEN class-in study -*ACC* most NEG
ha-Ø-nun-ta
do-AGR-PRES-INDIC
'Chelswu studies least in his class.' (=(11d))

b. *Chelswu-nun caki-uy pan-eyse ceil *ani*
-TOP self-GEN class-in most NEG
kongpwuha-Ø-nun-ta
study-AGR-PRES-INDIC (=(11a))

Once (19a) is employed for the UN+LV complex, we can eliminate sentences such as (20b) (=(11a)) because only the light verb *ha-* is expected to undergo Verb Raising across the negative postverbal adverb. This explains why *ani* must appear between the noun (i.e., *kongpwu* 'study') and the verb (i.e., *ha-*), as in (20a). If structure (19b) is selected for the UN+LV construction, not only will it be difficult to explain a string such as UN--*ani*--*ha-* as in (20a), but also sentences like (20b) will be incorrectly predicted to be grammatical.

4. SUMMARY AND CONCLUSIONS

In this paper, I have argued that the Korean NM *ani* is generated higher than the AGRP so that it can c-command subject NPI's in the SPEC of the AGRP at S-structure. Furthermore, unlike other adverbs, *ani* (along with *cal* and *mos*) is claimed to be generated postverbally, based on word order distribution. The surface structures are derived via Verb Movement, the generation of *ha-* determining Type 1 or Type 2 negation. Distinct properties are observed between the Japanese NM *na-* and its Korean counterpart *ani*. These differences lead to a proposal that Korean *ani* is generated in the SPEC position of the NEGP while the Japanese NM *na-* is generated as the head of NEGP.

The Verb Movement effect is visible in Korean owing to the presence of postverbal adverbs. Unlike Korean, however, Japanese lacks postverbal adverbs. Thus, Verb Movement will invariably be a string-vacuous process in Japanese.

REFERENCES

Aoun, J. and Y. Li. 1989. Scope and constituency. Linguistic Inquiry. 20.141-172.

Baker, C. L. 1991. The syntax of English NOT: The limits of core grammar. Linguistic Inquiry. 22.387-429.

Baker, M. C. 1988. Incorporation: A theory of grammatical function changing. Chicago: University of Chicago Press.

Choe, H. -S. 1988. Restructuring parameters and complex predicates: A transformational approach. Doctoral dissertation, MIT.

Chomsky, N. 1986. Barriers. Cambridge: MIT Press.

Chomsky, N. 1988. Some notes on economy of derivation and representation. MIT Working Papers in Theoretical Linguistics, ed. by I. Laka and A. Mahajan, vol. 10, 43-74.

Emonds, J. 1978. The verbal complex V'-V in French. Linguistic Inquiry. 9.151-175.

Fukui, N. 1986. A theory of category projection and its application. Doctoral dissertation, MIT.

Fukui, N. and M. Speas 1986. Specifiers and projection. MIT Working Papers in Theoretical Linguistics, ed. by N. Fukui, T. R. Rapoport, and E. Sagey, vol. 8, 128-172.

Han, H. -S. 1987. The configurational structure of the Korean language. Doctoral dissertation, University of Texas, Austin.

Harada, S. I. 1976. Honorifics. Syntax and Semantics: Japanese Generative Grammar, ed. by M. Shibatani, vol. 5. New York: Academic Press.

Jung, Y. -J. 1990. X-bar theory, SPECs, and directionality. NELS 21.

Kang, M. -Y. 1988. Topics in Korean syntax: Phrase structure, variable binding and movement. Doctoral dissertation, MIT.

Kitagawa, Y. 1986. Subjects in Japanese and English. Doctoral dissertation, University of Massachusetts, Amherst.

Koopman, H. and D. Sportiche 1988. Subjects. ms. UCLA, Los Angeles.

Kuroda, Y. -S. 1988. Whether we agree or not: A comparative syntax of English and Japanese. Papers from the Second International Workshop on Japanese Syntax, ed. by W. J. Poser. Stanford: CSLI.

Laka, I. 1990. Negation in syntax: On the nature of functional categories and projections. Doctoral dissertation, MIT.

Lee, J. -H. 1991. The Korean negative marker: Not a head but an adverb. ms. Graduate Center/CUNY, New York.

Lee, J. -H. (to appear) A derivational approach to two types of Korean negation. Proceedings of the workshop on Korean syntax and semantics: 1991 LSA Linguistic Institute, UCSC.

Mahajan, A. 1990. The A/A-bar distinction and movement theory. Doctoral dissertation, MIT.

May, R. 1985. Logical form: Its structure and derivation. Cambridge: MIT Press.

McGloin, N. H. 1976. Negation. Syntax and Semantics: Japanese Generative Grammar, ed. by M. Shibatani, vol. 5. New York: Academic Press.

Miyagawa, S. 1991. Case realization and scrambling. ms. Ohio State University.

Pollock, J. -Y. 1989. Verb movement, universal grammar, and the structure of IP. Linguistic Inquiry. 20.365-424.

Reinhart, T. 1976. The syntactic domain of anaphora. Doctoral dissertation, MIT.

Saito, M. 1987. Three notes on syntactic movement in Japanese. Issues in Japanese Linguistics, ed. by T. Imai, and M. Saito. Dordrecht: Foris.

Whitman, J. 1991. String vacuous V to COMP. ms. Cornell University.

Zanuttini, R. 1990. On the relevance of tense for sentential negation. ms. University of Pennsylvania.

The Syntax of Serialization in Korean

SOOKHEE LEE
University of Washington

The Syntax of Serialization in Korean[0]

Sookhee Lee
University of Washington

1. Introduction

One of the syntactic or configurational structures most actively discussed in the African linguistic literature for the last few decades may be SERIAL VERB CONSTRUCTIONS (SVCs). SVCs are constructions in which a sequence of verbs with tense/aspect agreement appears in a single clause without any markers of coordination or subordination, as in (1):[1]

(1) a. intransitive + intransitive
Zhāng-sān shàng-loú shuì-jiào (Mandarin, Li and Thompson 1973)
Zhang-san go upstairs sleep
'Zhang-san goes upstairs and sleeps.'

b. transitive + intransitive
Ajàó gbé àpótí wá (Yorùbá, George(1975))
Ajao took box come
'Ajao brought the box.'

[0] I would like to express thanks to my adviser, Joseph E. Emonds, for crucial comments and discussion, and to Heles Contreras, Karen Zgona, and Michael Rochemont for helpful suggestions. All responsibility for errors remains my own.

[1] In principle, serialization is a phenomenon that any number of verbs come together in a series. Therefore, there is no *a priori* group of verbs called serial verbs. In this paper, I discuss examples with only two verbs, even though more than two verbs can occur in a serial verb construction.

c. transitive + transitive
Kofi naki Amba kiri (Sranan, Sebba(1987))
Kofi hit Amba kill
'Kofi struck Amba dead.'

d. intransitive + transitive
ofóni-bi tọ́rụ fin bẹ́ịn-mị (Ị̀jọ, Williamson(1965))
bird river fly cross-Past
'The bird flew across the river.'

e. transitive + ditransitive
li pase liv-la bay mari (Haitian, Déchaine(1985))
3Sg pass book-DET give Marie
'S/he passed the book to Marie.'

The examples in (1) refer to a single overall event, even though the actions of two verbs may not be simultaneous.

SVCs do not seem to exist in Indo-European languages. They are found in the Kwa group of Niger-Congo languages in West Africa, in Caribbean creoles, in New Guinean languages, and also in East Asian languages such as Mandarin Chinese and possibly Thai. Among them, Ị̀jọ, spoken in the Niger Delta area of Southern Nigeria, has a unique word order (see Williamson 1963, 1965): it is the only serializing language with subject-object-verb (SOV) word order and all other serializing languages are of the subject-verb-object (SVO) type.

The constructions formed as [V-*e* V] in Korean have been traditionally considered to be complex predicates derived from a multi-clausal source or as compound predicates formed in lexicon (see Choe 1988; I. Yang 1977; and Suh 1990). In this paper, however, I claim that these are none of those predicates but rather SVCs and that Korean is also an SOV type serializing language. I first investigate the function of the morpheme -*e* which occurs between two verbs, and argue that it is just a DUMMY MORPHEME with no lexical meaning. Then, I propose that there are two types of SVCs in Korean, SVC1 and SVC2. I provide several empirical and theoretical tests to support this distinction. Accepting Baker's (1989) DOUBLY-HEADED VP structure, I formulate the configurational structures and thus show a structural difference between SVC1 and SVC2.

2. Properties of -*e* and Clausal Complex Predicates

Unlike SVCs in other serializing languages, SVCs in Korean have the morpheme -*e* between the first verb V1 and the second verb V2. Presumably, one might hesitate to approach Korean complex predicates from the perspective of SVCs, since -*e* has been overtly dealt with as an Infl (see Choe 1988) or a Comp (see H. Lee 1976 and D. Yang 1976) in the framework of generative grammar. However, let us start our discussion with an assumption that -*e* in Korean SVCs is just a dummy morpheme.

2.1. -E as a Suffix for Morphological Closure

The morpheme *-e* , which has no lexical meaning, is introduced right after V1, since every Korean verb is a bound morpheme and requires the presence of at least one verb-final suffix to stand alone. Kang (1988:78) also captures the same idea, and claims that Korean verbs, being bound morphemes, are subject to the following morphological principle:

(2) **Morphological Closure**
Bound predicates must be closed off by a set of suffixes belonging to the category C.
(C = verb-final suffixes)

Kang says that the Category C does not include the aspectual/tense/Agr/modal suffixes in Korean. This proposal is in accord with our assumption that *-e* is a dummy morpheme which is suffixed to make a bound verb free in a morphological sense.

Besides, according to Williamson (1965:53), the morpheme *-ni* suffixed to V1 in Ijo SVCs is just a LINKER with no lexical meaning. Korean *-e* also seems to function as a linker to connect two verbs. Even though Korean *-e* is morphologically oriented and Ìjo *-ni* is phonologically controlled, these suffixes seem to have the same function.[2]

The idea that *-e* is a linker leads us to predict that its suffixation to a verb causes no change of grammatical category of the verb. Since *-e* is a dummy morpheme, it is not expected to serve a significant grammatical function. In fact, this comes out when we compare *-e* with other verb-final suffixes, as in (3):

(3) a. Swuni-nun chayk ilk-ki-lul cohaha-n-ta
Swuni-Top book read-KI-Acc like-Pres-Dec
'Swuni likes to read a book.'

b. Swuni-nun ku chayk-ul ilk-ci-lul anh-ass-ta
Swuni-Top the book-Acc read-CI-Acc do not-Past-Dec
'Swuni did not read the book.'

In (3a) and (3b), the suffixes *-ki* and *-ci* play a role of nominalizer. The realization of an accusative Case after those suffixes implies that they change the grammatical category of the verbal stem *ilk*-'read' into a noun or of the whole verbal category including *ilk-* and its argument into a nominal one. Let us consider another verbal suffix *-nun*, given in (4):

(4) Swuni-ka t_i cohaha-nun chayk$_i$
Swuni-Nom like-Rel book
'the book that Swuni likes'

---

[2] In Ìjo, the suffix *-ni* is introduced usually when the next unit begins with a vowel and has no syntactic significance. See Williamson(1963, 1965).

In (4), *-nun* plays an important grammatical function, a relativizer, like 'which' or 'that' in English. However, *-e* just links and has no influence upon grammatical status. Therefore, I claim that *-e* is just a dummy-morpheme linker which is used to satisfy the requirement of morphological closure.

2.2. Is -e an Infl or a Comp?

It is still possible to regard *-e* as an Infl or a Comp. I will show somewhat indirectly that it is neither of these functional categories. That is, if a plausible candidate for an embedded clause shows no indication of clausehood, the candidate is not actually an embedded clause at any level of representation. In fact, there are several cases of sentences exhibiting a remnant of clausal embedding in deep structure. Causative sentences are such a case, given in (5):

(5) a. ku-nun Swuni-ka chayk-ul ilk-key ha-ess-ta
he-Top Swuni-Nom book-Acc read-Comp do-Past-Dec
'He made Swuni read the book.'

b. ku-nun Swuni-eykey chayk-ul ilk-key ha-ass-ta
-Dat
c. ku-nun Swuni-lul chayk-ul ilk-key ha-ass-ta
-Acc

In (5) *Swuni* is not only a semantic subject of the verb *ilk*-'read' but also a causee. While it has nominative Case in (5a), it has dative Case in (5b) and accusative Case in (5c). This arguably suggests that (5b) and (5c) are derived from (5a) which includes an embedded clause and that the verbal suffix *-key* is a Comp (see S. Lee (1990) for the detailed discussion of causative constructions in Korean).

Also, the first verb in causative sentences can be followed by an honorific morpheme *-si*, which is an explicit realization of an Agr in Korean, as in (6):

(6) ku-nun halmeni-lul TV-lul po-si-key ha-ass-ta
he-Top grandmother-Acc TV-Acc watch-Hon-Comp do-Past-Dec
'He made the grandmother watch the TV.'

This directly shows that causative sentences include an embedded clause.

In constrast, this kind of syntactic phenomenon never happens in SVCs. First, there is no subject of V1's own in SVCs; rather the subject of V1 is always the same as that of V2, as shown in (7):

(7) ku-nun (*Swuni-ka) kang-ul heyemchi-e kenn-ess-ta
he-Top Swuni-Nom river-Acc swim-L cross-Past-Dec
'He swam across the river.'

So, it seems to be unsupported to regard *-e* as a tenseless Infl (cf. Choe, H.S.(1988)).

Secondly, the V1 in SVCs is never followed by an honorific morpheme, as in (8):

(8) apeci-kkeyse cip-ey tol-(*usi)-e o-si-ess-ta
father-Nom(Hon) home-at turn-Hon-L come-Hon-Past-Dec
'The father returned home.'

Thirdly, a tense morpheme is never realized after V1, but there comes a tense morpheme after V2, as in (9):

(9) ku-nun koki-lul kwu-(*ass)-e mek-ess-ta
he-Top meat-Acc broil-Past-L eat-Past-Dec
'He broiled the meat and ate it.'

As shown in (7)-(9), V1-*e* involves no indication of an Infl and consequently represents a category smaller than CP and IP. Here we come up with two categorial possibilities: one is VP or V' and the other is a brand-new maximal category whose head is a functional category -*e*. But I have already shown that -*e* is too weak in its meaning and grammatical function status to have its own categorial value. Therefore, it is very natural to think V1-*e* to be a part of the verbal category for the whole [V1-*e* V2] and -*e* a dummy morpheme.[3]

To summarize, SVCs never behave as if they are multi-clausal structures. Neither is V1 a verb of an embedded clause, nor is V2 a verb of a main clause, and [V1-*e* V2] is not a complex predicate derived from a complex clausal deep structure.

3. Two Types of SVCs

3.1. SVC1

Bámgbóṣé(1974, 1982) maintains that there are two types of SVCs in Yoruba, spoken in the western part of Nigeria. Those are the modifying type SVC and the linking type SVC.[4] Even though I do not agree with his transformational approach to SVCs, I find his classification similar to my distinction between SVC1 and SVC2 in Korean. I cite his idea about modifying verbs below:

> '...when they occur in a minimal sentence, they have all the characteristics of a full verb; but when they occur in a serial construction, they take on a modifying function and do not have the full range of verbal characteristics. In other words, the difference in the behavior of a verb varies according to whether it occurs as the only verb or as one of a number of verbs in a sentence.'
> (Bámgbóṣé 1974:32)

That is, modifying verbs in Yoruba SVCs mainly modify or emphasize the meaning of main verbs, and sometimes their meaning is radically changed when

---

[3] I asume that the morpheme -*e* neither exists in the lexicon nor has a categorial value, but is inserted in syntactic process--before PF and LF--to make up for the deficiency of boundness of a verb.

[4] In his analysis, the former is derived from a single underlying sentence and the latter from two or more underlying sentences.

they occur in SVCs.

We also have this kind of verb in Korean and they have been traditionally called AUXILIARY VERBS. The following are examples with an auxiliary verb (the data in (10) have been chosen from Kim 1984):

(10) a. ku-nun sihem-ul phokiha-e peli-ess-ta
he-Top test-Acc give up-L throw away-Past-Dec
'He just gave up on the test.'

b. ku-nun 100-mite-lul 10-cho-ey talli-e nay-ess-ta
he-Top 100-meter-Acc 10-second-in run-L take out- Past-Dec
'He ran 100 meters in just 10 seconds.'

c. ku-nun cikum-kkaci cal sal-a o-ass-ta[5]
he-Top now-until well live-L come-Past-Dec
'He has lived a good life until now.'

d. ceswuci-uy mwul-i mal-a ka-n-ta
reservoir-Gen water-Nom dry-L go-Pres-Dec
'Water in the reservoir is drying up.'

e. ku-nun pang-ey tul-e o-ass-ta
he-Top room-at enter-L come-Past-Dec
'He entered the room.'

f. ku-nun san-ey ol-a ka-ass-ta
he-Top mountain-at climb-L go-Past-Dec
'He went up the mountain.'

g. ku-nun khun soli-lo chayk-ul ilk-e tay-ass-ta
he-Top loud voice-with book-Acc read-L supply- Past-Dec
'He continued to read the book in a loud voice.'

h. ku-nun umak-ul thul-e noh-ass-ta
he-Top music-Acc turn on-L leave-Past-Dec
'He had the music turned on.'

i. ku-nun Swuni-eykey pimil-ul malha-e cwu-ass-ta
he-Top Swuni-to secret-Acc tell-L give-Past-Dec
'He told Mary the secret (for her).'

j. ku-nun ku chayk-ul ilk-e po-ass-ta
he-Top the book-Acc read-L see-Past-Dec
'He tried reading the book.'

All the sentences in (10) involve a construction [V1-*e* V2]. They have a series of verbs in a single sentence without any conjunction marker.

[5] The realization of *-e/-a* is conditioned by the preceding vowel, which is a case of vowel harmony.

Interestingly, however, it is hard to assign an English gloss to some of them, because the meaning of V2 as a main verb in a simple sentence hardly shows up in this construction. Instead of fully expressing its own meaning, the V2 adds special meaning or aspect to the meaning of the whole sentence. For example, even though the verb *peli-* has the meaning 'throw away' by itself, it does not express its meaning in (10a), but rather means 'finish' or 'get through'. So, (10a) is not just the statement of an event that he gave up on the test but emphasizes the completion of the event. In the same way, in (10c), not just the fact that he lived a good life is described, but it is expressed that his state of living a good life has been continued from the past until now. That is, the verb *o-* 'come' adds the aspect of duration of the event but indicates no property of a motion verb.

The meanings modified by V2s are arranged in (11):[6]

(11)

V2 in (10)	The meaning of Ve as a main verb in a simple sentence	The modified or enriched meaning by V2 in [V1-*e* V2]
a) *peli-*	'throw away'	completion
b) *nay-*	'take out' 'put forth'	completion
c) *o-*	'come'	duration
d) *ka-*	'go'	duration
e) *o-*	'come'	direction
f) *ka-*	'go'	direction
g) *tay-*	'supply' 'draw into'	continuance
h) *noh-*	'put' 'keep'	retention
i) *cwu-*	'give'	benefaction
j) *po-*	'see'	trial

As illustrated in (10) and (11), the meaning of [V1-*e* V2] is different from the combination of the meaning of V1 and of V2 in simple sentences.

Now, let us consider why these combinations are a type of SVCs. First, all V2s are primarily independent verbs, whatever secondary function they may serve. They can be used as the only verb in a simple sentence, as in (12):

(12) a. ku-nun ssuleyki-lul <u>peli-</u>ess-ta
he-Top garbage-Acc throw-Past-Dec
'He threw away the garbage.'

b. ku-nun non-ey mwul-ul <u>tay</u>-ess-ta
he-Top rice paddy-in water-Acc draw into-Past-Dec
'He irrigated the rice paddy.'

---

[6] Since the meaning of auxiliary verbs on their own are so varied according to context, I list only some of their main meanings or the meanings possibly related to the ones in auxiliary verb constructions.

c. ku-nun Swuni-eykey chayk-ul cwu-ess-ta
he-Top Swuni-to book-Acc give-Past-Dec
'He gave a book to Swuni.'

That is, all of these so-called auxiliary verbs are not auxiliary at all when they are the only verb.

Nonetheless, one might suspect that V2s in (10) are auxiliary or even deficient in the sense that they do not project their argument structure and the arguments preceding [V1-e V2] seem to be all selected by only V1 but not by V2. This is true in some cases, but the other way around also holds in other cases: rather, some V2s project their own argument structure and consequently enrich the argument structure of the whole sentence. Let us compare the examples in (13):

(13) a. ku-nun nolay-lul pwul-ess-ta
he-Top song-Acc sing-Past-Dec
'He sang a song.'

b.*ku-nun Swuni-eykey nolay-lul pwul-ess-ta
he-Top Swuni-to song-Acc sing-Past-Dec
'He sang a song for Swuni.'

c. ku-nun Swuni-eykey nolay-lul pwul-e cwu-ess-ta
he-Top Swuni-to song-Acc sing-L give-Past-Dec
'He sang a song for Swuni.'

d.??ku-nun nolay-lul pwul-e cwu-ess-ta
he-Top song-Acc sing-L give-Past-Dec
'He sang a song (for whom??).'

The prepositional phrase *Swuni-eykey* 'to Swuni' is allowed in (13c) but not in (13b), and it is necessary in (13d) but not in (13a). This means that the addition of *Swuni-eykey* results from the influence of the verb *cwu*-'give' upon the argument structure of the whole sentence.

Secondly, all examples in (10) describe a single event, not a sequence of separate events. So the meaning of (10d), for example, is far from the sequence of two separate events (14a) and (14b):

(14) a. ceswuci-uy mwul-i malu-n-ta
reservoir-Gen water-Nom dry up-Pres-Dec
'The water in the reservoir dries up.'

b.*ceswuci-uy mwul-i ka-n-ta
reservoir-Gen water-Nom go-Pres-Dec
'The water in the reservoir goes away.'

Instead, (10d) describes the state of water drying up in the reservoir, and thus is just a single event not a combination of separate events. Remember that it is a general property that the two verbs together denote a single event.

Thirdly, the tense, marked only after V2 in (10), has a scope over the whole sentence and thus the two verbs are interpreted to have the same tense.

Fourthly, there is only a fixed number of auxiliary verbs, and their combination with another verbs is extremely productive. Even though there is sometimes a selectional restriction between two verbs which seems to be semantically controlled, all the V2s in (10) follow a quite large variety of V1s. For instance, as in (15), *nay*-'put forth', *tay*-'supply', and *noh*-'put' are not preceded by verbs describing mental or psychological state such as *nukki*-'feel' or *salangha*-'love' (see Kim 1984):

(15) a.*ku-nun Swuni-eykey sarang-ul <u>nukki-e</u> <u>nay</u>-ess-ta
he-Top Swuni-to love-Acc feel-L put forth-Past-Dec
'He felt love for Swuni.'

b.*ku-nun Swuni-lul <u>sarangha-e</u> <u>tay</u>-ess-ta
he-Top Swuni-Acc love-L supply-Past-Dec
'He kept loving Swuni.'

However, except a few cases of this kind semantic selectional restrictions which generally apply for most verbs, the combination of V1 and V2 is considerably free. Therefore, there is no need to assign them to a special unique category called AUXILIARY VERB CONSTRUCTIONS (AVCs). They may as well be included in more general one, SVCs, and syntactically derived. They are products of the syntactic phrasal projection of two verbs, not specific-class verbs which are lexically derived.

3.2. SVC2

In addition to SVC1, there is another type of SVC in Korean, SVC2. SVC2 is distinguished from SVC1 in several ways. First, while V2s in SVC1 are a small number of closed class verbs, V2s in SVC2 are an open class. Second, the meaning of SVC1 may not be compositionally deduced from the literal meanings of V1 and V2, since they usually express a modified meaning, even though there is a consistence in their modified meaning as shown in (11). But in SVC2 the meanings of V1 and V2 are independently expressed. Third, the argument structures of V2s are fully realized in SVC2, but not in some SVC1. That this division into SVC1 and SVC2 is on the right track will be thoroughly shown in section 3.3, both theoretically and empirically. For now, I provide and discuss some typical sentences of SVC2.

Based on the transitivity of verbs, SVC2s provide four types of combination of V1 and V2 as in (16)-(19):[7]

(16) <u>intransitive + intransitive</u>
ku-nun cip-ey <u>kel-e</u> <u>ka</u>-ss-ta
he-Top home-at walk-L go-Past-Dec
'He walked home.'

[7] The discussion of SVC2 with transitive V1+ditransitive V2 is not included in this paper. For this, see S. Lee's dissertation (in preparation:ch4).

(17) transitive + intransitive
ku-nun maul-ul thongkwaha-e o-ass-ta
he-Top village-Acc go through-L come-Past-Dec
'He came through the village.'

(18) transitive + transitive
ku-nun koki-lul kwu-e mek-ess-ta
he-top meat-Acc broil-L eat-Past-Dec
'He broiled the meat and ate it.'

(19) intransitive + transitive
ku-nun kang-ul heyemchi-e kenn-ess-ta
he-Top river-Acc swim-L cross-Past-Dec
'He swam across the river.'

Again, all sentences include a series of verbs with no marking of coordination or subordination, and the two verbs denote a single event. The tense marked on only one of the two verbs is understood to cover both of them. The lexical properties of both V1 and V2 are completely projected in all SVC2s in (16)-(19), and the meaning of a whole [V1-*e* V2] can be deduced from the meanings of its parts, V1 and V2.

3.3. Supporting Evidence for the Analysis

In this section I carry out some experiments to see whether SVC1 and SVC2 are also structurally different and consequently to support our classification into two types of SVCs.

3.3.1. -*Se* Insertion

The first test is related to the insertion of the particle -*se* 'by means of' after V1-*e*. The SVC1 verbs reject the insertion of -*se* and the SVC2 verbs allow it (see also Kim 1984).[8] Let us compare (20) and (21):

---

[8] The reason why SVC1 and SVC2 show a difference with respect to this insertion seems to be semantic in a way and is probably associated with the meaning relationship of V1 to V2 in SVC2. In SVC2, V1 in general tends to describe the way V2 is done, and thus we can use an SVC2 sentence, but not an SVC1 sentence, as an answer to a possible question with *ettehkey* 'how' and V2. Let us compare (i) with (ii):

(i) A: ku-nun ettehkey o-ass-ni? ((10c):SVC1)
he-Top how come-Past-Int
'How did he come?'
B:??ku-nun cikum-kkaci cal sal-a o-ass-e
he-Top now-until well live-L come-Past-Dec
'He has lived a good life until now.'

(ii) A: ku-nun cip-ey ettehkey ka-ss-ni? ((16):SVC2)
he-Top home-at how go-Past-Int
'How did he go home?'
B: ku-nun cip-ey kel-e ka-ss-e
he-Top home-at walk-L go-Past-Dec
'He walked home.'

(20) a.*ku-nun cikum-kkaci cal sal-a-se o-ass-ta (SVC1: duration)
he-Top now-until well live-L-SE come-Past-Dec
'He has lived a good life until now.'

b.*ku-nun san-ey ol-a-se ka-ss-ta (SVC1: direction)
he-Top mountain-at climb-L-SE go-Past-Dec
'He went up the mountain.'

(21) a. ku-nun cip-ey kel-e-se ka-ss-ta (SVC2: motion)
he-Top home-at walk-L-SE go-Past-Dec
'He walked home.'

b. ku-nun maul-ul thongkwaha-e-se o-ass-ta
he-Top village-Acc go through-L-SE come-Past-Dec
'He came through the village.'

Ka- 'go' in (20a) and *o-* 'come' in (20b) seem to be the same verbs as those in (21a) and (21b). But these apparently identical verbs are actually homophonous. In SVC1, they are used with a specific meaning of duration or direction, but in SVC2 with their original meaning of motion.[9] It is impossible to insert *-se* before 'go' or 'come' in SVC1, but possible in SVC2. Consequently, this *-se* insertion test shows that V1 in SVC1 is more tightly linked to V2 than V1 in SVC2 is.

3.3.2. Adverbial Insertion

A second test is based on the possibility of the occurrence of an adverb between V1 and V2. In both SVC1 and SVC2, an adverb can occur in front of V1, or, if any, in front of an object NP. Interestingly enough, an adverb can not occur between V1 and V2 in SVC1, but it can in SVC2. Let us compare the SVC1 in (22) and the SVC2 in (23):

(22) a.*ku-nun sihem-ul phokiha-e kapcaki peli-ess-ta (SVC1)
he-Top test-Acc give up suddenly throw away-Past-Dec
'He suddenly gave up on the test.'

b.*ceswuci-uy mwul-i mal-a cemcem ka-n-ta
reservoir-Gen water-Nom dry out-L gradually go-Pres-Dec
'The water in the reservoir is gradually getting dried up.'

(23) a. ku-nun koki-lul kwu-e masisskey mek-ess-ta (SVC2)
he-Top meat-Acc broil-L deliciously eat-Past-Dec
'He broiled the meat and enjoyed it.'

As in (i) and (ii), only an SVC2 sentence sounds natural as an answer to *ettehkey* 'how'.

[9] The directional V2s 'go' and 'come' are virtually universal in serializing languages (see Sebba 1987: 185-193).

b. ku-nun kang-el heyemchi-e tanswumey ken-ess-ta
he-Top river-Acc swim-L in a breath cross-Past-Dec
'He swam fast across the river.'

An SVC2 in general allows insertion of an adverb between V1 and V2 but an SVC1 does not. This again indicates that V1 and V2 are more tightly linked in SVC1 than in SVC2.

3.3.3. Scope of Negation

A third test is concerned with the scope interpretation of negation. In the so-called long form negation where the negation word *anh-* 'not' follows the final verb of the sentence, the negation scope in SVC1 is sometimes interpreted to be different from the negation scope in SVC2.[10] For instance, whereas the whole V1-*e* V2 is negated in SVC1 as in (24), only V1 can be negated in SVC2 as in (25):

(24) A: ku-ka sihem-ul phokiha-e peli-ess-ni? (SVC1)
he-Nom test-Acc give up-L throw away-Past-Int
'Did he give up on the test?'

B:*ku-nun sihem-ul phokiha-e peli-ci-nun
he-Top test-Acc give up-L throw away-CI-Cont
anh-ass-ci-man, peli-ki-nun ha-ess-e
do not-Past-CI-Del, throw away-KI-Cont do-Past-Dec
??He did not give up on the test, but threw it away.'

(25) A: ku-ka koki-lul kwu-e mek-ess-ni? (SVC2)
he-Nom meat-Acc broil-L eat-Past-Int
'Did he broil and eat the meat?'

B: ku-nun koki-lul kwu-e mek-ci-nun an-lass-ci-man,
he-Top meat-Acc broil-L eat-CI-Cont do not-Past-CI-Del,
mek-ki-nun ha-ess-e
eat-KI-Cont do-Past-Dec
'He did not broil the meat, but ate it.'

As in (24), V1 and V2 in SVC1 resist being separately negated. But the independent negation of V1 is possible in SVC2, as shown in (25). In this way,

---

[10] The response to an SVC2 sentence such as (i) may be marginal:
(i) ?ku-nun cip-ey kel-e nuckey ka-ss-ta
he-Top home-at walk-L late go-Past-Dec
'He walked home late.'
But the sentence sounds natural when there is a slight pause after V1-*e* or when -*se* follows it, as in (ii):
(ii) ku-nun cip-ey kel-e-se nuckey ka-ss-ta
he-Top home-at walk-L-by means of late go-past-Dec
'He walked home late.'

the difference of scope interpretation of negation supports the idea that V1 and V2 in SVC1 have a closer relationship than in SVC2, whatever that relationship is.

3.4. Structures and Theoretical Issues

Based on these three tests, I postulate that the form [V1-*e* V2] of SVC1 has a structure different from that of SVC2 at a certain level of representation, even though their deep structure representations are not different. In this section, I discuss their structural differences and related theoretical issues.

Accepting Baker's(1989) analysis of SVCs based on his Head Licensing Condition (HLC), I assume that Korean SVCs have a doubly-headed verb projection, and that both V1 and V2 are main verbs in an SVC. That is, a VP in SVCs has two verbal heads, V1 and V2, whose lexical properties are projected in syntax following the Projection Principle.

3.4.1. SVC1 Structure

Let us start with SVC1 first. The V2s in SVC1 are a fixed number of a closed class. They lose semantic and syntactic weight in SVC1, even though they are originally independent verbs: i.e., i) they sometimes enrich the argument structure of the sentence but often do not project their argument structures, as discussed in section 3.1, and ii) they lack of their original full meaning and instead add a special meaning or aspect to the meaning of the whole sentence. Here, I claim that this semantic and syntactic weakness of V2s in SVC1 triggers a head movement of V1 with full content. It is not suprising that a semantically minimal or weak verb triggers another verb to be moved and incorporated to it, as illustrated in head movement and incorporation phenomenon in causative sentences of many languages (see Baker 1988: ch4 and S. Lee 1990). At the deep structure, V1 and V2 are separate verbs, but V1 is moved and incorporated to V2 in syntax, as shown in (26):

```
(26) a. D-structure              b. S-structure
            VP                           VP
            |                            |
            V'                           V'
           / \                          / \
          V'  V2        ===>           V'   V*
         / \                          /\   /\
     (NP)  V1                     (NP) ti V1i V2
                                        |__↑
```

Following Baker's Head Licensing Condition, both V1 and V2 are equally heads of the maximal projection VP in (26a). The NP is q-marked by V1 under sisterhood in the sense of Chomsky's(1981, 1986b) theta theory in D-structure. The V2 in (26a) does not necessarily q-mark the preceding NP, since it is not in a sisterhood relationship to the NP.[11] The NP is Case-marked by the V*, which consists of V2 and V1 incorporated into it, under government based on Baker's (1988:65) Government Transparency Corollary (GTC).

The trace of V1 in (26b), known to exist by the Projection Principle, must be properly governed to satisfy Chomsky's (1981) Empty Category Principle (ECP).[12] For V1 to govern its trace, two conditions must be met: it must c-command its trace and there must be no barrier that intervenes between the two. The V* category formed by adjunction does not count. Since it is not a maximal projection, it is not a potential barrier and does not block V1's c-commanding t_i.[13] Therefore, V1 governs its trace and the ECP is satisfied.

As illustrated in (26b), after incorporation, V1 and V2 no longer look like separate verbs but one compound verb. This accounts for why V1 and V2 in SVC1 exihibit a very rigid link in the preceding tests.

3.4.2. SVC2 Structure

Following Baker's Head Licensing Condition again, SVC2 also has a doubly-headed VP. Let us compare four cases of SVC2 structure according to the transitivity of verbs in (27):

```
(27) a. (16)      VP              b. (17)      VP
                   |                            |
                   V'                           V'
                  /|\                          / \
              PP  V' V2                      V'   V2
             /_\   |  |                     /\     |
            home  V1 go                   NP  V1  come
                   |                      |    |
                  walk                 village go through
```

---

[11] This seems to be a reason why the argument structure of V2 in SVC1 is not fully realized.

[12] This means that it must be governed by the chain coindexed V1. Since V1 and V2 have no θ-relationship in that a lexical category usually θ-marks a maximal category (see Baker 1989:53), the trace of V1 is not θ-coindexed with V2. Actually in every SVC, V1 and V2 are not θ-related in the sense of the Revised θ-Criterion by Emonds (1985:78). Therefore, the trace must be antecedent-governed by the coindexed V1.

[13] I accept here Aoun and Sportiche's (1983) definition of c-command:

> α c-commands β if α does not dominate β and for every maximal projection γ, if γ dominates α then γ dominates β.

```
c. (18)     VP              d. (19)      VP
            |                            |
            V'                           V'
           /|\                          /|\
      NP   V'  V2                  NP   V'  V2
      |    |   |                   |    |   |
    meat   V1  eat               river  V1  cross
           |                            |
         broil                         swim
```

In (27a), both V1 and V2 are intransitive verbs which have no internal θ-roles to assign. The NP is a structural sister to V1 in (27b) and to V2 in (27d). Thus, NP is assigned a θ-role by V1 in (27b) and by V2 in (27d). The NP in (27c) is θ-marked by V2, which is a structural sister, and also by V1, which is a V'-internal transitive verb. This is an example of pure OBJECT-SHARING in Baker's (1989) sense. Baker (1989) argues that, in a doubly-headed VP of an SVC, there must be object sharing especially when the first verb is transitive. However, this is not the case, as we see in (27b). Rather, I notice that all examples of SVC2 given in (16)-(19) involve SUBJECT-SHARING rather than object sharing.[14] Both V1 and V2 percolate their external θ-roles to their maximal projection VP where they are assigned to the subject. In this way, the two verbs share a subject instead of an object. The subject sharing idea is further supported by all SVC1 data in (10), in which no object is shared.

In the light of Chomsky's (1986b) θ-Criterion, it is not problematic for an NP to receive more than one θ-role in the same position. His θ-Criterion prohibits a θ-marked NP from receiving another θ-role in another θ-position after movement. But in (27c) the NP gets two θ-roles in the same D-structure position.

In (27c), NP is supposed to be Case-marked by both V1 and V2, as it is θ-marked by both of them. This causes no conflict with any principles in the framework of Government and Binding Theory. The Case Theory and the θ-Criterion bar a Case-marked NP trace and allow Case to appear only on the head of a chain (see Chomsky 1986b:186-204), but they do not disallow a doubly Case-marked NP in the same D-structure position.

4. Concluding Remarks

In previous research, it has been taken for granted that Korean has a special class of verbs called auxiliary verbs and that they construct so-called auxiliary verb constructions. This is presumably because most research focus has been put only on the semantic and syntactic deficiency of these verbs (cf. I. Yang 1977 and Choi 1991).

However, in this paper, I have argued that auxiliary verb constructions are actually a part of serial verb constructions. I have also claimed that Korean is a serializing language, which has two types of SVCs, SVC1 and SVC2, and that auxiliary verb constructions correspond to SVC1. Unlike previous research of SVCs in African linguistics (cf. Bamgbose 1974, 1982; George 1975; Oyelaran

---

[14] Only if both verbs are transitive, must there be object sharing. See S. Lee's dissertation (in preparation: ch3).

1982; Schachter 1974; Stahlke 1970, etc.), typological dichotomy of Korean SVCs has been made based on purely syntactic and theoretical arguments.

References

Aoun, Joseph and Dominique Sportiche. 1983. On the Formal Theory of Government. Linguistic Review 2.3.

Baker, Mark C. 1988. *Incorporation: A Theory of Grammatical Function Changing.* Chicago: The University of Chicago Press.

Baker, Mark C. 1989. Object Sharing and Projection in Serial Verb construction. *Linguistic Inquiry* 20. 513-553.

Bámgbóṣé, Ayo. 1974. On Serial Verbs and Verbal Status. *Studies in African Linguistics* 4. 207-217.

Bámgbóṣé, Ayo. 1982. Issues in the Analyses of Serial Verbal Construction. *Journal of West African Languages* XII.2. 3-21.

Choe, Hyun-Sook. 1988. *Restructuring Parameters and Complex Predicates: A Transformation Approach.* Doctoral Dissertation, MIT.

Choi, Ki-Yong. 1991. *A Theory of Syntactic X^o-Subcategorization.* Doctoral Dissertation, University of Washington.

Chomsky, Noam. 1981. *Lectures on Government and Binding.* Dordrecht: Foris.

Chomsky, Noam. 1986a. *Barriers.* Cambridge: MIT Press.

Chomsky, Noam. 1986b. *Knowledge of Language: Its Nature, Origin, and Use.* New York: Praeger .

Déchaine, Rose-Marie. 1985. An Account of Serial Verbs in Haitian Creole: Argument Structure Coalescence. *Current Approaches to African Linguistics* 8. eds. by Newman, P. and Robert D. Borne, 237-251. Dordrecht: Foris.

Emonds, Joseph E. 1985. *A Unified Theory of Syntactic Categories.* Dordrecht: Foris.

George, Isaac. 1975. Typology of Verb Serialization. *Journal of West African Languages* 9. 78-97.

Kang, Myung-Yoon. 1988. *Topics in Korean Syntax: Phrase Structure, Variable Binding and Movement.* Doctoral Dissertation, MIT.

Kim, Young-Hee. 1984. *Kuke Tonsaku Kusungey Natananun Uymikwankey Yunku* (A Study on the Semantic Relations in Korean Verb Constructions). Doctoral Dissertation, Ewha Women's University, Seoul.

Lee, Hong-Bae. 1976. Notes on Pronouns, Reflexives, and Pronominalization. *Ehak Yunkwu.* (Linguistic Research). 12-2.

Lee, Sook-Hee. 1990. Two Kinds of Causative Construction in Korean. ms., University of Washington.

Lee, Sook-Hee. In preparation. *The Syntax of Serialization in SVO and SOV Languages.* Doctoral dissertation, University of Washington.

Li, Charles N. and Sandra A. Thompson. 1973. Serial Verb Constructions in Mandarin Chinese: Subordination or Co-ordination? *You Take the High Node and I'll Take the Low Node*, ed. by Claudi Corm, 96-103.

Lord, Carol. 1973. Serial Verbs in Transition. *Studies in African Linguistics* 4.3. 269-295.

Oyèlárǎn, Olasope O. 1982. On the Scope of the Serial Verb Construction. *Studies in African Linguistics* 13.2. 107-146.

Schachter, Paul. 1974. A Non-Transformational Account of Serial Verbs. *Studies in African Linguistics*, Supplement 5. 253-270.

Sebba, Mark. 1987. *The Syntax of Serial Verbs.* Amsterdam: John Benjamins.

Stahlke, Herbert. 1970. Serial Verbs. *Studies in African Linguistics* 1. 60-99.

Suh, Jung-Soo. 1990. *Kuke Munpupuy Yenku* (A Study of Korean Grammar). Seoul: Hankuk Munwhasa.

Williamson, Kay. 1963. The Syntax of Verbs of Motion in Ìjọ̣. *Journal of African Languages* 2.2. 150-154.

Williamson, Kay. 1965. *A Grammar of the Kolokuma Dialect of Ìjọ̣.* Cambridge University Press: Cambridge.

Yang, Dong-Whee. 1976. Korean Negation Revisited. *Ene* (Language) 1.1.

Yang, In-Suk. 1977. Parameters of Going-Coming Compound Verbs in Korean. *Papers in Linguistics*, ed. by Kim, Chin-Woo. Hornbeam Press.

Case Alternation and Word Order Variation in Nominal

CLAUSES YOUNG-SUK LEE
University of Pennsylvania

Case Alternation and Word Order Variation in Nominal Clauses

Young-Suk Lee
University of Pennsylvania

1 Introduction

The issue of whether scrambling is movement or base-generation drew much attention in the early 80's, under the name '(non)configurationality' ([Hale 1982]). However, most recent studies on scrambling in the "principles and parameters" approach to syntax (GB hereafter) have focused on the issue of scrambling as A or A-bar movement ([Webelhuth 1989], [Mahajan 1990], [Frey 1990], [Miyagawa 1990], [Saito 1992], etc.),[1] taking it for granted that scrambling is a movement process. Despite this, I will argue that analysis of scrambling as movement is not emprically well-motivated on the basis of the data concerning case array and word order variation in event nominal clauses.

[1]This research has been partially funded by DARPA N00014-90-J-1863. I have greatly benefited from presenting this work at the LSA Summer Institute Workshop on Korean Syntax/Semantics, Santa Cruz. It is a pleasure to thank Richard Campbell, Dong-In Cho, Stanley Dubinsky, Robert Frank, Sabine Iatridou, Jeong-Ryeol Kim, Anthony Kroch, Michael Niv, Peter Sells, James Yoon, for helpful discussions, and Young-Mee Cho, Eunjoo Han, Ki-Sun Hong, Sun-Hyun Hong, Chang-Bong Lee, Kenziro Matsuda, Hiroaki Tada, Saeko Urushibara for their native speaker's judgments, and Aravind Joshi for supporting this research financially. My special thanks go to Shigeru Miyagawa for encouraging me to pursue this issue by providing relevant material at various occasions. All errors and shortcomings are unfortunately my own.

A crucial theoretical motivation for a movement analysis of scrambling in GB is to observe the projection principle. This is intended to preserve the thematic structure projected from the lexicon at all levels of representation, which results a category VP in the X-bar system of the base.[2] The category VP posited this way, however, is a pure reflex of the thematic hierarchy of the arguments determined in the lexicon, cf. [Chomsky 1981, 127–129], begging for further syntactic justification. Given this, various linguists ([Saito 1985], [Webelhuth 1989]) have tried to justify scrambling as movement in two ways: One is by motivating the category VP in syntax, e.g. asymmetry in nominative/accusative case assignement, subject/object asymmetry in scrambling, facts concerning pronominal coreference. The other is by finding similarities between scrambling and other well-established movement phenomena such as wh-movement and topicalization in English, e.g. island effects, left-brach condition effects, various crossover effects.

[Young-Suk Lee, work in progress], however, argues that much of the evidence which has been given is either only apparent (subject/object asymmetry, island effects), or not decisive (various crossover effects and facts concerning pronominal coreference). In this paper, I will argue that even the remaining facts — asymmetry in nominative/accusative case assignment and left-branch condition effects — do not constitute evidence for scrambling as movement, which is based upon an analysis of a constrained set of data, event nominal clauses in Korean and Japanese.

As will be discussed at length in section 2, an event nominal clause where the head noun is followed by an aspect morpheme, exhibits various case arrays for the same argument structure, which apparently result different range of word order variation of the arguments ([Iida 1987], [Shibatani and Kageyama 1988], [Sells 1990], [Miyagawa 1990] for Japanese, and [Cho and Sells 1991] for Korean). The intricacy of the data serves to constrain certain details concerning case licensing which have been, so far, left underdetermined. At the same time, it permits a very simple analysis if we assume that arguments can be base-generated in any order.

After presenting the data in section 2, in section 3 I propose my analysis, and discuss the categorial status of an aspect morpheme, and a potential problem for θ-role assignment under my analysis. Finally in section 4, I dicuss some consequences of the analysis, which show that asymmetry in nominative/accusative case assignment, left-branch condition effects do not constitute evidence for scrambling as movement. Finally, section 5 is the summary of the paper. All the examples in this paper are given in Korean, but the arguments hold for Japanese as well, unless otherwise specified.

[2]The category VP in this case is a theoretical notion by which we distinguish subject positions from object positions, i.e. a subject position is external to VP, while an object position is internal to VP. Although it is perfectly legitimate to posit a category VP, without necessarily making a subject position external to it, for example, as in various instantiations of VP-internal subject hypothesis (cf. [Fukui 1986], [Fukui and Speas 1986], [Kitagawa 1986] and [Koopman and Sportiche 1988]), the category VP in this paper should be understood in its theoretical sense, unless otherwise specified.

2 Data Description

As discussed by [Iida 1987], [Shibatani and Kageyama 1988], [Sells 1990], [Miyagawa 1990] for Japanese, and [Cho and Sells 1991] for Korean, an event/process noun (event noun hereafter), as opposed to a resultative noun, has its own argument structure (cf. [Grimshaw 1990]), as shown in (1):[3]

(1) a. Kim kyoswu-uy wencahayk-uy yenkwu
Kim professor-GEN nuclear cell-GEN research

b. *Kim kyoswu-ka wencahayk-uy yenkwu
Kim professor-NOM nuclear cell-GEN research

c. *Kim kyoswu-ka wencahayk-ul yenkwu
Kim professor-NOM nuclear cell-ACC research
'Prof. Kim's research on nuclear cells'

(2) a. *Kim kyoswu-uy wencahayk-uy yenkwuhanta
Kim professor-GEN nuclear cell-GEN do research

b. *Kim kyoswu-ka wencahayk-uy yenkwuhanta
Kim professor-NOM nuclear cell-GEN do research

c. Kim kyoswu-ka wencahayk-ul yenkwuhanta
Kim professor-NOM nuclear cell-ACC do research
'Prof. Kim does research on nuclear cells.'

The event head noun *yenkwu* 'research' in (1) takes two arguments, i.e. subject and object, just like its verbal counterpart *yenkwuhata* 'to do research' in (2). The main difference between the two cases is that in (1) all of the arguments have to be marked genitive case, while in (3), verbal case.[4]

2.1 Case Array

However, when an event noun is followed by an aspect morpheme, such as *(to)cwung* 'during', *(cik)hwu* '(right) after', *(tang)si* 'when', etc., the arguments exhibit additional case possibilities, as illustrated in (3).[5]

[3]Event nouns are better known as verbal nouns ([Martin 1975]), and are typically of Chinese origin. Examples of resultative nouns are *chayksang* 'desk', *hakkyo* 'school', etc. In the glosses, I use the following abbreviations:

NOM	nominative	ACC	accusative	GEN	genitive
LOC	locative	ASP	aspect	CE	causative ending
TOP	topic	PL	plural	Q	question

[4]Verbal case is meant to refer to nominative and accusative case, as opposed to genitive case.

[5]Strings relevant for the present discussion are indicated by square brackets. The matrix clause *cencayng-i ilenassta* 'a war took place' is added to show that the subject of the nominal clause (*Kim kyoswu* in this case) does not have to coincide with the subject of the matrix clause (*cencayng*).

(3) a. [Kim kyoswu-uy wencahayk-uy yenkwu-cwung] cencayng-i ilenassta
Prof. Kim-GEN nuclear cell-GEN research-during war-NOM took place

b. [Kim kyoswu-ka wencahayk-ul yenkwu-cwung] cencayng-i ilenassta
Prof. Kim-NOM nuclear cell-ACC research-during ...

c. [Kim kyoswu-ka wencahayk-uy yenkwu-cwung] cencayng-i ilenassta
Prof. Kim-NOM nuclear cell-GEN research-during ...

d. *[Kim kyoswu-uy wencahayk-ul yenkwu-cwung] cencayng-i ilenassta
Prof. Kim-GEN nuclear cell-ACC research-during ...
'*During Prof. Kim's research on nuclear cells*, a war took place.'

The arguments may be marked not only all genitive case, as in (3)a, but also all verbal case, as in (3)b. Furthermore, some arguments may be marked with verbal case, and others with genitive case (mixed case array): In (3)c, the subject is marked nominative case, and the object, genitive case. The combination shown in (3)d, however, is ungrammatical, where the genitive subject is followed by the accusative object.

We observe the same kind of case possibilities with ditransitive event nouns. This is illustrated in (4)a–(4)f:

(4) a. Kim chongcang-uy swusekhaksayng-eykey-uy colepcang-uy swuye-cwung
president Kim-GEN best student-DAT-GEN certifacate-GEN pass-during

b. Kim chongcang-i swusekhaksayng-eykey-uy colepcang-uy swuye-cwung
president Kim-NOM best student-DAT-GEN certificate-GEN pass-during

c. Kim chongcang-i swusekhaksayng-eykey colepcang-uy swuye-cwung
president Kim-NOM best student-DAT certificate-GEN pass-during

d. Kim chongcang-i swusekhaksayng-eykey colepcang-ul swuye-cwung
president Kim-NOM best student-DAT certificate-ACC pass-during

e. *Kim chongcang-uy swusekhaksayng-eykey-uy colepcang-ul swuye-cwung
president Kim-GEN best student-DAT-GEN certificate-ACC pass-during

f. *Kim chongcang-i swusekhaksayng-eykey-uy colepcang-ul swuye-cwung
president Kim-NOM best student-DAT-NOM certificate-ACC pass-during
'during President Kim's passing the graduation certificate to the best student'

Just as in the case of a transitive head noun, all the arguments of the ditransitive head noun *swuye* may be marked genitive case (cf. (4)a), or verbal case (cf. (4)d). When the arguments exhibit mixed case arrays, they have to fit the descriptive generalization stated in (5).[6]

[6] In Korean, genitive case on the dative argument may be omitted without affecting the grammaticality of the string while genitive case can never be omitted in Japanese. In fact, many speakers of Korean including myself slightly prefer the case where genitive case is dropped.

(5) If an argument is marked genitive, all the other arguments to its right must be marked genitive case as well. Otherwise, the sentence is ungrammatical.

The ungrammaticality of (3)d, (4)e, and (4)f fall under this generalization.

2.2 Word Order Variation

In addition to the interesting case arrays they exhibit, the arguments in an event nominal clause may be permuted, with certain limitations. Consider the examples in (6) where the head noun is transitive, and those in (7) where the head noun is ditransitive.

(6) a.?[wencahayk-uy Kim kyoswu-uy yenkwu-cwung] ...
nuclear cell-GEN Prof. Kim-GEN research-during ...

b. [wencahayk-ul Kim kyoswu-ka yenkwu-cwung] ...
nuclear cell-ACC Prof. Kim-NOM research-during ...

c.*[wencahayk-uy Kim kyoswu-ka yenkwu-cwung] ...
nuclear cell-GEN Prof. Kim-NOM research-during ...

d.*[wencahayk-ul Kim kyoswu-uy yenkwu-cwung] ...
nuclear cell-ACC Prof. Kim-GEN research-during ...
During Prof. Kim's research on nuclear cells, (a war took place.)'

(7) a. colepcang-uy swusekhaksayng-eykey-uy Kim chongcang-uy swuye-cwung
certificate-GEN best student-DAT-GEN president Kim-GEN pass-during

b. Kim chongcang-i colepcang-uy swusekhaksayng-eykey-uy swuye-cwung
president Kim-NOM certificate-GEN best student-DAT-GEN pass-during

c. *swusekhaksayng-eykey-uy Kim chongcang-i colepcang-uy swuye-cwung
best student-DAT-GEN president Kim-NOM certificate-GEN pass-during

d. swusekhaksayng-eykey Kim chongcang-i colepcang-uy swuye-cwung
best student-DAT president Kim-NOM certificate-GEN pass-during

e. *swusekhaksayng-eykey colepcang-uy Kim chongcang-i swuye-cwung
best student-DAT certificate-GEN president Kim-NOM pass-during

f. *colepcang-ul Kim chongcang-uy swusekhaksayng-eykey-uy swuye-cwung
certificate-ACC president Kim-GEN best student-DAT-GEN pass-during
'during president Kim's passing the graduation certificate to the best student'

On examination of the examples in (6) and (7), we can find the generalization described in (8):

(8) 1. In the case where arguments are marked either uniformly genitive case or uniformly verbal case, all logically possible permutations of the arguments are grammatical: (6)a, (6)b, (7)a.
2. In the case where arguments show mixed case array, both (a) and (b) below should hold.

- The generalization stated in (5) holds: (7)b, (7)d, vs. (6)c, (7)c, (7)e.
- An argument to the left of a genitive argument cannot be marked accuative case: (6)d, (7)f.

Since the first item of the generalization (8) is a subset of (7), we can simplify the generalization as in (9).

(9) 1. If an argument is marked genitive case, all the other arguments to its right must be marked genitive case as well.
2. An argument to the left of a genitive argument cannot be marked accuative case.

Before moving to an analysis of the data, I will briefly comment on permutation among genitive phrases, since people's judgments on the data vary greatly. Most people including myself find (6)a to be worse than (6)b, as indicated by '?'. However, there is a clear contrast in grammaticality between (6)a and other ungrammatical examples. Also, adding a pause between the object and the subject improves the acceptability significantly. Moreover, (7)a is much more natural than (6), even though the ordering of subject and object arguments in the two is the same. Although it is not clear why (7)a should be any better than (6)a, examples like (7)a lead me to conclude that permutation among genitive phrases is syntactically possible. Finally, (10) below shows that adding an adverbial phrase *mikwuk-eyse-uy* between the object and the subject in (6)a improves the acceptability of the string.[7]

(10) wencahayk-uy Kim kyoswu-uy mikwuk-eyse-uy yenkwu-cwung ...
nuclear cell-GEN Prof. Kim-GEN America-LOC-GEN research-during
'during Prof. Kim's research on nuclear cells in America, ...'

3 Proposal: A Base-generation Analysis

In this section I propose an analysis of the data, and justify some assumptions I make on the categorial status of aspect markers and event nouns. I also discuss some potential problems concerning θ-role assignment under my analysis.

[7][Saito 1985, 228–235] claims that scrambling among genitive phrases is not possible in Japanese. However, he did not consider the cases like (7)a and (10).

3.1 Analysis

For my analysis, I assume the case licensing conditions in (11),[8,9] which requires the notion of 'licensing' and 'government,' as is defined in (12) and (13), respectively.[10]

(11) Case Licensing Conditions

a. Genitive case is licensed by [+N,–V] lexical head.
b. Accusative case is licensed by a [+V,+ACC] lexical head at S-structure.
c. Nominative case is licensed by a [+V] category at S-structure.

(12) α **licenses** β iff either (i) or (ii):

i. α governs β.
ii. α immediately dominates β.

(13) α **governs** β iff α m-commands β and there is no barrier between α and β (cf. [Chomsky 1986, 9]).

I assume the following with regard to argument order and aspect morphemes.

(14) a. Arguments are base generated in any order at D-structure.
b. An aspect morpheme projects a category with the feature [+V].

Now I propose (15):[11]

(15) **Proposal**: Case alternation and word order variation in event nominal clauses are derived from the interaction between

- the scope of an aspect morpheme, and
- the licensing conditions for nominative, accusative, and genitive case.

Let us consider a few examples to see how the current proposal accounts for the data.
Figure 1a is a schematic representation for (3)c, where the nominative subject precedes the genitive object. The genitive case on the object is licensed by the head noun. The nominative case on the subject is licensed by 'XP[+V]' which immediately dominates it.[12] Figure 1b is a representation of (3)b, where the

[8][Miyagawa 1990] gives a movement analysis for the same set of data in Japanese. The genitive case licensing condition here is directly adopted from his analysis.

[9]The question of which lexical head has [+ACC] feature is orthogonal to the main issue here, and the reader can refer to [Kim 1990] and [Hong 1991] for thorough discussions on the nature of [+ACC] verbs.

[10]As for the definition of 'barrier' and its related notions, refer to [Chomsky 1986].

[11]Accounting for various case possibilities in terms of the scope of an aspect marker here is hinted at [Abney 1987], where he explains the distribution of nominative, accusative and genitive subject of a gerundival clause in English in terms of the scope of the gerundival morpheme *-ing*, which has the feature [+N].

[12]The categorial status of XP will be discussed in detail in the next subsection.

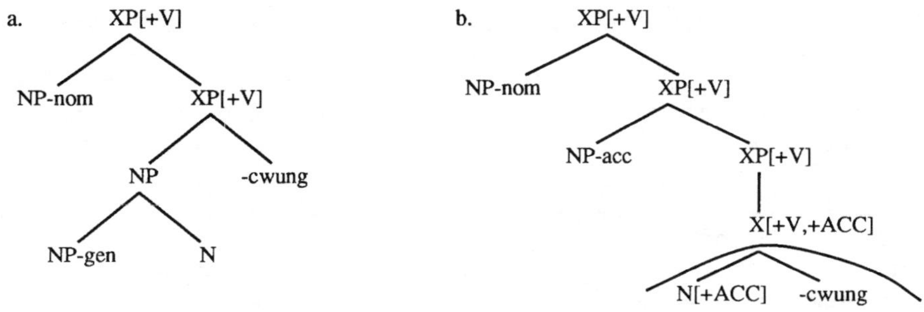

Figure 1: Derivation of 'NOM-GEN' and 'NOM-ACC' order

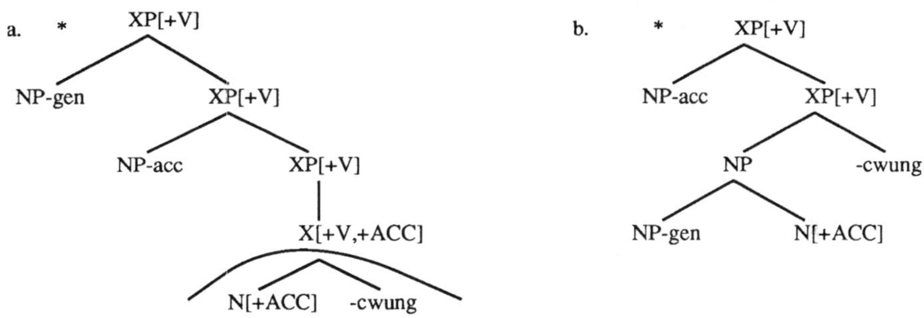

Figure 2: Derivation of 'GEN-ACC' and 'ACC-GEN' order

nominative subject precedes the accusative object.[13] The accusative case on the object is licensed by the [+V,+ACC] lexical head 'X', and the nominative case on the subject, by 'XP[+V]'.[14]

Figure 2a is a representation of (3)d, which is ungrammatical. This string is correctly ruled out since there is no N lexical head which can license the genitive case on the first NP. Figure 2b is a representation of (6)d, which is ungrammatical. Its ungrammaticality is due to the fact that there is no [+V,+ACC] lexical head which can license the accusative case on the first NP, even though the genitive case on the second NP is licensed by the head noun. The reader may easily verify the correctness of the analysis with respect to the remaining examples.

[13]As [Sells 1990, 12–13] points out, the default hypothesis for the category of an event noun would be that it is a verb, especially when the arguments exhibit verbal case array. In fact this is the position which [Ahn 1991] takes. Concerning this point, I do not have any strong argument for one or the other. Nevertheless the fact that arguments may be marked verbal case only when the event noun is followed by an aspect morpheme, seems to indicate that its category is always a noun, and that it is the aspect morpheme which affects the case possibility of the arguments.

[14][Sells 1991] convincingly argues that any morphological process which takes place in the lexicon is left-headed. If he is right, which I believe, then the lexical head 'X[+V,+ACC]' should be formed in syntax since the head of this category is an aspect morpheme, and hence right-headed.

3.2 Categorial status of an aspect morpheme and an event noun

In giving my analysis, I assumed that an aspect morpheme projects a category with the feature [+V]. I also implicitly assumed that the category of an event noun is a noun, regardless of the case array which the arguments exhibit. In this section, I discuss the motivation behind these assumptions.

The decision on the categorial status of an aspect morpheme is due to the distribution of nominative/accuative case in the data. As is clear from the contrast in case possibilities between (16) and (17) below, it is the aspect morpheme which is responsible for the occurrence of accusative and nominative case.

(16) a. Kim kyoswu-uy wencahayk-uy yenkwu
Kim professor-GEN nuclear cell-GEN research

b. *Kim kyoswu-ka wencahayk-ul yenkwu
Kim professor-NOM nuclear cell-ACC research

c. *Kim kyoswu-ka wencahayk-uy yenkwu
Kim professor-NOM nuclear cell-GEN research
'Prof. Kim's research on nuclear cells'

(17) a. Kim kyoswu-uy wencahayk-uy yenkwu-cwung
Prof. Kim-GEN nuclear cell-GEN research-during

b. Kim kyoswu-ka wencahayk-ul yenkwu-cwung
Prof. Kim-NOM nuclear cell-ACC research-during

c. Kim kyoswu-ka wencahayk-uy yenkwu-cwung
Prof. Kim-NOM nuclear cell-GEN research-during
'during Prof. Kim's research on nuclear cells'

I attribute this case licensing ability of the aspect morpheme to one of its features, [+V]. Since the standard view on accusative case assignment is the same as I assume here, cf. [Chomsky 1981, 170], my treatment of an aspect morpheme as a category with the feature [+V] for the purpose of accusative case licensing does not require further justification. With respect to nominative case licensing, however, a largely accepted view is that it is licensed by INFL or its component categories such as AGR or Tense, not by a category of [+V].[15] Despite this common view, below I give one piece of evidence which demonstrates that INFL is not responsible for nominative case assignment, indirectly supporting my view that [+V] feature is all that is required for nominative case licensing.[16]

In Korean, nominative case may occur in a small clause where there is no inflection/aspect morpheme. Consider the examples in (18) and (19):

[15]In his analysis of the same data, [Miyagawa 1990] treats the aspect morphemes as functional categories, and claims that both nominative and accusative case are licensed by a functional category.

[16]As for a more detailed discussion on the independence of nominative case from INFL in Japanese/Korean, refer to [Heycock and Lee 1989] and [Lee 1990].

(18) na-nun [aki-ka ulum-ul kuchi-key] hayssta
I-TOP baby-NOM cry-ACC stop-CE made
'I made the baby stop crying.'

(19) sensayngnim-i [Chelswu-ka kongpwu-lul kyesokha-tolok] seltukhasiessta
teacher-NOM Chelswu-NOM study-ACC continue-so that persuaded
'The teacher persuaded Chelswu to continue studying.'

(18) is an example of a causative construction, and (19), a control construction.[17] Both contructions require a tenseless complement clause, as evidenced by the absence of tense/aspect morphemes in each embedded clause. Nevertheless, the embedded subjects *aki* in (18), and *Chelswu* in (19), respectively, are marked nominative case. If the existence of a functional projection corresponding to an inflection/aspect morpheme is essential for nominative case, then the only way of explaining the data above would be by positing a functional projection with a null head, which is not desirable by 'null hypothesis.' On the other hand, if we adopt the assumption that nominative case is licensed by [+V] category, as is assumed here, then the nominative case of the embedded subjects in (18) and (19) is explained with no stipulation.

A question which might arise from assuming an aspect morpheme as a category with the feature [+V], which heads the projection 'XP[+V]' in figure 1 and figure 2, is how we explain NP-like behaviors of the category 'XP[+V]'. As [Sells 1990] correctly points out for Japanese, the category corresponding to 'XP[+V]' in Japanese behaves very much like an NP in the following sense: First, only nominal categories appear in front of the copula *da*, and the category at issue occurs in front of the copula. Second, the category can be followed directly by nominative/accusative case markers just like an NP.[18] Jeong-Ryeol Kim (p.c.) has also pointed out to me that the category at issue should be an NP since it may be followed by a postposition, as illustrated in (3)a–(3)c in section 2.

Even though the facts Sells and Kim point out are true, these facts don't necessarily lead to the conclusion that the category is an NP, since not only an NP but also a PP can be followed by a copula, cf. (20), by a case marker, cf. (21), and by another postposition, cf. (22).

(20) [nay-ka ne-lul po-n] kes-un hakkyo-**eyse**-**i**-ta
I-NOM you-ACC saw-MOD thing-TOP school-LOC-COP-DEC
'It was in school that I saw you.'

---

[17]Strictly speaking, (19) is not a control construction under the analysis given here, since there is no PRO in the embedded clause which is controlled by a matrix argument. I am calling this a control construction, since (1) the translation of the matrix verb corresponds to English *persuade*, which is a control verb, (2) the embedded subject *Chelswu-ka* may occur as a dative as well, and in that case the dative argument is better analyzed as a matrix clause argument which controls the PRO in the embedded clause.

[18][Sells 1990] actually discusses these facts to argue that the category of an event noun is an N not a V rather than the category of XP at issue. Although he also notes that it is the feature [+asp] in the aspect morpheme which licenses nominative and accusative case, he does not consider the possibility that an aspect morpheme is an independent category with its own projection. Instead, it is simply a suffix to the head noun, leaving the categorial status of the head noun intact.

(21) cikum-**pwute-ka** cinccata
now-from-NOM be effective
'(The/a thing) is effective from now on.'

(22) Chelswu-ka Seoul-**eyse-pwute** tallye oassta
Chelswu-NOM Seoul-LOC-from ran and came
'Cheswu ran from Seoul.'

From the examples (20) – (22) it seems reasonable to conclude that the category 'XP[+V]' is in fact a PP, and an aspect morpheme is a P. Nevertheless, this option is not viable in GB since the category P is a feature bundle [–V,–P], and I leave this question open here.[19]

3.3 Theta-role assignment

The analysis which I have given for case licensing and word order variation in event nominal clauses is very simple, and does not require any major revision to the theory of grammar. Under this analysis, however, we cannnot maintain the standard assumption on θ-role assignment, which is defined in terms of government by a θ-role assigner. Let us consider example (3)c, repeated here as (23), and its representation in figure 3.

(23) Kim kyoswu-ka wencahayk-uy yenkwu-cwung
Prof. Kim-NOM nuclear cell-GEN research-during
'during Prof. Kim's research on nuclear cells'

In figure 3, the genitive NP can be assigned its θ-role by the head noun via government. In the case of the nominative NP, however, a θ-role cannot be assigned to it since the 'XP[+V]' is a barrier for the government by the head noun.

[19] James Yoon (p.c.) has pointed out to me that when an event noun is followed by the morpheme *-cha* 'as an occasion', genitive case array is not allowed, as illustrated by the ungrammaticality of (a) below:

a. *[Bush taytonglyeng-uy incil mwuncey-uy hyepsang-cha] cwungtong swungpang kil-ey olassta
president Bush-GEN hostage problem-GEN to negotiate middle east visiting road-LOC rose

b. [Bush taytonglyeng-i incil mwungcey-lul hyepsang-cha] cwungtong swungpang kil-ey olassta
president Bush-NOM hostage problem-ACC to negotiate middle east visiting road-LOC rose

c. [Bush taytonglyeng-i incil mwuncey-uy hyepsang-cha] cwungtong swungpang kil-ey olassta
president Bush-NOM hostage problem-GEN to negotiate middle east visiting road-LOC rose
'President Bush is on his way on a visit to the Middle East *to negotiate the hostage problem.*'

If we assume that *-cha* is an aspect morpheme like other aspect morphemes discussed in this paper, I simply have no explanation for why only *-cha* behaves specially. On the other hand, Yookyung Kim (p.c.) points out that a nominal clause followed by *-cha* is different from other nominal clauses discussed in this paper in that they have to be obligatorily followed by a controlled clause (i.e. the subject of the matrix subject has to be the same as that of the *-cha* clause). If she is correct, then a nominal clause followed by *-cha* belongs to a different construction from that followed by an aspect morpheme. Still it seems worth exploring why the object argument in *-cha* construction may be marked either accusative or genitive.

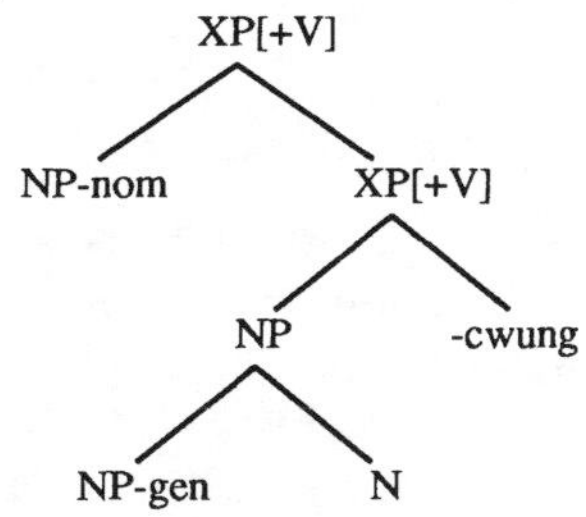

Figure 3: Representation of 'NOM-GEN' order

Given this difficulty with θ-role assignment in the current analysis, I will assume the following non-standard θ-role assignment for the time being. Namely, undischarged θ-roles are percolated up to the next maximal projection and the θ-role is assigned by the maximal projection via government. Note that this way of θ-role assignment is not consistent with the semantic compositionality, which is instantiated in the form of projection principle and the usual definition of θ-role assignment in GB. In fact, any analysis which assumes base-generation of scrambled word order cannot maintain the standard compositional θ-role assignment.

As mentioned in the introductory section, the main motivation for a movement analysis of scrambling is to observe the projection principle, and it is this principle which ensures the compositional θ-role assignment. Once we adopt the base-generation analysis of scrambling, the compositionality in θ-role assignment cannot be maintained, unless a separate lexical structure is assumed for θ-role assignment, in addition to the constituent (i.e. syntactic) structure, cf. [Chomsky 1981, 129]. The relevant question would be whether it is worth holding onto movement analysis of scrambling in the absence of any syntactic evidence for it, and satisfy the compositional θ-role assignment, or we give up the idea that θ-role is assigned compositionally in syntax. In the absence of any valid empirical motivation for scrambling as movement, I would take the view that θ-role assignment doesn't have to be assigned compositionally.

4 Consequences

In this section I discuss some consequences of my analysis. As will become clear shortly, they show that asymmetry in nominative/accusative case assignment, and the facts on pronominal coreference are not valid evidence for the existence of VP node. The left-branch condition effects on scrambling, which have been used to argue for scrambling being an operator movement, cf. [Webelhuth 1989], have an independent explanation based on genitive case licensing.

4.1 Nominative/Accusative Case Assignment

Asymmetry in nominative/accusative case assignment has been given as evidence for scrambling being movement, by motivating a VP node.

As is expressed in their licensing condition in (11), which is repeated below, there is an asymmetry between nominative and accusative case licensing.

- Accusative case is licensed by a [+V,+ACC] lexical head at S-structure.
- Nominative case is licensed by a [+V] category at S-structure.

However, the crucial point is that the same category projection — a projection of [+V] category — participates in nominative and accusative case licensing, contradicting the claim that a subject which is assigned nominative case should be separated from an object which is assigned accusative case by VP.[20]

Furthermore, my proposal on nominative/accusative case licensing contradicts the analysis of scrambling proposed by [Mahajan 1990], when applied to Korean. Assuming a highly articulated phrase structure along the lines of [Pollock 1989] and [Chomsky 1991], he argues that when it is A-movement,[21] scrambling is induced by the necessity of case assignment, i.e., an object moves to the SPEC of AGR-obj, and a subject, to the SPEC of AGR-sub, where they are assigned case appropriately. However, the data at hand and my analysis of them show that subject and object case assignment cannot be separated by different category projections. Moreover, accusative case licensing cannot be dissociated from a lexical head with [+ACC] feature, contrary to the claim that accusative case is licensed by a functional projection.

4.2 Binary Branching Structure and Pronominal Coreference

Another piece of evidence which is given for the existence of VP in Japanese by [Saito 1985] is facts concerning pronominal coreference. The paradigm for pronominal coreference in English, and its licensing condition, are given in (24) and (25), respectively, which are taken from [Saito 1985, 36].

(24) a. [$_S$ John$_i$ [$_{VP}$ loves [$_{NP}$ his$_i$ mother]]]
b. *[$_S$ He$_i$ [$_{VP}$ loves [$_{NP}$ John's$_i$ mother]]]
c. [$_S$ John's$_i$ mother [$_{VP}$ loves [$_{NP}$ him$_i$]]]
d. [$_S$ His$_i$ mother [$_{VP}$ loves [$_{NP}$ John$_i$]]]

(25) A pronoun cannnot be c-commanded by its antecedent.

[Saito 1985] takes the following step to justify the existence of VP in Japanese:[22]

[20]The question of how nominative case is assigned in Japanese and Korean has been very controversial, and a number of analyses have been proposed, e.g. default case analysis by [Kang 1986] and [Kim 1990], nominative case assignment by INFL or AGR by [Yim 1985], [Ahn and Yoon 1989], nominative case assignment by both V and INFL by [Whitman 1991], and nominative case as a marker for subject of syntactic predication by [Heycock and Lee 1989], to name a few. Among these different view, the current analysis is most consistent with the view that nominative case is assigned by default in a clause where the head is a verb. For further summary of different views on nominative case assignement and their criticisms, refer to [Heycock and Lee 1989] and [Ahn 1990, 332–339].

[21][Mahajan 1990] claims that scrambling is a non-unitary phenomenon: It is A-movement when it is substitution into the SPEC positions of functional categories, while it is A-bar movement when it is an adjunction to maximal projections. This is what causes the mixed character of scrambling.

[22]For a more detailed discussion on the pronominal coreference, refer to [Saito 1985, 36-47].

1. The paradigm in (24) is straightly accounted for by the condition in (25).
2. Japanese exhibits exactly the same pattern as English with regard to pronominal coreference.
3. Therefore, Japanese has VP.

Note, however, that step 3 does not necessarily follow from step 2. To satisfy the condition on pronominal coreference stated in (25), all we need is some kind of hierarchical phrase structure on which the notion of 'c-command' may be instantiated, not necessarily a phrase structure with a VP node. More specifically, any binary branching phrase structure will be adequate to account for the facts in terms of the condition in (25), and it is exactly the structure I have assumed throughout.

The current analysis assumes base-generation of arguments for scrambled word orders, which is similar to those proposed by [Farmer 1980] and [Hale 1982], among others. Contrary to these proposals which assume a flat phrase structure, however, I assume a binary branching phrase structure, which is crucial in explaining the data of mixed case array (cf. [Cho and Sells 1991]).

As it turns out, the binary branching phrase structure which is independently motivated for the case facts in event nominal clauses gives a simple solution for the facts on pronominal coreference, without invoking a VP node.

4.3 Apparent Left-branch Condition Effects

[Ross 1967] claims that 'left-branch condition,' as illustrated by the examples in (26), is a property of an operator movement, at least in English. [Webelhuth 1989] draws on this, and concludes that scrambling in German is an instance of an operator movement since it obeys the left-branch condition, among others.[23]

(26) a. *Whose$_i$ did you see [t$_i$ brother]?
b. *How$_i$ is John [t$_i$proud of his children]?
c. *How$_i$ did John leave [t$_i$ quickly]?

A scrambled counterpart of (26)a in Korean is also ungrammatical, as shown in (27)b, apparently obeying the left-branch condition.[24]

(27) a.

ne-nun	[nwukwu-uy	tongsayng]-ul	poass-ni
you-TOP	who-GEN	sister-ACC	saw-Q

b.

*nwukwu$_i$-uy	ne-nun	[t$_i$ tongsayng]-ul	poass-ni
who-GEN	you-TOP	sister-ACC	saw-Q

'Whose sister did you see?'

[23]Refer to [Webelhuth 1989, 338–345] for the details.

[24]I use a trace for Korean examples for expository convenience, without committing myself to any particular analysis.

If we follow Webelhuth's logic for scrambling in German, the ungrammaticality of (27)b should lead us to conclude that scrambling in Korean is an instance of operator movement just like English wh-movement, in spite of evidence to the contrary (cf. [Lee and Santorini 1991], [Lee 1991]). However, the licensing condition for genitive case proposed by Miyagawa, and adopted here, i.e. genitive case is licensed by a [+N,–V] lexical head, the ungrammaticality of examples such as (27)b is explained easily, without resorting to the left-branch condition. In (27)b, the genitive case on the scrambled NP cannot be licensed since it is disconnected from its licenser, i.e. the noun *tongsayng.*

Furthermore, grammaticality of (28) and (29), which are Korean counterparts of the ungrammatical (26)b, and (26)c, respectively, indicates that the left-branch condition is not operative in Korean, as it is in English or German, and therefore the ungrammaticality of (27) has to be explained by other principles of grammar, which turns out to be the condition on gentive case licensing.

(28) elmana$_i$ ne-nun ney casik-tul-i [t$_i$ calangsulep-ni]
how you-TOP your child-PL-NOM be proud of-Q
'How much are you proud of your children?', or
'You are very proud of your children, aren'you?'

(29) elmana$_i$ ne-nun [t$_i$ ppali] talil swu iss-ni
how you-TOP fast run can-Q
'How fast can you run?'

5 Summary

In this paper, I presented the data concerning case array and word order variation in event nominal clauses, and proposed an analysis based on the assumption that arguments are base-generated in any order. I also discussed some consequences of the analysis, which contradict some evidence which has been given to support the claim that scrambling is movement.

References

[Abney 1987] Abney, Steven, 1987. *The English noun phrase in its sentential aspect.* PhD thesis, M.I.T.

[Ahn 1990] Ahn, Sung-Ho, 1990. *Korean Quantification and Universal Grammar.* PhD thesis, The University of Connecticut.

[Ahn 1991] Ahn, Hee-Don, 1991. *Light verbs, VP-movement, negation and clausal architecture in Korean and English.* PhD thesis, University of Wisconsin–Madison.

[Ahn and Yoon 1989] Ahn, Hee-Don and Yoon, Hang-Jin, 1989. Functional categories in Korean. In et al., Susumu Kuno (editor), *Harvard studies in Korean linguistics III*, pages 79–88. Hanshin Publishing Company, Seoul.

[Cho and Sells 1991] Cho, Young-Mee and Sells, Peter, 1991. A Lexical Account of Phrasal Suffixes in Korean. Ms., Stanford University.

[Chomsky 1981] Chomsky, Noam, 1981. *Lectures in government and binding. Studies in generative grammar 9.* Foris, Dordrecht.

[Chomsky 1986] Chomsky, Noam, 1986. *Barriers. Linguistic Inquiry Monograph 13.* M.I.T. Press, Cambridge, MA.

[Chomsky 1991] Chomsky, Noam, 1991. Economy of derivation and representations. In Freidin, Robert (editor), *Principles and parameters in comparative grammar*, pages 417–454. M.I.T. Press, Cambridge, MA.

[Farmer 1980] Farmer, A., 1980. *On the Interaction of Morphology and Syntax.* PhD thesis, M.I.T.

[Frey 1990] Frey, Werner, 1990. *Syntaktische Bedingungen für die Interpretation.* PhD thesis, Universität Stuttgart.

[Fukui 1986] Fukui, Naoki, 1986. *A theory of category projection and its applications.* PhD thesis, M.I.T.

[Fukui and Speas 1986] Fukui, Naoki and Speas, Margaret, 1986. Specifiers and projection. *M.I.T. working papers in linguistics* 8:128–172.

[Grimshaw 1990] Grimshaw, Jane, 1990. *Argument Structure.* M.I.T. Press, Cambridge, MA.

[Hale 1982] Hale, Ken, 1982. Preliminary Remarks on Configurationality. *Proceedings of NELS* 12:86–96.

[Heycock and Lee 1989] Heycock, Caroline and Lee, Young-Suk, 1989. Subjects and predication in Korean and Japanese. In Hoji, Hajime (editor), *Japanese/Korean linguistics*, pages 239–254. CSLI, Stanford.

[Hong 1991] Hong, Ki-Sun, 1991. *Argument Selection and Case Marking in Korean.* PhD thesis, Stanford University.

[Iida 1987] Iida, Masayo, 1987. Case Assignment by Nominals in Japanese. In Wechsler, Steve and Zec, Draga (editors), *Working Papers in Grammatical Theory and Discourse Structure.* CSLI, Stanford.

[Kang 1986] Kang, Young-Se, 1986. *Korean Syntax and Universal Grammar.* PhD thesis, Harvard University.

[Kim 1990] Kim, Young-Joo, 1990. *The syntax and the semantics of Korean case.* PhD thesis, Harvard University.

[Kitagawa 1986] Kitagawa, Yoshihisa, 1986. *Subject in Japanese and English.* PhD thesis, University of Massachusetts, Amherst.

[Koopman and Sportiche 1988] Koopman, Hilda and Sportiche, Dominique, 1988. Subjects. Ms., University of California, Los Angeles.

[Lee 1990] Lee, Young-Suk, 1990. Is INFL universal? A case study of Korean. *Proceedings of ESCOL* 7.

[Lee 1991] Lee, Young-Suk, 1991. Scrambling and Pronoun Binding in Korean. Paper presented at Harvard Worshop on Korean Linguistics.

[Lee and Santorini 1991] Lee, Young-Suk and Santorini, Beatrice, 1991. Resolving Webelhuth's paradox: evidence from German and Korean. In *Proceedings of the Tilburg Workshop on Scrambling.*

[Mahajan 1990] Mahajan, Anoop, 1990. *The A/A-bar distinction and movement theory.* PhD thesis, M.I.T.

[Martin 1975] Martin, Samuel, 1975. *Reference Grammar of Japanese.* Yale University Press, New Haven, CT.

[Miyagawa 1990] Miyagawa, Shigeru, 1990. Case realization and scrambling. Paper presented in Tilburg Workshop on Scrambling, Holland.

[Pollock 1989] Pollock, Jean-Yves, 1989. Verb movement, Universal Grammar, and the structure of IP. *Linguistic inquiry* 20:365–424.

[Ross 1967] Ross, John Robert, 1967. *Constraints on variables in syntax.* PhD thesis, M.I.T.

[Saito 1985] Saito, Mamoru, 1985. *Some Asymmetries in Japanese and Their Theoretical Cosequences.* PhD thesis, M.I.T.

[Saito 1992] Saito, Mamoru, 1992. Long distance scrambling in Japanese. *Journal of East Asian Linguistics* 1:69–118.

[Sells 1990] Sells, Peter, 1990. More on light verbs and theta marking. Ms., Stanford University.

[Sells 1991] Sells, Peter, 1991. Korean and Japanese Morphology from a Lexical Perspecitive. Ms., Stanford University.

[Shibatani and Kageyama 1988] Shibatani, Masayoshi and Kageyama, T., 1988. Word Formation in a Modular Theory of Grammar. *Language* 64.

[Webelhuth 1989] Webelhuth, Gert, 1989. *Syntactic saturation phenomena and the modern Germanic languages.* PhD thesis, University of Massachusetts, Amherst.

[Whitman 1991] Whitman, John, 1991. String Vacuous INFL to COMP. Paper given at 1991 GLOW colloquium.

[Yim 1985] Yim, Young-Jae, 1985. Multiple subject constructions. In et al., Susumu Kuno (editor), *Harvard studies in Korean linguistics*, pages 101–112. Hanshin Publishing Company, Seoul.

Uniform Pro Subject Analysis of Japanese Sentences*

SHIGEO TONOIKE
Meiji Gakuin University and MIT

0. Introduction

In a series of papers I have suggested that the subject of a Japanese clause is *pro,* a zero pronoun, occurring in the postverbal position and functioning as a VARIABLE bound by an OPERATOR of the form NP-{*ga/wa/mo*}. This analysis, while it accounts for the apparent *pro*-drop characteristic of Japanese because the operator is optional, begs the question of why the specifier position of IP cannot host an overt pronoun, if it can host *pro.*

Chomsky (Class Lecture, 1990) suggests that subject agreement (AGR_S) is universal and that PRO has NULL CASE and is licensed in English by a semantically minimal AGR_S. If this proposal about the universality of AGR_S is correct, then AGR_S in Japanese should be not only semantically minimal but also empty of any ϕ-features. Then it should follow that Japanese AGR_S can license nothing but

* This paper is based primarily on the two earlier papers written in Japanese. I am grateful to the audience of the 2nd Workshop on Japanese Grammar held at the National Language Institute, Tokyo in December 1988 where I read the first version of Tonoike (1989) and the audience of the Southern California Japanese/Korean Linguistics Conference held at UC Santa Barbara in September 1991, where I read an earlier version of this paper for their comments, criticisms and suggestions. As is obvious from the exposition, the part about Japanese having PRO subject licensed by empty Agreement is a development since I came to MIT. I am grateful to Noam Chomsky, Ken Hale, Howard Lasnik, Alec Marantz, James Higginbotham, Noriaki Yusa for patiently listening to my ideas and giving me invaluable comments on them. The possibility that the Japanese empty subject might be PRO rather than pro was brought to my attention by a remark that Pierre Pica made in one of our many enjoyable discussions. He said, "Small pro? Why not big PRO?" This remark got me started on the track that has led me to this paper. I am grateful to Joel Bradshaw for the comments and stylistic improvements that he suggested for this final version. Any errors and mistakes that may be left in this paper are my own.

PRO in Japanese, and this will solve the problem of accounting for the non-appearance of any overt pronoun in the specifier of IP in Japanese.

After a brief discussion of the Japanese clause structure in Section 1, the UNIVERSAL AGR_S HYPOTHESIS will be introduced in Section 2, together with the UNIFORM PRO SUBJECT HYPOTHESIS. Section 3 presents evidence that shows that Japanese subjects are uniformly PRO. Section 4 discusses the status of PRO as a variable bound by an operator. Section 5 presents data suggesting that the Uniform PRO Subject Analysis is applicable to Korean and Chinese.

1. Japanese Clausal Structure

In Tonoike (1989, 1990, 1991) I have argued that the Japanese clausal structure is as shown in (1) below.

(1)

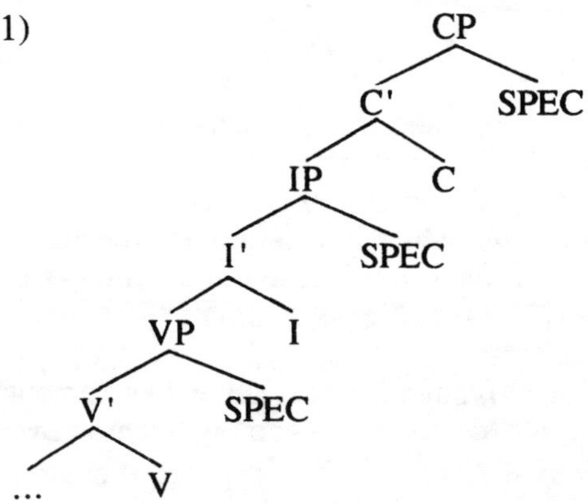

If this is correct, then it follows that Japanese cannot have an overt structural subject (S-SUBJECT, for short) because the S-subject position, namely the specifier position of IP cannot contain any overt element: nothing except certain particles can follow Inflection (i.e., tense morpheme) in an independent sentence. It also follows that what is usually considered as the subject of a sentence, such as *John-ga/wa/mo* in (2) below (which I shall refer to as O-SUBJECT, short for operator-subject, for convenience), cannot be the S-subject since it occurs to the left of the verbal element.[1]

1. In the gloss I will use the following abbreviations without committing myself to the correctness of the categorical status implied. In particular, I do not regard *wa* as the topic marker nor *ga* as the nominative marker, nor do I regard *koto* as a complementizer. Morphemes are given in their phonologically adjusted forms. top=Topic marker *(wa);* nom=Nominative marker *(ga);* acc=Accusative marker *(o);* Pres=Present tense marker *(ru/i);* Past=Past tense marker *(ta);* Neg=Negation *(nak);* Pass=Passive morpheme *(rare);* Subj=Subjunctive Inflection *(re);* Cont=Continuative Inflection *(te)* (sometimes called gerundive form); COMP=Complementizer *(koto, no);*

(2) John-{ga/wa/mo} kaet-ta
John-{nom/top/also} leave-Past
'John left' 'As for John, he left' 'John also left'

For this reason, I suggested an analysis in which O-subjects are treated as adjuncts functioning as an operator binding the S-subject, which I regarded as *pro*. Thus the examples in (2) are analyzed to have the schematic structure shown in (3) at S-structure.[2]

(3) [$_{CP}$ [$_{IP}$ John$_i$-{ga/wa/mo} kaet-ta pro$_i$]]

If we allow *pro* to occur as an O-subject (as a zero topic in the sense of Huang (1984)), this analysis accounts nicely for the fact that Japanese appears to be a *pro*-drop language, i.e., for the fact that 'subjectless' sentences such as (4) are possible in Japanese.

(4) a. pro$_i$ [kaet-ta pro$_i$] yo
come-Past I-tell-you
b. pro$_i$ [tabe-ta pro$_i$] yo
eat-Past I-tell-you

These sentences can be used in reference to somebody understood in the context, whether it is the speaker, hearer, or somebody or something else.

However, if *pro* can occur in the Spec of IP, then it is expected that an overt pronoun such as *kare* 'he' should be able to occur there, because it is generally the case that a zero pronoun and an overt pronoun are interchangeable as in (5).

(5) John-wa suika$_i$-o kat-te, hitoride {[e$_i$]/sore$_i$-o}
John-top watermelon-acc buy-Cont alone it-acc
tabe-ta
eat-Past
'John bought a watermelon and ate it by himself'

However, *pro* in S-subject position cannot be replaced by an overt pronoun.

Pol=Polite marker *(mas)*, etc.

2. I did not arrive at the structure shown in (3) immediately. At first I analyzed the 'subject' as a CP adjunct and *pro* as occurring to the left of the verb. Here I leave unspecified the exact structural relationship that the operator has with regard to IP.

(6) a. *Kaet-ta-kare yo
come-Past-he I-tell-you
b. *Tabe-ta-kare yo
eat-Past-he I-tell-you

The ungrammaticality of (6) remains a problem for the analysis of S-subject as *pro.* However, if S-subject is PRO, then no such problem arises. That is a possibility made available by Chomsky's recent proposal about PRO having Null Case and being licensed by semantically minimal AGR_S.

2. Universal AGR_S Hypothesis

Chomsky (Class Lecture, 1990) suggests that AGR_S is universal (call this the Universal AGR_S Hypothesis) and that PRO has Null Case and is licensed by a semantically minimal AGR_S. Thus in English two types of AGR_S can be distinguished, namely AGR_S with full ϕ–features, which can license a Nominative subject and AGR_s with minimum ϕ-features and therefore can license only PRO with Null Case. I will distinguished the two as AGR_S^{Full} and AGR_S^{Min}. AGR_S^{Full} cooccurs with Tense, whereas AGR_S^{Min} cooccurs only with infinitives and gerunds (and possibly N). This situation is illustrated in (7).

(7) a. John AGR_S^{Full} Past leave
b. John AGR_S^{Full} Past want [PRO AGR_S^{Min} to leave]

In (7a) and in the matrix clause of (7b) AGR_S^{Full} licenses the nominative subject *John,* while in the complement clause of (7b) AGR_S^{Min} licenses PRO with Null Case.

Now it is a well-established fact that there is no observable subject-verb agreement in Japanese. Therefore the only way AGR_S can exist in Japanese is by being empty, empty of any ϕ-features. It is less than the semantically minimum AGR_S^{Min} of English. Let us represent the empty Japanese AGR_S as AGR_S^E. Since AGR_S^{Min} can license only PRO, AGR_S^E cannot license anything but PRO. Thus since Japanese clauses have only AGR_S^E, it follows that the only S-subject that they can have is PRO. This accounts for the fact that no overt subject, neither a full noun phrase nor a pronoun, can occur in the S-subject position as shown in (6) above.

Under the Universal AGR_S Hypothesis, the examples in (2) should be analyzed as having the structure in (8) rather than (3), and the examples in (4) as having the structure in (9).[3]

(8) [$_{CP}$ [$_{AGRP}$ John$_i$-{ga/wa/mo} [kaet-ta-AGR$_S$E PRO$_i$]]]
(9) a. [$_{CP}$ [$_{AGRP}$ pro$_i$ [kaet-ta-AGR$_S$E PRO$_i$] yo]]
b. [$_{CP}$ [$_{AGRP}$ pro$_i$ [tabe-ta-AGR$_S$E PRO$_i$] yo]]

(9a-b) contain *pro* as the operator binding PRO. This corresponds to Huang's (1984) zero topic binding a variable. The only difference between this analysis and that of Huang is whether the S-subject is PRO or *pro*.

The Uniform PRO Subject Hypothesis, while it accounts for the non-occurrence of overt element in S-subject position, raises the following two questions.

(10) a. Do Japanese 'subjectless' sentences show properties attributable to the presence of PRO subjects?
b. Is the status of PRO compatible with the status of a variable?

These two questions are dealt with in the following two sections.

3. Evidence for the Uniform PRO Subject Hypothesis

3.1. Arbitrary PRO Interpretation of O-subjectless Sentences

If the Uniform PRO Subject Hypothesis is correct for Japanese, then sentences without O-subjects (overt or null) should show evidence that they contain PRO subjects. This prediction is born out by a number of classes of sentences, parts of which have already been noted by Saito (1982), Kuroda (1983), and Hasegawa (1985). Consider first the following generic statements without overt O-subjects.

(11) a. Nihon de-wa ie-ni hair-u PRO toki-wa kutu-o
Japan in-top house-in enter-Pre time-top shoes-acc
nugi-mas-u PRO
take-off-Pol-Pres
'In Japan people take off their shoes when they enter a house'
b. Toozi nihon-de-wa hutuu niku-o tabe-nak-at-
those days Japan-in-top normally meat-acc eat-Neg-be-
ta PRO
Past
'In those days in Japan people didn't normally eat meat'

---

3. Here I use a more articulated structure with IP reanalyzed as consisting of TP and AGR$_S$P.

These examples do not have overt O-subjects nor do they have a zero topic identifiable by the discourse. And their interpretations are such that they can be said to have an arbitrary PRO interpretation of their S-subjects qualified by the place and time adverbials. What is notable is that these sentences are not infinitival constructions. (11a) contains Present tense and (11b) Past tense.

Another set of examples exhibiting arbitrary PRO subject interpretation are directions such as below.

(12) Mazu tamanegi-o mizingiri-ni si-mas-u PRO Tugini ...
first onion-acc mince do-Pol-Pres Then ...
'First mince onions. Then ...'

Unlike English, where directions take the form of imperative sentences, Japanese uses O-subjectless indicative sentences. Here there is no natural candidate for an overt O-subject. Again these sentences contain Present Tense.

Embedded clauses denoting actions exhibit the same properties.

(13) a. Gohan ni misosiru-o kake-ru PRO no/koto-wa gyoogi-
rice on miso soup-acc pour-Pres COMP top manner-
waru-i
bad-Pres
'It is bad manners to pour miso soup over rice'

b. Uso-o tuk-u PRO no/koto-wa waru-i koto da
lie-acc tell-Pres COMP top bad-Pres thing is
'It is a bad thing to tell a lie'

It might still be argued that S-subject positions in the above examples are filled not by PRO but by *pro*. But there is a clear difference between PRO and *pro*. *Pro* occurs in the object position where it is governed by the verb and Case-marked by it. Consider.

(14) John-wa suika$_i$-o hitotu kat-te hitoride pro$_i$ tabe-ta
John-top watermelon-acc one buy-Cont alone eat-Past
'John bought a watermelon and ate it all by himself'

In this example *pro* occurs in the object position of the verb *tabe*. If the S-subject positions in the examples in (11-13) are occupied by *pro* with an arbitrary interpretation, then a gap in the object position should exhibit the same arbitrary interpretation as a gap in S-subject position. However, that is not the case. Compare the following pair of examples, where a gap is marked by ___.

(15) a. *Syusse su-ru _ to, minna-ga _ kira-u
get-promoted if everybody-nom hate-Pres
'If one gets promoted, everybody hates one'
b. Syusse su-ru _ to, minna-ni kiraw-are-ru _
get-promoted if everybody-by hate-Pass-Pres
'If one gets promoted, one gets hated by everybody'

The gap in the object position of the main clause of (15a) does not allow an arbitrary interpretation, whereas the gap in the passive S-subject position of the main clause of (15b) does allow an arbitrary interpretation. This subject-object asymmetry cannot be accounted for if all positions marked by _ in (15) are filled by *pro.* It falls out naturally from the PRO theorem in conjunction with the Uniform PRO Subject Hypothesis: PRO cannot occur in the object position because that position is governed by the verb.[4]

3.2. Expletive PRO

The fact that the English *it*-expletives do not have overt counterparts in Japanese may be cited as evidence for the Uniform PRO Subject Hypothesis. Nothing seems to prevent PRO from acting as an expletive. First consider the following examples involving meterological expressions.

(16) a. Kyoo-wa mus-u _
today-top steam-Pres
'It's muggy today'
b. Gasut-te ki-ta _
get-foggy come-Past
'It's getting foggy'
c. Kemut-te ki-ta _
get-smoky come-Past
'It's getting foggy/smoky'
d. Moyat-te ki-ta _
get-misty come-Past
'It's getting misty'

These examples do not have O-subjects. *Kyoo-wa* is not an O-subject but simply a time adverbial. Many of them, in fact, cannot tolerate an O-subject. Other meterological verbs such as *kumor* 'get cloudy' and *hare* 'clear up' may be cited as verbs taking expletive PRO subjects at least in one of their uses.

The same is true of adjectives denoting temperature and amount of light as used in the following examples.

4. Kuroda (1983) makes essentially the same point with a different pair of examples.

(17) a. Kyoo-wa {samu/suzusi/atataka/atu}-i _
today-top {cold/cool/warm/hot}-Pres
'It's {cold/cool/war/hot} today'
b. Koko-wa {kura/akaru}-i _
here-top {dark/light}-Pres
'It's {dark/light} here'

The following temporal and meterological expressions can also be regarded as containing expletive PRO subjects.

(18) a. Ima 3 zi des-u _
now 3 o'clock be-Pres
'It's 3 o'clock now'
b. Kyoo-wa {nitiyoobi/i-i tenki} des-u _
today-top {Sunday/good weather} be-Pres
'It's Sunday today' 'It's fine today'

Furthermore, such periphrastic modal expressions as given below may also be analyzed as containing expletive PRO subjects. Consider.

(19) a. [John-ga ika-nake-re _ ba] nara-na-i _
John-nom go-Neg-Subj if [can-be]-Neg-Pres
'(Lit.) It cannot be if John does not go=John must go'
b. [John-ga {it-te/ika-naku-te} _ mo]
John-nom {go-Cont/go-Neg-Cont} even-if
yo-i _
[all-right]-Pres
'(Lit.) It is all right even if John does not go=John need not go' or '(Lit.) It is all right even if John goes=John may go'

As indicated by bracketing and the literal translation, of the two S-subject positions in each example, the first is bound by the O-subject *John,* but the second is either free or bound by the complement clause, just like the expletive *it* and the complement *that*- and *if*-clause in the following examples.[5]

(20) a. It is necessary that you go.
b. It is quite all right if you don't go.

5. If the proposal that the above examples involve expletive PRO is correct, it constitutes a blatant counterexample to Jaeggli and Safir's (1989) generalization that PRO cannot be an expletive. It is not clear at this stage how the differences between Spanish, German, and English (which they based their generalization on) and Japanese may be accounted for.

3.3. Subject-Object Asymmetry in the Use of Resumptive Pronouns

There is an independent piece of evidence showing that the S-subject cannot be overt in Japanese, which will provide additional support for the Uniform PRO Subject Hypothesis. Generally, the so-called topic phrase, i.e., the sentence initial phrase marked by *wa* can bind either a gap or a RESUMPTIVE PRONOUN contained in the rest of the sentence. (It can also be related to the rest of the sentence by the 'aboutness' relationship, but that is irrelevant here.) First consider the cases of topic phrases consisting of non-subject elements.

(21) a. John$_i$-wa [Mary-ga {[e$_i$]/kare$_i$-o} hihansi-ta]
John-top Mary-nom him-acc criticize-Past
'As for John, Mary criticized [him]'

b. John$_i$-wa [Mary-ga {[e$_i$]/kare$_i$-ni} tegami-o kai-ta]
John-top Mary-nom him-dat letter-acc write-Past
'As for John, Mary wrote a letter [to him]'

c. Kono ie$_i$-wa [Sooseki-ga bannen-ni {[e$_i$]/soko$_i$-ni}
this house-top Souseki-nom late-years there
sun-da]
live-Past
'As for this house, Souseki lived [there] in his late years'

It should be clear from these that a resumptive pronoun can occur in a direct object gap, an indirect object gap, and a locative gap.[6]

With this much in mind, now consider the following pair of examples.

(22) a. John$_i$-wa [[e$_i$] Mary-o hihansi-ta]
John-top Mary-acc criticize-Past
'As for John, [he] criticized Mary'

b. *John$_i$-wa [kare$_i$-ga Mary-o hihansi-ta]
John-top he-nom Mary-acc criticize-Past
'As for John, he criticized Mary'

The PF string *John-wa Mary-o hihansi-ta* does have the interpretation indicated. Therefore, the usual practice is to assign it the structure in (22). The exact nature of the gap is a matter of some issue.

---

6. Topic phrases can occur without the particles that are associated with the position of the gap under certain conditions, while they have to be accompanied by appropriate particles under other conditions. It is not quite clear to me what conditions underlie this except that they seem to have something to do with the recoverability of the information of the particles. In any case, the exact conditions about the obligatoriness or optionality of particles do not affect the argument to follow. See Kuroda (1983, 1986) and Saito (1982, 1983a) for these and related issues.

Some regard it as a trace left by extraction of the topic, others regard it as a base generated variable, still others take it to be PRO. (Our analysis takes it to be PRO but places it after the Tense element.) In all of these analyses except the present one there is some way to mark an overt element by *ga*, should it occur in place of the gap, and nothing prevents a resumptive pronoun from occurring in that position just as in the other examples above. However, as the b) example shows, it is impossible to have a resumptive pronoun there.

This is a surprising fact if the Japanese subject occurs in the clause-initial position and there is some mechanism to assign *ga* to it. Any analysis having this property would have to resort to some *ad hoc* stipulation to ban a resumptive pronoun from the relevant subject position. Under the Uniform PRO Subject Hypothesis, however, the impossibility of a resumptive pronoun in that position is doubly accounted for. First, the only position in which a true subject (S-subject) can occur is in the specifier position of AGR_SP at S-structure, which is to the right of AGR_S. Therefore, if a resumptive pronoun should occur, it would have to occur to the right of V or AGR, never at the beginning of the sentence. Second, and this is crucial since the S-subject is PRO licensed by $AGR_S{}^E$ in Japanese, no overt element can take its place because it cannot be licensed by $AGR_S{}^E$.

The only way to allow a topic phrase to bind a resumptive pronoun in the clause-initial 'subject' position in the present analysis is by having both elements as O-subjects, one asymmetrically c-commanding the other as schematically shown below, assuming (non-crucially) that O-subjects are adjoined to AGRP.

(23) $[_{AGRP}$ $John_i$-wa $[_{AGRP}$ $kare_i$-ga $[_{AGRP}$ Mary-o hihansi-ta $PRO_i]]]$

Of the two operators, the second one *kare-ga* is completely superfluous. This violates the principle of full interpretation (FI) of Chomsky (1986:98):

(24) Principle of Full Interpretation (FI)
Every element of PF and LF, taken to be the interface of syntax (in the broad sense) with systems of language use, must receive an appropriate interpretation--must be licensed in the sense indicated.

Just as language does not allow free variables, as Chomsky (1989) notes in relation to the interpretation of the empty category occupying the object position of the verb *catch* in *John is too clever to catch,* so does language disallow 'free operators,' operators that bind vacuously. We can take either *John-ga* or *kare-ga* as a free operator because one of them binds PRO vacuously.[7] This situation does not change even if the resumptive pronoun is replaced by a zero topic. The gap will still have to be interpreted as a superfluous operator. Needless to say, such a problem never arises with non-subject resumptive pronouns.

The above three arguments should suffice to establish that Japanese clauses contain PRO as their S-subjects even when they lack an overt O-subject. Thus the answer to the question (10a) has turned out to be *yes*. Now, let us turn to the question (10b).

4. Variable Status of PRO

The Uniform PRO Subject Hypothesis treats PRO as a variable bound by O-subject when there is one. An argument against this hypothesis may be formed based on the Functional Determination approach to empty categories of Chomsky (1981, 1982). Chomsky (1982: 34-35) proposes that an empty category is functionally determined either as PRO, NP-trace, or variable by the following procedure.

(25) a. An empty category is a variable if it is in an A-position and is locally A'-bound.
b. An empty category in an A-position that is not a variable is an anaphor.
c. An empty category that is not a variable is a pronominal if it is free or locally A-bound by an antecedent with an independent θ-role.

Since the basic assumption here is that the three types of empty categories are distinct and in complementary distribution, this approach does not allow the possibility of PRO being a variable.

However, as has been pointed out by Epstein (1984), Safir (1985) etc., Chomsky's functional determination approach cannot be retained *in toto*. Safir (1986), for instance, proposes to drop (25b-c) and retain only the contextual definition of variable, i.e., (25a). His argument for this is based on the contrast of grammaticality between the following examples, first noted by Higginbotham (1980).

(26) a. ??who_i [did [his_i washing his_i car] upset e_i]
b. who_i [did [PRO_i washing his_i car upset e_i]

(25) would exclude the possibility of the empty category subject of

---

7. Or one could rule out (23) as a violation of the Bijection Principle of Koopman and Sportiche (1981), which requires that there be a one-to-one correspondence between operators and variables. In 23) PRO is bound by two operators.

the gerund in (26a) being PRO because, being locally A'-bound by *who,* it would be contextually determined as a variable by (25a). And if it is a variable, it must be properly governed to meet ECP. But the subject of a gerund is not a properly governed position as can be seen by the ungrammaticality of (27).

(27) *Who$_i$ did [t$_i$ washing his car] upset you?

Therefore the functional determination approach of (25) predicts that (26b) should be an ECP violation. Clearly this is a wrong prediction. Instead if we drop (25b-c) and assume that the values of the features [±anaphor] and [±pronominal] are intrinsic to empty categories and do not change throughout the derivation, then the empty category in the subject of the gerund of (26b) will be PRO contextually defined as a variable by (25a) since it is locally A'-bound by *who* and will not violate ECP because it is PRO. The difference between (26a) and (26b) is explained by the Parallelism Constraint on Operator Binding.

(28) The Parallelism Constraint on Operator Binding (PCOB)
If O is an operator and x is a variable bound by O, then for any y, y a variable of O, x and y are [α lexical].

(26b) meets the PCOB because the two variables PRO and e_i are both non-lexical, i.e., phonologically null, whereas (26a) violates it because one variable, *his* is lexical while the other, e_i is non-lexical.

Safir extends the same analysis to account for the cases involving variables bound by a quantifier.

(29) a. ??[his$_i$ washing his$_i$ car] upsets everyone$_i$
b. everyone$_i$ [[his$_i$ washing his$_i$ car] upsets t$_i$]

(30) a. [PRO$_i$ washing his$_i$ car] upsets everyone$_i$
b. everyone$_i$ [[PRO$_i$ washing his$_i$ car] upsets t$_i$]

(29a) is a weak crossover violation paralleling (26a). (30a) with PRO subject escapes weak crossover violation just as (26b) does. After Quantifier Raising (QR) at LF, 29a) and (30a) look like (29b) and (30b), respectively. The subjects of the gerunds are contextually defined as variable at LF. (29b) violates (28) because one variable, *his* is lexical and the other, t_i is non-lexical. (30b) satisfies (28) and hence grammatical.

What Safir has proposed for English is that an element can be contextually defined as a variable by (29a) at S-structure after Wh-Movement (26b), or at LF after QR (30b). Then it comes at no cost to allow PRO in (8) repeated below as (31) to be contextually defined as a variable at D-structure in Japanese, if no further movement of the operator takes place.

(31) $[_{CP}\,[_{AGRP}$ John$_i$-ga/wa/mo [kaet-ta-AGR$_S{}^E$ PRO$_i$]]]

That PRO can be contextually defined as a variable will remain unchanged even if there is LF raising of the operator possibly adjoining it to the righthand side of IP (AGRP) giving (32).

(32) $[_{CP}[_{AGRP}\,[_{AGRP}$ t_i [kaet-ta-AGR$_S{}^E$ PRO$_i$]] John$_i$-ga/wa/mo]]

At this stage I will leave open the question of which is the LF representation of the sentence. Thus, the answer to the question posed in (10b) has turned out also to be *yes.*[8]

---

8. H. Hoji pointed out that if the first *John* is an operator binding PRO in (i), the sentence should be a violation of Strong Crossover though this type of sentence is quite acceptable in Japanese as opposed to the typical case of Strong Crossover as in (ii).

(i) $[_{AGRP}$John$_i$-ga $[_{AGRP}$John$_i$-no hon-o yon-da PRO$_i$]
John-nom John-gen book-acc read-Pst
'John read John's book'

(ii) *{John$_i$/kare$_i$}-ga dare$_i$-no hon-o yon-da PRO$_i$ no?
{John/he}-nom who-gen book-acc read-Pst PRO$_i$?
'*Whose$_i$ book did {John$_i$/he$_i$} read?'

However, (i) is not a regular case of Strong Crossover: The variable, i.e., PRO is not c-commanded by the second instance of *John* in (i), whereas the variable left after (LF) WH-Movement of *dare* 'who' in (ii) is a violation of Strong Crossover because it is bound by PRO. The real challenge for the Operator-Subject analysis is to account for the distinction between (i) and the following ungrammatical example.

(iii) *$[_{AGRP}$Dare$_i$-ga $[_{AGRP}$John$_i$-no hon-o yon-da PRO$_i$ no]
who-nom John$_i$-gen book-acc read-Pst
'*Who$_i$ read John$_i$'s book?'

The only difference between the two examples lies in the O-subjects. Therefore, there must be a distinction between the operator statuses of (the first instance of) *John* in (i) and the wh-word *dare* in (iii). The relevant distinction may be one between 'true quantifier' and operator without true quantificational force as proposed by Stowell and Lasnik (1987). The first instance of *John* in (i) is an operator but does not have true quantificational force because it does not range over a nonsingleton set. It functions more like a restriction on existential operator: $\exists x{:}x{=}$John x read John's book. *Dare* in (iii), on the other hand, is a true quantifier because of its very nature as a wh-phrase. PRO is identified as a null name in (i) and as a true variable in (ii), if we expand Stowell and Lasnik's notions. Then we can capture the difference between i) and (iii) by saying that names can be bound by another name but not by a syntactic variable. This may be one of the cases covered by the following generalization proposed by Lasnik (1989).

(iv) A less referential expression may not bind a more referential one.

5. Implications for Other 'Agreementless' Languages

The logic of this paper has gone as follows: Since Japanese does not exhibit observable subject-verb agreement, it can only have AGR_S^E. Since AGR_S^E has less semantic content than AGR_S^{Min}, it can license only PRO. Therefore, every Japanese sentence can have only PRO as S-subject. The lack of observable subject-verb agreement is not limited to Japanese. Korean and Chinese are also known to lack observable agreement. If the assumptions and the flow of logic in this paper are correct, then it should also follow that the Uniform PRO Subject Hypothesis holds in Korean and Chinese. One empirical prediction that this hypothesis makes is that independent 'subjectless' sentences in these languages should exhibit arbitrary PRO interpretations of their S-subjects. Indeed, this prediction is borne out in its essence by the Korean data in (33) and the Chinese data in (34).[9]

(33) a. Hankuk-eyse-nun ceskalak-ul sse-se umsik-ul ip-ulo
Korea-in-top chopstick-acc use-ing food-acc mouth-to
kaceka-u-ta
carry-Pres-Ind
'In Korea people use chopsticks to carry food to their mouths.'

b. Imi tangsi-ey cencayug-eyse hwanyak-ul sayongha-ess-ta
already those-days war-in firearms-acc use-Past-Ind
'Already in those days people used firearms in war'

c. Wuseu yangpha-lul taci-seyo. Kulikonase, ...
first onions-acc mince-Imp Then, ...'
'First mince onions. Then ...'

d. Kecismal-ul {ha-nun-kes/ha-ess-nun-kes}-un nappun il-i-
lie-acc {say-Pres-Nom/say-Past-Rel}-top bad thing-be-ta
Ind
'It is a bad thing to tell a lie/One should not have told a lie'

(34) a. zai zhongguo yong kuaizi jia shiwu dao zui-li.
in China with chopstick clip food to mouth-in
'In China people use chop-sticks to carry food to their mouths'

b. na-shi [zai zhanzheng-zhong] yijing zhiyong huoqi.
that-time at war-during already use firearms
'Already in those days people used firearms in war'

c. xian qie yiangcong. zai ...
first mince onion then
'First mince onions. Then ...'

9. I am indebted to SooWon Kim for the Korean data and to Wei-tien Tsai and Paul Law for the Chinese data.

d. shuo huang shi huai shi.
tell lie is bad thing
'It's a bad thing to tell a lie'

Thus, the availability of arbitrary PRO interpretation seems to be basically the same in Korean and Chinese as in Japanese.

Korean (35) and Chinese (36) also share with Japanese the property of lacking overt *it*-type expletives and the consequent possibility that PRO may function as an *it*-type expletive.

(35) a. Onul-un (ralssi-ka) {tep/chwup/mutep}-ta
today-top (wether-nom) {hot/cold/muggy}-Ind
'It's hot/cold/muggy today: Today is hot/cold/muggy'

b. Onul-un ilyoil-i-ta: Cikum-un sey si-(i)-ta
today-top Sunday-be-Ind Now-top 3 o'clock-(be)-Ind
'It's Sunday today/Today is Sunday: It's 3 o'clock now'

(36) a. jintian hen re/leng.
today very hot/cold
'It's hot/cold today. Today is very hot/cold'

b. jintian xingqitian. xianzai san-dianzhong.
today Sunday now three-o'clock`
'It's Sunday today' 'It's 3 o'clock now'

6. Conclusion

In this paper I have proposed the Uniform PRO Subject Analysis of Japanese sentences and argued that all Japanese sentences contain a PRO subject. To support this claim I have presented three pieces of evidence: the availability of an arbitrary PRO interpretation in O-subjectless sentences, the apparent lack of *it*-type expletives in Japanese, and the subject-object asymmetry in the use of resumptive pronouns. It has also been shown that other agreementless languages such as Korean and Chinese exhibit essentially the same characteristics.

References

Chomsky, Noam. 1986. Knowledge of language. New York: Praeger

Chomsky, Noam. 1989. Some notes on economy of derivation and representation. MIT working papers in linguistics 10.43-74.

Epstein, Samuel. 1984a. A note on functional determination and strong cross-over. The linguistic review 3.299-308.

Epstein, Samuel. 1984b. Quantifier-*pro* and the LF representation of PRO_{ARB}, LI. 15. 499-505.

Hasegawa, Nobuko. 1985. On the so-called zero pronouns in Japanese. The linguistic review. 4.289-341.

Higginbotham, James. 1980. Pronouns and bound variables. LI. 11. 679-708.

Hoji, Hajime. 1985. Logical form constraint and configurational structures in Japanese. Doctoral dissertation, University of Washington.

Hoji, Hajime. 1986. Weak crossover and Japanese phrase structure. Issues in Japanese linguistics, ed. by Takashi Imai and Mamoru Saito, 163-201, Dordrecht: Foris Publications.

Huang, C. T. James. 1984. On the distribution and reference of empty pronouns. LI. 15.531-575.

Huang, C. T. James. 1987. Remarks on empty categories in Chinese. LI. 18.321-337.

Huang, C. T. James. 1989. Pro-drop in Chinese: A generalized control theory. The Null Subject Parameter. eds. by Osvaldo Jaeggli and Ken Safir, 185-214. Boston: Kluwer Academic Publishers.

Jaeggli Osvaldo and Ken J. Safir. 1989. The null subject parameter and parametric theory. The Null Subject Parameter. eds. by Osvaldo Jaeggli and Ken Safir, 1-44. Boston: Kluwer Academic Publishers.

Koopman, Hilda. and Dominique Sportiche 1982. Variables and the bijection principle. The linguistic review. 2.139-160.

Kuroda, Shige.-Yuki. 1965. Generative grammatical studies in the Japanese language. Doctoral dissertation, MIT.

Kuroda, Shige.-Yuki. 1978. Case-marking, canonical sentence patterns, and counter equi in Japanese. Problems in Japanese syntax and semantics. eds. by John Hinds and Irwin Howard. Tokyo: Kaitakusha.

Kuroda, Shige-Yuki. 1983. What can Japanese say about government and binding. WCCFL. 2.153-164.

Lasnik, Howard. 1989. On the necessity of binding conditions. Essays on Anaphora, by Howard Lasnik. Boston: Kluwer Academic Publishers.

Safir, Ken. J. 1985. Syntactic chains. Cambridge: Cambridge University Press.

Saito, Mamoru. 1982. Case marking in Japanese: a preliminary study. MIT.

Saito, Mamoru. 1983. Case and government in Japanese. WCCFL. 2.247-259.

Stowell, Tim. and Howard Lasnik. 1987. Weakest crossover. UCLA and University of Connecticut.

Tonoike, Shigeo. 1989. *Wa, mo, ga* no ronri-keishiki--bun-bunpou to danwa-bunpou no interface-- [LF representation of *wa, mo, ga*-- interface between sentence grammar and discourse grammar]. Meiji Gakuin Ronso. 446.51-75. Meiji Gakuin University.

Tonoike, Shigeo. 1990. *No* no ronri-keishiki--*wa, mo, ga* no ronri-keishiki ni tuzuite-- [LF representation of *no*-a sequel to LF representation of *wa, mo, ga*--]. Meiji Gakuin Ronso. 467.69-99. Meiji Gakuin University.

Tonoike, Shigeo. 1991. Comparative syntax of English and Japanese. Current English linguistics in Japan. ed. by Heizo Nakajima. Berlin: Mouton de Gruyter.

Whitman, John. 1991. String vacuous V to COMP. Paper read at 1991 GLOW.

Index